WITHDRAWN

★

THE GROWTH OF THE RED ARMY

★

THE GROWTH OF
THE RED ARMY

By D. Fedotoff White

PRINCETON
PRINCETON UNIVERSITY PRESS
1944

TO THE MEMORY OF MY FATHER

PREFACE

THIS is not a "definitive" book about the Red Army, nor is it an outline of its history. It is a study of the organizational growth of the armed forces of the Soviets, of the component groups within them, and of the conflicts and conflict situations among these groups.

The valuation of the Red Army has fluctuated a great deal during its comparatively short existence. In early 1918, very few "competent" Russian or foreign observers thought that the Red armed forces would ever develop beyond the stage of an armed mob, the nemesis of the propertied classes of Russia, but impotent against a brigade of regular troops.

On the eve of the Second World War the opposite was true. The Russians themselves told the world that they had the largest, finest, and best-equipped and best-trained army. Quite a few foreign observers agreed. Even one or two former White strategists were willing to concede that their erstwhile antagonists had succeeded in building up a powerful and efficient military machine.

The Russo-Finnish campaign, however, seemed to destroy the belief that a new paragon of armed might had arisen in the East, and that the proletarian doctrine, grafted on the body of Russia, had given birth to a superlative new military organization, to a new skill in the art of war.

As this preface is written it is clear that the Russian evaluation of the Red Army was the correct one and that most of the foreign observers (with a few notable exceptions) had completely missed the mark.

The Red armed forces have been in existence for over twenty years, undergoing several basic changes in that period. From the militia of the early Red Guards and the anarchistic bands of bluejackets and local guerillas, they grew into a large regular army with a professional officers' corps, a strict military discipline, a fighting tradition, battle-scarred banners and a distinctive organization.

The process of growth and change was not always a smooth one. Treason of generals and officers, mutinies of soldiers and seamen, ruthless execution of the rebellious element by the authorities—such vicissitudes accompanied the early years of the Red Army. A few years ago a violent crisis in army life found its outward expression in the execution of Marshal Tukhachevskii, in the "purge" involving more than a score of thousands of generals, officers and political

leaders of the armed forces of the Soviet Union. Permeated by the
political element, closely associated with the Communist party of
Russia, the army has reflected at various stages of its history the
infra-party struggle to which some of its ablest leaders have fallen
victim.

The elements of conflict among the several component groups
within the Red Army, between entire units of the armed forces and
the government, between some of the most prominent of the military
leaders and the ruling Kremlin group, were present in the early years
of the Soviet military forces, and (as evidenced by the "purge") in
recent years as well—although in a modified form. The reintroduction
of the institute of military commissars in 1937 was a definite indication of the desire of the Soviet Government to take a firmer grip on
its armed forces.

Aside from the abortive mutiny of the Socialist Revolutionaries of
the Left in 1918, only one of the rebellions of the Red armed forces
has threatened the régime. That was the Kronstadt revolt of the seamen, soldiers and workers of that dockyard citadel of Leningrad.
Other rebellions were devoid of first-rate political significance. The
wandering from the fold of such guerilla leaders as Grigoriev and
Makhno, the desertion to the peasant insurgents of some of the
troops sent against Antonov's guerillas in 1921, did not menace the
existence of the Soviet state. There were bands of steel to keep together the structure of the military might of the Soviets, bands sufficiently strong—and sufficiently flexible—to withstand the disruptive
forces of conflict, and to compel obedience to the, at times, somewhat
elusive general party line of the Communists.

The disruptive forces within the Red Army were, at certain periods
at least, greater than in any contemporary European army. But the
protective bands were also stronger and more cunningly devised than
in any European armed force.

This work does not guess at the future of the Red Army. Divina-
tion is a special gift rarely bestowed on students of social sciences.
The aim of the book is to examine how the Red armed forces have
come into being, how they were organized, what were the stresses to
which they were subjected, how the bands were fashioned to counteract these stresses, what flying buttresses were erected by the architect
of the tower of Soviet military strength, and under what circumstances in the past the dams built to stem the turbulent flow of conflict within the Red Army have failed their engineers and broken
down.

A few words about the methodological approach used in this work may be useful to the reader.

One may view an army as an organism harmoniously growing and developing along the lines laid down by the historic traditions of a country in handling its military affairs, or as a "superstructure" reflecting the economic conditions of the land, its technological level, the skill of its citizens, the viewpoint of its ruling class. Others may think of an army as a co-operative structure, an example of social harmony of leadership exercised by the commanders and the loyalty and will to be led generated in those commanded.

This book offers another approach: that of the study of an army as a complex of groups with conflicting interests, desires and wills, held together, in a measure, by a common interest more all-embracing, more essential than those which stimulate conflicts within it, and also by an organizational structure specially devised to meet these conflicts and conflict situations, and to overcome them.

The analysis of the Red Army, as a study of conflicts and conflict situations within it, seems to be particularly appropriate because of the peculiar origins of that army, because of the organizational plan adopted by the Soviet Government to overcome the antagonisms between the commanding personnel and the rank and file of the army. The government was not only conscious of that conflict, but openly acknowledged it and took organizational steps to counteract it. The same occurred at a later stage of development of the Red Army, only a few years ago. The sustained effort to increase the percentage of communists both among the commanding personnel as well as "other ranks" and the emphasis on the urban proletariat in recruiting the armed forces and its leaders, at least until the publication of the 1936 constitution, have exhibited the continued watchfulness of the communist ruling group of Russia, their awareness of the latent conflicts within the Red Army and their anxiety to devise means of keeping these conflicts latent, of canalizing them, or of extirpating them.

That these realistic attitudes have had definite advantages in maintaining control of the armed forces is borne out by the course of the Russian Civil War, as well as that of World War II.

The narrow social base of Lenin's dictatorship called for a certain organizational structure in the Red Army. From the very beginning problems of national defense in the building up of the military forces were subordinated to those of class and group dictatorship. This narrow base and the lack of traditional acceptance of its authority by the masses of the population led to emphasis on political reliability, even to the extent of sacrificing potential war strength.

The conflicts within the army had their roots in the origin and development of the Soviet dictatorship. In the microcosm of the army was reflected, in a measure, the greater world of Soviet Russia.

The morale of an army is an elusive quantity. It means different things to different students. It is clear, however, that—apart from the *material*, physical endowment of its personnel, or their military-technical skill—an army has to possess other qualities to be effective, to maintain its will to victory, to overcome the fear of death and mutilation lurking in the minds of its soldiers. Patriotism, love of one's country may be one of these factors. Great enthusiasm for a religion, for a social ideal, for a kingdom of God on earth, may supply other facets of an army's morale.

The Soviet armed forces, in theory at least, combine the defense of the "socialist Fatherland" with the idea of liberation of the working class the world over, with a vision of a classless society to be founded on the ruins of the now existing capitalist states. The element of national defense seems to be acquiring a greater prominence in Soviet Russia lately, crowding back the idea of liberation of the proletariat, of the world revolution. The support of the non-party and non-proletarian elements is necessary to the Soviet Government in the face of the supreme test. To these elements, of course, the appeal of national defense is more natural than the appeal of world revolution.

The separation of Russia from the rest of the world, particularly prominent in the last few years before World War II, has quite probably made for an insularity, a feeling of apartness, not only among the educated classes, but also among certain elements in the village. This sense of difference, of standing apart from the rest of the world, has probably contributed to the morale of the Red Army, making it feel that it is called to defend not merely the soil, but also a way of living, and that, in case of defeat, not only may territorial losses be involved, but the whole warp of life may be replaced by another.

Historic situations never repeat themselves in their entirety. There are, however, certain elements of similarity in situations occurring under the stress of quasi-elemental events such as war, revolutions, great epidemics. The study of these elements does not provide the practical military man or politician with a prescription for the course of action to be taken or even a blueprint of the likely course of events. Nevertheless, without the study of these repeating elements any other than intuitive judgment of current events or of future trends is impossible.

A general does not become a successful *Feldherr* merely by studying military history, history of military art, military sociology and kindred disciplines. It is, however, difficult if not altogether impossible to become a successful modern military leader without understanding the essentials of all these.

In the same way, without the awareness of the conflict history within the Red Army and of the organizational measures taken by the Soviet Government to counteract these antagonistic trends and to forestall their growth in wartime into full-fledged conflicts, it is impossible to appraise intelligently the Soviet military forces.

The core of this book—the four long chapters, IV, VIII, IX and X—contains the analysis of the changes in the principal groups within the Red Army. These groups include the commanding personnel in the narrow sense (its officers); the political personnel (the commissars and others connected with the political organs of the armed forces); the Communists and groups closely affiliated with them, such as the Komsomol (Communist Youth), organized in nuclei and collectives within the armed units and the administrative offices of the Red Army; and last, but not least, the rank and file soldiers. It also discusses tensions and stresses within these groups, between them and also between the groups in the armed services and the State.

The short chapters—I, II, and III—outline the inheritance received by the Red Army from the army of Imperial Russia and the early stages of the organization of the armed forces of the Soviets, with attention to the influences which shaped these forces. Chapters V and VI stand somewhat apart from the rest. The former deals with the Kronstadt Rebellion; the latter may be regarded as a laboratory test of conditions under which the Soviet military organization failed to maintain its loyalty to the ruling party group. The chapter is devoted to an analysis of these conditions. Chapter VI examines the early stages of the development of the Soviet military doctrine (the later stages were analyzed by the author in his "Soviet Philosophy of War" which appeared in September 1936 in the *Political Science Quarterly*). This development of the Soviet military theory offers a very interesting sidelight on the rivalries and aspirations of the several groups within the army. It furnished the expression of these trends in terms of military theoretical concepts. In some instances theories were mere verbalizations of a struggle for position and influence. Chapter VII gives a brief outline of the difficult transition of the Red Army from the Civil War structure to that of the New Economic Policy era.

The problem of armament and technical equipment of the Red Army has been deliberately left outside the scope of this study, with the exception of incidental remarks in the course of discussion of the Army's organizational growth. This is a study in military sociology and not an attempt to write a general history of the Red Army. However, the connection between the rapid industrialization of the U.S.S.R. and the expansion of the Soviet educational system under the consecutive Five Year Plans, as well as the growth of the Red Army, is briefly examined. Without the understanding of the inter-relations between these phases of the development of the U.S.S.R. and the up-building of the Red Army into a modern armed force, it is impossible to understand the strength of the latter. It is quite probable that the lack of appreciation of this inter-relation has made for the undervaluation of the Red Army by the foreign military "experts."

Analysis of changes which have occurred since the attack of Germany on Soviet Russia was not made a part of these studies. There is a dearth of objective documentary material available to students residing outside the borders of the U.S.S.R. concerning these changes. They are apparently so deep and important that only a special investigation after the war, when suitable documentary material will become available, could do justice by them. To attempt theoretical generalizations in the field of military sociology, on the basis of the study of one army only, seemed undesirable to the author. Such generalizations probably could be arrived at to better advantage upon a comparative study of the three "new" type armies—Russian, German and Italian. The author hopes to undertake such an analysis later. Meanwhile, only tentative and quite obvious conclusions have been drawn from the material examined.

Work on this volume was begun in the early spring of 1940. It was virtually completed (with the exception of certain parts of Chapter X) by the beginning of 1942. No attempt was made to review the manuscript in the light of recent developments on the Soviet front. The reader, it is hoped, will judge whether any revision was necessary.

The author is deeply indebted to Professor William Linn Westermann of Columbia University for his encouragement to return to the field of social studies. To Professor Geroid Tanquary Robinson of the same University the writer owes a debt of gratitude not only as a student of his incisive seminar in Russian History, but also for the many tokens of friendly helpfulness, for advice and criticism, which assisted greatly in the re-shaping of the author's viewpoint in the field of social studies. Professor Theodore Abel, also of Columbia University gave the idea for this work in 1940, when the author was following his course in Social Conflict, and by his interest in the development of the studies of the Red Army furthered their completion.

There is no bibliography attached to this work. Not merely economy of space made for the decision to omit it. Most of the sources used are in Russian and a bibliography would therefore merely add to the scientific apparatus without proffering any useful help to English-speaking readers. Those familiar with the Russian language will find sufficient bibliographic information in the notes—organized by chapters and placed at the end of the book.

Russian names of persons and places were, as a rule, transliterated, with certain simplifications, in accordance with the system widely used in this country by scholars in the Russian field. Names familiar to English-speaking readers, like Trotsky, are spelled in accordance with the established practice of the daily press.

A word of appreciation is due to the several librarians who have made the author's research a pleasant task. The head of the Division of Documents of the Library of Congress, Mr. James B. Childs, has given every assistance. Mr. George A. Novossiltzeff, of his staff, has taken endless pains to place available documents within the reach of the author.

Mr. N. R. Rodionoff, in charge of the Slavic Division of the same Library, and his staff have rendered valuable help by their suggestions and courteous attention to every request made. Dr. V. V. Gzovski, of the Law Library of the Library of Congress has offered useful advice and drew the author's attention to important documents. Mr. D. D. Tuneeff did not spare himself in checking the various available sources of information.

Dr. Sergei Yakobson of the Consultants' Service of the Library of Congress has given freely of his erudition and time to answer numerous questions. The Staff of the Slavonic Division of the New York Public Library have helped considerably by their courteous and friendly assistance on many occasions. The author is particularly beholden to Mrs. A. A. Heifetz of that Division for the many kindnesses in finding shortcuts to expedite his research work.

Mr. H. Glenn Brown, Reference Librarian of the University of Pennsylvania Library, put the author under considerable obligation by his untiring helpfulness and prompt attention to requests made to him.

Mrs. Catherine Sadlon has offered valuable suggestions, and the staff of Princeton University Press went out of its way to facilitate the preparation of the manuscript for publication.

D. Fedotoff White

Philadelphia, Pennsylvania
February 1943

CONTENTS

★

THE GROWTH OF
THE RED ARMY

★

★ I ★

THE HERITAGE

LENIN and his followers came to power in the fourth year of Russia's participation in World War I. They had plucked the control of the state from the hands of the Provisional Government which had not succeeded in reforging the old Imperial Army into the shield and buckler of the new-born Russian democracy.

The Provisional Government, on the other hand, had inherited from the Empire it superseded a vast, albeit insufficiently armed and inadequately equipped, military organization. With all its shortcomings, however, the old Imperial Army of Russia had been rugged enough, even as late as the summer of 1916, to inflict a disastrous major defeat upon the Austro-German forces opposing it. The Russian armies of the South West, led by General A. A. Brusilov, struck along a two hundred and fifty mile front on June 4, 1916. In a two months' campaign they had recovered about eight thousand square miles of territory, capturing over four hundred thousand officers and men from the enemy.

Thus the Russian Empire, even on the eve of its fall, still disposed of a powerful army capable not only of keeping the enemy at bay on the defensive, but also of carrying out large-scale successful offensive operations of great strategic significance.

There were, however, many signs of decay and decomposition in at least some of the component parts of the Imperial armed forces antedating the advent to power of the Provisional Government.

The process of deterioration of the Russian armed forces did not begin with the March revolution of 1917. There is a considerable body of evidence showing that this process was going on apace during the years of the war preceding that date.[1]

To cite an example: At a conference held at the Russian G.H.Q. on December 17-18, 1916, General Brusilov spoke of the 7th Siberian Army Corps as having arrived from the Riga front "entirely under the influence of propaganda." "Men of that corps refused to attack; there was rebellion within the ranks, and one of the company commanders was bayonetted by his soldiers." Order was restored by stern measures.[2]

The available data, however, do not lend themselves to the deduction that the process of deterioration was proceeding with a virulence and speed sufficient utterly to endanger seriously the strength of the

Russian arms in 1917. It fell to the March revolution of 1917, with its corollary of the weakening of state power, often bordering on paralysis, to develop the latent disease, to accentuate the antagonism between the leaders and the led, to add the new heady wine of freedom to the old bottles of wrath of the Russian peasantry in army great-coats. The *rapidity* of the downfall of Russian armed might was the result of these fruits of the revolution rather than of the internal development of its own forces of disruption.

There is ample evidence in the official military documents of 1917 confirming the adverse influence of the revolutionary upheaval on the fighting efficacy of the Russian arms.

A detailed analysis of the factors that had contributed to the rapid falling apart of the Russian Army in 1917 cannot be made here. This volume has as its task the study of the growth of the new—the Red Army—and not an autopsy of the old Imperial Army.

The Red Army sprang from the grafting of new organizational principles on the bole of army structure. The influx of large bodies of the armed workers of the Red Guard militia, of the revolutionary guerillas embracing workers and peasants as well as Cossacks, the powerful stimulus contributed by the revolutionary intellectuals who had donned army coats—all this had resulted in an armed force vastly different not only from the Imperial troops of Russia, but also from any contemporary army. The Red Army used the officers and the N.C.O.'s as well as the rank and file of the old army, but this numer-ous personnel was utilized as loose bricks to construct an edifice of a new and different design, not—with a few exceptions—in organized units that would maintain their own features. The process of change from the old army to the new was not that of evolution. It was de-cidedly a revolutionary one, and a clear break is easily seen between the agony of the first and the birth of the second.

Nevertheless, the manner of disintegration of the old army had a lasting influence on the process of growth of the Red Army. It seems, therefore, advisable to illustrate by a few examples the process of decay that had preceded the creation of the regular Soviet forces. These examples have been drawn from the ample evidence available with a view to showing the various aspects of deterioration in the Imperial armed forces. Space does not permit anything but a cursory treatment either of the factual material or of the deductions.

At a conference, held at the Army G.H.Q. on March 18, 1917, i.e. after the March revolutionary events, it was reported: "The fighting efficiency of the army has been lowered and it is very difficult to count on the army advancing at the present time." Factors of a moral character were aggravated by the decline in the efficiency of transport. It was stated at the same conference: "We are unable to transport to the front simultaneously sufficient food to provide daily rations and to permit the accumulation of reserves of supplies. Without the latter (covering at least the two weeks' requirements) it is impossible to begin any operations whatsoever."[3]

Under these circumstances, belts had to be tightened at the front as well as in the country at large. The Provisional Government obtained the support of the Executive Committee of the Soviet of the Workers' and Soldiers' Deputies for the reduction in the daily rations of the army. The proclamation of the Soviet supporting that measure was circulated by the organs of the military supplies service on March 20, 1917.[4]

It was recorded in an interesting compendium of the opinions of the senior commanding personnel of the armies of the Russian Western Front regarding the morale of the troops in the first days following the March revolution of 1917 that, in the opinion of the majority of those present, the discipline of the troops had deteriorated, confidence between officers and men undermined, the morale and the combat efficiency of the troops "considerably lowered." It was thought accordingly that: "At the present time troops are suitable for defense only; offensive operations will be possible only after one or two months' time." Almost all members of the conference pointed out that the large quantity of political literature that had flooded the army since the March revolution "was causing enormous harm" as "distracting military units from combat duty and unsettling them." The *Izvestia*, published by the Soviet at Petrograd, and the orders issued by the same Soviet, were especially singled out for their pernicious influence on the morale of the troops.[5]

On this background of pessimism, a secret telegram, dated March 18, 1917, and sent to the Minister of War by the several generals commanding at the different fronts, suddenly struck a note of optimism. The signatures include those of men of ability such as Stcherbachev, Brusilov and Kaledin. Therefore a statement such as: "The armies wish and are able to attack," coupled with a request that no steps be taken to approach the Allies with refusal to carry out obligations undertaken by Russia with respect to the conduct of war, sounds very surprising.[6] One may reasonably surmise that the generals who dispatched that telegram were prompted by political expediency rather than by an objective view of a military problem. It was accepted by the Ministry with more than a pinch of salt. This is evidenced by the endorsement by one of the highest officers of the Russian General Staff: "What happiness, should reality prove this to be true!"

That the telegram actually reflected conditions at the front is denied by a mass of evidence to the contrary. Thus, the commanding general of the Fifth Army wrote to his immediate superior, General Ruzskii, within a few days of the date of that optimistic message, that while regiments resting in reserve repeatedly stated their willingness to fight on to a successful conclusion of the war, they did not respond with any enthusiasm to orders to go to the trenches, and that it was impossible to find any unit willing to undertake even the simplest of combat operations, such as scouting. "There is no way whatever to make anyone move forward from the trenches. The combat morale has fallen to a low level. . . ." "Soldiers are not only unwilling to advance, but even simple stubbornness in defense has deteriorated to an extent which threatens the outcome of the war. . . . Even the replacement of one regiment in the trenches by another from the reserve has become a difficult undertaking as no one is certain that the replacing unit would not at the last minute refuse to occupy the trenches."[7]

The antagonism between the officers and the men is illustrated by a telegram sent by the Chief of Staff at the G.H.Q. to the Minister of War on March 24, 1917, regarding the arrest, and removal from their respective positions, of the colonel and the three battalion commanders of the 68th Siberian Rifles Regiment, by the deputies elected by the men and officers of that regiment. It is rather interesting to note that the arrest and removal from their position of these four senior officers, according to the telegram, had the approval of "practically all officers of the regiment." These acts were motivated by the antagonism to the revolution shown by the colonel, and the lack of confidence in the combat competency of the other officers removed, who were also accused of harsh treatment of their subordinates.[8] The symptom of cleavage not only between officers and men but between senior and junior officers referred to in the telegram will be examined later. It should be noted here that the conflict in the old army did not, by any means, imply a simple cleavage, with officers on one side and men on the other. The pattern of conflict was considerably more complicated.

The incident confirms the report of the general in charge of personnel matters at the G.H.Q. that "the uncrowned power of the commanding personnel of the army has no force to master the armed mob of soldiers."[9]

There is some evidence that at least in certain instances the committees formed in the military units of the front after the March revolution were endeavoring to supplement the efforts of the commanders in combating defeatism and general demoralization among the troops. Two members of the State Duma—the quasi-Parliament of the czarist régime—visited the front on a mission to promote harmony between officers and men and restore the morale of the troops. They reported on April 11, 1917, that they had obtained a favorable impression of conditions prevailing in the 5th Army Corps, ascribing this to the "intensive struggle of the committees against bolshevik propaganda."[10]

Apparently this evidence should not be taken as an indication of a general improvement in the condition of the army after its decline during the turbulent days following the March events. General Denikin's report to the Commander in Chief, dated June 11, 1917, spoke of the 2nd Caucasian Corps as "passing particularly painfully through the transition period from the old régime to the new." According to the estimate of the General commanding the army to which that army corps belonged, the 2nd Caucasian Grenadier Division, the 51st and 134th, because of the state of their morale, had no combat value. It was also mentioned in the same appraisal that the 1st Caucasian Grenadier Division was in better condition, while the 38th Army Corps was "calmer," and General Brusilov commented on the report with the remark: "With such a state of mind prevailing, is it worth while to prepare an attack?"[11]

Even the 38th Army Corps, reported to be "calmer," did not succeed in maintaining its reputation. Only a few weeks later, one of its regiments was reported to be disaffected, disgusted with the war, and antagonistic to its officers. Some of the latter were threatened with murder by the soldiers. One of the companies of that regiment attempted on the 1st of July to hold an armed meeting, carrying posters emblazoned with such sentiments as "Down with war," "Down with the minister-capitalists, the State Duma and the Soviet."[12]

There is some evidence that the removal by the Army G.H.Q. for political reasons of generals who whole-heartedly co-operated with the army committees, apparently as one of the steps in preparing the Kornilov rebellion—that inept attempt at a military coup, in September 1917—had an unfavorable influence on the state of affairs among the troops they had commanded.[13]

Meanwhile, the supply services had not begun to function any better than they did in March. A telegram from the head of the Military Traffic Service to the Chief of Staff at the G.H.Q. on October 27 speaks of an acute deficiency in food supplies for the front, caused by the resistance of the peasants to the removal of grain from their respective districts and looting by the soldiery.[14] In this respect, therefore, the Provisional Government had not succeeded in improving the situation which it had inherited from the Imperial régime. Rather to the contrary—the growing anarchy in the rural districts and the high-handed acts of some of the army units made it difficult to maintain the flow of supplies to the front at the same level as before.

After the failure of the Kornilov coup a still further deterioration took place in the army. A telegram from the Deputy Commissar of the Northern Front to the Minister of War dated September 22, 1917, advised that "as before the state of mind is unsettled, bolshevik ideas are gaining ground."[15]

A summary of reports on the morale of the army for the last two weeks of October, compiled by the Military-Political Department of the G.H.Q., referred to a very active fraternization on the front of one of the divisions of the 7th Army, as a result of which the Austrians had captured Russian soldiers and taken them to their lines as prisoners. The enemy officers were taking advantage of the situation by photographing Russian fortified positions and making a topographical survey of the Russian trenches. That summary speaks of some of the army units "anticipating the law permitting the election of the commanding personnel," and "bringing this right into effect prior to its official approval."[16]

For the conditions prevailing during the last weeks preceding the November revolution, a picture of the rapidly increasing rate of decay of the armed forces of Russia is given in a resolution of the officers of the Petrograd Guards Regiment on October 4, 1917. "Men made soldiers by force and sent to the trenches by force do not want to carry on with the war . . . the idea of the defense of the country is understood only by a few and accepted by still fewer. . . . Egoism, complicated now by hopes for a better future ('land') overrides everything else, and we, officers, forced to make them act against the voice of their own reason, have ceased to be near them or to be understood." After the retreat "the troops behaved like bandits, thieving, robbing, destroying . . . and murdering. We were mere spectators, unable to stop the pogrom. . . ." "with its present personnel, and administered under the present system, the army is unable to defend the state. On the contrary, the state will destroy itself when hunger, privation, the autumn and winter hardships, and, most important, the realization by the soldiers of complete impunity for their acts, will finally take the upper hand."[17]

Professor Miliukov, in his work on the Russian revolution, refers to the acquittal of Captain Dzevaltovskii, and calls this the last straw which made universal the feeling that seditious acts could be committed with impunity. The incident occurred when Kerensky, head of the Provisional Government, was addressing the Grenadier Guards. Captain Dzevaltovskii interrupted him, expressed the Guards' lack of confidence, and openly referred to himself as a bolshevik and a pupil of Lenin.[18]

Under these circumstances, it is not surprising that an official telegraphic report from the H.Q. of the Separate Army, on December 28, 1917, i.e. after the bolshevik seizure of power, stated: "Confirm fighting efficiency of the Special Army is equal to zero . . . in the 31st Corps there exists universal demand for peace and irresistible desire to go home without delay . . . high-sounding slogans would not induce soldiers to resume war. Decay of units in 44th Corps progressing apace."[19]

To the defeatist agitation of the Bolsheviki and other influences opposed to the prosecution of the war, the officers' corps were unable to exercise any effective counter-influence. General Denikin, in his book on the Imperial Russian Army, expressed the opinion that even at the time of the 1905 revolution it was felt that the Russian officers were not adequately prepared for the successful education of their troops in the complicated political situation which existed at that time. A course in political science and another on current political trends was introduced in the Russian military schools in 1907, but three years later this was abandoned and the courses replaced by one on "financial and police law." Denikin asserted that in the 1917 revolution the young army officers, as well as the old, found themselves unequipped and helpless to cope with the political and social problems that had suddenly confronted them. According to Denikin, in the political discussions so frequent in 1917, officers were unable to maintain their ascendancy even over the semi-educated soldiers of the ranks.[20]

The evidence of the Russian military documents referred to above is amply confirmed by the testimony of foreign military observers attached to the Russian Army. In a volume of memoirs, the head of the French military mission in Russia, General Niessel, described in detail the state of disorder in which the Russian Army found itself in October 1917. According to Niessel, the number of absentees from the army reached at that time the incredible figure of three million—if credence be given to the statistics of the G.H.Q. The more conservative estimate of the Ministry of War placed it at one and a half million. According to Niessel, the effective strength of the troops at the front in that period was about three and a half million.[21]

It is not necessary to adduce additional data to prove that the military organization of Russia was so seriously impaired by November 1917 that the armies at the front could not be regarded any more as effective combat forces. Whether there still was the possibility of restoring the lost military efficacy in some of the component parts of the Russian armed forces cannot be usefully discussed here. Some of the military among the Bolsheviki held that this was feasible, as will be referred to later.

What were the factors that had decisively contributed to the rapid rate of dissolution of the military power of Russia between the March and the November revolutionary upheavals is a subject of lively controversy among students of the problem.

The official Soviet view as to the causes of the rapid decay of the Russian Army in 1917, expressed in a preface to one of the collections of documents relating thereto, holds that the principal reasons for the breakdown were the uninterrupted military defeats, the constant lack of supplies, the great war-weariness of the troops, the ever-growing realization of the senselessness of the war from the viewpoint of the peasant soldier, and the persistent growth of hatred of the officers on the part of the enlisted men. According to the author of that preface, the soldiers regarded their officers as the representatives of the feudal régime of landlords' domination over the peasantry. In speaking of the committees formed in the army in 1917, the same preface states that these committees, which became such a prominent feature of self-government and administration of all army units after the March revolution, developed into a class organization of the peasantry. It is underscored that as early as March-April 1917 the official reports on the morale of the troops presented a picture of deterioration of discipline and of a rapidly mounting antagonism between soldiers and officers, the army being sharply divided into two fundamental classes—peasants guided by workers on the one hand, and the bloc of officers, bourgeois and noble, on the other. The author admits, however, that in the first days after the March revolution, defensist tendencies were fairly strong among the masses of the soldiers.[22]

According to that Soviet view, the rate of the process of decay of the army had increased greatly after the collapse of the Kornilov rebellion. From that time on, all relations of command-subordination were obliterated. The officers ceased to be commanders in fact. They became merely class enemies of the soldiers. At the same time, the soldiers' elemental yearning for land and peace was replaced by organized sympathy and help to the Bolshevik party, so that the committees had become either dominated by the members of that party, or, at least, by elements prepared to work hand in hand with the latter.[23]

One may easily discover in these views a desire to minimize the responsibility for the disruption of the old army on the part of the Bolsheviki, an intent to shift the blame onto conditions under the old régime, the resultant class antagonism between officers and men, the long and disastrous war, the material conditions of the army and the age-long coveting of the landlords' acres by the Russian peasant. To a certain extent, however, such a view finds support in the documentary evidence of the process of decay which began in the Russian Army after the first great defeats of 1914. At the same time, no objective student can fail to be impressed by the great difference between the rate of the process *before* and *after* the March revolution, between the period of 1917 before the Kornilov rebellion and afterwards, when the Bolsheviki succeeded in establishing their influence over the masses of the soldiers at the front.

It is true that, as referred to above, there were instances of serious decline of discipline and symptoms of defeatism in the army *before* the March revolution. At that time, however, the most flagrant cases of insubordination were immediately punished, and order was restored, so that the military forces of Russia remained in a large measure, in the beginning of 1917, a still usable instrument of war. The argument of war-weariness, material privations, realization of the senselessness of the war from the viewpoint of the peasant soldier etc., so strongly underscored by the Soviet spokesman, ignores the important fact that the March revolution did not begin at the front where all these conditions should obviously be more pronounced, but in the rear, among troops fairly well fed and clothed and comparatively comfortably housed in Petrograd barracks—as against trenches —the vast majority of whom had not fired a single shot against the enemy. True, the front had accepted enthusiastically the accomplished fact of seizure of power by the revolutionaries at Petrograd. But, here again, one cannot fail to notice that the conflict within the armed forces was lashed into fury at first not among the troops that suffered most from the rigors of war, such as the infantry in the trenches, but among naval units, where men were materially much better off and did not, in consequence of the war, have to undergo any hardships comparable to those that were the lot of their comrades in the trenches. Even within the navy, the crews of the submarines and the destroyer flotillas of the Baltic Fleet, who had borne the brunt of naval warfare, did not react to the virus of revolutionary propaganda as violently as the men of the battleships, the training ships and the personnel of the naval depots, who during the war were living almost under normal peacetime conditions.

Also worth noting: the conflict between officers and men and the consequent lapse in the efficiency of the naval forces was much more acute at Helsingfors in Finland than at Reval in Estonia; more acute in the Baltic Fleet as a whole than in the Black Sea. At Kronstadt, where the influence of war was hardly felt, the conflict and the ensuing anarchy was at its worst.

Obviously, one has to look for causes for this elsewhere than in the grounds enumerated by the author of the preface to the Soviet collection of documents on the decay of the old army. On the one hand, was the accessibility of Finland to agents of the German intelligence service, who could easily find allies among the friends and relatives of the Finnish *Jaegers* who volunteered to serve with the German armies in the hope of serving thus the cause of independence of their country. On the other—Kronstadt versus Sebastopol—the greater proximity of the large industrial center and the stronger influence of the bolshevik and internationalist elements in general, had, undoubtedly, a great deal to do with the violence of the conflict at Kronstadt, as against the orderly transition to the new régime at the principal dockyard of the Black Sea.

There has already been occasion to mention the Riga front as a "danger zone" with respect to defeatist propaganda. Here again it is possible to point to a specific cause for the deterioration of the combat efficiency of the troops in that sector. German propaganda found in Riga and vicinity numerous helpers among the German-speaking elements of the Baltic Provinces, while the Latvian group of the Bolshevik party was both energetic and numerous.

The class composition of the various parts of the Russian armed forces is also an important matter, not to be overlooked in the analysis of the process of degeneration of the old army. The large percentage of industrial workers among the seamen of the Baltic Fleet, which had made them since 1905 particularly susceptible to socialist propaganda, had a definite connection with the ready acceptance by a large part of the Baltic Fleet, in 1917, of the more extreme revolutionary slogans, leading to a complete cleavage between officers and men.

An analysis of the relative virulence of the revolutionary movement among the various services and arms of the Russian forces remains to be written. However, even a foreign observer such as the French General Niessel, could not fail to see the difference between the state of affairs in November 1917, among the artillery units as against the infantry he visited. He was struck on the same trip to the front by the excellent conditions prevailing among the personnel of the aviation units he came to know.[24]

At least in so far as the naval forces were concerned, the history of their previous participation in the revolutionary outbreaks since 1905, the proportion of reservists who actually took part or witnessed these outbreaks, had an important connection with the trend of events after March 1917. The personalities of the officers, their ability to adapt themselves to problems of leadership under new conditions, their influence with their men, the percentage of regular soldiers and non-commissioned officers in the ranks that had survived from the pre-war days (such as in the cavalry and some of the artillery units)—all these were not without influence on the development of events in the respective units in 1917.

Professor Miliukov ascribes considerable importance, prior to March 1917, to the defeatist propaganda carried on among the workers and soldiers by some of the Russian socialist groups, and states, in his work on the Russian revolution, that at the front the work of the Germans was added to that of the Russian socialists. The Socialist and Labor (*Trudoviki*) party deputies of the State Duma of the Empire had abstained from voting war credit,[25] although such important leaders as Plekhanov, of the Social Democrats, and Kropotkin, of the Anarchists, had come out openly for the defense of the country.

After the March revolution the famous Order No. 1,* issued by

* The text of Order No. 1, March 1 (14), 1917:
"To the garrison of the Petrograd District. To all soldiers of the Guard, army, artillery and fleet for immediate and precise execution, and to the workers of Petrograd for information.
"The Soviet of Workers' and Soldiers' Deputies has decided:
"1. In all companies, battalions, regiments, depots, batteries, squadrons and sepa-

the Executive Committee of the Petrograd Soviet, played a very important role as a stimulus of conflict between men and officers and a
powerful dissolvent of army discipline. Order No. 2, intended to offset the unfortunate effect of its predecessor at the front, failed to
achieve its aim. The commentary of a member of the Executive Committee of the Petrograd Soviet, V. B. Stankevich, that "war, as a real
task was alien to the members of the Committee, who looked at everything only through the prism of the problem of struggle with the old
government, and, also, were afraid of the unknown and mysterious
front,"[26] was an apt characterization of the frame of mind of the
leaders of the powerful body which *de facto* shared with the Provisional Government the control of policies of Russia during the first
weeks after the March events.

The manifesto of March 14, 1917, adopted by the Soviet as the
expression of its views on war, was under the strong influence of
Zimmerwaldian tendencies, and helped powerfully to spread among

rate branches of military service of every kind and on warships immediately choose
committees from the elected representatives of the soldiers and sailors of the above
mentioned military units.

"2. In all military units which have still not elected their representatives in the
Soviet of Workers' Deputies elect one representative to a company, who should appear with written credentials in the building of the State Duma at ten o'clock on
the morning of March 2.

"3. In all its political demonstrations a military unit is subordinated to the Soviet
of Workers' and Soldiers' Deputies and its committees.

"4. The orders of the military commission of the State Duma are to be fulfilled
only in those cases which do not contradict the orders and decisions of the Soviet
of Workers' and Soldiers' Deputies.

"5. Arms of all kinds, as rifles, machine-guns, armored automobiles and others
must be at the disposition and under the control of the company and battalion committees and are not in any case to be given out to officers, even upon their demand.

"6. In the ranks and in fulfilling service duties soldiers must observe the strictest
military discipline; but outside of service, in their political, civil and private life
soldiers cannot be discriminated against as regards those rights which all citizens
enjoy.

"Standing at attention and compulsory saluting outside of service are especially
abolished.

"7. In the same way the addressing of officers with titles: Your Excellency, Your
Honor, etc., is abolished and is replaced by the forms of address: Mr. General, Mr.
Colonel, etc.

"Rude treatment of soldiers of all ranks, and especially addressing them as 'thou,'
is forbidden; and soldiers are bound to bring to the attention of the company committees any violation of this rule and any misunderstandings between officers and
soldiers.

"This order is to be read in all companies, battalions, regiments, marine units,
batteries and other front and rear military units."

"PETROGRAD SOVIET OF WORKERS' AND SOLDIERS' DEPUTIES"

("The Revolution of 1917, Chronicle of Events," Vol. I, pp. 186-187.)
quoted from Chamberlin, William Henry. *The Russian Revolution
1917-1921*, v. I, (Macmillan Company, New York, 1935), pp. 429, 430.

the soldiers the idea that peace could be achieved by means other than the continuation of military activities.[27]

An attempt by Guchkov, then Minister of War, to persuade the Military Commission of the Soviet to abstain from further agitation of peace and war aim problems, in order to preserve the combat efficiency of the army, met with Sukhanov's reply that the Soviet "cannot sacrifice itself, i.e. the interest of the revolution . . . to the maintenance of the efficiency of the army. . . . The Fatherland has rights, interests and problems other than defense."[28] True, in April 1917, the Soviet adopted a proclamation to the army directed against a separate peace.[29] In the meanwhile, the ideas of soldiers' self-government, of peace, of antagonism against the officers had already not only taken strong root, but found expression in overt action.

Leon Trotsky said in 1921 that the offensive of June 18, 1917, organized by Kerensky, was the heaviest blow delivered to the Russian revolution, and that the Brest-Litovsk peace was the result not only of the policies of czarist diplomacy and the Kerensky régime, but of the June 18 offensive as well; that the peace signed by Lenin's government was merely a payment on a bill of exchange endorsed by Nicholas II, Miliukov and Kerensky.[30]

In another speech, made on March 22, 1918, upon the occasion of the celebration of Red Army day, Trotsky, in answering a hypothetical question as to whether the destruction of the old army and the consequent defenselessness of the front was necessary, said: "I also ask was it necessary? However, it is possible to admit that what was predictable was unavoidable,"[31] which of course evades the problems of the bolshevik responsibility for their share in the disruption of the old army.

To sum up: the factors enumerated by the author of the preface, referred to above, were undoubtedly present, and formed the background for the rapid decay of the old army in 1917, although its defeats were by no means "uninterrupted," as he asserted.

The shortsighted policy of the Provisional Government in 1917 had also added to the acceleration of the process of degeneration of the Russian armed forces. To hope for the success of the June 18 offensive was to give proof of political blindness and a lack of understanding of military realities.

The various socialist groups represented in the Executive Committee of the Petrograd Soviet had their share in sowing the seed of discord and disintegration at the front.

The impact of the Kornilov affair sharpened the conflict between officers and men, and making the former, if not actively inimical, at least indifferent to the fate of the Provisional Government.

The fact remains, however, that after March 1917, the only *conscious,* sustained and important effort to break up and annihilate the old army was made by the Bolsheviki, as freely admitted by one of the bolshevik military leaders, N. I. Podvoiskii, in his report, which will be discussed in the next chapter.

The problem of the defense of the country was definitely and deliberately subordinated to the interest of the party, of class and of the world revolution. The seeds of the Civil War, the immediate reasons for Russia's inability to resist the extortionate terms of the Brest-Litovsk peace treaty—all these in a large measure grew out of the stand taken by Lenin with respect to war and the old army, and the subsequent activities of his party at the front. The responsibility of the Bolsheviki for their share in the weakening of the power of resistance of Russia in 1917 cannot be rightfully shifted to other shoulders or dismissed as a mere detail in the general elemental process of disruption inherited from the old régime.

Writing as late as 1929, F. Blumenthal, in his book on political work during wartime, had to combat ideas of fraternization—derived from the 1917 practice advocated at the time of the Bolsheviki—advanced as one of the means of overcoming the resistance of an enemy army by Soviet forces. His admission is significant for the understanding of the rôle fraternization propaganda played in the degeneration of the old army. "Admitting that fraternization had a very strong influence on German and Austrian soldiers, even then their commanders very quickly succeeded in taking the matter in hand and attempted to *use* fraternization for their own ends . . . fraternization simultaneously demoralized Russian units. This was, of course, one of the aims of fraternizing. As a result . . . a colossal explosion of revolt against war among the Russian soldiers."[32]

All available evidence clearly indicates that:

At the time the Provisional Government was going through its agony, the old army ceased to be a reliable and adequate armed force even for defensive purposes. The rate of deterioration of the Russian armed forces between March and November 1917 was rapid, and struck at the very vitals of these forces.

In the meanwhile the Bolsheviki were taking steps toward the organization of an armed force of their own.

★ II ★

BOLSHEVIK FORCES BEFORE NOVEMBER 1917

THE Bolsheviki gave a great deal of thought and organizing effort to the formation of a nucleus of military forces loyal to the party. This work began during the very first weeks following the March 1917 events.

One of the most important components of these forces was the Red Guard, an industrial workers' militia that came into being soon after Lenin's arrival in Russia in the spring of 1917. By July, when Petrograd's proletariat made their abortive attempt to wrest power from the Provisional Government, there were some ten thousand of these Red Guards, organized in tens (which paradoxically included thirteen men each), platoons, companies, and battalions. On the eve of the November rebellion, a Staff of the Red Guard was formed at Petrograd to co-ordinate and direct these workers' battalions.[1]

The threat of General Kornilov's putsch provided a strong impetus for the recruiting of the proletarian militia, and swelled it to about twenty thousand men.[2] Moscow and other industrial centres also had Red Guard units varying in strength and efficiency.[3]

In the days of Kornilov's rebellion in September 1917, the units of the Red Guard were drilling every day near the buildings housing the Regional Committees of the party in Petrograd, "studying all battle exercises, the use of weapons and the military formations, with the greatest eagerness," according to the testimony of an eye-witness, V. Bonch-Bruevich.[4]

The Regional Committees became centers of the bolshevik military forces during the time preceding the overthrow of the Kerensky government. Red Guard units took turns of duty there, armed patrols circulated near them, a signal service was maintained, and passwords were exchanged every day. Bruevich maintains that in these companies "the military ordering of life reached great strictness."[5] The militiamen were well armed with rifles, revolvers and hand grenades.

According to the official Soviet view, the Red Guard was the principal and decisive armed force in the November rebellion.[6] It was *par excellence* the military organization of the proletariat, which was fostered and developed by the Bolsheviki in 1917, in preparation for the armed rebellion they were planning.

A. Geronimus, the communist military sociologist, points out that the upbuilding of an efficient Red Guard, as well as the undermining of the old army organization, was approached and solved by the Bolshevik party from the standpoint of preparation for a successful uprising. The problem of national defense, in face of the thunder-clouds of the German Army hanging over Russia, was thus definitely subordinated by the Bolsheviki to the struggle for power with the Provisional Government.[7]

Another pillar of Soviet might in the early days of its existence was the Latvian Rifle Regiments. At the All-Russian Military Conference of the Bolsheviki, which opened on June 16, 1917, Comrade Iurevich, representing the military organization of the party among the Latvian Rifle units, stated that the Bolshevik party collective of the Latvian Rifle Brigades numbered 1,537 members, about 10 per cent of whom were old revolutionaries. He said that each company and detachment had a bolshevik nucleus. Iurevitch claimed that the entire elective organization of the Latvian Rifles was controlled by the Bolsheviki.[8]

At the Northern Regional Congress, which met shortly before the November uprising, the representative of the Latvian Rifles was reported as saying that their forces and their armed might were at the disposal of the Congress—not of the Provisional Government.[9] That this statement was not mere verbiage was proved after the November uprising, when the Latvian Rifle Regiments almost to a man passed into the Red Army and thus played a great rôle in the upbuilding of the Red Army forces of the Petrograd Military District.[10] The Bolsheviki headquarters at the Smolny Girls' College in Petrograd were guarded in the end of 1917 by a picked detachment of Latvian Rifles. To this detachment Lenin thus entrusted his own and his principal followers' safety during the turbulent early months of the existence of the Soviet state.[11]

Perhaps the most picturesque of the various groups of the supporters of Lenin's régime in 1917, and certainly the most dreaded by the Bolsheviki's enemies, was that formed by the bluejackets of the Russian Navy, the famous "ornament and pride of the revolution."

In the early days after the March 1917 events, the Bolsheviki succeeded in building up an enthusiastic following not only among seamen stationed at the principal navy yard of the Baltic—Kronstadt—but also at Helsingfors, where the main battle forces of the Russian Baltic Fleet were concentrated. At the first meetings of the Helsingfors Soviet, in March 1917, a small nucleus of Bolshevik bluejackets was already active. With the arrival of a group of experienced bolshevik agitators, which included the well-known Antonov-Ovseenko, later so prominent in Spain, a large part of the bluejackets fell under the sway of the Bolshevik party.[12] As a consequence, a large contingent of Helsingfors sailors left for Petrograd to participate in the November rebellion jointly with the Kronstadt seamen. Flotillas of destroyers sailed thence into the Neva to support Lenin's thrust for power, and to supplement the help given to the uprising by the guns of the cruiser *Avrora*, moored below the bridges.

There were also other units of the old armed forces that the People's Commissars could count on in an emergency: some Chasseurs, and other Guard Reserve units, as well as a part of the companies of the Naval Guards and the Second Naval Depot located at Petrograd.[13] The armored-car detachment, quartered at the Peter and Paul citadel, "a firm, highly disciplined military unit," commanded by an ex-czarist officer, played an important rôle in maintaining such law and order as the Soviet Government were able to exercise at Petrograd in the last months of 1917.[14]

The official history of the Russian Civil War estimates that of the millions of soldiers of the old army, only some thirty to fifty thousand "remained under the banners of the Revolution," or, in plain English, for various reasons were willing to support, for the time being at least, the Bolshevik régime. This estimate—such as it is—embraces, among others, the Latvian Rifle regiments, the bluejackets, the armored-car detachments, and some of the army units in the Far East.[15]

Such were the more or less reliable armed forces at the disposal of the government headed by Lenin in the first weeks of its existence. This comparatively small group of armed men was like an insignificant island in the turbulent sea of the millions of soldiers of the old army intent on getting home and forgetting all about war and military discipline.

The Bolsheviki work among the ranks of the old army aimed, in 1917, not only at the destruction of it as an efficient armed force, but also at the revolutionizing of the masses of the soldiers with a view to establishing their influence over them.[16] In the first respect, they were entirely successful, as they were merely giving a hand to an elemental movement for peace and land among the war-weary muzhiks in soldiers' uniforms. In the second, they soon found that their influence, powerful enough in adding to the chaos and destruction, was not adequate for turning the old army to their own uses in the early months of 1918, when the Soviet Government was anxiously casting about for armed force to meet the German advance after the interruption of the Brest-Litovsk peace negotiations.[17]

It is claimed by the Bolsheviki—and their claim seems to be justified by the results—that of all the Russian political parties in 1917
they had the clearest understanding of the importance of an organizational support for their influence in the army. The Bolsheviki
formed special party machinery to deal with military problems, which
later expanded into a large organization within the army. They
achieved this in advance of the Socialist Revolutionaries, the Mensheviki (the moderate wing of the Russian Social Democratic party)
and the middle class party of People's Freedom (*Kadety*, as they were
popularly known at the time). Of all the Russian political parties, the
Bolsheviki, it is claimed, were the only one that succeeded in creating
a military newspaper of national importance in their *Soldiers' Truth*
(*Soldatskaia Pravda*).[18]

The Petrograd Committee of the Bolshevik party appointed a
Military Commission which had as its goal the unification and co-
ordination of the activities of all soldiers and officers belonging to the
party. As early as March 31, 1917, a meeting was held which laid the
foundation for a military organization which was first attached to
the Petrograd Committee, and later became connected with the Central Committee of the party. At the All-Russian Party Conference of
the Bolsheviki held at the end of April 1917, reference was made to
military organizations of the party existing at Moscow, Rybinsk,
Ivanovo-Voznesensk, Lugansk and some other places in the Don industrial region. Helsingfors and Kronstadt Bolshevik party organizations were at the time filled almost entirely with bluejackets and
soldiers. At all these points, with the exception of Moscow and Petrograd, the military organizations were still numerically very weak, just
beginning to take shape. Their work among the armies of the front
was at its inception, except in the Twelfth Army, where they had a
better foothold.[19]

The Bolshevik party press played a very important rôle in spreading Lenin's ideas among the soldiers at the front. At first, the general
party newspapers, such as the *Pravda* of Petrograd and the Moscow
Sotsial-Demokrat, and later the special military newspapers, the
Soldatskaia Pravda, already mentioned, the *Okopnaia Pravda* published in Riga, and others, were daily sent to the soldiers at the front,
and in the rear, in hundreds of thousands of copies—which was for
Russia of that period a very large circulation.[20]

Soldiers' clubs, opened in Petrograd and other cities, also had their
part in the indoctrination of the armed men of Russia with bolshevik
ideas. It was found that workers' gatherings as a rule did not attract

large numbers of soldiers. A club opened for the use of the members of armed forces in the building occupied by the Bolshevik Military Organization at Petrograd was an immediate success, and attracted many soldiers of the Petrograd garrison as well as delegates from front units, which at the time were crowding the streets of the national capital.[21]

The summoning of the conference of delegates of the party military organization lent further impetus to the spread of the bolshevik influence in the army. Almost simultaneously with the call for the election of delegates to the conference, there sprang up new military party organizations at Kharkov, Kiev, Ufa, Krasnoiarsk and Kazan. At the opening of the conference on June 16, 1917, one hundred and twenty-five delegates were present. With those that arrived later, and the Petrograd representatives, the number of participants exceeded one hundred and fifty. According to a fairly reliable report, these delegates represented forty-three front, and seventeen rear military organizations.[22] The membership of the conference thus reflected the rapid spread of the bolshevik influence in its army. It was estimated that about thirty thousand soldiers were represented at the conference, although one of the authorities makes reference to twenty-six thousand as being represented. Most of the delegates were private soldiers. There were only a few commissioned officers at the conference. The civilian element was almost entirely absent. The majority of the delegates joined the party after the March revolution of 1917, and had thus belonged to it only for a few short months, or even weeks. There was, however, among the delegates, an influential group of party members who had belonged to the Bolsheviki for several years.[23]

The speeches of the delegates throw some light on the scope and relative strength of the party influence in the different component parts of the army. In the Twelfth Army, for instance, in the 109th Division, the Bolsheviki were particularly strong—the *Okopnaia Pravda* was in fact started in that division. However, only eight regiments of that army had party organizations, some of which numbered up to one hundred members. The delegate from Minsk emphasized that the mass of the local military organizations was formed of private soldiers and that officers were very few within its membership.[24]

The aims of the military organization of the party were outlined by N. I. Podvoiskii, in his report to the conference, as the destruction of the standing army and the arming of the entire people. Another important leader of the conference, Nevskii, brought up the question of the creation of the Red Guard and of the arming of the workers, stressing that that problem could be solved only with the assistance of the soldiers. The Fourth Part of the resolution passed at the conference cautiously and cryptically suggested the formation from "army revolutionary democratic elements" following the leadership of Social Democracy of a "material revolutionary bulwark of the revolution," or, *anglice*, the building up of an armed force for the coming uprising.[25]

The draft of the regulations of the All-Russian military organization of the party discussed at the conference prescribed the formation of nuclei in each army unit, such as company, squadron, etc. All party members of that unit were instructed to belong to the nucleus. This famous feature—the cellular structure of the military party organization—was a unique characteristic of the bolshevik system; no other Russian party adopted it.[26]

It is interesting to observe that at that time the bolshevik military organization advocated the replacement of all commissioned officers by elected representatives of the people.[27]

At that first conference on military affairs since the March 1917 revolution, there came to the surface opinions differing from those advanced by the spokesmen of the party hierarchy. Thus, among soldier-delegates, a strong dislike was discernible for the arming of the workers and their formation into separate armed units. The bolshevik soldiers saw in this a certain lack of confidence in the revolutionary army on the part of the party. The national defense viewpoint was also represented—some of the delegates considered it undesirable to disorganize the old army.[28] Apparently their feelings for national self-preservation had not as yet been entirely uprooted by the views of the Central Committee of the party.

These heretical views, of course, could not prevail against the steam-roller of the party machine, and resolutions were dutifully passed advocating an immediate arming and organization of workers' battalions of the Red Guard from workers of both sexes, the Red Guard to be self-governing and at the disposal of elective workers' regional organizations of the large proletarian centres.[29] The expression of these views, however, marks the beginning of conflict within the party military organization as to policy and tactics. These conflicts, sometimes latent, at times open, became an integral part of the military life of a régime under which the army was deposed from its position of political aloofness and made politics-conscious—at times acutely conscious of the political disputes within the party.

The advocacy of the so-called democratization of the army was a Trojan horse with intent at its disruption. The Bolsheviki admit this themselves. Election of officers and self-government of the lower ranks were proposed as the basis for the construction of a "revolutionary and democratic" army. Even military operations were to be controlled by the lower ranks, while military courts were to be replaced by "Comradely Courts," not necessarily presided over by officers, to whose jurisdiction both officers and men were to be subjected.[30]

The discussions and resolutions of the conference give an indication of the direction in which Lenin's plans were developing. He was still moving along the same general lines laid down in his *Letters from Afar*, penned while he was still abroad.

In accordance with resolutions passed at the conference, the military organization of the party participated in the building up of the Red Guard units, assigning instructors to them and obtaining for them arms and ammunitions. Special fighting detachments of revolutionary army soldiers were also energetically prepared against the day of rebellion.[31]

It would seem that even at that period Lenin and his collaborators still regarded the Red Guards as the basis of the future armed forces of their state. The old army, apparently, was viewed by them merely as a reservoir of men and material to be drawn upon for the upbuilding of the Red Guard and the formation of fighting detachments to be used in the struggle against the Provisional Government.

Nevertheless, the course of events after November 1917 brought about a radical change of view as to the organizational structure of the armed forces on the part of the rulers of the Soviet State.

★ III ★

THE EARLY DAYS OF THE SOVIET REGIME

MINOR difficulties, to overcome which the newly established Soviet Government needed the use of armed forces, were successfully met. The memoirs of the bluejacket Dybenko, who later rose to command a Soviet army, shed some light on the relative military efficiency of the various component parts of the Soviet forces at the time of their first test, after the bolshevik uprising. Dybenko brought with him from Helsingfors three thousand seamen. Fifteen hundred more, with two batteries of artillery, were on their way to Petrograd to help the Soviet Government at the time of General Krasnov's attempt to recapture the capital with a small body of Cossacks on November 10, 1917. On that day, Dybenko discussed the situation with one of the bolshevik military leaders, Podvoiskii, at the party headquarters at Smolny. He found the latter "nervous"; information as to what exactly was going on at the front was lacking. Dybenko then went to the scene of action himself, passing, on the way, small groups of armed workmen—the Red Guard—trudging in both directions along the macadam road leading to the erstwhile Imperial residence. He noted: "The detachments moving hither and yon were entirely unlike any really organized military units." As he reached Pulkovo, Dybenko discovered that the person directing the attack of the proletariat was an ex-czarist officer by the name of Walden assisted by another ex-czarist officer fully armed with pistol and sword.[1]

Having looked over the situation at the Pulkovo front, Dybenko summed up his views: "What are the Petrograd regiments now? Not one of them is able to put up a fight." He pointed with pride to the five thousand bluejackets whom he had already concentrated at Petrograd.[2]

The Red Guards at Pulkovo also were aware of their shortcomings. "Where are the bluejackets? How soon will they come to help us?"[3] And the gray-coated seamen turned the tide at Pulkovo for Lenin.

Of course, Dybenko's testimony must be taken with a grain of salt; being a seaman, his picture of the contrast between other armed forces and his doughty bluejackets was drawn in black and white. Other information, however, supports the trend of Dybenko's views; the ten to twelve thousand Red Guards concentrated at Pulkovo against the puny forces at Krasnov's disposal could not achieve any decisive results until the bluejackets arrived and led the charge.[4] It would seem that at the end of 1917 the bluejackets were, perhaps, the best fighting element at the disposal of the Soviet Government, apart from the Latvian Rifle Regiments and armored-car detachments of the Petrograd citadel. The Red Guards were poorly trained and led, while the regiments of the Petrograd garrison were in a state of demoralization and dispersal.

The trouble with the bluejackets was not their lack of will to fight —they went for the hated counter-revolutionaries with all the zest one would expect of young men cooped up on battleships during the years of war, spoiling for a fight that never came. But when fighting was over it was next to impossible to keep them in hand. As Dybenko puts it: "the bluejacket is an eternally rebellious soul, striving at freedom. Only a week after the revolution he could not get reconciled to a 'safe haven.' His mutinous spirit stormed forward . . . driving him to action."[5] A sociologist would, no doubt, find a less mystic explanation for the lack of restraint shown by the bluejackets after the revolution—the removal of the tight, restraining fetters of the Imperial naval discipline left them emotionally unprepared to conduct themselves as behooves free citizens.

Lenin's admiration for these doughty allies began to wane, as soon as he found out that the anarchistically-minded among the seamen took matters in their own hands at Petrograd, arresting in the streets people of whom they disapproved for one reason or another, conducting searches of apartments and houses without proper authority, even kidnaping and holding for ransom some of the wealthier citizens. Matters came to a head when these seamen arrested three naval officers and murdered two of them in spite of the efforts Smolny made to save the officers from the bluejackets' clutches.[6]

"From anarchy to counter-revolution there is only one step," said Lenin, when confronted with convincing proofs that the "ornament and pride of the revolution"—the seamen stationed at Petrograd— were honeycombed with anarchistic organizations and had fallen under the influence of the prominent leaders of anarchism residing at Petrograd. Matters went so far that the seamen-Anarchists at the Naval Depot Barracks terrorized the rest of the bluejackets there. They showed a particular dislike to the Bolsheviki among their colleagues, considering them sea-lawyers and spineless moderates.[7]

Bonch-Bruevich relates in his memoirs his experience with a detachment of seamen quartered temporarily at the War College. In spite of all efforts to introduce strict discipline among them, some of the seamen began to destroy furniture and to make a general nuisance of themselves. The culprits were arrested and sent under escort of their fellow-seamen on board their ships, with instructions to have them disarmed and dismissed from the service.[8]

Later on, a large number of seamen were disarmed by the Latvian Rifles.[9]

These conflicts with the sailors were repeated during the Civil War, and ultimately culminated in the mass rising of the seamen at Kronstadt in the spring of 1921. They mark the beginning of antagonisms leading to the use of force among the component parts of the Soviet armed units.

Despite these internal frictions, the armed force at the disposal of Lenin's government was at first adequate for the purpose of maintaining his group in power and suppressing the more violent forms of disorder in the capital. At times there were difficulties, as during the period, called by Bonch-Bruevich that of "the drunken pogrom agitation," when demoralized soldiery of the Petrograd garrison smashed up wine cellars and liquor stores, staging a peasant kermess of wild carousal and license.[10] These disorders, however, were never a real threat to the existence of the Soviet Government.

The first real crisis that confronted the armed forces of the Soviets came when the Germans interrupted the Brest-Litovsk peace negotiations and began to move their troops eastward, threatening Petrograd.

In one of his *Letters from Afar*, written in the end of March 1917, Lenin confirmed his view that the Bolshevik party should stand for the revolutionary utilization of revolutionary forms of the state; that they needed the state for a certain period of transition. However, the state he wanted was not of the kind in existence in the capitalist countries, with organs of power in the form of police, army, bureaucracy, "distinct from and opposed to the people." He wanted, in accordance with his interpretation of the Marxian formula, to destroy the state machinery of Russia, replacing it by another, "*merging* the police, the army and the bureaucracy *with the universally armed people*." Lenin advocated that the proletariat organize and arm *all* the poorest and most exploited sections of the population, so that "they *themselves* may take into their own hands all the organs of state power, that they *themselves* may constitute these organs."[11]

Lenin, however, was careful to say that the idea of laying out any "plan" for a proletarian militia would be absurd. He stated that "when the workers, and all the people as a real mass, take up this task in a practical way, they will work it out and secure it a hundred times better than any theoretician can propose."[12] He also advanced the thought that such a militia would be a proletarian militia, because the industrial and the city workers would "just as naturally and inevitably" assume in it the leadership of the masses of the poor, as they took the leading position in all the revolutionary struggles of the people in the years 1905-1907 and in 1917." He felt that such a militia would guarantee absolute order and "a comradely discipline practiced with enthusiasm."[13]

If this is not a "plan," it is, at least, a nucleus of one. The new armed organization of the state is viewed as an array of the "oppressed" classes led by the urban proletariat. A great deal of importance and room is given to the initiative of the masses themselves, while the discipline described as "comradely" is obviously radically different from, and opposed to, the hierarchically enforced discipline of the armies of the capitalist states. The idea of a national army led by professional officers seems to be thus rejected as unsuitable for the purposes of the revolutionary proletariat.[14]

At the same time, Lenin advocated pacifistic attitudes among the soldiers of the old army. He wrote in *Pravda* on May 11, 1917: "It is as well that the soldiers curse the war. It is well that they clamor for peace. It is well that they begin to feel that war benefits the capitalists. It is well that they, breaking the prison discipline, themselves begin to fraternize on all the fronts." This and similar utterances of Lenin and his collaborators might easily be taken—and no doubt were taken—by the masses of Russian soldiery as a stand against war in general, pacifism as an essential political principle. However, then as later, pacifism was never taken over by the Bolsheviki as a fundamental principle of their creed.[15] They believed in force as an instrument of policy.

A very interesting and somewhat obscure facet in the history of the change of the bolshevik viewpoint as to the organization of armed forces, is Lenin's position with respect to the remnants of the old army still under arms in the anxious days after the breaking up of the Brest-Litovsk conference.

Erich Wollenberg, in his book on the Red Army, points out that after the November revolution Lenin again and again insisted that since their advent to power the Bolsheviki had become defenders of their country, of the "socialist fatherland." He quotes Gusev, a prominent communist military writer, to the effect that the leaders of the new government had to execute a complete change of front: from disorganizers of the old army, they had to become organizers of the new. Wollenberg insists, however—and his views have the support of other evidence reviewed—that only in a few isolated instances (the Latvian Rifle regiments, the Fourth Cavalry Division, some armored-car detachments) did the Bolsheviki succeed in reorganizing units of the old army into efficient formations of the new.[16]

The late Eugene Behrens, formerly in command of the Soviet Navy, and a member of the Revolutionary Military Council of the Republic, told the writer that very shortly after the November uprising he and Admiral Altvater had a number of conferences with Lenin and Trotsky on reorganization of the armed forces of Russia. Behrens was surprised by the clear understanding of the urgency of reestablishing strict military discipline shown by Lenin. As an illustration, Behrens mentioned that when Altvater presented at one of these conferences a draft of some military or naval regulation to Lenin, the latter criticized it as too mild, too reminiscent of the Kerensky régime committee system of army government.

The stenographic report of the proceedings of the Seventh Congress of the Russian Communist party held on March 6-8, 1918, contains some clues as to Lenin's trend of thought regarding the old army, and his reasons for supporting the acceptance of the harsh terms of peace insisted upon by the Germans. These minutes were kept secret for a number of years and apparently faithfully reflect the heated discussions which took place at that Congress, which, according to the preface to the report, was broken up into factions, "reflecting the state of our entire party, of the entire working class, of all of Russia. . . . It was a depressing picture, it was a hard time."[17]

Iakov Sverdlov, President of the All-Russian Central Executive Committee of the Soviet Government, said at the March 6 meeting that "as we have no troops" military organizations of the Bolsheviki and the division which heretofore existed between the workers' and soldiers' branches of the party structure should become a thing of the past.[18] In his speech the next day, Lenin also mentioned that "we have no army, while we have to live side by side with a spoliator armed to the teeth . . . whom of course our agitation for a peace without annexation and contributions could not bring to reason."[19]

Apparently at that time the responsibility for the demoralization of the army began to suggest itself at least to some of the delegates present at the Congress. There is no definite indication of that in the text of the report, but there are quite a few hints corroborating such a view in the speeches of the members of the opposition.

Lenin parried the danger of such an implied accusation by pre-
tending that the party was unanimous in its wish to destroy the old
army: "How did it occur in general that not one of the currents, not
one of the trends, not one of the organizations of our party opposed
this demobilization? Are we completely demented? Not at all. Officers,
non-Bolsheviki, kept saying even before October that the army could
not fight, that it was impossible to hold it even for a few weeks at
the front. After October this became obvious to anyone who wanted
to see facts, the bitter, ugly reality. . . . There is no army, it is impossible to retain it. The best that can be done about it is to demobilize
the army as soon as possible." A still more acrid tone permeates
Lenin's further remarks: ". . . even previously it was impossible to
close one's eyes to the evidence that decomposition had reached unheard-of lengths, even to the sale of artillery guns to the Germans for
a few pennies. . . . We knew that through the fault of the army we
had to make peace with the imperialists."[20]

Lenin urged that the respite granted by the peace of Brest-Litovsk
should be used to educate the nation in developing self-discipline, in
inculcating among the people the idea of the necessity of the armed
struggle, so that an army could be created that would be ready to
face even "unheard-of suffering." "All will come in time; start now
with self-discipline; obey at all costs so that there shall be exemplary
order; workers should study how to fight at least one hour each day."
"Because I am for national defense, because I stand for the up-building of the army—even if this must be done far behind the lines, where
the present demobilized sick army is being healed." Lenin pointed out
that when the German Army was within a few days' march of Petrograd, the bluejackets and the Red Guard formed by the Putilov
workers "with all their enthusiasm" were not able to stem the onslaught of the enemy, since they were left unsupported.[21]

So far the general trend of Lenin's argument seems to indicate
that he supported the acceptance of the harsh terms of the Brest-
Litovsk treaty because there was no way of resisting the onslaught of
the German Army, what with the demoralization of the old army and
the insufficiency of the efforts of the bluejackets and the best of the
Red Guard. Lenin repeatedly emphasized the fact that he stood on the
platform of defense of the country, but that because of the inadequacy
of the means at the government's disposal there was no choice but to
sign a peace with the "imperialists," and that revolutionary war was
utterly impossible.

Later in the discussion, however, Lenin lifted the veil and revealed the real reasons for his opposition to the continuation of armed opposition to the Germans: "The Russian bourgeoisie and all her hangers-on . . . are sicking us on into this war . . . to declare war now on Germany means to give in to the provocation of the Russian bourgeoisie . . . this is the best way to overthrow us now."[22]

Other grounds for signing the peace are shown in the speeches of Lenin's supporters. Sverdlov made the very interesting statement that when he and his colleague were following day by day General Bonch-Bruevich, who was at the time their principal military adviser, marking on the military map positions assigned to detachments of the Red Guard, they came to the conclusion that to the General these proletarian units were just so much cannon-fodder which had been fed into the maw of enemy cannon for the past three and a half years. They thought that for the General the loss of five to ten thousand proletarians meant nothing. On the other hand, Sverdlov and his party colleagues felt that by "letting these detachments perish we are cutting the limb on which we are sitting."[23] Of course Sverdlov's statement could be interpreted in more than one way. Either the sacrifice of the better elements (from the bolshevik viewpoint) of the Petrograd proletariat was too great an offertory on the altar of defense of national territory, or, more probably, the loss of these Red Guard detachments endangered the safety of the dictatorship of the party and anything was better than a threat to the continuance in power of Lenin's followers.

Further on, Sverdlov stated that the workers did not show any strong wish to continue the armed struggle with Germany. Some other delegate developed this thought by explaining that a marked change had occurred during the fortnight preceding the congress in the views of the Petrograd proletariat regarding the revolutionary war: "At present the same is happening in the working class districts of Petrograd as happened in Moscow and all over the country. One after another, workers come forward and say: 'Two weeks ago I said this, but now I look at the matter differently.' "[24]

The question is posed whether the change in the feelings of the proletariat occurred spontaneously under the impetus of the bad news from the front, or, perhaps, was somewhat influenced by the propaganda of those of the party members who followed Lenin in his wish for peace. Whatever the cause, available evidence seems to point in the direction indicated by Sverdlov: one of the speakers referred to the statement by a comrade from Moscow who claimed that sixty thousand workers had joined the Red forces in Moscow and were spoiling for a fight, but explained that later it was established that only 2,830 volunteered.[25]

It is interesting to contrast this alleged lukewarmness of the Moscow proletariat toward the revolutionary war with the zeal displayed by the peasantry of the provinces invaded by the Germans. Sokolnikov spoke at the Congress about peasants, furious at the Germans for requisitioning horses, cattle and other property, attacking the enemy soldiers, and referred to the development of peasant guerilla warfare against the Germans. Other information bears out Sokolnikov's statement. Thus, in the province of Pskov, entire townships voted to mobilize all males from 18 to 40 years of age. G. Pukhov in his book on the growth of Soviet armed forces in the Petrograd military district, speaks of the recruiting bureau at Velikie Luki being swamped by volunteers anxious to serve in the Red Army, the majority of these recruits coming from territories occupied by the Germans.[26]

It is worth while noting that in contrast to the pessimistic remarks at the Congress about the defeatist attitude among the workers in the beginning of March, figures of recruiting of volunteers at Petrograd show up to March 1 a rather rapid influx of recruits, which continues also in March, although at a slower rate. Thus, up to February 25, there were recruited 5,500 men, on the next day the total rose to 9,600, by the 28th to 12,320, and on the first day of March the number of volunteers reached 15,300. During the entire month of March, on the other hand, less than ten thousand new volunteers joined up.[27]

The training of these volunteers left, of course, much to be desired. Smilga spoke at the Congress about his conversation with a Red Guard who, in reply to the former's question whether the Red Guards underwent a period of instruction in military matters, replied: "We came direct from the factory. We received rifles and left."[28]

These reports do not seem to indicate faint hearts among the peasants and workers. Apparently, in spite of the war fatigue and disillusionment, there were still large numbers of young Russians in factories and border villages willing to give their lives in a fight against the invading armies of the German Emperor. Smilga provides the real answer: "In view of the present conditions, a few military routs would unavoidably undermine and destroy our political power and lead to the restoration of whomever you please." Radek added to this a very pertinent analysis of the way the disbanding of the Constituent Assembly lessened the chances of the Bolsheviki to obtain the active support of the German working class: "I am asking all comrades in our party, who thoughtfully approach the events of the day: Did we strengthen our chances in Germany by disbanding the Constituent Assembly? No, by this we have given material for agitation against us as men of violence, we have strengthened the opinion that we are sitting on bayonets—and, nevertheless, we had to disband the Constituent Assembly," as otherwise the party would have lost power over the state.[29]

Thus the situation is well delineated in the course of the heated debate at the Congress. The very method of preparation for the seizure of power by violence, which involved the demoralization of the old army, helped greatly to make the country weaker with respect to its enemy.

The numerical weakness of the Bolshevik party cadres was a factor of great importance in shaping Lenin's course with respect to armed resistance to Germany. There is the testimony of one of the party leaders—A. Shliapnikov—that the Petrograd Committee of the party represented during World War I, before the March resolution, about 3,000 members. The official party data estimate that on January 1, 1917, the party was composed of 23,600 members, and by January 1, 1918, of 115,000 members.[30] A small party ruling through violence was not in a position to suffer severe defeats at the hands of the German Army. To call in the moderate socialists and the middle-class parties in the face of the national danger, to rouse the peasants to a patriotic defense of the land, would have meant the abandonment of the dictatorship of the proletariat, or rather, the rule of Russia by Lenin and his small group of party associates.

The national interests conflicted here with the party interest, and the former were sacrificed to the latter. A universal arming of the people implied democratic methods of government in a country where the state apparatus was weak and poorly organized. And this the party would not concede. Also, from then on the idea of militia was abandoned, at least for the time being, for that of a regular army with a hierarchical structure especially adapted to a minority party rule. The fifth of the Ten Theses discussed at the Congress already mentions the creation of an armed force of workers and peasants, "the least torn asunder from the people." . . . "The organized state of general national armament, as one of the first steps toward complete realization of the arming of the entire people."[31] Such were the words that introduced the New Model Army of the Soviets. Born in the conflict of Marxian ideas, Lenin's revolutionary tempo and the realities of Russian life, the Red Army started on a momentous career.

★ IV ★

THE RED ARMY DURING THE CIVIL WAR

Organization

LEON TROTSKY, speaking at a meeting of the All-Russian Central Executive Committee on April 23, 1918, gave a thumbnail outline of the organization of the Red Army as it was shaping itself at the time.[1]

The old Ministry of War, inherited from the Imperial régime via the brief tenure of power by the Provisional Government, was re-named the People's Commissariat for Military Affairs. It concerned itself largely with matters pertaining to the old army, its rapidly dis-solving personnel and its still important vast matériel. Within the framework of that bureaucratic machine functioned the "All-Russian Collegium for the Organization of the Workers' and Peasants' Red Army." The Collegium came into being on December 20, 1917, and existed until May 8, 1918. Then it was replaced (together with sev-eral other bureaus) by the All-Russian Supreme Staff. Five members of the Bolshevik party, including N. I. Podvoiskii and N. V. Kry-lenko, were guiding its work. Gradually, from a small beginning, it came to dominate the entire Commissariat.

As Trotsky puts it: "At the present we are merging . . . the depart-ments of the All-Russian Collegium for the organization of the Workers' and Peasants' Army with the respective departments of the Commissariat of War, the latter still reflecting the old army which no longer exists."[2]

This reorganization of the central machinery of military adminis-tration was supplemented by the upbuilding of local military bureaus in townships, counties, provinces, and military districts. A uniform type of organization was adapted for these military administration offices, called "Commissariats for Military Affairs." Each of these offices was headed by three functionaries. One of these was a military specialist, drawn from the officer personnel of the old army, flanked by two "commissars for military affairs" selected for their political affiliations and reliability from the Soviet viewpoint. According to Trotsky, in purely military matters, in all operations, work and com-bat problems, the last word was left in these offices to the military specialists. The political commissars were instructed not to interfere with operation orders of the military specialists. Their signatures on military documents merely signified that the given order was not a counter-revolutionary device.

Actually, the order of April 6, 1918, which defined the functions of commissars, stated that these officials were not responsible for the expediency of purely military operation orders. For these the military specialists were to assume full responsibility. In case a commissar felt he could not approve of a purely military order, he had no right to delay its execution or its issuance. All he could do was to report his disapproval to the immediately superior military body. An exception was made with respect to operation orders suspected on definite grounds of being motivated by counter-revolutionary intentions.[3]

Simultaneously with the recruiting of the officers of the old army for command and administrative positions in the New Model, an effort was made to train new Red officers. Trotsky mentioned 2,000 Red cadets trained in military schools established for the purpose.

The principle of electiveness of commanders by soldiers, one of the shibboleths of the 1917 propaganda of the Bolsheviki, was definitely discarded. As Trotsky said in his speech: "The undoubted danger of electiveness is that tendencies of the so-called army syndicalism could penetrate into the army, i.e. that the army would regard itself as an autonomous body, which gives itself its laws."[4]

Trotsky ascribed great importance to the decree on compulsory military education, which he supported before the Central Committee. This decree was adopted on April 22, 1918. It provided for the military training of workers and those of the peasants who did not employ any hired labor. The plan of the training was divided into three stages: 1) for school children, 2) preparatory, for persons from 16 to 18 years of age, and 3) regular, for those between the ages of 18 and 40. The training of the school children was left to the People's Commissariat for Education in co-operation with the People's Commissariat for Military Affairs. The other two stages were placed under the auspices of the latter. The course of training was to comprise eight weeks with at least twelve hours of military studies weekly, or a total of 96 hours for the entire course. Trotsky himself admitted the possibility that the period of training was too brief.[5]

The class principle was proclaimed by Trotsky as fundamental in the Red Army. He argued that as the workers had taken power into their hands, they had to create *their own* army. He concluded by pointing out that from the objective military standpoint the requirements of defense of the country under the conditions of the Soviet régime called for the up-building of the army on a class basis.[6]

N. Kakurin in his work on Civil War pointed out that the G.H.Q. of the old army also took part in the organization of the Red Army, paralleling thus the work carried out by the central organs of the People's Commissariat for Military Affairs. On January 26, 1918, the G.H.Q. had issued its own instructions as to the formation of the Red Army. The duty of forming units of the Red Army was laid on the military departments of the local Soviets. Voluntary enrollment was indicated as the source of recruiting. Companies of "about 150 men" were recommended as the basic type formation. Authority was given to local Soviets to draw on the supplies of the military stores in their respective territories. The full control over the forces of the Red Army was handed over by this instruction to the local Soviets. It was also left to them to determine the number of troops to be raised in their territories. Transfer and direction of the military forces was placed at the discretion of the provincial and regional Soviets. It was stipulated, however, that these Soviets should if necessary, place their military forces at the disposal of the central government.[7]

This instruction of the G.H.Q. gave expression to its extreme decentralizing views. It even did not provide for any co-ordination from the center of local efforts of raising the Red Army. Kakurin maintains that the "creative initiative" of the local Soviet authorities developed at first along the lines of that instruction.

The fruit of these local efforts was the heterogeneous armed units, which, joining with detachments formed from the remnants of the old army, became the bricks with which the original "screens"* were built. Behind these screens the recruiting and the training of the regular Red Army proceeded apace.[8]

Some of the local Soviets were very ambitious in their plans to raise military forces on their own initiative. Thus the Soviet of Nizhnii-Novgorod decided to organize a whole army, the nucleus of which should be one infantry and one cavalry regiment, a battery of field artillery, an armored-car detachment and an automobile column.[9]

How well organized the military departments of the local Soviets were is a matter of conjecture. No doubt, however, the average were not functioning as well as the Military Commissariats organized by the central authorities. Even those, or at least some of them, were not functioning on a high level of efficiency. Pukhov draws a rather dark picture of the Petrograd County Commissariat in January 1919. According to him, a committee appointed by the district office of the Military Economy Inspection was unable to proceed with its audit of

* Covering detachments facing the German and Austro-Hungarian armed forces.

that Commissariat, as there was no order or method of keeping accounts. It was found that the cashier kept official funds at his home, and that no provision was made for a money chest at the office of the Commissariat. There was a shortage of over three thousand rubles in the funds entrusted to the cashier. On a later occasion, on December 23, 1919, another inspector, visiting the same Commissariat, reported that "disorder and desolation" reigned at its bureaus, and that many of the leading functionaries were not possessed of the proper qualifications for their work.[10]

After all, conditions at a Commissariat at Petrograd should be, by all counts, better than in some remote provincial county capital.

N. Kakurin rightly assigns great importance to the fact that the Red Army, inheriting only a few fragments of the organized armed units of the old army, became heir to the entire vast machinery of the central and local military administration of old Russia. The personnel of these administrative organs was absorbed and utilized in the new bureaus formed by the organizers of the Red Army.[11] Altogether over ten thousand former civil servants of the old Russian military bureaucracy were incorporated into the office force of the Red Army.[12] This number does not include army officers, who, under the old régime, had specialized in bureau work and were also taken over by the Red Army. This trained and experienced office personnel played a very important rôle in keeping the machinery of the Red Army working during the Civil War.

The military organization with its parallelism of locally created and centrally appointed bureaus was further complicated by the establishment on March 1, 1918, in Petrograd, of the Supreme Military Council which concerned itself with the operation work on the theater of external war—with the Germans—and left the conduct of war on the internal front outside the scope of its work. Its principal usefulness was in the introduction of a measure of organizational uniformity into the motley detachments comprised in the "screens." The latter were divided into regions and sections.[13]

The date when the local Military Commissariats were established by decrees of the Soviet of People's Commissars was more than a month later than that of the formation of the Supreme Military Council: these decrees appeared on April 8 and April 20, 1918.[14]

Only as late as May of the same year an Operation Department was organized by the People's Commissar for Military Affairs in Moscow for the direction and central control of operations at the various fronts of Civil War.[15]

The sequence in which these various organs came into being had great importance in gaining the services of a number of excellent officers of the old army for command positions in the Red Army.

Many of these officers of the old army were ready to take part in the defense of their country against Germany even under the red banners of the Soviets. They considered it their duty to serve their country against an external enemy even under a government whose ideas and methods were repugnant to them at the time. They refused, however, during that period to enter the Red Army for service on the internal front of the fratricidal Civil War. In this manner the activities of the Supreme Military Council in forming and regularizing the "screens" of Russia's defense against the Germans drew into the service of the Red Army a large number of former czarist army officers. These officers became a reserve of command personnel. Gradually they became accustomed to the idea of serving their country under the red flag. With the spread of the Civil War they were psychologically prepared to take command of Red Army units on internal fronts as well.[16]

Some of the ablest leaders of the Red Army began their service under the flag of the Soviets in these "screens." Among them were the Commander in Chief of the Red Army, S. S. Kamenev (a former colonel of the Imperial General Staff), and A. A. Svechin, a former major general of the Imperial General Staff, who later became the head of the All-Russian Supreme Staff, and subsequently occupied with great distinction the chair of Military History at the War College.[17]

The organization in Moscow of the Operation Department attached to the Moscow Military District, which was supposed to take charge of the co-ordination of operations on the internal fronts of the Civil War, did not at first yield any considerable results in the way of unification of strategy of the Red armed forces engaged at these fronts. The local organizations continued to flourish and to assert their own initiative. The numerous local "commanders in chief" and "army commanders" were loath to give up their freedom of action and to follow the dictates of Moscow.[18] In the Ukraine alone there were several "commanders in chief" who actually were more on the order of guerilla leaders than commanders of regular army units.[19]

Trotsky bitterly complained in 1918 of the difficulties encountered in overcoming the local tendencies to disregard the center in its efforts to gather together the threads of military administration throughout the country. He thundered against "local patriotism," the efforts of the local Soviet organs to appropriate and to conceal military matériel of every description. "Every county, almost every township, believes that the Soviet power can be best defended by concentrating on the territory of the given township as much as possible of aviation matériel, radio equipment, rifles, armored cars. All try to conceal this matériel—not only in the provinces, but even in the centers, nay, even in the regional organizations of Petrograd." Trotsky mentioned in the same speech that telegrams and complaints, pointing out this state of affairs to the local authorities, did not meet with any support among the local Soviet officials.[20]

Was this pulverization of military effort the result of the G.H.Q. instructions mentioned above or were the instructions merely a reflection of the strong decentralizing tendencies of the local Soviets, the local party organizations and the local leaders? The persistency and the universality of these anti-centralist trends seems to indicate that the latter was the case. Further evidence bearing on this point will be examined at the end of the present chapter.

In March 1918, Trotsky was appointed to lead the military organization of the Soviets. The work of centralizing the control of the administration and operative activities of the Red armed forces was then begun in earnest. On July 8, the command of all the armed forces of the Republic was entrusted to a Field Staff, headed by a Commander in Chief. On September 2, 1918, the Revolutionary Military Council of the Republic was created with the functions of co-ordinating all operation, administrative and supply work of the Red Army both at the front and in the country at large. Trotsky was made the chairman of that Council.[21]

On November 30, 1918, the Council of Workers' and Peasants' Defense came into being, with Lenin at its head. The raising and the organization "of all forces of the Soviet Republics for defense against the attacking counter-revolution" was made the province of its activity.[22]

It took, thus, a full year for Lenin's government to complete the building up of the machinery of national defense.

The decree of the Central Executive Committee dated November 30, 1918, which had established the Council of Defense included a preamble which asserted that: "Under these conditions of universal brigandage, plunder and violence, only one country stands out as the genuine abode of the independence of the working class, as the protector of the weak and exploited peoples, and as the fortress of social revolution. That country is Soviet Russia." As colleagues of Lenin, the following were appointed members of the Council: Trotsky, Nevskii, Briukhanov, Krassin and Stalin. The powers given to that body were enormous: "The Council of Defense is to have full power in matters pertaining to the mobilization of the forces and resources of the country in the interests of defense. The decisions of the Council of Defense shall be absolutely binding upon every department and institution, both central and local, and upon every citizen." However, the direct control of the army and the navy was left in the hands of the Revolutionary War Council, the bureau of which at the time consisted of Trotsky, I. I. Vatsetis (an ex-czarist Colonel of the General Staff, a Latvian, Supreme Commander in Chief), and S. E. Aralov.[23]

Within the Revolutionary War Council, the Commander in Chief was placed in a very strong position, though his orders had to be approved by at least one member. As the decree of the Central Executive Committee, dated October 30, 1918, ran: "The Supreme Commander in Chief is entirely independent in all questions of a strategic-operative character. His orders must be countersigned by a member of the Revolutionary War Council."[24]

The chairman of the Revolutionary War Council was at the same time the People's Commissar of War and the Navy, and the Collegium of the People's Commissariat for War was included in the membership of the Revolutionary War Council.[25]

So it came to pass that the immediate direction of all the military operations of the young Soviet Republic was entrusted to a czarist colonel of average ability, under the supervision of his bolshevik colleagues on the board of the Council.

While the machinery of direction, administration and supply of the armed forces was thus taking shape and assuming forms that were to persist for many years, the plan for the recruitment of the ranks of the Red Army was gradually evolved.

The All-Army Conference concerned with the problem of demobilization of the old army, which opened its sessions on November 27, 1917, "found it necessary to begin the organization of a socialist army by means of voluntary recruiting upon recommendation of the recruits by revolutionary socialist parties and organizations of workers, soldiers and peasants." The old army, with the exception of certain age-groups, was to be demobilized. An instruction drawn along these lines was signed by Krylenko on December 23, 1917.[26]

Upon further study of the problem, new difficulties were found in the path of forming an army along the lines advanced by the Congress. Thus, Nevskii, at a meeting of military organizations, attached to the Central Committee of the Bolshevik party, expressed the thought: "it is difficult to organize a socialist army" and that "it must be created not from workers alone, but from all laboring classes." Podvoiskii, even at that late date, thought that the solution of the problem could be found in "pouring fresh elements" into the old army units, in using the framework of the old army for the absorption and training of the volunteers.[27]

By January 1, 1918, several principles were established by the Collegium for the organization and the formation of the Red Army, which became the cornerstone in the up-building of the armed forces of Soviet Russia. They were: The Red Army was to be an army of workers and peasants, recruited from volunteers among the "revolution-conscious" workers and peasants, with the object of defending the interests of the toilers of the world and of helping revolutionary movements the world over. The Red Army soldiers were to be in the service of the state and to receive pay for their services. The families of the soldiers were to be provided with all necessities by issues in kind by authorities. The *Regulations for the Organization of the Socialist Army*, issued on January 1, 1918, contained the modification of one of these principles. It was decided to introduce the principle of voluntary service among the troops at the front *only gradually*.[28]

B. Thal, in his history of the Red Army, points to December 29, 1917, as the date on which the Petrograd Soviet, upon the plan and proposal of the Collegium for the organization and the formation of the Red Army, began to organize the first units of the regular Red Army, as distinguished from the Red Guards.[29] The lead of Petrograd was followed in other cities. Units of the Red Army came into being at various points within the Soviet Republic.

Under these circumstances, the famous decree of January 15 (the 28th by our calendar), 1918, issued by the Soviet of People's Commissars,[30] does not really mark the day of the foundation of the Red Army. It laid down the statutory basis for work already begun by local bodies along lines suggested by the Collegium and the G.H.Q. of the old army in its instruction already referred to on page 35 above.

The official Soviet history of the Civil War speaks in disparaging terms of the discipline and training of the troops raised during the first months of the existence of the Red Army: "There was no time for training. Discipline was built on shaky foundations; meetings and discussions of orders were of frequent occurrence. The commanding personnel was confronted with many impossible claims on the part of fighters. There were no regulations, no instructions, to guide the internal organization and discipline."[31]

The volunteer movement drew recruits mainly from the urban population. The village did not send soldiers in any considerable number to swell the ranks of the Red Army. As a Soviet military historian, F. Nikonov, remarked: "Because of a faulty organizational principle, all the burden of the struggle thus fell upon the workers' class, which was perishing in an uneven struggle."[32]

On May 29, 1918, the All-Russian Executive Committee resolved that "the transition from the volunteer army to the enforced mobilization of workers and the poorest peasants is urgently dictated by the whole situation of the country, for the struggle for bread as well as for defense against internal and external counter-revolution now becoming prevalent because of famine."[33]

On June 26, 1918, Trotsky submitted to the Soviet of People's Commissars a plan for universal military service for the toiling classes, providing for the calling up of the corresponding age-classes of the bourgeoisie for service in the rear in special labor detachments. Prior to formal approval and the promulgation of decrees on obligatory military service, workers and peasants not employing hired labor were conscripted in fifty-one counties of the Volga, Ural and Western Siberian provinces, and it was also decided to mobilize the workers of Petrograd and Moscow.[34]

The All-Russian Central Committee adopted, on May 29, 1918, a resolution regarding obligatory recruitment of the Red Army. On June 12, the previously mentioned mobilization of five age-groups (21 to 25 years of age) of the fifty-one counties of the twelve provinces was decreed. On June 17, the workers of Moscow and of the suburbs of that city born in 1896-1897 were mobilized for the army, and on June 29 the same age-group of the Petrograd workers were called out. According to the official Soviet history of the Civil War, these mobilizations were well organized and were carried out successfully. In Moscow alone, 12,000 men reported for service, 9,000 of them being accepted for the Red Army.[35]

In addition to these mobilizations, organized and carried out by the central military authorities, there were a number of other mobilizations of workers and peasants of various provinces by local government organs on their own initiative. According to the same official commentary these mobilizations were unsuccessful, as they were not well planned and were carried out largely under pressure of war necessity. On July 10, 1918, such locally initiated mobilizations were definitely prohibited by the Commissar for Military Affairs, who made exception to the rule only for "exceptional circumstances."[36]

By the decree of the Soviet of People's Commissars of June 29, 1918, all males of ages from 18 to 40 were declared liable to military service.[37]

Thus, from the very introduction of the principle of compulsory service in the Red Army a definite policy had become noticeable: the urban proletariat of the large cities was used to leaven the masses of mobilized provincial workers and poor peasants.

By November 1, 1918, the number of persons mobilized for service in the Red Army included 164,000 private soldiers, 110,000 former non-commissioned officers, and about 23,000 former officers and civil servants of the military bureaus of the old army.[38]

The political supervision of the large personnel of the Red Army, entrusted to political commissars, was co-ordinated by the establishment, in April, 1918, of the All-Russian Bureau of Military Commissars.[39]

The various elements thus utilized in the construction of the Red Army were not only heterogeneous, but often definitely antagonistic to each other. The officer called to command the workers and peasants was the same officer who only a few weeks before was pointed out to the groups from which his subordinates were drawn as the greatest enemy of their class, as a relic of a feudal land-owning state machine and an active counter-revolutionary. The commissars, recruited among Bolsheviki, Socialist Revolutionaries of the Left, and sometimes among other radical groups, were regarded by the officers as agitators in 1917 who had urged on the soldiery to persecute and torment them, as possible agents of the German intelligence service and as tools of a governing clique which openly and assiduously persecuted social strata closely allied with many of the officers. The non-commissioned officers looked upon officers as competitors for command positions which they felt by revolutionary right, should fall to them, the sons of the classes which had come out victorious in the revolution. The peasant soldiers, on the other hand, were often not too willing to accept military service in any regular army or to show obedience to officers or commissars. The old state structure, overthrown in 1917, had not as yet been replaced by an accepted and firmly established régime in the minds of the peasants and even of certain groups of workers. The new state had yet to prove its durability, its claim to the allegiance of the nation, to kindle emotional responses and to establish emotional ties among the millions of its citizens. The process of molding the Red Army developed against a background of acute antagonism, of latent conflicts often developing into open conflicts, into rebellions, treason and desertion en masse. To understand the origin of these conflicts, the course they took and the reason the Red Army survived them, it is useful to examine the component parts of the Red Army structure separately.

Commanders

The very name of "officer" was considered so odious to the masses by the Soviet government in 1918 that the commanding personnel of the Red Army was given other appellations such as "military specialists," "instructors," "commanders," and "red commanders."

General Denikin, in analyzing the position of the career officer of the old army, stated that the social composition of the Russian officers' corps changed very greatly in the nineteenth century. Instead of a homogeneous noble officers' group, closely linked with the ruling strata of society, as well as the intellectual circles of the day, the Russian army officers evolved, toward the end of the nineteenth century, into a corps of diverse social origin, with only a few connections with the ruling stratum 'or with those participating in the intellectual movement.[40]

In the beginning of the twentieth century, one of the contributors to the columns of the official army newspaper, the *Russian Veteran* (*Russkii Invalid*), attempted to extol the virtues of the nobles' army of the *War and Peace* period as opposed to the depravity of the plebeian army as described by Kuprin in his *Duel*. Such an attempt could only evoke a feeling of consternation among the officers of the line regiments of the army.[41]

A statistical analysis of the social origin of cadets of the Alexis Military School of Moscow, prepared by Colonel Sventsitskii, gives an interesting illustration of the rapid change which took place in the recruitment of the Russian army officers' corps between the years 1864 and 1913.[42]

This School was not one of those sought after by the aristocracy for the education of their sons for a military career. On the other hand, it stood higher in the scale of social acceptability than some of the so-called Junkers' Schools. It may be, perhaps, regarded as slightly above the average with respect to the military schools of the Empire in reference to the social origins of its pupils—according, of course, to the standards of social values of the old régime.

During the period of 1864-1869, i.e. immediately following the liberation of the serfs, 81 per cent of its cadets were young men of noble origin. Nine per cent were children of the so-called "personal nobles"—these did not inherit the rank and privilege of nobility— and 10 per cent were descendants of the honorary citizens. By 1876-1877, the percentage of descendants of hereditary nobles fell to forty-three, that of the personal nobles (junior army officers, minor civil servants, school teachers, etc.) to thirty-three. The merchants and burghers were represented by 13 per cent, while the children of the clergy (in Russia definitely not an aristocratically-connected group) made a showing of 11 per cent. In the period of 1888-1889 the nobles were represented by 12 per cent, the personal nobles' descendants increased to 57 per cent, the merchants and burghers to 16 per cent, honorary citizens formed 5 per cent, children of the clergy dropped to 5 per cent, while the children of peasants represented 5 per cent. In the years 1906-1907, statistics show a slight increase of the nobles to 13 per cent, a decrease of the personal nobles to 38 per cent, an increase of the merchants and burghers to 27 per cent, and of honorary citizens to 11 per cent. At the same time the number of the children of the clergy diminished to 3 per cent and the number of peasants rose to 8 per cent. In the period immediately preceding the World War, 1912-1913, the figures were: 9 per cent for the nobles, 30 per cent for the personal nobles, 28 per cent for the merchants and burghers, 19 per cent for the peasants, 4 per cent for the clergy and 10 per cent for the newly appearing group of "personal citizens."

The contrast between 1864-1869 and the 1912-1913 periods is striking indeed. The nobles dropped from 81 per cent to 9 per cent and became outnumbered by the peasants, represented in the latter period by 19 per cent, who were not among the cadets at all in the former period. The group of the rapidly growing urban middle class rose from 10 per cent to 38 per cent, illustrating the rapid rise in the importance of the commercial and industrial classes of the population. The descendants of the personal nobles increased from 9 per cent to 30 per cent, corresponding to the influx of the non-noble elements into the lower ranks of the bureaucracy and the army officers' corps. It is noteworthy that the personal nobles' element was on the decline numerically during the period immediately preceding the World War, as against the years 1888-1889, when they constituted the majority. Apparently the children of persons of that class (mostly impecunious intellectuals or semi-intellectuals) were not attracted to the military career as strongly as they were a quarter of a century before. Should the nobles, personal nobles and clergy be grouped together as representing the intellectual classes, one would find that they accounted in 1912-1913 for 44 per cent, while the urban middle class and the peasants outnumbered them with 56 per cent.

General Denikin maintains that, in spite of its heterogeneity, the Russian army officers' corps was strongly welded together by the military tradition and was definitely conservative in its political view. According to him, the officers' corps in the years preceding the World War stood aside from the intellectuals, who were as a rule in opposition to the régime and its political concepts. These intellectuals looked down upon the officers' epaulettes.[43]

Some parts of the armed forces of Russia—the Guards, the Navy, and, in a large measure, the Cavalry—continued to maintain the aristocratic character of its officers' corps. There was a certain amount of antagonism and jealousy between the less-favored officers of the line regiments and the Guards officers, who enjoyed very important privileges as to promotions and higher appointments.

The higher ranks of the officers were to a large extent filled either by the graduates of the War College or of other military colleges, or from officers of the Guards. In 1892, 45 per cent of the Russian generals were graduates of these colleges.[44]

Among graduates of the War College in 1912 there were 80.9 per cent officers of the line, and 19.1 per cent officers of the guard. Nobles represented 48 per cent.[45] In other words, even among the aspirants for the highest military positions of the state, the nobles were already in a minority.

The officers' corps was recruited from graduates of the Military Schools and the Junkers' Schools. The pupils of the former were largely drawn from pupils of the Cadet Corps (military academies) and had one or two years of seniority in the first officers' rank upon promotion. They were mostly sons of army officers or of the nobility.

The Junkers' Schools were established to provide an opening for young men of the various social classes who were not educated in the Cadet Corps. The graduates of these schools were not given officer's rank immediately upon completing their studies. They entered the army as warrant officers. There were opened a few military schools of an intermediate type (1888, 1890, 1892 in Moscow, Kiev and Elizavetgrad respectively) with the program of Military Schools, but intended for short-term volunteers with a completed college or secondary school education. From 1913 all Military Schools became open to children of persons of all classes or estates.[46]

In the 'eighties the proportion of officers originating from Military

Schools and those from Junkers' Schools stood at 26 per cent and 74 per cent respectively. In the 'nineties it changed to 45 per cent and 55 per cent. In 1901 the Junkers' Schools were radically reformed, and their course was lengthened from two to three years. From 1904 on, the cadets of the Junkers' Schools began to be promoted to the first officers' rank as against that of the warrant officer as before. In 1902, 3,200 young men took part in the entrance examinations. More than 1,500 of them passed the examinations satisfactorily, and 740, or 23 per cent of the applicants, were admitted. In this period, then, the supply of available young men of satisfactory scholastic standing was in excess of the number of vacancies in the Junkers' Schools— they ceased thus to be the refuge of the scholastically incompetent, as they had often been in the preceding century. Between 1907 and 1911, the Junkers' Schools were gradually transformed into Military Schools, so that the whole system of officers' training was unified three years before the beginning of the World War.[47]

In the 'nineties, 80 per cent of the infantry officers were graduates of the Junkers' Schools. During the same period, 83 per cent to 92 per cent of the field officers (lieutenant-colonels and colonels) were graduates of these schools, in the infantry, and 73 per cent to 88 per cent in the cavalry. A few of them made their way by sheer energy and tenacity through the War College, in spite of their often very defective general education. Seven to ten per cent of the graduates of the War College came from their ranks. Some of the leading generals of the World War, such as M. A. Alekseev, Count Keller, Lechitskii, Sievers, Gerngross, were graduates of the old Junkers' Schools.[48]

General Denikin, speaking of his fellow cadets at the Kiev Junkers' School of the intermediate type, remarked: "I believe we had no wealthy people among us. At least within the walls of the school, social and financial differentiation was not noticeable and never divided us. There were, however, some homeless cadets and some from very poor families, who had to rely upon the government pay to cover their sundry petty needs. The pay then amounted to 22½ to 33 1/3 kopeks per month.* These cadets had no money to buy tobacco, a toothbrush or a stamp. . . . They carried their difficulties stoically. I do not recall any cry-babies, or toadies."[49] These schools, apparently, tended to build up will-power and character.

On the other hand, the highest military institution of learning, preparing future leaders of the army, the War College, was not con-

* 11 to 17 cents U.S. currency.

ducive, according to Denikin, to development of men of great will and of firm character. As Denikin says: "the War College of that time taught its pupils to assume a 'protective coloring'." To this he ascribes the ease with which some of the officers of the General Staff had adapted themselves to the Soviet régime. His argument is worth quoting: "Obviously men educated in the tradition of all-mightiness on top and absolute obedience below were unable to understand that 'regulations and order' are written for all—not only for the little men, like company commanders . . . but for the military high dignitaries as well."[50]

According to Denikin, 90 per cent of the army line officers had no other means of support than the scanty army pay. Promotion was slow. It took them on the average fifteen to sixteen years to obtain the command of a company. The political opinions of these economically ill-favored men were, as already stated, stanchly conservative. According to Denikin, after the revolution it came to light that the Social Democratic party had practically no following at all among the army officers, while Socialist Revolutionaries were represented only "by a very limited number of officers who had little importance in the party."[51]

Denikin stated, however, that in the years preceding 1917, the prejudice against the parliamentary system was gradually fading among the Russian army officers.[52]

The revolutionary elements had a bitter grudge against the officers' corps. An article which appeared in 1907 in Paris in the émigrés' newspaper *Red Flag* (*Krasnoe Znamia*), contained the admission that revolution failed in 1905 because of the firmness of the officers and their influence over their men.[53]

The line officers had a number of reasons for feeling that their careers were subordinated to those of the officers of the Guards. In 1910, among the commanding officers of infantry line regiments, there were 51 Guard officers and 145 army line officers. In the regular cavalry the Guards were even more favored: 18 Guardsmen against 22 officers of the line. In 1903, among those commanding the artillery of divisions, there were 20 Guardsmen and those enjoying Guard privileges (such as the graduates of the Artillery College had) against six officers of the line.[54]

These officers of the line, despite their low economic status and poor career prospects, were, according to Denikin, ardent patriots. They were devoted to their country almost by instinct, without analyzing their feelings and without studying the people and its interests.

Social problems did not attract the young officers—they looked upon them as matters alien and without interest to them. Denikin characterized the officers' corps as: "living in a semi-closed circle of persons and ideas, without showing interest in social and popular movements. With prejudice against politically moderate circles of society, suspecting those, without any good reason, of 'shaking the foundations' and in a greater or lesser ideological estrangement from these circles."[55]

During the World War the whole physiognomy of the Russian army officers' corps changed very considerably. It is estimated that on the eve of the war in 1914 there were in the army 50,300 career officers. As a result of the mobilization, 35,000 officers, largely of reserve, non-career origin, were added to that number. In the course of the three years of the war, altogether some 214,000 young officers entered the army, swamping the original nucleus of career men, many of whom were killed, maimed or captured in the course of the hostilities.[56]

Instead of officers, educated for military service in Cadet Corps from the age of 10-11 years, or at least trained for three years in Military Schools, the average wartime officer passed through only a few months of military training and was, no doubt, representative of the aspirations and characteristics of the young educated Russians of the World War period. The shortage of officers of noble origin was so great that even all except two regiments of the infantry of the Guards had to abandon their traditions with regard to the recruitment of their officers and began to accept young men of non-noble families. Some of these officers were active members of revolutionary parties.

Among these youngsters in officers' uniforms there were many university and technical college graduates, as well as former undergraduates of these institutions of learning. What their political convictions were by 1917 is very difficult, if not altogether impossible, to determine. However, there is extant a summary of a questionnaire on political affiliation, filled out in 1909-1910 by students of the Technological Institute of St. Petersburg. According to this questionnaire, 25.3 per cent of the students belonged to the Social Democratic party, 3 per cent to the Anarchists and 12.4 per cent to the Socialist Revolutionaries. All rightist groups were represented by a mere 5 per cent, while the liberal Constitutional Democratic party (regarded by the average cadre officer at the time as dangerously radical) had the allegiance of 20 per cent of the students. Thus 40.7 per cent of the student body were definitely affiliated with active revolutionary groups as against 5 per cent belonging to conservative parties. Such groups as the non-affiliated "leftists" with 10.1 per cent and 20 per cent without party affiliation whatsoever completed a picture which clearly indicates a definite radical trend among the students.[57]

It is quite possible that by 1914 the average Russian college student was not as radical as the contents of the above questionnaire would indicate—the crest of the revolutionary wave among the Russian intellectuals had passed its highest point several years before the beginning of the war. Nevertheless, it is clear that, with the influx of hundreds of thousands of young wartime officers, different ideas and patterns of behavior had entered the Russian army officer corps. It ceased to be a group of professional military men of a definitely conservative, if not reactionary, viewpoint in politics, and became, at least in its lowest ranks, a cross section of the Russian educated class, as well as the semi-educated youth of the war period. The influence of the regular army officers with whom they came in contact imposed on them a somewhat superficial veneer of the officer behavior pattern. In the navy, the cadre officers remained the dominant element on board warships, the temporary officers serving mainly on board naval auxiliaries and in the shore establishments of the navy.

One may safely say that in the years immediately preceding the war, revolutionary tendencies were conspicuous by their absence among the Russian cadre officers.

On the other hand, there has already been occasion to mention, on page 6 above, the part taken by some of the junior officers in the conflict between soldiers and the older regimental officers in 1917. There is a considerable amount of documentary evidence of antagonism between the cadre officers and some of the temporary wartime officers. Thus the report of the two members of the State Duma, Maslennikov and Shmakov, relating to events in April 1917, contains mention of the speeches made by two temporary officers of the Guard Rifle Division against the cadre officer of their regiments, whom they accused of antagonism to temporary officers and enlisted men.[58]

G. Graf in his book on the participation of the Russian Baltic Fleet in the World War describes the disputes between the cadre officers and the temporary ones at the First All-Russian Congress of the officers of the army and navy at Petrograd in 1917. He states that a group of young officers, "mostly college undergraduates, already infected with socialism at college," put forward the suggestion that the delegates define their attitude to the revolution. The congress broke up into three parts—one voicing support to the Provisional Government, the second declaring itself for the Soviet, and the third expressing itself as entirely outside of politics.[59]

Such members of the Bolshevik party as Ensign Krylenko and Sub-Lieutenant Raskolnikov are well-known exponents of revolutionary tendencies among the wartime officers of the Russian armed forces.

Trotsky's statement in a newspaper article published in 1918 that officers were educated in reactionary-monarchist views, while true of the cadre officers, does not seem to reflect the exact situation insofar as the war-time officers were concerned.[60] His other statement, made in November 1918, that the old officer class was closely connected "in all its past" with the ruling classes, does not find support in the evidence examined. A very curious commentary as to the social standing of the wartime officers is to be found in a memorandum addressed to the Director of Military Education of the old army under the date of December 22, 1915. This memorandum refers to the report submitted to the Emperor by General Adlerberg upon the results of the latter's inspection of the reserve depots battalions: "Most of the ensigns belong to elements extremely undesirable as material for the recruitment of the officers' corps. Among them are common laborers, locksmiths, stonemasons, floor-waxers and butlers. As I was informed, soldiers offer themselves for examination even without asking leave to do so. Under these circumstances, entirely unsuitable soldiers obtain the ensign's rank." The Emperor's thoughtful marginal note reads: "This should be given earnest attention."[61]

General Niessel describes his visit to a School of Ensigns at Kiev in 1917, where soldiers from the ranks were trained for officers' commissions after having served in the army at the front.[62]

Certainly these scores of thousands of graduates of wartime Ensign Schools had very little in common with "the ruling classes." The gradual infiltration of the peasantry and the lower class urban element into the Military Schools of pre-war days has already been examined. These poverty-stricken infantry officers of low-class origin had very little in common with the rich land-owner class or the upper strata of the bureaucracy. Their contacts with the industrial and wealthy trading classes were also far from close.

The important factor making for the conflict between officers and men in the Russian Army in 1917, outside of the strain nearly always latent in the relationship "superior-inferior" in any military hierarchy (and aggravated by the long war, the revolutionary events, and the desire of the peasant soldier to go back to his village, to which he considered the officers a definite obstacle) was the difference in culture between the mass of the peasant soldiery and the intellectuals and semi-intellectuals in officers' uniforms. Professor Miliukov quite rightly stresses the great cultural differentiation between the Russian educated classes and the masses of the Russian people in the nineteenth century.[63] In the first years of the twentieth century that gap was not by any means filled. Thus, culturally, the officers were almost aliens to their gray-coated subordinates. To the peasant-soldier, every educated man, every officer was still a *barin*—a gentleman—not because of the latter's wealth, social position or rank, but merely on account of the great cultural chasm dividing the westernized classes of Russian society from the inhabitants of the village.

In many respects, the old cadre officer was psychologically nearer to the peasant-soldier in the ranks than the young college graduate with all his radicalism and socialism. There was something earthy, essentially Russian, about the infantry line company commander of the old army, whose western veneer did not always conceal the Russian popular behavior pattern. And, after all, through years of dealing with the peasant-soldiers, these old-time officers learned a great deal more about the latter's habits and behavior than the youngsters in temporary officers' uniforms could possibly absorb from their contacts with the "people."

In 1918, there were drafted into the Red Army over 22,000 former army officers in the Red Army in addition to 2,500 medical and veterinary officers. By April 1, 1919, the number of officers grew to 28,410, that of the medical and veterinarian personnel to 4,395. Altogether, from June 12, 1918, to August 15, 1920, 48,409 former officers were drafted in the Red Army. Quite a number of these saw service in the White Armies before joining the Red. In 1921, a total of 14,390 former White Army officers were found in the Red Army.[64]

Next in importance to the old army officers among the commanders of the Red Army stood the former non-commissioned officers of that army.

In 1918, there were 128,168 former non-commissioned officers of the old army enrolled in the Red Army, as well as 9,713 of the lower medical and veterinary personnel. By April 1, 1919, their numbers had risen to 165,191 and 15,365 respectively. The total number of non-commissioned officers who entered the Red Army between June 12, 1918, and August 15, 1920, amounted to 214,717, and of the lower medical and veterinary personnel, 26,766.[65]

In making its bid for the allegiance of the former non-commissioned officers of the old army, the Soviet Government waved a magic wand before their eyes—the marshal's baton. Trotsky's order of August 3, 1918, called the former N.C.O.'s to occupy command positions in the Red Army. "You are yourselves sons of the toiling people. The Workers and Peasants' Army is your army. . . . You will create indestructible cadres of the socialist officers' corps of the Soviet Republic."[66]

Every former N.C.O. in the ranks of the Red Army, volunteers as well as those drafted into it, was given the position and the privileges of a platoon commander, i.e. of a subaltern officer. This mass promotion to commissioned officers' positions of the N.C.O.'s had, no doubt, a great psychological effect upon them.

By the decree of August 3, 1918, the Soviet of People's Commissars, in addition to the mobilization of workers born in 1896-1897 from the six industrial provinces, proclaimed also the mobilization of workers born in 1893-1894/5 from the same six provinces who had served as N.C.O.'s in the old army. The preamble of the decree spoke of the rapid creation of a new officers' corps by attracting to positions of command "honest and valiant sons of the people from among the former non-commissioned officers."[67]

In the fall of 1918 Trotsky said: "We can now tell our enemies we have created a new officers' corps. We have called on the non-commissioned officers and on all advanced, conscious fighters in whose breasts pulsates the ardent wish to defend the Soviet Republic on all fronts."[68]

The impression created by these pronouncements was that practically all command positions were to be handed over to the non-commissioned officers, whose class origin made them more acceptable to the Soviet Government, as well as to the soldiers, than was the case with commissioned officers tainted by "bourgeois" or "noble" origin.

Whether Trotsky meant anything of the kind is another question. In examining his order and his speech, one has to bear in mind that at the time he was, on the one hand, under the influence of a bitter disillusionment caused by numerous defections of the former czarist officers from their posts in the Red Army, particularly in the Archangel-Murmansk area and on the Volga, and on the other hand he had to face a loud and angry clamor of large sections of the party and the army in the field against the employment of former army officers in command positions in the Red Army.

In his article, "Military Specialists and the Red Army," written on December 31, 1918, Trotsky refers to the discontent pervading the lower, middle and upper ranks of the party, caused by the fact that the lack of military leaders among its partisans made it necessary to call in the services of those "not of *our own.*" As symptoms of this discontent, there appeared articles in the *Pravda* on November 29, 1918, and December 25, 1918, by V. Sorin and by Kamenskii (the latter a member of the All-Russian Central Executive Committee) denying the need for the employment of trained military men on the ground that military science and military art were of no value.[69]

In a "Letter to a Friend" (published in the military magazine *Voennoe Delo* in February 1919), written on January 10, 1919, Trotsky again spoke of the "passions aroused by the problem of military specialists." He mentioned that in one of the armies it was considered the sign of "supreme revolutionism" to mock the military specialists. Trotsky claimed that the originators of this antagonism were: "the worst among the 'new' commanders," "military semi-educated, semi-partisans, semi-Communists, who did not want to tolerate next to themselves party workers, nor earnest workers in the field of the military profession." According to Trotsky, these commanders were always seeking the explanation of their own failures and defeats in the treason of others.[70]

Stalin's attitude, as expressed in a note to Lenin on July 7, 1918, from the Tsaritsin front, is an important characteristic of this opposition to Trotsky's policies in employing former officers in the Red Army. "The work is complicated by the fact that the H.Q. of the North Caucasus Military District is entirely unadapted to the conditions of the struggle against counter-revolution. It is not only that our 'specialists' are psychologically unfit to wage a decisive war on counter-revolution, but also that the 'staff' workers know only how to 'draw schemes' and propose plans . . . they are absolutely indifferent to operation activities . . . in general they feel themselves to be strangers, guests. The military commissars have not succeeded in filling the gap."[71]

On the other hand, the trial of Admiral Stchastnyi, who commanded the Baltic Fleet, the attempts to arouse rebellion in the Destroyer Division of that fleet made by Lieutenant Lisanevich, the defection of Rear-Admiral Vikorst at Archangel, General Bogoslovskii and the Colonel of the General Staff Makhin at the Eastern Front—who all had held important positions in the Red Armed forces—had undoubtedly a great deal to do with the angry and disappointed statement of the People's Commissar for War in his speech at Moscow on July 29, 1918: "As far as members of the highest commanding personnel are concerned, we have too few officers who are devoted to the Soviet Government and are honestly carrying out their duties."[72]

Be that as it may, the Red Army badly needed lower commanding personnel, and mobilization of a large number of the former N.C.O.'s filled that need. The former officers alone obviously could not supply the need in leaders of the rapidly growing Red forces. The N.C.O.'s did not by any means obtain the monopoly of command positions as might be implied from Trotsky's clarion call. But many of them rose to the highest positions in the Red Army, and Marshal Budenny, in 1943 still alive and in possession of his baton, is the living testimony to the fact that "the path of glory" opened to the N.C.O.'s of the old army led, if not *ad astra*, at least to a place on the reviewing stand during the November parade of the Red Army in Moscow. The official Soviet history of the Civil War states, however, that: "during the period of the Civil War, the number of former officers formed an overwhelming majority among the commanding personnel of the Red Army."[73]

According to Denikin, the N.C.O.'s of the old army were almost entirely drawn from the peasant class. Their relations with the men were much more cordial than was the case in the old German and Austrian armies. In the Russian barracks under the old régime there was no trace of hazing and mocking of recruits.[74]

A. Zaitsov, in his book on the Red Army, points out, on the other hand, that the vast majority of the former N.C.O.'s were unfit to occupy even the lowest officers' posts. He asserted, however, that the N.C.O.'s were at that better trained than the young Red commanders graduated from the numerous military schools established during the Civil War. A former Red brigade commander, who passed later to the Whites, an ex-officer of the old army, stated in his report to the White Army authorities: "The lower commanding personnel up to company commanders, at the front even up to deputy regimental commanders, are former N.C.O.'s or even privates (of the old army). These commanders fall into two groups: a smaller one, definitely devoted to the interest of communism with which it is connected by personal interest, and a larger one, mostly consisting of those mobilized, almost inimical to bolshevism. Both of these groups have a poor military training, and are not a particular menace. . . ."[75]

A good many of these former N.C.O.'s, particularly those who were sergeant-majors in the old army, had the habit of command and knew well how to handle men. Appointed to command positions, they were jealous of their rights and had sufficient will-power to impose their personalities on their subordinates. There is extant a very curious reminiscence of Marshal Budenny, an ex-czarist cavalry N.C.O., on an incident in 1918, when he commanded a cavalry detachment of the Red Army. Some soldiers organized a meeting and were addressed by a speaker who advocated the reestablishment of committees in the army. Budenny stepped forward and remarked to the orator: "Comrade, you had better get going from here while everything is all right with you . . . it is necessary to build now, the committees should not be organized." Turning to the crowd of Red Army soldiers he added: "If you do not disperse, I shall cut you down with my sword."[76] He had his way in a situation where very few of the old army officers could succeed in 1918, and the young "Red officers" were very likely to fail.

In the cavalry, the former N.C.O.'s took over much more important positions than in the other arms. From the lowest to the very highest, commands in the cavalry were predominantly occupied by the former N.C.O.'s, or even privates, of the old army cavalry. There were only very few former regular army cavalry officers in the mounted units of the Red Army. They were encountered there only as an exception. A few infantry officers, also a small minority, held some of the staff posts.[77]

The Red cavalry was recruited largely from volunteers, and included a large proportion of the more active and warlike elements of the Red forces. Their commanders were called upon to give the highest personal example of daring and bravery under fire. Not only squadron and regimental commanders, but commanders of brigades and divisions took part in the charges with their men.[78]

Babel's *Cavalry Army* contains some excellent descriptions of the fighting and life of these Red horsemen, led by the N.C.O.'s. In some respects the Red cavalry described by Babel was more like some horde of the Zaporog Cossacks, so vividly portrayed by Gogol in his *Taras Bulba*, than a part of the regular army of a proletarian state.

The problem of the training of officers "of their own" began to occupy the attention of Soviet Government at an early date. Some of the Command Courses, where the Red cadets were trained, began to function some two months before the official date of the founding of the Red Army in February 23, 1918.[79]

The post of the Commissar in Chief of the military educational institutions was created by a decree of the Soviet of the People's

Commissars, dated November 14, 1917, only a few days after the conquest of power by Lenin.

This functionary inherited from the old régime not only the buildings and matériel of the old Military Schools and Colleges, but also organized bodies of cadets with their instructing personnel.[80]

The first steps, after the disbanding of these cadets, were made in the direction of recruiting the new body of Red cadets from among the more revolutionary elements of the soldiers of the old army. Very soon afterwards, an effort was made to attract to the courses workers who had served in the Red Guards. In 1918, the workers formed 37 per cent of all the cadets.[81]

It is noteworthy that until the end of 1918 the Command Courses were in practice self-governing bodies, with soviets and committees of cadets exercising authority over the internal discipline of their respective schools. In other words, the state of affairs which existed in the old army after the revolution and in the Red Guards continued to flourish there long after the discipline of the regular units of the Red Army was established on an entirely different foundation.[82]

A great deal of attention was paid to the political education of the future Red officers. The communist collectives were a very important factor in shaping the organization and training of the Red cadets. This was particularly important since, until October 1918, even the general lines of discipline to be enforced in the Command Courses had not been officially laid down. D. Petrovskii, a former Director of Military Education of the Red Army, stated that the first wide discussion of the basis of military discipline of the cadets took place in October 1918. It had among its ends not only to define methods of discipline, but also to answer the fundamental question—whether the revolutionary army needed any formal discipline at all.[83]

This utopian trend did not persist for long, and at the time of the opening of the Sixth Congress of Soviets in November 1918, it was decided to abolish the soviets and committees at the Command Courses and to hand over the government of the cadets and their instructors to commissars jointly with the directors of the Courses. The latter were former old army officers. The relationship between commissars and directors was at first rather indefinite. Trotsky's speech of October 14, 1919, seems to indicate that the People's Commissar for War was hesitant to introduce in the Command Courses the system adopted in the combat units of the Red Army. It is somewhat difficult to follow his trend of thought as expressed in that speech, but it would seem that he admitted at the time the possibility of some commissars taking full charge of the Command Course to which they were accredited. On the other hand, he also visualized some of the "military specialists" (a euphemism for "old army officers") taking over, as directors, complete charge of the Courses, without even the supervision of a commissar.[84]

In February 1918 ten Command Courses were in existence. By January 1919 their number had risen to sixty-three, while on January 1, 1920, the Department of Military Education, despite "re-organizations and disbandments," had one hundred and five military educational institutions under its supervision.[85] By January 1921 that figure had further increased to one hundred and fifty-one.

As early as 1918, instructors in tactics were directed by the Department of Military Education to follow closely events at the Civil War front, and to offer to the cadets commentary as to tactics used. This, however, was not followed up to any degree. D. Petrovskii ascribes the failures of the instructors to discuss with the cadets the course of the Civil War and the new tactical problems arising during its operations to the lack of interest in the Civil War on the part of the instructors, who often were of the opinion that the lessons of the Civil War were of no consequence for the conduct of future external wars.[86]

Practically all these instructors were taken over from the various Military Schools and Ensign Schools of the old army. Aside from the circumstance that these instructors did not feel at home in their new surroundings, teaching the revolutionary youth, they were probably of the opinion that the low level of their students' general education was jeopardizing their chances of acquiring enough of the rudiments of the military arts and sciences to become adequate subalterns.[87]

It is also possible that quite a number of the instructors were steeped in their teaching routine to the extent that they would not adapt their courses to the new conditions and different audiences.

General Niessel, in commenting on his visit to the Kiev Constantine Military School, remarked that most of the instructors were men who had specialized in teaching in military educational institutions, many of them of a fairly advanced age. None of them had served at the front. He characterized their teaching as bookish and ultra-formalistic, without practical exercises which would require on the part of the pupils any effort to understand and solve command problems.[88]

According to Niessel, the instructors did not take into consideration the experience of the war years.

Should we assume that the personnel of the Constantine School was typical of the Russian military educational institutions of that type, one would have to admit that it would be a great deal to expect that a teaching personnel which persisted in its routine throughout the World War would suddenly enthusiastically absorb, digest and proffer to the Red cadets the lessons of the Civil War.

The original plan devised by the Soviet Government provided for three types of military educational institutions. The schools of the lower type (First Step) were to be followed by the middle-type schools (Second Step) and the education was to be completed at the Third Step schools or military colleges, where the education of the commanders of the Red Army was to receive the final touches.

The First Step schools had for their end a complete practical training for the lowest officer posts (platoon commander), as well as a practical acquaintanceship with the duties of the next command (company commander). It was planned that regardless of the arm in which the young cadet was to serve upon graduation, he was supposed to acquire a general understanding "about war and the forces working in it." The First Step schools were planned to train officers for one arm of the service only. Some were thus designated to educate infantry officers, others cavalry, and still others artillery.[89]

The Second Step schools were to provide the means of perfecting their students in all phases of military science necessary for the efficient direction of detachments comprising the three arms—infantry, cavalry and artillery—as well as to enable them to direct the operations of such detachments in practice.[90]

The Third Step schools—*Akademii* or Military Colleges, such as the War College, the Artillery College, the Engineers College, etc.—were to prepare highly trained specialists in their respective fields of military science and art.[91]

These, however, were long-range plans. The actual application of them did not begin until the end of 1921, i.e. well after the end of the Civil War.

The Command Courses, which multiplied so rapidly during the Civil War, were not comprised in the plan, although they continued to exist until 1924. After the end of the Civil War they were directed to concern themselves with the training of the reserve officers, while the Military Schools provided for the plan were to educate the regular officers.

During the Civil War years (1918-20) altogether 39,914 cadets were graduated from Command Courses.[92] Of these, 26,585 were graduated in 1920, so that during the height of the Civil War (1918-19) only about thirteen thousand graduates of these schools were appointed to command positions.[93]

By June 1920 a higher type of Command Courses was opened. They had a twelve months' period of training. Some of these schools were reorganized into normal military schools as provided by the plan.[94]

The political training, first introduced for cadets only, was later extended to include the instructors as well. However, in the second half of 1919, when the great demand for commanders brought about a shortening of the already too brief period of training of the cadets, the political education was seriously curtailed.[95]

Most of the cadets entered upon their period of training during the Civil War period without any party affiliations. Most of those graduating had become members of the Communist party, while at school. Thus these courses were important breeding-grounds for new Communist party membership. Their graduates carried with them the elementary communist ideas into the army with all the zeal of the neophytes and without any critical understanding of the various problems they heard about at school, because of the low general education they had received before entering.

The apprehensions of the instructors as to the ability of the Red cadets of the Civil War period to absorb enough of the military science to become useful junior officers were apparently justified. D. Petrovskii admits that the Red commanders promoted during the Civil War were for all practical purposes merely well-trained private soldiers with a well-developed sense of duty.[96]

The commissars of the courses were apparently a very important factor in the functioning of these schools. Their duties were three-fold: to serve as a check upon the anti-bolshevik elements among the instructors and cadets, to guide the Red element, and to provide the impulse and the enthusiasm for the day-by-day life of the courses.[97]

That the first part of these duties was not a mere formality was evidenced by the arrest for counter-revolutionary activities of some of the instructors of the crack Command Courses located right in the Kremlin of Moscow, in the very heart of the Soviet and party stronghold.[98]

The young "Red commanders," as they were then known, upon promotion to their respective army units, had often to serve under and with the former old army officers, known then as "military specialists." Thus the two groups were opposed one to the other as distinctly differentiated within the Red Army officers' corps, separated even by the barrier of a different appellation. After the Civil War, both groups became known as "commanders of the Workers' and Peasants' Red Army." During the early years of the Red Army they were thus sharply differentiated and often in conflict with each other.[99]

Extracts from letters written by the young Red officers were published in *Military Science* (*Voennoe Znanie*) in 1920. They provide a good picture of the aspirations and disappointments of the graduates of the Command Courses. Despite the very short term of studies, a strong attachment and loyalty to their school is typical of these letters. Commissars, instructors and fellow cadets are remembered with a friendly, almost tender feeling. In this respect these Red cadets did not differ from the cadets of the old army military schools—the *esprit de corps* was already present and school loyalty very definitely had its place in the emotional complex of the young Red commanders. For many of them, be it remembered, the Command Courses constituted the first school where a definite social ideal and group loyalty was presented to them. These youngsters had very much at heart the prestige of their respective courses. Upon joining an infantry battalion, the soldiers of which were mostly "ignorant young Ukrainians, who not only do not understand the policy of our Soviet Republic, but have never even heard of it," the young communist officer took upon himself the political enlightenment of the soldiers.[100]

So far so good. But here appears the *bête noire*: "The higher commanding personnel of the regiment are by a long shot not good comrades of ours. They have a strongly developed feeling of self-love and egotism. Very often they misuse their power . . . we were educated differently . . . and we have begun through the intermediacy of the Political Department a struggle with the evil done by the old commanding personnel."[101]

Both in the staff offices and in the regiments the young Red officers were confronted with the "mysterious natures" of the old régime officers—complex, and to them incomprehensible, personalities, also by commissars "with square insignia" who by their speeches and by their acts "threw us into complete confusion." "I am confused and surprised," wrote one of the fledgling Red commanders, "by all I have seen with my own eyes. I am not complaining of my fate—it is more than favoring me. . . . You taught us to introduce among the Red soldiers a conscious comradely discipline. Unfortunately, here people insist on something else. Everywhere a feeling of fear is present—not for conscience' or duty's sake, but solely because of the cudgel which is always right before one's nose."[102]

Another former Red cadet writes: "We are looked upon with contempt, because we have brought with us a revolutionary discipline, not the cudgel type . . . soldiers are always ready to flock around to listen to us, but the old commanders drive them off on paltry errands, often not even in the line of duty . . . the commander of the regiment says with a snigger: 'When Red commanders arrive I shall give them sections to command—let them run around' . . . he sends into the firing line only those of the commanders who are Communists. Those who box the soldiers' ears he keeps at his discretion in the reserve. . . . Tell all the Red cadets that the Red Army no longer trusts the former officers, the army is waiting for the proletarian officers—conscious, honest workers. The army is throwing out the egotists and woe to a commander who infringes on revolutionary discipline."[103]

This defiant epistle is followed by another: "We are received here as recruits were formerly taken in . . . our regimental commander never speaks to us Red commanders. He regards us in general as small fry. We have a military science society. He speaks there on tactics, always along the old fashioned lines, and does not tolerate any objections." A correspondent from Turkestan writes: "Some commanders behave exactly like old officers . . . how can they be tolerated within the Red Army?"[104]

On the other hand, testimony of the former officers who served in the Red Army was pungent. A former Brigade Commander of the Red Army, who later passed over to the Whites, wrote in his report in 1919: "As regards the so-called Red officers, the whole mass of them are men without education. Although most of them belong to the party, they have little stability . . . their average general and military training is below that formerly acquired in a good regimental N.C.O.'s school."[105]

The Command Courses were recruited through the method of assignment of certain persons to be trained there. There was no competitive entrance examination. The army units were told to send a certain number of men to be trained as cadets, and the candidates were selected without reference to their own wishes to become commanders. Petrovskii remarks that those sent to the courses were by no means always the best Red soldiers. An order of the Revolutionary Military Council, dated March 15, 1919, offers an interesting commentary in this respect: "Be it ordered to send to study in the abovementioned courses only carefully selected candidates who are able to satisfy the following conditions: They must be able to read, write and know the four rules of arithmetic; they must be in possession of documents testifying to their loyalty to the Soviet Government (such as a recommendation from a political commissar). For the infringement of this order the commanders of the army units will be held responsible in the full measure of severity of the laws of the revolutionary epoch." That this order was necessary implies that some of the cadets sent by the army were deficient in the very modest educational requirements set forth by the order. Petrovskii's testimony offers some concrete examples of this deficiency: in some of the regiments of the 45th Rifle Division, several of the cadets-designate were entirely illiterate. Some of them had not expressed any wish to enter the courses. Petrovskii goes on to say that in his experience similar unsatisfactory appointments to the courses continued to occur up to 1923. In that year it was definitely established that in so far as the recruitment of the normal military schools was concerned, the voluntary principle should be adhered to instead of appointment by way of drafting the candidates into the schools.[106]

The percentage of members of the Communist party among the graduates of the Command Course was: In 1918—70 per cent; in 1919—54 per cent (a drop probably due to a larger influx of peasants); in 1920—62 per cent; in 1921—65 per cent. The proportion of those that remained in the Red Army by January 1923 was as follows: graduates of 1918—53 per cent, 1919—16.4 per cent, 1920—11.3 per cent, 1921—26.2 per cent. Petrovskii intimates that a large number of the Red commanders were killed during the course of the Civil War, and that a large number became political workers and thus abandoned the career of arms. The first suggestion for the rather small percentage of the Red officers remaining to serve in the Red Army after the end of the Civil War does not seem to be borne out by the trend of the figures. The large percentage of 1918 graduates, who were exposed to the risks of the war for at least a year longer than those of the latter years, as well as the lesser percentage of the 1920 graduates as against those of 1919 seems to indicate those of the Red commanders promoted in the early days of the Civil War adapted themselves to the command positions in the Red Army and had obtained sufficient practical experience during the campaigns of that war to be considered valuable. It would seem that those who attended the abbreviated courses of the second half of 1919 and 1920 were found wanting even from the viewpoint of the then very modest requirements of the Red Army and dropped into a sphere of activity where promotion could be obtained on the grounds of revolutionary enthusi-asm, rather than for reasons of efficient leadership of troops in the field.

Of the total number of graduates from 1918 to 1922 inclusive, only 18 per cent remained in the Red Army in 1924.[107] In a way this is a judgment on the qualities of the Red cadets of the Civil War period and their ability to carve a career for themselves in the army.

The Red cadets were often used as shock troops in periods of crisis. Both the communist as well as the non-party elements marched enthu-siastically to the front as rank and file fighters in the battles for Petrograd in 1919, in the storming of Kronstadt in 1921, and on numerous other occasions.[108]

Petrovskii, in summing up the reports about the military ability of the Red commanders wrote: "In 1920 during a tour of the fronts . . . everywhere praise was given to the revolutionary firmness and self-sacrifice of the young *kraskomy* [abbreviation for "Red com-mander"]. At the same time everywhere it was added: 'They do not know how to give a command, they do not have the necessary will-power to command.'" It would seem that those of the cadets that were sent to schools from the front units made satisfactory subalterns. Those who had previously occupied platoon and section commanders' posts became excellent officers. The civilians without previous army experience prior to entering the Command Courses usually produced poor and even entirely unsatisfactory commanders.[109]

The former Director of Soviet Military Education claims that during his visits to the front he had frequently noticed that the senior commanders were unduly critical of the former Red cadets. This attitude found its expression in an article in the magazine *Revolution and War* (*Revoliutsiia i Voina*), published by the G.H.Q. of the Western Front of the Red Army.[110]

The antagonism between the old army officers and the Red com-manders sometimes found expression in the drastic re-examinations of the Red officers after a period of service with their army units prior to their confirmation in their quality of full-fledged commanders. "Old officers often cruelly flunked workers and peasants, who went to the front full of enthusiasm, anxious to give their energies to the defense of the Republic."[111]

Apparently the relations between the old officers and the Red com-manders were not merely antagonistic. Certain opinions and patterns of behavior of the officers of the Czar began to take root in the mentality of their proletarian colleagues. Petrovskii states: "Within the walls of the military school we encountered the old régime view of the peasant about the rôle of the officer with respect to the mass of the private soldiers. We had also noticed a certain trend to the upper class traditions of the cadets of the czarist military schools." He continues: "Professionalism is the scourge which lashed morally officers of all times and in all countries. . . . Our Red commanders would graduate from Command Courses, would leave for the front . . . should they show knowledge and enthusiasm for their work they were sent to the highest military school. . . . They became members of the new officers' group, and no agitation whatsoever, nor beautiful speeches about the necessity of contact with the masses would be of any avail. The conditions of existence are stronger than kind wishes."[112] Later on these "professionalistic" tendencies were to become even more pronounced. This will be discussed in a later chapter.

There was a fourth group that furnished commanders of the Red Army: old professional revolutionaries with an aptitude for leadership, men of the old fighting squads of the revolutionary underground parties of czarist days, chieftains of guerillas, born leaders who developed among the Red Guards—all these provided commanders of a wide range of ability and efficiency. On the one hand there were such men as Frunze, who later rose to occupy Trotsky's place as the People's Commissar for War. He was, perhaps, the most talented among the old professional revolutionary intellectuals who chose the profession of arms. Voroshilov, who also became the incumbent of Trotsky's post, is a prominent representative of fighting squad chieftain who later turned into a guerilla leader.

There was, however, an entirely different brand of guerilla leader: the innumerable Ukrainians, headed by Makhno and Grigoriev, embracing the chieftains of the north Caucasus groups, and the Red Cossack captains.

To what extent these *guerilleros* had become a thorn in the side of the regular Red Army is appropriately illustrated by Trotsky's order to the Third Army, issued on April 23, 1919: "It is necessary to cleanse ruthlessly the commanders of the Third Army . . . in some units of the Third Army there are still surviving the habits of guerillas or *ataman* to discuss combat orders and to fail, under all kinds of pretexts, in carrying them out."[113]

In an instruction to the leaders of the Fourteenth Army, dated August 1919, the People's Commissar for War again dwelt upon "the necessity of cleansing the commanding personnel. In the Ukrainian units there are too many Petlura guerillas and *ataman* elements, such as Bogunskii, Lopatkin and so on. Even the best of these guerilla commanders still do not understand what an order means and consider that disobedience to an order is the most natural thing."[114]

One of the principal inconveniences of having the guerilla leaders with their men in the Red Army was the strong personal influence of these chieftains over their "armies," renamed into brigades or even divisions of the regular Red Army. Their actions were often difficult to predict. Their defections occurred sometimes at the most critical moments. Thus Makhno's withdrawal from Nikopol into the Znamenskii Forest in July 1919 endangered the retreat of the 58th Division. Grigoriev's rebellion in May of the same year jeopardized the operations of the Third Army, while the abandonment of their positions by the two regiments of the Bogunskii Brigade resulted in the capture of Poltava by the Whites.[115]

Old intellectual revolutionaries, like Frunze, had of course little in common with the anarchistic peasant chieftains like Makhno. The one uniting link was that of their strong personal ascendancy over their men, the magnetism of their personalities. Besides, both these groups came into the Red Army, not because of their professional qualifications and military training, but on account of their qualities of initiative, leadership and ability.

On the other hand, Voroshilov and some of the lesser workmen guerilla leaders had shown, during the Civil War more than one trait in common with the Ukrainian *ataman*. They were also opposed to the centralized control of military affairs from Moscow, to the appointment of commanders by the central military organs, and the direction of military operations by former czarist officers.

The history of Trotsky's struggle with Voroshilov at Tsaritsin (now Stalingrad) over the problem of central control is an outstanding episode of the series of conflicts between the decentralizing guerilla tendencies constantly flaring up at the various fronts and the successful effort of Trotsky to create a New Model Army that could be directed from Moscow. R. Gul's book on the Red Army leaders may contain a great deal of apocryphal material, but his story of the Trotsky-Voroshilov feud has a ring of truth. Another colorful episode, the attempt of the cavalry leader Dumenko to assert his independence, which resulted in the killing by Dumenko of the Commissar Mikeladze, is quite well known.[116]

The analysis of the component groups of the commanding personnel of the Red Army shows thus clearly that it contained antagonistic elements that were sometimes in open conflict with each other as well as with the Soviet Government. It was, probably, a less homogeneous officers' corps than that of any European army since the days of the French army of the revolution. Some of the antagonisms and conflicts were rooted in the contradiction between the class warfare principle of the Communists and the practical necessity of using the "class enemies" of the proletariat—the officers, the peasant N.C.O.'s (some of whom were of kulak origin) as well as the kulak guerilla chieftains as commanders of their army. The army itself was predominately recruited from peasants.

The Russian proletariat at the time of the Civil War was not sufficiently strong—numerically or intellectually—to fight its battles on the external and the internal fronts. It had, however, had ample will-power in the persons of the chiefs of the Bolsheviki. That will ruthlessly bent or broke the representatives of the hostile groups of the population incorporated among the commanding personnel of the Red Army.

As long as the Civil War lasted it was easy to trace the internal antagonism and conflict within the officer personnel of the Red Army.

On the other hand, the commanding personnel, as a whole, often stood in an antagonistic relationship to their subordinates. The underlying causes for this will be examined later in this chapter. Some of the conflicts between the commanders and the soldiers will be described immediately below.

At the time of the organization of the so-called "screens" in March 1918 the appointment of former old army officers to leading positions was mistrusted and misunderstood by the local authorities and the soldiers. Not only the men in the ranks, but their commanders, who prior to that were elected to their posts by the rank and file, were definitely displeased to see former generals and colonels forced upon them in positions of authority by the central government. The local Soviets, which had developed their own military departments and had established their own armed detachments, as already mentioned on page 35 above, were also in opposition to the new-fangled ways of Moscow. At least in one instance billeters sent to Kaluga by the H.Q. of one of the "screens" had to return empty-handed with a warning that the staff of the screen had better keep away from Kaluga. The incident was ultimately solved by direct negotiations between the commanding officer of the "screen" and the the chief of the troops of the Kaluga "republic."[117]

A number of former officers were killed in the struggle for the establishment of an adequate discipline in the ranks of the troops of the "screens." The official history of the Civil War cites five names of such victims of their sense of duty. Some of the officers sought to escape the difficulty of the situation by deliberately offering to occupy posts in the Red Army far below their former rank and experience. Thus a former Major General of the old army, who had lately commanded a brigade of artillery, took over the duties of a platoon commander in an artillery train. The more successful of these officers, such as Getmantsev, overcame the antagonism of the elected commanding personnel and the mutinous disposition of the troops, and turned their detachments into efficient combat units.[118]

One of Trotsky's comments on the old army officers who had joined the Red forces, refers to the antagonism displayed toward them by the rank and file. It is an apt illustration of the conditions that prevailed at that early period of the existence of the Red Army. "Of the old officers, there remained with us either the high-principled and idealistic ones, who understood or at least sensed the meaning of the new era (these, of course, were in an insignificant minority), or time-servers, inert, without principles, who had no energy to go over to the Whites; there remained, finally, quite a number of active counter-revolutionaries, who were caught unawares. . . . Fundamentally the spirit of their class-resistance was broken. Nevertheless the hatred against them of the rank and file was still intense and became one of the sources of guerilla tendencies; within the framework of a small local detachment there was no need for qualified military workers."[119]

In the end of December 1918 the People's Commissar for War wrote that the "wholesale, often unjust attacks on military specialists from the ranks of the former cadre officers, who are now working in the Red Army, create among a certain part of the commanding personnel a mood of indetermination and perplexity. On the other hand, officers occupying staff posts in the rear are afraid of transfers to the Red Army, because of lack of confidence in them, which is artificially fostered by unbalanced elements within the Soviet ranks. It is clear how such phenomena unfavorably affect the interests of the army in the field."[120]

A telegram sent to Trotsky by General Novitskii reflects the feelings of those of the old officers who considered that the state of affairs in the Red Army made it impossible for them to accept command positions in the armed forces of the Soviets without loss of their professional and personal dignity"; . . . collaboration of military specialists should be made possible by confidence in them and the observance of guarantees of their professional and human dignity . . . on which, as Mr. Novitskii says, they cannot count at present"— thus Trotsky sums up the gist of the message addressed to him by the former Commander in Chief of the Armies of the Northern Front.[121]

Blumenthal even goes so far as to state that during the Civil War the commanding personnel of the Red Army worked to a large extent because of fear.[122] This seems to be a very narrow interpretation of the motives of the former old army officers who accepted command positions in the Red Army, although there was no lack of reasons for them to feel that their lives were in two-fold danger— from the enemy before them and from their own men behind.

On the Northern Front, where the Red Army was confronted not only by the White Russian troops, but by Allied armed forces as well, the feelings of the Red soldiers against their commanders, who formerly were czarist officers, ran so high that several of these officers were actually killed by their own men during action against the enemy.[123]

At that front the dislike of the Red soldiers for the former old army officers who were sent to command them was fanned into flames of bitter hatred by the frequent instances of treason on the part of these officers. As the official Soviet history of the Civil war has it: "the officer personnel had difficulty in comprehending how they could go into battle against the Allies, with whom, as the saying goes, they fought side-by-side against the Germans, and who 'helped' us a great deal by sending us artillery."[124]

The situation at the Northern Front became so acute that it was decided to remove all the commanding personnel recruited from old army officers from the front units, with very few exceptions. They were replaced by N.C.O.'s and those of the Red private soldiers who had distinguished themselves.[125]

The memoirs of the participants in the Northern Front campaigns contain a number of references to episodes of treason or suspected treason on the part of the old army officers who served there in command positions in the Red Army.

Andrei Lychkov describes how in 1919 an ex-officer by the name of Katz persuaded a company of the 6th Soviet Regiment to surrender to the enemy. The next day after that, one of the Red soldiers reported to the communist detachment that the commanding officers had decided to take over to the Whites also some of the other companies of the regiment. The Communists surrounded the house where the officers were assembled, disarmed them and organized a meeting of the soldiers of their regiment in the village street. It was decided at the meeting that the officers were under arrest and that the soldiers should elect their own commanders.[126]

A. P. Shelekovskii reports the crushing by a guerilla detachment in August 1919 of an officers' conspiracy in the 3rd Petrograd Regiment on the same front. According to Shelekovskii, the officers of that regiment had planned to raise a rebellion, to open the front in the sector of Sheleksa, to cut off the advance positions of the Red Army on the railway by blowing up the railway bridge over the river Emtsa, arresting the H.Q. of the brigade to complete the disorganization of the Red forces in that sector. As a result of the conspiracy and the subsequent arrest of the officers, the entire regiment became demoralized.[127]

These reports seem to indicate that both in the 6th and 3rd regiments the former old army officers had a great deal of influence over their peasant soldiers. Arrests had to be made by outsiders—the guerillas—whose ranks contained many Communists—and not by the soldiers of the regular Red Army.

The extent to which the "conspirators," leaving aside the treason of Katz, were really intending to accomplish the various plans ascribed to them, and the rôle played in these incidents by the hatred of the guerilla elements against the old officers are matters for conjecture. The fact of the conflict remains, with its trail of disorganization and loss of efficiency in the units involved.

These real and alleged instances of treason were by no means isolated cases. There was a real galaxy of conspiracies and treason on the part of the old officers who served as commanders in the Red Army.

To cite a few additional examples: in the H.Q. of the North Caucasus Military District at Tsaritsin, out of the three principal military specialists, one—Nosovich—deserted to the enemy and a second was convicted of treason and executed.[128]

R. Gul rather shrewdly ascribes to Trotsky (*se non e vero*, etc.) a remark allegedly thrown out to Voroshilov: ". . . as to the desertion of Nosovich, are you certain that the cause of his running away to the Whites does not lie in your throwing him into the Cheka instead of giving him a chance to work?"—hinting at Voroshilov's highhanded action with respect to the military specialist sent by Moscow to help in the organization of the military district. Voroshilov handed

Nosovich over to the Cheka for imprisonment on board a lighter anchored in the Volga.[129]

In more than one instance the persecution of the former officers by the guerilla type communist leaders had undoubtedly a great deal to do with the former deserting to the enemy. On the other hand, we know that General Novitskii, whose telegram to Trotsky was already referred to on page 67 above, served with great distinction with Frunze at the Eastern front. Very probably his informed and well-trained mind was the source of a good many of the fruitful decisions of Frunze which led to the success of the armies under the latter's command. An educated man, Frunze treated Novitskii with consideration and tact, in contrast to Voroshilov's treatment of Nosovich and other former officers who had the misfortune to serve at Tsaritsin.

One of the principal causes of conflict between the former officers serving in the Red forces and the Soviet Government was the widespread suspicion that the bolshevik leaders were agents of the German General Staff and had done their work of breaking up the old army not only because they were revolutionary internationalists, but also on account of the source of their financing.

The fate of Admiral Stchastnyi, who commanded the Baltic Fleet, is a case in point. In his speech on March 12, 1922, Trotsky said: "When we, a decried, a defamed and an illegal party, crawled out from the Kerensky underground, the entire world stood up against us. . . . Some regarded us as mercenary agents, others as murderers, but all were against us."[130] Small wonder, then, that many of the officers of the armed forces of Russia, including some of the most energetic and patriotic among them, should have shared these beliefs.

At the time of Stchastnyi's arrest in the spring of 1918, there were found in his possession several documents, allegedly counterfeits. One of them purported to be a copy of what looked, on the face of it, like a communication addressed to the head of the government of the Petrograd Commune by the Intelligence Officer of the German Army. It contained the statement that the German Intelligence Service was informed that a group of Kronstadt anarchist seamen had decided to hand over a part of the Baltic Fleet to the Finnish revolutionaries to help them defend Viborg and Björke against General Mannerheim's troops. The communication went on to intimate that the Intelligence Office understood that this decision of the seamen had the approval of the Petrograd Soviet and warned that such an act would be construed as a sufficient reason to occupy Petrograd and to insist upon the disarmament of Kronstadt and of the naval vessels located there.[131]

Trotsky further mentioned, in his accusatory speech at the Stchastnyi trial, that another document found in the latter's possession purported to be a communication from the German Field Staff to Lenin, chiding the head of the Soviet Government for the appointment of Blokhin to the post of principal commissar of the Baltic Fleet, as the latter was, allegedly, hindering the execution of German plans.[132]

Whether these documents were forgeries (possibly they were prepared by the German Intelligence to increase the mutual mistrust between the Fleet Command and the Soviet Government—Trotsky intimated in his speech at the trial that they were fabricated by some officers of the navy), or whether they were true documents, is a matter which some future historian of the Russian revolution may establish. However, there was more than one reason for a man of Stchastnyi's antecedents and mentality to accept these documents at their face value, and to regard them as another proof of the Lenin government's subservience to the German High Command. That certain groups of seamen, nay, even some of the leaders among the co-partners of the Bolsheviki in the government at the time—the Socialist Revolutionaries of the Left, as well as some of the Bolsheviki, were inclined to give all the help they could to the hard-pressed Finnish Reds, was well known. That certain elements in their own government were inclined to go to extreme lengths to bring about a break with Germany was later shown by the murder of the German Ambassador at Moscow by the Socialist Revolutionaries of the Left. There was, therefore, nothing improbable *per se* in the accusation contained in the communication that certain groups of seamen of the Baltic Fleet were anxious to help the Finns to defend the Karelian Peninsula. Nor was there anything particularly surprising in the protest addressed to the Soviets by the German Intelligence Office.

As Trotsky himself said: "Some regarded us as mercenary agents." To those who so regarded the Soviet Government, the documents were a mere confirmation of their views and quite in line with what they thought of Lenin and his followers. When it is remembered that the accusation of being willing tools of the German Intelligence Service was recently levelled at many of the old bolshevik leaders in Soviet courts and in the Soviet press—the *Kommunist*, in its September 1937 issue, qualified the followers of Trotsky and Bukharin as "agents of Japano-German fascism"[133]—it is easy to see that in 1918 the accusation was readily accepted by those opposed to the communist leadership. The recent accusations prove at least that even at this late date there are elements in Russia ready to accept the statement that Trotsky and some of the other principal personalities of the Communist party were German agents. How many more were ready to believe this in 1917-1918!

The author remembers well a conversation with Stchastnyi in the beginning of 1918 on the ice of the Helsingfors harbor, when the fate of the Baltic Fleet hung in the balance, and the danger of the warships falling into German hands was great: "The Bolsheviki are German agents, they are going to try to hand over the fleet to the enemy so that they can use it against the Allies. Something is going to happen, however, which will stop them. . . . The Baltic Fleet made the bolshevik revolution possible, the Baltic Fleet will also bring the bolshevik power to an end." Such was the gist of his remarks.

This mistrust of the motives of the Soviet Government led to the attempted rebellion by the Destroyer Division of the Baltic Fleet at Petrograd led by Lieutenant Lisanevich, and, according to Trotsky, approved and sponsored by Admiral Stchastnyi. The latter's execution, and the attempt to arrest Lisanevich, who was hidden by his men and helped by them to escape, alienated many of the naval officers and confirmed them still more strongly in their belief that the Soviet Government was merely a servant of the German High Command. What better proof of their subservience, they thought, than the execution of the man who saved the Baltic Fleet from the clutches of the enemy? Even at this date there are among Russian naval officers residing abroad a few men deeply convinced that Trotsky and his group were acting at the time as German agents. In 1918, this feeling not only led to an acute conflict among a large number of the naval officers serving in the Red Navy, but also involved a substantial group of the Baltic Fleet bluejackets. Some of them were in the Popov detachment in Moscow, which raised the banner of rebellion against Lenin on July 6, 1918, and arrested the dread head of the Cheka, Dzerzhinskii.[134]

These few illustrations may be of some help in forming an idea of the various conflict situations which divided the commanding personnel of the Red Army among themselves, separated a part of it from the men, and threw them in opposition to the Soviet Government.

One of the measures adopted by the Soviet Government to overcome these disrupting tendencies among the commanding personnel and to crush the incipient conflict situations was the establishment of the institution of military commissars. Their work in the Red Army during the Civil War will be examined below.

Military Commissars

In a resolution passed by the Fifth Congress of Soviets on July 10, 1918, the rôle of the military commissars was defined in the following manner: "The military commissars are the guardians of the close and inviolable internal bond between the Red Army and the workers' and peasants' régime as a whole. Only irreproachable revolutionaries, stanch champions of the cause of the proletariat and the village poor, should be appointed to the posts of military commissars, to whom is handed over the fate of the army."[135]

The military commissars were not a novelty in the Russian armed forces in 1918. The Provisional Government had appointed a number of front commissars to the armies. Kerensky had approved, in July 1917, the statute of front commissars, drafted by the well-known terrorist Savinkov. The personnel of these commissars of the Provisional Government was recruited from heterogeneous elements. Besides Savinkov, who had occupied for a time the post of commissar of the South Western Front, they included other members of revolutionary parties that supported the Kerensky Government. A number of these commissars were army officers of revolutionary tendencies (such as V. B. Stankevich, commissar of the Northern Front, and Dubois, commissar of the Twelfth Army). Some of them took an energetic part in the effort of the Provisional Government to rebuild the morale of the old army, while others (for instance, Dubois) became mere intermediaries between the army committees and the higher command personnel.[136]

The work of these commissars was in the direction of restoring discipline, or rather rebuilding it on new foundations, and combating the defeatist tendencies fostered by the Bolsheviki. At times their activities brought them in sharp conflict with the rank and file of the soldiery. In one of the army corps of the Fifth Army, the Corps commissar barely escaped with his life after attempting to persuade an infantry division to take part in the July offensive.[137]

During the period of an acute conflict between the army command and the Provisional Government at the time of the Kornilov putsch in September 1917, some of the commissars, through their influence with the army committees and the rank and file, helped a great deal to bring about the collapse of the rebellion. Thus Savitskii, who acted *pro tem* as the commissar of the Northern Front, made it impossible for General Klembovskii, a partisan of Kornilov, to render any effective help to the latter.[138]

In other words, the Provisional Government front commissars were the political representatives of that government in the army, appointed to improve the military efficiency of the troops under the new order of things, where officers had in large measure lost control over their men. They were also to ensure the loyalty both of the commanding personnel and the troops to the régime, although the latter functions do not seem to have the all-important aspect they assumed with respect to the military commissars of the Soviet régime.

According to General Niessel, the principal commissar of the army was subordinated to the Chief of Staff of the Supreme G.H.Q. Instructions to the commissars of the various armies were supposed to pass through his hands. However, as asserted by Niessel, the latter had the right to correspond directly with the government.[139]

Strangely enough the decree of December 16, 1917, which laid down the principles of administration of the army upon the advent to power of Lenin's government, made no attempt to reintroduce in a new form the institution of the front commissars.[140]

The order of the People's Commissar for War dated April 6, 1918, was the first document issued by the central Soviet authority to define the functions of military commissars.

The order stated that the military commissars were the immediate political organ of the Soviet Government in the army and that the commissars were to be appointed from "irreproachable revolutionaries, able to remain the embodiment of the revolution under the most difficult circumstances." The persons of the commissars were declared inviolate, and an insult offered to a commissar while on duty was proclaimed equal to the most heinous crime against the Soviet Government. "The military commissar shall see to it that the army does not become a thing apart from the entire Soviet system and that the various military establishments do not become foci of conspiracies or instruments against workers and peasants." The commissars were instructed to take part in all forms of activities of the military specialists and were to receive jointly with the latter all reports and letters. Theirs was the duty to countersign all orders. Only orders so countersigned were to be considered valid. At the same time the responsibility for the efficacy of the purely military—operation and combat orders—was left to the commanding personnel. The commissars' signature on such orders merely meant that there was no reason to suspect a counter-revolutionary motive behind the intentions expressed in the order. At the same time the commissars were made responsible for the prompt execution of all orders.[141]

"The commissar shall see to it," went on the order, "that all workers of the Red Army, from the top to the bottom, fulfill their work faithfully and energetically, that all funds are disbursed economically and under the most stringent supervision; that all military property is preserved with all possible care." Among the duties of the commissars was the liaison service between the Red Army establishments and the central, as well as local, institutions of the Soviet Government. They were responsible for obtaining effective co-operation of the latter with the Red Army.[142]

The highest ranking military commissars (at the time of the issuance of the order, those of the Supreme Military Council) were to be appointed by the Soviet of the People's Commissars, those of the District and Regional Councils by the Supreme Military Council in agreement with the respective local soviet.[143]

There are several noteworthy points about the order. In the first place it refers to appointments of commissars to central and local administrative institutions of the Red Army, and does not mention at all the procedure of appointment of commissars to front units of the Red armed forces. Secondly, while the principle of appointment of the commissars by the central military authorities is clearly established, contrary to the libertarian bases of the army self-government, as outlined in the decree of December 16, 1917, a certain concession to the decentralizing tendencies is admitted in the guise of the concurrence of the local soviet organs to the appointment of candidates selected by the central military authority.

With regard to the responsibility for the conduct of military operations, the line of demarcation is sharply drawn. The commanding personnel is left with full authority as well as the responsibility for the efficacy of their dispositions.

In a manner, this order illustrates the limitations of the central military authorities' practical jurisdiction at that time—it did not reach beyond the newly established military commissariats and the units they were about to organize.

It would be erroneous, however, to conclude from the text of the order, that there were no military commissars in the forces of the Soviet Republic during the period antedating it.

Niessel refers in his book to Posern, the commissar appointed by the Soviet Government to the H.Q. of the Northern Front, as performing his duties in January 1918. He also mentions a seaman, who was at the time the commissar of an army cavalry corps, commanded by General Svechin at the same front. The Commissar of the Fifth Army at Dvinsk, spoken of in Niessel's memoirs, was at his post considerably earlier than the date of the Trotsky order.

The selection of these early commissars seems to be somewhat haphazard—the one at the cavalry corps "made appearances only to obtain from the medical officers prescriptions for alcohol under the guise of medicine, and spent his time getting drunk and running after loose women."[144]

Attempts at the political guidance of the front units were apparently made as early as December 1917. The official Soviet history of the Civil War makes mention of the establishment of a political department (*politotdel*) at the H.Q. of the Commander in Chief of the Soviet troops in the south. This department published a politico-military paper. In this way, at a very early date, the political control of the army units began to develop, not along the lines of the decentralized, or "territorial" system, but by means of special military-political organs.[145]

On January 15, 1918, an organization and propaganda department was added to the structure of the All-Russian Collegium for the creation of the Red Army. This department did not aim to embrace the political guidance of all the armed forces of the Republic, and its activity was mainly along the lines of propaganda for the establishment of a regular Red Army. It opened a short-term school for agitators who were to act as recruiting officers to help the local authorities to obtain volunteers for the Red Army.[146]

The official Soviet history of the Civil War confirms that even during the first months of the existence of the Red Army there were military commissars who served as organs of political control of the army.[147]

I. Petukhov, in his book on party organization and party work in the Red Army, considers that because of the acute antagonism between the Red soldiers and the old army officers appointed to command them during the early days of the Red Army, the first thing the commissars had to accomplish was to overcome that antagonism. Petukhov says: "As between the commander (who only a few days before had been 'in faith and truth' serving the Czar) and the Red soldiers, there hung a 'precipice,' the rôle of the commissar, as the political organ of the Soviet Government in the army, had to be reduced to the establishment of the necessary bond of confidence between them."[148]

Trotsky in 1918, in outlining the rôle of the commissar in the army, said: "The military specialists will direct the technical end of the work, purely military matters, operation work and combat activities. The political side of the organization, training and education, should be entirely subordinated to the representatives of the Soviet régime in the person of its commissar."[149]

Here the problem of the political education of the troops, of their indoctrination with Soviet ideas, is brought up. It was not included in the order defining the commissars' functions.

Petukhov states, however, in his book already referred to above, that while until January 1919 there was no special document issued by the central authorities entrusting the commissars with party-political functions, in fact as early as in the first half of 1918, the commissars functioned and were regarded as the representatives of the party in the army, as the organizers *par excellence* of the party and political work in general within the units to which they were attached.[150]

For instance: In June 1918, at the all-city meeting of Communists serving in the Red Army establishments and units of Moscow, it was urged that in all institutions of the army there should be formed party cells. The commissars were to be entrusted with the establishment of the party machinery in all the military institutions and offices located in Moscow.[151]

In the reports of the military commissar of the Kazan Workers' Regiment and those of the commissar of the Simbirsk group of troops, dated June 1918, reference was made to the appointment of all Communists, as well as the transfer of them from one unit to another by the commissars. Also that the commissars were in fact directing the activity of the party organizations in the regiments.[152]

Beginning with the earliest days of their work, the commissars were drawn into propaganda and agitation activities. They also had to take interest in the so-called "cultural-enlightenment" work in the Red Army. Clubs and libraries were established in the Red Army, and served to circulate government-inspired newspapers and books. These were supplemented by discussions and lectures on political subjects, sponsored in many cases by the commissars.[153]

As A. Geronimus states in his essay on the cardinal moments in the development of the party-political apparatus in the army in the years 1918-1920: "it was impossible to arouse the peasant masses for a new war without preliminary intensive organizational work in the village, without introducing the class struggle of the village poor against the kulaks."[154]

Detachments formed in such proletarian centers as Petrograd and Moscow arrived at the front with a well-organized and tightly-knit party nucleus. In other units, formed in the agricultural provinces or from guerilla detachments, such nuclei were lacking. Thus, according to Geronimus: "the principal burden of the political work in the front units fell upon the political commissars. . . . In a number of units the relations between the commissars and the party cells were of an indefinite character. In some units commissars were even chosen by the party collective—the remnants of the traditions of the first post-October months."[155]

It would be erroneous to suppose that the commissars in the army from the very beginning were all Communists. The statute establishing the institution of the military commissars merely insisted that they should be recruited from "irreproachable revolutionaries" reflecting thus the heterogeneity of the personnel which was already performing the functions of local political control in the Red armed forces.

It is obvious that as the functions of the military commissars developed so as to embrace not only the supervision of the actions of the commanding personnel, but also the direction of the political work of the Communist party in the Red Army, none but Communists became eligible for these posts.

In fulfillment of the order of the People's Commissar for War of April 6, 1918, the All-Russian Bureau of Military Commissars was organized to co-ordinate the work of the commissars, to publish instructions for their guidance and to call, "if necessary," congresses of these commissars.[156]

With the growth of the work of the military commissars, that Bureau was replaced by the Political Department of the Revolutionary Military Council of the Republic, headed by a member of the Central Committee of the Communist party.[157]

The gradual extension of the scope of activity and influence of the military commissars found an expression in a note drafted by Trotsky in the fall of 1918. "There do not exist and did not exist any orders telling the commissar 'thou hast no right to interfere in any dispositions whatsoever of the commanding personnel.' . . . The sphere where the commissar has least 'rights,' is the domain of operations, of command. . . . But nobody ever prohibited the commissar from expressing his opinion regarding operation problems, giving advice, controlling the execution of an operation order, etc." This "liberal" interpretation of the order of April 6, 1918, was followed by the remark, that on his own part, the commander also has a right to take interest in political work : "a good commander cannot fail to take an interest, as the state of political work has a tremendous influence on the fighting efficacy of the unit."[158]

One may see in these remarks a trend toward the interpenetration of the fields of activity of the commissar and the commander, toward the synthesis of these originally opposed elements of Red Army leadership.

The same thought is developed still further in a letter addressed by Trotsky to the Revolutionary Military Councils of armies and fronts on July 12, 1919, in which he wrote: "the commissar, of course, is not called upon to *replace* the commander of the regiment or the head of the supply service, not even less to *dislodge* them, but he is called upon to *supplement* them, not only through a vigilant control . . . but also by direct initiative, a direct creative effort, hand in hand with the commander or head of the supply service."[159]

This evolution of Trotsky's views as to the rôle of the commissar reflected partly the actual state of affairs in the Red Army. On the other hand it had roots in the discussions of the problem in party councils.

The Eighth Congress of the Communist party, held in March 1919, placed the military commissars in a very strong position by passing a resolution, which in part read as follows: "the commissars in the army are not only the direct and immediate representatives of the Soviet Government, but are first of all the bearers of the spirit of our party, of its discipline, firmness and courage in the struggle for the realization of the proposed aim." Problems of administration and supply were placed under the joint authority of commanders and commissars. The latter were also granted the right to inflict summary punishment (including arrest) and the right to bring offenders to trial.[160]

I. Petukhov's comments on the relations between commanders and commissars in 1919 are very enlightening. According to him, at the time, a part of the commanders were working very closely with the government ("our party," as Petukhov has it), and were fulfilling their duty faithfully and with zeal. That group began to express open dissatisfaction with its position because of the important authority vested in the commissars. In the second year of the Civil War, these commanders were not reconciled to the abridgement of their own authority as commanders of armies or of lesser units by the supervision and control of their every action by the commissars. They regarded this interference as an obstacle to the development of their own creative initiative. On the other hand, a certain number of commissars had a definite tendency to acquire practical command experience and military education. They tended actually to take over the functions of commanders and cherished the hope of eventually dispensing altogether with the services of the military specialists, and concentrating in their own hands full military authority and leadership. According to this historian of political and party work in the Red Army during the Civil War, I. Petukhov, by the end of 1919 and in the beginning of 1920 a definite type of "good" commissar had emerged. A man who knew the details of the supply service and could adjust its shortcomings, who was well acquainted with the commanding personnel and knew the administrative machinery of his unit "as well as his five fingers," who did not lose his head in action, and who, if necessary, could replace the commander in a critical moment—such was the *beau idéal* of the military commissar of the period.[161]

In other words, the most loyal (from the Soviet viewpoint) and energetic commanders, recruited from old army officers, came into conflict with those of the commissars who felt themselves best fitted for the profession of arms and were anxious to command the troops in the field in their own right, to use their own military knowledge and experience, rather than merely to supervise the military specialists.

This trend led to a spirited campaign for the complete scrapping of the institution of military commissars as it was originally established, and of the forms it assumed in the second part of 1919. One of the arguments used by the partisans of unity of military command was founded on their estimate that the military political departments had by then developed into a well-organized and influential party-political machine in the army, and were thus fully able to take over all matters pertaining to the political supervision and control of the Red Army.[162]

These political departments were brought into legal existence by the statute of political departments of the Revolutionary Military Councils of Fronts and Armies, published in December 1918. Some of the Soviet historians consider, however, that the origin of these departments should be sought in the Organization and Propaganda Department of the All-Russian Collegium for the creation of the Red

Army or in the All-Russian Bureau of Military Commissars already referred to above.[163]

The latter institution seems to have a better claim to the legitimate ancestry of the Political Departments. The Bureau's most important work was centered in the Agitation-Enlightenment Department, headed in the first months of its existence by the well-known old Bolshevik Enukidze (who later fell victim to one of the "purges") and the Department of the Schools for Military Commissars. During the first period of their activity the schools of agitators and instructors graduated several hundred students. These graduates were "to assist in the organization of communist cells in the units of the Red Army." Petukhov concludes from this that the Bureau, from its inception, was regarded not only as a state institution, but also as a part of the party machinery as well.

Support for this view could be found in the order of the Revolutionary Military Council of the Republic "Concerning the Political Departments of the Revolutionary Councils of the Fronts," where reference was made to the Bureau, as "acting in closest contact with, and under the direction of the Central Committee of the Russian Communist party."[164]

The Political Departments of Armies and Fronts actually had come into being several months before the appearance of the statute published in December 1918. The one of the Eastern Front was organized in the first days of July 1918. As Petukhov writes: "Political Departments of Fronts, Armies and Divisions came into being at the initiative of the individual members of the Revolutionary Military Councils and Commissars."[165]

A. Geronimus states: "The order of the Revolutionary Military Council of the Republic, No. 357, dated December 5, 1918, in its essence merely gave sanction to their formation."[166]

In the field of development of a unified political control of the Red Army, as in some of the other spheres of its growth, local initiative thus preceded the action of the legislator.

The main function of these Political Departments were: "cultural enlightenment"—meaning political as well as general education, the instruction of Communists sent to the army and their distribution among the various units, and publication and distribution of pamphlets and newspapers. They were also concerned with political work among the local population of the territories in which their respective army units were located. The Political Departments did not become universally established in army divisions until the spring of 1919. At first they existed generally at the Front and Army H.Q.'s.[167]

It is important to note that this centralization of the political control of the Red Army, which was the counterpart of the military centralization, had met with a measure of opposition on the part of the elements both within the army and in the party councils who favored "democratic" methods of control dubbed by their opponents as "army syndicalism."

At the same time the direction of the Special Departments of the Cheka (concerned with work in the Red Army) and of the Military Tribunals was also concentrated in the hands of the Revolutionary Military Councils and the respective military commissars.[168]

In this manner all phases of Red Army activity were gradually coordinated and became controlled in a centralized and hierarchical fashion through appointees of the central government, building up a system completely opposite to that provided for by the decree of December 16, 1917.

At the Eighth Congress of the Russian Communist Party the authority of the commissars over the commanding personnel was strengthened by means of a system of attestations which were to be conducted by the commissars.[169]

A. Geronimus points out that the military division of the Communist party program, while stating in its fifth paragraph the necessity of "concentrating political direction of the army and comprehensive control over the commanding personnel in the hands of the workers' class," did not contain any reference to the institution of commissars as exercising *par excellence* this control. Geronimus stresses that this omission of the control functions of the commissars from the party program was not accidental. In his view, even at that time the control functions of the commissar were regarded by the party as a temporary expedient, and by no means as the only possible form of party supervision of the commanding personnel.[170]

It is interesting to observe that all reference to the commissars was also omitted from the Service Regulations governing the ordering of the internal relations of the personnel of the Red Army. Trotsky, in an order dated March 2, 1919, had given as a reason for this omission that these Regulations were prepared to meet the needs of the Red Army not only in the immediate future but in a later period, as well, when unity of direction would be introduced in the Red Army. His view seems to give support to that expressed by Geronimus.[171]

What was the relative importance of the institution of military commissars in bringing about the victories of the Red Army? Here opinions differ.

On the one hand, D. A. Petrovskii claims that it is wrong to ascribe its successes to the correct solution of the organizational problems, and even denies the novelty of the principle involved in the establishment of the military commissars in the army. "If we examine," he says, "the basic institutions of the Red Army, we shall see extremely little originality in them. All revolutionary governments have had recourse to the institution of commissars. In so far as the political work is concerned, such work was the foundation of revolutionary building of all times and in all countries . . . we have to turn, not to the commissars and not to political departments, but to the communist cells, to find the key to the understanding of the successful organization of the Red Army and its victories in the field of battle." This statement of the eminent Director of Military Education is somewhat offset by another of his remarks to the effect that while the commissars were not supposed, according to regulations, to interfere with orders issued by commanders, the institution of commissars "taken in the broadest sense of the word"—whatever this may mean—"did partake very importantly in those daring operations, which form the pride of the Red Army."[172]

Another witness of the activities of the commissars, the ex-czarist Colonel who commanded a brigade of infantry in the Red Army, Kotomin, left a comprehensive report analyzing the group of men who filled the posts of the commissars during the Civil War. "Commissars are the best of the Communists," he wrote in a memorandum submitted to the White Command, after his desertion from the Red Army. According to Kotomin, 5 per cent or even less of these commissars are Communists by conviction "strongly believing in the idea of socialism." This group is energetic, giving the best they had without sparing themselves and working "to the limits of human endurance." The other 95 per cent or more were exploiting to the limit the privileges of their position, while the first group was entirely selfless and did not seek any advantages for themselves.[173]

Trotsky's commentary on this characterization was that Kotomin had included in the second group the commissars of working-class origin. He defends them by saying: "of course the aim of communism is the betterment of the position of the toiling masses, of the toilers of town and village . . . but this does not mean at all that each worker Communist . . . fights for personal advantage."[174]

This, however, is a moot question. It should be thoroughly examined by some historian of the Russian revolution. In later chapters evidence will be adduced to show how keenly interested were large groups of Communists in establishing and maintaining a privileged position in the Soviet state. It is at the same time quite probable that a revolutionary puritan like Trotsky had idealized at the time the non-intellectual elements of his party and had failed to appreciate the great dynamic urge of self-interest hidden behind the collectivistic verbiage of the congresses, conferences and discussions of the Communists of the early NEP period.

Kotomin was particularly struck by the tireless energy of the military commissars and by their ability to work. He explained this partly by their youth, partly by the fanatical faith of their leaders, which was a source of inspiration to the commissars; also by the stringent party discipline and the strict accountability to which their superiors held them for every sin of omission. Kotomin also mentions "the desire to make a career and the fear of denunciation, as spying on one another is prevalent among them in the most persistent and merciless degree."[175]

This sleuthing was, of course, also extended to their political wards, the commanding personnel. The commissars roomed with the commanders to whom they were attached. They accompanied them wherever they went, so that each step made by the commanders was immediately known to the commissars. It is true that at the same time the commissars, according to Kotomin, watched over the prestige of the commanding personnel. Commissars of lower degrees were drastically punished for any "demagogic" gestures against the commanding personnel.[176]

It is quite natural that such energetic "muscular Communists" would antagonize various groups in the Red Army. There is evidence that some of the commissars went very far in extending their authority in the fields of military administration and supplies. Some of them began to issue orders of their own in these spheres of activity without the signature of the commander. The youthful Commander of the Soviet Armies, Tukhachevskii, already a Communist at the time, complained that such orders were issued by commissars and members of the Revolutionary Military Council of his army.[177]

The campaign for the abolition of dualism in the administration and command of the Red Army began in December 1919. Its first noted advocate was the old Bolshevik, Smilga. His speech at the December 1919 congress of the political workers of the Red Army is

considered a landmark in the history of the long struggle for the unification of leadership in the Soviet armed forces. Smilga demanded
the abandonment of the collegiate system of the Revolutionary Military Councils of Armies and Fronts, proposing to replace them by a
special commissar who would have charge of the political department,
the special department of the Cheka and the revolutionary tribunals.
The rewarding for meritorious service was also to be in their hands.
This measure was to be followed by the extension to the commanders
of the right of issuing orders on their own responsibility without the
endorsement of the commissar. The posts of commissar were to be
abolished altogether in units commanded by men of proved loyalty.
Smilga's paper on the unity of command was published in No. 2 of
Military Thought (*Voennaia Mysl*) in 1919.[178]

Trotsky, in commenting on Smilga's proposals, remarked in December 1919 that in principle he believed that each unit should be
headed by a commander and that the division of authority was wrong.
In his opinion the commander should have authority not only in the
sphere of command, but also in the field of politics and ethics, if not
in that of party activities.[179]

It is interesting that, in support of his view that it would be a mistake to insist that in all instances authority should be centered in hands
of Communists to the exclusion of non-party elements, Trotsky
brought up the example of the Military Sanitary Administration,
where the rule of appointment of Communists only to responsible
positions was strictly adhered to . . . "one has to admit that this is the
most rotten institution we have."[180]

The thought embodied in the order of April 6, 1918, was developed
by Trotsky in the same speech: the commissars were created to serve
as political guarantors for the commanding personnel. As long as the
mass of the Red Army soldiers mistrusted, virtually to a man, the
commanding personnel, the commissars were intermediaries between
the commanders and the Red soldiers. At the same time Trotsky, admitting the desirability of unity of command, promised the political
workers he was addressing at the time that no immediate change
would be made in the arrangements regarding the functions of commissars. He expressed himself as opposed to the issuance of an order
abolishing posts of commissars in units commanded by Communists.
The People's Commissar for War pleaded that such an order would
create a difficult situation for the non-communist military specialists,
and that in practice it would be hard to decide in each individual instance whether commanders who had joined the party only recently

should be placed in the same category in respect to abolishing the posts of commissars in their units with those of old party standing.[181]

Trotsky, thus, at the time took the middle path, eschewing the recommendation of Smirnov at the Eighth Party Congress to increase the influence of the commissars by granting them authority not only in administrative and organization matters, but also in the field of military operations as well.[182] He did not side with Smilga, who represented the opposite viewpoint. Apparently he had felt that, for the duration of the Civil War, it was advisable not to alter radically a method which was giving good results so far.

In the performance of their duties, commissars came at times into violent conflict with the soldiers. Commissar Bych was killed near Lgov in July 1918, during the disturbances created in the Red Army units in that district by the agitation of the Socialist Revolutionaries of the Left for an offensive against the Germans in the Ukraine.[183] One of the members of the Revolutionary Military Council of an army of the Eastern Front, Lindov, was killed by the mutinous soldiers of a division, where the guerilla tendencies were still strong.[184]

An order, dated August 30, 1918, of the People's Commissar for War, records a conflict between the commissar personnel and the higher military authorities. It refers to the execution of several commissars of the Fifth Army for "abandoning positions entrusted to them." At this period, the Red Army was still poorly organized and disciplined. The military commissars, as well as the commanders executed with them, fell victims to a general condition existing in the army at the time. Their execution ended a period of lax discipline and made clear to the political personnel of the Red Army that they would be held to the strictest accountability for the conduct of their units.[185]

The line of demarcation between the functions of the commissars and those of the Political Departments was not definitely drawn until the Eighth Congress of the Party in March 1919 made a decision in this respect. Their mutual relationship prior to that date was governed in a large measure by the personal qualities of the commissar and the Chief of the Political Department, respectively—this, at least, is the opinion of I. Petukhov. At the time it was not clear who was to select and to appoint subordinate commissars of a division—the military commissar of that division or the Political Department. The resolution of the Eighth Congress of the Party settled that question by empowering the political departments "under the immediate guidance of the Central Committee of the Communist party" to select the personnel for commissar posts "weeding out from their midst the vacillating or careerist elements and all who were admitted by accident."[186]

An important work of organization and revision of the party political machinery was accomplished by the Congress of the Political Workers of the Red Army called by the Political Administration of the Republic (PUR), which in May had replaced the Political Department of the Revolutionary Military Council of the Republic.

By this time the political departments of divisions had become the principal carriers of political work at the front. Similar departments of the armies and the fronts retained only directing functions.[187]

The new instruction to party cells prepared by the Congress was later in December of the same year approved by the Central Committee of the Party. According to Petukhov, this instruction was the first document, approved by the central party authorities, defining the place of the political departments in the whole system of the party— political organizations of the Red Army. The first part of this instruction squarely subordinated all party activity in the divisions of the Red Army to the divisional political departments : "the general guidance of the activity of all cells of the Russian Communist party and the co-ordination of the political enlightenment work in the units of a division is entrusted to the divisional political departments."[188]

In this manner another victory was gained for the centralistic control by appointees from above of an additional sphere of activity in the Red Army.

The Political Department of the Republic (PUR) prepared the statutes governing the political departments of fronts, armies, divisions, and military districts. These were published by the Revolutionary Military Council of the Republic in an order appearing in January 1920. They defined the aims, the functions and the powers of each category of the political departments. As already mentioned, the divisional political department became and remained the cornerstone of this political ziggurat of the Red Army : "the political department of a division" it was ordained, "is to be regarded as the immediate creator of political, party and cultural life in the units of the division."[189]

In this way, from a small beginning, originating in the necessity of control of an ideologically alien commanding personnel, the institution of political commissars developed into a complicated party-political body which became the "direct and immediate" representative of the party, the standard-bearer of its slogans and directions in the Red Army.

While this highly centralized and powerful organization filled with personnel appointed by the central authorities was taking shape, the commissars, at least in a number of units, were losing interest in the political work. At the same time, a definite trend appeared among some of the Communists in the Red Army favoring the transfer of the direction of all "political enlightenment" work in the units of the army to party collectives. This movement was given a great deal of impetus by the tendency of many commissars to forsake political work for operation and administration activities. This lack of interest on their part in the political phase of their duties had created a vacuum and offered an invitation to the more energetic of the secretaries and presidents of the party collectives to take upon themselves the tilling of this field that had remained fallow.

An order of the Revolutionary Military Council of the Twelfth Army issued in July 1920 offers a striking commentary on this situation: The Political Department of the Twelfth Army, Order No. 120, drew the attention of the military commissar personnel of the army to the necessity of developing an intensive political activity. Notwithstanding this, information coming from the front indicated that many of the military commissars had failed to understand the all-importance of the problem and were absorbed by operations work exclusively. In some of the divisions the fitness of the military commissars was evaluated only from the viewpoint of their combat qualities. . . . It was ordered: In promoting military commissars to the more responsible posts, appointments should be made not only because of courage, but, mainly, on account of organizational ability and skill in promoting party work. All military commissars failing to measure up to these requirements should be systematically replaced.[190]

This order was a King Canute command. The flood continued to run irresistibly in the direction of appropriation of operations and administrative functions by the commissars.

The tendency discussed was one of the important factors leading to the general decline of political and party work in the Red Army, and to a measure of disorganization of the political and party machinery within it.[191]

The dissatisfaction of a portion of the Communists in the army with this stagnation of the political life furnished material for the appearance of the so-called "army opposition of 1921." During the wide discussions that preceded the Tenth Party Congress, two separate streams of oppositional ideas took shape. One stood for a radical change involving the complete abandonment of the system of political machinery in the political departments and for handing over the direction of the party work in the army to the local party committees. The second was willing to preserve the apparatus of political control in existence, but only on condition of the electivity of the directing personnel.[192]

The Tenth Party Congress resolved that: "the agitation of certain groups and of individual comrades for the change in the system of the present organization of the Red Army by introducing electivity, the subordination of commissars to the respective cells, etc., is entirely inadmissible."[193]

Thus the edifice of centralized autonomous political control of the Red Army survived the Civil War and succeeded in keeping its scarlet robes undefiled by civilian contamination.

In examining the short history of the commissars of the Red Army, one cannot fail to be struck by the remarkable feature of the evolution of that institution. The undoubtedly ardent and earnest political enthusiasm of the commissars of the early days gradually (at least among a large section of them) ran into channels entirely unforeseen by its originators. The ancient rhythm of army life was seemingly in conflict with the rôle of an observer and political auditor. The energetic young Communists cast for this rôle were men of action. The combat, the planning of strategic maneuver, the administrative details of a detachment, held a strong allure for them during the war. The "political enlightenment" and even political work among the greenhorn Communists in the ranks, who were fumbling with the basic tenets of Marxism, was a tame pastime in comparison with the "glory" of the battlefield, and the exercise of authority in the everyday life of the camp.

In other words, a curious conflict suggests itself here: that between the new-fangled institution breaking up the sacrosanct principle of unity of military leadership and the general *gestalt* of army life. While the Red Army was still an inchoate body composed of elements mechanically thrown together, the institution of commissars had its place and useful function. As soon as these elements grew into the chemical structure of the army, the crystal of the commissar institution did not fit into its new shape. It is as if the institution of commissars had only a very limited span of life and that its cycle had run its course by the end of the Civil War. As soon as the Red Army had become a regularly organized armed force, commanded by men welded into it by the fire of battle, the commissar had no place in it.

To understand how the political and party life continued to pulsate and to circulate within the body of the Red Army, without a great deal of impetus on the part of a large number of commissars, one has to turn to an examination of the development of the party collectives in the armed forces of the Soviets.

Rank and File Communist Organizations

In comparing the Red forces with those of the Whites, Trotsky said in December 1919: "Here, the workers are directing, and among them—the most conscious revolutionaries—the Communists. There, the officers, the college students—the most conscious representatives of the bourgeois interests—are directing." In the earlier part of the same speech, Trotsky spoke of the institution of the commissars as "securing" this directing rôle of the workers' class in the army.[194]

At that time, the workers' element, according to Trotsky, was rather less than more than 15 to 18 per cent of the total numbers of the Red Army. In estimating the number of Communists in its ranks, Trotsky said at the Seventh Congress of the Soviets, that there were more than one hundred thousand of them in the Red Army. He quoted the testimony of the commanding personnel, at that time still predominantly non-communist, in support of his statement that without that communist leaven, without the self-denial, without the exemplary valor of the representatives of the workers' class the "army would have fallen to dust." Trotsky also mentioned that whenever the military situation on a sector of the front or of an army became critical, the commanding officers sent requests to the Revolutionary Military Council to detail to the threatened part of the battle-line an adequate number of Communists to bolster up the morale of the troops.[195]

The official Soviet history of the Civil War places the total number of Communists in the army by October 1, 1919, at 180,000. It is estimated that during the Civil War more than 50,000 Communists perished at the front. By the end of the war, the total number of Communists in the army, both at the front and in the rear, reached 280,000 persons, grouped in seven thousand cells.[196]

Trotsky concluded, in comparing the communist element in the army with the Samurai class of Japan: "I must say that in the person of our commissars, the foremost front-fighter Communists, we have obtained a new communist order of Samurai, which—without any caste privileges—knows how to die and teaches others to die for the cause of the workers' class."[197]

D. A. Petrovskii's opinion that the study of the communist cells was the key to an understanding of the successful organization of the Red Army and its victories in the field, has already been referred to.[198] This view, if correct, implies that the activity of the local communist organizations in the various army units was more important in achieving victory in the Civil War than the centralizing effort of the Moscow headquarters.

The Soviet military historian, F. Nikonov, suggests that during the Civil War the units of the Red Army were classified with respect to their combat efficiency in accordance with the percentage of Communists within their ranks. He estimates that those with less than 4 to 5 per cent of Communists among their personnel were regarded as ineffective. Detachments with 6 to 8 per cent were looked upon as satisfactory, with an average combat efficacy. Units with 12 to 15 per cent of Communists were considered shock troops.

As Nikonov states, the Soviet Government, instead of forming special élite troops, established the principle of pouring shock complements of the communist and proletarian element into units chosen to bear the brunt of the most important military operations.[199]

In the early days of the Red Army the situation was different. The majority of detachments had no organized party collectives. This was true even of those units where there were individual party members in the ranks. Many of the bolshevik cells formed in the old army units ceased to exist after its demobilization without having become nuclei of reorganized Red forces.[200]

I. Petukhov describes the initial formation of communist cells in the Red Army units as a spontaneous process, undertaken upon local initiative. Individual members of the party in the armed forces of the Republic, feeling acutely the need of unification, without any direction from above, began to prepare rosters of Communists in their respective units and to call meetings of Communists in their detachments. These meetings proceeded to adopt resolutions to organize cells or, as they were sometimes also called, party fractions in the army.[201]

Among the levies formed in the more advanced industrial regions, such as Petrograd, Ivanovo-Voznesensk and Moscow, local party organizations had laid the foundations of party collectives in the detachments of the troops raised in their localities before these were sent to the front.[202]

The Petrograd Conference of Bolshevik Red Army Soldiers resolved, in April 1918 that the problem of the day was "the immediate formation of party collectives in all units and detachments of the Red Army and the furthering of energetic activity of these collectives." The Regional Party Conference of the Northern Region decided in July of the same year "to organize immediately, in all units and sub-divisions of the Red Army, party cells of Communists."[203]

The resolution of the Petrograd Conference of Bolshevik Red Army Soldiers defined the aims of the military party collectives in the following terms: "a) To organize meetings, lectures and gatherings; b) To exercise control over the recruiting of the detachment and its purging of all undesirable elements; and c) To direct the political, cultural and economic life of the detachment. For this, the cell should establish close contact with the Soviet political commissar, should also suggest and obtain the election of candidates for all elective positions, and, as well, direct and control the activity of the elected officials.[204]

All this tends to support the view of I. Petukhov as to the spontaneity of the development of the party machinery within the army. On the other hand, there is evidence extant that the military organization of the party, attached to the Central Committee of the Bolshevik Party, had adopted as early as December 1917 the decision to organize party cells in all military units, so that these cells would become the backbone of the new revolutionary discipline in the armed forces of the Republic.[205] It may be well to note here that this decision antedates the decree relating to the foundation of the Red Army, and may therefore be considered as referring only to the Red Guard and the old army.

By the end of 1918, largely because of local initiative, party cells in a number of units grew so powerful that they took upon themselves the direction of the administration and even aspired to elect the commissars. They also exercised a direct control over the commanding personnel, interfering even in the purely operational work of the latter. By adopting the general party practice, these cells began to build a hierarchical party organization within the army by electing divisional and army collectives or bureaus. These organs of party government were sanctioned at party conferences in the majority of divisions and armies in the fall of 1918 and in the winter of 1918-1919. Their immediate functions consisted of the guidance of party work in the narrow sense of the word. In a number of instances they also undertook to guide the "cultural enlightenment" work. In divisions where there were no political departments in existence, their functions were assumed by the party collectives.[206]

At the H.Q. of the Eastern Front a party fraction was formed. In the end of 1918, and in the beginning of 1919, it sat for hours discussing questions of appointment and transfer of commanders and other responsible officials, as well as the organization and structure of the H.Q. apparatus.[207]

In addition to cells consisting of regular party members, cells of "sympathizers" were also formed in Red Army units. By the end of 1919, their total number had reached 1,500. The recruitment of members of these cells in a number of regiments was conducted by the commissar by the simple method of asking those so inclined to join the cells, without the formality of an application on the part of the candidates. In many units, decisions as to the establishment of the sympathizers' cells were carried at general meetings of the personnel. In other words, non-party members took part in deciding matters concerning party machinery alongside the regular party members.[208]

During the entire year of 1918, there were no general regulations or instructions issued by the central authorities relating to the functions of party cells in army units on active service.[209]

This chaotic state of affairs extended also to the scope of activity of the cells. A considerable number of them concentrated their attention on administrative and operational work, others on cultural and political activities among the soldiers. In this way, until 1919, the overwhelming part of the cells were the sole judges as to the limits of their duties and authority. Petukhov claims that some of the cells, led by a strong nucleus of qualified party members, were, in fact, completely in command of their respective units, and decided both for the commander and the commissar not only administrative, but also operation matters.[210]

In contrast to this energetic control exercised by some of the cells, there were army units where, until September 1919, party members were not brought together into collectives at all.[211]

A. Geronimus draws a parallel between this growth of decentralized political action by the local party collectives in the Red Army and the guerilla tendencies. He says: "The interference of the cells in the directing functions of commanders and commissars side by side with a wide infra-party democracy . . . became more and more a contradiction to the general aims of party direction of the army. Guerilla tendencies, which the party was burning out in the army with red-hot iron, had a rebirth within the party organization in the singular form of army syndicalism.[212]

In other words, there was not merely a struggle for authority between the commissars (and, in a measure, commanders) and the party collectives for the direction of the life, administration and even operation of the army units, but also there was a conflict between the general centralizing tendency advocated by Moscow and the decentralization activities of the groups of Communists in the various army units.

To follow the Marxian concept of change, one might say that the dialectical process, after having exhausted its possibilities in the struggle for control of the army between the local Soviets and the Soviet of the People's Commissars, began, in a way, to function on a different level—within the ranks of the Communist party itself, where the chiefs were imposing centralization on the army, while the rank and file organizations had virtually become a law unto themselves in some parts of the armed forces. This process of struggle for power by the local army cells may also be viewed as the rebirth in another form of the army committees of 1917, this time within the framework of the party which had destroyed them.

The Instruction on Party Cells, published in January 1919 by the Central Committee of the Communist Party, imposed a definite veto on these decentralizing tendencies. It prohibited the creation of any kind of elective army committees or bureaus of the party in the army. Those in existence were either absorbed by the already established political departments or were reorganized into political departments themselves.[213]

It may be worth noting that in this manner the politically active personnel of the elective army party committees was transferred into the offices of the centrally controlled organizations. One may surmise that these men did not entirely abandon their views or become entirely reconciled to their translation from the position of political leaders in their respective party groups to that of officials of a bureaucratic machine.

The principal aim of the party cell, as defined by the above-mentioned Instruction, consisted in the creation "in the unit, of a sturdy nucleus of Communists and sympathizers imbued with the consciousness of the significance of victories at the front for the socialist fatherland, able, at the necessary moment, to give an example of readiness to sacrifice one's own life for the sake of victory, to carry along with them the less conscious comrades—Red Army soldiers— and to oppose themselves everywhere to the spreading of alarmist rumors and panic."[214]

The attempts of the cells to interfere with the operation and administration fields of activity were definitely prohibited: "Party cells do not interfere in activities and dispositions of the commanding personnel. . . . They must assist the commander with all their energy in the struggle against infringements of Red Army discipline and themselves show an example by its observance."[215]

The resolutions of the Eighth Party Congress included a paragraph to the effect that the work of the commissars could be fruitful only if it were founded on the immediate support of cells of soldier-Communists. However, this resolution endowed the commissar and "all generally-speaking mature party workers" in the army with authority to see to it that "unstable elements in pursuit of imaginary rights and privileges" be kept out of the cells.[216]

Another part of this same resolution stated that "respect for the communist cells will be higher and more steadfast the more clearly each soldier understands, and becomes convinced by experience, that membership in the communist cell does not give the soldier any special rights, but only imposes upon him the duty to be a most self-denying and valiant fighter."[217]

That a declaration of such character was made a part of the resolution seems to indicate that there existed in the army a fairly widespread feeling that, apart from the stern duties imposed on the Communists by the very fact of their membership in the party, there were valuable privileges extended to, or appropriated by them; that, in fact, the Communists had definite advantages as to promotion and general betterment of their position, as against the non-party members, will be made clear by the analysis of the situation in the army during the period of the New Economic Policy.

The resolution was approved by the Congress against the opposition of a minority group that advocated the conduct of political work in the army on a combined basis of activities of appointed, as well as elected, functionaries of the party. The Instruction of the Central Committee to the party cells was approved by the Congress "in general and on the whole." This Instruction also legalized in the army an entirely new party organ—the party commissions. Such of these commissions as were attached to political departments of divisions consisted of three persons appointed by the head of the Political Department of the Army. The party commissions attached to the political departments of armies had two of their members appointed by the party members of the Revolutionary Military Council of the front or the army, and one person delegated by the local party committee.[218]

The duties of the party commissions were "to solve problems raised by the regimental cells or by the commissar as to expulsion from the party of its members, and also of dissolution of cells, and confirmation of new party members accepted at regimental party meetings."[219]

Later in the same year the Party Week in the Red Army resulted in increasing the number of the Communists in the ranks by thirty-five to forty thousand new members. Geronimus regards this as "the best index of the influence which the party succeeded in acquiring among the masses of the Red Army soldiers." This measure may also be regarded as an attempt to swamp the decentralizing elements among the Communists in the army by a ground swell of politically illiterate new members likely to be malleable in the hands of the commissars and other appointees of the central authorities.[220]

It would seem that these methods of extinguishing the attempts at self-government within the Red Army party collectives had much more far-reaching effects than its instigators imagined in 1919. The manipulation of party affairs by appointees of the center, and the swamping of the oppositionist elements (consisting often of the older party members) by mass recruiting into the party of politically immature elements, was later used on a wider theater of action by those in charge of the central machinery of the party government. Perhaps some historian of the Russian Communist party may trace to these measures of 1919 the gradual extinction of infra-party democracy by the ever-growing power of the centralistic bureaucracy at the head of it.

The above-mentioned Instruction to the party cells stated: "the regimental cell has, in the person of the commissar, a director empowered by the highest party institution to guide the party activity at the front. In case of dissention between the commissar and the party cell, the latter has the right to appeal to the higher party organ . . . upon the party cell devolves the duty to support by every means and strengthen confidence in the commissar as the political director."[221]

At the same time the commissar was made personally responsible for the expediency of the decisions of the cell "having any relation whatsoever to life at the front."[222]

In some parts of the Red Army, attempts at party self-government were short-lived. Thus in the First Army of the Eastern Front there were elected bureaus representing collectives of all units of every division of that army. These bureaus were headed by the party committee of the army. However, the latter held only four meetings and then disbanded, handing over its functions to the newly-organized army political department.[223]

In other armies, these divisional bureaus or committees continued to exist longer, and were not abolished even on the appearance of the political departments. I. Petukhov quotes a report of the delegates of the 29th Division at the communist conference of the Third Army to the effect that in October 1919, there was called a divisional party conference which discussed a number of questions and elected a committee. "We believe," ran the report, "that in the future joint work of the divisional committee and of the political department is necessary."[224]

The December 1918 Order about the political departments and the January 1919 Instruction to Party Cells did not settle the problem of organization of political life within the divisions. I. Petukhov considers that the weakness shown by the political departments of fronts and armies in guiding the political work of the lower units, and the lack of instructions definitely prescribing the method of organization of political machinery in the divisions, led to the appearance of tendencies calling for the concentration of direction of party work not in the hands of the Revolutionary Military Councils or Bureaus of Military Commissars, but in those of elected collegia. This trend was particularly pronounced at the Eastern and the Northern Fronts.[225]

According to Petukhov, elected divisional bureaus continued to exist until the end of 1919 in many army divisions. However, in 1919 they could be founded only by the decision of the political departments of the armies.[226]

The new Instruction to Party Cells prepared by the Congress of the Political Workers of the Army in December 1919, and approved later in the same month by the Central Committee of the party, definitely placed in the hands of the divisional political departments the direction of the activities of all cells and the regulation of "political enlightenment" work in the units of a division.[227]

It seems justifiable to believe, on the ground of the evidence examined, that the active life of the cells was furthered by the most zealous of the revolutionary party element, and that those Communists who were not interested enough to establish party collectives in their units were very probably either less energetic or less convinced supporters of communism.

On the whole, the new Instruction had set the framework of the relationship between the appointed political workers and the party cells and collectives in the army for a long period. The relationship of these party organizations with the commanding personnel was already clearly established by the January 1919 Instruction, which underscored the fact that party cells should not interfere with the activities of that personnel.[228]

It would seem that this triumph of centralized party bureaucracy in the Red Army had a painful effect on the political life within the army. Petukhov refers to "a marked decline of political and party work in the units and the disorganization of political and party machinery" in the end of 1920 and the beginning of 1921. Of this period a pertinent illustration may be found in the thesis of the political administration of the Caucasian Front: "the infra-party crisis finds its most striking expression in . . . the unusual universal decline of party life, in the conflicts between the commissars and cells, which, by their frequency, have assumed the character of an epidemic."[229]

These internal dissensions, apparently, did not have any unfavorable effect on the military efficacy of the Communists in the Red Army.

That the Communists in the army during the later part of the Civil War were in the foremost rank of the firing line there is a great deal of evidence. G. Pukhov cites instances during the Iudenich advance on Petrograd, when the front lines were held by Communists only. He quotes one of the commanders of divisions defending that city: "comrade-Communists go to their death in the same way as they went to the factory to fulfil an important and a difficult task—without any excitement or heroics."[230]

The Instruction to Communists at the Front published by the Political Department of the Seventh Army emphasized this element of self-denial. One of the principal points of this Instruction may be summed up as follows: The Communist is the foremost fighter of the Red Army. The place of the Communist is in the firing line. The Communist must serve as an example of a patient and steady bearing under all the privations and difficulties of combat life.[231]

In 1920, during the Soviet-Polish War, Trotsky, in one of his proclamations, called the Communists "the soul of the Workers' and Peasants' Army." This may smack of idealism, but it aptly expressed the thought of the leaders of the Red Army at that time.[232]

The testimony both of the White as well as the Red participants in the Civil War agrees in conceding a high degree of valor at the front to the Communists. They were beyond doubt the backbone of the Red Army, the energizing element, the collective "father of victory."

They were injected, like red corpuscles into a blood stream, into the Soviet forces whenever the situation became dangerous. A very interesting summary of mobilization of Communists during the

Soviet-Polish War is contained in the stenographic report of a speech made by Krestinsky at the Tenth Party Congress. During a six months period party mobilizations for war work sent about 25,000 Communists into the front lines.[233]

That important party members were not spared the ordeal of battle is quite clear. Besides the several special mobilizations of responsible party workers mentioned above, there is a great deal of evidence to that effect.

To conclude the examination of the rôle of the Communists in the Red Army, it is fitting to give attention to the order issued by Trotsky in May 1920 to the Commissar and commanding personnel of the Western Front. By that time the Red Army organization had already assumed a definite shape, and its life was regulated by the pattern acquired during the years of the Civil War, as well as molded by the unceasing effort of the central authorities to make it conform to a prescribed standard. The rôle of the Communists in the army is viewed, in the text of that order, as one of paramount importance.

The following quotations from Trotsky's order shed a clear light on the conception the People's Commissar for War had of that rôle:

". . . It is necessary that in each platoon, section and squad there should be a Communist, even if a young one—but devoted to the cause. He should observe the morale of the nearest fellow-fighters, explain to them the problems and the aims of the war, and, in case he is himself perplexed, approach the commissar of his unit or some other responsible political worker for elucidation. Without such internal, unofficial, personal, day-by-day and hour-by-hour agitation under all conditions of the combat situation, the official agitation through articles and speeches will not give the required results.

". . . *The conduct of Communists* in the Red Army has a decisive significance for the morale and the battle efficacy of units. It is necessary, therefore, to distribute Communists in an organized way, to guide them attentively and to keep careful check of their work. . . . Revolutionary military councils and political departments of the armies, commissars and political departments of divisions, commissars of brigades and regiments should carefully check up on the behavior of all Communists subordinated to them with respect to combat functions after each new battle ordeal, ruthlessly casting out those lacking in decisiveness and meting out stern punishment to cowardly egotists.[234]

A spy, an agitator, a brave soldier, an obedient tool in the hands of the politico-military functionaries—such is the portrait of the Communist in the Red Army drawn by the principal organizer of the Red Army of the Civil War epoch.

That all these activities were necessary will be seen from the following summary examination of the most numerous part of the Red Army—the private soldiers.

Soldiers

One of the yardsticks to measure the enthusiasm of the soldiers for the cause in which they are fighting is the number of desertions from the army during the course of the war. This is not by any means a perfect yardstick, as a good many other reasons, apart from the disposition of the soldier to risk his life at the behest of the state, enter into the determination of a rise or a decline in the number of desertions in wartime. It is, however, an important index of the morale of the army.

The official Soviet history of the Civil War states that the principal reasons for the avoidance of military service and the desertions from the Red Army lay in the lack of understanding of the character of the war by the so-called "middle" peasant, the great mass of the rural population economically situated between the rich kulaks and the pauper elements.[235]

Several additional, less important causes are also enumerated by F. Nikonov in that history. They were: 1) insufficient development of political work in the village; 2) general want of order in the rear of the armies and the ineffectiveness of the local military machinery; 3) confusion in the minds of the population provoked by the rapid change of governments (particularly in the Ukraine); 4) impunity for avoidance of military service and desertions; 5) unsatisfactory food and cold barracks in the winter; 6) weakness of the state apparatus, particularly in the village; and finally, 7) poor work of the social security organs, resulting in a lack of confidence on the part of the soldiers that their families would be provided for by the state in their absence on military duty.[236]

These causes may be summed up under the following headings: 1) lack of enthusiasm of the peasant masses for the Civil War; 2) weakness of the state and the low level of its organization; 3) economic exhaustion resulting from the World War, the Revolution and the Civil War. Another reason may be adduced: experience in desertion from the old army and the almost complete impunity for mass desertions from the army in 1917 under the Provisional Government.

F. Nikonov estimates that by February 1917, there were about one and a half million deserters from the ranks of the old army.[237] On page 10 above, mention was made of the desertions from the army in 1917, which had assumed truly homeric proportions.

The prestige of the state power had fallen low by the beginning of 1918. The peasant had learned by experience that the chastising arm of the state did not always succeed in reaching the culprits. Trotsky, in a speech delivered in March 1918, drew a picture of the human personality set free by the revolution and the subsequent growth of extreme individualism and anarchistic tendencies: "Revolution, which had awakened the human personality . . . naturally, at first, gave to this awakening an extreme, if you wish, an anarchistic character. This awakening of the most elemental instincts of the personality had frequently a crudely egotistical, or, speaking in philosophical terms, 'egocentric' character. Only yesterday the man of the masses was nothing—a slave of the Czar, of the nobility, of the bureaucracy, a cog in a factory machine. In peasant life he was merely the object of taxation. Today, freeing himself of all this, he has felt himself for the first time a personality and begun to think that he is all, that he is the center of the cosmos. He strives to take for himself all he can, thinks only of himself and is not inclined to consider the popular class viewpoint. Hence the flood of disorganizational tendencies, of individualism, anarchism, rapaciousness that we are observing, particularly in the wide circles of the *déclassés* elements of the country, in the milieu of the old army and also in certain elements of the working class."[238]

The accent on the *déclassés* elements may be demagogy. However, the mood of the Russian masses of the period is certainly well reflected in these sentences.

Another speech of the People's Commissar for War, delivered in April 1918, emphasizes the lowered prestige of the state power which was prevalent then in Russia. "Because of the natural psychological reaction, the existence of this pre-October lack of confidence in the government and its orders among us has led to attempts by all to pass each order, each regulation, through the apparatus of their own criticism, their own distrust and judgment, which held up the fulfillment of the order, was destructive to work and should not happen because of the interests of the toilers themselves."[239]

The mistrust of the governmental activity, this acutely critical attitude to the government, was unquestionably a real objective fact in the life of the masses of the Russian people during the Civil War period. But was it entirely a survival of the pre-revolutionary and the 1917 period?

F. Nikonov refers to desertions from military trains reaching 25 to 30 per cent of the total numbers, and in some exceptional instances soaring up to even 50 to 70 per cent. He states that as a rule reinforcements reached the front at about two-thirds of the strength they had at the time of departure.[240]

On the basis of official statistics, F. Nikonov has prepared a very interesting table giving the number of *apprehended* deserters, during the different periods of the Civil War. The grand total of such deserters for the period from January 1, 1919, to January 1, 1920, amounted to 2,846,000 in round numbers. During the year 1919, 1,753,000 deserters were brought back into the fold.[241]

At the same time, the total numbers of the Red Army by February, 1919, was about one million men. It rose by January 1, 1920, to about three million men.[242]

To understand the picture of the Red Army for that period, it is useful to remember the statement of the Commander in Chief of the armed forces of the Republic, Kamenev, that for each fighter at the front there were ten men on the army ration in the rear.[243]

In this way the fighting units of the Red Army at the fronts of the Civil War in 1919 were actually a "thin red line" encompassing masses of parasites on the army rations—and these included a large number of "political workers"—and hundreds of thousands, nay millions, of apprehended deserters.

Analyses of the figures of some of the armies at the front result in a very enlightening illustration of a situation where even the front line units were losing more of their personnel by desertion than by death in action. Thus the 35th Rifle Division, in the month of September 1919, lost only 26 men killed in action, while the number of those listed as "disappeared without report," in the official verbiage of the day, totalled 1,115 men. For the Fifth Army for the same month the losses are given as 518 killed and 2,627 "disappeared without report." Undoubtedly a large part of the latter were deserters.[244]

In the Petrograd Military District, 119,390 deserters were forcibly apprehended during 1919. This figure is particularly striking in juxtaposition to the total number of troops of the district by May 1, 1919, given as 116,410, and by September 1 of the same year, 193,-445. (These figures were the highest and the lowest for the monthly figures of the year.) During the six-months period from October 1, 1919, to April 1, 1920, 116,317 deserters were brought back into the army. Of these 75,127 were forcibly apprehended and 41,180 had returned voluntarily to the Army, under pressure of the various sanctions and of propaganda against desertion.[245]

Figures for the French army during the First World War offer a thought-provoking comparison. According to a report presented by L. Marin, from August 1914 to the end of December of the same year the number of deserters from the entire French army amounted to 509. In 1915, the figure for the entire year stood at 2,433. In 1916, it rose to 8,924. In 1917, there was a sharp increase to 21,714 (which is ascribed by the French military sociologist, Charles Coste, to the influence of defeatist propaganda). In 1918, the total number of deserters fell to 13,302.[246]

Charles Coste gives figures for avoidance of military service for the later years of the French Revolution, when there was a strong disinclination of the masses of the French people to heed the call to arms. Thus, of the 200,000 men ordered to join the army in September 1798, only 24,000 presented themselves.[247]

The fantastic numbers of deserters from the Red Army were beyond doubt a symptom of a deep and acute conflict between the will of the Communist-controlled state and the masses of the Russian peasantry, in the same way that the large number of desertions from the old army was an outward sign of the aversion of the peasant to giving his life for aims which he did not understand in a war in which Russia sacrificed the lives of millions for the cause of the Allied victory.

G. Pukhov ascribes the numerous desertions in the Petrograd military district to socio-political factors, to the political tendencies predominating within the villages of the district. He places next in importance the poorly-organized life of the army, coupled with material privations. Among the factors that in his opinion made for the high percentage of deserters, he mentions also the inadequate political work in the units, particularly those at the front, and the low percentage of Communists in the ranks. Pukhov includes among these factors the "fairly active" anti-soviet agitation by the various White and socialist (anti-bolshevik) organizations.[248]

The People's Commissar for War, speaking in March 1920, described the soldiers of the Red Army. He stated that in each unit there were soldiers of three descriptions. A small group of "spoiled" soldiers, "debauched" by the "bourgeois-noble régime" who had lost moral ties with the toiling classes. Trotsky characterized that group as egotists whose interests were limited to themselves and to whom the future of the workers' class was of no concern. This set was opposed by Trotsky to another, also a minority, of "conscious, revolutionary soldiers," who had struggled against the czarist régime before the revolution and who were "entirely consciously prepared to give their lives for the cause of the toiling people." Between these two extremes were the average soldiers, "in character honest, rural and urban workers still not sufficiently conscious, still without understanding of the significance of the revolution and of the problems of the Soviet Government." According to Trotsky, this great mass of "average soldiers" at times came under the influence of the group of "egotists," at other times under that of the revolutionary soldiers. As a result the morale of a unit was apt to change rapidly. A growth in the influence of the revolutionary element transformed a regiment reputedly of a low combat efficacy into one of good fighters, within a fortnight.[249]

This analysis by Trotsky is obviously devised for didactic purposes. The Manichaean picture of the struggle for the soul of the "average soldier" drawn by the People's Commissar for War oversimplifies the real situation as it existed in the Red Army during the Civil War. The problem of the morale of the troops of the Red Republic was undoubtedly more complicated than that.

The source of recruitment had a great deal to do with the regiment's zeal for the cause of the Soviets. In discussing the Makhno guerillas, Trotsky admitted, in 1920, that in the Ukraine, for instance, the kulaks had succeeded in capturing the leadership in the village and opposed it to the town. "It seemed," said Trotsky, "as if all the mass of the peasantry was unanimous in its enmity to the proletariat and the Communist party. On this base all the Ukrainian petty-bourgeois kulak parties were formed." He pointed out that both Petlura and Makhno had endeavored to find support in the *united* village, juxtaposing it to the proletariat, and that the unification of the village was achieved by the kulaks.[250]

Under these circumstances Soviet troops drawn from Ukrainian villages were not likely to show themselves stanch supporters of the proletarian cause.

At times the Soviets took special steps to ensure the loyalty of certain bodies of troops through provisions regulating the method of their recruitment. In August 1920, Trotsky had instructed the military districts to begin to form "immediately and with exceptional energy" cavalry units (squadrons, platoons and mounted machine-gun platoons), prescribing that these formations be recruited predominantly from Communists, sympathizers and volunteers "entirely devoted to the Soviet Government."[251]

Class origin of soldiers had a great deal to do with the combat efficacy of troops. An article in *Military Messenger* (*Voennyi Vestnik*) in 1928 analyzed the percentages of workers in the units of the Red Army in 1920. In the divisions that had distinguished themselves in action, the percentage of workers ranged from 26.4 (8th Red Cavalry Division) to 19.6 (28th Rifle Division). In Budenny's famous First Cavalry Army the percentage of workers was 21.7. On the other hand, in the 9th Rifle Division, regarded as one of low combat value, the workers were only 10.5 per cent of the total number. In penal detachments, workers were 9.7 per cent of the total, in the detachments from apprehended deserters, 3.8 per cent. For the Red Army as a whole the percentage of workers at the time was 14.9; in the field units at the front it amounted to 16.5, while in the rear it fell to 11-13.[252]

Some of the measures taken by the Soviet authorities for the improvement of the morale were on the propaganda level. Trotsky wrote in May 1919: "It is necessary to create such a situation, such a frame of mind in the country, that a deserter could find no place to lay his head, like Cain, who betrayed his brother."[253]

Other measures were aimed directly at the soldiers themselves. As early as August 1918, capital punishment upon verdicts of military courts was used against desertion and abandonment of posts. Trotsky's order of August 30, 1918, mentions the shooting by verdict of a court-martial of "cowardly liars" who simulated illness; also of several deserters who refused to atone for their crime by re-entering the ranks of the army.[254]

Whenever soldiers attempted to oppose their will in an organized manner to the dictates of the Soviet Government, drastic and swift punishment was administered. In an order dated January 27, 1919, the People's Commissar for War spoke of the regiments of the Volsk Division who had refused obedience: "Of them not a trace is left ... the Soviet Republic admits of no mercy for traitors and scoundrels." He threatened the Nikolaevsk Division which had rebelled and deposed its commissars and commanders that within twelve hours all those who remained in the ranks of the rebels would have as their fate "ruin and death."[255]

The old companion of the armies on the march—the dread drumhead court-martial, dispensing capital punishment to recalcitrants—was thus incorporated into the *mores* of the Red Army. The Bolsheviki resisted its reintroduction into the old army by the Provisional Government in 1917. Now, they found it a useful means of improving the morale of the Red Army.

The interests of the workers and the "middle" peasants were not by any means identical during the Civil War. At times these interests were in definite conflict. Under these circumstances, different slogans had to be used to prevail on members of these classes to lend their support to the Civil War, and to influence those of them in the Red Army. In July 1918, Trotsky, in addressing a large and representative gathering in Moscow, presented the Civil War as a campaign for bread for the children, the old, the workers, and the Red Army. He exclaimed: "Long live the campaign of workers and peasants for bread and for union with the poor peasant." The resolution of that meeting stated: "the mobilization of hungry workers and their training and arming, their brotherly alliance with the village poor, their joint campaign against the kulak and speculators—these are the only means of collecting supplies of bread at prices accessible to the people, and of making the toiling people secure until the next harvest."[256]

This was a thinly veiled appeal to the city proletariat to loot the rich rural districts. "If you want your family to eat, help the Red Army to empty the bins of the village," was the catchword for the workers in the ranks of the Red Army and outside of it.

Such propaganda, of course, could have no useful effect on the "middle" peasant, who later became the "average" soldier of the Red Army. In a letter addressed to these "middle" peasants on February 6, 1919, and published in the Moscow *Izvestia*, Trotsky assured the peasants that the Soviet Government did not intend to force the "middle" peasants to change to the communistic form of economy. He told them that in the field of taxation policy, the Soviet Government saw its problem as placing the main burden of taxation upon the shoulders of the kulaks, thus lightening that burden for the "middle" peasant. He admitted that at times the "little conscious" among the Red soldiers had molested the local population including the "toiling peasants," but pleaded that, with better organization and greater successes of the Red Army in the field, its attitude to the "toiling population" was becoming "better, more solicitous, friendlier."[257]

Kulaks were not permitted to enter the Red Army or to send their sons there. No doubt there were many exceptions to this rule, as numerous army officers were of kulak origin, and so were the even more numerous N.C.O.'s who came to occupy command positions in the Red Army.

In March 1919 Trotsky wrote: "The kulaks should not be given military training. Watch in the strictest possible way that in addition to workers only honest toiling peasants are mobilized . . . for the kulaks, together with the sons of the bourgeoisie—the Rear Militia. Let them do the common, the hardest work in the interest of the army and the defense of the Soviet land."[258]

Thus a new class of helots came into being in the rear of the Red Army. Men who were too low in the new social scale or too unreliable to be given arms to defend the Soviets in the ranks of the Red Army (commanded largely by their class comrades), were forced to become hewers of wood and drawers of water to the new proletarian aristocracy.

The Statute of the Rear Militia, published by decree of the Soviet of the People's Commissars on July 20, 1918, ordained that all citizens not subject to mobilization into the Red Army were subject to simultaneous call with their respective age groups to serve for one year in the Rear Militia. They were to be organized into labor battalions to do such work as trench-digging, road-building, loading of railroad cars, etc. In this group were included persons from 18 to 45 years of age belonging to widely different classes of Russian society. Those living on incomes derived from sources other than personal work, those employing labor of others for profit, members of the boards of industrial trading and agricultural enterprises, were herded together with barristers, solicitors, notaries, newspapermen formerly on the payroll of the bourgeois press, monks and clergy of all denominations, members of the so-called "free professions" ("if they did not perform socially useful functions"), former officers, civil servants and persons without definite occupations.[259]

In this manner practically the entire educated class of Russia, including painters, writers, sculptors, architects, was rejected as unfit to serve in the Red Army and thrust into the outer darkness of the Rear Militia. The inclusion of newspapermen, writers, painters and other intellectuals, who could not possibly be classified as capitalists according to the Marxist terminology, with the bourgeoisie and the former bureaucracy, was somewhat surprising. What was the object of this amalgam? Were the Soviet military leaders afraid to have educated men in the ranks of the Red Army and did they prefer to fill those with the illiterate peasantry lorded over by the commissars and shepherded by the Communists and industrial workers? Or was this the punishment of the Russian educated class for their boycott of the Bolsheviki in the early days of the Soviet régime?

This deliberate elimination of a large proportion of the educated population of the country from service in the Red Army had undoubtedly the effect of making it difficult to staff services of the army requiring educated minds. In this instance, as in many others, the needs of the army were sacrificed to the political security of the party. The conflict between the party interest and the state interest is evident here, as it was in the work of destruction of the old army carried out in 1917.

In practice, the decree was not applied literally, and numerous members of the helotic classes either made their way into the armed forces of the Republic, under one guise or another, or escaped the effects of the decree by making themselves "indispensable" in the countless Soviet institutions.

Among "the lower ranks" of the Peasants' and Workers' Army, the kulaks (with the exception of such temporary allies as Makhno guerillas, Grigoriev's "army," etc.) were not present in any considerable numbers. Members of the new ruling class, the workers and their temporary allies, the "middle" peasants, formed the bulk of the rank and file of the army together with the poor peasants. In that respect, if not in that of its commanding personnel, the army justified its name.

Charles Coste, in his study of the social psychology of war, suggested that, during war, more than under any other circumstances, the feelings of the average man are plunged into the depths of his social environment. As he says: "in these historic moments, 'epochs eminently social,' man is subject more than ever to the impact of collective forces and lives in full accord with the needs of his social environment."[260]

Coste felt that the problem of the morale of troops during war should be considered from the viewpoint of moral ties attaching the fighting men to their national group, as well as from that of the strict military discipline, which keeps them within the fold of the social organization especially strengthened for the purposes of armed struggle.[261]

Coste considered that the "military spirit" was created and maintained by the spontaneous tendency attaching the citizen to his nation, and also by the constraining power of the state.[262]

The French Combat Instructions for Small Units issued in 1919 maintains that: "the military virtues are sustained by the exaltation of two sentiments: those of honor and patriotism." Another set of French army regulations, published in 1920, also placed love of the fatherland at the summit of the moral life of the troops.[263]

In a civil war, of the type fought in Russia in 1917-1921, the appeal to patriotism, as such, has no place. In the propaganda of the Soviet Government in the Red Army, a substitute was offered, that of love for the socialist fatherland. General Verkhovskii, of the old army, who offered his sword to the revolution, wrote in his work *On the Aims of the Military Schools*: "The most important driving impulse in the struggle we have lived through was the *yearning of the workers and peasants to maintain their life and their wealth*, as well as the position acquired during the revolution and the land seized, from attack by the old dispossessed classes. This is the basic motive which guided the masses in the struggle. The best, the advanced, the most idealistically inclined men went in the name of the idea of the struggle for socialism, for the new world and liberated labor. The *enthusiasm* of these men was the organizing force around which rallied all the forces of the Republic opposed to the efforts of the counter-revolution. . . . This created the *will to victory* which welded the Red Army, and, despite the terribly heavy privations and defeats, crowned the struggle by a victory of historic importance of the first order."[264]

The above extract was quoted with approval by Trotsky in his work on the Civil War.

The workers did not want to see the return of the capitalist owner of the factory in which they were working, and which, at least at the time, they regarded as belonging to them. The peasants wanted to continue in undisturbed possession of the acres they had seized from the landlords and the Church. There was, therefore, a very definite bond of common material interest which made a large portion of the rank and file of the army ready to fight the White armies, whose victory, they thought, would restore capitalistic economy in industry and landlordism in rural life.

For the duration of the Civil War, this bond of common interest, this fear of the return of the dispossessed *barin*, proved stronger than the disruptive forces of conflict, such as between the "middle peasant" and the worker. This was the "socialist fatherland" which held the army together instead of the feeling of patriotism exalted in the French army regulations. The second important force, that of military discipline, was also present in the Red Army during the Civil War, although it assumed shapes different from the traditional forms prevalent in the European armies of the nineteenth and the beginning of the twentieth centuries.

The introductory remarks in the Disciplinary Code of the Red Army, published in 1919, stated that the Red Army had achieved its final victory, not because of the fear of punishment nor through the allurement of rewards. "The feeling of revolutionary duty and the instinct of the struggling proletariat will give the army that strength which will completely destroy the oppression of capitalism and lead to the triumph of communism."[265]

The same remarks concede, however, that from the very beginning of the Red Armed forces "despite completely comradely equality," necessity had introduced even in these early detachments "the strictest military discipline." In these early days "there were among the Red Army soldiers some that did not understand the necessity of obedience to a single will." With such soldiers they dealt in their own fashion. The punishments inflicted were either too drastic or too lenient, "very often unjust and always diverse for the same kind of offenses."[266]

Discipline is defined by the Code as "order established by the laws of the Republic in the Red Army. It is founded on respect for all laws of the Republic and unstinted devotion to the socialist Soviet régime as well as realization of the necessity of the heaviest sacrifice for the complete liberation of all toilers from the oppression of the capitalist order and for the consolidation of socialism."[267]

"The revolutionary military honor" is defined in the Code as the consciousness of personal dignity in men as fighters, revolutionaries of the Red Army and citizens of a free country conscientiously fulfilling their duty. This dignity cannot be allowed to suffer insults on the part of anybody.[268]

All those in military service, prescribed the Code, were to bear responsibility for infringements of their military duty in accordance with the provisions of the military laws. No one could be punished otherwise than by verdict of a court or in accordance with the prescriptions of the Code.[269]

Rewards were established for distinguished service in the form of the Order of the Red Banner, promotion, and public recognition of such service. "He who knows more, and does more, will be made the commander"—this was the promise of the marshal's baton to the humble private.[270]

Subordinates were commanded to fulfill punctually and "without hesitation" all orders of their commanders in the line of service, with the exception of "orders directed against the Soviet Government."

Upon receiving such an order—"an obviously criminal order"—subordinates were to report it immediately to their commissar or to the nearest Military Commissariat, and to the commander next in order of seniority above the one who had issued it. In combat conditions, it was the duty of the commanders to compel obedience from their subordinates by all means at their disposal, including the use of armed force, the latter with the knowledge of the military commissar. The use of armed force was authorized "if such non-fulfillment of orders might prejudice the successful solution of a combat problem."[271]

The right of arrest was granted to commanders and soldiers on special duty for any infringement of discipline, provided the act was committed in the line of service or within the zone occupied by the unit, and the arrest aimed to stop "the disturbance of order or to prevent the commission of a crime." The commissar had to be immediately notified as to measures taken.[272]

In addition to these powers conferred on the commanders and men on special duty for the purpose of immediately bringing to an end violations of discipline, and for the prevention of crimes, the commanding personnel were invested with authority, "for the maintenance at the proper level of revolutionary military discipline, spirit and honor," to extend to their subordinates rewards for "distinguished conduct while on duty, for zeal and for knowledge of their duties," as well as to impose summary punishment on those lacking in zeal or misbehaving themselves.[273]

The rewards which commanders and commissars were authorized to extend to their subordinates ranged from verbal and written public recognition of their achievements to special leave and other privileges. Summary punishments they were authorized to impose varied from warning and reprimands of all shades and forms to imposition of extra turns of duty, not to exceed ten days, stopping of leave and detention in barracks for not more than two weeks, as well as removal to lower positions (platoon and higher commanders were to be removed only with the concurrence of the commissar). Section *e* of paragraph 44 of the Code also authorized all other measures of repressive action which might arise from conditions and circumstances and would not contradict the spirit and character of the Red Army.[274] Complaints as to the severity of punishment were not permitted.[275]

There are two very striking features about the punishments that the commanding and commissar personnel were given leave to impose on their subordinates: removal to lower position, which would be equiva-

lent to reduction in rank in armies where ranks were definitely established (as in the case of Soviet armed forces today) and the remarkable latitude given by section *e* of paragraph 44.

The Code placed in the hands of the commanders (to a certain
extent under the supervision and control of the commissars) very
large powers of coercion, including the use of arms against recalcitrants in action. The commissars were also given very considerable
penal powers in the field of summary punishment. It would seem,
therefore, that in spite of the statements in the introductory remarks
of the Code, discipline in the Red Army was to be maintained by
measures as harsh as in any army, with powers of summary punishment granted to commanders broader even than in quite a few armies
of the capitalist countries. Whether *in fact* the commanders could
actually always impose such punishments is open to conjecture. What
is known about the activities of the communist cells in some of the
units of the army would seem to indicate that in a substantial part
of the Red armed forces disciplinary control did not rest in the hands
of the commanders in the manner prescribed by the Code. As was
the case in a great deal of Soviet legislation in other fields in the early
years of the Republic, the Code was more in the nature of a blueprint of a building the Soviet authorities expected to erect in the
future.

What is worth noting, however, is that the elements mentioned by
Coste as paramount in the moral life of an army, the feeling for the
fatherland and the fear of punishment, are both very much in evidence in the Code, although the fatherland "pure and simple" was
replaced by the "socialist fatherland," the evolution of the concept
of which will be traced in subsequent chapters. Even *l'honneur* of the
French military statutes had found its place in the Soviet Code, although it assumed a different guise. The step from the declarations
of the decree of December 16, 1918, to the provisions of the Disciplinary Code of 1919 was very great indeed. The Code had a greater
resemblance to the humdrum statutes of capitalist armies (omitting,
of course, the flamboyant revolutionary verbiage) than to that decree.

According to the former "all plenitude of power in each military
unit and their aggregates belongs to the respective soldiers' committees and soviets."[276]

In the Code of 1919, the Comradely Court of the Company was
permitted to extend its competence only over misdemeanors, outside
the sphere of military service requirements, which did not result in

any damage to the state. In other words, it dealt only with misdemeanors pertaining to everyday life.

This Comradely Court consisted of three members and two substitute members, elected for three months by secret universal and equal ballot of the men. The court elected from its own midst a president and a secretary. These courts initiated proceedings upon receiving information from commissars and commanders, as well as individual soldiers and private citizens. It judged such offenses as, for instance, insults offered by one soldier to another, which were not accompanied by serious physical violence and had occurred during off-duty periods; drunkenness, gambling, reprehensible behavior while off duty. The courts had powers to inflict punishments within the same limitations as established for the summary disciplinary rights of the commanders and commissars. The company commander could not be brought to trial before these courts, although the courts could ask the commissar and the commander of the unit to bring the company commander to trial.[277]

The differentiation between the lower commanding personnel, such as platoon and section commanders, and the company commander, is thus sharply drawn. While the former were subject to trial by the Company Court, the latter was exempt. The higher-placed, such as battalion and regimental commanders, were entirely outside the scope of activity of these courts, and the same was true of the military commissars.

These courts were, to an extent, survivals from the armed forces of Russia in 1917, and the early units of the Red forces, which were in practice self-governing in matters of discipline, as well as several others.

During the early days of the regular Red Army, committees continued to flourish. For instance, the order No. 19 of the Petrograd Military District, dated March 28, 1918, even prescribed the formation in companies and regiments of "Red Army soldiers' committees." Summary disciplinary punishment did not exist. Special disciplinary courts were established by the order No. 48 of the Military Commissariat of the Petrograd Commune on April 27, 1918, at the H.Q. of the districts of the Red Army. These courts consisted of two soldiers and one member selected from the personnel of the Regional Council. They were empowered to impose arrests up to fifteen days, and to expel soldiers from the service.[278]

That the ideas of military anarchy propounded in the decree of December 16, 1917 (which really merely reflected conditions already

existing in most of the units of the old army at the time), did not
entirely disappear from the Red Army, is shown by the incident
which occurred in the 15th Rifle Division in January 1919. The units
of the division had left the field of battle in a manner described by the
H.Q. of the Ninth Army as "shameful flight." The commanding personnel of the division, who were threatened with dire consequences,
owing to the unseemly behavior of their units, disagreed with the
H.Q. of the Army in the evaluation of what actually occurred, and
had called a meeting of commissars, members of communist collectives' bureaus, of the battalion, company, squadron and battery
cells. The meeting proceeded to examine the accusation, levelled at
the 15th Rifle Division by the H.Q. of the Ninth Army, of fleeing
ignominiously from the battlefield. It then passed to the examination
of the proposed replacement of the commanding personnel of the
division by other commanders. The policy of the army H.Q. and of
its Revolutionary Military Council also came up for discussion, and
measures were debated to "liquidate the painful situation." Finally,
the meeting proceeded to examine the "necessity of calling a conference of the collectives of the front."[279]

The Old Adam of 1917 refused to die. Here the commanding personnel and the communist collectives resuscitated the practice of the
army committees and soviets of 1917 by wrangling with the High
Command. It imitated the practice, fairly widespread in the early
years of Civil War, of battalion cells reprimanding commanders of
divisions for such things as carelessness in the observance of rules
governing confidential military correspondence, or taking issue with
military supply organs as to the weight of the pig slaughtered to
provide an evening meal for their battalion.

This anarchy of the communist cells, of the commanders and of
the commissars, could not but influence the attitude of the men in the
ranks. One can hardly speak of a uniformly enforced discipline, particularly off the actual field of battle, in the Red Army of the Civil
War period.

A report submitted by a member of the Revolutionary Military
Council of the Southern Front in April 1919, in commenting on the
poor discipline prevailing in the Thirteenth Army, quoted a memorandum of the commander of the Starobelsk Regiment: "Soldiers
categorically declare that they are unable to continue to fight since
they are, first, hungry, second, barefoot, naked, and devoured by
parasites, because from the first revolt of our organization until now
no supplies have been issued." The Deputy Commander of the Army

was arrested and barely escaped with his life.[280] The Commander of the Starobelsk Regiment was thus apparently taking the easiest way out and under the influence of the mutinous men of his unit preferred to report to his superiors the state of the regiment rather than take any steps to restore discipline.

The factor of physical privation, so strikingly commented upon in the above report, had a profound influence on the discipline and the combat efficacy of the units of the Red Army during the Civil War.

In commenting on Red Army units, a participant in the defense of Petrograd against the Iudenich offensive wrote: "Their outward appearance is miserable. They are dressed in all kinds of garb. Military greatcoats are mixed with civilian overcoats and jackets, khaki caps alternate with civilian hats and caps. As to footgear, they have boots, shoes, and about half of them wear bast slippers."[281]

Another eye-witness, a member of the Communist Youth Union, stated: "Worn out, hungry soldiers, angered by the general refusal of peasants, ceased to ask, or even to demand, and started thorough searches which often became but little different from pillage. Boars and chickens made their appearance and fires began to send up sparks."[282]

The failure of the supply organs to furnish the men with rations, and the lack of initiative of the commanding personnel in obtaining food from the population in an organized way, led thus to a plundering of the peasantry by the hungry Red soldiers, destroying all semblance of military discipline.

One can cite endless examples of the deficiencies in the material side of life of the Red Army, and of their influence on the morale of the soldiers. E. A. Stchadenko speaks of a report of the commander of the 5th Division in May, 1919, to the effect that his men were "naked and barefoot," and that underwear and uniforms were urgently needed. The commander expressed his concern that, unless wearing apparel was sent promptly, his units might pass over to the rebel Grigoriev, whose soldiers were well provided with uniforms and footgear.[283]

Stchadenko asserts that the underclothing, boots, shoes and other wearing apparel requisitioned from the civilian population of Odessa for the needs of the Red Army, made possible the change in the morale of the troops, and permitted the Red command to maintain possession of Odessa.[284]

In 1920, in the Twelfth Army, men were fed irregularly and

horses were famished because of lack of fodder. Instead of boots, men were issued bast slippers or defective shoes.[285]

The care of the sick and wounded was very unsatisfactorily organized. Under the heading "Shame and Disgrace," Trotsky wrote in June 1919 about the transport of wounded his train encountered at one of the southern railway stations. The men were lying on the bare boards of the car floors without any bedding whatsoever. Many of them were clad only in filthy underwear. Those with infectious diseases were placed alongside the wounded. One of these sanitary, or rather insanitary, trains stayed from early morning till evening at a railway siding. During that time the wounded were not once fed. Medical personnel, nurses and échelon commanders were absent. The People's Commissar for War came to the conclusion that the military sanitary organization of the Southern Front was in bad shape.[286]

The material deficiencies had a certain influence on the strategy and tactics of the Red troops during the Civil War. Priority in taking over a city or town assumed great importance. Taking possession of a town meant affluence to the unit achieving it. The supplies seized and confiscated from public stores and the civil population brought an immediate improvement in the well-being of the men. Army units, therefore, keenly competed for the privilege of entering the town first. In spite of regulations governing the disposition of trophies, each unit, after the occupation of a town, endeavored, and usually managed, to keep for itself and conceal whatever it had seized.[287]

Articles of prime necessity were lacking in the front units, although the army was using up a very large part of the total supplies at the disposal of the state. In 1920, according to the estimates of the annual plan, the army was to receive 25 per cent of all flour at the disposal of the Soviet Government, 40 per cent of grain and fodder, fats, soap and cotton goods, 50 per cent of grits, 60 per cent of meats, fish and sugar, 90 per cent of men's footgear and 100 per cent of all tobacco.[288] The army was thus consuming a very large part of the available resources of the country. Despite this, the wounded and the sick were but indifferently cared for, and men at the front often went without essentials.

In 1918 the budget of the Soviet state was placed at 28 billion rubles. The army was given two-thirds of the total. At that time the Red Army had not as yet grown into the enormous organization it became in 1920.[289]

The late Commander in Chief of the Red Army, S. Kamenev, maintained that on the whole, the Red Army soldiers were satisfac-

torily fed, even better than was provided for by the standards established by the supply organs. He admits, however, that soldiers had
suffered from lack of tea, sugar, soap, tobacco, matches and cigarette
paper. Kamenev ascribes this to the general shortage of these articles
in Russia at the time. He admits that the supply organs had failed to
organize the feeding of the combat units at the front until the very
end of the Civil War. The divisions in the field had to feed their men
as well as they could, exploiting the resources of the front zone. As
an exception, the Western and Northern fronts (the latter until it
began to move forward) were fed entirely by the supply organs.[290]

Kamenev did not attempt to deny that whenever stores of materials
suitable for uniforms and other articles of consumption were captured
during an attack on a town, the army units used these supplies for
their own needs. He says that only in isolated cases were such stores
pillaged, and that, as a rule, the Red Army soldiers respected what
they regarded as state property.[291]

It would seem, therefore, that whatever pillaging was done, was
on behalf of the collective needs of the units that had entered the
captured town first, rather than by individual soldiers for their own
account.

This manner of "living on the towns," seems to be another manifestation of the decentralizing spirit and the guerilla tendencies so
strongly in evidence in the Red forces during the first years of the
war. It is obviously in conflict with the centralizing tendencies of
Moscow, and the inordinately large powers extended to the officials
of the supply organs, some of whom were granted the rights and
privileges of commanders of fronts and armies.[292]

Undoubtedly the tremendous numerical preponderance of the non-
combatant personnel of the Red Army over the comparatively small
numbers of the front soldiers had a great deal to do both with the
enormous proportion of the produce of the country consumed by the
army and with the lack of essentials at the front. The personnel
of the tremendous rear apparatus consumed most of the supplies and
only a trickle reached the front.

The appearance of the Red Army soldiers, particularly during the
early period of the Civil War, was far from martial, or even tidy.
One of the old army generals who had served in the Red forces left
his impressions of these soldiers in 1918: "With unshorn hair, caps
thrust on the back of the head, in unbuttoned soldiers' greatcoats, with
rifles slung on the bandoliers . . . they shuffle along the Petrograd
sidewalks in a noisy crowd. . . . A group of mounted men, just as

unkempt and dishevelled, on poorly groomed horses, gallop on the cobblestones of the Petrograd streets, without any mercy for their mounts' feet. . . . Sentinels, at their posts, sit on stools or on steps of porches, with rifles between their knees, talking peacefully with the passers-by."[293]

It is small wonder that Trotsky, in a speech delivered in March 1918, fairly screamed that "at all costs, and at any price, it is necessary to implant discipline in the Red Army."[294]

Lenin himself was very displeased with the manner in which Red Army units presented themselves at the Red Square parade in November 1918. Bonch-Bruevich quotes him: "Look at them, how they march . . . like bags of sand." Lenin, according to Bonch-Bruevich, while glad to see the ranks of the revolutionary army, was very grieved that the soldiers were so poorly clothed and badly disciplined, that the units were obviously hastily thrown together and deficient in the niceties of military drill.[295]

Even later in the Civil War, men were sent to the front without any proper training. A. Ziuzin says in his reminiscences of his experience in an attack: "We lay on the ground, firing without aim." Another participant in the Civil War reminisces: "Even when given a target, we would not always hit it, because during the few days of instruction we had not learned how to handle the rifle properly."[296]

Addressing himself to the sailors of the Volga Armed Flotilla in August 1918, Trotsky said that he was stunned by what he saw on board its ships. In his presence Commissar Markin ordered an engineer to start a motor. When the latter refused to be started, Markin remarked: "It's always the same with us . . . when it is necessary to leave a position, motors work satisfactorily; but when we need to go to a position, motors immediately go on strike." Trotsky expostulated: "Comrades, sailors, with such an order of things the fleet has no combat efficacy, it cannot live. And it is with good reason everyone remarks that your new Volga flotilla works exceedingly indolently, lazily, without energy and without success."[297]

The martial ardor of units of the Red Army differed greatly, according to whether they were formed by the central military organs in the rear, or grew up in the process of civil strife from local Red Guard units or volunteer detachments. Trotsky admitted this freely, although he was responsible for the training of the latter. He ascribed the difference, in October 1919, to the fact that in the former most of the soldiers were mobilized recruits, commanded by old army officers, while in the latter there was a large percentage of Communists, with a prevalence of volunteers in the ranks, and very few former old army officers in command positions.[298]

The mood of the local population whence the recruits were drawn had obviously a great deal to do with the military qualities of the respective army units. Thus it is stated that in December 1918 reinforcements consisting of route battalions and companies of mobilized peasants of the Viatka and Perm provinces were considered an "extremely unstable element," and even demoralized the fighting front units they were sent to reinforce. The peasantry of these provinces were far from enthusiastic for the Soviets at that time. In February 1919, on the Western Front, divisions formed in the rear were found wanting in combat qualities—"after the first action they had ceased to exist as combat units." Matters had reached such a pass that it was decided not to send divisions from the rear, but to form from their personnel route companies to be sent for the reinforcement of the veteran fighting units of the front.[299]

N. Kakurin states that the bottom of all the "troubles" in the rear of the Red Army were the tendencies prevalent among the "middle" peasantry. As Kakurin puts it: "these peasants, no longer seeing in their immediate vicinity the landlord whose acres they had appropriated, thought to avoid the burden of the Civil War. They were vexed by its exigencies, forcing them to give recruits to the Red Army, and to surrender their food supplies to the government, without receiving anything of equivalent value in return." The same author maintains that the anti-Soviet mood of the peasants was promoted by the unsatisfactory relationship between town and village in the early period of the war, and also by the effort of the kulaks to extend their influence and leadership over the masses of the "middle" peasants. True, in regions that were occupied by the White armies, or had experienced their domination, the mood of the peasantry frequently underwent a rapid change in favor of the Soviet régime.[300]

Central and Northern Russia were also not free of peasant insurrections during the Civil War. In the Ukraine, the peasant rebellions flourished throughout its duration like the proverbial green bay tree.

To give a few examples: In July 1919, in one of the counties of the Iaroslav province, about ten thousand peasants took part in an armed rebellion which was crushed by armed force during the same month.[301]

A meeting of mobilized villagers, some five hundred strong, held in an Archangel township in 1918, resolved not to obey the call to serve in the Red Army, and even attacked an armed detachment of

Latvian Rifles, who were escorting several arrested members of the Party of People's Freedom, liberated the latter and put the Latvian Riflemen in fetters.[302]

During the year 1919, on the territory of the five provinces of the Petrograd Military District, there were altogether 64 instances of "troubles" and disorders. Of these, the province of Pskov had 24, and that of Novgorod, 14. In April 1919, in one of the counties of the province of Pskov, armed bands of deserters from the Red Army had succeeded in arousing against the Soviet Government the population of the county's three townships, who took up arms.[303]

It is not surprising, therefore, that units of the Seventh Army, which was defending Petrograd against Iudenich's onslaught, were in 1919 considered deficient in combat qualities. Its units were to a large extent recruited in the provinces where the conflict between the peasantry and the Soviet state had often reached the pitch of open rebellion. Here are the reports about some of the units of that army. The 2nd Rifle Division, "combat efficacy low, particularly in the artillery"; the 6th Rifle Division, "temper of the troops unstable, desertions observed, particularly in the 50th Rifle Regiment"; in the 46th and 51st Rifle Regiments there were instances of Red Army soldiers passing over to the enemy; in the 19th Rifle Division "combat efficacy low"; in one of its regiments there was an instance of refusal to obey orders and there also were desertions; in the troops of the Petrograd Fortified Zone in the 161st and 169th Rifle Regiments "there were instances of Red Army soldiers passing over to the enemy."[304]

In the decisive action of the Iudenich campaign for the Pulkov Heights, the Petrograd workers and Communists who were sent to reinforce the troops were the foremost factor in bringing about a change in the morale of the soldiers. Even at that, there were instances of self-inflicted wounds and desertion.[305]

A Ukranian peasant soldier, drawn from provinces where the village was in open opposition to the Soviet régime, was definitely regarded as unreliable material for the Red Army.

That the peasant soldier in the Red Army was regarded as inferior by the commanders and the commissar element, and that he was sometimes brutally treated, is reflected in a speech delivered by the People's Commissar for War at a conference of political workers of the Red Army in December 1919. Trotsky said: "I have received letters to the effect that in some units soldiers are thrashed. One of these communications came from Maxim Gorky, saying "we are being manhandled." Even some Communists told me frankly: "I hit him in the teeth with the butt of my revolver."[306]

That these were not isolated cases may be judged from order No. 2248 of the Revolutionary Military Council of the Republic, dated December 22, 1922, stating that "there was often observed rough treatment of Red Army soldiers" and "there were established instances of commanders boxing the ears of soldiers, and those guilty did not by any means suffer appropriate punishment."[307]

That at least some of the commanders and commissars were not above taking an undue advantage of their official position, regardless of the impression this made on their men, was reflected in a letter addressed by Trotsky to the Revolutionary Military Councils of Fronts and Armies, which said that government automobiles were used by those in authority for "gay parties right before the eyes of the tired Red Army soldiers." Instances were also cited when "commanders dress with extreme elegance, while the fighters go half naked." Trotsky concluded: "such facts cannot but provoke exasperation and discontent among the Red Army soldiers." The puritan People's Commissar for War pointed an indignant finger at drinking bouts he said were organized by commanders and political workers and in which women took part.

In that letter, Trotsky had expounded his aim: "Without setting the impossible goal of immediate elimination of all and sundry privileges in the army, to endeavor to reduce these systematically to the actually necessary minimum."[308]

To what extent these *pia desideria* of the founder of the regular Red Army were fulfilled will be discussed in subsequent chapters. Meanwhile, the examined data clearly indicate that the peasant soldiers (even after the exclusion of the kulak element from the army) were not always willing partners of the proletariat at some of the fronts of the Civil War.

Manhandling, beating with revolver butts in the face and "suitable" punishment as provided for by section *e* of paragraph 44 of the Disciplinary Code, were the outward expression of the conflicts in the Red Army between the anarchistic, anti-centralist tendencies of the village and the centralist, dictatorial trends of the Communist party. It was not merely a conflict between groups with different economic and political interests. It was a deep-rooted antagonism between two ways of living, two different cultural practices and concepts.

An extreme illustration of the lengths to which antagonisms between Red Army units of different social origin and belonging to different arms could go is the episode described by I. Babel in his remarkable *Cavalry Army*—remarkable not merely for its brutality, but also for an uncanny realism and accuracy of observation. It deals with an attack of a brigade of Budenny's Cavalry Army on trenches occupied by peasant infantrymen of the Reds. The cavalry charged these trenches in sheer bravado, thrashing the peasant soldiers with their heavy whips, to assert their superiority over mere foot-sluggers.[309]

Conclusions

The countless conflicts criss-crossing the Red Army, like thunderbolts in a storm over the great plains of the Ukraine, leave one wondering that any army could survive such tremendous internal stresses and achieve a victory on the internal fronts.

What then was the key to the Red Army victories? Professor P. Miliukov, in his work on the Russian revolution, has expressed the thought that the Red Army had three formidable advantages over its White opponents. One was its social composition. The masses of the peasant population felt themselves much closer to the peasant soldiers of the Red Army than to the "gentry" of the Whites. Secondly, the Red Army was moving from the hungry North to the abundance of the South. In such a movement, the personal interests of the fighters coincided with collective interests, while the Whites, advancing from the south to the north, had to carry with them food not only for themselves, but also for the population of the territories wrested by them from the Reds. Personal advantage could thus find its satisfaction only in a direct plundering of the population of the occupied regions. This, of course, did not serve to attract the sympathies of the populace to the Whites. The third advantage consisted, according to Miliukov, in the geographical position, which permitted the Red Army to operate on internal lines. Thus, the army, in using railroads, could regroup its effectives and move them from one front to another.[310]

In his foreword to the official history of the Civil War, A. Bubnov maintains that the Soviets' victory came because "we had learned to defend ourselves," and had created the Red Army, because "in the organization of the Red Army were splendidly realized the logical sequence and firmness of the proletarian direction in the alliance of the workers and toiling peasants against all exploiters," as stated by Lenin. To this, Bubnov added another suggestion, also borrowed from Lenin, that victory was achieved on account of "the correct relationship between the directing Communist party and the revolutionary class—the proletariat and the mass, i.e. the entire totality of toilers and exploited."[311]

Trotsky said in 1923 that "we conquered because of the limitless self-denial of the revolutionary vanguard and our innumerable peasant reserves . . . all our shortcomings in the sphere of organization, training, and supplies we made up for by the numerical strength of the reserves and the unstinted heroism of the vanguard."[312]

In 1922, Trotsky suggested that the Red Army had won because of the support given by the peasant to the worker against the landlord and the capitalist. "In this social fact is rooted the final cause of our victories," said the Red war lord.[313]

In comparing Miliukov's views with those of Trotsky, one cannot fail to notice that the former laid great stress on the social composition of the Red Army from the viewpoint of the influence of that factor on the civil population. He seems to disregard the conflict between the "middle" peasant and the proletarian interests, and the tenacious hostility of the Ukrainian village to the communist state. Trotsky also viewed the "support" by the peasant of the worker as the cornerstone of victory for the Red Army.

The geographical factor, in its part involving the difference in abundance of food supply in the South as against the North, was taken by Trotsky into consideration in his speech already referred to on page 106 above. In that respect there are elements of similarity in the views of the anti-bolshevik Miliukov and those of the People's Commissar for War.

The advantages of operating on internal lines are of course considerable. The importance of the large reservoirs of recruits for the Red Army in the villages of the territory held by the Soviets cannot be minimized. And yet, it would appear that Lenin's remarks about the firm and thorough guidance reflected in the organization of the Red Army may, perhaps, point to the most important factor of all.

Both sides, indeed, had antagonized the peasantry. The majority of the village population, quite probably, had little love either for the Whites or for the Reds. Their sympathies had fluctuated from one side to the other, mostly in accordance with the latest experience the village had had in the hands of Whites or Reds.

The masses of the former soldiers of the World War, both in village and town, still thought of the officer, with his gold or silver tinsel shoulder straps, as their enemy who in 1917 had tried to prevent them from leaving the trenches, and going home to seize the landlord's acres or the capitalist's factory.

The prestige of ruling from Moscow and having possession of Petrograd, as against issuing decrees from such new-fangled "capitals" as Omsk, Ekaterinodar, or Archangel, was also not without some influence. With some sections of the Russian population it carried with it the idea of "fatherland." This often became important during the Polish War and in some phases of the Civil War, when the foreign interventionists were particularly active. Some Irkutsk merchants were overheard in early 1920 to say with hope and relish: "Now that Kolchak is defeated we are going to have a chance again to trade with Moscow."

The apparatus of the old central government, which became available to the Soviets in Petrograd, and later in Moscow, also, no doubt, played its rôle in helping them in the technical side of the organization of the state and the army, while their opponents had to be satisfied with the rag, tag and bobtail of the provinces, assisted by such persons as succeeded in escaping from the capitals to join them.

Whether all these technical advantages would be sufficient to outweigh the internal stresses examined above, and to overcome the violent conflicts within the Red Army, is open to doubt.

On the other hand, the Red Army and the Red state, let us remember, had an important advantage: their forces were directed from one center, there was one consistent plan of operation for the Red Army, applied by men of more than average ability (S. Kamenev and Lebedev). Theirs was a clean-cut program of political action. Intelligent and vigorously conducted propaganda and agitation provided a powerful impulse for the "dispossessed" classes to defend what they had acquired, or thought they had acquired, against the onslaughts of what they regarded as the forces of those whom they had dispossessed.

Furthermore, the great tool of Lenin, which had helped him to achieve his victory, was the disciplined and ruthless phalanxes of the party he created. Here was a new class, avid for distinctions, not averse to personal privilege, ambitious to secure and to hold the key positions in the army and in the state. These men were moved, not by personal interest alone, not merely by a traditional devotion to duty, or by a desire to find a niche for themselves in the world, although, of course, all these motives entered into their emotional and mental *gestalt*. They were crusaders for a new idea, they had before their mental eyes the blueprint of a new world, a bonny world, worth living and dying for. There was great dynamism in their fervor, a feeling of being fully and entirely right, of deserving to win because of what they thought the consequences of their victory might be, not only for Russia but for the entire world. This element—call it religious or revolutionary enthusiasm, as you prefer—was undoubtedly the great stimulus, the tremendous force that sustained the Red Army during the Civil War.

There was a certain unity in the desires and aspirations of the Communists of that period, while their opponents were held together merely by a negative feeling, the hatred of the Soviet régime.

True, there were antagonisms within the party: *vide* Tsaritsin, *vide* the fiasco of the Polish campaign.[314] At the same time, as long as Lenin lived, and was able to guide the destinies of the party, the unity of control was maintained, and hundreds of thousands of Communists permeated the blood vessels of the Red Army, like a myriad of red corpuscles, to meet their White enemies, wherever the brains of their leaders directed them. The flexibility, and, at the same time, the adequate discipline of the party, permitted the Red Army to withstand heavy blows and losses during the terrible years of the Civil War.

The personality of the leaders—of Lenin, of Trotsky, of Frunze, of Stalin—had also unquestionably a very great importance. Statements, such as those Colonel Fedor Makhin of the old army made in his book on the Red Army, that Trotsky's practical activity was far below the importance of his official position, and that the latter limited his mission to the appointment of the higher personnel of the Commissariat for War and the army high command, are, of course, unmitigated twaddle. Trotsky's rôle in the organization of the army along regular lines was tremendous, and everyone who had a chance to observe his activities during the Civil War knows perfectly well to what extent Trotsky was the Soviet *père de la victoire*.

Thus the personal element of men of extraordinary, if unequal, ability, will power, and indefatigable application, had also, beyond question, an important influence in keeping the Red Army together and in guiding it to victory. But the very fact that there was a concise program to fight for, something that could be translated into words comprehensible to the most illiterate worker, to the "darkest" peasant in the army, was of untold value to the Red cause. One cannot merely shout "Down!," one must show to the masses the image of what they are asked to fight for. Not merely an abstract idea, like world revolution, but a state of toilers right then and there, in their own homeland. Acres to be held, factories to seize—that was a tremendous cause for which to risk one's life, and give to that life a singleness of purpose.

The Communists were, then, the electric current that charged the vast machine of the Red Army, and supplied the driving power of the leaders' will, translating it into action. Whoever they were, commissars, commanders, rank and file soldiers, their will to victory provided the unifying cement, the iron frame, that held the Red Army together, despite its internal conflicts.

After the victory was garnered, dissensions within the party, and opposition to the ruthless, centralized control of wide circles of the population opened up latent conflicts. The boom of the Kronstadt guns brought to an end the heroic era of military communism, and ushered in the dull New Economic Policy. This had a profound influence on the organization and efficiency of the Red Army. In the next chapter, the causes of the violent outbreak of conflict within the Red Armed forces stationed at Kronstadt will be examined, and an attempt made to analyze the background of these events, to show why the internal stresses became powerful enough to break the bonds that welded the Red forces together during the Civil War.

★ V ★

KRONSTADT

LENIN, speaking at the Tenth Party Congress on March 8, 1921, at the time the Kronstadt rebellion was at its height, stated: "I have no doubt that this rebellion, which has rapidly exhibited to us the familiar figure of the White Guard generals, will be liquidated in the nearest day . . . but it is necessary for us to weigh carefully the political and economic lessons of this event. . . . What does it mean? The passing of political power from the Bolsheviki to an indefinite assortment or alliance of variegated elements, seemingly only a little to the right of the Bolsheviki, perhaps even to the left of the Bolsheviki. . . . At the same time it is beyond doubt that White generals, as you all know, have played an important rôle in this. This is fully proven. . . . It is entirely clear that this is the work of Socialist Revolutionaries and of White Guards residing abroad. . . . And at the same time the movement has resolved itself into a petty-bourgeois counter-revolution, into a petty-bourgeois, anarchic element. In that there is something new."[1]

Trotsky in 1921 stressed the fact that as the Baltic Fleet was not in a position to play an active rôle, its personnel had deteriorated. He said that a large number of revolutionary bluejackets, who had played an important part in the November 1917 revolution, had been transferred to other fields of activity. Those who replaced them were, in a large measure, "fortuitous elements," and included a comparatively large number of Latvian, Estonian and Finnish seamen, who "regarded their service as a temporary occupation," and were mostly indifferent to the revolutionary struggle. Trotsky pointed out that this circumstance had facilitated the conspirators' work. They had taken advantage of a particular conflict and enlarged its frame, so that for a part of the seamen there was no way of retreat from the position they had taken up. The mutineers had succeeded in taking possession of the powerful artillery of the fortress, and the two battleships, while the garrison and the populace had remained passive bystanders, and had not even had time to realize what was going on.[2]

The official Soviet history of the Civil War describes the background of the Kronstadt rebellion in somewhat broader terms. At the end of February 1921, a section of the Petrograd workers "had given in here and there to the frenzied anti-Soviet agitation and begun the so-called 'bag-pipe' (*volynka*)." This new-fangled word stood for the old-fashioned "strike."[3]

The movement, according to the Soviet historian, had developed under the influence of an acute food crisis and had encouraged counter-revolutionary elements to change their propaganda, conducted by means of a large quantity of leaflets distributed to the Petrograd proletariat, from the advocacy of "freely elected non-party Soviets" to the openly proclaimed slogan of "Down with the Soviet Government! Long live the Constitutional Assembly!"[4]

According to this official version, the Red Army and the Red Navy units, as well as the crews of the naval vessels at Kronstadt, were filled with the "dregs of the Petrograd Port," as well as high school students, and war prisoners (ex-followers of Makhno of Ukrainian guerilla fame or of the Denikin White Army). Among the Kronstadt garrison, the propaganda was carried on under the guise of the defense of "honest, freely-elected non-party Soviets," against the "bolshevik usurpers," in the name of the Third Revolution.[5]

N. A. Kornatovskii, in a paper on the Kronstadt rebellion published in a volume edited by him on the occasion of the tenth anniversary of that event, wrote that the immediate causes of the Kronstadt rebellion lay in the change which had taken place in the social composition of the seamen element of the Baltic Fleet, the inefficiency of the local civil and military governmental agencies, together with the unsatisfactory state of the Kronstadt party organization and the absence of a firm party guidance from Petrograd.[6]

Another contributor to the same volume, M. N. Kuzmin, pointed an accusing finger at the followers of Trotsky—Raskolnikov (who then commanded the Baltic Fleet) and Hessen. According to Kuzmin, these two had used the naval apparatus for the heinous purpose of "fractional" work within the party, multigraphing and distributing at all public meetings Trotsky's theses, Bukharin's speech and other "oppositional material." In the words of Kuzmin: "they had worked to discredit the party direction of the Petrograd organization"—*vide* Zinoviev and his friends.[7]

Zinoviev's proclamation, broadcast over the radio, was republished by the *Izvestia* of the Provisional Revolutionary Committees of Kronstadt on March 6, 1921. It attempted to persuade the population of Kronstadt that the leaders of the rebellion were mere puppets, pulled hither and yon by strings in the hands of the "czarist general Kozlovskii," some other old army officers and "known White

Guards." "Really you are fighting not for democracy but for the Czar's generals"—so ran the proclamation.[8]

The various statements referred to above were made for different reasons and were aimed at different goals. This, of course, had a great deal to do with their contents. Lenin, for instance, was analyzing the situation for the benefit of the party congress. Trotsky was obviously trying to reduce an event of tremendous political and social signifi- cance to a mere military uprising fostered by a few conspirators. One must remember that his views were given to the representatives of the foreign press at the time when a trade treaty with Britain was hanging in the balance.[9] Kuzmin's aim, very probably, was to make political capital by pointing to the "Trotskist gangrene," so danger- ous, according to him, even in 1921. Other authors mentioned above try to draw a sharp line between the "revolutionary seamen of 1917" and the "dregs of the Petrograd Navy Yard" of 1921, pointing to the change in the social composition of the crews of the Baltic Fleet, which supposedly had occurred between the years 1917 and 1921. Zinoviev's crude distortion of the Kronstadt situation was so obvious at the time that the mutineers had ventured to reprint it in their own press as another example of the mendacity of the bolshevik leaders.

To understand the conflicts which led to the Kronstadt rebellion it is necessary to analyze, however briefly, the general situation of Soviet Russia after the end of the Civil War, the trend of opposition to Lenin within the Communist party and the rising antagonism be- tween the "upper" and the "lower" strata of party membership. That the Kronstadt seamen in 1921 were radically different socially and in their general pattern of behavior from the Baltic bluejackets of 1917 —"the ornament and pride of the revolution"—is also an assumption worth looking into. Ultimately an analysis of the program and tactics of the rebels may yield some useful material.

W. H. Chamberlin, in his excellent history of the Russian Revolu- tion, wrote that the basic difference between the crisis of 1920-1921 and the two previous major crises that had confronted the Soviet Government since its seizure of power, lay in the fact that the latter had had roots in war (the first was brought about by the advance of the Czecho-Slovaks in 1918, the second by the march of General Denikin's forces on Moscow in 1919), while the former was a crisis of the whole economic and social system of war communism and did not involve any military problem.[10]

As Chamberlin says, the specter that haunted the Kremlin at the end of 1920 and the beginning of 1921 was that of a collapse from within, "as a result of the profound mood of disillusionment and dissatisfaction among the masses." He pointed out that "In some respects the conclusion of peace with Poland and the elimination of Wrangel were psychologically disadvantageous" to the Communists. It was impossible from then on to bolster up the morale of peasant soldiers by holding up to them the bogey of Russian and Polish landlords. Class hate of the workers for the old-régime ruling and wealthy classes could not be exploited any more in the interest of the Communist party, nor was there the convenient symbol of Civil War available any more to serve as an excuse for the privations the country was undergoing.[11]

The poor harvest of 1920 made grain stocks smaller in the village. The peasants' dislike for the forcible requisitioning of foodstuffs for the needs of the Soviet state became even more acute than before. Living conditions in cities and towns also took a turn for the worse in 1921. On January 22, 1921, a cut of one-third in the beggarly bread ration was announced for Moscow, Petrograd, and other large towns.[12]

An extremely severe fuel crisis led to the closing of sixty-four of the largest factories in Petrograd. As Chamberlin wrote: "This midwinter economic crisis was all the more severe because the Soviet authorities, very badly informed about the country's actual resources in food and fuel, had adopted a too ambitious program of restarting factories, without reckoning with their ability to keep them open."[13]

The attitude of industrial workers underwent a very marked change. Such a stronghold of proletarian enthusiasm as the metal workers' union, at a congress held in Moscow in February 1921 exhibited a mood of extreme bitterness among its non-party delegates. On the first day of the congress pro-communist speakers were shouted down.[14] At the congress of the workers of the waterways, the commissars had to turn to non-party technicians to cope with the open antagonism of rank and file delegates to the Communist party leadership. In a number of election meetings in Moscow, open anti-communist trends were evident.

The report of the Control Commission presented by Aaron Soltz at the Tenth Party Congress makes very enlightening reading. Soltz said that many communications received by the commission from party members had deprecated the general tone of the party, which, they said, compelled them to leave the party, "or to despair of the situation in which, according to them, the party finds itself, because of the unhealthy phenomena taking place within it."[15]

Soltz added that these communications showed that the rôle played in the party by many privileged persons, occupying important positions and freed from party control, made for a situation where the actual state of the party differed widely from their concept of what the party should be. As a result, the authors of the letters felt themselves unable to remain within its fold. The privileged position of the Communists invested with authority led to their estrangement from the masses of the rank and file party members and to a peculiar view as to the authority vested in them. As Soltz puts it, "I am invested with authority and am responsible only to that organization which has conferred on me that authority. I do not recognize any duty to give account to the party masses." Soltz also mentioned that there were reports of some responsible workers exploiting their position to their own material advantage, but stated that instances of such abuses were much less frequent than the refusal to give heed to the voice of the local party organizations.[16]

It was pointed out in the statement made by the Central Control Commission to the Central Committee of the party that the leading party workers were attempting to reduce discussions of principle to personal squabbles. At the same time a letter from the important Petrograd party organization definitely warned of the danger of a schism and offered to take the initiative in organizing the pre-congress campaign in the sphere of struggle around the problem of the rôle of the trade unions. The Central Control Committee's statement interpreted this as an indication that the Central Committee of the party refused to undertake the guidance of the pre-congress campaign. The Commission's report asserted that this gave the impression "that we have not a party, but separate communist groupings, which will conduct a struggle among themselves at the Congress."[17]

Osinskii, a delegate affiliated with the group known as Democratic Centralists, characterized the crisis as follows: the weariness and discontent of the worker and peasant masses; the fact that the party lost touch with the masses in some respects; and that solidarity within the party was weakened, and there were many groupings. He claimed that there were syndicalist trends within the party, proof of which he saw in the insubordination shown by the local party organs as against the orders of the center. Osinskii stressed the destructive rôle played by the so-called Workers' Opposition within the party. "The noisy Workers' Opposition," he said, "is taking advantage of the turbulence in the factories, which is at present observable. It is blaming

everybody, exposing Panama scandals,[18] and attempting to play the
rôle of the overthrower of cabinets."[19]

Another delegate, Milonov, made the assertion that the grave crisis
the party was living through was due to the "fouling of our party by
elements alien to her (peasantry, intellectuals)" and that the "healthy
proletarian elements" were leaving it. According to Milonov, this was
overwhelmingly evident during the party re-registrations, which, he
said, were undertaken purely on formalistic grounds. As a result, an
upper crust began to harden and to change into a caste. As Milonov
expresses it: "there is a tendency to prefer authoritarian leadership
to the methods of spontaneous activity of the masses." Sosnovskii
considered that the main danger was that the party organization was
being flooded by the peasantry. He cited at the Congress the case of
the Ekaterinenburg party organization, in the heart of the industrial
Ural region, two-thirds of the membership of which consisted of
peasants.[20]

The well-known woman Communist Kollontai also gave expression
to the idea that the principal cause of the crisis was to be found in the
change of social composition of the party: "a number of alien elements have sneaked" into the party, as she put it. On the other hand,
Krestinskii, in challenging those who had levelled the accusation that
the party was being swamped with intellectuals, stated that in forty-
two provinces the maximum percentage of intellectuals did not exceed
18 to 19, and was below that for the party as a whole.[21]

The stormy petrel of the Congress, Shliapnikov, the leader of the
Workers' Opposition, apostrophized Lenin, shouting that the party
had lost the internal cohesion which it formerly had possessed. He
stated that among the metal workers at Petrograd less than 2 per cent
belonged to the Communist party. At Moscow, figures for forty-one
metal works employing twenty-two thousand men indicated that there
were only 4 per cent party members. Shliapnikov stressed that the
party was growing, not because of the influx of members from the
ranks of the industrial workers, but from those of the peasants and
the white-collar employees.[22]

Comrade Rafail took issue with Lenin, challenging the latter's
statement that the discussion about the rôle of the trade unions was a
luxury which the party could ill afford at the time. He retorted that
the mistake lay not in the fact that the discussion was permitted, but
in the manner in which it was conducted: "for two months the whole
party staged an all-Russian 'gab-feast,' into which that very discussion degenerated."[23]

The reasons for the acute discontent of the peasants with the Soviet policies were summed up by Lenin, who said that during the war it was unavoidable for the Soviet state to confiscate the surpluses of food in the village. The continuation of this measure did not, however, answer to the requirements of peacetime conditions. "When we direct all our attention to the reconstruction of economic life," said Lenin, "we have to know that before us stands the petty agriculturalist, the petty proprietor, the petty producer, who works for the commodity market until the complete victory of large scale production. . . . This is a matter of many years, no less than a decade, and in our penurious condition probably for an even longer period. Until then, for long years, we shall have to do business with this petty producer, as such, and the slogan of free trade will be unavoidable."[24]

The discontent of certain party circles with Lenin's centralistic policy did not originate at the Tenth Congress or immediately before it. Some of the speeches held at the Ninth Congress, which took place from March 29 to April 4, 1920, give evidence of considerable opposition to that policy.

At the March 31 meeting, Sapronov pointed out that the trend developed by the party, under Lenin's guidance, led to the dictatorship, not of the party, nor of the proletariat, but of the party bureaucracy. Turning to Lenin, Sapronov asked: "Do you believe that in machine-like obedience lies the salvation of the revolution?"[25]

Preobrazhenskii declared that the party was in danger. At the previous Congress, held in March 1919, the party numbered over two hundred thousand members, while "at present we have represented at this congress more than half a million; and the enrollment of the new members into the party has created an exceedingly menacing situation, since there are comrades attending our party meetings who are not drawn politically into our work and are not educated. . . . in status they are equivalent to those who for ten or twenty years, or from the beginning of the revolution, have worked with the party . . . in this sense they cannot possibly be equal, though enjoying formally an equal status." Syrtsov sarcastically spoke of the political departments in the army bringing in new Communists "by platoons into the party cells," and claimed that these departments were unable to absorb or to educate these newcomers. Syrtsov taunted the Central Committee of the party with self-conceit: "those in authority know best," he parodied its attitude. "This self-conceit leads unavoidably to bureaucracy," was his verdict.[26]

Trotsky, in opposing Sapronov, used as his strongest argument the allegation that the latter's supporters were mostly Ukrainians. "We know well," said he, "that our party organizations in the Ukraine, in their worst part, reflect the same illnesses . . . in the Ukraine I would meet, in one town or another, limitless criticism, grumbling and chatter, but when the time came to mobilize workers for the front, five men went, while ninety-five deserted."[27]

Trotsky's argument was adroit demagoguery, but it hardly answered the charge of the bureaucratization of the party raised by his opponent.

At the time of the Tenth Congress, the issue became of great importance. The attention of the rank and file members became attracted to the real (and, perhaps, also to some imaginary) privileges of the "upper" strata of the party membership, those who occupied the so-called responsible posts in the party machine and in the Soviet Government.

That the antagonism was not restricted to Kronstadt is evident from the contents of the articles published by Aaron Soltz in *Pravda* in January and February of 1921.[28] He quoted from a letter of a Communist who had recently resigned from the party: "I do not believe in the realization of communism in view of all the privileges which are enjoyed by those Communists who occupy responsible posts."[29]

Chamberlin mentions, in his book on the Russian revolution, that another contributor to *Pravda*, a certain Speranskii, had declared that the hostility of some workers and rank and file party members toward responsible party functionaries had become so great that at times it reached the intensity of "class hatred." Speranskii said that any hostile reference to the way in which the commissars lived was applauded at the meetings.[30] Anyone who lived in Moscow and Petrograd at the time had opportunity to observe that Speranskii's statement had ample foundation in the mood of the masses.

The discussion of the proper functions of the trade unions, which had preceded the Tenth Party Congress, developed against the background of acute jealousy and animosity of the "lower" strata against the communist leaders. This antagonism was made even more pronounced by the acute economic crisis the country was passing through. After the decision of the Central Committee of the Party on December 24, 1920, to open up a free discussion of the trade union issue during the period preceding the convocation of the Tenth Congress, eight platforms were put forward by groups and individuals. Of these, three attracted considerable support. One of the latter was sponsored by Lenin and nine members of the Central Committee of the party, who had sided with him; another was advanced by Trotsky, who also had a group of supporters in the Central Committee, albeit a smaller one than that of Lenin; the third was that of the Workers' Opposition.[31]

The latter group proposed to concentrate in the hands of the trade unions "the entire management of economic life," and to inaugurate a system under which factories were to be managed by elected factory committees, each member of which would attend to some particular branch of administration.[32]

Lenin believed that the trade unions should have educational and propagandist powers, while Trotsky wanted to bring the unions into close contact with the problems of economic management, but desired to reach this end by controlling the unions entirely from above.[33]

As Chamberlin rightly points out, behind this controversy was the larger problem of the future course of the communist economic policy. Trotsky's ideas were in line with the development of the system of war communism, while Lenin, apparently, had already lost faith in the feasibility of war communism under peace conditions, and was groping for new methods to achieve economic recovery. The very fact of an open, and at that, bitter, dispute between Lenin and Trotsky was, no doubt, a matter of deep concern to the rank and file of the party.[34]

Under these circumstances, it is impossible to regard the Kronstadt rebellion merely as a local event, due entirely, or even principally, to conditions prevailing at Kronstadt. In that microcosm of the navy yard was reflected what was going on in the entire Soviet world.

Chamberlin considers that the same factors which in the past had tended to make Kronstadt the center of revolutionary agitation against the Provisional Government in 1917, operated to produce the rebellion of 1921. "A hatred of privilege and authority was ingrained in the spirit of the place, where the population consisted almost entirely of workers and sailors," he says. Chamberlin also points out that anarchy had many adherents in Kronstadt in 1917 and concludes with the assertion that "it was natural that this sailors' fortress should be especially restive under the new yoke of the communist commissars."[35]

The contrast between Chamberlin's view and those expressed by Trotsky, Zinoviev and even Lenin, is profound indeed.

The examination of the several angles of the problem may prove useful in judging whether Chamberlin's assertions are better founded than those of the official Soviet spokesmen.

One of the most interesting points is that of the so-called change in the social composition of the seamen of the Baltic Fleet between 1917 and 1921. As the situation is presented by the Soviet side, the very fact of disloyalty of the Baltic Fleet, or for that matter of any Russian bluejackets, to the Soviet leaders, was something without precedent, something new, which had to be explained by a radical change in the attitude, but also in the social origins of the crews of the ships at Kronstadt. There is, nevertheless, considerable evidence to the contrary.

Dybenko, reminiscing about the early months after the November revolution, wrote that the first attempt to undermine the influence of the ships' committees and to appoint commissars on board men-of-war, provoked "a storm of indignation, not only among the rank and file seamen, but among a part of the members of the Central Committee of the Baltic Fleet as well." To meet the situation, the President of the Central Committee, Izmailov, was made the chief Commissar of the Baltic Fleet. Dybenko says: "this appointment did not pass without incidents. Anarchy was growing in the fleet."[36] And this was still 1917.

In the summer of 1918, the crews of several vessels of the Destroyer Division had adopted a resolution, proposed by Lieutenant Lisanevich, calling openly for a rebellion against the Soviet Government, and accusing it of an intention to destroy the Baltic Fleet in subservience to Germany's wishes. The resolution advanced the idea of the dictatorship of the Baltic Fleet. The crews of the Destroyer Division even sent their delegations to the battleships and cruisers, but failed to obtain the support of the latter.[37]

This should not be so surprising, provided one recalls that at the Second Congress of the Delegates of the Baltic Fleet in the end of September 1917, the presiding body had included two Socialist Revolutionaries of the Left, and one Anarchist, in addition to the four Bolsheviki. In other words, at that time the relation of the Bolsheviki to other revolutionaries in that body (and libertarians at the same time), stood as four to three.[38] At the second meeting of the Central Committee of the Baltic Fleet, held soon after the outbreak of the March Revolution in 1917, out of thirty-three members, only five were Bolsheviki and six were regarded as their sympathizers.[39] In other words, the relative strength of the Bolsheviki to other parties and groups in the Committee stood then as one to three. There were in 1917 large and vocal groups of Baltic seamen, who did not follow the banners of bolshevism, although, temporarily, they were willing to co-operate with them against what they regarded as their common enemy—the Provisional Government and the vestiges of the old régime.

Stchadenko, in his paper on the Grigoriev guerilla, spoke disparagingly of the large number of utterly demoralized bluejackets at Odessa. From their number, Zhelezniak succeeded in forming only one armored train crew. Even Zhelezniak himself was for a while not quite certain as to his stand with respect to the Soviet Government. Stchadenko wrote: "He did not agree for a long while, but later came to the understanding that it was necessary either to defend the revolution or to fight it. After he grasped that, he remained a faithful champion of the revolution till the end."[40] And this was during the Civil War, in the spring of 1919!

A large number of bluejackets sided with the Grigoriev guerilla at the time of the latter's rebellion against the Soviet Government. At Nikolaev and Kherson they terrorized the civilian population, plundering and devastating these towns. Stchadenko tells of a detachment of four hundred bluejackets sent from Odessa to reinforce loyal Soviet troops who passed over to the Grigoriev guerilla. Stchadenko adds significantly that these seamen were "anarchistically-minded bandits."[41]

Bonch-Bruevich mentions in his memoirs that as early as March 1918 Lenin had changed his mind about the Baltic Fleet bluejackets, when it came to his knowledge that the latter had refused to carry out combat orders on board men-of-war at the time when the German expeditionary force was helping the Finnish Whites to suppress the proletarian movement. According to Bonch-Bruevich, the seamen had "refused, out of cowardice, to open fire on German troops, being afraid of an attack from the sea, and in this manner indirectly helped the Germans and the Finnish counter-revolutionaries."[42] The notation of the change in Lenin's attitude is important. The reason for this change may have different roots than those described by Bonch-Bruevich.

During the rebellion of the Socialist Revolutionaries of the Left in July 1918, at Moscow, the bluejackets proved by their conduct that Lenin was right in his opinion of them. Armed seamen belonging to the detachment of Popov raided the Cheka and arrested some of the leading Chekists.[43]

The resolution adopted in October 1918, at the mass meeting of bluejackets of Petrograd at the barracks of the Second Depot of the Baltic Fleet, had a definitely anti-Leninist and even an anti-communist character. It advocated the tearing up of the Brest-Litovsk treaty, the immediate armed assistance of the Ukraine against the German troops of occupation, and demanded that the seamen be sent to the front all in one group.[44] In this manner the influence of the Communists over the Baltic Fleet seamen was already on the wane in 1918.

G. D. Kondakov, enumerating causes that had to do with bringing about the Kronstadt rebellion, referred to the tendencies of the Revolutionary Military Council of the Baltic Fleet to place in responsible positions "inexperienced party workers from the ranks of the old 'shell-backs' (in a special way stressing that on board ship only a seaman can command respect. . . .)"[45]

Commissars Nazarenus and Posern had to give up their seats on the Council because they did not come from the ranks of the bluejackets. Zof and Kuzmin, who replaced them, also were unable to maintain themselves at their posts "in the atmosphere of intrigues and squabbles." As Kondakov puts it: "Tactless acts, sometimes demagogical speeches by Communists of the 'old-sea-dog' variety deprived them of all influence."[46]

In other words, the bluejackets did not want to take orders from civilian Communists, whom they considered outsiders. The seamen constantly asserted their independence against the appointees of the center who had not seen service afloat.

That the Kronstadt movement had found ready support among the seamen in the Petrograd naval barracks is confirmed by one of the contributors to the already-mentioned volume on the Kronstadt rebellion.[47]

In the same volume there is also material in refutation of the official view that the change in the social composition of the crews of the Baltic Fleet was responsible for the anti-bolshevik movement among them. F. M. Nikitin wrote of a conversation he had with a seaman from the Cruiser Brigade. The latter stated that his ship, the cruiser *Rossiia*, had joined in the decision to reelect the Kronstadt Soviet and in the meanwhile to take authority into their own hands. In deploring the situation, Nikitin said: "The crew [of his detachment] consisted mostly of old seamen. It was possible to attract them to the side of the Communists. However, Communists did not show any activity, did not do anything, did not take any steps."[48]

After all it is not altogether surprising that the old seamen, the men of 1917, took a hand in the overthrow of the communist dictatorship at Kronstadt. Evidence examined above shows clearly enough that, even from the early days of the November Revolution, the bluejackets were an independent lot, difficult to manage, and were far from constant in their support of the Soviet Government in the period between 1917 and 1921. That they were imbued with a strong revolutionary spirit did not necessarily mean that they were willing to lie patiently on the Procrustean bed of the communist dictatorship.

It would seem, therefore, that Chamberlin's reference to the fact that the very regions which rebelled most violently in 1905 and 1917 had later become centers of uprising against the communist régime, may be applicable to Kronstadt as well.[49] Common to all these localities was the fierce libertarianism, which, of course, did not pass away after the Bolsheviki took over the reins of government.

The record of the Baltic Fleet seamen since 1917 was such that it was nothing out of the way that Kronstadt crews responded more violently than any other to the stimuli of anti-centralistic tendencies, to the dissatisfaction not only of the peasants, but of the urban proletariat as well, with war communism. The seamen did not have to change for that. The characteristic of the Russian bluejacket, already mentioned above "as a soul in rebellion, striving toward freedom," still held true. He could not, a week after the revolution of November, nor in 1921, reconcile himself to a "safe haven," he was still in search of action—a libertarian *par excellence*.

Another important problem is that of the Communist party membership at Kronstadt. Soviet commentators make a great deal of the social origins of the Kronstadt Communists.[50]

On March 1, 1921, there were 2,126 members and about 500 candidates in the Kronstadt party organizations. Of these members, 684 were attached to the regional party committee, while 1,442 came under the tutelage of the Kronstadt political department. In other words the naval and military Communists outnumbered the civilian party element by more than two to one. According to the official data, about 85 per cent of the Kronstadt Communists were of working class or peasant origin.[51] These statistics suggest that the vast majority of these Communists came from the lower classes of Russian society—from the viewpoint of the old régime.

G. D. Kondakov made an attempt to disprove that evidence, by analyzing the Kronstadt party membership in the light of entries in their party tickets under the heading: "What special qualifications do you possess?" This analysis, according to Kondakov, had established that the majority had stated under that heading: "clerking," "office-work" or "was a scribe." Such qualifications came up with particular frequency in the party tickets of the naval and military Communists. Kondakov did not give in his paper any figures as to the percentage of persons with those and analogous qualifications among the Kronstadt Communists. However, he drew the conclusion, based on his analysis, that among these Communists, petty bourgeois elements had predominated, such as the semi-intellectuals, like clerical workers, who were "purely petty bourgeois in their ideology."[52]

In the upper strata of the Kronstadt communist circles, according to Kondakov, the worker element was almost entirely absent. Of the nine members of the local party committee, six were intellectuals and one a worker. The total was made up by "two others" (who these "others" were, is not clear).[53]

The same volume contains an interesting paragraph on the party membership at Kronstadt in August 1920. It is stated that at the time there were 4,435 members of the party there. In other words, half a year before the rebellion there were twice as many members as in March 1921. Of these, 25 to 27 per cent had voluntarily resigned from the party during the party re-registration of September 1920. According to the same source, immediately after the re-registration (apparently another word for the more up-to-date one of "purge"), the Kronstadt communist organization comprised 635 civilian members and 1,500 naval and military members, as well as about 500 candidates. It is also mentioned that of these, about 50 per cent were peasants, about 40 per cent were workers, and only about 10 per cent intellectuals and white-collar workers. There were very few Communists of long-standing party affiliation among them. Only three of the civilian Communists had joined the party before 1917, against 61 who had joined prior to November 1917.[54]

Of the twelve members of the Kronstadt party committee at the time, only two were assigned exclusively to party work. Even these two were given additional "loads." One of them was elected to the post of Vice-President of the Kronstadt Soviet, while the other occupied the position of editor of the Kronstadt *Izvestia*.[55]

During the rebellion, 497 members (about one-quarter of the total membership) had voluntarily resigned their memberships, 211 were excluded from the party after the crushing of the rebellion, while 137 did not report for re-registration, which had followed it. (Apparently they regarded themselves as having no chance to pass the re-registration test.)[56]

It is reported that when attacks were made at party general meetings or among the populace, on the privileges enjoyed by the commissars, the political police constituted themselves champions of the vilifiers of the commissars, and came to regard as its principal duty, spying on the activities of the local leading Communists.[57]

Apparently there were some attempts made among the rank and file of the Kronstadt Communists to take cognizance of the critical situation created by the strikes in Petrograd and the mood of the masses. Such attempts were cut short by the commissar. According to Kondakov, that dignitary shouted: "I will not permit the spread of the revival of the committee habit," hinting at the anarchistic army committees of 1917. The leaders themselves, it seems, did not take any steps to consolidate the position of the government forces in the face of the approaching storm.[58]

A letter published in the *Izvestia* of the committee of the Kronstadt rebels by a communist seaman, Rozhkali, repeated the motive of antagonism between the rank and file Communists and the "bureaucracy"—the leaders. "We have marched into a terrible bog. We were led into this bog by a small group of communist bureaucrats, who, under the mask of Communists had built themselves warm nests in the Republic. . . . Is it possible that our brethren's blood would be shed for the interest of these Communist-bureaucrats. . . . True Communists must not press their ideas by force, but should go hand in hand with the entire toiling mass."[59]

The resolution of the Communists of the fort *Rif*, in declaring their allegiance to the revolutionary committee of the rebels, ran thus: "During these entire three years many egotists and careerists have joined our party; as a result of this, bureaucracy developed."[60]

Another resolution, that of the Communists of the battleship *Sevastopol*, also contained a reference to "egotists and careerists," responsible for the bureaucratization of the country and the alienation of the workers and peasants from the communist cause.[61]

Similar feelings were voiced in the resolution of Communists in the anti-aircraft defenses of Kronstadt, of the collective of the Communists of the Signal Service of the fortress, as well as in that of the Communists employed at the local office of the Workers' and Peasants' Inspection.[62]

One of the most interesting letters to the editor of the *Izvestia* of the rebel committee was signed by an ex-bluejacket of the Russo-Japanese war era, who rose from the ranks of the workers in the naval arsenal to become the head of the town's municipal financial department: "In the provinces henchmen of commissars and other responsible workers were doing ugly deeds. From all directions complaints poured in against individual party members. . . . I have noticed all the injustice of the leaders of the party infected by bureaucracy and torn apart from the masses."[63]

This brief examination of the conditions of the Kronstadt party organization clearly indicates that there is no reason to regard the social composition of the party membership as peculiarly "petit bourgeois," or radically different from the composition of the average party organization of the period. For that matter, the percentage of working class Communists after the September 1920 re-registration, standing at 40 per cent, compares favorably in that respect with some of the large industrial centers. As mentioned above, Sosnovskii stated at the Tenth Congress, that at Ekaterinenburg, in the heart of the industrial Ural region, two-thirds of the party membership were peasants. At Kronstadt the peasants, after the re-registration of September 1920, constituted only about 50 per cent. The relative number of intellectuals and white-collar workers was also not particularly high at Kronstadt. According to Krestinskii's statement in defense of the party leadership, when he had no interest in exaggerating the percentage of intellectuals in the party ranks, a figure of 18 to 19 per cent was given as prevalent in some of the provinces. In other words, Kronstadt intellectuals and office workers, estimated at 10 per cent at the time of re-registration of September 1920, were relatively less numerous than was the case at least in some of the provinces, where, of course, in urban organizations, the percentage of such persons was higher than for the whole province.

The first party census was made in 1922. Statistics relating to the party as a whole for the earlier years are, therefore, approximations at best. The Statistical Department of the Central Committee of the party established certain data for the year antedating the 1922 census on the strength of information obtained during that census on the party status of the members covered by the census, making reasonable allowances for death and other losses in the membership for the different age and sex groups. According to such approximations the party contained, in 1921, 41 per cent of workers, 28.7 per cent of peasants, and 30.8 per cent of white collar employees and "others." Those that had joined the party during 1921 were divided as follows: workers, 29.7 per cent, peasants 41 per cent, white collar employees and "others" 29.3 per cent. Thus percentage of workers in the Kronstadt party ranks was, on this basis, close to the average for the entire party, and there does not seem anything abnormal in the relative number of workers in its ranks. It was, in fact, considerably higher than the average given for the party accretion for the year 1921. The white collar members were three times less than the average for the entire party, and stood approximately in the same relation to the total of 1921 accretions. The only deviation in a direction regarded by the communist leaders (particularly the oppositionists of the time) as undesirable, was in the percentage of the peasants. It is considerably higher than for the party as a whole and even larger than the unusually high percentage of peasants among the members who had joined the party in 1921. If this large percentage of peasants is taken as the cause for the remarkably rapid demoralization of the Kronstadt party organization, then the oppositionists, who had pointed out the danger of filling the party with peasants, were right in their apprehensions. That the relative strength of the white collar element had anything to do with the behavior of the Kronstadt party collectives seems to be disproved by the comparison with the official party statistics, such as they are. There is, however, another point in evidence—that of the small percentage of old party members among the communist civilian element at Kronstadt. For the party as a whole, for January 1922, there were estimated to be 9.1 per cent of members who had joined before 1917, and 16.5 per cent who had joined prior to 1918. Whether many old party members had resigned or were expelled during the September 1920 re-registration it was impossible to establish.[64]

Kondakov's analysis along the lines of the "special qualification" has little value, as it does not offer any definite figures and thus does not provide any basis of comparison with the personnel of the party as a whole or with the urban organizations elsewhere.

Another allegation of Lenin and his fellow communist leaders— that about the rôle of the White Guard generals in the Kronstadt movement, also needs looking into.

The order dated March 2, 1921, signed by Lenin and Trotsky jointly, called the Kronstadt movement "the rebellion of the former General Kozlovskii," and began with an assertion that it was the handiwork of the French counter-espionage service. The resolution adopted by the meeting on board the battleship *Petropavlovsk* was stigmatized as a "black-hundred—Socialist Revolutionary" one. The order mentioned that beginning with the morning of March 2, "the group of the former General Kozlovskii (chief of the artillery) openly appeared on the scene. Former General Kozlovskii, with three officers whose names have not as yet been ascertained, had openly assumed the rôle of rebels. . . . In this way, the meaning of the recent events is completely clear. Again on this occasion a czarist general was behind the socialist revolutionaries."[65]

Zinoviev's proclamation even more definitely stressed the fact that the leaders of the Kronstadt rebellion were mere puppets in a show directed by the "czarist General Kozlovskii, Captain Burkser, Kostromitinov, Shirmanovskii and other well known White Guards. . . . You are being misled. You are told that you are struggling for 'democracy.' . . . Two days have not gone by—yet you can see that in reality you are fighting not for democracy, but for czarist generals."[66]

The mass meeting held on March 1, 1921, in the Square of the Revolution, was attended by about ten thousand people—sixteen thousand according to rebel statements. Among those who addressed the meeting there were no czarist generals or officers. At least there are no records of such addresses. The addresses were followed by a speech by the seaman Petrichenko, a leader of the bluejackets of the battleship *Petropavlovsk*, who suggested that the meeting adopt as its own the resolution passed by the crew of that ship.[67] The adoption of that resolution, which had a definitely anti-communist trend, and the action taken the next day at the meeting of delegates, marked the beginning of the rebellion.

The delegates who attended the meeting on March 2 were elected in accordance with an official notice, which had appeared in the *Izvestia*, published at Kronstadt by the Soviet Government. A number of these delegates were Communists. The latter, however, did not constitute the majority of the delegates. The proceedings were opened by Petrichenko. The presiding body was elected by open vote, as was customary at the time at Soviet meetings. The first speakers were the President of the Executive Committee of the Kronstadt Soviet, the Communist Vasiliev and the Commissar of the Fleet, Kuzmin. According to the testimony of one of the members of that presiding body, "the meeting consisted exclusively of seamen, Red Army soldiers, workers and employees of Soviet institutions. There were no generals, colonels or any other officers among them. The 'Soviet' character of the meeting was well pronounced."[68]

The Commandant of the fortress of Kronstadt, a Communist, left Kronstadt and his post upon the formation of the Provisional Revolutionary Committee, to which were elected in a body the presiding officers of the delegates' meeting of March 2. According to regulations, his duties devolved upon the next in line of succession in the military hierarchy, the chief of artillery of the fortress, who happened to be the ex-czarist general, serving in the Red Army, Kozlovskii. The latter declined to assume the duties of Commandant under the pretext that the old rule was not applicable under the circumstances, and the Committee appointed to the post of Commandant the ex-officer Solovianov. Kozlovskii was left to look after the technical end of artillery. According to Kozlovskii, his name was used by the Communists in their proclamations because he happened to be the only ex-czarist general at Kronstadt. The names of the other three officers linked with him were those of Burkser, Kostromitinov and Shirmanovskii, who were all serving under him in the artillery department of the fortress. One of the two latter, according to Kozlovskii, occupied the humble position of a draftsman.[69]

Among the fifteen members of the Provisional Revolutionary Committee there was not one ex-czarist officer. It consisted of six seamen, three workers, one telephone operator, a school principal, two white-collar employees, one assistant physician and one merchant marine mate. There were, in this manner, nine seamen and workers out of the total fifteen members. This, from the Soviet viewpoint, was more desirable than the composition of the Kronstadt Party Committee, which, as already shown, included only one worker and six intellectuals.[70]

Military specialists took part in the discussion of problems of defense of Kronstadt on board the *Petropavlovsk* on March 3. Several other meetings were held by the Provisional Revolutionary Committee with the participation of ex-officers, who attended them in their capacity of military specialists. However, the advice tendered by these ex-officers, to take the offensive immediately, and thus exploit the confusion among the Communists, was turned down by the Committee. According to the assertion of the authors of the *Truth about Kronstadt*, published in Prague by the participants after the rebellion, the movement originated in the deep conviction of the seamen that all Russia would take up the fight and that Petrograd would join the revolt forthwith. The authors of the book argue that the rebellion was not a result of a deliberately conceived plan, as in that case the moment for it would have been delayed until the breaking up of the ice in the Gulf of Finland, when Kronstadt would have become impregnable to land forces.[71] Soviet sources also confirm the fact that the suggestion of the officers to enlarge the base of the rebellion by undertaking military operations on the mainland was rejected by the Committee.[72]

The author was in Petrograd a few days before the outbreak of the rebellion and had a long talk with a naval officer, Geizig, who served as chief gunnery officer on board one of the battleships at Kronstadt. This officer, a former shipmate and a close personal friend of the author, had every reason to be frank with him. Not a word was said during the course of the conversation about an impending rebellion.

The Whites as well as the Russian socialist organizations abroad were apparently taken unawares, as they were unable to send any force to help Kronstadt, although at the time they had at their disposal considerable financial means and could easily have mustered on short notice a fairly large number of fighting men. It is true that Captain Wilken, connected with one of the White Russian organizations, came to Kronstadt on skis from Finland during the rebellion, but according to all accounts, including his own, he acted merely as an observer and did not take part in the defense of the fortress. Naval officers connected with the various offices of the central organs of the navy at Moscow, who were frequently visiting Kronstadt and seeing their friends serving there afloat and ashore, had no inkling whatsoever of the possibility of the development of any serious conflict. Army officers, like Kozlovskii, after all, were not likely to obtain much influence with the bluejackets of the battleships, who were extremely clannish, even to the extent of refusing to accept the authority of commissars who had not come up from shellback ranks.

It would seem that the rôle of the sole general present at Kronstadt, Kozlovskii, as well as of the other ex-czarist officers, was not more important than that of military specialists, technical advisers, whose counsels, at that, were not really followed by the Committee. In the attacking government forces, ex-czarist officers, very likely, played a more important rôle—such, for instance, as that of Tukhachevskii. It is worth noting, that a number of ex-czarist officers at Kronstadt refused to take part in the rebellion, even in the capacity of military advisers, and declared themselves neutral. Such was the case of Captain Saltanov of the navy. This neutrality did not save those of them who remained at Kronstadt after the crushing of the movement. Some of them fell victims to the heavy hand of Soviet justice and were executed.

All this tends to confirm the fact that the officers were not the prime movers of the rebellion, and that the helm of the movement was not in their hands. It was important, politically, for Lenin and his friends, to maintain among the Soviet population the idea that the Kronstadt movement had the earmarks of the White Guard movements of the past. This fiction was maintained even in the short published list of those executed after the fall of Kronstadt. Of the large number of those done away with, only thirteen names were included on that list, which was headed by five names of ex-officers of the *Sevastopol*, all of whom were hereditary noblemen. The rest of the list included one ex-priest and seven peasants.[73]

Chamberlin considers that the mere publication of the program of the Kronstadt insurgents is a sufficient refutation of the "absurd propagandist falsehoods which were immediately put into circulation by the Moscow radio station."[74]

The political platform of the rebellion has the earmarks of a libertarian leftist movement. In more than one way it is a return to the grass roots of the Russian revolution.

The resolution adapted by the crew of the battleship *Petropavlovsk*, which was passed by the mass meeting of March 1 (officially the meeting of the crews of the First and Second Brigades of Battle-ships) reflected the trends of oppositional opinion both within the Communist party and in the country at large. Paragraph 3 advanced the thesis of freedom of the trade unions from governmental control; paragraph 7 called for the abolition of the political departments in the armed forces—they were to be replaced by locally elected Cultural Enlightenment Commissions.[75] These themes were, of course, the subject of discussion at Communist party congresses and there found a ready support on the part of some of the delegates.

The reelection of the Soviets was placed at the head of the program. Secret ballots were insisted upon, as well as the freedom of pre-electional agitation. This freedom was to be restricted to workers and peasants only. Freedom of speech and the press "for workers and peasants, Anarchist and Left Socialist parties," was also demanded. The freedom of meetings and peasant associations was incorporated into the platform. The liberation of political prisoners belonging to socialist parties, also of "all workers, peasants, Red Army soldiers and seamen held in prison in connection with working class and peasant movements."[76]

In the field of economic reconstruction it was advocated that all "barrier detachments"—units placed on railroads and other ways of communication to prevent traffic in foodstuffs by individuals for gainful purposes—should be abolished. The rations were to be equalized for all, except workers engaged in occupations harmful to health. The principal part of the economic program called for the removal of state control over the exploitation of land by the peasants. These were to have full freedom to decide upon the methods of using the soil and were free to own cattle. Hired labor, however, was not to be permitted. Cottage industries, also without the use of hired labor, were to be permitted to function free of state control.[77]

To get rid of the threat of communist domination, communist armed detachments in the armed forces as well as in the factories were to be abolished. Assignments of Communists for special duty service at factories were to be done away with.[78]

This resolution was adopted by the mass meeting, according to the minutes, "unanimously, with two abstaining from voting." The President of the Kronstadt Soviet Executive Committee, Vasiliev, and M. I. Kalinin, voted against it, according to the report of the Commissar of the Fleet, N. Kuzmin.[79] At the delegates' meeting on March 2, the same resolution was passed by an "overwhelming majority."

Articles in the *Izvestia* of the insurgents' committees developed this program. In the March 8 issue, there appeared an editorial headed "What are we fighting for?" The main burden of it is the protest against the dictatorship of the Communist party. "Upon achieving the October Revolution, the working class was hoping to obtain its liberation. In the result an even further enslavement of human personality obtained. . . . The power of the police-gendarmerie monarchism passed into the hands of the usurper-Communists, who brought the toilers, instead of freedom, an ever-present fear of being dragged into the torture-chambers of the Cheka, which exceeds by many times in its horrors the Gendarmerie Administration of the czarist régime. . . . The glorious escutcheon of the workers' state— the sickle and hammer—the communist authorities have in fact replaced by the bayonet and the prison bars, for the preservation of the calm, unruffled life of the new bureaucracy of the communist commissars and civil servants . . . but the most abominable and criminal of all is the moral bondage created by the Communists: they have laid their hand on the internal world of the toilers, forcing them to think only in accordance with their dictates. . . . The workers were made serfs of the machine tools by means of state-controlled trade-unions, making work not a joy, but a new thraldom. To the protest of the peasants, reflected in elemental uprisings of workers, forced to strike by the very conditions of life, they reply by mass shootings and a blood-thirstiness which has nothing to borrow from the czarist generals."[80]

In a letter "to the comrades, workers and peasants," published in the rebel *Izvestia*, the editors state: "We do not want a return to the past. We are not the servants of the bourgeoisie, not the hirelings of the Entente. We are the defenders of the power of all toilers, but not of an unbridled tyrannical power of any one party. . . . Comrades, peasants, you, more than any one, were misled and robbed by the Bolshevik Government. Where is the land you had wrested from the squires, land you have dreamed of for hundreds of years? It was given to the communal farms or taken for Soviet farms and you can only look on and smack your lips. From you was taken all that could be carried away. . . . With hungry bellies and gagged mouths, barefoot and naked, you are forced to do the will of the new nobility."[81]

In the last issue of *Izvestia* there was published the editorial *Socialism in Quotes* which lashed out at the communist dictatorship. "The power they stole, the Communist replaced by commissar overseership and arbitrariness over the body and soul of the citizens of Soviet Russia. Against reason and contrary to the will of the toilers, there began a persistent upbuilding of bureaucratic socialism with its slaves, instead of the free czardom of labor. . . . From a slave of the capitalist, the worker has become the slave of the state-owned enterprises. . . . Each expression of free thought, every just criticism of the actions of the criminal rulers has become a crime, punished by imprisonment and often even by the firing squad. . . . We received a bureaucratic socialism with Soviets consisting of bureaucrats, obediently voting according to the orders of the committee of the party and the infallible commissars. . . . The slogan "who does not work shall not eat" was turned inside out . . . everything for the commissars! For the workers, the peasants, and the toiling intellectuals, there remains only endless burdensome labor under prison conditions." The leaders of the movement conceived their task as that of laying the foundation for a new phase of the revolution. "Here in Kronstadt we have laid down the first stone of the third revolution, have knocked off the last fetters of the toiling masses and have opened up a new, wide road of socialist creation. . . . This new phase will set in motion the toiling masses of the east and west, will give an example of new socialist building."[82]

It is a far cry from these slogans, from these aspirations of the Kronstadt mutineers, to the plans of the White Guards for the restoration of the old régime. It was a thoroughgoing libertarian interpretation of the ideals of the Russian revolution and, as Chamberlin says, it expressed pretty faithfully the more or less conscious desires of the majority of the Russian working-class and peasant masses. Part of the economic program of the insurgents, their demands for the greater economic freedom of the peasant, and for the abolition of the more oppressive features of war communism was adopted by the Tenth Party Congress, and became embodied in the New Economic Policy.[83]

The spokesman of the insurgents wrote after the suppression of the rebellion: "The Kronstadt rebellion has forced the Communists to give up their economic policy, i.e. the very communism for the sake of which—allegedly—the October revolution was achieved, seas of blood were shed, and Russia was destroyed."[84]

This, of course, is only partially true. There were trends within the directing groups of the Communist party toward the discarding of war communism. Lenin himself, as already referred to, was searching for a new way out of the economic and political impasse. Kronstadt accelerated the change and strengthened the hand of those of the leaders of the party who were opposed to the continuation of the war policy in peacetime. It is also possible that Kronstadt sounded the death knell of Trotsky's ambitions to become the head of the Communist party and the ruler of Russia. His stand for the continuation of war communism and the subsequent bloody retribution handed down to those of the insurgents who fell into the hands of the government forces left a deep impression in the minds of many Communists, marking him as a man lacking in practical political judgment.*

That the Kronstadt movement was not an isolated intrigue fostered by foreign agents and White organizations is abundantly clear, not only from the survey of their program, but also from the manner in which it affected the Soviet policy. The examination of the course of events at Petrograd antedating the meeting of March 1, 1921, will provide evidence of the close connection it had with the trends and moods of the working class of the large industrial centers of Russia.

Apart from the speeches at the Tenth Party Congress emphasizing the open hostility of large groups of workers to the Soviet régime, and the figures quoted by Shliapnikov regarding the lack of inclination on the part of the metal workers of Moscow and Petrograd to join the Communist party, ample data are available to show that at the end of February 1921 the Petrograd workers were at the end of their patience and were ready to resort to overt action against the government.

* Trotsky himself had later denied that he had any share in the executions of the Kronstadt rebels.

E. Wollenberg in his *The Red Army* wrote that at the time the industrial proletariat vacillated during the Kronstadt movement, and that its sympathies inclined to the camp of the insurgents "whom it supported openly by means of mass strikes in Petrograd and other large towns. . . . The bolshevists now found themselves isolated for the first time since their victory in October 1917." He also stresses the fact that the workers had exercised a strong influence on the rebels, remarking that a large number of the Kronstadt Communists and practically the entire population of the island of Kotlin, consisting mainly of fishermen and metal workers, took part in the rising. An eye-witness, A. Baranov, in his reminiscences about the Kronstadt rebellion, described how a train with a detachment sent from Petrograd to reinforce the government forces attacking Kronstadt, was delayed on its way to Oranienbaum. "We had all reasons to believe that there was evil intent" behind the constant halts of the train en route and its slow pace. One could reasonably conclude that the railroad workers were not too anxious to see the loyal forces strengthened for the impending attack against the rebels' stronghold.[85]

An official memorandum on the behavior of the workers and the spread of the strike movement at Petrograd between the dates of February 25 and March 5, 1921, preserved in the Leningrad archives, contains very valuable information on the anti-bolshevik mood of the proletariat of the erstwhile citadel of communism.

In the Petrograd sector, the workers of the Artillery Depot assembled in groups and discussed the events. Some were overheard shouting, "The commune has come to the end of its rope." In the Vasileostrovskii sector the workers of the Trubochnyi Factory, who went out on strike on February 23, staged on the next day an anti-Soviet demonstration, and were assisted in this by some of the other enterprises located in that sector. On February 25, the following works were on strike: Baltiiskii, Trubochnyi, the Laferm cigarette factory, Pechatkin's, Brusnitsyn's and the Kabelnyi Factory, as well as the St. Petersburg Mechanical Works and Rosenkrantz'. The memorandum states: "On the following day the strike either attenuated or grew worse in the enterprises of the sector. There were instances when, for example, the workers of the Baltiiskii plant, on the morning of February 28, showed up for work, but after calling for the immediate convocation of the Assembly [apparently the Constituent Assembly] and the liberation of those arrested, went home, with the exception of four hundred men. On March 1, small groups of Baltiiskii's workers (five or six men) even attempted to persuade workers at other enterprises to down tools."[86]

The strike lasted in that sector until March 3, although part of the workers of one or two factories began to work on February 28, while the Baltiiskii plant remained on strike until March 7.

In the second city sector the strike movement affected the Old Admiralty and the New Admiralty shipbuilding yards. Between March 1 and 4, workers of the New Admiralty came to the yards, but did not actually do any work. The Old Admiralty men were on strike on February 27, and partially resumed work on March 1. They returned fully to work on March 2.[87]

In the Viborg sector, the Arsenal works were the first to go on strike, on February 25, having elected on the same day a commission to find out what was going on at the other industrial enterprises. On the same day a meeting of the women workers of the Nitochnaia Factory adopted a resolution advocating the freedom of trade. On March 1, the workers of the Rosenkrantz, the Parviainen, the Ognesklad and the Petronitka went out on strike. By March 2 all enterprises of the sector had resumed work.[88]

In the Obukhov sector, where the large armament factory of the same name was located, on February 26, only maintenance men went to work at the Obukhov Works. On February 28, about two thousand workers broke into the premises and demanded that a general meeting be called. On March 1, only 700 men came to work, while about one thousand stood outside the gates of the works.[89]

In the Moscow sector, at the Skorokhod shoe factory, men refused to work on February 28. At the Rechkin factory a group of about 200 workers (of a total of 700) assembled and demanded the release of those arrested. The Pobieda factory did not work the whole day, and the same was true of the Arthur Koppel works.[90]

In the Narva-Peterhof sector, the workers of the Putilov shipbuilding yard struck and attempted to persuade men of the other departments of that huge enterprise to join them. However, the latter refused. In the Smolny sector the Nevskaia Nitochnaia and the Bumagopriadilnaia factory struck on February 26.[91]

The report of an instructor of the 79th Rifle Brigade, dated March 23, 1921, commented on the close affiliation between the seamen and the civilian population of Kronstadt, and that the latter were influencing the frame of mind of the garrison and particularly of the young seamen.[92]

The mood of the inhabitants of Petrograd is described by N. A.

Stepanov. During the march to Smolnyi of the detachment of the Red military cadets to which he belonged, they were hailed with shouts: "Trotsky's cadets are going to shoot the working class!" According to Stepanov, single Red cadets did not dare show themselves in the streets of Petrograd at the time. But even these shock troops of the revolution, the Red cadets, were not entirely immune from the virus of disaffection. Stepanov mentions that a conspiracy was discovered among the Peterhof Command School cadets, and that several of them were apprehended by the political police and taken under escort to Petrograd.[93]

The same Stepanov narrates that on March 16, on the eve of the decisive attack on Kronstadt, the regiments of the 27th Rifle Division stationed at Oranienbaum had rebelled, expelled from their ranks all their commanders, and adopted the slogan: "Let us go to Petrograd and beat up the Jews!" This moment, according to Stepanov, was quite alarming for the Government forces at Oranienbaum. However, the rebellion was quickly suppressed by specially picked detachments, and these mutinous regiments even took part in the final attack on Kronstadt.[94]

V. Gromov reports instances of mass desertions to the enemy of the men of the regiments of the 187th Brigade "under the influence of the latter's demagogical agitation," during the first large-scale attack of March 8. Even Red cadets he commanded (these were partly from the Peterhof and partly from the Moscow Command Schools) were among those who deserted to the enemy after the failure of the attack.[95]

M. Kuzmin makes mention of the election of a revolutionary committee by the crews of the icebreakers and salvage vessels at Petrograd and that "in other units such attempts were prevented." It is also characteristic that the proclamation of the Provisional Bureau of the RKP (i.e. the organization of the Communists who had sided with the insurgents) was transmitted to Petrograd over the telephone by the Signal Service of the navy and distributed to all naval units at Petrograd.[96]

The connection between the Petrograd strikes and the movement among the industrial workers of that city on the one side, and the Kronstadt movement on the other, is well established by these data culled from Soviet sources. The rebels themselves claim that on February 25, a part of the Petrograd garrison informed the authorities that it would not act against the workers and was disarmed; also that on February 24, there was a brush between a crowd of workers some two thousand strong and a detachment of Red cadets; that workers' meetings were dispersed by armed force. Chamberlin says: "The Petrograd strikes . . . represented the spark that set off the powder magazine in Kronstadt." That this explosion did not touch off, in its turn, the smouldering mood of rebellion at Petrograd, is no doubt partly the result of the inertia of the Kronstadt committee who did not agree to the plans for an offensive on the mainland laid before them by their military advisers. There is a curious similarity between the passive resistance of the Kronstadt rebels and the armed revolt in 1825 known as the Decembrist rebellion. In both instances lack of resolute leadership lost the day.

In analyzing the conflict which resulted in the armed uprising at Kronstadt, one cannot fail to notice that the initiative came from the bluejackets and their leaders. The local land forces of the Kronstadt garrison merely fell in and joined the seamen. The 160th Rifle Regiment located at Kronstadt, consisting of about twenty-five hundred Ukrainian lads, recruited in the regions particularly friendly to the Makhno guerillas, had less than 2 per cent of Communists in its ranks. There were altogether only forty Communists and candidates among its personnel.[97] The regiments stationed at Oranienbaum, which later took part in the suppression of the rebellion, did not seem to be much different from it. The soldiers were also disaffected and had no love for the Communists and the commissars. They were, at the same time, unable to formulate their grievances clearly and delineate the issues at stake, either to themselves or for the benefit of others. They did not have it in them to formulate a plan of action. All that was done of importance at Kronstadt was the work of the bluejackets, who were the backbone of the movement.

The crews of the men-of-war at Kronstadt were much less affected by the permeation of their ranks by outside Communists than was the case of the Red Army land units. There were no Red commanders on board ships to leaven the mass of the men with their Soviet enthusiasm and discipline acquired at the Command Schools, as was the case in the army. The ships were still commanded and officered by former Imperial naval officers, warrant officers of the old navy and a few men promoted from the ranks. These officers were passively loyal to the Soviet régime and had little influence politically over their men, who had been accustomed, since 1917, to disregard completely the political views of their officers. These officers were well trained technicians, living apart from the mass of the men, and were suspected by the latter of counter-revolutionary tendencies. With very few exceptions they lived completely aloof from the political trends, ambitions and aspirations of the men serving nominally under their command. The tradition of elected committees of 1917 did not die out in the navy, as it did in the army, and the trends of 1917 were still fairly vigorous in this respect in the Baltic Fleet. Commissars were appointed largely from the ranks of the seamen, did not enjoy very much authority, and shared many of the latter's views and prejudices.

A large number of old ex-seamen, employed in the industrial enterprises of Kronstadt, had ample opportunity to discourse on the "good old times" of 1917 with the younger element among the seamen, who also easily fell under the spell of the swashbuckling, devil-may-care, older men they served with on board ships.

Since 1917 the Baltic seamen regarded the revolution as their particular ward and responsibility. Had they not carried the day both at Petrograd against Kerensky's forces and at Pulkovo, barring the road to Krasnov's Cossacks? They had taken matters into their own hands against the czarist Government in March and against the Provisional Government in November 1917. Why not continue the tradition and blaze the trail for a third, libertarian, revolution in 1921?

The level of intelligence of the seamen, particularly among the men who had served as qualified technicians in the old navy, was much higher than that in the ranks of the infantry regiments of the Red Army. They were better educated, more widely read, accustomed to act on their own initiative, and, what is particularly important, had learned the value of independence and freedom. A good many of them had had ample experience in organizational and political work since 1917. A number had long-standing associations with Anarchists and the Socialist Revolutionaries of the Left.

The lack of effective political control of the seamen through commissars' or Communist commanders of political experience and education and the type of officers that were in command, made the Baltic Fleet a relic of the conditions of 1917. Those particularly zealous for the communist cause, or endowed with great personal ambition, had left the ships since then and were either serving in the Red Army or were employed in Soviet institutions elsewhere.

The survival of the libertarian pattern of 1917 in a naval station fairly well insulated from non-naval communist influences made it possible for the bluejackets not only to formulate, but to carry out a plan of action, no doubt under a certain amount of influence of the Anarchists, and those who had left the party in such large numbers during the September 1920 re-registration.

The large percentage of industrial workers among the naval crews made for a close relationship between the proletarians of Petrograd and Kronstadt. The seamen had numerous friends among the workers of the Baltiiskii, Putilov, Admiralty and other shipyards of Petrograd, as well as the workers of the large armament plants, such as Obukhov. There was a constant interchange of information and influence between the industrial workingmen and the men on board the gray-hulled ships at Kronstadt. This was also the case during the czarist régime when this intercourse helped to revolutionize the seamen. In the same way, these influences continued to hold sway in 1921, this time to the disadvantage of the Soviet Government.

The ferocious mood in which the communist leaders began to square their accounts with the mutineers after the capture of Kronstadt by the loyal troops, left no doubt of their intention to destroy, root and branch, the vestiges of the old libertarian tradition of the Russian Navy.

The rebels had refrained from taking any communist lives. The Soviet Government, on the other hand, as early as March 3, already had executed forty-five seamen at Oranienbaum—a quite heavy proportion of the total personnel of the men at the Naval Aviation Detachment. These men had voted for the Kronstadt resolution, but did not take arms against the government. This mass execution was merely a prelude to those that took place after the defeat of the mutineers. These "preliminary" executions exceed the total of 36 seamen who had paid with their lives for the two large rebellions of the 1905 revolution—at Kronstadt and Sveaborg—and left out of the running the small total of three bluejackets executed at Vladivostok after the important uprising of 1906.[98]

A German commentator makes reference to the execution of each fifth man of a regiment that began to waver and refused to move against the insurgents. He also says that, immediately after the capture of Kronstadt by the government forces, five to six hundred wounded prisoners taken, with arms in hand, in the forts and houses of Kronstadt, were summarily shot. That this information is not improbable, seems to be confirmed by the testimony of a participant in the attack on Kronstadt, I. Iustchuk, who describes how upon the capture of Fort No. 6, at the entrance to one of the casemates, he found a heap of bodies of insurgent seamen and was informed that these men were killed, after they had surrendered, by a comrade who "was having his fun" and who was with difficulty restrained by the Red cadets from wiping out the rest of the prisoners.[99]

The Kronstadt rebellion took place not only at a time of acute dissatisfaction both among the peasants and the industrial workers with the Soviet Government's policies, but also at a period when the Communist party itself was splitting into several factions openly campaigning against each other. The two great Civil War leaders—Lenin and Trotsky—were in sharp opposition to each other on the most important issue of the day. The combination of all these factors produced, in the peculiar atmosphere on the gun-decks of the battleships, the electric discharge which set off the mutiny.

The Kronstadt rebellion not only had inaugurated the New Economic Policy. It also brought to an end the old navy, which had outlived the old army by more than three years. On the other hand, the New Model army not only established, in the course of the Civil War, its peculiar hierarchical structure, but began to formulate its own military doctrine, claiming for it not only originality, but also faithfulness to Marxian concepts of society. A brief summary of the clash of views regarding this doctrine may prove useful toward a better understanding of the mentality and aspirations of the Red Army leaders.

★ VI ★

THE BIRTH OF A DOCTRINE

THE ardent discussion of what the doctrine of the Red Army should be took an important place in Soviet military life after the end of hostilities of the Civil War and the Polish campaign. This discussion translated to a different plane some of the conflicts and antagonisms of the Civil War period. The struggle between Trotsky, who found support for his ideas in the views of some of the ablest military thinkers of the old army, on the one hand, and the energetic group of self-made strategists produced by the Civil War, headed by the talented Frunze, by Voroshilov, Gusev, and Tukhachevskii, on the other, had a very considerable significance for the subsequent fate of the Red Army—perhaps even for the outcome of the struggle for power among Lenin's successors. It was one of the phases of the struggle for the control of the Red Army in the post-war period.

The young Red commanders, victorious in the field against their White enemies, thought that they had discovered the foundations of a new revolutionary doctrine of the proletariat, which relegated to the scrapheap the theories of the old army generals, based on the experience of the World War and the study of its history.

In following the discussion of doctrine, conducted in Soviet Russia with the zeal and fervor of the early ecumenical councils, one cannot help wondering whether Trotsky had realized at the time that his popularity with the communist element in the Red Army command and the more ambitious communist Red Army commanders was bound to suffer because of the stand he had taken in that debate. And these were the men whose political opinions counted with the army.

Is it possible that in this instance Trotsky was carried off his feet by his own logic and the fierce joy he had in laying low his opponents in a theoretical joust, with complete disregard for the immediate, as well as the more distant, political consequences to himself.

Very few beacons were lighted by the founding fathers of Marxism to guide the footsteps of the debaters.

Karl Marx's contribution in the field of <u>military doctrine</u> is exceedingly meager. The principal legacy he left in that field is his view that the development of forces of production and of relations of production postulates the development and the conditions of military art.[1]

Engels, on the other hand, had penned some remarkably trenchant observations on the military art.[2] He taught that the emancipation of the proletariat would create new forms of warfare. With a great deal of common sense and insight into the problem, he had warned, at the same time, that the first attempts at new methods of warfare by a proletarian state would be far from the ultimate military art of the emancipated working class.[3] In other words, he saw clearly that it would take time and experience to introduce into the bourgeois methods of warfare any drastic changes that would be of value to the proletarian state.

Military art, according to this collaborator of Marx, must be the logical development of the new social relations, as in the case of the French revolution and Napoleon. He was obviously opposed to producing the chickens of military theory from an ideological incubator. Engels firmly maintained that every new development in the art of war must be predicated on the impact of the forces of production.[4]

In short, Engels believed that the organization of the armies, their method of operation, their victory or defeat, were dependent on material economic factors, which include human material and armament; in other words, on the quantity as well as the quality of the population, and the state of technological development reached by the country.[5]

Generally speaking, this is not very different from the accepted view in at least some of the capitalist countries.

There was not, therefore, any ready-made revolutionary theory handed down by the founders of Marxism, which could be used to regulate the shaping of military doctrine for the armed forces of Russia in the early post-Civil War period. There was, of course, the traditional social-democratic program of popular militia and the promises made by Trotsky during the course of the hostilities, that the militia ideals were not abandoned forever and that the future organization of Soviet military might would be based on units coinciding with factories, villages and townships, these units to be trained outside of barracks.[6]

As early as 1919, Tarasov-Rodionov published in the military periodical, *Voennoe Delo*, his theses attacking the employment of former old army officers in command and staff positions in the Red Army, expressing the belief that their mental processes, formed under the influence of the position-warfare of the World War, made them unfit to meet the new conditions of the Civil War, with its emphasis on local initiative and bold offensive operations. Tarasov-Rodionov insisted that the relatively small forces of the Red Army, as well as of its opponents, made position war impossible and that maneuver was the keynote of the Civil War. He urged that military Communists should form their minds by reading histories of past wars which had a maneuver character. He believed that the organization of the Red Army should be adapted to suit the specific nature of Civil War campaigns, and advanced a number of practical suggestions, such as the formation of numerous cavalry with horse artillery, of mobile machine-gun detachments, of armored-car and armored-train units. "Generals and general staff officers, since they do not understand and do not recognize the class policy of the proletariat . . . cannot be of any use to the Red Army,"[7] was his conclusion.

There was, thus, a very definite claim in these theses, that a thorough understanding and adherence to Marxian principles was necessary for the successful planning and execution of the campaigns of the Red Army. In other words, the theses attempted to establish an intrinsic dependence of strategy and tactics, as well as of military administration, on Marxian theory.

Trotsky called these theses ludicrous, and dismissed them with a rhetorical shrug.[8] Some of the suggestions advanced by Tarasov-Rodionov, such as those dealing with the expansion of the cavalry forces, mobile machine-gun detachments, armored cars, etc. were, however, embodied later into the practice of the Red Army and became an important factor in helping it to defeat its enemies.

At the other extreme stood the views of the former Major General of the old army, A. Svechin, who later wrote the well-known treatise on strategy that went through several editions in Soviet Russia. In the pages of the same *Voennoe Delo*, Svechin's paper on cultural-class types of armies expressed the view that the army of the Soviet Republic could be successfully built up only on the basis of principles which, in the days of the Thirty Years' War, were made the foundation of Wallenstein's Camp. Svechin treated as pusillanimous the fear of bonapartism, of "the general on a white horse," and uncompromisingly rejected the militia type of army as an improvisation. He disparaged the military councils and the system of military expert advisers, clamoring for full powers of authority for commanders and in particular for the Commander in Chief, whom he wanted to free from the tutelage of the Revolutionary Military Council. In the midst of an acute political strife and persecution of groups differing ideologically from the communists, he raised the standard of toleration in the Soviet Army in all matters religious, political and social. Svechin's idea was thus of a national, not a class army, subordinated to the government, of course, but left free to develop what he called the specifically soldierly viewpoint, instead of being permeated with political ideas and influences. Such an army, imbued with a professional military attitude, was, of course, the very antithesis of the militia of the social-democratic program. The logical leaders for this professionalized army, by implication, were to be the old army officers willing to serve the Soviets.[9]

Trotsky, in rejecting the first set of suggestions as utopian, treated the second as reactionary. The subsequent history of the Red Army shows, however, a certain strange blend of the ideas—or at least of some of them—expressed both by Tarasov-Rodionov and Svechin during these early skirmishes in the field of doctrine. The element of professionalism appeared in it, as well as the jealous exclusion of any but the communist viewpoint. These discussions were merely preliminary skirmishes between the representatives of the antagonistic groups in the field of military theory. The principal battle of the war doctrine did not start in earnest until the end of the Civil War.

As early as 1921, a group of the leaders of the Red Army of the Ukraine, headed by Frunze and Gusev, had prepared an outline of what they believed to be the new proletarian concept of the science of warfare. The central point of their theses was the urgent advocacy of a uniform military doctrine for the Red Army. As the authors wrote at the time: "One of the basic conditions for the securing of the maximum of potency of the Red Army is to transform it into a monolithic organization, welded together from top to bottom not only by the common political ideology, but also by the unity of views on the character of the military problems facing the Republic, on the method of solving these problems, as well as on the system of combat training of troops."[10]

According to A. Bubnov, Lenin did not share the early enthusiasm for a proletarian military dogma. He is reported as saying to Frunze: "You [military Communists] are wrong here," and remarking that the approach used by Frunze and his group was a correct one if looked upon from the viewpoint of long-range perspectives, but "should you come out right now with a theory of proletarian art, you would fall into the danger of communist coxcombry."[11]

Trotsky vigorously opposed Frunze's views. He acknowledged in 1921 that it was quite natural that attempts were made to establish a military theory "filled with a class content" in view of the sharp turn taken by history in the development of the revolutionary class struggle. He objected, however, that it was too early as yet to formulate and to accept any such doctrine. "It is necessary," said he, "to exercise the greatest vigilance in order to escape falling into some mystical or metaphysical trap, even though such a pitfall were covered up by revolutionary terminology." While Trotsky was ready to admit that the Soviet Government was more inclined to theorizing than any other existing government, he asserted that: "We want a concept concrete, precise and filled with historical content."[12] The controversy over the urgency of the adoption of a military doctrine was joined by the representative of the Russian academic military thought from the angle of advocacy of freedom of military thought as the *sine qua non* for a successful maturing of modern views on warfare.

A. Svechin felt that as soon as such a dogma were officially approved military theorists differing from it would be penalized and their work would become impossible. Svechin thought that official censorship clamped down would interfere with the progress of military thought.[13]

While Trotsky made light of that fear of the heavy-handed intrusion of the strong arm of communist authority into the field of theoretical military thought, subsequent events offered ample justification for Svechin's apprehensions. Witch-hunting became later the accepted practice in debates on military and naval doctrine after the death of Lenin.[14]

Svechin expressed the view that a revolutionary epoch is an era of empiricism; that changing conditions did not permit the formulation of an adequate stable doctrine. This, of course, could not find any support with Frunze's group and went further than the position taken by Trotsky.[15]

The latter, to be sure, had expressed himself at times with a great deal of contumely with respect to the revolutionary military dogma. One of the most striking remarks made by him during the course of the discussion of that doctrine was: "That we have achieved victories was not an accident. There was a will to victory—it was founded not in a military dogma, but in the definite historic problem which gave a meaning to the entire contemporary epoch."[16] This remark has not lost its pungency even today.

In later days, Trotsky's position in that debate was vulgarized by his political opponents into a mere denial of the possibility of establishing an even relatively stable military doctrine and the advocacy of the replacement of it by a "rapid balancing up of a changing situation, of new groups and combinations" and "endless tacking" under the pressure of the daily occurrences, i.e. the replacement of a scientific approach to military problems by acquired reactions and intuition. The denial of the value of the experience of the Red Army during the Civil War for the development of the Soviet armed forces was also held against him, as well as his alleged identification of the political aspect of war with the strategical one.[17]

It has been freely admitted by Trotsky's opponents that the discussion of the military doctrine was the reflection of the "dissatisfaction of the best part of the military workers with the guidance of Trotsky" in the field of military reconstruction during the period of transition from war to peaceful conditions.[18]

What Trotsky was accused of—the denial of the possibility of forming a stable military doctrine—fits A. Svechin's views much better than those expressed by the People's Commissar for War.

In his *Strategy* Svechin maintained that it was very difficult to foresee the circumstances of the next war that the Soviet Union would have to fight and that, therefore, one should deal with the greatest circumspection in matters tending to narrow down the content of military theory. "For each war," wrote Svechin, "it is necessary to develop a special line of strategic behavior, each war represents a particular case, which calls for the establishment of its own peculiar logic, instead of applying the same pattern, albeit a red one. . . . In the broad framework of the general theory of contemporary warfare, dialectics permit a clearer characterization of the line of strategic conduct which should be chosen in a given instance than could be achieved even in a theory specially formed to cover that specific instance."[19]

Trotsky's viewpoint differed considerably from these thoughts of an ex-general of the old army. He considered that the Marxist theory was sufficient as a basis for the theoretical considerations of military problems, and that, therefore, there was no call to amplify it by a special theory concerned with military problems only. "And to invent something better than the *tachanka** one had to take lessons from the bourgeoisie."[20]

Trotsky's conception was, then, that the Marxian theory provided the means for general orientation in problems of war, and that a thorough study and the digestion of the military thought of the bourgeoisie should precede any attempt at formulation of a proletarian military dogma. In other words, he was opposed to any attempts at improvisation in the field of military theory by persons not familiar with the contemporary developments in the field of military thought

---

* A light horse-drawn carriage of the Ukraine peasantry, used in the Civil War for mounting machine guns that were fired from this moving platform during attack.

abroad, and those inherited from the old régime. "One should learn the ABC," he went on mercilessly, "if military doctrine goes to the point of saying : 'We shall obliterate you under a rain of Red caps'— we shall have no use whatever for it. We must throw out coxcombry and revolutionary superficiality. When strategy is developed from the viewpoint of young revolutionaries, the result is chaos."[21]

All the low esteem of an old revolutionary exile for young party members, the disdain of an intellectual for half-trained minds daring to oppose him, comes to the surface in these sentences.

In explaining his own approach to the problem of the creation of the Red Army, Trotsky stated that his point of departure was not a military doctrine understood as the sum total of dogmatic proposi- tions, but the Marxian analysis "of the requirements of self-defense of the working class, which had taken power into its own hands," had to arm itself, to disarm the bourgeoisie, to defend its power from the encroachments of its enemies. He pointed out the concrete problem that confronted the Soviet leaders—that of inducing the peasantry to follow the working class in the struggle against the landlords, as well as the forestalling of the efforts of the "kulak democracy" to arm the peasantry against the proletarian state, and last, but not least, the forming of a reliable body of commanders for the Red Army. "We have created the army from that historical material which was on hand. The whole work was unified by the viewpoint of the workers' state, struggling for its preservation, for its consolidation and devel- opment." Trotsky then threw out one of his brilliant epigrams in calling doctrine a word "tainted with metaphysics," and saying that it was possible to assert that by the very fact of the creation of the Red Army, the armed force on a new class foundation, was by the same token the establishing of a new military doctrine. "Despite the variety of practical means and the changes in the manner of approach, there was no place in our military building for empiricism devoid of ideas, or for subjective arbitrariness : all the work from beginning to end was unified by the single class revolutionary goal, the unity of the will directed toward it, the unity of the Marxian method of orienta- tion."[22]

This explanation offered by Trotsky himself comes much closer to defining correctly his position than the summaries of his view made later by his enemies.

To the attempts toward creating a special communist military doc- trine, Trotsky opposed the military art in its historical development. He argued that the subject of war is man; that man has certain stable anatomical and psychological characteristics and a certain habitual pattern of behavior. Man acts in a relatively stable geographical environment. In this way, Trotsky concluded, in all wars, of all times and peoples, there were certain common, relatively stable (although by no means absolute) characteristics. On the basis of these characteristics, historic military art was developed. Its methods and practice change, as well as the social conditions determining it (such as technology, class structure, forms of political organization). From this proposition Trotsky developed the next, to the effect that military doctrine calls for a relatively stable condition both at home and abroad. With a great deal of acumen he advanced the thought that while, obviously, the struggle against Soviet Russia should appear as a sufficiently stable element in the "military doctrines" of all capitalist states, this did not conform to the actual facts in the situation. The complex and conflicting interests and, even more important, "the lack of stability in the social basis of the bourgeois governments" exclude the possibility of carrying out even that doctrine consecutively. "The only doctrine for us," he concluded, "is to be on the alert and keep our eyes wide open."[23]

At a later date, in 1923, Trotsky came to emphasize the importance of critical thought in the army. There is a certain similarity in the views expressed by him in October of that year with those of Svechin in 1921. He then conceived the army as a critically thinking organism, able to appraise the situation for itself. According to him, this did not exclude the existence in the army of strict discipline. He thought that the "truly revolutionary stern discipline could be founded only on the critical thought of the entire army." He spoke bitterly of his dream of an army that did not hurriedly sign resolutions presented at meetings, but formed its opinion after a thorough appraisal of the facts of the situation. Then "the increased internal cohesion, the comradely spirit and criticism" could be well combined with strict discipline. In Trotsky's opinion, this would not only place the army on a higher level, but would initiate into the political life "the sluggish masses of the peasantry."[24]

A change in Trotsky's political fate brought about this emphasis on freedom of criticism within the army. While Svechin advocated the freedom of thought within the narrow limits of purely military speculation, Trotsky came out for a much broader concept as to the permissible range of critical thought within the armed forces.

While he was, undoubtedly, driven into this position by the logic of the infra-party struggle, there is an ideological nexus between his opposition to the saddling of the Red Army with a dogma in 1921 and his advocacy of the critical attitude of mind in the army in 1923. The common denominator was his opposition to regimentation of thought within the army in the post-war period.

In 1921, he took the stand on his assertion that it was necessary to give up the attempts at building up "an absolute revolutionary" strategy on the ground of the limited experience of the Civil War. Trotsky even invoked the authority of Clausewitz, so well respected by the founding fathers of Marxism, in support of this assertion.[25]

In April 1922, Trotsky criticized Frunze's position at great length. That such an abstruse subject as the military doctrine should be brought up at a party congress speaks for the great importance ascribed to this discussion in party circles. It had ceased to be a purely military matter and had acquired a considerable political importance, leading also to a general discussion of the applicability of the Marxian method to the development of military and other arts.* This debate between Frunze and Trotsky deserves attention. It not only brought out a very interesting interpretation of the Marxian theory and its limitations by the People's Commissar for War, but apparently had some influence on Frunze's own views as evidenced by his utterances in later years.

To bolster up his views, Frunze quoted Engels's writings of the 'fifties to the effect that the conquest of power by the proletariat and the development of the socialist society would create the premises for a new strategy. Trotsky voiced his agreement with the principle enunciated by Engels, and said that should Soviet Russia be constrained to wage war with a capitalist country after reaching an advanced stage of development of socialist economy, its strategy would be entirely different from the conventional pattern. This, nevertheless, did not, in Trotsky's picturesque parlance, provide any reason "for sucking today a proletarian strategy out of one's thumb." He foresaw that the New Model strategy would grow out of the effort to improve the practice of warfare, but did not admit that it could come from the "naked yearning to say 'something new'." Using a homely simile, Trotsky gibed: "This would be tantamount to a situation where a person who appreciated original people should pose himself the problem of becoming an original person. Of course, he would be unable to accomplish anything but the most pitiful, apish tricks." Only by de-

* At the Tenth Party Congress Frunze and Gusev had brought up their theses but withdrew them because of Trotsky's opposition. See Trotsky, L. *"Kak Vooruzhalas Revoliutziia"* Vol. 3. Book 2, p. 242.

veloping the socialist economy, by improving the cultural level, as well as internal cohesion of the working masses on one hand, and by developing the qualification of the personnel of the Red Army, its technical equipment and its cadres "we shall beyond doubt enrich the military practice by new approaches, new methods," concluded Trotsky. With a rapier thrust at his enemies, he followed this up: "to place before oneself the solution of the problem of the new strategy by a speculative method from the revolutionary nature of the proletariat means occupying oneself with the doubtful task of turning the French Field Service Regulations inside out—and unavoidably getting mired."[26]

Trotsky's own blueprint for a plan of action for the immediate future was elementary in its simplicity: to organize thoroughly and develop the primary cell of the army—the section, to sum up the Soviet military experience in a manner permitting the section commander to understand it and make it his own, to bring to a higher level the self-consciousness, as well as the knowledge, of these commanders.[27]

A few weeks later, Trotsky tackled the basic problem of the theoretical approach to problems of warfare by Marxists. He came out quite definitely against the tendency to attempt the solution of every problem by the method of historic materialism already in evidence at that time in certain communist circles in Russia.*

"Even should one agree that 'military science' is a science, it is impossible to assume that this science could be built according to the method of Marxism," Trotsky argued. "Historical materialism is by no means a universal method for all sciences. . . . To attempt to apply it in the special domain of military affairs would be the greatest fallacy, no less a one than an attempt to move military science into the group of natural sciences. . . . Do not let us encumber our discussions of aviation problems by trite Marxist terminology, high-sounding words, grandiloquent problems, which as often as not would turn out to be shells without kernel or content."[28]

Old Army officers were ready to cheer these views of the People's Commissar for War. The young zealots, fresh converts to the gospel of Marx, were enraged. They were told, and had come to believe, that there was a universal sesame at their disposal to solve any new problem in a revolutionary bolshevik way. And here was Trotsky saying that the key could not open the book of war! That instead of a logical

* Later these tendencies became accepted by the leaders of the party and led to a development of a peculiar Marxian scholasticism.

well rounded-out theory of a Marxian science of war, the conquerors of Denikin and Wrangel had to be content with drilling sections and waiting patiently for the Soviet economic life to rise to a higher level. And at that time the level of production kept itself obstinately well below that of the effete days of czarism.

Frunze and Gusev, on the other hand, had a program much more to the taste of the doughty warriors, particularly those who had served in the capacity of commissars and as members of the numerous staffs of the various political departments of the Red Army. They asserted, in fact, that under "the conditions of the developing world revolution," in order to prepare for the future civil and semi-civil wars, which, according to them, were most likely to develop "within the near future" the problem of formulation of the unified military doctrine could not be entrusted to the narrow specialists in the field of military affairs. In their view, the correct solution of that problem could be reached only through the joint effort of the military specialists and the political workers of the Red Army who had acquired sufficient experience in military affairs and the conduct of warfare.[29]

In a later article in the periodical *Army and Revolution* (*Armiia i Revoliutsiia*), Frunze again repeated his conviction that a unified military doctrine should be adopted and that no other doctrine should be permitted to exist alongside of it. He urged that this military doctrine should be the expression of the will of the new governing class —the proletariat. He defined the military doctrine as a system establishing the character of the organization of the armed forces of a country, the methods of combat training of the troops, their direction on the basis of views predominating in the state as to the character of the military problems confronting it, and the methods for their solution. These views flow from the class character of the state, and are determined by the level of development of the forces of production. He summed up his program in a statement that all military affairs of a given state, including its military doctrine, on the basis of which are built its armed forces, are the reflection of the entire order of things predominating in that state and, in the final analysis, of its economic life, the first source of all strength and resources.[30]

Frunze's thought was very clumsily formulated, but the import of it is quite clear. He did not regard armed forces as something having a separate existence regardless of the prevailing conditions of a given state and in a given period. Frunze considered that the military system of the state was determined by the general conditions of life in that state, and that the military doctrine of any given state was determined by the "general political line" of the social class which was at the head of it.[31]

According to Frunze, the principal condition for the formulation of an adequate military doctrine was its strict co-ordination with the general aims of the state and the material and spiritual resources at its disposal. He admitted that it was impossible to invent such a doctrine, that all of its elements were clearly given in the environment, and that the work of theoretical thought must consist in discovering these elements, in bringing them together into a system in accordance with the basic teachings of military science and the requirements of military art.[32]

Apparently Frunze did not occupy the most extreme position with regard to the problem of the paramount importance of the Civil War experience for the reconstruction of the Soviet military forces. At one of the meetings of a conference of the Military Scientific Societies held in May 1922, he spoke of a "part of the military workers who were trained right in the ranks of the Red Army and were socially and politically connected with the working class and the peasantry," which was inclined to over-estimate the value of the experience of the Civil War and to insist upon the advancement to the first place of the study of its lessons.[33]

In the theses, submitted to the Eleventh Party Congress upon the initiative of Frunze and Voroshilov, the whole problem of the training and education of the Red Army was examined. The theses insisted that these should be based on a unified system of views thoroughly permeating the entire army. This system was to embrace the formulation of the problems set to the Red Army, the principles of its organization as well as the methods of its operations. "The sum total of these views brought together into a system with the help of the Marxian method of analysis of social phenomena, should be impressed upon the Red Army by means of regulations, orders and instructions. It would give the army the indispensable unity of will and thought."[34]

This formulation was more subtle and less open to attack than the first set of theses prepared by Frunze and Gusev. Trotsky readily admitted at the Congress that the new proposal was better thought out, but expressed the view that it was even more dangerous and harmful than the first.[35]

What, then, was the concrete content of this military doctrine advanced by Frunze, Gusev, Voroshilov and other opponents of Trotsky?

The seventh thesis of those presented at the Eleventh Party Congress stressed the fact that the Civil War had a predominantly maneuver character. "This was the result, not only of the purely objective conditions (the enormous theaters of the military operations, the relatively low numbers of the troops, etc.), but also of the internal qualities of the Red Army and of the revolutionary spirit, the impetuousness in battle, as manifestations of the class nature of the proletariat that was leading it."[36]

The eleventh of these same theses, dealing with the tactics of the Red Army, also had emphasized its active character. "The tactics of the Red Army were and will be permeated with spirit of activity in the sense of daring and energetically conducted offensive operations. This flows from the class nature of the Red Army, and, at the same time, coincides with the requirements of military art."[37]

The *leitmotif* of Tarasov-Rodionov's theses, the maneuver, the impetuous attack, all this is present in the program submitted by Frunze and Voroshilov. The defensive-position warfare was definitely thrown out on the dust-heap. The valiant ex-Sergeant Major Budenny even advanced the explanation of the strategy of the World War, with its lack of daring strategic solutions, by the simple expedient of ascribing it to the lack of decisive leadership: "There was no real genius among the war leaders."[38]

The advocacy of offensive strategy and tactics was not limited to a small group of Frunze, Voroshilov and their friends. Tukhachevskii, so different from them in his upbringing, education and temperament, also came out unreservedly for the "derring-do" methods of warfare, allegedly peculiarly adapted to the revolutionary troops of the Soviets.[39] That this approach to military problems had roots in the historic development of the Red Army there is no gainsaying.

Trotsky admitted that his opponents' viewpoint appeared as early as 1917 in the Red Army. Even at the very beginning of the organization of the Red Army forces, suggestions were made that the structure of the Red Army be made to correspond to the strategy of maneuver. Army corps, divisions, even brigades were declared to be too ponderous organizational units. It was urged that the whole army be reduced to separate detachments composed of the different arms, or of regiments.[40] The practical deductions from these premises, their translation into concrete suggestions, into methods of warfare for which to train and equip the Red Army, were much weaker than the theoretical formulas themselves.

Frunze deduced from his strategic views that fortresses should play only an entirely insignificant rôle in the future operations of the

Red Army, and that an important means of struggle with enemy armies superior in technical equipment lay in a thorough preparation of guerilla warfare on the territory of the probable theaters of war. He gave cavalry a very prominent place in future wars and considered that the training and development of that arm should be made one of the first tasks of the Red Army.[41]

It is very interesting to observe how a man of the obvious ability, nay talent, of Frunze, did not escape the usual snare of the average successful general: that of visualizing the next war in terms of the last. And the war Frunze had fought on the Russian plains, was, in character, very far removed from wars between modern, well-trained armies equipped with technical means.

In Frunze's speech delivered in March 1922, one cannot fail to notice that his discussions of the theoretical military problems had led to a modification of his position with respect to the all-exclusive importance of the maneuver principle. He pointed with disapproval at thinkers who believed that by making their own the principle of maneuver the Red Army could completely dispense with position strategy and tactics of defense, as well as the accumulated experience of the World War. "Such a conclusion," said he, "would be the greatest delusion and would become a great danger to the Red Army." He limited his own concept of offensive strategy to making of it the basic, but not the only, principle, which, according to his explanation, meant that the position forms of warfare, characterized by the immobility of the troops, and the stability of the front lines, could not in any case become the predominant fundamental form of the next military operations of the Red Army. He stoutly maintained, nevertheless, that the attack and the offensive, all other conditions being equal, were always more advantageous than defense.[42] The suggestions advanced by Tukhachevskii, another partisan of the offensive military dogma, are permeated by the zeal of a neophyte. The young guardsman who passed from the officers' mess of the aristocratic Semenovskii Regiment into the ranks of the Bolshevik party also took an extreme position in approaching problems of warfare. Class struggle, help from the proletarians of the capitalist countries in wars Soviet Russia was likely to conduct, played an important rôle in Tukhachevskii's military thought of that period.

Tukhachevskii shared with Frunze the latter's low opinion of the value of fortified positions.[43] He emphasized the growing importance of loss or gain of territory in the conduct of war, pointing out that the occupation of land belonging to the enemy might seriously alter the relative strength of the contending forces and make possible the expansion of the aims of war. In another place Tukhachevskii had made the assertion that the mass training of nations in the rudiments of war contained in itself the fatal germs that would destroy the capitalist state, when the bayonets of the toilers would turn against the "exploiters." There is an obvious connection between these two statements: Tukhachevskii had hoped that the Red Army, upon occupying an important part of enemy territory, would be able to recruit into its ranks the proletariat of the nation attacked.[44]

These premises put a premium on the offensive principle in strategy. Tukhachevskii kept to it at a date when he had already strongly modified his view as to the probability of a long period of trench warfare in wars of the future. According to him, to deny the possibility of achieving the aims set to war by policy through the defeat of the enemy's forces was tantamount to the denial of the use of force. He considered that a military defeat of a capitalist state would accelerate the revolutionary movement latent in it and would advance the hour of the final defeat. Then the proletarian state would be able to make a real lasting peace with the new revolutionary government emerging from the ruins.[45]

These views have shown their vitality by the application (in a somewhat vulgarized manner) in the last Russo-Finnish campaign of the Red Army, when the Kuusinen government was set up, although before, and not after, the victory. The first important offensive was directed to districts that during the Finnish Civil war of 1918 had shown themselves favorable to the Reds.

The historic military science was ably represented in this controversy by A. Svechin, who advanced some ideas that later became embodied in his "Strategy." He held that the strategy of attrition did not negate in principle the annihilation of the armed force of the enemy, as the aim of the operations. Such a strategy conceived that goal only as a part of the problem set before it, and not the entire task. He called short-sighted those of the Soviet military thinkers who looked upon the evolution of the World War toward the strategy of attrition as a result of mistakes and lack of foresight on the part of the general staffs. He thought that the strategy of attrition in that war was the result of historic necessity.[46]

Svechin disagreed with the assertions that each delay at the front turns to the disadvantage of the side pursuing positive aims. He asserted that the political offensive aim could be connected with a strategic defense; that a strategic defensive, resulting in a series of combined operations with a negative aim may pursue a final positive end. Svechin cited, in support of his theory, the success of the blockade of Dagestan by the Russians, the English continental blockade of Napoleon's empire and of William II's Germany.[47]

His earlier views, expressed, for instance, during his debate with General Velichko at the meetings of the Military Historic Committee at Moscow in the winter of 1920-1921, were more pronouncedly in favor of a strategy of defense, of the exploitation of the wide spaces of the Russian territory with its forests and swamps, the use of it as of a shield against an enemy better equipped with the technical means of warfare. His pessimism as to the possibility of a fairly rapid development of an up-to-date military industry in Russia (justified at the time), had, no doubt a decisive influence on his theories of the period. The intervening years of the New Economic Policy probably had an influence on his views in that respect. At the same time his thoughts on the strategy of a defensive war by Russia in 1921 were not, really, in conflict with his later concepts, since he, as already mentioned above, considered that for each war it was necessary to develop a special line of strategic conduct. And these lines might be different for the exhausted Russia of 1921 and the somewhat re- cuperated Russia of 1927.

Trotsky vigorously attacked the particular claim on, and the adapt- ability of, the Red Army for maneuver warfare and the principle of offensive, to the exclusion, or relegation to second place, of its antithesis, the defense. He also denied the inherent internal connec- tion between the social class character of the Red Army and the maneuver-offensive forms of warfare.

In his paper on military doctrine, published in December 1921, Trotsky stated that in principle, the Soviet Government would always be for an offensive revolutionary war under conditions when such a war could lead to the liberation of the toiling classes in other countries. He contended that with Soviet Russia, exhausted by the World and the Civil Wars, the Government's aim was to encourage military studies, to create and arm a large well-trained army, all for defense purposes. Trotsky flatly denied that the Red Army was the first to adopt the maneuver strategy in the Civil War. He maintained that the Whites made it their own also, that maneuver strategy became the rule because of objective reasons, such as the enormous spaces of the theaters of war and the relatively small size of the opposed armed forces, also on account of the weak development of the means of communication.[48]

In criticizing his opponents, Trotsky did not mince words or spare epithets; vainglorious was not the strongest adjective used by him in describing their frame of mind. He added another reason for the rapid forward and backward flux of the Red Armies in the Civil War. And that reason was not of a nature to endear him to the Red commanders. Trotsky said that the middle commanding personnel was insufficiently prepared for their task, while the lower was decidedly weak. Because of these shortcomings of the commanding personnel, military concepts, even the best, broke down in the process of execution and resulted at times in rapid and deep retreats. "Practically at all our fronts we had to fight the war twice, sometimes three times over. Why? Because of the quantitative and qualitative deficiency of the cadres." He thought that there was no doubt that in a civil war in Western Europe, the element of position warfare would assume a much more important place than was the case in Russia.[49]

Trotsky twitted the authors of the theses at the Eleventh Congress with their attempt to combine the class nature of the proletariat with the requirements of military art, as a form of reinsurance policy in the field of theory by invoking the authority of the French Field Service Regulations of 1921 in support of their emphasis of the offensive principle in strategy. He clearly realized the inadequacy of the technical equipment of the Red Army for the conflict with forces of the Western European states. The advantage of a better transportation system of the potential enemies in Western Europe would permit them to complete their mobilization promptly ahead of the Red Army. This would mean that in the first period of war, Soviet forces would have to resort to defense in order to gain time to complete their mobilization, he said.[50]

"The aim of war is the complete defeat of the enemy. This defeat cannot be achieved without the offensive. The strongest will is shown by one who creates the most favorable conditions for the offensive and exploits them to the end. But this does not mean that in order to manifest will it is necessary to be the first to attack. The material conditions of mobilization do not permit this. I should be a hopeless formalist and a dolt should I found my plan on the proposition that I must be the first to attack," Trotsky summed up.[51]

The People's Commissar for War also opposed the introduction of the doctrine of revolutionary war as a measure of political education of the troops, advanced by those who admitted that an immediate application of the offensive doctrine was impossible under the current political and economic conditions. This trend of thought tacitly conceded that the Soviet Republic's paramount interest was to maintain peace, but considered it of great importance from the viewpoint of revolutionary indoctrination of the Red Army, to inculcate the doctrine of revolutionary war as a part of its training.[52]

In discussing the arguments advanced by the supporters of this trend, Trotsky bared the political reasons for his opposition to the doctrine of revolutionary war and also to the offensive military doctrine. He pointed out that the Soviet policy had for its immediate object the bettering of relations with the peasantry and that the peasant problem was particularly acute in the Red Army. The elimination of the danger of the landowners' return and the delay in the beginning of the revolution in Europe had made it impossible to unite the more than one million men in the Red Army, nine out of ten of them peasants, under the banner of an offensive war for the cause of the proletarian revolution. Propaganda for such a war would fall on deaf ears, he concluded.[53]

Here, then lies the crux of the reasons behind Trotsky's opposition to the offensive military doctrine. He considered, correctly, that the wave of the world revolution was receding in Europe and that the bond between the peasants and the proletariat, which existed during the Civil War and was founded on a certain temporary common interest, was not by any means as strong when peace was reached. The peasant was no longer afraid of the return of the landlord. Kronstadt, no doubt, also taught a lesson as to the limits to which peasantry could be driven. Under these conditions, a defensive doctrine—that of the protection of the soil of Russia against foreign invasion—was the only possible platform on which the proletarian leadership and the peasant rank and file of the Red Army could be united on the ground of a common interest. "The failure of our August campaign and the defeat of the September movement in Italy have changed the balance of power in favor of the bourgeoisie throughout Europe," said Trotsky.[54]

Trotsky's thought was formulated even more clearly in a speech delivered in April 1922: "You wish [turning to his opponents] that the peasant should be ready at any moment to fight on the international fronts for the cause of the workers' class on the grounds of the proletarian doctrine. To educate the Communists, vanguard of the workers, along those lines, is our plain duty. But to believe that on this basis it would be possible to build up an army founded as an armed union of workers and peasants, is to be a doctrinaire and a political metaphysician. The peasants accept the idea of the necessity of the

Red Army only in so far as they realize that despite our deep yearning for peace and our great concessions, enemies continue to threaten our existence."[55]

The fifth of the theses, submitted to the Congress, insisted that the Red Army would in future perform its military functions in the conditions of revolutionary war, either defending itself against the onslaught of imperialism, or attacking jointly with the toilers of other countries in a common struggle. Trotsky pointed out that the two problems were placed by the authors of the theses on an equal footing, and were viewed by them as equally important for the current period: "How would you tell a Saratov peasant: 'Either we shall take you to Belgium to fight the bourgeoisie or you will have to defend the Saratov province against an Anglo-French landing expedition at Odessa and Archangel'? Is it feasible to approach the problem in this manner?"[56]

Tukhachevskii made a suggestion to the Communist International to organize under its auspices an international general staff, in other words to furnish the Communist International with a body of experts to plan, direct and carry out the application of overt force in the interest of the world revolution. Trotsky objected that an international general staff could be created only on the foundation of the national staffs of *several* proletarian states.[57] There was apparently a disinclination, not only on Trotsky's part, but on that of other important Soviet leaders of the time, to place such a dangerous weapon in the hands of the Communist International. They were inclined to preserve the control of armed force in their own hands. On the other hand, the work of establishing peaceful diplomatic and trade relations with Western Europe would undoubtedly have been placed in jeopardy by the organization of such a general staff.

Notwithstanding Trotsky's opposition, the offensive dogma continued to be the favorite doctrine of the commanding personnel of the Red Army. Trotsky readily admitted this himself in a speech made in September 1921, when he analyzed a tactical exercise of the Red Army. He said that the predominant view on military operations in the Red Army was founded on the width and boldness of strategic conceptions, on the extreme mobility of the troops, on rapid marches and impetuous attacks. Trotsky warned that in a war in the West, Soviet strategy would have to deal with ponderous masses of troops, and that it would by that very token acquire a tendency to position warfare and would have to abandon its predilection for bold, rapid maneuvering.[58]

Trotsky, in opposing the notion that the principle of maneuver was essentially revolutionary or connected with the class nature of the proletariat, said that the centralization of control over military affairs, particularly the centralization of the direction of the movements of troops and of the choice of the place and time for decisive action in the hands of the central military organs of the Soviet Government, was the real secret of the success of the Red Army.[59] This, of course, was a very narrow view and should be regarded, probably, merely as parrying the claim of the partisans of guerilla tendencies in the Red Army, who were prone to ascribe the mishaps in the course of the Civil War to faulty instructions from Moscow.

At the same time, Trotsky was not opposed to the close examination of the accumulated experience of the Civil War and to the incorporation into military regulations of the value of that experience. "It is necessary, while the memory of the combat operations, large and small, is still vivid, to compare that experience with the regulations, and each commander should conscientiously ask himself whether these words answer to the practice or not, and if they differ, should decide where the difference lies. To collect all this systematized experience, to sum it up, to evaluate it at the central headquarters through the application of higher experience in strategy, tactics, organization and politics, to clear the regulations and programs of all out-of-date, superfluous material, to bring them closer to the army and to make the army feel to what extent they are necessary to it and to what extent they should replace improvisation—this is a great and essential task."[60]

This stressing of the importance of unifying the Red Army regulations was answering a real need. It was freely admitted by Soviet commentators that commanders (and this was especially true of the self-made military men) were apt to "create" their own brand of tactics right on the field of battle. As a result of this mass improvisation, the Red Army had many tactics, and this plurality of tactical views was carried over into the tactical training of troops in peacetime. The problem of uniform tactical training of troops became quite acute. As a Soviet writer said: "The Red Army officially did not know of any field service regulations; it made its own regulations. . . ."[61]

This statement is purely an exaggeration. The majority of former commissioned and non-commissioned officers of the old army had carried over with them into the Red Army their experience and their training, so that the old Imperial army field service regulations were undoubtedly a powerful influence that helped to mold the tactical thought of a large proportion of the Red Army commanders.

In conducting his main campaign against the supporters of the "revolutionary military doctrine," Trotsky had found time to combat ideas arising in entirely different quarters—those of the old army officers who were advancing their ideas through the medium of the military periodical *Voennoe Delo*. In condemning their views on what discipline in the Red Army should be, Trotsky admonished them that "in the field of social, political and historical problems you, in a majority, do not know anything at all, and even worse, all you were taught is old rubbish, discarded long ago by the development of human thought."[62]

At times, drastic measures were taken against the attempts of these "unreconstructed" czarist officers to give expression to their views— clearly showing that the Old Adam of Russian nationalism was still alive under the Red-starred cap of the Soviet army which they were wearing. Thus the military periodical *Voennoe Delo* was closed by Trotsky for printing an article commenting on Marshal Pilsudski's activities, where the "natural jesuitism of the Poles" was contrasted with the "honest, straight-forward spirit of the Great Russian people." Prompt retribution was visited upon the heads of the editors of that periodical, the publication of which was suspended "pending radical changes in the editorial board."[63]

While this battle over strategic principles was raging, some attempts were made to discredit the discipline in the Red Army, to bring back the ideas on conduct of military administration, as well as practices of the guerilla detachments and of the days of the Red Guards.

As late as the end of 1921 there still was a tendency in the Red Army, carried over from the early days of its existence, which deemed strict military discipline unnecessary and asserted that there was no necessity to command, that it was enough to obtain ascendancy over the men through personal authority, and that suasion was more important than blunt military orders. There was, of course, nothing new in this. During 1917, after the March revolution, the ideas and practices of the old Army tended this way in so far as the enlisted personnel and at least some of the committees were concerned. These thoughts were expressed very succinctly in April 1918, by the Socialist Revolutionary of the Left, Ranchevskii, at the regional Communist party conference at Petrograd, devoted to the problem of organization of the Red Army: "There should not be any permanent and regular army and we should abandon, categorically and forever, all methods of warfare based on old foundations, i.e. waged with the help of a regular army and fortresses. . . ."[64]

Suggestions of similar nature were made in the end of 1921 at a meeting of the Military Scientific Society of the War College at Moscow. In countering them, the People's Commissar for War said: "Is it possible to do anything about this with one stroke of the pen, faced as we are with differences in cultural levels and with ignorance?"[65]

Apparently this tendency was already rapidly declining, as there is little trace of it in the discussions of Red Army problems after the Civil War. The centralistically controlled army with a well-defined military discipline, investing with authority commanders and commissars, became the established form of the armed forces of the Soviets. The social-democratic program of the people's militia was definitely shelved. The reasons for this will be clear from the contents of the next chapter.

In this discussion of the military dogma one can easily discover traces of several important conflicts of the time. The inadequacy of the proletarian basis of the communist power and the necessity of maintaining a compromise with the peasantry made it impossible to develop ambitious plans for world revolution along the lines hoped for at the time of the Russo-Polish war.

On the other hand, the ardent communist element was not prepared emotionally to give up these plans or at least the training of the army for the execution of these plans in the future, and to settle to the dreary routine of "form squad right" of garrison life or its Soviet equivalent. The world was their oyster and they wanted to pry it loose with the bayonets of the Red Army.

Against the background of these aspirations a clash of group interests developed. Should Trotsky's advocacy of the historic military art triumph, the old army officers, particularly the old War College graduates, would establish their ascendancy and would appropriate to themselves the solution of all the important problems of reorganization and training of the Red Army. The self-made military men, the former non-commissioned officers commanding army divisions in the Soviet forces, could not compete with them in that field.

To maintain their position in the army, the importance of the old "bourgeois" military art had to be denied and the paramount importance of a revolutionary military doctrine based on the experience of the Civil War, and the teaching of the apostles of Marxism had to be asserted.

The problem became particularly important with the curtailing of the army personnel at the end of the war. Who was to command the few remaining divisions, the now not so numerous regiments?

With the trend toward unity of command, those of the commissars who had a flair for military life were anxious to find a place for themselves in the military hierarchy. They often knew more of Marx's teaching than of Clausewitz' and Suvorov's. From their viewpoint a revolutionary military theory had great practical advantages. Instead of going to school to study the ABC of the military art, there was a chance to develop and to expound a new doctrine.

In the struggle for political control, these interests were important levers. Groups of people, influential both in the army and in the party organizations could be rallied under the banner of the military dogma.

For an educated officer of the old school, like Svechin, the freedom of theoretical discussion of military problems was a decided advantage. With his knowledge of military history he had the whip hand over people who rarely even knew before the Civil War that there was such a science at all. His chair of military history at the War College, in order to maintain its influence on the students, had to have freedom of military thought. From the standpoint of his opponents that was a definite disadvantage. They had to combat better-trained opponents on their own field. A revolutionary doctrine would silence all these heretics most effectively and leave the field to the young theoreticians of the *Scientia Nuova* of war.

Behind a *seemingly* purely theoretical discussion, there was in reality a struggle for power, for position, for influence. And all these appetites played into the hands of Stalin, Voroshilov and Frunze. By advancing the classical military viewpoint as the right one, for the time being, until the development of a socialist economy and culture, Trotsky placed himself in the position of defending views which seemed reactionary and suspect to the many Communists in the Red Army who throughout the Civil War regarded with the greatest suspicion the old army officers with whom they were associated. The very idea that the latter's views were upheld by Trotsky in the purely military field gave a sharp weapon to his political opponents.

In looking back after almost twenty years on this controversy, one cannot fail to notice that there was a great deal to what Trotsky maintained. The means of the country, the international political situation, the lack of properly educated communist military cadres, did not permit of any correct solution other than the one he proposed. At the same time, one cannot but notice that apparently he failed to see, or at least was unwilling to admit, an intrinsic connection between an ardent enthusiasm for a cause, whatever the cause may be, sufficiently widespread in an army and its leaders, and the offensive form of warfare.

Nations that are lukewarm about their own forms of government and the underlying social philosophy are not prone to develop a real offensive spirit, regardless of the verbiage that may be spun out by the military theoreticians. In the current war, the example of France has clearly shown that there was an intrinsic connection between the defensive campaign and the lack of enthusiasm for the basic ideas of French democracy, widespread, apparently, both among the generals and the rank and file, although for different reasons. Liddell Hart's theory of warfare is hardly that of a crusader, it is merely that of a supporter of the *status quo*.

A defensive doctrine would hardly have suited the leaders of Moslems in the first century of the Hegira. There was a fanatical belief in their rightness, in their having a mission to fulfill. The same was true of the Russian Communists in 1921. A defensive military doctrine, or any military doctrine short of a definitely offensive one, did not correspond to their emotional *Gestalt*, it was out of place in their viewpoint.

Trotsky's views, which had a great deal to commend them from the abstract military standpoint, failed to take into consideration this emotional element, worked up during the years of the Civil War. To suggest ending the wild-eyed adventure for the conquest of Europe for the cause of communism in drilling squads was tantamount to one of the early Khalifa ordering his ragged troops to study the niceties of the Byzantine drill. No doubt the drill was superior to the indifferent manner in which Arab warriors maintained their formations; Arab warriors, however, who time and again vanquished the regular troops of the *Romeis*, thought of further conquests and not of devoting themselves for an indefinite period to the imitation of their foes in the niceties of troop movements.

In academic theory (military theory) Trotsky was right; in practice (political and also military) Trotsky was wrong. To dam this revolutionary enthusiasm, to tell these victors to their faces that they did not know the rudiments of warfare, was detrimental to the morale of the Red Army—and that army at the time had to live through a very difficult period of readjustment.

That in the long run the offensive theories of the self-made Red Army leaders were vindicated by the recent events on the continent of Europe, adds to the many illustrations in military history of how dangerous it is to dogmatize and to sublimate the experience of the last large-scale war. In that respect Svechin was right in his view that each war requires a special strategic approach.

In going counter to this emotional urge for the offensive of the Red Army, in refusing to recognize its potential value, Trotsky, no doubt alienated a large number of the most enthusiastic leaders of that army and, perhaps, also weakened his political chances for undisputed leadership. The task of post-Civil War reorganization of the Red Army was exceedingly arduous. Every possible effort was needed to help to maintain the morale of the cadres during the painful transition period which will be discussed in the next chapter. In disparaging the advocates of "Red" military doctrine Trotsky had thrown aside an important means to bolster up that morale.

★ VII ★

THE REORGANIZATION OF THE
RED ARMY

Two important factors made difficult, even painful, the process of demobilization of the Red Army after the end of hostilities. They complicated its reorganization into a permanent force on a peace footing.

The years of Civil War, added to those of the World War, spread weariness and dislike for military life, not only among the peasant rank and file soldiers but also among some of the communist element in the military and political hierarchy of the army. The war was over and the weary soldiers wanted to take off their uniforms and turn to peaceful occupations.

Years of war communism were coming to an end. The transition from the days when the entire country was stripped to enable the Red Army to carry on were fading into the dusk of the New Economic Policy, with its attempt to balance the budget, its stable currency, and accent on reconstruction of the economic prosperity of the country.

The army was deprived of the privileged position it held during the war years, and ceased to be the principal consumer of food and other supplies the Soviet Government was able to lay its hands on.

At the height of its expansion, the Red Army numbered 5,300,000 men. Trotsky said in December 1921, that the Red Army, as well as the naval forces, the detachments of the political police force, and the cadres of the universal military training system were reduced to 1,595,000 men. Of this number the army proper accounted for 1,-370,000 men. The central and local military bureaus absorbed as much as 34 per cent of this still large force, while 66 per cent made up the active field forces. The latter comprised 95 rifle brigades and 49 cavalry brigades.[1]

During 1921, thirteen age groups were fully demobilized (1886-1898). Only three age groups were left in the army (1899, 1900 and 1901).[2]

This rapid reduction in personnel made it extremely difficult to continue training. As Trotsky said: "Were we to look back at the passing year of intensive demobilization and ask ourselves, how did the Red Army live, I should have to say that it went hard with the army." He also added that the army's hope was to see the process of reorganization completed as soon as possible, so that its life could stabilize itself, so that the army could acquire a definite establishment and could devote itself to the training and education of the troops.[3]

Trotsky linked the problem of material demobilization and its effect on the army with that of the "spiritual demobilization" trends in the country. He ascribed to these causes the difficulties experienced by the army throughout the year 1921. He stressed the fact that the inadequacy of shelter, of fuel, of equipment caused the Red forces to suffer "heavy privations."[4]

The privileged position of the army during the Civil War had apparently caused a considerable amount of dissatisfaction even among the industrial workers of Russia. In October 1920 the People's Commissar for War had to address a circular letter to the front and army headquarters which read, in part: ". . . the mass of workers, living on hunger rations, cannot but watch closely that the army shall not demand for itself more than is actually necessary, and that all supplies to the army shall be actually delivered to their proper destination. Since, in this respect, of course, all is not well, there exists in the workers' masses a natural dissatisfaction with the irregularities, with injustices and abuses of some of the organs of the military administration." At that time Trotsky proposed as a remedy to bend every effort to reduce the various advantages and privileges enjoyed by the commanders and the political personnel of the army.[5]

The trend pointed out by Trotsky assumed an even greater importance among the civilian population as time went on. In November 1921 Frunze wrote that it was impossible to miss the radical turn in the psychology of the workers with respect to the valuation of the Red Army for the present and for the future of Russia. The relations between the civil offices and the military bureaus left a great deal to be desired. There were frequent instances of lack of attention or even of gross neglect of the army's needs. Local Soviet organs were often lacking in zeal in rendering assistance to the demobilized soldiers in the latter's efforts to readjust themselves to civilian life.

Frunze summed up his impressions: "The party and the working class . . . have turned themselves spiritually to peace; in their inner valuation of the current situation of the country, the moment of assurance as to its stability and durability clearly predominates."[6]

Things did not improve during the next year. Frunze wrote in March 1922: "Lazily and drowsily move the wheels of the military machine." He felt the army had lost its best and most active elements and was placed in very difficult material conditions, as well as being neglected by the party.[7]

The Red Army ceased to be the petted child of the Soviet Government and of the Communist party. This was confirmed by other well-informed observers.

Bubnov, speaking at the Sixth Congress of the Komsomol in 1924, in discussing the period of the reorganization of the Red Army (1920-1923) quoted Trotsky's admission that during that period many serious mistakes aggravated the situation. As Bubnov put it: "there was no foresight, even in matters which could be anticipated." "Accidental," unplanned reductions in the establishment of the army further emphasized the lack of stability in the army life during the course of the demobilization. The element of "fluidity," which later caused so many difficulties in Soviet industry, was present at that time in the Red Army. "The greatest inconstancy" in the drafted element of the army was resulting in a radical undermining of the regularity and adequacy of supplies. It was also hindering the tactical training and other phases of military education of the troops. Political work in the army was seriously deteriorating.[8]

Trotsky pointed out in 1922 that the indefiniteness of the reorganization, the lack of a well-defined plan and the constant re-grouping of the personnel was particularly painful for the Red Army. He considered that even a drastic reduction in the numerical strength of the army would be better than such uncertainty, provided the army could be given a stable budget, so that it would know what to count on.[9]

Another handicap under which the army was laboring was the heavy load of guard duty which absorbed a great deal of time of the commanders and men. The Soviet Government at the time lacked a suitable organization of watchmen, and Red Army guards had to mount sentries to guard cars with freight belonging to the government and warehouses of all kinds.[10]

The transition from the methods of supply in kind, in use during the period of war communism, to those in line with the monetary practice of the New Economic Policy, was not completed in so far as the army was concerned until 1924.[11]

Petukhov also confirmed what Frunze had said, that with the shifting of the focus of attention of the party and the government from military problems to the field of economic and cultural reconstruction, the supply service of the army had suffered severely and that "this had undermined the base for the development of the political work."[12]

An even darker picture of the material conditions of Red Army life during the period of reorganization was drawn by Frunze in a paper published in 1922. He spoke of "unheard-of difficulties in material conditions of existence, with the eternal worry about the satisfaction of the elementary needs of one's unit, one's family and one's self." These material deprivations were adding fuel to the smoldering fire of "demobilization tendencies" in the army, exercising a painfully depressing influence on the spirit of the personnel of the Red Army.[13]

The central military organs were indicted by Geronimus for their lack of vision and experience in handling demobilization problems. He stated that the task was approached in a routine bureaucratic way without a definite plan. As a result, army units were repeatedly reorganized, merged and shifted from one locality to another. Insufficient barrack accommodations and inadequate heating, coupled with the lack of uniforms and underclothing, had accentuated the discomfort experienced by the army during the demobilization and had interfered with its military efficiency.[14]

These material insufficiencies had a definite effect on the influx of Communists into the military cadet schools. D. Petrovskii wrote at the end of 1922 that in the preceding eighteen months the percentage of Communists in cadet schools had declined quite perceptibly. He ascribed this to the "cleansing" the party had undergone during that period and the extreme caution exercised in accepting new members. He mentioned that the personnel in charge of training and supervision of the cadets were constantly confronted with a "decadent frame of mind" and pacifist leanings. In plain words, peasant youngsters had found conditions in the village under the New Economic Policy more agreeable to them than those in the army. The usual reaction setting in after most large scale wars was also having its effect, and bringing in its wake distaste for military life and war.[15]

In commenting on the disinclination of proletarian and peasant youth to enter military cadet schools, Petrovskii admitted that this was connected with the bad material conditions of existence both of the cadets and of the commanders of the Red Army.[16]

Even as late as 1925, when conditions for commanding personnel were brought to a higher level, Frunze spoke of the "beggarly" position of the Red Army and of its political and commanding personnel.[17]

The following table illustrates the considerable decline in the percentage of Communists among the Red commanders graduating from military cadet schools:[18]

1918	70%	1921	65%
1919	54%	1922	45%
1920	62%	1923	42%

The position of a Red Army commander in peacetime was not regarded as particularly enviable. During an investigation conducted by D. Petrovskii, he was told that "a commander's life is not a life but a brass kettle," "a commander's life is penal servitude." Petrovskii drew the conclusion that in order to attract workers and peasant youths to study for a military career, to dispel their fear of becoming commanders, it was necessary to improve the conditions of Red Army commanders.[19]

The drab routine of army life in peacetime, against the background of the disillusioning effect of the New Economic Policy on the more enthusiastic Communists in the army, made the commanding personnel affiliated with the party impatient of the humdrum garrison life and the dull everyday work. Even that bulwark of the party in the army was reported as infected with the virus of the "decadent frame of mind."[20]

By the end of 1921, the army had—against 1,430,000 men on its ration—73,000 Communists (including 30 per cent of candidates for party membership). This compares with the situation as of August 1, 1920, when 64.5 per cent of the party membership was in the Red Army, according to Geronimus's estimates, indicating that there were altogether 278,000 Communists at the time in the Red Army (including 30 per cent of candidates).[21]

Geronimus says that the slow tempo of demobilization and the difficult conditions of life laid the groundwork for a "counter-revolutionary" movement in the Red forces during that period; that these trends were fostered by "anti-Soviet" tendencies present among certain elements of the commanding personnel. He describes agitation among the private soldiers for equalization of material conditions of service with the commanding personnel, for the abolition of the political departments and the Special Departments—the army branches of the political police—and the refusal of some army units to participate in the suppression of the peasant rebellions and even some instances, such as in the Tambov province, of their passing over to the side of the embattled peasantry.[22]

A committee appointed by the Central Committee of the party in 1924 to review the condition of the Red Army reported that the Red

Army "as an organized, trained, politically educated force supplied with all essentials for mobilization" did not exist at that time. "At the present time, the Red Army has no combat value."[23]

The report of the committee may have been influenced by political considerations in order to show the inefficiency of Trotsky's administration. Other evidence, however, seems to indicate that the condition of the Red Army was unsatisfactory and that neither its morale nor its fighting efficiency were at a high level at the time.

The rate of decline in the numerical strength of the Red Army between the years 1921 and 1923 may be seen from the following table :[24]

March 1921	4,400,000
December 1921	1,430,000
December 1922	610,000
— 1923	562,000

There was a serious conflict among the Soviet leaders and the Red Army chieftains as to the organizational forms the Soviet armed forces should assume after demobilization.

An attempt was made by the partisans of the traditional social democratic program of militia to bring about a radical change in the organizational structure of the Red Army along the lines of that program. The issue was fought out at the Tenth Party Congress.

The internal condition of the country, seething with peasant rebellions, was such that this attempt could not succeed. As Geronimus wrote, to build a militia under conditions of antagonism between the workers' class and the peasantry, while hunger stalked through town and village, and in face of an epidemic of peasant rebellion (euphemistically called "banditry" by the Soviet writers) was to court disaster. It was in the eyes of the ruling group of the Communist party equivalent to giving arms to the enemies of the proletarian dictatorship.[25]

Certain anti-communist trends were of course filtering into the standing Red Army also. It was, nevertheless, considered at the time that it would be much easier to counteract these influences and keep the peasant soldier in line. Under these circumstances the Tenth Party Congress resolved that "for the present moment the agitation of some comrades for the factual liquidation of the existing Red Army and the immediate transition to the militia is wrong and dangerous in practice."[26]

At the other wing of the Congress there were groups of delegates who considered the militia system unsuitable for the period of proletarian dictatorship. Some of these laid stress on the purely military advantages of the standing army *versus* militia for the conduct of the revolutionary wars of conquest in which they expected the proletarian state would be involved. Others objected to militia on the grounds of internal political and economic consequences. The second group had found considerable support among army political workers, as well as in local party organizations. Geronimus says that the Moscow party committee had adopted the thesis advanced by Smilga supporting these views. The same thesis had already received the approval of the conference of the army political workers during the Eighth Congress of Soviets.[27]

Smilga's thesis criticized the militia plan in the following manner: "The militia system, of which the basic characteristic is the territorial principle, is faced with an insuperable obstacle in the path of its introduction in Russia. Given the numerically weak proletariat in Russia, we would not be able to ensure proletarian guidance in these units. Even greater objections to the introduction of the militia system arise from the viewpoint of strategy. With the weakness of our railroad system, we should not be able, in case of war, to concentrate forces on the threatened directions. . . . Furthermore, the experience of the Civil War has incontrovertibly shown that territorial formations *were entirely unsuitable*, and that the soldiers deserted. Therefore, the return to this organizational form would be a crude, unjustifiable error."[28]

This decision of the Tenth Congress went counter to the plans elaborated by the preceding party conclave.

At the Ninth Party Congress in April 1920, Trotsky, in discussing the militia system, took as his point of departure the thesis that the army reflects the basic traits of the political régime of the country, and, moreover reflects these traits in their most accentuated form. He insisted that the organizational form of the army does not determine its class essence. Trotsky also thought that the maintenance of a militia type of army would not be cheaper than that of a regular standing army. His advocacy of it was not on the grounds of economy.[29]

The People's Commissar for War advanced the thought that a regular standing army was in contradiction to the requirements of the economic development of the country. Militia, according to his thought, had the advantage of not separating labor and defense, because the militia system did not tear the workers and producers away from the economic life, at least not for long periods.[30]

At the same time, Trotsky admitted that for a very considerable term it would be necessary to maintain, in the most threatened directions, fully mobilized units, possibly even entire armies, kept constantly in readiness. He thought that these standing forces could perhaps be recruited through voluntary enlistments, giving in this manner an outlet for soldiers who had become professionalized in the course of their war service.[31]

Trotsky proposed that the beginning of the change be made through the distribution of the cadres of the existing army divisions, brigades and regiments throughout the country in accordance with the locations of the industrial enterprises. In his thought, every industrial worker having charge of a shop, or a member of the board of an enterprise, or a member of the local Soviet organs, should attend command personnel courses and take on the duties of an officer in one of the local militia units. He thought that the cadres had to maintain the closest possible touch with the trade unions and that commanders should be appointed in co-operation with the latter.[32]

This plan was certainly a very interesting one. Its proposal to place the leadership of the militia in the hands of the most active politically, or most prominent in the sphere of trade union work and of industrial administration, was a very daring assertion of the dictatorship of the proletariat in the practical control of the armed forces directly by the leading local proletarians. This merging of political, administrative and economic leadership with the military command would have resulted in giving control of the local military forces to the local proletarians, and, in a way, would make for a certain measure of decentralization in the control of the armed forces, at least in peacetime.

A certain parallel with the feudal type of military organization suggests itself. Those in control of the economic and political life were to have direct control of the military forces as well.

The Congress resolved that the essence of the militia system should consist in bringing the army closer to the production process, i.e. that the manpower of the various economic districts should be at the same time the manpower of corresponding militia units. The distribution of militia divisions, brigades and regiments was to be coordinated with the geographical distribution of the industrial centers of the country, so that an industrial center with its agricultural periphery would form the foundation of the militia unit.[33]

The personnel of the cadres of the militia was to be gradually renewed with the aim of establishing the closest possible connection with the economic life of the district, so that the commanding personnel of a division located, for instance, in the territory of a group of mining enterprises, would consist "of the best elements of the local proletariat."[34]

In other words, the Congress had accepted the outline of the militia organization proposed by Trotsky. The program envisaged the elimination from the commanding personnel of all non-proletarian elements (i.e. not only of the former czarist officers who were serving in the Red Army but also commanders of peasant origin), placing command of the militia units entirely in the hands of the industrial workers. It was actually a proposal to form armed camps of the numerically weak proletariat throughout the country, so that through its working-class commanding personnel, the party could exercise the dictatorship of the proletariat in the countryside.

To develop the already-mentioned likeness with the feudal system: instead of knights and members of nobility, the functions of leadership in the armed levies were to be exercised by the proletarians who had risen in the industrial or administrative hierarchy. This organization had, of course, the earmarks of an open class domination, by one class, a small minority in Russia, of the armed forces of the country.

In the discussion regarding the relative military value of militia, Trotsky took the position that militia was not a weaker form of military organization than the modern standing army; that, founded on the base of a universal military training and schooled in the art of war outside of barracks, locally, militia would develop into the ideal army of the Soviet state.[35]

In his later writings, Trotsky maintained that the problem of reorganization of the army consisted in changing the Red Army to a militia foundation. He said at the time that it was impossible to give up the educational and cultural work conducted at the barracks without bringing up the economic and cultural level of the village and strengthening its ties with the town.[36]

The pious hopes of the Ninth Congress were shattered by the Tambov insurrection, by the Kronstadt rebellion, by the wave of peasant uprisings in the Ukraine. As Frunze wrote in 1922: "It is clear that under the conditions of the weakening of the union between the workers' class and the peasantry . . . the militia system could become a weapon in the hands of the counter-revolution. This circumstance was fully realized by the Communist party, and, therefore, regardless of the liquidation at the end of 1920 of the external fronts, we did not do anything in that sphere as yet."[37]

A. Svechin had opposed the militia system as early as 1919 and his paper in the *Voennoe Delo* criticized that system as inefficient. Rather curiously, he also expressed the thought that the concept of militia is a survival of democratic ideology, hinting that the supporters of the militia plan were still under the influence of the ideas of the Second International.[38]

In his spirited reply on the pages of the same *Voennoe Delo,* Trotsky wrote that apparently Svechin had not succeeded in mastering the programs of all three Internationals, thinking, as he seemingly did, that the Communist party had come to power to "replace the tricolor barracks by red."[39]

Apparently Svechin's blow was well aimed. One is rather inclined to think that the idea was suggested to him by some military Communist. His accusation that the supporters of the militia plan were trying to keep burning the fires lit by the Second International hit the mark.

Trotsky heaped all the ridicule of which his pen, at its vitriolic best, was capable, on the head of the military theoretician. However, in the long run it was Svechin, not Trotsky, who was proved to be right by the course the Red Army evolution took. In later years Svechin's idea of the cadre army became part of the official program of the Soviet Government at the time when the danger of the Nazi invasion reared its head over the western border of Russia, i.e. when the Soviet Government began to need a really efficient army ready to meet the onslaught of a formidable enemy.

The discussion of the military advantages and deficiencies of the militia system assumed after the end of the Civil War very considerable proportions. Those who had followed it in Moscow in the winter of 1920-1921 remember the attempts of some of the old army general staff officers to trim their sails to follow in the wake of the People's Commissar for War. In a paper read at a meeting of the Military Historical Commission, one of these officers, in extolling the advantages of the militia system, even brought up the battle of Sempach, fought in the Middle Ages (1386), as an instance of the greater efficiency of the militia (Swiss) as against the regular army (Austrian). After a remark from the floor, that, after all, the knightly cavalry could hardly be considered as a regular army in the modern sense of the word, and that the battle in question was really fought between two militias, the chairman of the meeting apologized for not stopping the speaker earlier, and addressed some withering remarks of his own to the unfortunate victim of his own theoretical flexibility. Generally speaking, however, most of the educated military professional people were opposed to the militia system for various reasons. Tukhachevskii was particularly vehement in his attacks on it.

No doubt, quite apart from theoretical considerations, the fact that the better informed professional officers realized that in the militia, organized along the original lines suggested by Trotsky, there would be no room for their professional careers, had something to do with their opposition to the plan.

At the same time, it is interesting to note that the territorial militia plans, as introduced later by the Soviet Government, had met with the approval of a number of ex-czarist officers in the ranks of the White émigrés. Thus Colonel Piatnitskii (who wrote a very informative book on the Red Army) explained his reasons for devoting a considerable amount of space in his work to the problem of the territorial troops' organization: "We believe that the decision taken by the Red Army with respect to the organization of the armed forces would be unavoidable even in the future National Russia which would be, in the first stages after its re-birth, poor and surrounded on all sides by enemies."[40]

The application of the new blueprints of the militia plan of army reorganization had to wait until the acute phase of conflict between the proletarian element, or rather those who followed the ruling group at Moscow, and the peasantry, had passed. The New Economic Policy—the famous NEP—laid the foundations for the elimination of a great deal of friction, and in 1922 Frunze, in his article on the regular army and the militia in the *Armiia i Revolutsiia* journal, was able to say: "The friction which existed at one time (Kronstadt, the Tambov rebellion) between the workers' class and the peasantry is eliminated now."[41]

With the political change, the reorganization of the Red Army along the lines advocated by Trotsky became possible. However, the lessons of the 1921 crisis had left a heavy impression on Soviet military administrators. The plan, as actually brought into effect, was a compromise between the "pure" militia design and the regular army pattern. The details of the application of the militia plan also were different from Trotsky's vision of the proletarian feudal levies.

The motivation behind the advocacy of the militia plan, in its turn, underwent a very considerable change. Thus, in 1925, in a paper in the *Na Novykh Putiakh*,* Frunze frankly admitted that should there be a practical possibility of making a choice between a regular army, numbering from a million and a half to two million men, and the

* "On New Paths." At that time Frunze was the People's Commissar for War.

combined plan, embracing a comparatively small regular army and a large territorial militia, the first would have, from the military viewpoint, all advantages on its side. He stated, however, as an obvious generally known and accepted truth, that there was no such choice possible for the Soviet Government.[42]

As the following pages will make clear, the principal obstacle to the adoption of the first of the plans mentioned by Frunze—that of a large standing army—was the economic impossibility of carrying it out because of the economic weakness of the Soviet state in the early 'twenties.

Frunze also advanced the thought that the enlargement in the personnel of the regular army might be interpreted abroad as a proof of "Soviet imperialism," and would thus furnish a weapon in the field of propaganda to the enemies of the Soviets abroad, a weapon which might have an effect even on a part of the proletariat of Western Europe. "It would be politically inexpedient," said Frunze, "were we to give food to that agitation, were we, by our practice, to instil apprehensions as to our imperialism."[43]

The slogan "look toward the village," which was prominent in that period, was translated by Frunze, in terms of practical activity of the Soviet Government, as work in the direction of improving the economic conditions of the peasantry. In his opinion, there were "entirely satisfactory premises for the strengthening of the ties between the workers and the peasants," and "this is the most important element, which should define the possibility of a positive achievement in our work among the territorial militia units."[44]

The comparison with Trotsky's original argument in favor of the militia system and these thoughts of Frunze's is quite interesting. The first were exceedingly theoretical, included claims that had no foundation in objective facts (the suggestion, for instance, that militia was as effective, in a military way as the regular army), while the second was based on a number of practical considerations, the principle of which was rooted in the economic limitations which confronted the Soviet state at the time.

That at least some of the military people still regarded the relatively small regular army as the main military force of the Soviet state is clear from Frunze's attack on these views, which he made in 1925. "Some still retain the view that the main point lies not in these formations [territorial militia] but in something else. That our regular cadre units, located in our borderlands are the warp of the combat strength of the Red Army."[45]

In other words, the plan of the militia army, even in its modified form, did not find a universal acceptance as yet; there was a group in the Red Army opposed to it, and the theoretical conflict was not outlived as late as 1925.

In the earlier years (1923, for instance), such opposition was not only openly expressed, but was able to find material for its arguments in some of the practical results of the first experiments in the field of application of the militia plan.

Trotsky admitted in 1923 that before the muster of the territorial divisions (which was arranged for that year) there were many doubters as to the possibility of making the change to the militia system during a revolutionary period. According to Trotsky the muster of the ten territorial divisions passed off successfully. He accepted this as proof that the socio-political premises for the militia plan were, on the whole, favorable, and that the military administrative machinery, with the aid of the state apparatus, was able to cope "on the whole and in general" with the problems that faced them in the sphere of the territorial military work.[46]

It is worth noting that in the same speech Trotsky had made a serious issue of the exclusion in the most drastic fashion of "traders and kulaks," i.e. of the economically strong elements of town and village during the NEP period, from the territorial divisions as well as from the entire Red Army. He urged those responsible for the recruitment of these divisions to exercise the greatest vigilance in that respect.[47]

That the muster discussed by Trotsky was not entirely successful is shown by another part of the speech above referred to. He had spoken about the Bessarabian Division, where there were during the muster 50 per cent of desertions of its total personnel, "who, it seems, even had organized armed bands." For all of the mustered divisions deserters averaged 2 per cent.[48]

It would seem, therefore, that at least in one part of Russia, the peasants were not as yet reconciled to their proletarian governors, and the attempt to form territorial militia divisions from these recalcitrant peasants was met with an opposition which led even to armed insurrection. No wonder, then, that there were still doubting Thomases in the Red Army who were clinging to the then unfashionable idea that there was a basic qualitative difference between the regular Red Army divisions and those of the militia.

"One should not view the matter as if the field divisions of the Red Army and the militia ones were the embodiment of opposite principles," wrote Trotsky. "Really the problem consists of gradually and 'from both ends' transferring the Red Army, as it was historically created, to the militia system basis."[49]

This dream of Trotsky has not been realized as yet in Soviet Russia and the tide began to move in the opposite direction, as soon as a serious danger to the Soviet state appeared from powerful neighbors instead of the bogeys that were raised from time to time for political purposes by the Soviet authorities themselves. The military deficiencies of the militia system on the Russian plan became so obvious that the whole system was virtually scrapped. This, however, had happened at a much later stage of the evolution of the Red Army, which will be the subject of the subsequent chapters. During the NEP, the territorial militia system not only came into being, but was very considerably developed and perfected.

Trotsky argued in his later writings for the militia plan on grounds of the economic necessity "in the period of transition of the armed forces to a peace footing, the army and the navy fall into the most direct dependence on the general economic condition of the country."[50] He also admitted earlier an intense desire on the part of the masses of the people to lighten the burden of supporting the large standing army which had grown so rapidly during the Civil War: "Of course it is true," said Trotsky in January 1921, "that our enormous military machine has put everybody's back up, particularly the workers and peasants . . . everyone is dreaming of reducing it to a minimum."[51]

Tukhachevskii was not satisfied with defending the idea of the regular army in Soviet press and at Soviet meetings. He carried his arguments into the international revolutionary field. His spirited attack on the militia type of army was published in 1921 at Leipzig, under the auspices of the *Russische Korrespondenz*.

The comparison of the contents of his pamphlet with Svechin's reasoning in the *Voennoe Delo* in 1919 shows a very remarkable similarity of thought in its part relating to the tradition of support of the militia plan by the socialist parties of the Second International. The thought was more fully developed by Tukhachevskii, but the kernel of it is the same as in Svechin's paper. Whether the suggestion originated with the brilliant communist military leader, or with the better educated and more profound mind of the erstwhile general of the old army, is not clear from the evidence available.

As worked out by Tukhachevskii, the reasoning ran as follows: the militia plan had found favor with the leaders of the Second International because of the peculiar conception these leaders had of the coming struggle of the proletariat against the bourgeoisie. This idea envisaged what Tukhachevskii calls "a passive half-battle," and undermined the thought of revolutionary activity among workers. The struggle of the proletariat against the bourgeoisie was placed within limitations undesirable from the military viewpoint. "The Second International had inoculated the conception, that such an attack [of the proletariat against the bourgeoisie] is permissible within the narrow frontiers of one state only."[52]

Tukhachevskii opposed to this idea his own concept. He advanced the thought that whenever a socialist revolution was achieved it had "as a matter of course, the right to expand." Through direct action on all neighbors it would endeavor to encircle the globe. "Its most important weapon would naturally be its military might."[53]

From this blueprint of revolutionary expansion by the might of arms, Tukhachevskii concluded that the army of the socialist revolution should be capable of offensive operations not only within the borders of its own country, but, under favorable circumstances, outside of those as well. Tukhachevskii thought that the structure of the army should be dependent on the political goal set before it, as well as on the method of its recruiting. He rejected both the idea of an "armed nation" and that of militia, as unsuitable for a revolutionary socialist state. According to his views the revolutionary army should be recruited only from the ranks of the proletariat (in the case of Russia from the ranks of the poor peasants as well). "Permeated by a strong class consciousness and the revolutionary impetus of victory, this army would quickly become a regular and bellicose army." Furthermore, militia would be useless for the purpose of putting down peasant rebellions.[54]

This concept may have had considerable attraction for many strata of Russian Communists before the Warsaw *débâcle*. With the change of policy to the NEP, with the attempts to establish "normal" economic and diplomatic relations with Western Europe, Tukhachevskii's line of argument was utterly out of step with the thoughts of the ruling Kremlin group. He wanted to raise a specter of terror, which they were anxious to hide, at least for the time being.

Small wonder, then, that by 1924, 75 per cent of the infantry divisions were turned into territorial militia formations. From that time until 1934 the personnel of the Red Army (including the navy and air force) was limited to 562,000. It is true that in addition to these regular troops there were in Soviet Russia about 150,000 troops of the political police and about 100,000 frontier guards—which in the end of the 'thirties were organized into seven completely motorized divisions.[55]

The economic limitations and political considerations connected with the foreign policy of Soviet Russia made it desirable to limit the size of the regular forces of the Red Army. The militia idea was not entirely abandoned by any means, but was modified in the light of the experience of the 1921 rebellions. This compromise plan remained in force for over ten years, until the threat of Nazi military power on the one hand and the enlarged industrial base of Soviet Russia resulted in a considerable increase in the size of the regular army.

The discussions of the type of army Soviet Russia should adopt had bared conflicting trends of thought among the military leaders. The ardent international revolutionary military group, as represented by Tukhachevskii, was anxious for Russia to retain the pattern of the regular army, as they hoped, under favorable circumstances, to expand the field of application of the Soviet practice into other lands by means of military action. On the other hand, the professional army officers were supporting the regular army idea, both because they regarded it as the more efficient from the military point of view and also because they thought that their talents and education would have less scope in a militia, particularly one organized along the lines of the original Trotsky plan. The opposition came from quarters interested in taking full advantage of the "breathing spell" given to the Soviet Union for a complete recovery in the economic and cultural fields, also from those who had cherished for many years the concept of militia as the only right form of military organization in the socialist state. In this manner, these discussions reveal deep conflicts of thought among the communist and the non-party element within the army as well as without.

This sketch of the controversy around the basic concept of military organization may lead to a better understanding of the following outline of the practical steps in the upbuilding of the military might of the Soviet during the NEP.

★ VIII ★

FRUNZE'S ARMY

Trotsky did not succeed in completing the post-war reorganization of the Red armed forces. This task was accomplished by M. V. Frunze, who became the *de facto* head of the Red Army in the beginning of 1924.

This able communist military leader had a wide military experience during the Civil War, conducting the operations of the important armed forces entrusted to his command with skill and success.

Frunze conceived the Red Army not as a national army but as an army aiming to defend the interests of the toilers the world over.[1]

The erstwhile head of the Political Administration of the army, A. S. Bubnov, defined the basic principles of reform carried out by Frunze in the Red Army: the sweeping out of the army of the "survivals" of war communism, the introduction of greater accuracy in planning the defenses of the country, and, lastly, the re-grouping of the personnel of the military organs to permit a more rapid advancement of the young military communists and of the young "Red commander" element trained in the Soviet military schools or promoted to command positions from the ranks during the Civil War.[2]

The "liquidation of the survivals of war communism" in the Red Army was interpreted by Bubnov as meaning the introduction of a monetary economy. The NEP was gradually permeating the Red Army in the affairs of daily life as well as ideology.[3]

Bubnov pointed out with pride that the Red Army had already acquired trained staff officers of its own (as distinguished from the old army general staff officers within its ranks) as well as an élite of Red Commanders, trained since the revolution.[4] To make possible a rapid career for these young military people, regarded as "their own" by the Soviet state, as well as the party, the third part of Frunze's reforms furnished adequate foundations.

Kamenev's speech at one of the meetings of the Thirteenth Congress of the Communist party was quoted by Bubnov as follows: "We have come out of the period of landslides, sudden violent commotions, of catastrophes, we have entered the period of slow processes, which one should know how to observe." Bubnov thought that stability in the economic sphere should be accepted as the most essential premise for the planned reconstruction of the Red Army. The existence of what he called the "pacifist democratic era" in the life of Western

Europe, served, in his opinion, as a guarantee against a sudden war. "We must tell ourselves: we have actually a relatively lengthy respite." This respite permitted them to envisage an "era of organic reconstruction of the armed forces" of the Soviet Union.[5]

In so far as the navy was concerned, the reconstruction began with the building up of a new personnel to replace the old seamen inherited from the czarist régime, the rebellious "ornament and pride of the Revolution."[6] The new element drawn into the navy was chiefly taken from the ranks of the Communist Youths—the *Komsomol*.[7]

Bubnov's summary of Frunze's reforms is not complete, as he omitted some of the most far-reaching measures, introduced by the latter. Thus an important move was made in the direction of restoring the unity of command in the army. The actual process of concentration of all the powers in the hands of commanders of units was at first moving ahead rather slowly. As Frunze himself explained, it was necessary first to pave the way for the utilization of the influential commissar element. Some of these were to be re-trained for command duties, others prepared to handle administrative or economic duties in the army organs. However, as Frunze had said in April 1925 the matter was settled in principle "in an entirely precise and definite manner." Seemingly the dual control of the army units was on its way out.[8]

A very well-sustained and far-reaching effort was made by Frunze to improve the discipline in the Red armed forces. In this respect there was considerable room for improvement, as discipline was at a very low level after the end of the Civil War. This was true even of the elementary outward discipline in the ranks of units on parade or drill.[9]

The old shortcomings of the Red Army with respect to regulations and manuals for combat training were being rapidly mended, so that Bubnov could announce in 1924 that within that year the army would be supplied with all the essential regulations and manuals.[10]

During the Civil War and the first years following it the Red Army did not have a corps of non-commissioned officers, though many of the lower commanders were really, in their training and experience, as well as in the level of their ability, of the non-commissioned type, and tended to perform duties usually entrusted to N.C.O.'s. Also, graduates of the short-term command courses were, on the average, at best suited only for the duties of non-commissioned officers in the first months of their service with the army. From 1924 on, the training of the "lower command personnel" was entrusted to regimental schools opened for that purpose. Frunze had hoped that these schools would be the means of considerably strengthening the entire military system of the Soviets, particularly the militia divisions, by supplying the crying need for instructors for the young soldiers.[11]

The material side of army life was also given attention. The pay of the commanding and political personnel was raised considerably in 1924. Funds for this were obtained by a drastic reduction of the establishment of the central organs of the military administration. The axe fell on about 40 per cent of the employees of these offices. The local military administrative organs also were re-grouped with the aim of reducing the number of persons on their pay-rolls.[12]

The soldiers in the ranks were better looked after than in the preceding years. They began to receive more adequate uniforms, more nourishing food, and somewhat more satisfactory housing. In the matter of housing, conditions were, nevertheless, not as good as in other respects.[13]

The reform of military education, begun in 1921, was by 1924 on a fair way to fulfillment. The short-term command courses of the Civil War type could be dispensed with, so that the training of command personnel was entrusted to normal military schools with a much longer course and a wider program of military education.[14] Gradually, the total number of military educational establishments was reduced to 68, which number included 44 military schools for the training of young officers. By 1927, about 2,000 officers had graduated from the War College and other higher military schools. There were six of these colleges then, besides the five military departments of civil colleges.[15] The new "Red" officer corps was rapidly turning into a professionalized group of men, trained in the art of war, to the theoretical study of which they had devoted a number of years.

Upon the reorganization, the Red Army comprised the regular standing forces, numbering 562,000 (including the personnel of the navy and of the air force) and of the territorial militia enrolled in 43 divisions. The regular army accounted for two-fifths of the infantry and artillery, four-fifths of the cavalry, as well as the entire personnel of the technical troops (air force, tank and armored-car detachments, engineers, signal service troops, etc.). The length of service in the regular army was set at two years for the basic arms. The entire army (including both the regular as well as the territorial militia) included 71½ infantry and 16½ cavalry divisions. The personnel of territorial units consisted of the cadres, numbering from one-tenth to one-sixth of the total strength serving for two years, and the alternating personnel, serving for five years in theory, but completing its military training during short one to three month periods, and returning to civilian activities in the intervals.[16]

The development of the so-called "national" formations of the Red Army also had received a greater impetus under Frunze's guidance, although even by 1927 the program was carried out only with respect to the Ukraine, White Russia and Transcaucasia. Such parts of Russia as Turkmenia, Uzbekistan and Kazakstan had only embryonic organization of national military forces in the latter year.[17]

Frunze in the last years of his life fully understood the importance of modern technical means in warfare, and while the still sluggish tempo of Russian industry did not permit him to carry out sweeping improvements in respect of the mechanization and rearming of the army, he took steps to pave the way for the reconstruction of the equipment and training of the Red Army as a modern fighting machine supplied with the up-to-date technical facilities. "The war of the future in a considerable measure, if not entirely, will be the war of machines."[18] Such was his slogan in planning for that future.

In examining the brief but fruitful term of his administration, one cannot fail to be struck by the firmness with which Frunze laid down the foundations on which the Red Army continued to develop during a long period of years. He stood closer than Trotsky to the fighting element of the army and its lower political personnel, and his turn of mind was much less theoretical than that of his predecessor. He grasped well the essential practical problems of the army. Under his guidance, the Red Army emerged as an organized military force, growing organically and gradually improving in its efficiency as a fighting machine. One must not forget, however, that the beginnings of the many improvements by Frunze were made under Trotsky, although in the last years of his régime Trotsky was engaged in an active political strife, which, no doubt, took a great deal of his time and energy away from his work in the military field. The considerable improvement of the economic conditions of the country during the years of respite of the NEP, when the shorn lamb of Russia—the peasantry—was again permitted to grow some wool, provided a favorable background for the betterment of the material conditions of the army. The lean and bitter years of war communism were over and more temperate winds were blowing over the Russian plain.

It would be wrong to think that the conflicts in the Red Army during the Civil War period had completely exhausted themselves. There still was a great deal of material for antagonisms among the various component groups in the army, and it was affected to a certain extent by the political struggle and the class antagonisms in the country at large.

The army was becoming more like the commonplace Western European armies but it retained many unique features, and remained a class army designed not only as an instrument of military defense of the country, but also as a tool of class control. To what extent the change in form affected the content, and what influence, if any, this change had on the policies of the Communist party and the Soviet Government would be interesting to know. Limitations of space prevent any but the most cursory glimpses into these aspects of the military problem.

Since the end of the Civil War the commanding personnel had undergone a momentous evolution. The changes that took place at the time of Frunze have not lost their importance even today.

Commanders

During the period of Frunze's reforms there still were among the commanding personnel of the Red Army the several groups that were present during the Civil War, i.e. the old army officers, the former N.C.O.'s of the old army, the military communists, the former Red Guards and former private soldiers, who had received their military training immediately on the battlefields of the Civil War, as well as the graduates of the Soviet short-term command courses—the Red Commanders.

An additional group came into being after the first mass graduation from normal military schools in 1923 of Red Commanders, who had received a fairly adequate military training, and could, in a measure, be compared in this respect, if not in actual experience and general education, with the graduates of the old army military schools.

The numerical strength of these groups had been rapidly changing since the end of the Civil War. The most numerous groups—those of the old army officers and of the old army N.C.O.'s, was declining in strength, while the Red Commanders, the former commissars and others without a professional military training, were proportionally gaining in relation to the total number of the commanding personnel.

By the end of 1921, the commanding personnel of the Red Army (beginning with those occupying the posts of platoon commanders, i.e. excluding section commanders) contained 43.4 per cent of commanders without any military education whatsoever. There was a group about 13 per cent strong of the former N.C.O.'s of the old army, another of about 10 per cent of Red Commanders graduated from the short-term Soviet military schools, 22.1 per cent of former temporary old army officers, about 6 per cent of former army civil servants and 5.6 per cent of old army cadre officers.[19]

There were thus 63.3 per cent of the commanding personnel in the group termed by Trotsky as "most democratic . . . from the lowest walks of life," opposed to 36.7 per cent belonging largely to the former upper and middle classes of the Empire, if not by descent, at least through their former personal status. Only 5.6 per cent of the total—the former cadre officers of the old army—could be regarded as professional military officers, although, perhaps, some of the temporary old army officers, because of their long service in the field, both in the World War and the Civil War, had become professionalized, through actual training they had received.[20]

Less than 20 per cent of the commanding personnel belonged in 1921 to the Communist party, as against the 10 per cent of Communist party membership for the entire Red Army. The percentage of Communists among the commanding personnel of the army was substantially reduced during the great party "cleansing" of the fall of 1921.[21]

In the same year the Soviet War College graduated for the first time since its foundation, about one hundred Red general staff officers.[22]

In 1921 the commanding personnel was purged of its least reliable (from the communist viewpoint) elements. More than 14,000 former White officers were registered separately, and about 4,000 of these were handed over to the People's Commissariat of Labor and given an indefinite furlough from military duties. Another 8,415 were also furloughed indefinitely by a special order of the Revolutionary Military Council of the Republic.[23]

It is rather interesting to note that in 1921 there were 1,681 deserters from the ranks of the commanding personnel and 1,896 from those of the administrative personnel of the Red Army.[24]

There were further drastic reductions in the commanding and administrative personnel during the subsequent years. The tables on the next page show at a glance the reasons for removing these men from the Red Army.[25]

The number of those removed for political reasons seems to be much higher in 1924 than in 1923, even if only persons in the groups "former Whites and similar reasons" and "insufficient political qualifications" are included in that category.

In spite of these purges, a certain number of former White officers

In 1923

	Age	Reductions in the establishments	Illness	Unsatisfactory attestations	Former Whites	Death	Reasons not indicated	Total
Commanding Personnel	1,561	77	18	107	32	8	103	1,906
Administrative Personnel	1,183	518	4	39	23	7	77	1,851

End of 1924

	Age	Former Whites and similar reasons	Insufficient training and lack of utility	Insufficient political qualifications	Other reasons	In all	Plus	Total
Commanding and Administrative Personnel	2,742	1,584	2,149	535	1,772	8,782	608	9,390

remained in the Red Army's commanding personnel. Those whose service record and gallantry in action was considered of a sufficiently high level to warrant regarding them as devoted to the Soviet cause, were officially relieved of the stigma "former White officers," and given full rights of Red Army commanders.[26]

The social origin of the commanding personnel fell into the following groups :[27]

	WORKERS	PEASANTS	OTHERS
1923	13.6%	52.7%	33.7%
1926	16.%	57.2%	26.8%
1927	22.4%	56.%	21.6%

In other words, while the number of members of the former middle and upper classes diminished perceptibly during the four-year period under consideration, persons of proletarian origin had increased—without, however, becoming a majority. The largest group, in 1927, as in 1923, remained that of persons of peasant origin. Thus, on the eve of the first Five Year Plan, the majority of the Red Army commanders were men with close ties with the village.

These general figures for the entire commanding personnel are perhaps not as interesting as those shown in another table, given below, presenting the break-up for the various categories of the commanders for the year 1926.[28]

	WORKERS	PEASANTS	OTHERS
Highest commanders (comparable to generals)	7.3%	31.2%	61.5%
Senior commanders (field officers)	9.3%	46%	44.7%
Middle commanders (comparable to captains and subalterns)	18.0%	61.4%	20.6%

While one could say that during the Civil War the Red Army was predominantly officered by the former officers and N.C.O.'s of the old army, the above table seems to indicate that as late as 1926, after Frunze's reforms had run their course, considerably more than half of the generals of the Red Army were still men who came from the ranks of the Czar's officers. In the group of the middle commanders, the percentage of men of peasant origin was very high, almost exactly equal to that of the "others" among the generals. This was probably because of a large number of former N.C.O.'s of the old army among that group.

Party affiliation during the term fluctuated as follows:[29]

	1924	1927
Members of the Communist party	24.4%	38.7%
Candidates for Membership in the C.P.	6.2%	10.9%
Members of the Komsomol	1.2%	5.8%
Without party affiliation	68.2%	44.6%

While between 1921 and 1924 the percentage of Communists among the commanders increased only slowly, it grew quite rapidly in the next three years, so that in 1927 the Communists, the candidate Communists and the Komsomols already formed the majority of the commanding personnel of the Red Army. From the communist viewpoint this was a favorable situation at the time when social cleavage again assumed an acute form during the Five Year Plan and compensated for the large percentage of peasants and "others" among the commanding personnel at that time.

In 1923 there still were 43.4 per cent of commanders without any military education. By 1926, thanks to a well-developed network of schools and refresher courses, as well as removal of the "unteachable" element, as exemplified in the table for 1924 above, only 4 per cent of commanders were without any special military training.[30]

Whether those who went through the various short-term schools as adults without much general education and without mental habits developed by school attendance in youth really became adequately educated military officers is open to doubt.

What Trotsky said in November 1921 was probably still true even at the end of the NEP period of the large percentage of former guerilla leaders, Red Guards, bluejackets, and private soldiers of the old army who rose to command positions in the Red Army and remained in it after the end of hostilities. "Nobody would deny," said Trotsky, "that a new commanding personnel has appeared, which is realizing the aspirations of the toiling people, although it is building the army with errors against Russian literacy and against military literacy. Our misfortune is that the land is illiterate, and, of course, years and years are necessary until illiteracy disappears and the Russian toiling man becomes associated with culture."[31]

These words could hardly endear Trotsky to the large group of Red commanders concerned. It is quite likely, however, that the situation he described continued well into the late 'twenties or even later. In peacetime conditions, this group of unlettered commanders who prided themselves on being the core of the army, as veterans of the revolutionary struggle, was a great handicap to the development of the military efficacy of the Red Army.

In so far as the reserve commanders were concerned, matters were even worse. In May 1925 Frunze frankly admitted that, because of budgetary limitations, it had been impossible to call out the reserve commanding personnel for refresher training even once since the end of hostilities. "This reserve commanding personnel of ours," he remarked, "is characterized by a complete military backwardness." In the meanwhile, the Red Army had adapted new tactical methods, and new regulations were introduced. The reserve commanding personnel were almost entirely ignorant of these changes.[32]

During the NEP period there was a tendency to represent, in public utterances and in the press, the commanding personnel of the Red Army as a monolithic group, where the differences between the old army officers and those who rose from the ranks and were promoted from the short term military schools had disappeared. The difference between the party and the non-party element was also toned down.[33]

The actual situation was quite different. There was considerable friction and antagonism between the various component groups of the commanding personnel in that period. Frunze's frequent utterances denying the existence of the rift were merely symptoms of the existing friction.

In discussing the Red Army at its eighth anniversary, Voroshilov had said: "We have at the present very many old specialists working for us. But should one ask me to say conscientiously what is the difference between N. N. Petin, commanding the Siberian Military District, and other district commanders, party members, I should have difficulty in answering. There is hardly any difference. . . . They are comrades alike and would die in the same manner at the first order of the Workers' and Peasants' Government at their combat posts, as their other, party, comrades would."[34]

Frunze's remarks, published in the *Red Star* on January 1, 1925, probably come nearer to revealing the actual situation. In discussing the retiring of a part of the commanding personnel, he admitted that this measure was commonly regarded as directed especially against the "old specialists" and indicating a new attitude toward them on the part of the authorities. Frunze denied demobilization measures were directed exclusively against old army officers, and stated that while "a certain group" of older commanders was retired from the army, this was done merely because those so affected had reached the retiring age as specified in army regulations. "Our attitude toward the old specialists," said he, "did not change for the worse, and we consider that even the separation of them into a distinct group has no sense whatsoever after the lengthy joint work in the ranks."[35]

A glance at the age limitations of the statutes that were in force prior to 1928 would immediately show, however, that they were made quite low and were quite obviously aimed at the former officers and non-commissioned officers of the old army.

These age limits were: for the generals, 45 years, for the field officers 36 to 40 years, for the "middle commanders" only 29 to 36 years. Room was very definitely made for the young graduates of the Soviet normal military schools, who were supposed to be both reliable from the Soviet viewpoint as well as sufficiently educated in the arts of war.

The correct interpretation of Frunze's words in that interview may be found in some of the notes found in his archives. "A wider way for the Red Commander—this is the basic watch-word. . . . Does this mean the persecution of the old military specialists and the admission of their uselessness for the Red Army? Nothing of the kind. Those who worked and continue to work in the Red Army among the old general staff, those who gave all their strength and knowledge to the work of upbuilding, have a perfect right to recognition of themselves and their services on the part of the Workers' and Peasants' state . . . the old are far from being really 'old,' and the young have a great deal still to learn."[36]

The trained old general staff officers were still indispensable for staff work and the administration of the central bureaus of the army. The new brood of War College graduates was yet lacking in experience. Hence Frunze's plea for the retention of the old army officers in the Red Army. However, in spite of his assurances to the contrary, these old army officers were considered by the "Red" element of the commanding personnel as standing apart from them, forming a separate group. Frunze himself had admitted it. In 1922, he had pointed out that "our old commanding personnel that came to us from the old czarist army, in its majority, could break with its habitual former concept only with the greatest difficulty to come over to the new viewpoint. It stood for the principle of the national army. In practice this principle meant the domination of the exploiting classes." He admonished these old officers not to feel that they were mere military specialists concerned with technical military problems only, and not to stand aloof from politics.[37]

The concept of the national army, so dear to many of the old officers, did not mean, of course, the domination of the army by the "exploiting classes" who were already economically annihilated by that time in Russia. But it did mean the negation of the subservience of the army to a party, the Communists, to a minority dictatorship.

That in the daily life of the Red Army there was considerable difference between the position of a commander without party affiliation (and such overwhelmingly were then the old army officers) and the communist commanders, was made clear by Frunze himself in his article on "The balance sheet and the prospects of military building." Speaking of commissars' relations with commanders, Frunze pointed out that when the latter were not members of the party (this was true of practically all the old army officers), these relations led to a gradual diminution of rights and functions of commanders. "The commander gradually loses the most precious qualities of every good commander —the will-power and ability to make independent, quick decisions."[38]

These non-party commanders were thus becoming "yes-men" to their commissars, and were unable, psychologically, to exercise command. In peacetime, commissars could take liberties with commanders they could ill afford in war.

In the meanwhile the attitude of these old army officers to the Red Army and the Soviet Government was undergoing a great change, as against the days when most of them were forced into the Red Army almost literally at the point of the gun. It is impossible to devote here sufficient space to the examination of this adjustment of the ex-czarist officers to the service in the Workers' and Peasants' army. A few illustrations, however, may be of some use.

The element of military professionalism, the habit of military life, of the camp, of the barracks, had its part in this process, together with pride in one's military craftsmanship.

E. Wollenberg, in his book *The Red Army*, brought up the case of an ex-colonel of the old army, who was hauled into the Red forces, and upon receiving from a commissar a copy of Trotsky's decree for the mobilization of former officers, was informed that his wife and children would be held responsible for any treachery he might commit. A few minutes later he was riding in a staff car, already invested with the command of a Red rifle regiment. Upon reaching his unit, he was given the cold shoulder by the former N.C.O.'s who had heretofore occupied all posts of command in the regiment. Two days later his regiment went into action. The ex-colonel grabbed a rifle and rushed at the enemy's positions at the head of his men. From then on he had the moral ascendancy over the commanders and men of the regiment, and all opposition to him ceased.[39]

The above-mentioned Kotomin's memorandum refers to Staff Captain Riakin, a Knight of the Order of St. George, who commanded a Red rifle regiment and served "zealously, risking his life at every step." According to Kotomin, the regiment was held together by this ex-czarist officer, although there were many Communists in it.[40]

Trotsky devoted a brief article to the memory of the ex-czarist general, A. P. Nikolaev, who commanded a brigade in the Red Army and was executed by the White army command upon being captured in 1919. Trotsky wrote: "The former general of the czarist army not only did not deny his connection with our Red Army, but on the contrary, threw the gauntlet in the face of his executioners and died shouting: 'Long live the Workers' and Peasants' Government!' "[41]

The war with Poland had made quite a change in the attitude of the old army officers. Those who heretofore had stood aloof from the Red Army offered their services to the Soviet Government. In May 1920 Trotsky reported at a Moscow meeting that one of the best known leaders of the czarist army, General A. A. Brusilov, had addressed a letter to the chief of the army staff, suggesting the desirability of raising to a higher level the feeling of national patriotism, judging it impossible without this to create an effective army. He had offered to call a conference of men of "wide military and practical experience" to discuss recruiting, training, the better utilization of the transportation system and the possibility of improving the supply services. Brusilov's offer was accepted by the Soviet Government and he was made the chairman of the Special Conference. Other members appointed to it were generals prominent in the administration and command of the old army, such as Polivanov, Klembovskii, Baluev, Gutor and Zaionchkovskii.[42]

This conference was an emotional bridge between the old Russian army leaders, who still retained a great deal of moral influence with their younger fellow-officers, and the Soviet Government. They had themselves taken that step, and it was recognized as a patriotic move on their part by the Soviet leadership.

Wollenberg asserts that patriotic feeling was the main motive inducing officers of the old army to offer their services in good faith to the Soviet Government. He brings up the example of Admiral Altvater at the Brest-Litovsk peace conference, who told Trotsky: "I came here because I was forced to. I did not trust you. But now I shall help you and do my duty as never before, for I sincerely believe I shall be serving my country in so doing."[43] The writer's own impressions confirm Wollenberg's views regarding Altvater. To an even greater degree this was true of the former Commander in Chief of the Soviet naval forces, Captain Eugene Behrens, who offered his services to the Soviet Government from the highest motives of patriotic duty.

However, these volunteers were comparatively few, and until Brusilov's offer, the old army generals as a group were more or less openly inimical to the Red Army. The end of the Civil War, the quicker pulsation of the feeling of national duty during the Polish campaign, the belief that the Soviet Government had come to stay and had no real rivals for the rule of Russia—all these motives made for a very definite change in the mood of the old army officers in command positions in the Red forces. Belief in the Soviet Government's certainty of survival played a rôle even as early as 1918. Thus the present Soviet Ambassador at the Court of St. James, who was at the time one of the leaders of anti-bolshevik forces on the Volga, has reported a conversation with an old army general, who told him that he regarded the bolshevik government as firmly established and considered attempts to overthrow it as mere adventurism.[44]

A good many Russians who had surreptitiously emigrated from their native country in the early 'twenties, in the NEP period, will remember how their friends among the old army and navy officers, suspecting their intentions, begged them never to write and not to count on them for any participation in counter-revolutionary activities. The break with the mood of 1917-1920 was definite.

Frunze wrote in 1925 that the deciding factor in matters relating to promotion of commanders was that of their combat record and that there would be no change in this respect in the future. "Preference will be given to those who rose from below, who have a large combat experience and have retained the freshness of their vigor."[45]

These elements "who rose from below" were given preference in admission to the War College, this door to highest career in the army. In December 1924, Frunze was able to state that 72 per cent of the students belonged to the worker and peasant classes, while the balance of the vacancies were filled by the "toiling intelligentsia." The latter term, no doubt, covered a good many sins and included some of the former old army officers.[46]

In April 1924, Frunze delivered a significant speech at the War College, explaining his ideas as to the changes in the higher command personnel of the army. He claimed that in his actions he was not guided by any lack of political confidence in those removed from their posts. He gave, as the motive for his changes, the new vigorous elements rising from below, new cadres of workers seeking employment for their abilities. He condemned Trotsky, by innuendo, for not providing a sufficient outlet for these new elements in the army, and accused him of being slow in admitting them into positions of control and authority. "Had we gone by this path more firmly earlier, probably, there would be no necessity now for this general shake-up which is at present being carried out." In his view, these forces, accumulated in the lower strata of the army commanders and political personnel, were searching for employment and found it during the reorganization of the military machine carried out after the ousting of Trotsky from the control of the Red Army.[47]

In practice, this really amounted to the replacement of men loyal to Trotsky, or at least apolitical, by Trotsky's opponents. This was the first "purge" of the Red Army. The ambitions of the young commissars and the "Red" commanders made them willing allies of those who were perpetrating the purge. In later chapters there will be occasion to dwell in greater detail on the method of that operation and its effect on the morale of the commanding and political personnel.

In his memoirs, Trotsky refers to the arrival at Sukhum in January 1924 of a delegation of the Central Committee of the party to co-ordinate with him the changes in the personnel of the Commissariat for War. "Essentially, this was already the purest comedy," he wrote. "The renovation of the personnel was going on at full speed for a long time behind my back."[48]

Trotsky ascribed the removal of the Deputy People's Commissar for War, Sklianskii, from his post, to Stalin's vengeance. While he had a great deal of regard for Frunze, he considered him as a military administrator considerably inferior* to Sklianskii.[49]

* Whether Trotsky was right in this, is doubtful. Frunze was a man of considerable talent.

That the new element "from below" had serious defects, Frunze was the first to admit. "To the number of these negative sides, I count first of all the excessively great self-confidence in one's own capacities," he said. This self-confidence often turned into self-conceit and bombast. According to Frunze, these were not uncommon traits among the rising young forces.[50]

One is inclined to believe that Piatnitskii was right in classifying the Red Army commanders according to their acceptability to the Soviet Government in the following sequence:

1) Commanders belonging to the party. 2) Commanders candidates for party membership of working class origin. 3) Commanders belonging by their origin to the urban proletariat. 4) Commanders of poor peasant and rural laborer origin (regarded as a necessary evil in a country with a predominant peasant population). 5) Commanders whose class origin branded them as "class enemies," the "socially alien element," the former officers of the old army who were still indispensable because of their military-technical qualifications, and could not be replaced as yet by the proletarian elements.[51]

Of the 50,000 or thereabouts of old army officers who had served in the Red Army, only 4,500 had remained within it in 1930. Their percentage to the total number of the commanding personnel fell from 76 per cent in 1918 to 10 per cent in 1930.[52]

This constant pressure from below of the young "Red" element among the commanders had made for a cleavage and an antagonism between the communist element and the old army officers, who were gradually being crowded out of the army. Some of the former N.C.O.'s and soldiers of the old army who were unable to acquire the required minimum of information and to broaden their general cultural horizon sufficiently to compete for advancement with the graduates of the normal military schools established by the Soviets were, probably, also far from happy in the highly competitive atmosphere of the army.

Voroshilov had to admit in 1927 "that in our army we do not have as yet a real fusion among the commanding personnel." He went on to describe the mood of some of these commanders who "fall into despair" because of being passed in promotion, or—perhaps even more characteristic and important—"because he did not have the ordinary opportunity of sharing his feelings with some one among his comrades, to discuss his affairs."[53]

This was certainly a strange state of affairs, as described by the then People's Commissar for War. In military life there develops, as a rule, a very close-knit regimental or brigade group of officers, who become intimate friends and come to share their joys and sorrows with their comrades at arms. Anyone who was a member of a Russian wardroom or a regimental mess of the old army would vividly recall the friendly and mutually helpful life of these groups.

The reason for this estrangement of the commanding personnel of the Red Army was given by Voroshilov in the same speech: "Had we always had a comradely collective fusion, had there existed a setting in which it were possible to open one's soul to each other . . . we should not have had these situations, where a commander did not know where to turn and, as a result, fell into despair sometimes for quite petty reasons. . . ."[54]

That disparity in class origin and cultural level had a great deal to do with the lack of comradely spirit, and this obviously antagonistic atmosphere existing among the commanders of that period, is also proved by Voroshilov himself in his analysis of the social origins of students of military schools: "Into our schools come, mainly, worker and peasant youth. But to this healthy strata unite themselves other, undesirable, strata. We have, on the one hand, the rising percentage of 'others,' and now these 'others' are not what they were before . . . we have men who go into military schools because of lack of work, the unemployed, and, usually we receive a considerable number of those who had suffered one or other failure in their life course."[55]

This sharp differentiation between the "others" and the "desirable" elements, clearly shows the attitude of the Soviet authorities to these two categories among the commanding personnel of the Red Army. True enough, the pill was coated, in so far as the older commanders belonging to the "others" group are concerned, by the explanation that the "others" seeking admission into the military schools during the last years of the NEP were not as good as those of the same category who had joined the Red Army during the Civil War years.

It may be useful at this stage to examine the new group that began to enter the ranks of the commanding personnel after the NEP, that of the graduates of the Soviet normal military schools.

These schools had a three-year course for infantry and cavalry, and a four-year course for those specializing in other arms.[56]

The general education of the applicants for admission was considered unsatisfactory by the military authorities because of the decline in the educational standards of the Russian secondary schools since the revolution. The head of the military education, D. Petrovskii, plainly stated: "That our school—I am speaking of civil schools —is functioning badly, this we all know."[57]

To remedy this, Petrovskii even proposed the re-establishment of military secondary schools to replace the old czarist Cadet Corps, where children of the old army officers were receiving their education under the Empire.[58] He pointed out that such a school was already functioning at Baku, opened on the initiative of the Azerbeidzhan Republic. A conference of the commanding personnel of the Ukraine and the Crimea had adopted a resolution in 1922 advocating the opening of these military secondary schools.[59]

Among the reasons advanced in favor of militarization of a certain number of the secondary schools was that of better prospects of obtaining, through these means, students for the normal military schools who would be devoted to the career of arms. Petrovskii had intimated that the young workers and peasants entering the latter schools were first of all guided by their thirst for a better general education and were willing to study the special military subjects only because of the chance of broadening their general education.[60]

This plea for Soviet Cadet Corps met with a decided setback at the hands of those responsible for Soviet public education, and did not bear fruit at the time.[61]

The NEP tendencies, with their anti-war and anti-militarist bias, had a serious influence on the students of the Soviet military schools. Petrovskii complained that at times it was very difficult to "digest" the youngsters entering these schools during the NEP period. As he puts it, they were coming "from the street," thoroughly permeated with NEP tendencies, conflicting with the traditions and aims of Soviet military education.[62]

To offset these trends brought into the military schools by young men without any military background, by 1925 special efforts were made to attract to these schools "middle" commanders and members of the political personnel of the same rank—i.e. persons who would occupy positions in the army corresponding to lieutenants and captains—who were not in possession of any rounded out military education. It was suggested at the time that all such commanders should pass through the normal military schools. The other group urged to enter the schools was that of the graduates of the command courses of Civil War times. Volunteers who had joined the army as privates were also considered as desirable material for the schools, although it was admitted that not all of them were suitable commander timber, as not possessing the "firmness of will" necessary for a commander, and that many of them were lacking in a real interest in the military career and were on a "low level of political development."[63]

The young men "from the street" who were entering the normal military schools in the first years of the NEP were obviously very different from the standard of the command courses of the Civil War period. They were better educated, and the comparatively long course of studies in the normal military schools gave them an incomparably better chance to acquire the rudiments of military theory and practice.

Trotsky wrote in 1924 that these young men entered the military schools without any revolutionary or fighting experience behind them. The Red Army had already crystallized itself into an organization with a definite regimen and traditions. The authority of the older commanding personnel stood very high among these youngsters— theirs were the laurels of the revolutionary wars and the halo of revolutionary heroes. So high was this respect for the older comrades at arms that Trotsky was apprehensive lest that authority depress or even terrorize the young men into conformance with the established pattern.[64]

That the young commanders were thus molded into a military caste, on a Soviet pattern, was very distasteful to Trotsky at the time, as he appealed for support to the young against what he called the "party bureaucracy." "The army," he then wrote, "as a fighting mass organization, needs not bureaucratic toadies, but men morally well tempered, permeated with the feeling of responsibility."[65]

The social origin of the students of normal military schools continued to change in the direction of a greater proletarization of the student body. The number of students belonging to the "others" category was falling off.[66]

	WORKERS	PEASANTS	OTHERS
1921 (February 1)	31.4%	48%	20.6%
1923 (April 1)	33.6%	50%	16.4%
1925	33%	52%	15%
1927	38%	51%	11%

Party affiliation of these students shows a trend toward increase in the non-party element among them between 1921 and 1923 and a rapid falling off between 1923 and 1927:[67]

	1921	1923	1927
Communists	51.8%	30.7%	30%
Without party affiliations	48.2%	50.5%	29%
Komsomols	—	18.8%	41%

These figures show that the change in the social origin of the students of the military schools of Soviet Russia in that period had certain similarities with the direction of that change under the last decades of the old régime. While the number of peasants increased very markedly (compare with 19 per cent in the Alexis Military School in 1912-1913) and the number of "others" fell off very considerably (from 79 per cent at the same old régime school in 1912-1913) the latter group continued to be represented, with the general direction of the trend being the same: from the upper social classes to the lower.

The student body was thus changing pronouncedly in the direction of becoming the "workers and peasants" cadets not only in name but also in fact.

Piatnitskii had expressed the thought that the rapid proletarization of the normal military schools resulted in giving the Red Army an almost illiterate, uncultured officers' corps, whose primitive minds were not able to grasp and to digest the more complicated phases of military sciences and of the art of war.[68]

This may be so in a measure, but one must not lose sight of the fact that the change for the better in these respects from the average of the Civil War period command courses was very definite, and represented real progress.

The normal military schools had in view to prepare young commanders fully qualified in theory as well as practice, to occupy the post of platoon commander, and to have sufficient knowledge and training for the command of a company. It was stressed that regardless of the arm selected by the student, he should have a sufficiently rounded out general military education to understand the art of war on the whole and to possess the knowledge of the dynamics of war. The normal schools were introduced in the end of 1921 and the beginning of 1922. Commanders of each arm of the service were to be educated in separate schools.[69]

The training of commanders of the so-called "national" troops was entrusted to ten "unified military schools," each of which prepared commanders for the infantry, for the cavalry and for the artillery. Of these, one, named after Unschlicht, was designated for training men of Polish nationality to provide against the possibility of the formation in the future of the Red Army of Poland. The length of the training period varied from three and a half to four and a half years, depending on the arm for which the students were trained.[70]

The low educational level of the classes from which the Soviet Government sought to draw the students of the military schools made it necessary to set the entrance requirements well below those insisted upon in the old army. Until 1928, the certificate of graduation from the lower schools (schools of the first degree) was sufficient for admission. After 1928, the nominal educational requirements were raised somewhat, but until 1935 these new rules were not applied strictly, particularly with respect to the lower commanding personnel (sergeants and corporals) who sought to enter the schools. In 1935, 15 per cent of those admitted had an education below the requirements provided for in the regulations.[71]

The contrast between the NEP realities of Soviet life and the traditions of the Red Army created difficult psychological problems for the communist commanders, and resulted in "decadent moods," as Petrovskii calls them, among the students of the military schools. The peasant element among those felt strongly the "call of the land," and the students in general were affected by the pacifistic tendencies that were flourishing at the time in the villages as well as the towns.[72]

Probably the greatest organizational factor making for cleavage between the various groups of the commander element was the method by which the principle of unity of command was introduced. Its practical result was the creation of several categories of the commanding personnel endowed with different rights and having activities of varying scope.

The desirability of concentrating in the hands of commanders the full powers of authority in the fields of operations, administration and supply made itself felt early in the life of the Red Army.

Thus, I. Smilga, in a speech delivered before the first All-Russian Congress of army political workers in 1920, stated that he considered it feasible to grant to commanders the right to issue orders without endorsements of commissars, and to liquidate the institution of military commissars in units commanded by "proven men," in which class Smilga included not only communist commanders, but also those of the non-party element in command positions "who by their work had proved their devotion to the Soviet government."[73] However, it was not until 1924 that the principle of unity of command came to be applied in the Red Army. Frunze stated in December of that year that after the latest "compression" of the army which left in it "the best part of the commanding personnel," it had become expedient to envisage practical steps in the direction of concentration of authority in the hands of commanders.[74]

Three different approaches to reach that end were suggested by Frunze: 1) Concentration in the person of the commander of not only combat, administrative and supply functions, but of political guidance and education of the troops as well. 2) Investing commanders with full powers in the spheres of combat, administration and supply. 3) For administrative bureaus the concentration of authority was considered the easiest to achieve. It was planned not to have there any special political organs at all, and to let the party nuclei, under the guidance of the nearest political military organ, conduct the political work in their bureaus.[75]

The first pattern, according to Frunze, was to be an exception, and not even all of the Communists among the commanding personnel were expected to be endowed with powers provided for under that head. The second was to be the typical arrangement. Party members, as well as non-partisan commanders, were supposed to be granted powers provided for in that category. An exception was made for the navy, where it was considered inadvisable to hurry with the introduction of the new plan. The social origins of the senior commanders of the navy and the scarcity of "Red" commanders in positions of authority on board ships no doubt provided the reasons for this exception.[76]

In 1927, Voroshilov stated that the application of the principle of unity of command had given an opportunity to the commanding personnel to study all phases of political army work and to become active political workers themselves. Also that the measure had called for a higher level of military training on the part of the members of the political organs of the army. He concluded by saying that, by and large, the principle of unity of command was already practiced "in a significant measure" and had given "serious results." In 1926 he said he hoped that within a year or two the unity of command might become universally applied.[77]

There were, nevertheless, some difficulties. In the same year, Voroshilov had occasion to point out that the application of the principle of unity of command had led to a tendency evident among some of the commanders to brush aside the political workers of the army and to assert their own primacy, as well as the paramount importance of the command functions over the political ones. Some political workers, on the other hand, had reached the conclusion that their functions were restricted merely to political work alone, and were not paying any attention to combat, administration and supply. In Voroshilov's view, both of these trends were wrong—the commanding personnel should not leave all political work to political organs, and party guidance should permeate "the entire life of the Red Army." He also condemned the tendency of many political workers to overburden the commanders with political work, insisting that the latter lecture to their men about "all Changsolins and Poincarés." Voroshilov felt that, with this political load, commanders had no time left for rest or relaxation.[78]

This overburdening of commanders with political work undoubtedly decreased the efficacy of the commanding personnel, who had little time to improve themselves in the purely military aspects of their duties. And it was precisely there that room for improvement was still very considerable.

In 1925, Frunze pointed to the low level of discipline among the commanding personnel of the army and to the lack of military bearing—he even cited moving in the ranks on parade.[79]

On the other hand, the political workers were not inclined to lend a hand in maintaining discipline. According to Frunze, at that time the burden of discipline enforcement rested entirely upon the shoulders of the commanding personnel, while political workers preferred to play the rôle of defenders of soldiers from oppression on the part of commanders.[80]

In 1924, Frunze spoke of the slovenliness in dress of the commanders and the political personnel of the army. At the time he drew attention to the frequent failure to carry out orders given in the line of duty, or the execution of such orders only upon repeated insistence upon them. He spoke, as well, of the discussion of commanders' orders by subordinates.[81]

As he stated elsewhere "instead of a firm and categorical insistence on the fulfillment of duty, there exists an unprincipled 'playing up to' the Red Army soldiers, the wish to show one's own exceptional 'democratism.' " He ascribed this phenomenon to the dual control which served to deprive commanders of will-power and initiative.[82]

That the situation did not improve in this respect, even by the end of the NEP, seems to be indicated in Voroshilov's remarks in 1927 that some commanders were inclined to believe that it did not pay to spoil their reputation as good fellows by entering into conflict with the masses of the soldiers among whom "many are no worse than I."[83]

Wollenberg also testifies to these "democratic" tendencies among the commanding personnel at the time. He states that communist commanders seldom wore the badges of their rank when off duty and frequently dispensed with them even when on duty. He cites a case of a company commander who had refused in 1925 to ride in a motor bus, on the ground that it was not fitting for a proletarian commander to ride in a "motor."[84]

That Wollenberg does not exaggerate seems to be proved by several items in the *Red Star* in 1925. One speaks of commanders tending to disregard "their rights and obligations in matters of discipline." Another quotes a letter to the editor (possibly of inspired origin) speaking of a discussion of commanders' ethics at a regimental meeting—for instance, whether it was ethical for a commander to have overstuffed furniture, to own geese, to be personally tidy and to wear well-cut clothes, also to wear rings and to drink beer. The editorial reply to these queries was not less curious than the questions asked. It began by stating that there was no need for a special ethical code for commanding personnel, and then proceeded to say that the commander should be a paragon of all the virtues, and should give the best possible object example to the soldiers. As to overstuffed furniture, the problem was solved by a counter-question asking "Where would a commander get the means to buy such furniture?" Rings were unconditionally condemned, as well as dandyism in clothes. Beer was considered permissible in moderate quantities. Geese ownership was declared *per se* permissible, but should commanders devote too much of their time and energy to geese-breeding, then geese ownership would be against the better interests of the service.[85]

The extreme naïveté of this discussion does not hide the conflicts involved between the more cultured group and those who rose from the ranks or came from the work bench, as well as the puritans of proletarianism; between the lovers of flesh-pots and the ascetic element inherited from the early Civil War days. The levelling down, the egalitarianism of the prevailing official tendency is obvious.

There were no special officers' messes, and the commanding personnel's food was prepared in the same kitchen as that of the private soldiers.[86] The reason for this lay in the policy of trying to provide for rest and relaxation of the commanding personnel and members of their families within the walls of the Red Army clubs, where the private soldiers spent their hours of leisure. It was regarded as undesirable to isolate commanders from the rank and file even during the rest period. This close personal contact with the men in the ranks was regarded as the safeguard of a closely-knit army personnel.[87]

That there were difficulties in this respect one can see from some indications in Soviet sources. Thus the *Military Calendar* for 1924 states that in order to enable the commanding personnel to spend their off-duty hours at the Red Army clubs, these should be so organized as to attract, to be of interest as well as of use, to the commanders and their families. As examples of suitable adaptation of Red Army clubs to commanders' needs, the *Military Calendar* points to the so-called Red Army and Navy Houses, at Leningrad, Moscow, Kharkov, Kiev and other important garrison centers. While all ranks of the Red Army were admitted to these houses, their functions were planned with a view to suit the interests and needs of the commanding personnel and their families. It would seem that these houses were really officers' clubs, admission to which was not denied, for certain political reasons, to the rank and file of the army.[88]

This problem of providing for the leisure hours of the commanding personnel was a very important one, because of the difficult economic situation they had found themselves in under the NEP.

Frunze wrote in 1922 about the "unheard-of difficulties in the material conditions of existence" of the commanding personnel. Even for years later such an urgent matter as that of pensions for retired commanders was still hanging in the air.[89]

Wollenberg speaks of the army corps commander's pay in 1924 as equalling 150 rubles a month.* This roughly corresponded to wages earned by a well-paid metal worker and was 25 rubles per month below the so-called "party maximum," i.e. the largest monthly salary permissible for a party member at the time.[90]

The official Soviet sources confirm Wollenberg's statement:[91]

| | RED ARMY | | | | | |
| | UNTIL AFTER | | | | | |
	DEC. I 1925	DEC. I 1925	POLISH ARMY	ENGLISH ARMY	GERMAN ARMY	FRENCH ARMY
Platoon commander	42	65	76	212	62	57
Company commander	53	78	116	343	84	110
Battalion commander	61	85	150	488	114	152
Regimental commander	85	120	204	614	163	211
Army division commander	110	150	323	1020	280	321

The table shows that there was a great disparity between the pay of officers commanding battalions or larger units in the U.S.S.R., as against those in the Western European armies, where the economic stratification of the officers, according to their rank, was much more marked than was true of the Soviet army during the NEP.

Voroshilov commented on this in 1926, stating that the Soviet

---

* The part of the table showing officers' pay in Western European countries was taken over from Soviet sources and not checked. They probably do not represent accurately the actual picture, as the purchasing power of the Soviet ruble did not correspond to its artificially maintained foreign currency value. It should be regarded merely as a crude approximation.

commanders do not aspire to "generals' remunerations," although they are aware that their economic well-being would improve with the general change to the better in the economic conditions of the U.S.S.R.[92]

In 1925 only 30 per cent of the commanding personnel were housed in a manner regarded by Frunze at all as tolerable. Seventy per cent had housing facilities below that level. Frunze spoke of various localities where several commanders with their families had only one room among them. In other words, each family had only a part of a room at its disposal.[93]

The reserve commanders, when called for re-training outside of the ranks of the army, were remunerated for their work on a basis which would not look attractive to a Chinese coolie. Those employed or belonging to the peasantry were paid five kopeks per hour, while the unemployed among them were paid nine kopeks per hour, for the time they were engaged in their studies.[94]

In the first years of the NEP the pay of the commanding personnel was considerably below that shown in the table on page 222. In 1924 there were two increases in the pay, one in May, the other in December, which benefited mostly the junior and the middle commanders.[95]

Frunze said in April 1925 that the economic conditions of the commanding personnel was improved by from 30 to 40 per cent. This improvement was achieved at the expense of the reduction of the Red Army from 610 thousand to 562 thousand. Under the NEP, the Soviet state could not afford both a numerous and a well-paid army, and the improvement in the economic position of the commanding and political personnel could be achieved only by reduction in the size of the Red Army. This makes clear the economic reasons for the introduction of the territorial militia system.[96]

Frunze was hoping that it would be possible to introduce further improvements in the economic situation of the commanding and political personnel—up to 20-25 per cent. The increases in pay were partly offset by the cancellation of the rights of the commanders to obtain their fuel supply free and the imposition of the burden of payment out of their pay for the public utility service of which they availed themselves.[97]

One can well imagine under these circumstances the material plight of the Red Army commanders in the years 1922 and 1923.

One of the reasons for the low remuneration rate of the commanding personnel lay in the increased proportion of the whole army consisting of commanding and political personnel. In April 1925,

Frunze remarked that while the Red Army was smaller in numbers than the old Imperial Army in peacetime, it had at least the same number of commanding personnel as the old army. This remark followed directly upon the heels of his statement that the beggarly condition of the commanding and political personnel of the army was a well-known fact.[98]

The relations of commanders with the soldiers in the ranks were not always smooth. There was, apparently, a considerable amount of practice in these relations that differed from what was laid down by Soviet theory. Thus, in February 1925, Frunze had pointed out that the Red Army soldiers were very sensitive to the attempts by the commanding personnel to exploit them for non-duty work. What he calls the element of "batmanship," the tendency of making personal servants out of soldiers, was observable in the Red Army at the time. He insisted that all such trends would be strongly opposed by him. Under the Red Army practice, soldiers had the right of sending complaints to agents of the Military Prosecutor's office. The number of complaints grew from year to year: In 1925 the average number of complaints filed monthly with these agents amounted to 1,892; in 1926, to 1,923; in 1927 to 2,082.[99]

This tendency of the Red Army soldiers to file complaints against their commanders was apparently encouraged by the Military Prosecutor.

As examples of the kind of friction that occurred, the following items drawn from Soviet sources may be of interest:

A commander was transferred to take over a detachment. He had arrived at his new unit, accompanied by his family and household goods. Upon reaching his unit's H.Q. he told the soldier on duty to tell off several men to carry his baggage from the railroad station to his new apartment. A certain amount of dissatisfaction was evident, but only one of the men refused to proceed to carry out the order. The commander took down the name of the soldier who had refused, but, apparently, did not inflict any punishment upon him. As time went on, the new commander continued to exploit his men for such purposes as splitting cord-wood for his apartment stoves, sending them to borrow money from his subordinates, etc. When a junior commander wrote letters to the editors of newspapers to expose him, he succeeded in ousting his public-spirited subordinate from the Red Army. Ultimately that commander was brought before a military tribunal and severely punished.[100] As he was also convicted of rape, it is not quite clear from the newspaper item whether the punishment was severe because of the crime or because of his attempts to exploit his subordinates for non-service purposes. However, the very fact that he was able to carry on his practice of using soldiers as his servants, and even borrowing money from them, without any interference from his superior officers or any attempt on the part of the communist element to bring it immediately to a halt, seems to indicate that the practice of using soldiers for non-service purposes was well established at the time, and did not provoke strong opposition on the part of commanders and the political personnel. That the difficult economic situation of the commanding personnel had a great deal to do with this is very likely.

It would seem that one of the characteristic traits of the period was the lack of a definite pattern in the relations between the commanders and the men in the ranks. As often happens in military life, the lack of such a generally accepted pattern made for conflict. Voroshilov, speaking in 1926, referred to the lack of skill on the part of commanders in their treatment of soldiers, and said that, in some instances, commanders were too familiar, leading to a lack of respect and even to breakdown of discipline. Others, on the contrary, were too harsh in the application of their disciplinary powers. For 1922 there exists, as already mentioned, an official admission, in an order of the Revolutionary Military Council of the Republic, that rough treatment of the soldiers by commanders was a common occurrence, and that there were instances of beating up of soldiers by commanders. The statement regarding the latter was accompanied by a comment that culprits did not all, by any means, suffer suitable punishment. This seems to indicate that the practice was condoned in certain groups of commanders and even political workers, who did not take stringent measures against the transgressors.[101]

Graduates of the normal military schools did not seem to be any different from the rest of the commanders in these respects. Petrovskii even speaks of the element of old régime ideas of the peasantry among them as to the rights and privileges of the officers with respect to the civilian element, and the "other ranks." He adds that these graduates also had a feeling of superiority toward the Red Army commanders who had not undergone regular military schooling.[102]

The lack of a generally accepted pattern affected even such usually rigidly regulated spheres of military life as close-formation drill. Frunze says that, within the same regiment, different companies followed the inclinations of their commanders in this respect. He ascribes

this deviation from the prescribed routine to survival of the old guerilla habits.[103]

In some of the territorial militia units, commanders apparently had
considerable difficulty in enforcing even a most rudimentary discipline.
Frunze mentions an incident concerning a company on march. It fell
out of ranks and spread out in a long column of stragglers, in spite of
all the efforts of its commander. Finally, the latter, a member of the
party, admonished his men in strong language. The Communists
among the militiamen thereupon called a meeting of indignation and
declared their censure of the commander's action.[104] Another instance
mentioned by Frunze deals with a company of sappers. At a practice
spanning of a bridge by the company, its commander ordered one of
his men to enter the water. The latter at first refused, and complied
with the order only upon being admonished by the commissar.[105]

To what extent the non-party commanding personnel had adapted
their general viewpoint and political convictions to those insisted upon
by the Communist party, it is difficult to say. There were obligatory
courses for commanders which were supposed to offer them political
training. However, in 1925 these were discontinued on the grounds
of lack of time at the disposal of commanders, also because of a
shortage of suitable textbooks and sufficiently experienced instructors.
Communist commanders and the political workers were urged to draw
the non-party commanders into debating societies, obviously in order
to influence their views in the fields of politics, religion and philosophy.[106]

As to the general average of the military technical knowledge and
ability of the commanding personnel of the Red Army, Frunze admitted in 1925 that it was definitely below the standards of other
European armies.[107]

At the same time the promotion to higher command positions of
the young graduates of the normal military schools was very rapid.
Petrovskii thought that the necessary minimum was: two years in the
command of a platoon, one year as a senior subaltern, three years as
company commander, two years in command of a battalion and three
years in command of a regiment.[108]

It is doubtful whether young men, far from well educated, could
master the modern army technique rapidly enough in these short
periods of service in the respective posts to become, on the average,
better than mediocre incumbents in the higher posts.

With the low average level of military technical information among
the commanding personnel, the problem of entrance examinations and

programs of the higher military educational establishments—the War College and the technical military colleges—became a very acute one.

Until 1924, the faculties of these colleges continued to apply fairly severe requirements at examinations. From that year on, the entrance examinations were reduced to the level of the programs of the normal military schools. This was done by the faculties under considerable pressure from above. The measure was intended to give a better chance—to the graduates of the normal military schools as well as to the less well educated among the balance of the commanding personnel—to enter the colleges and thus have a chance of quicker advancement to the highest staff positions and the command of the larger army units.[109]

Generally speaking, this measure was unfavorable to the former old army officers and the better educated elements among the commanding personnel of the army. Instead of a stiff competitive examination, which sifted those better educated from the general run of the mill, mediocrity had an even chance under the new rules with men on a higher cultural level.

S. R. Steinmetz, in his interesting book on the philosophy of war, remarks that in the modern army, as well as in modern industry, class origin should not give a right to leadership. Retribution for giving preference to the less able for class reasons may come in the form of the defeat of the army so situated. Steinmetz, in writing his book, had in view the German nobility, a class brought up in the traditions of successful military leadership for generations. In Soviet Russia, the principle of "gangway for talent" proclaimed by Napoleon, was sacrificed in the interest of the proletarian elements, who were unable to compete in the field of theoretical knowledge with the better educated scions of other classes.[110]

Steinmetz thought that times had changed, and that whoever wanted to win the wars of the future, must have soldiers who think, and officers who are superior to them in the efficiency of their thought processes.[111]

Because of its class structure and tendency, the Red Army had deliberately lowered the intellectual requirements for the candidates for admission to the normal military schools, as well as to the military holy-of-holies—the War College. The conflict between the requirements of modern army technique and those of the dictatorship of the proletariat was solved in favor of the latter.

The life of communist commanders was further complicated by their relations with subordinates, who also were party members. As

Wollenberg points out, a communist commander who behaved in what was considered as unsuitable (from the communist view) manner, on service or in private life, had to answer for his conduct to the communist cell, the secretary of which might possibly be a private soldier or his direct military subordinate. These communist commanders were supposed to give an example to the others by leading a strictly Spartan mode of life.[112]

To sum up: There was evidence during the NEP of the development of a new professional military class. The process was far from completed. The commanding personnel was anything but homogeneous and consisted of elements standing on different levels of cultural development and military technical training. The obvious advantages enjoyed by the communist commanders given "single command" privileges promoted dissension and envy. The right of soldiers in the ranks to file complaints with the Military Prosecutor's office added to the feeling of uncertainty. Economic conditions were still difficult, particularly for those with families to support. Nevertheless, from the Soviet viewpoint, the commanding personnel was more reliable than during the Civil War, and contained more elements closely akin to the party and Soviet civilian circles.

The communist element in the army had become more favorably disposed to the old army officers who were retained in the Red Army service. While Blumenthal might still rant, in the late 'twenties, at former officers, who, according to him, had served during the Civil War only because of fear of the Soviet terror, Smilga's views, expressed as early as 1920, probably were more representative of the change in this respect. He said: "When we had attracted the former officers' corps into the Red Army service, we were exceedingly poorly informed about that corps. We did not know it. We regarded it as a counter-revolutionary body, inimical throughout. Closer contact with it has shown us that this was not so. . . . We have dissected the officers' corps into layers and have separated all these elements that were able to go together with the Soviet government. And such elements existed among the officers' corps . . . together with princes and counts there were sufficient numbers of peasants and burghers . . . the Communists themselves, in coming into contact with the military world have undergone a very considerable evolution." According to Smilga, the military Communists were influenced by former old army officers in such matters as the principle of electing officers, discipline, strict insistence on execution of orders, etc. In other words, there was a certain amount of give and take between the military Communists and the former army officers, serving in the Red Army. Voroshilov's remarks, made in the early 'thirties, also indicate a much better understanding of the trends within the old army officers' corps, than was shown by Soviet leaders in the earlier years of the Civil War.[113]

Whether Smilga was right in looking to class origins of the old army officers for variations in adaptability for service in the Red Army is a moot question. After all, most of the leaders of the White forces, such as Denikin, Kornilov, or even Kolchak, were not exactly descendants of the lineage of Rurik.

One thing is clear, however ; instead of a mechanical fitting together of heterogeneous elements, as during the Civil War, there was evidence during the NEP of gradual reciprocal influence of the various groups of the commanding personnel. In spite of conflicting tendencies, there seems to emerge the beginning of a generally acceptable body of ideas, common to the personnel as a whole.

Commissars

According to Smilga—and he was well informed—a substantial part of the commissars and other political workers of the Red Army had passed during the Civil War from political and supervisory work to command duties. Among these, no doubt, were many of the more energetic and strong-willed, those who had felt the urge to exercise power directly, to lead, to command, instead of controlling and checking.[114]

This reflux of the more enterprising element came at the time when the commanding personnel, including a large number of old army officers, began to assert itself, to grasp for the substance of military authority. Thus the chief of the political department of the 25th Rifle Division wrote toward the end of 1920: "The next stage in the work of military building will be characterized by the strengthening of the rôle of the command personnel."[115]

The trend in the direction of abolition of commissars, which began to assume serious proportions in 1920, could not fail to have an influence on the morale of those among the political personnel who were not inclined to abandon the field of political activity for command and administrative duties.

In this connection, the resolution of the First Congress of the Turkestan Front political workers is characteristic. The delegates had declared themselves against any weakening whatsoever of the institute of military commissars, and insisted that commissars should continue to be appointed to units commanded by Communists also. The historian of the party work in the Red Army, I. Petukhov, saw in this attitude the influence of the so-called Left Communists "inclined to replace revolutionary practice by a revolutionary phrase."[116]

Perhaps one could see in that resolution the desire of persons disinclined to exchange their positions of power and influence for the drudgery of an administrative job or a minor command post. It is well to remember that as early as 1920 Smilga spoke of the signs of decay of the institution of military commissars.[117] The Turkestan political workers, possibly, had felt like men making a desperate defense of a doomed cause.

In 1921, the so-called "Army Opposition" among the Communists, at the discussion of the commissar problem opened before the sessions of the Tenth Party Congress, brought forward the suggestion that the political organs of the army be liquidated or curtailed. The more extreme wing of that opposition stood for the handing over of the functions of guiding the party work in the army to the local (civilian) party committees. The more moderate thought it possible to retain the machinery of the political organs of the army, but on condition that they be made elective. Purely political work, as well as agitation and propaganda, were to be centered in a separate organ—*Politprosvet*—which was to be independent from the commissars and the political organs of the army.[118]

Aside from these internal dissensions among the party men in the army, the difficult economic situation had its effect on the functioning of the institute of political commissars and of military political organs.[119]

The Tenth Party Congress had rejected the suggestions of the "army opposition," regarding the introduction of the elective principle with respect to the heads of the political organs and the placing of the military commissars under the control of the communist cells. It advocated, however, more widespread transfer of commissars to command and administrative posts. The autonomy of the military political and party organs from the local civilian committees was also upheld by the congress.[120]

In 1921, there was a great deal of friction and difficulties among the political personnel of the army and the communist element in it in general. Instances of violation of party discipline, utilization of important service positions among the political workers of the army for personal ends, mass expulsions from the party—all this had occurred among the party element of the army. These difficulties continued until 1923.[121]

As late as that year, articles appeared in the Soviet military press advocating the scrapping of the system of political guidance of the army, as it grew up during the course of the Civil War, and the handing over of that work to the local party committees. Thus N. Glagolev (an employee of the PUR), in an article published in the *Voennyi Vestnik* asserted that with the transition to the territorial militia system the field work of agitation and propaganda in the army should be handed over to the local party committees and the organs of the department of political enlightenment. Another military political worker, Gamov, advocated in the military press the reorganization of the military political organs into institutions concerned with the work of political enlightenment only. Their functions concerned with the guidance of party work in the army were to be transferred to the local communist organizations.[122]

These discussions culminated in the famous circular No. 200 of the Political Administration of the Republic (PUR), which authorized the army party organizations and the army political organs to discuss all problems of party work in the army. I. Petukhov remarks in that connection that a large part of the leading personnel of the PUR stood at the time on the platform of the opposition. The publication of that circular, which had appeared without the sanction of the Central Committee of the Party, had permitted the opposition element to advance, at party cell meetings, such proposals as the election of the political organs of the army, restriction of the functions of these organs to "political enlightenment" work, the handing over of the guidance of the party work to elective party commissions, etc. In some instances there were suggestions to permit the discussion of military orders.[123]

The XIIIth Party Conference condemned the activity of the opposition in the army, and circular No. 200 was annulled by the PUR. A new circular (No. 32, dated February 3, 1924) was issued under the signature of the new head of the PUR, Bubnov. It was pointed out that the application of democracy within the party must be limited by the peculiarities of army life, which, in the first place, admitted election of party organizations only in so far as company and regimental cells, as well as the so-called party commissions, were concerned, while the rest of the party apparatus was appointed from above.[124]

The annulling of Circular No. 200 marked an important turn for

the Red Army. It is, in a way, the end of the tendencies which survived in the armed forces of the U.S.S.R. from the days of 1917.
From then on, the army was supposed to carry out political directions
received from above and even the communist element within it lost the
right of developing lines of political action apart from that laid down
by the PUR.

The attitude of the political workers toward the problem of unity
of command also was far from homogeneous. During the 1924 discussion there were advocates of making the military commissars the
only persons clothed with full responsibility for the units. They
thought that commanders should be mere assistants to the commissars
in the field of combat and training functions.[125]

These extreme enthusiasts of army political control had failed to
achieve their aims. At the time when the Organizational Bureau of
the Central Committee of the party had in principle, in June 1924, decided to introduce the unity of command leaving the forms and dates
of the application of its decision to the organs of the Red Army, the
discussion of the reform in the Red Army press reflected a considerable opposition to it among the political personnel of the armed forces.
Mention has already been made of the passionate debates which had
taken place at the conference and meetings of the political personnel
of the different military districts.[126]

I. Petukhov states that these discussions took place in an atmosphere of tension on the part of the political personnel, and that there
was no unanimity among its members as to the carrying out of the
resolution of the Organizational Bureau.[127] The decision of the
plenary session of the Revolutionary Military Council of the Republic
laid down in November 1924 that in the military districts (fronts
and armies) the system of revolutionary military councils was to be
preserved. These councils were regarded by Smilga as early as 1920
as showing signs of decay. He thought that the very fact that their
political members had acquired in the course of the war a modicum
of military learning and experience had made them act in critical
moments as *Soviet* meetings, reaching compromise decisions in cases
of dissension. And Smilga rightly regarded compromise as inadmissible in military matters. At the same time the project of the transition
to the unity of command system presented by Bubnov was approved
in principle. The presiding body of the Council was empowered to
work out the final text of the instructions.[128]

The decision reached by the Council may be described as a compromise which preserved the authority and the interests of the rank-

ing members of the political personnel of the army and at the same time did not antagonize the rank and file of the political army workers, giving them time to adapt themselves to the new conditions and a hope for future advancement.

In a manual published in 1926, the functions of the military commissars were defined as embracing "the guidance and immediate execution of party-political work, as well as assuring the training and education of the personnel in the spirit of class solidarity and communist enlightenment."[129]

The same manual had emphasized the fact that the military commissars were not only the political representatives of the Soviet Government in the army, but also—and first of all—representatives of the Communist party. They were regarded as co-equal with the commander in responsibility not only for the politico-moral state of their units, but also for securing, through the system of "party-political influence and guidance," the successful execution by the commanding personnel of their military and administrative functions.[130]

The liaison work with the party, the state, trade union and Komsomol organizations was entrusted to the commissars. Instead of being isolated representatives of the political control in the army, as they were in 1918, they had become heads of ramified organizations. The regimental commissar had the regimental bureau of the party, headed by a secretary, to work with; there was also the organizer entrusted with work among the Komsomols, and each company and detachment of the regiment had a political director. Those in charge of the regimental school, club and library were also under him.[131]

The field of the regimental political organs' activities comprised: a) assistance to commanders in maintaining military discipline; b) organization of studies in the field of politics as well as general enlightenment, hygiene, military science, the guidance of the soldiers' discussion circles; c) a certain amount of political work among the local civilian population; d) direction of the work of committees of economic assistance; e) rendering help to the Red Army personnel in the field of improvement of their standard of living, and—last but not least: f) accepting complaints and depositions of the personnel of the regiment.[132]

Activities described under c) seem to be a survival from the period when the military commissar during the Civil War was at times the only representative of the political arm in localities recently taken over by the Red Army. On the other hand, the complaints and depositions were likely to permit interference by the commissars with the work of the commanders and to constitute a source of endless friction.

The junior political personnel—the political directors attached to companies—were made responsible for the political education and training of soldiers of their respective companies. They were subordinated to the military commissar in so far as their work of political enlightenment was concerned, and in matters of military service to the battalion commander. In other words, they were entirely independent of the company commanders. They looked after the mobile company library, the "propaganda wagon" and the "Lenin corner." Their duties also included assisting the company commander in matters of military training and education of the soldiers. Company commanders, members of the party and qualified to conduct political work, were permitted to unite in their hands the functions of political directors of their own companies, and were given assistants to carry out the details of that work.[133]

A speech made by Frunze on April 15, 1925, shows clearly that the slow rate of transition to the adaptation in practice of the unity of command system was in a large measure caused by the desire of those in control of the military policy of the Soviets to avoid antagonizing the political workers of the army by a rapid abolition of a considerable number of posts of military commissars and other important functionaries in the political machine of the army. These people had to be taken care of, either by transfer to command or administrative duties or by absorption into the civilian apparatus of the state.[134]

The following table shows the trend in that respect between the years 1925 and 1928. The table deals only with commanders who were at the time members of the Communist party.[135]

	April 1925	January 1926	September 1926	March 1928
Corps Commanders	41.1%	70.6%	82.3%	100.%
Division Commanders	14.3%	48.3%	54.7%	71.9%
Regimental Commanders	35.8%	37.8%	38.6%	53.6%
Company Commanders*	0.0%	18.5%	37.7%	

In studying these figures, one has to bear in mind that with the increase in the number of commanders possessing full power, the number of positions for military commissars was declining at the same rate. In other words, there was less chance for promotion, less opportunity to rise to more important positions and greater power within the framework of the political service of the army.

* In September 1927 there were 41.7 per cent of the company commanders upon whom the privileges of unity of command were conferred.

Political workers were fighting rear-guard actions against these encroachments.

I. Petukhov reports instances of a "haughty attitude" on the part of party members among the commanders to those one or several steps below them in the military hierarchy. He comments : "The communist commanders must realize, to understand, that within the party organization he is merely a member of the party, the same as all other comrades. The only difference is that, upon whom more is laid, of him more is asked."[136]

In 1927 the opposition elements within the Communist party were warning that the Red Army was getting ripe for bonapartistic adventures, for the appearance of "Russian Chiang Kai-Sheks" etc.[137]

What was really occurring was quite different. Gradually the incompatibility of the principle of equality of party members *qua* party members, regardless of their position within the military hierarchy, with its age-old foundations of military discipline, was becoming obvious. The more strong-willed, the more ambitious of the communist commanders were attempting to dominate the meetings of party members as they were accustomed to dominate their military subordinates on duty. The political workers felt the heavy hand of these communist commanders and did not like it. They saw themselves crowded out of positions acquired during the Civil War, relegated to a secondary rôle.

That at least some of the commissars had also transferred into the sphere of party relations, habits acquired while in the military service, is suggested by S. Gusev in his book on "The Civil War and the Red Army." He reports the instance of a party cell in the North Caucasian Military District where its secretary called upon the party members to rise and stand at attention whenever the commissar came to a meeting of the cell.[138]

The circular of the Central Committee of the party dated March 6, 1925, describing the two forms of unity of command, stated that the commissars were freed of the daily routine control of the military administration and the economic functions of the commanders. They had retained only those of political guidance and party work, together with the responsibility for the moral and political state of the unit. It was the duty of the commissar to assist the commander "by all his influence and authority" to strengthen and to improve the combat training as well as the economic and administrative state of the unit. Under this form of unity of command, the commissars, while bereft of many of their functions, remained paramount in the field of political and party guidance. There was, however, another form. Under it, the really plenary form, the functions of commissars were entirely handed over to the commanders judged able to direct party-political work.[139]

In the navy and the so-called national units, the introduction of the principle of the unity of command was postponed. The institution of military commissars continued to function there as before.[140]

The final text of the new regulations, which were approved by the Central Committee of the party,[141] laid down that the general guidance over all party and political work in the army and in the navy should be the province of the PUR. The latter was to carry out its work under the immediate guidance of the Central Committee of the party, as its military department.[142]

The execution of the PUR's plans was to be carried out by the political departments of the military districts, fleets, armies, divisions, etc. The liaison work with the civilian party organization was placed upon the local organs of the PUR. The heads of the local political departments as well as the military commissars were to become members of the local party committees.[143]

In this form the political control of the army, while placed directly under the Central Committee of the party and not under the People's Commissar for War or the Revolutionary Military Council of the Republic, became autonomous from the control of those specifically responsible for the defense of the state. On the other hand, the local party organizations had no power over the political organs of the army in their respective territories. In practice, this meant the development of a powerful political machine permeating the military forces, independent from the leaders of those forces and free from control of the local party organs.

The form the organization assumed was very likely shaped in a considerable measure by the course of the struggle between Trotsky and the Kamenev-Zinoviev-Stalin groups.[144]

It is a far cry indeed from the views expressed by Frunze's collaborator, Gusev, in 1918, to the highly centralized control over the political activity in the army. Of the two trends, "centralism," as Gusev called it, and "democracy," the former had won hands down, not only in the sphere of the purely military organization, but also in that of party-political work in the army.[145]

A comparison of the new formula with the resolutions of the Tenth Party Congress concerning the Supreme Political Enlightenment

Department would show the great change of viewpoint as to the functions of the political organs of the army.[146]

From the organizational viewpoint, the immediate guidance by the party of a body closely interwoven with such a typical organ of the state as the army presents a very interesting development.

The institute of military commissars, with the above-mentioned restrictions, survived thus through the NEP period. K. Voroshilov in analyzing the rôle of these commissars, stated that the functions of control and those of observation of the commanding personnel—which formed in the early days of the Red Army the principal functions of the military commissars—were in the process of withering away. The rôle of the political organs of the army was described by him as consisting of party-political and cultural-educational work. This work, according to Voroshilov, was of "enormous importance" in the combat training of the army. Characteristically, Voroshilov had added that the "general situation" required the intensification of party and political enlightenment work in the Red Army.[147]

In the meanwhile, there is sufficient evidence to show that the political personnel devoted a very considerable part of their energy to watching of the political trends among the rank and file of the Red Army. In July 1925, *Red Star* carried an article by A. Safronov suggesting methods for keeping track of what the soldiers thought. The best method, according to Safronov, was to gather periodically the rank and file Communists and Komsomols of the unit and to obtain the results of their observations. Thus the party element was to be used for spying on the non-party soldiers. Questions and remarks made during the political hour by soldiers are also mentioned as an excellent source of information. Men on duty at the so-called "Lenin corners" were said to receive many questions from soldiers. It was suggested that these questions be systematized and analyzed. Correspondence, particularly with demobilized soldiers who had returned to their villages, was pointed out as a mine of information. Finally there were the wall papers: the items submitted by the soldiers, both used and rejected, are stated to contain valuable data. It also was recommended questions asked by soldiers at company and regimental meetings should be recorded.[148]

A characteristic institution of the period was the control bureau of soldiers' letters, attached to the PUR. This bureau had its branches in the political departments of the military districts, army divisions and regiments (in the latter it was represented by special delegates).[149]

The relations of the political personnel with commanders apparently left a great deal to be desired. Frunze wrote in January 1925 about instances he described as shocking, of commanders and political workers following conflicting courses of action, and of political workers withholding their support in matters involving the prestige of the commanders in the performance of their duties.[150]

An article in the *Red Star* in July 1925 seems to indicate that the lower political personnel were apt at times to take a formalistic attitude with respect to soldiers, and even to decline to answer in a satisfactory manner questions put to them in the so-called "Question and Answer Books."[151]

Perhaps one of the principal reasons for the deficiencies of the political personnel of the period lay in their low cultural level.

The military-political schools of the Military Districts which were entrusted with the task of training that personnel, insisted only that the prospective students should be able to read and write, know the constitution and be familiar with the most important current events. Those who had served six months in the army or had worked in the party apparatus or the "enlightenment" field outside of the army were eligible, provided they were party members or "conscious sympathizers." The latter had to be recommended by the commissar and the bureau of the party cell of their units. Students remained in these schools for twelve months only.[152]

Political workers for technical units (aviation, armored troops, signal and engineers' troops) were trained at the Central Military Political School where the course was longer, lasting eighteen months.[153]

There was also a Central Turki Military-Political School which trained political workers for army units with a predominating Turki personnel, also with a twelve months course. The candidates were required to know at least one of the Turki languages.[154]

It is obvious that the general cultural level of graduates of these schools was low. The admission requirements were on the level of those of the Command Courses of the Civil War period. They were way below those of the normal military schools. With a shorter period of training than the latter they could not fail to produce graduates of a much lower level of general education.

This fact is particularly important as the political organs of the army, while living within it and supported by means derived from the military budget, were entirely independent of the organism within which they led their "parasitical" existence.[155]

There is evidence that the military were not satisfied with that situation, and that in 1924 there had appeared within the Red Army trends favoring the subordination of the political organs to the military headquarters. The Revolutionary Military Council of the U.S.S.R. cut short these tendencies at their very incipience. They were qualified as "most noxious and most dangerous." The autonomy of the political organs was unequivocally upheld, and the possibility of reorganizing them into departments of military headquarters was rejected.[156]

In territorial militia organizations the political organs had extended their work also to the young men undergoing their preliminary military training.[157]

That the opposition to the principle of unity of command did not cease even as late as 1927 is clear from K. Voroshilov's remarks at the Fourth Congress of Soviets of the U.S.S.R., when he accused "some of the comrades" of attempting to "muddy the waters" and warned, among others, especially the army political workers not to forget that it was the party's privilege to cancel or to modify any measure.[158]

In the meanwhile, the Revolutionary Military Council of the U.S.S.R. decided in favor of retaining the principle of unity of command and established the following regulations:

1. The commissars were not to sign orders, with the exception of those connected with political work.

2. The general political guidance of a unit was entrusted to the commander, should he be invested with plenary powers. The immediate execution of party-political guidance was to be in the hands of the commander's political assistant, under whose orders was placed the political personnel of the unit. The practical work in the party-political field was also to be carried out by that assistant.

3. The political assistant was to report to the commander about the political state of the unit, about the party-political work of the political personnel and about "all basic directives received by him from the higher political organs."

4. The political assistant was to maintain a direct relationship with the higher standing political organs, as well as with the political personnel of the unit.

5. In case of differences between the commander and his assistant in matters concerning political work, the dispute was to be placed before the higher political organ and its decision confirmed by the Revolutionary Military Council of the District.[159]

It is obvious that the political personnel had won in its struggle against the essence of the principle of unity of command. The commanders, endowed with what on the surface looked like plenary powers, had obtained merely a formal control over the political work in their units. Not only were the political assistants authorized to deal directly with the higher-placed political organs as well as with the political personnel in the subdivisions of the units, but disputes in matters concerning political work were to come before political and not military organs. As to the confirmation of the decisions by the Revolutionary Military Councils of the Districts, this also did not offer to the commanders any protection, as the councils themselves could hardly be regarded as purely military organs, permeated as they were by the political personnel.

Thus, on the eve of the first Five Year Plan, the process of unification of command had received a severe setback, and the antagonistic relationship between the military commander and the political worker of the army remained, in spite of the great change in the class and political affiliations of the former. The political apparatus of the Red Army had remained a state within the state and endowed with a life of its own, not integrated with the rest of the armed forces.

F. Blumenthal wrote in the late 'twenties that no one among the Communists visualized the army as separated from the party any more, from the politics of the workers' class. Such thoughts did not exist at the time, he said, even among the non-party commanding personnel.[160]

In this manner the direct party control exercised by political organs leading a parasitical existence within the body of the armed forces became the accepted principle of the organization of the Red Army. As A. Bubnov has formulated the problem of the party work within the army, it consisted of: "securing victory, organized in conformance with the class policy of the proletariat." He visualized political work as a function of the party. It enters the framework of the military organization serving the aim "of keeping the army both Red and effective militarily."[161]

Whether these two aims were compatible within the framework laid down for the exercise of political control, seems to be answered in the negative by subsequent events.

It is necessary to examine here, however briefly, the so-called Trotsky opposition in 1923 in the Red Army, in so far as the political workers of the army were concerned.

Geronimus stated in his book on the Communist party and the Red Army that the oppositionists drew support mostly from the ranks of the political workers and those attached to army staffs. He claimed that these men were mostly intellectuals or people of petty-bourgeois origin. He also says that the young communist college students drafted into the army had furnished recruits to the opposition.[162]

Should we accept this statement as reflecting correctly the situation, it would seem that the political workers did not prove to be the mainstay of the ruling group of the party and had sided with the man whom they regarded as the creator of the Red Army. The support which they seemingly had received from the better educated communist youths in the ranks is also interesting and significant.

Geronimus maintains that the opposition comprised a considerable part of the ranking Communists of the army, as well as members of the leading political organ of the army, the PUR, which had resulted in building up within the army an opposition party organization. Geronimus accuses the opposition of having prevented the reorganization of the army and of bringing chaos into its life. He states also that the opposition had transferred the struggle into the non-party masses of the rank and file, as well as of the commanding personnel.[163]

The crisis was solved by the replacement of the personnel of the PUR and by the appointment of A. S. Bubnov, instead of Antonov-Ovseenko, as the head of it.

In 1925, the directing organ in charge of the political activities within the army—the PUR—had concentrated in its hands all the party, political, as well as political-enlightenment work in the army. Its activities were regulated by decisions of the Central Committee of the party, by those of the Supreme Political Enlightenment Department, and by the orders of the Revolutionary Military Council of the U.S.S.R. Its circle of activity embraced: 1) training of cadres of political workers in the army, the control of their activity, their appointment, transfer and retirement; 2) procurement of supplies for the various phases of activity of the political workers and the financing of these activities; 3) political guidance of the military press; 4) organization of propaganda among the civil population; 5) inspection tours for the study and readjustment of the political apparatus of the army.[164]

A special Conflict Commission was attached to the PUR for preliminary investigation of conflicts that were supposed to come before the Central Control Committee of the party. A Permanent Political

Council was created under the aegis of the Chief of the PUR to co-ordinate the work of the various political organs of the army, and to work out the "single political line" for the guidance of the work of the local political organs.

The Chief of the Political Administration of the Military District was made an *ex officio* member of the Revolutionary Military Council of the District. The latter had plenary powers in guidance of the troops of the district.[165]

The PUR had charge of the judicial and police work in the army. The "Special Departments" of the OGPU, which were part and parcel of the police and punitive apparatus of the army, were not subordinated to the respective political departments. The head of the Special Department of the OGPU was placed immediately under the collegium of the latter. The work of these departments was coordinated with that of the political departments of the army, not through a chain of subordination, but through the "line of party-political guidance," by means of military political conferences attached to the political departments.[166]

There were, therefore, three systems functioning within the Red Army: the military commanders, the army political service and the organs of the OGPU. The latter were the ultimate means of control through which the ruling group of the party maintained a firm grip over the army's life.

The selection of members of the commanding personnel for promotion was in a large measure controlled by the political organs of the army. These had their representatives on every attestation commission, which ruled the fate of the commanding personnel. The attestations of the commanders were prepared also with the participation of the political organs.[167]

Promotion of commanders was thus greatly influenced, if not entirely controlled, by the opinion of them held by the members of the political organs of the army. Unless commanders were on good terms with the commissars, their chances for promotion were slim, to put it mildly.

It is interesting to observe that apparently as late as 1923 a large proportion of political workers on the rolls of the departments of party building in the military political organization, consisted of non-proletarian elements. Their class origins, at least in some of the military districts, marked them as having even less of the "toiler" element in their midst than was the case of the commanders. Thus, out of 38 political workers of these departments in five military districts, only

13 were workers, while 18 belonged to the category of "others" and seven were peasants. Their party affiliation was also of comparatively recent date. Five had joined in 1917, seven in 1918, and 26 in 1919. Among them there were seven who had formerly belonged to other political parties—*vide*, Mensheviki, or Socialist Revolutionaries.[168]

This brief sketch will serve to illustrate the remarkable growth, articulation and increased scope of activity of the political organs of the army. What the commissars had lost in influence because of the introduction of the forms of unified command they had gained in other directions. Perhaps one of the most striking features was the right granted to the military commissars to stop on their own authority the execution of the resolutions of the party cells in their respective units, with the obligation, it is true, to report the incident to the higher-standing political organ. The centralistic principle had won, hands down, in the field of political work, in the same way that it won the victory in the sphere of military organization. Not only the days of the guerillas were over, but those of party democracy in the army as well.[169]

Rank and File Communists

The end of the Civil War and the beginning of the economic reconstruction of the country in the post-war period had a serious effect on the numerical strength of the Communists in the Red Army. This coincided with a decline in the influence of party members on the non-partisan elements in the armed forces.

A well-informed commentator stated that by September 1921 there remained in the Red Army 90,000 party members and candidates for party membership, i.e. only 30 per cent of the number of Communists who were carried on army rolls on August 1, 1920. The same commentator made a special point in stating that a large proportion of the Communists who had left the army in that period belonged to the category of those "irregularly demobilized." This irregular transfer from army to civilian work was carried out by the provincial and county party organizations by agreement with the army political departments. In some instances, even the latter formality was not observed.[170]

What accentuated still further the influence on army life of that reflux of party membership to civilian activities was that those who had remained were not the most seasoned party element. Even some of the important party posts in the army came to be occupied by very young Communists with a brief party standing. According to S. I.

Gusev, not only the rank and file of the young Communists, but even a certain part of the political workers occupying responsible posts in the army were "weaker" than those who had left the army. The average party standing of the military Communists continued to fall in 1921.[171]

The new accretion to the strength of the Communist party, which had swelled its ranks by 1922, was not considered entirely satisfactory by those in charge of the armed forces of the Soviets at the time. Trotsky had referred in 1922 to complaints that a certain percentage of the young Communists drafted into the army could not be regarded as first-class material. Apparently one of the difficulties was that the new recruits, before joining, had carried on fairly important government work, and therefore were not satisfied with their lowly status in the ranks of the army.[172]

Trotsky had cited in the same speech a report of the Party Commission of the 44th Kiev Army Division that the young Communists drafted into the army and recently sent to join that division "had shown all the negative characteristics of rank egotists and deserters." The stenogram of the Congress reports that a voice from the ranks of the delegates claimed that the major part of the young Communists drafted into the army were unsatisfactory. This, however, was denied by Trotsky.[173]

Trotsky characterized the young soldiers in the army as imbued with the ardent desire to study, to increase the scope of their activity, "to rise up regardless of cost." No doubt, the young Communists in the army reflected that tendency to an even greater degree than the non-party element. The competition for promotion, the wish to rise rapidly in the military hierarchy, found a reflection in a contention that military competence should be subordinated to political loyalty in the matter of choice of commanders.[174]

Whether the trend away from the proletarian cadres to membership based on a wider class foundation had anything to do with this tendency to careerism is a legitimate question to pose, although space does not permit of developing the answer conclusively. In a pamphlet published in 1924, Trotsky, in advocating the establishment of "healthier" relations between old party cadres and the majority of the party membership consisting of persons who had joined it after the November revolution, had stressed that the problem was much wider than that of relationship between different age groups. He had pointed out that upon seizing power the Bolsheviki had had first of all to create a state apparatus. This led to the weakening and dilution of the basic cadres of industrial workers in the party and the exceptionally rapid growth within it of "administrative" elements, which included non-proletarian elements as well. In other words, the social base of the party underwent a serious change.[175]

Trotsky claimed that in 1924 less than one-sixth of the party membership actually consisted of proletarian workers at the bench.[176]

That conditions in the Red Army fully reflected that trend, the party census of 1927 bears witness. It includes some typical instances revealing not only a non-proletarian majority in the ranks of the military Communists in the units examined, but also the tendency of a considerable proportion of Communists to conceal their bourgeois origin.

The table given below shows at a glance the changes introduced into the statistical returns dealing with social origins of Communists serving in three army units by the data of the census.[177]

	BEFORE CENSUS	AFTER CENSUS	INCREASE	DECREASE
UNIT A				
Workers	39.6	39.3	—	0.3
Peasants	45.0	34.9	—	10.1
Others	13.8	23.2	9.4	—
UNIT B				
Workers	40.7	36.4	—	4.3
Peasants	49.7	32.2	—	17.5
Others	9.6	31.4	21.8	—
UNIT C				
Workers	45.1	45.1	—	—
Peasants	40.5	31.3	—	9.2
Others	14.4	23.6	9.2	—

The rôle of the so-called Party Commissions, representing in the army the Central Control Commission of the party was of great importance in molding this heterogeneous mass of people of widely differing class origin into a pliable instrument of party policy. A competent student of the Red Army has stated that the fate not only of the political workers but of the rank and file Communists in the army as well was entirely in the hands of these commissions, or, rather, in the hands of their secretaries, before whom the political cadres of the armed forces of the Soviet stood in awe.[178]

The personnel of these Party Commissions, obviously, had to be selected with care. The Statute of Party Commissions, formulated by a conference of the leading political workers of the army called by PUR in 1921, was later confirmed by the Central Committee of the party. It established that Party Commissions had to be elected at divisional and army conferences, and were to consist of three members and two candidates. Only those with a party standing of not less than three years could be elected to divisional Party Commissions. The higher standing Party Commissions were open for membership only to those who had joined the party before the November revolution. It is important to note that chiefs of respective political departments had the right to cancel the elections of members; also that all resolutions of Party Commissions could be executed only upon agreement with the respective chiefs of political departments.[179]

Thus these *elective* bodies were subordinated to *appointees* from the center. The higher posts in these commissions were reserved for the party aristocracy—the veterans of pre-November days.

An interesting departure from the policy of the Civil War period took place in 1922 with respect to the recruitment of the naval forces. The Kronstadt rebellion was obviously the reason for this new policy.

In 1924, the head of the PUR, Bubnov, emphasized the rôle of the Communist Youth Organization—the Komsomol—in the sphere of reconstruction of the Soviet armed forces, particularly of the navy.[180]

As Frunze wrote in an article published in the *Red Star* in 1925, the acceptance of the patronage over the navy by the Komsomol had marked a radical change in the life of the naval forces of the Soviet. The Komsomol was encouraged to strengthen further its ties with its off-shoots in the army and the navy, and, under the guidance of political organs, to labor to make these branches into an instrument of further improvement of discipline, as well as technical progress.[181]

Bubnov had stated that the reconstruction of the navy had to begin by building up new cadres of seamen. As he put it, the problem was to create a strong and politically sound cadre of the navy. The main body of this new cadre was recruited from the ranks of the Komsomol.[182]

At the Fifth Congress of the Komsomol, held in 1922, the following aims were placed before its membership:

1. The strengthening of ties between the navy and the toiling masses, and the establishment of the political influence of the Komsomol in the naval forces.

2. The recruitment of personnel of the navy and of the naval schools by young proletarians.

3. The propaganda of the idea of upbuilding of the navy and its importance for Soviet Russia among the toiling masses of the population.[183]

Of these three, that of recruitment of the personnel from the ranks of proletarian youth was set apart by Bubnov as the most important one. By 1924, three contingents of this youth were drafted into the navy. By social origin these contingents were very desirable from the communist viewpoint. They contained 75 per cent of workers, 23 per cent of peasants and only 2 per cent of "others." A large percentage came straight from the work bench: there were 63.5 per cent metallurgists, 2.5 per cent woodworkers and 19 per cent common laborers. Seventy-four per cent of these youths were Komsomols, 13 per cent members of the Communist party, 12 per cent were candidates for membership in the party—almost a full 100 per cent affiliation with the party and its ramifications.[184]

There were difficulties, however. To begin with, the level of literacy of the drafted Komsomol was low. Bubnov rightly considered this a drawback in the mastering of the navy technique by the young recruits. The criterion became party loyalty instead of the technical qualifications making for easier adaptability to the requirements of naval training. Also, the Komsomol youngsters were physically weak. And they wished to acquire certain technical skills, showing a lack of interest in branches of naval service which did not offer technical training of the kind likely to be useful in civil life.[185]

Apparently these first contingents of the Komsomol were unable to overcome at once the influence of the older bluejackets cast in the libertarian tradition of 1917. Bubnov referred to inadequate work of the naval political organs in 1922-1923, which resulted in the abandonment of the Komsomol by some of the young recruits. These became a non-party element and were thus lost as an instrument of political influence. Others, while maintaining a nominal membership, had lost their characteristic Komsomol traits and were absorbed by the human environment instead of becoming an active factor in shaping the naval personnel along the lines laid down by the party.[186]

The adjustment to naval discipline was a painful process for a part of the Komsomol, in the same way that earlier the young Communists found it difficult to become reconciled to the limitations of army draft in peacetime. Bubnov mentioned a considerable percentage of deserters among the Komsomol in the early stages of the new system of recruitment of the navy. He claimed, however, that by 1924 there were practically no desertions among the Komsomol. There was also a tendency to oppose naval discipline among a certain part of the Komsomol young seamen. They regarded that discipline as unduly harsh and could not understand the need for it. But here again, in

1924, Bubnov could claim that by that time the Komsomol had become the best disciplined part of the naval forces.[187]

The naval schools were also filled with the Komsomol. In the preparatory school of the naval college the Komsomol formed in 1924 95 per cent of the total student body. In the training schools for the non-commissioned naval specialists they represented 85 per cent.[188]

This influx of young proletarians into the navy made for a high percentage of persons of proletarian origin among its personnel. Bubnov gives the following figures for 1924: workers 42 per cent, peasants 50 per cent, others 8 per cent.[189]

Bubnov could, therefore, with a certain amount of justification, claim that the navy had the best personnel from the class viewpoint and could be regarded as one bone and one flesh with the workers' class.[190]

The navy had thus become *par excellence* a stronghold of the party and its offshoots. The old libertarian tradition of the bluejackets was definitely on the way out.

Apparently, it was not so easy to maintain among the Komsomol the interest in military and naval affairs. The general atmosphere of the NEP period, with its accent on the economic reconstruction, was unfavorable to this. Only a few members of the Sixth Congress—and those in military uniforms only—had acknowledged themselves as readers of the *Red Star*, official newspaper of the armed forces. Bubnov had to admit that in the second half of 1923 there was a marked falling off of interest in the patronage over the navy.

Anyhow, the naval branch of the armed forces of the Soviets was singled out for an intensification of the proletarian and party-affiliated element in its personnel. It became, in fact, the Red equivalent of the officers' battalions of the White Army. This concentration in certain units was a reversal of the policy of distributing the communist element widely through many units.

By 1927, about 10,000 members of the Komsomol had been drafted into the navy. There was, however, a certain falling off in the percentage of workers in the navy personnel. Thus Voroshilov, in his report to the Fourth All-Union Congress of the Soviets, spoke of 29.39 per cent of workers, 60.47 per cent peasants and 10.14 per cent of others. While party members and candidates formed 20.36 per cent and the Komsomol 21.48 per cent of the total personnel of the navy, these party-affiliated elements were outnumbered by the non-party personnel, which stood at 58.16 per cent.[191]

The thorough purge of the party-affiliated elements of the navy after the Kronstadt rebellion, and the special care exercised in re-cruitment, had apparently a definite influence on the views of the naval Communists and Komsomols. Bubnov stated in 1924 that al-though the Komsomol as well as party members had participated in the party-wide discussions, there was no opposition movement no-ticeable at all in the navy.[192]

Permeation of the land forces by Komsomol recruits was relatively lower than that of the navy. Bubnov had stated that before 1924 the Komsomol stood at 35 to 50 per cent of the party membership of the army. After the 1902 age group draft joined the army, that per-centage rose to above 70 per cent.[193]

In so far as the land forces were concerned the aim set before the Komsomol was that of becoming the immediate active assistant and collaborator of the Communist party in matters of political enlight-enment. Komsomol work had to become part of the party work. The Komsomol recruits were to establish connections with company and regimental party cells, in the activity in which they were to take part "systematically and uninterruptedly."[194]

The lowest rung of the political ladder of the army—that of the political instructor—was available to the Komsomol. Bubnov had pro-claimed the slogan: "Komsomol, give us the political instructor."[195] Thus a definite goal was set for the ambitions of the young Kom-somol in the land forces—that of reaching into the party-political bureaucracy.

A wide campaign for the replenishment of party and Komsomol by new members from the ranks of the armed forces was carried on. In the beginning of 1927 there were 49,160 party members and 28,840 candidates, or a total of 78,000 party-affiliated persons in the Red Army.[196]

The number of the Komsomol in the army was on the increase. In 1925, 64,056 applications for Komsomol membership were filed in the army. During nine months of 1926 it was 42,000. This against a total of 20,000 drafted into the army with the age group of 1902. When the latter group passed from active service into the reserves it included 49,739 Komsomol. In other words, its Komsomol member-ship of the age group of 1902 more than doubled during the period of active service in the army. By 1927, the total number of the Kom-somol in the armed forces had reached 117,181, i.e. they outnumbered the party members and candidates by more than 50 per cent.[197]

Despite this considerable accretion in party numerical strength, the non-partisan element still continued to exceed the former in numbers in the Red Army, even at the end of the NEP period.

The following table may serve to illustrate the process of change in the party and Komsomol relative numerical strength in the armed forces :[198]

DATE	KOMSOMOL	PARTY MEMBERS	NON-PARTY
Apr. 1, 1925	10.7%	12.1%	77.2%
Dec. 17, 1926	16.3%	13.6%	70.1%

During the same period the commanding personnel was becoming permeated by the party to a much greater degree than the army as a whole.

DATE	PARTY MEMBERS	KOMSOMOL	NON-PARTY
Apr. 1, 1925	40.9%	2.4%	56.7%
Dec. 17, 1926	49.7%	3.8%	46.5%

It is well to remember that at the time the rank and file of the army was still predominantly of peasant origin. In this manner, the mass recruitment of party and Komsomol from its ranks meant in practice bringing large numbers of non-proletarians into the ruling group.

The above table shows that in the closing period of the NEP a commanding personnel, predominantly affiliated with the party, was superimposed on a rank and file still largely non-partisan. At the same time, the combined strength of the party-affiliated and Komsomol soldiers was becoming relatively important, and had already very considerably exceeded the relative strength of the Communists in the army during the Civil War. In this manner, the weakening of the communist element in the army, noticeable in the first years of the NEP, was definitely liquidated toward the end of that period, and important progress made in the direction of making the army Red not only in ideology as well as in name.

The following table gives the numerical strength of the party-affiliated and komsomol element of the army between 1924 and 1928 :[199]

Year	No. of Communists and Candidates	No. of Komsomols	Total with party affiliation	Increase in one year	Percentage of party-affiliated with respect to total army personnel
1924	51,800	36,700	88,500		16%
1925	57,700	58,000	115,700*	21,500	19%
1926	72,300	98,000	170,300	54,600	30%
1927	78,200	119,800	198,000	27,700	36%
1928	82,000	120,000	202,000	4,000	37%

* Obvious typographical error in the source used where the figure 110,000 is given.

The remarkable increase during the year 1926 presented a strong contrast with the situation in 1928, when the rate of increase had fallen to a mere fraction of the average for the period under review.

The actual induction into the party in the Red Army was shown in the following figures :[200]

1925	29,900 men
1926	26,000 men
1927	28,500 men
1928	33,429 men

There was, by 1927, a considerable difference in the social origins of the Communists in the army as against the party as a whole :[201]

	Army	*Party as a whole*
Workers	39.7%	55.7%
Peasants	35.2	19.0
Employees	22.5	22.6
Others	2.6	2.7

The proletarian element was in the minority in the army party organization, while it formed a majority for the party as a whole. In the army the peasant element within the party almost equalled the workers.

In the army the party was organized into relatively small cells, which in 1925 had averaged 15 members each, in 1928, 14.9 members. The total number of these army cells grew from 3,942 in 1925 to 6,443 in 1928.[202]

Trotsky, in one of his pamphlets published in 1924, remarked on the danger of influence or even infiltration of kulak elements into the party through army cells, but saw an antidote to this in the differentiation of the peasantry into groups on several economic levels. This strength of the peasant element in the army party organization was reflected in the relatively low cultural level of the army Communists.[203]

An article in the *Red Star* in 1925, commenting on the Communists who had joined the army with the draft of the 1902 age group, had stated that the majority of these party comrades belonged to the so-called Lenin conscription group, and were politically illiterate, without any idea as to party work in the army. This resulted in a dearth of party members for the lower positions in the party apparatus. The Ukrainian Military District had reported forty instances of party candidates acting as cell secretaries. Similar situations were also known to exist in the Siberian Military District.[204]

It is small wonder, then, that under these conditions, the active rôle in the army party organization had gradually passed into the hands of the commanding personnel. The PUR, commenting on the state of party organs in the army in the fall of 1926, had pointed out that the most characteristic trait of that apparatus was that two-thirds of positions within it were occupied by commanders, who thus had concentrated in their hands the guidance of the party masses in the army.[205]

Gradually, party members and candidates became associated with the commanding personnel, while the Komsomol was predominantly rooted in the rank and file of the army.[206]

The low cultural level of army Communists made it necessary to pay particular attention to the development of the chain of party schools to train these men politically.

In 1927, this school system provided training facilities for almost one hundred and fifty thousand students distributed in the following manner:

	NO. OF SCHOOLS	NO. OF STUDENTS	% OF PARTY MEMBERS	% OF KOM-SOMOL	NON-PARTY
1st Step Schools	2,031	48,569	55.1%	37.5%	7.4%
2nd Step Schools	1,347	29,396	83.8%	10.2%	6.0%
Komsomol Schools	2,720	66,505	—	88.9%	11.1%
	6,098	144,470	35.6%	55.6%	8.8%

The non-party students came from the ranks of those who were preparing themselves to enter the ranks of the party or of the Komsomol.[207]

The political bureaucracy of the army continued to make steady inroads on party organizations within the army. Thus the new Statute of Party Commissions in the army approved by the Central Committee of the party on November 16, 1922, had not only increased the membership of these Commissions to five active members and three candidates, but, "in the interest of greater co-ordination of the work of the party Commissions with that of the Party Sections of the Political Departments," the chiefs of these sections were admitted into the Party Commissions with the right of "consultative voice."[208]

Even as early as in 1921 the Instruction to Communist Cells in the Red Army ordered these cells to see that every cell member regularly carried out all his obligations in the line of military duty, to help translate into action as rapidly as possible all orders and instructions of the commanding personnel, to cut short all attempts at agitation tending to weaken the military efficiency of the unit, and by all means to promote the better military training of soldiers.[209] Thus, gradually the cell was becoming an instrument of the Political Departments of the army, a tool to promote military discipline and military skill among the rank and file.

In practice, however, until 1923 all these instructions largely remained on paper, and did not translate themselves into actual practice. The army party life was going through a difficult period. I. Petukhov has called the state of affairs at the time "the internal crisis." Party discipline was observed in the breach; members were expelled from the party *en masse*. Even as late as 1926 the PUR had reported the expulsion of 2,500 military Communists from the party during the preceding six months period.[210]

The material examined does not give sufficient clues to estimate to what extent the struggle between Trotsky and the majority of the party disrupted party life among the rank and file military Communists. Bukharin, then affiliated with the dominant group, made an attempt to connect the so-called military conspiracy and the discovery of an illegal printing plant of the opposition, with oppositional activities in the army, verging upon incitement to a rebellion. He spoke of military groups, aspiring to bring about a military *coup d'état* where some former Kolchak colonels were supposed to be associated with an opposition Communist.[211]

The army press published in 1925 a number of items reporting discussions in connection with the oppositional activity of Trotsky in the army and navy party circles. In every instance that had come to the attention of the writer, Trotsky was condemned.[212]

No doubt there was another side of the picture, but it did not find any expression in the material examined.

It would seem, however, that the army rank and file Communist may have had difficulty in absorbing Marxist theory—in 1923, 32.2 per cent of Communists in the Ukrainian Military District were reported showing unsatisfactory results in their political studies. In the Petrograd Military District the percentage so reported had reached 52.3. They were, however, apparently largely on the side of the Central Committee, and even the deviation of the PUR from the straight and narrow path of party discipline in the matter of issue of the famous Circular No. 200, did not seem to have any lasting appreciable results on the loyalty of the party masses of the army to the Central Committee, who had remained in the party fold after the various expulsions. At least, the material examined does not indicate any such deviation. In any case, A. Geronimus testifies that during the discussion which had preceded the XVth party Congress in November 1927, 96.6 per cent of the 39,000 participants in the respective party meetings in the army and navy had voted for the policy of the Central Committee, the famous "party line." Nevertheless, there were attempts of the Trotskyist opposition to work among the military Communist rank and file, and special Military Bureaus were formed by the opposition.[213]

There was a period when the fact that the majority of the ranking functionaries of the PUR had belonged to the Trotskyist opposition themselves, had activated oppositional trends among Communists in army units. These Communists, finding a springboard for their activities in the already-mentioned Circular No. 200 of the PUR, had advanced demands for the election of the commissars, as well as of the commanding personnel, the subordination of the political organs of the army and of the commissars to the control of the party cells and conferences, and the handing over of the functions of the Political Departments of the army to the Party Commissions. They also clamored for the right to discuss at cell and conference meetings all phases of party life and military Communist representatives on local civilian party committees.[214]

Thus the tradition of the "army syndicalism" of 1918, of the groups of "democratic centralism" and that of the "workers' opposition" of 1921 had an echo in the activities of the 1923 opposition. The leaders of the latter found support, according to A. Geronimus, among the Communists employed on staffs and in political organs, mostly men with an intellectual background, also among former communist college students drafted into the army. The party masses, according to the same author, did not participate in the movement, although an attempt was made to form a fraction recruited from the ranks of army Communists.[215]

Geronimus stressed the danger to the party from this fractional activity, because of its tendency to involve in a struggle within the party the masses of non-party soldiers and commanders, creating thus a possibility of a split of the army into two camps. As Geronimus can hardly be regarded as an impartial witness, he may greatly exaggerate this feature of the oppositional activity. Be that as it may, the replacement of the leadership of the PUR by order of the Central Committee and the cancellation of the Circular No. 200 was followed by the prohibition of party discussions in the Red Army cells and conferences. This brought the oppositional activities to an end, or at least drove them underground in so far as the army was concerned.[216]

The influx of politically inexperienced young party members made the army Communists pliable material in the hands of the political organs and the communist commanding personnel, who were now more or less permanently entrenched in the seats of power and influence in the army party organizations. The rank and file came and went with the ebb and flow of the drafts, and had to fit itself into a pattern laid down for it by those with a durable army connection. They had become the object of political influence from above rather than active factors in party life, a very useful adjunct to the vast political bureaucracy of the army, its sounding board, mouthpiece, eyes and ears.

The struggle between the commissar element and the rank and file party organizations of the army had definitely come to an end with the complete victory of the former. The antagonistic relationship between the commanding personnel and the party cells so often in existence during the Civil War was replaced by the domination of the army party life by the communist commanding personnel.

The party members and the Komsomol were still privileged groups within the army, but they were groups that knew their place and were accepting guidance from the political organs of the army instead of trying to compete for power, as during the Civil War and immediately afterwards. The torrent was tamed, canalized and made to work the mills of army routine life.

Soldiers

Bubnov referred in 1924 to the 1902 age group draft as "peasant youth," which had come into the army with a set of what he called "prejudices." According to him, some came wearing crosses or ikons, quite a few did not comprehend the March revolution, or, for that matter, had they any clear idea about that of October (November). He warned that these "prejudices" should be carefully taken into consideration by the party in planning its work in the army.[217]

With respect to the anti-religious propaganda, Bubnov had suggested extreme circumspection. Only a gradual "assistance" was to be extended to these peasant youths to enable them to free themselves of "prejudices." The recruits should not be antagonized or mocked because of their religious convictions.[218]

Two years earlier, in 1922, the conference of the military delegates to the XIth Party Congress had passed theses prepared by Trotsky in co-operation with Rabichev, which explained to the soldiers why they were drafted into the army—the cornerstone of the propaganda among the young soldiers. First of all, these theses stated, the soldiers should know why they were called to serve in the army. The explanation should be based on "concrete conditions of the current day," and not on the theory of the class struggle. The young soldiers very definitely should not be treated as students attending a course on class struggle, but as young citizens preparing themselves to go to war.[219]

At the same Congress, Trotsky had formulated the program of indoctrinization of recruits as follows: the young peasant lad from Saratov or Penza, taken by the proletarian state from his village to serve in a regiment first of all should know why and for what he was drafted. This explanation should be given him "concretely, politically and not 'pedagogically.' "[220]

As a means of perfecting the education of the young soldier, Trotsky advocated giving to the Red Army well trained corporals— section commanders, in the parlance of the day. In his view, these new corporals would be both commanders and educators of the soldiers. Without these new section commanders Trotsky deemed it impossible to bring to a higher level the military as well as the political qualifications of the soldier. As the prejudice against the N.C.O. grades was still strong, Trotsky advanced the plea that the section commanders should be the lowest rung in the hierarchy of commanders—Red Army officers, and not non-commissioned officers, as in the capitalist armies.[221]

While the need in the lower commanding personnel was a very real one in the Red Army, the solution proposed by Trotsky was not a practical one. The large number of section commanders could not be supplied by the normal military schools. The solution was arrived at in the same way as in the old army, by training the lower commanding personnel in regimental schools.

Voroshilov stated in 1926 that regimental schools were expected to produce annually about 75,000 of the lower commanding personnel. These were thus definitely placed in a different category from the rest of the commanding personnel by the markedly lower standard of their general, as well as military, education. They reproduced, in the conditions of the Red Army, the old army N.C.O.'s and not the junior commanders as Trotsky has planned.[222]

It is true that the door to promotion to higher positions on the ladder of command was not entirely shut to the section commanders. Special facilities were offered them to enter the normal military schools upon undergoing preparatory training. However, as Voroshilov had to admit, the hundred thousand or so men of the junior command personnel were too numerous to permit of this mass being moved up the steps of the military hierarchy. Only a small part of them had found their way into the normal military schools.[223]

Voroshilov was able to state in 1927 that the Red Army had acquired trained junior commanders and had filled the gap which had existed in the Red Army structure during the Civil War period.[224]

The solution arrived at was more practical than that suggested by Trotsky, to whom, nevertheless, should go the credit for focusing the attention of those interested in army affairs on the urgency of the problem of creating a numerous and adequately trained lower commanding personnel.

In the same way, the latter's suggestions as to propaganda among soldiers were also cast to the winds. An article in the *Red Star* in January 1925 had stressed the motto "Political training in 1925 must be built on the watchword: the Russian Communist party is the leader and the organizer of victory of the Red Army." The author of the article advocated making this program (directed against Trotsky as the Russian Carnot, responsible for the successes of the Red Army) even more narrowly partisan by introducing lectures on the fight against Trotskyism. He also spoke for the complete abandonment of any ties between political training and general educational work in the army. The author condemned the views of those who thought that the most important aim of political education should be the broadening of the general cultural horizon of the soldier and were leaving to political indoctrination only a supplementary, secondary rôle.[225]

The very fact of the appearance of an article of that character in the strictly censored official organ of the Red Army shows how far ideas on political training of soldiers had traveled from 1922, when Trotsky was still firmly in the saddle.

This political training was directed at soldiers 81.6 per cent of whom were peasants and only 11 per cent workers.[226] The peasant lads, particularly in the divisions of the Territorial Militia, were, naturally, deeply interested in rural problems, and their views reflected the political moods of the peasantry. Such questions as taxation, agrarian reconstruction, co-operatives, rural credit, etc., were of great concern to them, and attempts were made by instructors at hours devoted to political training to discuss these matters with the soldiers. In 1925, it was deemed advisable to publish in the *Red Star* an article deprecating such discussions as useless.[227]

On the other hand, there is evidence that before 1925 there was a strong trend toward regarding political work as a part of the general "cultural enlightenment," of the effort to heighten the cultural level of the soldier. Thus the conference of the political workers of the 15th Army Division's artillery resolved that the political hour as well as the enlightenment hour, the political instructor as well as the school worker, were doing the same task, that of improving the cultural, and accordingly the political, level of the Red Army soldier. Other sources refer to this tendency for the political work to dissolve itself in cultural enlightenment. Thus, Permskii wrote in 1924 in one of the Red Army periodicals, that political work "in spite of the energetic opposition of all political workers" was becoming an apolitical educational training.[228]

The official *Military Calendar* for 1924, a manual published by the Army Headquarters at Petrograd, had definitely stated that "enlightenment" work among the army soldiers was a part of political work. Its aims were described as first of all teaching the soldiers how to read and write. The illiterates of a given unit were concentrated in one of its companies. For three to six months, in addition to military and political training, these illiterate soldiers were taught elementary arithmetic, geography and natural science, as well as reading and writing. In some of the military districts this purely cultural work among them was reported to have assumed a wider scope and as having embraced not only the illiterate and the semi-literate, but also the better educated. The program of studies was also correspondingly enlarged in these districts.[229]

This was not a new departure in Russia. There were literacy schools in the Russian Army in the nineteenth century. From 1902 on, in the infantry and field artillery, obligatory literacy schools for recruits was made the order of the day. This was no mean task: in 1905 there still were 59 per cent of illiterates among them as against 95 per cent in 1865.[230]

The systematic political indoctrination of soldiers was, however, an entirely new feature of Russian army life. The feeble attempts at a patriotic and monarchist propaganda among soldiers during the so-called "oral" instruction periods in the old army cannot be regarded as anything approaching even a rudimentary political training.

A. Geronimus explains that the demands of soldiers upon the Red Army as to fulfillment of their cultural and economic needs grew at the time in line with the general upswing of the political activity of the toiling masses of Russia. He claimed that these demands had become detrimental to the pursuit of the immediate aims of military and political training and that they led to a tendency to regard the army as a school offering general education and not as an awe-inspiring organization trained for fighting.[231]

The so-called "peasant moods" in army units were traced by Geronimus to the anti-Soviet trends in the village. They found outward expression in "jealousy" of the privileged position of the workers, dissatisfaction with the prices of manufactured goods, and the rates of rural taxation. Frunze, writing in 1925, confirmed the fact that these difficulties existed, that the peasantry had begun to "knock persistently at all doors," to look for an outlet for its needs and for a guarantee of the defense of its interests. He regarded this as a warning to be extremely cautious in extending any training in the use of arms outside of the framework of the army.[232]

In other words, the peasant was becoming politically articulate and was not reconciled to his position as a step-child of the Soviet State.

These trends were especially noticeable in the Territorial Militia units. They had led to the weakening of discipline and deterioration of relations between the soldiers in the ranks and the commanding personnel.[233]

S. Gusev, in his paper "Our differences in the field of Military Affairs," admitted that the ideological success of the kulak in the village was greater than that of the proletarian. The peasant ideology had remained the same as before the November revolution. The kulaks had become the personification of the capitalist tendencies in the development of the privately owned peasant economy. He concluded by remarking that the political—"ideological," as he calls it—influence of the kulak in the village was far out of proportion to his economic strength.[234]

Frunze drew a correct conclusion: as the Soviet army at the time was predominantly a peasant army, it would be strong only if the general policy of the Soviet Government answered the demands and served the interests both of workers and peasants. Only when the peasants, as well as the workers, were imbued with the conviction that the policy of the Soviet Government was fulfilling their interests would the army be a real force.[235]

The point of this conclusion was directed toward Trotsky and his plan for the collectivization of the village. The task of the propaganda campaign was to overcome the kulak trends, and to imbue the soldier with faith in the righteousness of the governmental policy. As an enthusiast of political propaganda in the army, F. Blumenthal wrote in 1926: "The assurance of the fighters that the ideas propagandized by the party are correct will make the soldiers follow with confidence and fearlessly the commander, the Communist leading in the attack. . . ." Blumenthal urged that political work should continue even under fire, because propaganda would cement fissures caused by conditions of relationship between peasants and the Soviet state in combat as well as in peacetime.[236]

The kernel of these ideas was expressed by S. Gusev in his paper on the political enlightenment work in the Red Army published as early as 1921. At that time he bluntly stated that army barracks could become the school of communism for peasant youth.[237] As he saw it, this was impossible to achieve without destroying the hold of the land and the sway of religion over these youths. Without uprooting these two influences, Gusev deemed it impossible to make the army an efficient fighting force, as well as a school of communism.[238]

Under these circumstances, the heightening of the general cultural level of the soldiers was not desirable *per se*, were it not connected with a corresponding deeper permeation of the soldiers with communist propaganda. Bubnov, the head of the PUR, openly acknowledged this in 1924, definitely demanding that the heightening of the cultural level of the soldier should not proceed more rapidly than the growth of his "political consciousness."[239]

Political propaganda was not considered a panacea for the weaknesses of the army, resulting from the dissatisfaction of the village with the policies of the communist dictatorship. Instruction regarding the distribution of the proletarian element among different arms proves this.

Armored troops, as well as railroad troops, were allocated an obligatory minimum of 50 per cent proletarians in their personnel. The air force was given 40 per cent, the signal troops 30 per cent, the cavalry only 12 per cent, while the infantry was left with a mere 8 per cent. The troops of the OGPU were allocated an average of 25 per cent for all arms.[240]

In this manner the arms which could be and were most effectively used in the suppression of peasant rebellions—the armored units, the air force and the OGPU troops—were guaranteed a respectable core of proletarian elements. The safety of communications and military transport was also taken care of.

The "non-toiling elements," principally the kulaks, were excluded during the Civil War—at least in theory—from service in the armed units. With the abolition of the labor battalions after the Civil War, representatives of these groups began to find their way into the ranks of the troops. According to Frunze they became there a source of "decay and dissatisfaction."[241]

This infiltration of "non-toiling" elements was brought to a stop by the introduction of the statute of obligatory military service. As Frunze summed it up: the duty of defense of the socialist fatherland was laid upon all citizens, but the duty of bearing arms in its defense was confined to toilers only—the workers and the peasants. All "non-toiling" elements were deprived of the right to bear arms in the defense of their country.[242]

But even this was not deemed sufficient for the protection of the sheep (toilers) from the goats (non-toilers). The latter were admitted into the so-called service detachments only. The kulaks and others serving in these detachments did not enjoy any privileges of the regular soldiers. They were in practice menials of the latter, and clergymen, drafted together with other "non-toiling" elements, were to be seen peeling potatoes while on kitchen detail. The *Nepy*, as members of these detachments were called, behaved themselves with a great deal of circumspection and did not make any attempts at agitation among the soldiers. Their material well-being was not a matter of great concern to the state. They were not even given uniforms. Since not all of these *Nepy* came from well-to-do groups, tatters and bare feet were not exceptional among them. But their meekness did not divert suspicion. As the commissar of one of the military schools remarked: "Give them a finger and they will tear off your arm."[243]

This curious symbiosis of these modern helots with the members of the ruling classes in the army was a striking development of the proletarian state. These helots belonged to the classes which L. Kamenev had called in 1923 "in a measure . . . our economic fellow-travelers . . . without whom we are unable to do at present."[244]

There is some evidence, however, that even as late as 1928, sons of wealthy kulaks were able to find admission into the ranks of the soldiers of the Red Army. In that year it was reported that in one regiment there were found fifteen soldiers whose families were paying taxes indicating a very substantial wealth according to the Soviet standards of the period. The same report stated that these soldiers were "of course" engaged in anti-governmental propaganda, and were attempting to prove to the poor and middle peasants in the soldiers' ranks that the then current taxation laws were detrimental to rural economy.[245]

Some of the economically strong peasants obviously knew the way to go around the legal obstacles in the path of their sons' entry into the Red Army.

A tabulation for 1927 of the so-called "insufficiently trustworthy" elements of the population who were not permitted to serve in the Red Army shows that a considerable proportion of the total population was for this reason excluded from military service. In 501 cities and towns, 565,545 persons were deprived of franchise, i.e. 6.8 per cent of about seven and a half million enfranchised urban population. The rural inhabitants in the same category had numbered 1,338,158 persons of 3.3 per cent of the enfranchised rural population. This adds up to 1,903,703 persons, equaling about 20 per cent of the reserves of the armed forces of the U.S.S.R.[246]

In addition to these "insufficiently trustworthy" persons, there was a large number of those regarded as entirely untrustworthy, such as registered counter-revolutionaries, political prisoners and those doing forced labor. A figure of two and a half millions is given in one of the works on the Red Army for persons in these categories. This figure may be an exaggeration for 1927, but, very likely, the number of persons included in the latter categories exceeded that of the previous one.[247]

Whatever the exact figure may be, the material examined clearly shows that millions of Russian citizens were legally excluded from military service for political reasons, so that the army was really not recruited on the basis of a universal service.

What actually occurred with respect to admission to the Red Army is difficult to ascertain definitely. There is, however, evidence, in addition to that already adduced above, that because of the army's attraction to persons not regarded as full-fledged Soviet citizens (they had hopes of attaining full civic rights through army service) there was during the NEP period an infiltration of disfranchized, "class enemies" and "socially dangerous" elements into the Soviet armed forces. The laxity of the organs controlling the selection of recruits provided the necessary loopholes. It is unlikely, nevertheless, that the numbers of these "undesirables" was at all considerable.[248]

S. Ivanovich, in his well-documented book on the Red Army, draws attention to the interesting fact that in 1926 the army of the Soviet Revolution drew its soldiers predominantly from the same social groups as the army of the Czar.[249]

	PEASANTS	WORKERS	OTHERS
1913	69.3%	14.1%	16.6%
1926	71.3%	18.1%	10.6%

In examining Soviet statistics of social origins of the soldiers one must bear in mind that the recruits had various reasons for "improving" their social origins by claiming that they were workers or poor peasants. The *Red Star* gives a striking example of the extent to which these statistics were unreliable. From a certain region recruits were drawn for four regiments. In one regiment poor peasants among that lot of recruits were reported to number 22.6 per cent of the draft, in another 66.4 per cent. Middle peasants were reported to number 20.2 per cent in one and 73.7 per cent in another. Wealthy peasants in one 1.4 per cent, in another 22.7 per cent.[250] As there was no reason to believe that the social origins of recruits for these regiments differed in so far as the individual regiments were concerned, the conclusion is obvious.

The attractiveness of the service in the Red Army from the viewpoint of bettering one's social and legal status may have had some influence on the decline in desertions during the NEP period.

Thus, in 1923, deserters had made up 7½ per cent of the total personnel; 5 per cent in 1924; only 0.1 per cent in 1925. These figures illustrate the defeat of the village in its struggle with the proletarian state in 1921-1923, and the better organization of that state. The improvement in the material conditions of army life also very likely, had its share in reducing desertions to a mere fraction of the Civil War figures.[251]

The Soviet state was hard pressed in 1923 to supply sufficient funds to cover even the minimal requirements of the Red Army. As Voroshilov stated in 1927, the budget of 1923-1924 was insufficient to provide for "even the minimal needs of the war departments." Frunze spoke in 1924 about the general penury of the state and the limitations this imposed on defense expenditures.[252]

In spite of these financial difficulties, Frunze was able to announce in May 1925 that the army ration had 3,012 calories per diem, as against 2,714 in the Rumanian, 2,797 in the Polish, 3,330 in the Italian and 3,658 in the U.S. army.* While Frunze was not satisfied with this state of affairs and had asked for an increase in the calory content for the ration for 1926, the fact that the Red Army ration was ahead of the Rumanians and the Poles speaks for itself. Bedding was still deficient and only 60 per cent of the soldiers were supplied with blankets. Barracks were out of repair: funds appropriated covered only 15 per cent of the needs.[253]

---

* These figures were taken from Frunze's book and were not checked with the sources of the respective countries mentioned.

In 1927, the army ration was increased to 3,242 calories. Both meat and vegetables were issued in larger quantities, and macaroni was included in the soldiers' menu. While even that ration was below the 3,388 calories of the old army ration, it was considerably more satisfactory than the ration of the early years of the NEP. Even the bedding and blanket deficiency was fully liquidated in 1926 in so far as the standing Red Army was concerned (apparently the Territorial Militia units did not fare as well at the time). Clothing, however, was not improved to a sufficiently high standard. Even in 1927, cloth uniforms were issued only to the junior commanders—the N.C.O.'s. The rank and file had to continue to be satisfied with the light cotton uniforms, supplemented by warm underwear.[254]

Of the barracks, only one-half were brought into satisfactory condition by 1927. This, no doubt, had an influence on the state of health of the soldiers. The number of those reported sick stood in 1925-1926 at 134 per cent of the sick in the old army in 1913.[255]

The soldiers' pay was low. Even the increased pay of 1927 was only one rouble 55 kopeks per month. It compared with 93 kopeks per month in the old army, and represented a decided improvement on the 1924-1925 pay of 38 kopeks, and a slight increase over the one rouble 30 kopeks paid in 1925. One must remember that pay in most of the European drafted armies was small and that the Soviet low pay merely conformed to the rule.[256]

The material conditions of army life were helped out by the so-called patronage system. As early as 1920, a number of cities and territorial sub-divisions declared themselves ready to take upon themselves immediate responsibility for improvement of the well-being of the troops stationed in their respective areas or those which had gained special distinction during the Civil War. This arrangement was formalized by a decision of the Revolutionary Military Council of the Republic and by a decree of the Central Executive Committee of the Republic, published on November 17, 1924. These patrons did a considerable amount toward making the barracks more livable and providing soldiers with some elementary comforts, improving their rations, supplying books and magazines for the soldiers' libraries.[257]

The table below, borrowed from S. Ivanovich's book *The Red Army* gives a comparison of the distribution of the hours of the working day of the Red Army as against that of the old army.

	RED ARMY	OLD ARMY
Sleep	8.5	8.
Military Training	5.5	8.5
Chores	2.	2.5
After-dinner rest	2.	1.5
Free time	1.5	3.5
Political studies and general enlightenment work	4.5	
	24.0	24.0

The time allocated to purely military training is thus considerably less in the Red Army as against the old army (47 per cent), although in the period under review the average length of service under the colors in the former was only half as long as in the latter.[258]

Voroshilov, in his report to the Fourth All Union Congress of the Soviets in 1927, had enlarged upon the place of the political studies in the training of soldiers. He stated that for two hours a day for five days per week soldiers and junior commanding personnel had to attend classes on political and general cultural subjects. By that time the program of these studies embraced the explanation to the men of the duties and problems of the Red Army, the rights and obligations of the soldier, the policy of the party and the Soviet Government, the policies of the capitalist countries with respect to the U.S.S.R. In its last phases the political training included acquainting the soldier with the practice of the Soviet work, co-operative and public activities in the village and town. Voroshilov summed up by saying that the program of the political studies was built around the axes of militarization, internationalization and sovietization of the soldier. The instructors for the classes of political studies were largely drawn from the ranks of the platoon commanders (70 per cent).[259]

That soldiers were often unable to follow intelligently these instructions in political and cultural subjects because of lack of basic education, pages of Soviet newspapers for 1927 and 1928 bear witness. Instances were recorded of attempts to find out to what extent soldiers understood the meaning of the words widely used in the current bolshevik argot. In one of the army units ten soldiers (including two Komsomols) were asked the meaning of words then in common use in Soviet press and during political instruction hours. Only one out of ten knew what Gomindan stood for. Who Chicherin was, was known to two. The word "discussion" was understood by two, "opposition" by three, "fraction," "production conference" by two. "Komintern" and "trust" were known to three. Even such a well-known abbreviation as TSIK (for Central Executive Committee) was not comprehended by all of the ten. In another unit, out of twenty-four soldiers examined only four understood the word "electrification," eight knew what "industrialization" stood for. Even among the Komsomol some thought that the then common abbreviation "es-er" (for Socialist Revolutionary) was derived from the English word "sir," and that the party name originated because it was a party of sirs, a body of aristocrats.[260]

The length of the terms of active service in the standing army was fixed by order of the Revolutionary Military Council of the Republic No. 2405 of 1922. They were for the infantry and artillery one and one-half years, for the cavalry, horse artillery and technical troops two and one-half years, for the air force three and one-half years and for the navy four and one-half years.[261]

In the later period of the NEP these terms were revised by the order of the same Council* No. 419 of 1924 and the statute of obligatory military service of September 18, 1925, which provided for two years' service for the infantry, artillery and cavalry, three years for the specialists of the air force and the same term of service for the coastal defense forces. For the navy and the naval branch of the OGPU the term was fixed at four years.[262]

The one and one-half year term of service had the serious disadvantage of leaving the standing army every fall depleted of soldiers. An attempt was made to remedy this in 1922 by calling to the colors in the fall, for six months' service, those recruits who were entitled to shorter terms of service (because of their educational status, for instance). A decree of the Central Executive Committee of the Republic and of the Soviet of the People's Commissars of September 28, 1922, was issued to introduce this measure. However, it coincided with the reduction in the numerical strength of the army by some 200,000 men, and was abandoned as impractical in any case.[263]

In the Territorial Militia in the early years of the NEP, tactical training was hampered by the lack of uniforms and equipment. Voroshilov spoke of the necessity of making one set of uniforms do double duty—the uniforms were taken from one unit after the training period was over and handed over to the other, beginning such a period. By 1927, however, all territorial units were fully supplied with uniforms, although camp equipment was still 20 per cent short of the requirements. Even as late as 1926, the lack of funds made it necessary to shorten the already brief term of training. For those serving their first year, it was reduced from ninety days to seventy,

* At that time styled the Revolutionary Military Council of the U.S.S.R.

for other years from thirty days to twenty-one. In 1927 it was possible to provide for the full terms of training.[264]

Under these circumstances, the decision of the conference of the Revolutionary Military Council of the U.S.S.R. with those of the military districts in January 1927, to the effect that the Territorial Militia had shown a sufficient degree of training and cohesion, and, generally speaking, was on the level of the standing army in this respect, makes strange reading.[265]

The full term of active service of the Territorial Militia, except that of its cadres, was very short.[266]

Infantry, Artillery and divisional H.Q.'s	8 months
Cavalry	11 months
Engineers and other technical troops	9 months

The approximate distribution of hours of work during the first year's term of training of a recruit in the Territorial Militia included :[267]

GENERAL STUDIES

Political Training	72 hrs.	
Hygiene	12 hrs.	
Barrack duties	16 hrs.	(for scouts and signal detachments, 12 hrs.)
Garrison duties	20 hrs.	(for mounted scouts, 15 hrs.)

PHYSICAL TRAINING

Physical culture	36 hrs.	

TECHNICAL TRAINING

Weapons	40 hrs.	(for signal detachments, 18 hrs. for chemical warfare troops, 20 hrs. for mounted scouts, 26 hrs.)
Military Engineering	14 hrs.	
Military Chemical Work	15 hrs.	(except for chemical warfare troops)
Care of Horses	—	(for mounted scouts only, 10 hrs.)

TACTICAL TRAINING & MUSKETRY

Tactical training	159 hrs.	(for signal detachments, 50 hrs. for chemical warfare troops, 70 hrs. for mounted scouts, 172 hrs.)
Musketry	136 hrs.	(for heavy machine gunners, 152 hrs. for signal detachments, 46 hrs. for chemical warfare troops, 81 hrs. for mounted scouts, 76 hrs.)
Topography	20 hrs.	(for signal detachments, 14 hrs. for chemical troops, 40 hrs.)
		Special studies, signal detachments, 239 hrs. Chemical warfare troops, 159 hrs.
TOTAL	540 hrs.	

The cadres of the Territorial Militia division were of 12 per cent to 17 per cent of their total strength, roughly about 1,400 men per division.[268]

The pre-army service military training took a well-planned character about the middle of 1922, when the department concerned (the VSEVOBUCH) decided to set for itself the goal to provide a general military training program for young men of eighteen years of age and a specialized military training for those of nineteen. By October of that year, 520,000 lads born in 1902 had received their training, while 105,000 born in 1903 were also so trained. The physical culture work, which was considered as a preparation for performance of military duties, also began to take on sizable proportions. By January 1922 there were 420 regional and sectional sport centers, serving as rallying points for some 1,500 sport organizations with about 160,-000 members.[269]

The pre-army training aimed at: a) developing political consciousness in young men of pre-draft age and inculcating military ideas among them; b) developing skill in handling of weapons, learning how to care for them (combined with an elementary course in musketry); c) tactical training for work within the limits of the section; d) close-formation drill; e) acquaintance with basic army regulations; f) physical development. The program envisaged 420 training hours in two years; 210 hours each year. The age for the beginning of the application of this program was later fixed at nineteen. The plan of distribution of the hours of training follows:[270]

	INFANTRY	CAVALRY	ARTILLERY	ENGINEERS	SIGNAL CORPS
Political Training	75	75	75	75	75
Military Hygiene	6	6	6	6	6
General Information & Army Regulations	20	20	20	20	20
Weapons	75	15	18	15	15
Chemical Warfare	6	6	6	6	6
Physical Culture	45	45	45	45	45
Drill & Tactical Training	73	44	39	50	44
Musketry	110	77	36	77	77
Military Engineering	10	10	6	—	10
Special Training	—	122	161	126	122
	420	420	420*	420	420

Simultaneously with the physical examination the pre-draft youths were also sorted out on the grounds of their social origins by special committees with the participation of the representatives of the OGPU and party organizations. In the earlier years of the NEP they were

* Adds up to 412, apparently some mistake in the figures of the source used.

not furnished rations or uniforms, and had to maintain themselves at their own expense. Exceptions were made for paupers or those who were not able to keep their positions in their places of employment. Beginning with 1925-1926, these pre-draft trainees were granted funds for rations, and the whole system of training was stabilized and perfected. Such a considerable improvement in the organization and training methods was achieved that it was found possible to reduce the training period from the original two months to one month.[271]

With the short terms of service under colors on the Territorial Militia, this pre-draft training played an important part in preparing reserves for the army, as well as in relieving the army from the more elementary forms of training of recruits.

The large public organizations (of course sponsored by the party and the state and controlled by them), such as the Military Science Society, the Volunteer Society for the furthering of Chemical Defense, the Society of Friends of the Air Fleet, the Society for the Furthering of Defense, etc., were merged into one enormous organization—the Society for the Furthering of Defense, Aviation and the Chemical Upbuilding of the U.S.S.R (OSOAVIAKHIM).[272]

These organizations were a necessary adjunct to the facilities of the Red Army and the pre-draft training in inculcating rudimentary military knowledge in the masses of the population. The standing army, as well as the Territorial Militia could not provide (because of financial limitations) military training for all able-bodied men of military age.

In 1925, Frunze estimated that each year there grew up about 1,200,000 young men reaching military age. Of these 850,000 to 900,000 were physically fit for service. The standing army could take over the training of 270,000 per annum.[273] The Territorial Militia divisions took care of another 250,000.[274] This left 350,000 to 400,000 physically suitable human material without military training in the ranks of the army. Frunze had announced in the same year that 842,-000 young men of the 1903-1904 age group were given pre-draft training, i.e. practically the entire physically suitable contingent. He regarded the results of this training as entirely satisfactory. In analyzing some of the groups trained, he said that at the Leningrad Military District, 16.17 per cent were passed as "good," 71.7 per cent as "satisfactory" and only 12.13 per cent as "poor." In the Ukrainian Military District, 65 to 70 per cent were passed as satisfactory, 30 per cent as "poor."[275] A question naturally arises whether the same standards were applied in each of these districts. These figures, no doubt, should not be regarded as anything approaching an accurate, uniform estimate of the results of training. However, Frunze's conclusion should not be disregarded, as he was a man of sober and realistic judgment.

The rôle of the Osoaviakhim will be discussed in the next chapter. The combined results of the pre-draft training and the Osoaviakhim's work had led to the mass militarization of the Soviet population, which made possible the rapid filling in of gaps due to losses in war, as well as to the formation of a tremendous reservoir of semi-trained manpower for new army divisions to be created in the course of a war.

Frunze had given a great deal of thought to the problem of discipline in the army of the first proletarian state. He was not entirely pleased with the practical application of disciplinary action in the army, and had admitted that not all of the commanders succeeded in guiding themselves by the fundamental principle that firm discipline can be created only on the basis of the moral and professional ascendancy of the commanding personnel on the one hand, and the thorough understanding by the soldiers of the obligations imposed by military service on the other. He felt that the combination of these two elements would provide the foundation for making the Red Army invincible. What he had called "mechanistic methods" of discipline, wide application of disciplinary punishments and other forms of administrative pressure were still, he said, frequent.[276]

Frunze had made an attempt to analyze the basis of the remarkable cohesion and indomitable combat stubbornness of the Russian troops of the eighteenth and the beginning of the nineteenth centuries, "of the days of Suvorov and later." He saw the foundation for these qualities of the Russian Army in the social and economic life of the Russian village commune, with its wide application of the various forms of economic co-operation. Frunze believed that the permeation of the Russian village by capitalism had an adverse effect on the qualities of the Russian soldier, and that the latter did not exhibit the qualities of firmness and indomitable spirit in the face of adversity during the last wars of czarist Russia to the same extent as his forebears. Frunze hoped that the reconstruction of the Russian economy by the Soviet state would provide the foundation for a new form of discipline. He did not, however, expect this to take effect in the near future.[277]

In the meanwhile Frunze did not see any contradiction between the exterior smartness, the requirements for the outward soldier-like bearing of the troops and the principle of revolutionary discipline. He felt that the latter should find its outward expression in soldierly smartness. Even the word "drill," so odious to the revolutionary elements in Russia, held no terrors for him. What he insisted upon, however, was that these outward forms should not be turned into a basis for discipline.[278]

Very considerable disciplinary rights were concentrated in the hands of commanders and commissars. The commander of a regiment (as well as the regimental commissar) was empowered to stop leave for a fortnight and to impose arrest for the same period, as well as give extra turns of duty for ten days. From the viewpoint of the N.C.O.'s the most formidable weapon was the right of reducing the subordinates to lower positions. In other words, commanders could make privates of them. Even the company commander could reduce to the ranks section commanders on his own authority and stop leave for five days, as well as impose arrest for the same number of days.[279]

An unusual feature of the disciplinary code was the provision that, in addition to punishments regularly provided for in the code, others could be inflicted which would be appropriate "under the conditions and circumstances, and would not be in contradiction with the spirit and character of the Red Army." Among such punishments, strangely enough, was placed the right to transfer subordinates to disciplinary detachments for a second absence without leave of less than six days' duration and for the first such absence in excess of that number of days.[280]

Those under arrest were held confined in solitary lighted cells and were given full rations. In case of shortage of solitary-confinement cells, prisoners could be grouped with others in one room.[281]

By 1924, the private soldiers had to wear uniforms on duty as well as off, while the commanding personnel were permitted to don mufti off duty.[282]

These features of "administrative pressure" did not distinguish the Red Army from those of capitalist states, as much as the remarkable effort even during the NEP period to influence the morale of the soldiers by other means.

In 1923, there were already 643 army clubs with 3,518 circles; by 1924, the number of clubs rose to 762, that of the circles to 6,288. In 1923, 82,000 men took part in the activities of the circles; the next year they had reached 111,943 in number. The so-called "Lenin corners" reached the figure of 2,917 by May 1, 1924. By November

1 of the same year there were 3,352 of them. Lectures, theatrical performances, concerts, excursions—there were 9,828 of them given in the Red Army in 1924 for the standing army, and 1,313 for the soldiers of the Territorial Militia. There were 4,763,800 books in soldiers' libraries by October 1, 1924. Of these, 20 per cent were on political subjects, 21 per cent fiction and 19 per cent volumes on military subjects. In 1926, there were 11,158 circles with 203,000 members, 757 clubs and 5,348 "Lenin corners."[283]

The clubs had as their aim political education of the soldiers, the "organization of their leisure" and the men's "cultural, comradely intercourse." The educational work fell into: a) primary; b) circle work; c) mass work; and d) library work. The primary work had as its aim the organization of leisure and providing answers to the current events problems, the awakening of interest in studies and preparation for club work. The "Lenin corners" in the companies, which had small libraries attached to them, were organized for the purpose of this work.[284]

The circles were divided into: a) political; b) military (circles of military science); c) physical culture and sports; d) dramatic; e) choral; f) painting and sculpture.[285]

It must not be overlooked that each party and Komsomol cell was also an important link in the effort to influence the thoughts and to build up the morale of the soldiers.

The federal organization of the Soviet state had raised a very serious problem: how the federal principle should find its expression in the organization of troops on a national basis.

Frunze had frankly admitted that while from the purely military viewpoint it might be better to have ten divisions recruited from Russians, all well trained and disciplined, rather than five good divisions and five of inferior quality recruited on a national basis, the importance of the revolutionary movement of the colonial peoples in their struggle for their national independence could not be overlooked. There was a connection between the plan for national troops and the hopes pinned by the Soviets on the unrest among the colonial peoples.[286]

In other words, the formation of national units first of all had in view revolutionary aims, internationalist aims, and not the strengthening of the Soviet armed forces as such.

In September 1922 the Russians in the army overwhelmingly outnumbered all other nationalities:[287]

	PER CENT		PER CENT
Russians	77.17	Latvians	.67
Ukrainians	8.85	Bashkirs	.29
Germans	.59	Others	4.8
Jews	1.61	Unclassified	2.87
Tatars	3.15		

These figures must be treated with caution, as until 1923 the statistics of nationalities in the Red Army were poorly organized. Ukrainians, for instance, were often counted as Russians.

By 1925, the Russians represented 64 per cent. The Ukrainians were at 22 per cent, White Russians 4 per cent. All other nationalities constituted 10 per cent. In other words the Russians (apparently Great Russians) had considerably declined in proportion to other nationalities.[288]

The problem of national army formation was the subject of a heated debate as early as 1917. Opinion ranged from bitter opposition to all national formations to the support of a separate Ukrainian army. At the military conference of the Bolsheviki held in 1917, Stalin had offered a resolution to the effect that the formation of national regiments was not in the interest of the toiling masses. He did not, however, deny the right of formation of such regiments by each nationality, but expressed the hope that the proletariat of the Ukraine would struggle against the transformation of the Ukrainian national regiments into a permanent separate army. This resolution was adopted by the conference.[289] In November 1924, the plenary session of the Revolutionary Military Council of the U.S.S.R. worked out a plan for national formations, which was approved in May 1925 by the Third Congress of the Soviets. This plan was carried out promptly with respect to nationalities which were subject to military services in czarist Russia (Ukraine, White Russia, Transcaucasia). Divisions, regiments and other subdivisions were formed in respect of these on a national basis. There were cadres of commanders of these nationalities. With respect to nationalities that were not subject to military service in pre-revolutionary Russia, considerably less progress was achieved because of lack of commanding personnel of the same national origins.[290]

Conclusions

A great deal of work was accomplished during the NEP period toward organizing the Red Army on a firm basis. Considerable advance was made in the field of training of officers. The introduction of the N.C.O.'s in the guise of junior commanders trained in regimental schools was also an important step in the right direction.

The pretences of the communist cells to interfere with the commanding and the political personnel were cut short and the authority of commanders and commissars considerably reinforced. The friction between different groups of the commanding personnel did not cease, nor that between the commanders and the commissars. However, the process of adjustment was going apace. The two main groups facing each other in the NEP period in the army were: the new military hierarchy—commanders and political workers on the one hand, the rank and file on the other. The cleavage was still deep, as it was based on a difference in the cultural background, the disparity of the economic interests of the respective social backgrounds of the groups as well as a difference in the political aspirations and viewpoint.

The soldiers were carefully watched for signs of political opposition. The sports circles, the theatricals, even the movies—all these were means of influencing the soldiers in order to change their viewpoint.[291]

Every letter addressed to a soldier was read by his superiors before being delivered. The same was true of letters sent by the soldiers. The resolution of the XIIIth Congress of the party had even demanded that the letters of the soldiers should be used as means of bringing the village closer to the understanding of the current problems of the Soviet state; at least in one army unit this went so far as the printing of a standard letter to be used by soldiers writing to folks in the home village.[292]

In this manner the soldiers were watched over, worked over, molded into the pattern set by the party. Whether all this effort was quite successful is open to doubt. H. G. Wells, with a great deal more sagacity than most of the observers of the Russian scene wrote: "The Russian mind is not a docile mind."[293]

The declaration of Frunze that the Russian Army was not a national army, but a force which had set as its goal the defense of the interests of the toilers of the whole world,[294] sounds today more like wishful thinking than an objective statement of fact. Particularly in the years of the NEP this was not likely to reflect the true picture. At that time the bulk of the soldiers and a large part of the commanders were peasants closely connected with the economically and culturally conservative village of that time, which, in temper, as S. Ivanovich said, had become socially much more conservative than was the case in the last decade of czarism.[295]

Almost ten years after the birth of the Red Army, relations between the soldiers and their commanders were still far from harmonious.

This is evident, for instance, from Voroshilov's speech in 1927. He referred then to the inattentiveness of commanders to soldiers, and the heightened sensitiveness of the soldiers to "the slightest injustice." Voroshilov had admonished his hearers to give urgent thought to the problem of "coming close to one's subordinates," to cement, in fact, the new forms of relationship between the chiefs and those in the ranks, to work out in practice a "comradely fusion," as well as to reach the feeling of mutual confidence.[296]

Thus, the commanding personnel, rising from the midst of the workers and peasants, seems to have encountered considerable difficulties in establishing moral ascendancy over their subordinates. It is not unlikely that the main difficulty lay in the fact that the commanders, as well as the commissars, were inevitably regarded by the peasant soldier in the end of the NEP period as tools of the state, the claims of which were inimical to the way of life on the land which he preferred and to achieve which he helped so mightily toward the success of the November revolution. Commanders and soldiers were really mere pawns in the greater conflict, that between the policy of the Soviet state and the private-ownership-minded village.

That the army in the NEP period was deficient in combat efficiency was freely admitted at the time by its responsible leaders. Thus Frunze had stated in 1925 that the training of the Red Army was still below the level even of the old Russian Army, that its commanding personnel was backward in the military technical knowledge and training, and that 10 per cent of the commanders were still without any military education whatsoever.[297]

Even Voroshilov, a much less frank person than Frunze, admitted in 1927 that the Red Army had to do a great deal of work both in the field of training the individual fighter and in that of the tactical training of troops to achieve satisfactory results. He had expressed the hope at the time that this goal would be reached in a year or two.[298]

It is a moot question whether one should take seriously Voroshilov's statement made at the height of the intra-party struggle that in 1923-1924, because of the lack of attention on the part of Trotsky's opposition, the army was not in a condition to provide for an adequate defense of the country in an emergency.[299] There is no doubt, however, that the army at the time was far from strong.

Trotsky himself wrote of military oppositionists standing daily guard over one of the leaders of the opposition, Beloborodov. It would seem, however, that Trotsky did not make any actual attempts to use the army for an oppositional *coup d'état*. He had left the post of the People's Commissar for War in January 1925 without a fight, in the same way that he had permitted the removal of his *alter ego* in military affairs, Sklianskii, from the post of Deputy Commissar for War.[300]

One is inclined to think that the weakness of the Red Army prior to 1925 was the outcome of much more complex causes than oppositional activities or Trotsky's negligence. Economic difficulties of the early years of the NEP, the still stormy sea of peasant rebellions, and the process of demobilization of the huge army of the Civil War period —all these made it impossible to build up a satisfactory army in these years.

Gradually, the Soviet Army began to emerge from the difficulties of the reorganization period. Its training methods began to take shape and its combat qualities underwent an improvement. By Western standards it was still a poorly equipped and inadequately trained army, beset by all the difficulties of maintaining modern standards in an industrially backward nation. But the foundations for further growth and development were firmly laid down by Frunze.

The problem of modernization of the armament and the equipment of the Red Army was closely connected with the industrial development of the U.S.S.R. The impact on the Red forces of the intensive industrialization by the leaders of the Soviets, under the so-called Five Year Plans will be traced in the following chapters.

THE IMPACT OF INDUSTRIALIZATION

THE inauguration of the Five Year Plan is rightly considered by W. H. Chamberlin as one of the three important dates in post-revolutionary Russian history, alongside those of the bolshevik revolution on November 7, 1917, and the adoption of Lenin's New Economic Policy in March 1921.[1]

The effect on the army of the intensive industrialization of Soviet Russia under the several Five Year Plans was great and manifold.

On the one hand, the rapid development of metallurgy had provided a suitable base for a military industry on a truly large scale. On the other, the creation of a Soviet automotive industry and the development of production of the internal combustion engine laid the foundation for the building up of aviation and the mechanization of several of the arms of the Soviet military forces.

But what perhaps will be regarded as equally, if not more important, was the geographical redistribution of the industrial centers of Soviet Russia and the new industrial growth of the Urals and Western Siberia. As Chamberlin noted down in 1934, the great chain of industrial plants stretching from Magnitogorsk in the south to the Berezniky in the north, lies from 1,200 to 2,000 miles away from the Soviet Western frontier. This position makes these plants secure against air raids, at least in the initial months of war, and turns them into the reserve arsenal of the Red Army should Russia have to abandon most of the territory west of the Volga.[2]

In his lucid *Russia's Iron Age*, Chamberlin emphasized the fact that according to the second Five Year Plan, the eastern regions of Russia (Siberia, the Ural Territory, Kazakstan and Central Asia) were to produce by 1937 one-third of the country's pig iron, as against a fourth in 1932; about a fifth of the electrical energy, as against 6.5 per cent in 1932; a tenth of the output of machinery as against a twentieth in 1932.[3]

The collectivization of the village with the upbuilding of the mighty system of tractor stations throughout the countryside had provided a large reservoir of men acquainted with the care of the internal combustion engine and made possible the creation of a large reserve of trained drivers and mechanics for the armored and motorized forces of the Red Army.

The expansion of industry under the successive Five Year Plans had vastly augmented the industrial proletariat of Russia. This laid a broader foundation for the rule of the Communist party. At the same time, on the other side of the ledger, the drive which Stalin felt strong enough to launch in 1928, against the private-ownership-minded peasant, had resulted in a tremendous conflict and a great tragedy for rural Russia. The terrible famine of 1932-1933 was the climax of that great drama. This conflict made more acute the antagonism between the peasant and the state and created considerable additional internal friction and tension in the Red Army. It also led to the more rapid proletarization of its personnel.

Frunze pointed out that the Soviet military industry was unable to satisfy the needs of the army with respect to internal combustion engines, tanks, automobiles and in several other respects, as to both quantity and quality. He admitted that there was no reason to expect that the army could equal in technical equipment western armies, as the resources of Soviet industry rendered impossible any rapid or radical changes in this respect.[4]

However, in the last years of his life, Frunze was awake to the importance of building up the technical equipment of the army and educating its personnel in the use of the modern implements of war, as well as training it in the tactics and strategy resulting from the wide application of the internal combustion engine in warfare.[5]

By 1927, Frunze's successor, Voroshilov, was acutely aware of the changes wrought in the methods of warfare by technological progress. He had stated then that in his opinion the next war would be more mechanized than the preceding one. He had to admit that the technological means of the Red Army were still below that of the western armed forces. Nevertheless he pointed with pride to the work of the Soviet aviation constructor, Tupolev, as a harbinger of a great future development of the Soviet air forces. He quoted figures to illustrate what was done to improve the technical equipment of the army. The production of the aviation industry, for instance, had increased from 1923-1924 to 1925-1926 at the rate of 351 for airplanes and 574 for engines as against 100. In 1923-1924 all engines built were trainers. Fifty per cent of the airplanes were also trainers. In 1925-1926 trainer engines constituted only 20 per cent of the output, while the number of combat planes had increased six and a half times as against 1923.[6]

At the end of the same year Voroshilov made a very interesting assertion: that the Soviet state had actually begun to consider the problem of preparing the country for war as of "actual significance" only with the spring of 1927. He gave as a reason for this increased concern with the country's state of preparedness, the current policy of England, which he described as "openly threatening" with respect to the U.S.S.R. He pointed out that in order to cope with this new situation, the Council of Labor and Defense had again regained its defense functions, which had lapsed after the end of the Civil War. The Council began again to meet regularly under the chairmanship of the President of the Soviet of People's Commissars to decide all questions connected with protecting the country from an attack from without.[7]

In addition to this new lease of life given to the Council there were created mobilization departments at all of the People's Commissariats. A special office of industrial mobilization was added to the organization of the VSNKH (Supreme Council of National Economy), and a section of the Gosplan (State Planning Commission) was formed and entrusted with the task of considering the needs of national defense in the planning of national economic development.[8]

In discussing the various phases of Soviet life important to national defense, Voroshilov pointed to metallurgy as the worst bottleneck, and cited statistics showing that only 70.5 per cent of pig iron and 81 per cent of steel of the quantities produced in 1913 were manufactured in 1926. The shortage of aluminum—the Soviets at the time did not produce any at all themselves—was a severe handicap, Voroshilov said. Zinc and lead had to be imported from abroad in the ratio of seven to one with respect to the home production. Even copper production was insufficient to satisfy the need, and a large quantity (50 per cent of the home production) had to be brought in from abroad. The chemical industries, and particularly the manufacture of explosives, were also insufficiently developed. The automobile industry was in its infancy. Only 300 cars were built in 1925-1926 and 500 in 1926-1927. There were altogether only about 22,000 passenger cars and trucks (including damaged) in Soviet Russia at the time. Voroshilov advocated the planning of new tractor plants in the interest of defense.[9]

Voroshilov frankly stated that the building of army tanks was in its earliest stages. He pointed out that in the western armies "the tank is one of the fundamental means of armament." He advocated an earnest effort to supply the army with a sufficient number of tanks.[10]

The state of the military industry (in the narrow sense of the word) was described by Voroshilov as the weakest spot of Soviet economy. "Chaos," "morass," "eyesore," were words freely used by the Commissar for War with respect to that industry's state prior to 1926. Even at the end of 1927, according to Voroshilov, the quality of production of military equipment was below that of the western countries.[11]

The state of the railways, the deficiencies of the macadamized roads, the uselessness of the non-surfaced roads for motor transport, were regarded by Voroshilov as great handicaps in the defense of the country.[12]

In outlining the suggestions for the Five Year Plan with respect to the defense of the country, Voroshilov underscored the fact that its first and principal aim was to increase as much as possible the technical means of the Red Army, leaving its numerical strength at the same level as before. All additional funds made available for defense purposes were to be allocated to the strengthening of the army's technical means and to the building up of the stocks of war supplies.[13]

Voroshilov postulated that the Five Year Plan should take as its point of departure the inevitability of an armed attack on Soviet Russia. From this followed the urgency to organize a defense of the country that would be adequate for the warding off of an onslaught of the united forces of all "probable enemies." He stressed the fact that the industrialization of the country made for the combat efficiency of the U.S.S.R. He drew from this the conclusion that military considerations should be included in the plan for building up Soviet industry under the Five Year Plan.[14]

The goal set by Voroshilov was that of bringing Soviet technical and combat efficacy to the level of the first-rate European armies.[15]

Detailed planning of the conduct of the national economic life in wartime was advocated by him as an urgent requirement to promote adequate defense.[16]

Apparently there was a trend of thought in Russia in 1928 which reasoned that it would be better to concentrate on the creation of a large military industry without a wide upbuilding of the entire metallurgical industry of the country. This trend was condemned by Voroshilov as leaving out of consideration the tremendous problem of supplying adequately the front and rear of the armies in wartime.[17]

Quite obviously, an army abundantly supplied with modern military technical equipment required a different commanding, as well as rank and file personnel from that of the poorly equipped army of the Soviets in the NEP period. Voroshilov, speaking in 1934, freely admitted that the Red Army had very few qualified trained technicians among its cadres in 1929-1930. A tremendous work had to be accomplished to re-train the commanders and to obtain non-commissioned officers and soldiers able to use intelligently and to maintain at a high level of efficiency the various new engines of war the Red Army had received in the course of the first Five Year Plan. By 1934, almost 50 per cent of the entire personnel of the Red Army were, according to Voroshilov, "technical specialists." As he said: "Our army had become a different army, that of technique."[18]

The training of commanders and the education of soldiers was entirely reorganized. The focal point of that training had become the study of the new technical means of war, both from the viewpoint of their technical exploitation and from that of their tactical application.[19]

That there were doubts in the minds of some of the leaders of the Red Army as to whether the commanders and the soldiers would succeed in mastering the new complicated technique was revealed in one of Voroshilov's speeches of 1934.[20]

Before proceeding to the examination of the changes in the doctrine, the modifications in training and the alteration of the social origins of the army under the impact of industrialization, it may be advisable to summarize, however briefly, the features of the first Five Year Plan more immediately concerned with the interests of the army, also the actual results of the application of those parts of the plan.

The blueprint of the industrialization of Russia was developed by the State Planning Commission for the years 1928-1929 to 1932-1933 on the foundation of directions given by the XVth Congress of the Party and the plenary meeting of its Central Committees.[21]

Two variants were developed: the minimal and the optimal. In both of these variants the effort for the immediate development of the defense of the country was planned practically on the same level,[22] although the plans differed by almost 20 per cent, or roughly by one year of development.[23]

The general problem set by the authors of the plan was the now famous "to catch up and overtake" the level of the advanced capitalist countries in order to assure the triumph of the socialist system of economics "in its historic competition with the economic system of capitalism."[24]

It was a tremendous task. During the first World War imports from abroad had provided 85 per cent of motor cars; 80 per cent of shells for heavy guns (over 8-inch); 75 per cent of aeroplanes; 72 per cent of heavy guns (over 6-inch); 63 per cent of machine guns; 62 per cent of explosives; 56 per cent of hand-grenades; 48 per cent of rifles; 38 per cent of small arms ammunition; 30 per cent of army boots; 30 per cent of cloth; and 25 per cent of chemicals for the manufacture of gas.[25]

In addition to this, the entire consumption of aluminum and tin had to be covered by imports; 98 per cent of lead; 70 per cent of copper and 50 per cent of zinc.[26]

At the same time, the total production of the national economy in 1927-1928 in milliards of rubles at pre-war prices was not very far ahead of that of 1913, as indicated in the following table.[27]

	Value of entire industrial production	Production by factories and mills included	Entire agricultural production	Total
1913	8.43	6.39	11.61	20.04
1927-8	10.08	8.14	12.26	22.34

In some of the essential phases of industrial production the U.S.S.R. was still substantially behind Russia of 1913.[28]

Thus, in so far as iron ore and pig iron were concerned, there was still a long way to go to catch up with the pre-war production:

	1913	1927-8	% of 1913
Iron ore (millions of tons)	9.2	5.7	61.9
Pig iron " " "	4.2	3.3	79.1

In the field of agricultural production, grain was also lagging behind the level of 1913:

	1913	1927-8	% of 1913
Grain (millions of tons)	81.6	73.1	89.5

However, in other fields important for national defense a considerable measure of progress was achieved:

	1913	1927-8	% of 1913
Coal (millions of tons)	28.9	35.4	122.5
Oil " " "	9.3	11.7	125.8
Peat " " "	1.6	6.9	446.2
Internal combustion engines (1000 H.P.)	26.5	106.9	403.4

In view of the deficiency in the field of production of iron ore and pig iron and the need of greatly increasing the engine-building industry, it is not surprising that out of the 11.8 billion rubles appropriation, under the minimal, and 13.5 billions under the optimal plan budgets for capital investment in the national industry, 3.5 billions and 4.0 billions respectively were earmarked for the development of the metallurgy and engine-building industry. This was more than was allocated for any other branch of the industry, including the program of electrification.[29]

The production of the non-ferrous metals, which had to be imported during the first World War to such a large extent from abroad, was to be increased at a very rapid pace. The program is summarized in the following table:[30]

	1927-28	*1932-33* *(minimal)*	*1932-33* *(optimal)*
Copper (thousands of tons)	28.3	65.0	85.0
Zinc " " "	3.15	38.0	77.0
Lead " " "	2.97	28.0	38.5
Aluminum " " "	—	—	5.0

To make possible the increase at a steep pace of the production of metallurgical enterprises, the fuel base also had to be greatly expanded. The plans accordingly provided for a vast development:[31]

	1927-28	*1932-33* *(minimal)*	*1932-33* *(optimal)*	*% of increase* *(minimal)*	*(optimal)*
Coal (millions of tons)	35.5	68.3	75.3	192.4	212.1
Oil " " "	11.7	19.0	21.7	162.4	185.0
Peat " " "	7.2	14.0	16.0	194.5	222.0

The Five Year Plan concerned itself with the human element as well, and some estimates were included as to the probable increase in the proletariat because of the industrialization of the country and the socialization of a part of the rural economy. The following figures were set down:[32]

	1927-28	*1932-33* *(minimal)*	*1932-33* *(optimal)*
All hired labor (in thousands)	11,350	14,781	15,764
Omitting agricultural labor (in thousands)	9,226	11,976	12,897

In other words, it was estimated that the proletariat of the U.S.S.R. would increase by 3.4 millions or 30 per cent, according to the minimal, and by 4 millions, or 39 per cent, according to the optimal plan. The urban proletariat was expected to grow by 30 per cent according to the minimal, and 40 per cent according to the optimal plan.[33]

Tractor-building was to be concentrated at the Putilov Works at Leningrad (up to 10,000 per annum) and at a new plant at Stalingrad (up to 40,000 per annum). The optimal version of the plan provided for establishing another large tractor-building factory beginning in 1929-1930.[34]

Automobile construction was to be increased up to 130,000 units per annum. Of these, up to 100,000 cars per annum were to be produced at the new plant at Nizhny-Novgorod.[35]

While the plan* had achieved considerable results, it fell behind the schedule in some of the more important phases of industrial production essential to the development of the technical base of the army.[36]

1932 (actual production)		1932 (actual production)	
Iron Ore (millions of tons)	12.1	Aluminum (thousands of tons)	0.9
Pig Iron " " "	6.2	Tractors (thousands of units)	50.6
Steel " " "	5.9	Automobiles " " "	23.9
Copper (thousands of tons)	46.6	Coal (millions of tons)	64.3
Zinc " " "	14.8	Oil " " "	22.3
Lead " " "	18.8	Peat " " "	13.3

The lagging behind of the iron ore, pig iron, steel and the non-ferrous metals production, also of the tractors and automobiles, was a serious handicap to the development of a powerful wartime military industry and the mechanization of the army in peacetime. Nevertheless, the results were impressive.

On the other hand, the proletariat grew in numbers more rapidly than anticipated. It actually reached 22.8 millions—more than 100 per cent increase.[37]

In summing up the results of the first Five Year Plan for 1932, Dr. M. T. Florinsky stated that the fuel industry had achieved 99.8 per cent of the assignment, the metal industry 127.2 per cent, the cotton industry 54.2 per cent. Within the metal industry group the deviations from the plan were even more considerable. Pig iron was at 62.0 per cent, steel at 56.7 per cent and iron ore at 62.9 per cent while machine-building and metal goods reached 181.2 per cent of the assignment.[38]

Probably the most far-reaching effect was caused by the deviation from the plan in agriculture. The goal was set to increase the area under crops of the "socialized sector," that is, of the land occupied by the state farms and the kolkhoz farms from 2.7 per cent of the total area under crops (in 1928) to 17.5 per cent (in 1932). Actually, by 1932, 78 per cent of the area under crops was in the hands of the state and the collective farms.[39]

This rapid collectivization of the village, achieved by ruthless methods, had a profound influence on the attitude of the village to the Soviet state and accordingly found its reflection not only in the views of the peasant soldier of the Red Army, but also in those of a certain section of its commanders and rank and file Communists.

The tendency to industrialize the more backward and remote parts of the country found its expression in the plan's provisions to increase

---

* The optimal variant of the plan was approved for execution. There were several revisions of the plan during its execution.

the relative weight of these parts of the U.S.S.R. in so far as industry was concerned.

Kazakstan's place in the industrial life of the country was to rise from 0.94 per cent to 1.79, Central Asia from 1.47 per cent to 2.52, Siberia from 1.28 per cent to 3.2, the Urals from 4.3 per cent to 10.4.[40]

A competent military commentator, T. Adamheit, summed up the practical results: the first Five Year Plan succeeded in creating a large armament industry.[41]

In the opinion of another German commentator, during the Five Year Plan period, the Soviet Army was not only placed in a privileged position with respect to assignment of the best manufactured, semi-manufactured goods and raw materials, but also was given first call on the best trained men. In his view, the army had kept in advance of the rest of the sectors of Soviet life, not only in the economic, but in the cultural field as well.[42]

During the first Five Year Plan, the Red Army did not increase numerically. It consisted of 71 infantry and 16½ cavalry divisions, with artillery and technical arms to match. Of these, 29 infantry and 12½ cavalry divisions belonged to the standing army, while 42 infantry and 4 cavalry divisions were in the Territorial Militia. The infantry divisions were formed into 21 rifle corps, while cavalry was organized into 4 cavalry corps. A few infantry divisions and several cavalry brigades were left outside the framework of the corps formations.[43]

The territory of the U.S.S.R. was divided into eight military districts (Moscow, Leningrad, White Russia, Ukraine, North Caucasus, Volga, Siberia, Central Asia). In addition to the districts there were also two separate armies: of the Caucasus and the Far Eastern.[44]

Two-thirds of the total infantry and cavalry divisions were concentrated near the frontiers. Almost the entire standing army (90 per cent) was stationed near the borders, as a covering force. The Far Eastern Separate Army consisted of 7 divisions of infantry and one of cavalry.[45]

The national formations grew apace, and there were 10 Ukrainian, 3 White Russian, 4 Transcaucasian (consisting of 2 Georgian, 1 Armenian, 1 Azerbeidzhan divisions). Apart from these were other national formations in the Volga, North Caucasus and the Central Asia districts, as well as within the territory of the Far Eastern army.[46]

Bearing in mind that the old Russian Army, upon mobilization in 1914, comprised 115 infantry and 38 cavalry divisions with 7,900 guns, the Red Army during the period under review was by no means numerically excessive for a country politically isolated and bordering on several of its frontiers with unfriendly nations.[47]

At the head of the organization of the armed forces of the U.S.S.R. remained the Revolutionary Military Council, the chairman of which (K. M. Voroshilov) was also the People's Commissar for the Army and the Navy. Directly subordinated to the Council were: 1) the staff of the land forces; 2) the administration of the army personnel and military education; 3) the navy department; 4) the air force department; 5) the department of supplies; 6) the sanitary-veterinary department; and 7) the political administration of the armed forces.[48]

The unified administration and command of all arms, on land as well as on sea and in the air, was thus maintained as heretofore.

The basic statute governing the organization and training of the armed forces was that of August 8, 1928, which had supplemented the statute of 1925. According to these statutes the defense of the U.S.S.R. was the duty of all citizens. However, the actual *armed* defense was laid only upon the so-called toiling elements among the citizenry. The non-toilers were to carry out functions in promoting the defense of the country in a manner which would not require bearing arms.[49]

For the recruitment of the armed forces, universal military obligatory service was introduced for all male toilers aged nineteen to forty. This service consisted of: a) pre-army service training; b) active military service; and c) service in the reserves. The pre-army service military training embraced all toilers of the male sex reaching the age of nineteen by January 1 of the respective year, and continued for two years.[50]

The active military service fell upon men reaching the age of twenty-one in the respective year, and continued for five years. It could be of three kinds: some served in the standing armed forces, others in the Territorial Militia, while still others were to undergo military training outside the framework of the armed forces.[51]

In the standing army the soldiers were to serve actually in the ranks without interruption, for two to four years, depending on the arm they were assigned to. The balance of their five years' service consisted of a furlough from one to three years, with refresher training periods not to exceed one month for privates and two months for non-commissioned officers during the entire duration of the furlough.[52]

In the Territorial Militia, the soldiers (exclusive of cadres), underwent training for periods not in excess of eight to twelve months, the period of service with the colors depending on the arm. The time between the training periods was spent on furloughs.[53]

Training outside the framework of the armed forces was to be carried out during training periods not to exceed six months altogether, the balance on furlough.[54]

Citizens on active military duty were given the honorable designation of Red Warrior (Redarmist or Redfleetman). Toiling women were accepted for service in the armed forces on a volunteer basis. In wartime the Council of the People's Commissars of the U.S.S.R. had the right to draft toiling women into military service for special duties.[55]

While non-commissioned officers were still included with commissioned officers within the commanding personnel brackets under the style of junior commanders, the statute stated specifically that they were to fulfill their service terms on the same basis as privates.[56]

For the non-toiling element, the Rear Militia, the Soviet labor battalions, still provided the only outlet for fulfillment of their military duty.[57]

According to an acute student of the Red Army, S. Ivanovich, the part of the Soviet citizens deprived of the right to defend the U.S.S.R. with arms in hand was identical with the category of citizens deprived of franchise, and did not exceed 8 per cent of the total population. For the youth of draft age, this percentage was considerably lower. Taking into consideration the already-mentioned tendency among sons of the disenfranchised to pass themselves off as "toilers," S. Ivanovich came to the conclusion that the Red armed forces recruited themselves, broadly speaking, on the same basis as the armies of other countries with obligatory military service.[58]

Another Russian émigré commentator, Colonel A. Zaitsov, concluded that the conscription laws of the Red Army were not unlike the pre-revolutionary Russian laws. He saw the principal difference between them in the treatment of exemptions on family status grounds. Under the Soviet laws the interest of the army predominated over that of the population in this respect.[59]

Some of the privileges accorded in pre-revolutionary Russia to persons with higher education were not extended by the Soviet statutes. The better educated recruits (graduates of secondary schools and colleges) were drafted into the army to serve in the ranks of combat units, and were obliged to prepare themselves for the examination for the reserve commissioned rank.[60]

A very important and significant feature of the statutes was that concerning the re-enlistment of non-commissioned officers. As an inducement, those of them who re-enlisted were permitted to come up for examinations for commissioned positions in the army, without passing through military schools.[61]

Full rights of citizenship were preserved by those on active service in the armed forces.[62] At least this was so in theory.

A very important rôle in the military training of the population outside of the ranks of the armed forces, was assigned to the huge military volunteer defense organization—the Osoaviakhim, which, as mentioned already on page 269, absorbed within itself several other volunteer defense organizations in June 1927.

Osoaviakhim

The Osoaviakhim was rapidly expanded during the years of the first Five Year Plan. It laid the foundations for the truly universal military training of the entire population fit to carry arms, with accent on the training of the urban population first, and of the kolkhoz peasants of the collectivized sector of rural Russia next. One cannot overestimate the truly gigantic task undertaken and carried out by that society, which had anticipated by many years the various forms of mass civil defense of Western Europe. The record of the Osoaviakhim is very little known outside of Russia. No doubt many features of this organization could have been made part and parcel of the civilian defense training in this country.

While the detailed study of the Osoaviakhim is outside the scope of this work, a brief discussion of its features during the years of the first Five Year Plan may help to elucidate the scope of the effort of the U.S.S.R. to strengthen its defense on the base of the growing industrial capacity of the country. There is no doubt that the Osoaviakhim contributed to the ability of Russia to withstand, without collapsing, the onslaught of the most powerful and best trained army in the world.

N. S. Unschlicht stated the problem bluntly in 1931 : "The forces of the Red Army alone would not enable Soviet Russia to achieve victory. The entire population would have to take part in the next war, and, accordingly, the entire population must be prepared for it. Technique does not recognize battlefronts or frontiers."[63]

In line with the mechanization and motorization of the U.S.S.R. and its armed forces, the Osoaviakhim concentrated upon the study of technical means—and of the latest technical military means—in the first place. One of the tasks set before it was to attract into the orbit of its work the intellectuals engaged in the technical work in the industrial enterprises. These, admittedly, were insufficiently interested as yet in the study of military problems and of the military technique.[64]

While until 1927 the center of gravity of the activities of the Osoaviakhim lay in the field of propaganda and agitation, making the population "defense-conscious" and organizing drives for various defense purposes, after that year it concentrated on actual military training.[65]

The resolution of the second plenum of the central committee of the Osoaviakhim in 1931 called for organizing the work in the field of military training around special training centers. This had become possible during the first Five Year Plan with the growth of the material base of the society in the guise of the numerous "houses of defense" training centers, schools and rifle ranges, built up by the society. Previously the work had to be carried on by study circles, often without any meeting place of their own.[66]

The direction of military training was also changed to conform with the advance in technical equipment. The study of the new technical means of warfare was made the cornerstone of that training. This, of course, called for retraining of Osoaviakhim instructors.[67]

In the field of agitation and propaganda carried on by the society, a new note was sounded by stressing the propaganda of military technique. A decision was made to publish a number of pamphlets popularizing new army equipment.[68]

The rapid growth of membership of the Osoaviakhim during the years of the first Five Year Plan was a remarkable phenomenon. By October 1, 1927, it embraced 2,950,000 persons. Two years later it had almost doubled, reaching 5,100,000 members. In 1931 there were 11,000,000, and it was anticipated at that time that by the end of 1932 membership would reach 20,000,000. The budget of the central body alone had reached in 1931 the 50,000,000-ruble mark.[69]

A good illustration of the growth of the work in the field of military education by the Osoaviakhim may be found in the field of marksmanship training. In 1928 there were 12,117 Rifle Circles. In 1929 their number had grown to 15,500. In 1929 there were 4,080 rifle ranges established by the Osoaviakhim. The membership of the rifle circles grew from 113,000 in 1927 to 341,000, i.e. almost tripled in two years. In 1930 it reached 560,000 and in 1931 it was 651,000. Of these, in 1930, 60,000 were trained at ranges only, as against 250,000 in 1931. Fully trained riflemen with experience under field conditions were 67,000 in 1930 and 86,000 in 1931. Even snipers were trained, although in small numbers as yet: 274 in 1930, 1,029 in 1931.[70]

The cadres of the Society consisted of active volunteer workers. In the primary cells of the society were 330,000. There were also 85,000 leaders of study circles, schools and detachments. Altogether 425,800 persons were engaged in the active work in the Society in 1929.[71]

The predominantly urban character of activity of the society in the above years was reflected in its membership, which in 1929 included 34 per cent of workers, as against 32 per cent of peasants, with 16 per cent Communists and 17 per cent Komsomols.[72]

In the field of aviation, the Osoaviakhim had, in 1931, 14 glider stations, 40 flying fields, 139 emergency landing fields. A large central airfield and a glider factory were under construction. In addition to these, there was a vast network of flying schools, avio-laboratories, shops for airplane model building and other centers for the training of pilots, aviation mechanics and sundry aviation specialists, as well as for the propaganda of military aviation among the population.[73]

It was planned to train several thousands of pilots, several thousands of flying mechanics, as well as experts in gliding and constructors of airplane models. The glider plant was geared to produce several thousands of machines per annum.[74]

The recruitment of volunteers of the Soviet air force was energetically taken in hand by the Osoaviakhim. It was claimed in 1929 that the recruits supplied by the society formed the main bulk of the volunteers entering military aviation schools. The popularization of these schools among worker and peasant youth was placed upon the shoulders of the cells of the Osoaviakhim jointly with the local cells of the Komsomol.[75]

In addition to this work, the Osoaviakhim was engaged, in 1931, in collecting a twenty-million ruble fund for construction of dirigibles and was assisting in organizing a dirigible base.[76]

It may be of interest to discuss briefly the program of the primary circles of military science of the Osoaviakhim as it was laid down in 1928. The program was designed to provide primary military training for persons without information or experience in military matters, largely for young people of the pre-army training age or younger. The aim was to supply the initial impetus and to create an interest in continuing military studies.[77]

The students were supposed to receive training in marksmanship in using the small caliber rifle and the training pellet cartridge in the regular army rifle, to become expert in taking apart, cleaning, greasing and assembling small arms. They were also trained to estimate distances, to orient themselves by the sun and the stars, as well as by compass and to read the simpler kinds of maps.[78]

The students were supposed to acquire the knowledge of all duties required of the individual soldier and to master the primary elements of military tactics. They were to be able to observe and to fire while wearing gas masks. Primary information regarding resistance to the modern means of warfare, such as enemy tanks, aviation, chemical warfare, etc. was also imparted. The simplest methods of first aid were taught.[79]

Political education was not left out by any means, and such topics as the international situation with respect to the U.S.S.R. and the current problems of the Red Army were included in the circle of studies.

All teaching was to be made as interesting and attractive to the students as possible, the subjects to be taught by sight wherever possible and the initiative of the students themselves to be encouraged. As a test of the knowledge of the students, it was recommended that tactical exercises, combined with a march, small two-sided maneuvers, or similar field exercises be used.[80]

In the center of the whole problem of adapting the armed forces to the new conditions created by the industrialization of the country, was the task of obtaining a commanding personnel able to meet the new challenge offered by the change from sluggish, outmoded hosts of foot soldiers and horse-riding cavalry, supported by a none-too-modern artillery, to modern mobile, highly mechanized armies, supplied with powerful aviation and lavishly outfitted with the latest technical means of warfare.

Commanders

In February 1928, Voroshilov surveyed the situation in the army with respect to the military education of the commanding personnel. It consisted at the time of the following groups :[81]

Graduates of the normal Soviet military schools	23,889
Graduates of the short-term Command schools	4,125
Graduates of the re-training courses	7,341
Persons without any adequate military education (former non-commissioned officers and privates of the old army, who failed to improve their military education)	3,968
Officers of the old army	4,418
Graduates of military colleges (including colleges of the old army, numbering 465)	2,126

The bulk of the personnel was composed of the graduates of the normal military schools, who were, no doubt, in their education and theoretical military training, much superior to the graduates of the Civil War period Command Courses, as well as the N.C.O.'s of the old army. However, there were several groups with deficient military education even by the somewhat low standards prevailing in the Red Army in that period. These included the graduates of the Command Courses, of the re-training courses, as well as the N.C.O.'s and privates of the old army who had failed to supplement their scanty educational equipment. All these totalled up to 15,434 commanders.

Voroshilov had to admit that it was too early as yet to assert that the Red Army possessed a finished type of Red commander. The diversity was too obvious. He qualified his statement by remarking that the situation concerning the commanding personnel was on the whole satisfactory.[82]

Voroshilov failed to bring up, in that discussion, the great dilemma which confronted the Red Army at the time, that of reconciling two opposing trends.

As the People's Commissar for War had stated in 1928, the party took as the point of departure for the work of building up armed forces from the "immutable principles," that of combat efficiency of the army being the direct function of the level of political consciousness and moral resilience of its rank and file and commanding personnel.[83] In terms of 1928, that meant that the social origins and the party allegiance of the commanders were of paramount importance.

As matters stood at the time, the requirements of filling the ranks of commanders with workers and poor peasants, with Communists and Komsomols, stood in direct contradiction to the urgent need to get the best educated elements into the military schools to enable the latter to master the theoretical studies required to prepare them to use successfully the complicated new technical means of warfare the Red Army was acquiring during the first Five Year Plan.

In May 1928, Bukharin outlined the situation in the secondary schools. In the lower forms in the beginning of the school year, the percentage of the proletarian element reached 46 to 50 per cent, which, from Bukharin's viewpoint, was a satisfactory state of affairs. However, by the end of the school year the percentage of proletarians fell to 10 to 15 per cent of the remaining students. He gave as a reason for this that the students of proletarian origin, children of agricultural laborers, of poor peasants, could not get a sufficient support from their families, and were unable to maintain themselves at school. According to Bukharin, the schools had become sieves, retaining the children of the better-off elements. An article in the *Izvestia* in 1929 admitted that secondary schools had become educational institutions for the children of the white-collar employees and that it was impossible to speak about the training of proletarian children for the proletarization of the universities and technical colleges.[84]

Because of this situation, the insistence that military school students be recruited from the ranks of the children of the proletariat could be satisfied only by a radical lowering in the quality of the product of these schools. About 87 per cent of students of military schools in 1929 had education below seven years of schooling, as against nine and ten years of the full course of the secondary schools.[85] In other words, the situation had become worse than that which had existed in the military schools of the old army before the abolition of the so-called Junkers' Schools.

The Soviet military schools were accordingly faced with the problem of preparing commanders able to cope adequately with command problems in the modern complicated army from elements which the *Red Star* called "almost illiterate" youngsters, in three to four years' time. This led to an overburdening of the courses with general educational subjects and a heavy strain on the students, who were not educationally equipped to follow the program. One of the results was "a large percentage of neurasthenics" among graduates of military schools.[86]

The antithesis of "educated" and "socially reliable" had thus become the nightmare of those responsible for the recruitment of military schools.[87]

The second factor was clearly winning over the first in the years of the first Five Year Plan. Thus, in 1928, the social origins of the complement of the military schools was vastly more "proletarian" in character than in the years before.[88]

	WORKERS	PEASANTS	OTHERS
1928	56.0%	34.4%	9.6%
1925	35.5%	56.8%	7.7%

The remarkable growth in the percentage of workers and the rapid falling off of those of the peasantry was a fitting illustration of the ever-deepening rift between the village and the Soviet state.

Among the candidates sent by the army itself, 92 per cent had only primary education and only 6 per cent had a complete secondary education. Two per cent were self-taught. The candidates sent forth by the various organizations included 86 per cent with primary education, 1 per cent of self-taught, and only 13 per cent of persons with complete secondary education.[89]

As S. Ivanovich aptly said: ". . . the socially dependable young commander had vanquished the culturally and scientifically educated commander."[90]

The next year there was little improvement and the *Red Star* wrote editorially that the general education of the candidates for admission to the military schools still left a great deal to be desired and was causing considerable difficulties in the functioning of these schools. The official Red Army paper bluntly stated that the general educational level of the commanders who had graduated from military schools in the few preceding years was not answering fully to the requirements of their work in the army.[91]

To help out the meager educational equipment of the students, additional courses in the Russian language and mathematics were introduced in the military schools. It is characteristic that in that year—1929—elements of higher mathematics were introduced for the first time in the programs of studies of artillery schools. In other words, in previous years, graduates of artillery schools managed to leave their alma mater without any knowledge whatever of higher mathematics.[92]

Red Star mournfully commented that in the Moscow district the general level of candidates preparing to enter military schools was still low. Those sent forth by the Red Army and the recruitment commissions were particularly so, falling behind the young men who came up for examinations on their own initiative.[93]

In order to improve the general educational level of the workers (both industrial and agricultural), as well as poor peasants, selected by the recruitment commissions, special brief training—rather, cramming—courses were opened.[94] In 1929, 25 per cent of all vacancies in military schools were filled by men who had passed through these courses.[95]

Altogether, in 1929, 19.8 per cent of those admitted to military schools had completed a secondary education (as against about 15 per cent in 1928) ; 70.7 per cent had completed only a primary education. This left 9.5 per cent of persons without any formal education whatsoever. As the *Red Star* admitted, only one-half of those accepted had received a general education sufficient to enable them to study profitably in the military schools.[96]

On the other hand, the proletarization of the schools went on apace. Of the students admitted in 1929, there were 55.5 per cent industrial workers and 11.8 per cent agricultural workers, or a total of 67.3 per cent proletarians. The peasants numbered only 24.2 per cent, others 8.5 per cent. Students who came up for the examinations on their own initiative were less satisfactory than the average from the class viewpoint. Only 54 per cent were workers. On the other hand 31 per cent were peasants and about 14 per cent were "others." They were, however, definitely the better educated element and included 33 per cent of persons with completed secondary education. As the army newspaper wrote, this was a tempting tid-bit for the technical military schools. The infantry schools obtained only 10 per cent of men with secondary education.[97]

The party element was particularly strong among the contingent of students drawn from the army. There were 56.2 per cent party members and candidates, as against only 10 per cent among the students sent forth by the recruitment commissions and a mere 7 per cent among those who came forward on their own volition. The average was 24.8 per cent as against 28.5 per cent in 1928.[98]

Women were for the first time admitted to military schools in 1929. The number of women students was small. Three entered the Topographers' School and one the Signal School.[99]

To obtain better trained commanders from the poorly educated students, authorities had lengthened the period of studies at the military schools. For infantry and cavalry schools it was extended from three years to three and one-half years, for the artillery, engineer and signal schools from four to four and one-half years. Lectures and discussions were to occupy only 20 per cent of the study periods. Fifty per cent of the time was earmarked for work on problems set to students, with the balance of the time left to the latter's discretion.[100]

In the meanwhile, the Central Committee of the party and the Revolutionary Military Council of the U.S.S.R. were fully aware of the educational deficiency of the commanding personnel in the face of the ever-growing mechanization of the army. The former had resolved in February of 1929 that it was imperative to press by every possible means the furthering of the increase in the special military qualifications of the commanding personnel, which was to parallel the technical progress of the army.[101]

As shown above, in spite of the urgency of obtaining a better-trained commanding personnel, military schools were filled by poorly educated men, unequipped to take full advantage of the courses offered to them.

At the same time, the upper crust of the commanders was also abounding with men without sufficient general education to enable them to adapt themselves promptly to the new tasks set before them by the new technical equipment bestowed on the army.

The highest commanding personnel (generals) included 81 per cent of men with combat experience preceding 1918. The senior commanders (colonels, lieutenant-colonels, majors) had 79.3 per cent of such persons among them. The middle commanders (captains and lieutenants) had only 39.6 per cent. Since, among those with combat experience antedating 1918, there were non-commissioned officers of the old army as well as privates, it is apparent that among the two senior categories there was a large percentage of men with a meager educational background—the Budennys and Voroshilovs and their fellow commanders—who had risen to exalted positions during the Civil War.[102]

The picture is still further elucidated by a glance at party membership. By 1930, there were 76 per cent of Communists among the highest commanders, 50 to 52 per cent among the senior commanders and 60 per cent among the middle commanders.[103]

The high percentage of party allegiance is an indication that many of them were not from the ranks of the officers of the old army. Graduates of the normal military schools had not yet had time enough to reach that group. It included a large number of people whom the fortunes of the revolution and Civil War had thrust up into their exalted positions within the army from groups of the population where education was scarce. As Voroshilov said in 1928 of some of these veterans of the Civil War: "literacy was harder than the storming of the Perekop" to them.[104]

For the commanding personnel as a whole, the percentage of workers rose from 12 per cent in 1921 to 28.5 per cent in 1929 and 29.9 per cent in 1930. Among the platoon commanders that percentage had already reached 36 per cent. The commanding personnel was moving at a substantial rate toward proletarization.[105]

It did not call for much perspicacity to see that the further continuation of these methods of recruitment of military schools would result in filling the army with commanders largely unfit, because of inferior general education, for duties under the new complex conditions of warfare.

An important step was taken to fill the ranks of secondary schools with proletarians. While class distinction existed in schools prior to the inauguration of the first Five Year Plan, it was intensified during its course. The so-called "class-mobilization for the front of learning" introduced recruitment by local communist leaders for diverse schools. At times, members of the local communist groups were sent to schools to improve their education. As a result, only few vacancies were left to persons not belonging to the favored groups.[106]

The head of the Political Administration of the army, A. Bubnov, was appointed People's Commissar for Education in September, 1929.[107] During the period of his incumbency, a drastic reorganization of civil education had taken place. It was decided by the authorities to introduce, by January 1, 1933, a new program with a view to increasing hours devoted to mathematics in the primary and secondary schools, expanding the programs of physics, biology, chemistry, geography, Russian language and literature, introducing compulsory study of one foreign language in the secondary schools and changing completely the methods of teaching sociology, language, literature and geography in the direction of increase of historic elements in education. And even more important, return to the lesson as the basic method of training was ordered, and, to ensure the actual predominance of the teacher in questions of education, the principle of yearly examinations was reintroduced, and school discipline enforced.[108]

The system in effect prior to the reform was roundly condemned by the party in the decree of August 25, 1932, which stated that the main defects of the Soviet school—insufficiency of general knowledge, defective preparation for higher technical training and an almost complete absence of knowledge in such fields as physics, chemistry, mathematics, the mother tongue and geography—had not yet been removed.[109]

This decree may be interpreted to mean that secondary education in Russia before this was entirely out of step with the technical progress of the industry, that the students came badly prepared for studies at technical colleges and by the same token, at the technical military schools, where mathematics, physics and chemistry were of such great importance.

The reorganization of the civil education and the recruitment of schools from elements socially acceptable for the Soviet régime offered a solution to the heretofore insoluble problem discussed above. It must not be overlooked also that the number of pupils in primary schools grew from 11,697,000 in 1929 to 19,163,000 in 1933, while that of secondary schools rose from 2,453,000 to 6,674,000.[110]

W. H. Chamberlin has described the typical Soviet school between 1921 and 1931 in his *Russia's Iron Age*, suggesting something of the nature of a joyous bedlam where discipline was so lax as to be almost non-existent, and the authority of the teacher was at a minimum. Marks and examinations were discarded. The teaching of separate subjects was replaced by the so-called "complex" method under which a class was supposed to work on a given theme—a city street, for instance, or the season of the year—learning in the process a bit of geography, a bit of arithmetic or history. As Chamberlin says: "Such methods produced a scrap-heap, a hodgepodge knowledge on the part of the children who were subjected to them."[111]

Under Bubnov's aegis, the "complex" method had been cast out, and teaching by individual subjects reintroduced. The desirability of testing the individual capacity of each student was recognized. Mr. Chamberlin, visiting Soviet schools in 1933 and 1934, was able to carry away the impression that the pupils were working hard and acquiring definite knowledge—"something which could not have been said of the Soviet schools a few years ago."[112]

From the standpoint of obtaining students for military schools suited to the exigencies of the modern armies, the reform of civil education was a great boon. It had made possible a definite improvement in the quality of the student material in so far as general education was concerned, as well as habits of discipline. The great expansion of secondary education provided a large reservoir of potential candidates for these schools. However, the reform came too late to influence the situation in the military schools during the first Five Year Plan period.

For the retraining of commanders, the army had introduced compulsory one-year training courses for those in line of promotion for the command of battalions, artillery battery groups, etc. and another, also of one year duration, for candidates for the command of regiments. As Colonel Zaitsov says, similar courses in other armies are usually designed to broaden the knowledge of the students, while those of the Red Army were chiefly intended to supplement the deficiencies in their previous training. On the other hand, every encouragement was extended to commanders graduating from the Staff College.[113]

At the same time, the proletarization policy had led to the reduction in the educational standards of the military colleges themselves. According to Colonel A. Zaitsov, in 1929 three-quarters of those who had entered the War College had only a primary education; 90 per cent of them were Communists and 60 per cent came from the ranks of the workers.[114]

Besides the War College there were five other military colleges: Naval, Technical (Engineering, Artillery and Chemistry), Aviation, Political and Medical. There were also military departments in some of the technical civil colleges, such as those of Transport, Electrotechnics, Technology, etc.[115]

Those responsible for the military policy were not ignorant of the inability of a large part of the proletarian graduates of the military colleges to pursue theoretical creative work in the respective fields. This was brought out by a very interesting investigation conducted by the PUR in 1929.[116]

Upon investigating 243 commanders who had contributed to military literature in the U.S.S.R., the PUR had established that 81.5 per cent of them were officers of the old army. Some of them were men well in the middle age group, as 38.7 per cent of them had achieved the general or field rank in the old army and 12.1 per cent had served on the general staff of the old army. Forty-five per cent of the authors were descendants of nobles, clergymen and merchants. The only consolation, from the communist viewpoint, was that 32.1 per cent of the authors were members of the party. The same investigation had also shown that such matters as strategy, tactics, military engineering, artillery, mobilization, etc. were predominantly studied by former old army officers, who numbered in these fields over one hundred authors, while there were only twenty-one commanders of the revolutionary vintage among writers on these subjects.

As the author of the article, analyzing the results of that investigation, remarked: "The social origins of our authors *en masse* are too bad for words . . . the figures do not jibe at all with the fact of the twelve years' existence of the Red Army."[117]

With the end of the NEP, the military schools had become popular, and conditions such as had existed in 1927, when only 45 per cent of commanders promoted from one of these schools had declared themselves as having any interest in military affairs, were rapidly becoming a thing of the past. The *Red Star* observed in September 1929 that in the Leningrad military district there were six candidates for every vacancy in the military schools of the district. A large percentage of students had come from the ranks of the Red Army. Thus for 410 vacancies, 149 of those accepted were re-enlisted non-commissioned officers, 79 were non-commissioned officers of the regular service term and 34 were the so-called "one year" men with better education. Altogether the army contingent numbered 262.[118]

The professional army commander's career had become attractive not only to persons with scant general education from the ranks of the army, but for the better educated elements of the country at large.

There were several reasons for this popularity. With the introduction in 1928 of the statute of the middle, senior and highest commanding personnel's promotion and service regulations, the process of crystallization of the officer corps of the Red Army had achieved a very substantial success.

The order of the Revolutionary Military Council of the U.S.S.R. No. 225, of 1928, which had announced the statute, gave as an explanation for the measure, the desire of the government to guarantee the stability of the service positions to the commanding personnel by confirming their rights to the service qualifications they had obtained. Also the wish to create for the commanding personnel definite service career prospects on the basis of firmly regulated rules of promotion. The service record containing the opinions of the superior officers was to be conducted with particular care, subject to communication to the person concerned. It was to be used as the main instrument for judging the fitness of the commander for further promotion.[119]

The first paragraph of that statute laid down that the commanding personnel of the Red Army consisted of those persons on military service who were in possession of the respective military or special education. The commanding personnel was divided into military commanders *proprio dictu*, the political, administrative, medical and veterinarian personnels.[120]

The central point of the statute was contained in paragraph 13, which defined the term "service category" as the expression exclusively of the service qualifications of the respective person. The service category was to be appropriated to the commanders simultaneously with their appointment to the respective positions.[121]

The service qualification was to be a function of such factors, as the previous service and positions filled in the army, the educational record and ability, as reflected by the opinions expressed in the above-mentioned service record.[122]

This was supplemented by paragraph 24, which stated that the respective quality of the commander was to be retained by him not only while on active service, but in the reserves as well.[123] The very word "quality" (*Zvanie*) was characteristic of the statute. It came close to the famous "rank" (*rang*) of Peter the Great, or to the even better known *chin* of the czarist service.

Another considerable boon was bestowed upon the commanders by the revision of the age limits for active service. They were considerably extended—for the highest commanders from 45 to 50, for the senior from 36 to 40-45, for the middle from 29-36 to 40.[124]

This feature of the statute is quite interesting. While the low age limit previously introduced was used as a weapon against the old army officers in the Red Army, so the new higher age limits were a favor conferred upon the graduates of the normal military schools and the self-made men in the army. These limits, however, were still lower than those in any other army and made for rapid promotion and the building up of a reserve officer corps composed of experienced men still relatively vigorous. Upon reaching the age limit for active service duties, commanders were transferred to the reserves where they remained for another ten years.[125]

The only fly in the ointment was the provision that the quality conferred could be taken away by the People's Commissar for the Army and the Navy, i.e. in an administrative way and not by a court decision.[126]

The same Commissar was empowered to retain commanders on active service until the expiration of the age limits established for the obligatory military service of the commanding personnel of the respective categories (i.e. for another ten years). The commanders themselves were permitted to petition for retention on active service beyond the active service age limits. Such requests were supposed to be acted upon favorably in instances where there were no suitable candidates available for filling the respective positions.[127]

By this token, the People's Commissar for the Army and the Navy was given a wide latitude, enabling him to favor those of the commanders whom he considered suitable to remain on active service beyond the active service age limits

For each category, in the middle and senior group brackets, a definite time limit was established for the maximum time an incumbent was permitted to remain in that category. These limits were six years for platoon and deputy company commander, as well as regimental commander, five years for others.[128]

A definite rate of pay was attached to each of the service categories.[129]

All promotions from one category to another were for merit only. There was no provision for promotion on the basis of seniority. The promotion of the ablest and the removal from active service of the unsuitable commanders was based on the service record, i.e. written valuations of the qualities of the person involved. The following points were especially considered: 1) data on past service and positions occupied; 2) personal qualities; 3) political suitability; and 4) condition of the unit commanded by, or work performed by the person involved.[130]

The qualities valued particularly in commanders may be judged in a measure by the questions asked by the Central Committee of the Society for Promotion of Defense in an instruction published in 1927. The first of these questions was connected with the social origin of the commander: who were actually making better commanders, workers, peasants or intellectuals? In other words, the class origin had a great deal to do with the valuation of the usefulness of the commander even in a period as comparatively calm as 1927.[131]

First in the list of qualities stood discipline. Apparently this characteristic was regarded as very important, to achieve first place on the list. Next followed will-power and tenacity, with ability to show initiative in the line of duty. Sixth and seventh on the list were presence of mind and ability to observe. Respect of subordinates held the fifteenth place, knowledge of the respective special branch of the service, eighteenth, preceded by ability for self-improvement.[132]

The statute provided that the middle commanding personnel was to be recruited from graduates of normal military schools, as well as from junior commanders (N.C.O.'s) who had re-enlisted and had distinguished themselves in action or by meritorious service in peace time.[133]

As S. Ivanovich has it, even the junior commanders had a marshal's baton in their knapsacks, by the provisions of the army regulations, and not—as in the Civil War—by the wish of the revolutionary element. As he says, there was a considerable difference.[134]

Erich Wollenberg wrote that during the years 1931-1933, the international spirit and the socialistic basis of discipline in the Red Army were swept away. The natural and easy relationship between officers and men in the Red Army had also gone overboard in these years.[135]

While it is difficult to argue with an eye-witness, one is inclined to think that the statute of 1928 was the real dividing line, and that what followed was the development of a trend already well established. Some evidence to that effect will be adduced in the following pages.

Meanwhile, it is worth noting that the provision authorizing the promotion to middle commander categories of the non-commissioned, re-enlisted officers had kept open the door for the further lowering of the general educational level of the army commanding personnel. Commanders who had graduated from refresher courses and the so-called "courses of perfectionment" were placed on the same level with the graduates of the normal military schools.[136]

Commanders who did not pass through the normal military schools or their equivalent in the old army were permitted to ask to be sent to the abbreviated one-year courses of military schools for improvement of their military education.[137]

Graduates of military colleges were given considerable advantages. Middle and senior commanders, after graduating, were appointed to the next higher category. These in the categories of platoon and battalion commanders were even taken up two steps at a time. Only the generals were not given higher categories upon graduating from college.[138]

Considerable space was devoted in the statute to the problems concerned with the service record. These were to be prepared jointly by the immediate superior commander and the commissar of the respective unit. Should the commissar disagree, he could append his own opinion. The higher standing commanders in the order of subordination were to give their conclusions in writing in the record on the opinion of the immediately superior commander. The record was to be prepared as much as possible on the basis of documentary evidence, such as orders referring to the conditions of the respective unit, opinions of the respective commander's work at tactical exercises, reports and works submitted by the latter himself.[139]

All service records were to be forwarded for analysis to the respective Service Records Commission. The person concerned had the right to protest against an opinion expressed in his record by writing to the commander standing immediately above the one who had confirmed the record.[140]

In other words, commanders had certain guarantees against the use of personal animus by their immediate superiors. On the other hand, the remote control exercised by the Service Record Commissions boded ill at least for those of them who did not belong to the politically favored groups.

The Statute of 1928, if not the Magna Carta of the commanding personnel of the Red Army, was something closely akin to the Petrine Table of Ranks, and provided for that personnel a very substantial anchor, a tenure of privileges obtained by service, which was absent in many other departments of the Soviet Government service.

This was not the only important advantage they had gained. Under the economic conditions prevalent during the first Five Year Plan, the fact that commanders were clothed and fed (and quite well, according to the Russian standards of the period), meant that they were considerably less affected by the loss in the purchasing power of the ruble than was true of the overwhelming majority of the population. While the commander's monetary income was not impressive, when expressed in rubles of pre-war purchasing value, his economic situation was well above the average. Even the much more modest scale of living of the rank and file of the Red Army had become so desirable in the eyes of the population that those entitled to liberation from military service because of physical disabilities made efforts to conceal their defects in order to obtain admission into the ranks of the army. As Piatnitskii comments, by 1932 this had reached the proportion of a mass phenomenon.[141]

The same situation explains the overwhelming tendency among the N.C.O.'s to seek re-enlistment. In certain regiments this had reached the 100 per cent mark by the fall of 1931.[142]

In the straitened conditions of Russian life of the time, the comparatively modest monetary remuneration received by the commanders, equalling in purchasing power, according to Piatnitskii, 28.5 pre-World War I rubles per month for platoon commanders and 45 rubles per month for company commanders, placed the latter of the two categories on the economic level that the warrant officers had occupied in the old army in the period immediately preceding the World War. In spite of this, the great mass of the population had every reason to envy their economic security, their good clothes, sufficient food and modicum of shelter.[143]

The proportion of commanders to the total personnel of the army was relatively high. Without the junior commanders (N.C.O.'s) that personnel reached 9.5 per cent of the total of the army, as against 7.9 per cent in Poland and 4.9 per cent in France. In this manner there was one commander for each unit of 9.4 rank and file soldiers, as against 12 in Poland, 19 in France, and 24 in the old Russian Army.[144]

The gradual transformation of Red Army Houses into Officers' Clubs was exemplified by what was going on in Kronstadt in 1929, as reported by the *Red Star* of November of the same year. One of the two Red Army Houses of Kronstadt was earmarked for the use of commanding personnel and of the "activist" element among the seamen.[145]

S. Gusev, in his book published in 1925, found it necessary to stress the antagonism between the new Red Army officers of revolutionary vintage, who came from command courses and the normal military schools, and the former officers of the old army. Thus he made reference to the report submitted to the Central Committee of the party by the communist cell of the War College. It spoke of the influence of the old ex-czarist officers' caste, of the strengthening of the ideological sway of the specialists, of the alleged monopolization of military science in the hands of the old army officers, etc. He was "viewing with alarm."[146]

During the period under review, the antagonism seemed to be no longer between old army officers and young revolutionary commanders, but rather between party members and the non-partisan elements among the commanding personnel. The Soviet military press contains numerous references confirming the existence of this antagonism.

Thus, in one of the September 1929 issues of the *Red Star*, S. Rabinovich wrote about the lack of good understanding between some of the non-partisan commanders and the Communists among them. In one of the regiments, a non-partisan commander had openly stated that the cell and the Communists as a rule did not pay any attention to the non-partisan commanders, and made no serious effort to bring these commanders into the ambit of public activity. This statement, Rabinovich says, was reflected in the utterances of other commanders as well.[147]

A concrete example of what this "lack of attention" on the part of the military Communists actually meant in practice was brought out in another article in the same publication in October 1929. A non-partisan platoon commander had found out that the secretary of the communist cell (himself a platoon commander) was assigning party work to a communist soldier of the former's platoon, entailing absence from that private's regular duties. The commander had asked the cell secretary to let him know in the future whenever the latter charged soldiers of his platoon to perform party work which took them away from service duties. As a result, the non-partisan commander became the object of persecution by the secretary of the regimental party collective, who accused him of all kinds of heinous sins. The commander decided to leave the Red Army, feeling that a non-partisan officer had no chance to make his way in it.[148]

Another instance, cited in the same *Red Star* in October 1929, describes a conflict which took place between the commander of an artillery battery and a political instructor. The starting point was the commander's refusal to permit the use of a battery horse by the political instructor.[149]

That these incidents were not isolated occurrences is confirmed by an article by A. Kogan, published in the *Red Star* of December 1, 1929. It describes conditions prevailing in one of the military schools of the White Russian Military District, where non-party commanders were at times definitely treated as inferiors. The examples Kogan brings up include such instances as negligence in advising the commander when his subordinates were sent to another town on party business; of a secretary of the cell countermanding orders of the battery commander; of cell meetings held during rest hours without advising the commander. Matters came to such a pass that some of the non-party commanders even began to disregard offenses against discipline and neglect of duty by party members and the Komsomol in order to escape being attacked by Communists at meetings. Party cells made attempts to regulate promotion of the junior commanders. Under these circumstances it is not surprising that, according to Kogan's statement, a certain part of the non-communist commanders of the school came to the conclusion that the days of officers non-affiliated with the party were numbered, that they were mere transient guests in the Red Army.[150]

These feelings found their counterpart in the minds of the students of the school. One of the cadets, a candidate for party membership, was not approved for full-fledged membership. He wrote to party officials that should the party harbor any doubts about him, he would prefer to be excluded from candidacy, and concluded by saying that he had in mind to leave the military school altogether, should he fail to be made a party member, since "the situation of the non-party commanders is clear to me." A. Kogan says that at that school the opinion was fostered that the non-party commanders (who formed about 40 per cent of the commanding personnel) were second-rate and had no chance for advancement in the army.[151]

The army command apparently became quite alarmed by this trend and made an earnest effort to stop it. The newspaper campaign was obviously only a part of that endeavor.

Probably the most significant step in that direction was taken when a delegation of the highest-ranking non-party commanders, who had served in the Red Army since its inception, was admitted to the XVIth Congress of the Party, in November 1930. It was headed by B. M. Shaposhnikov (now Marshal of the Soviet Union), who spoke against the slackening of the tempo of industrialization and urged solidarity and harmony within the party, siding with the general party line and expressing a criticism of the opposition.[152]

The oppositional elements within the party were making a great deal of the social origins of the commanding personnel, claiming that it was formed of old army officers and kulak peasants. They intimated that the army contained elements which made it susceptible to bona-partist trends. Voroshilov quoted in one of his speeches from a state-ment by the Left Opposition in 1927, which claimed that the Red Army was threatening to become a tool of a bonapartist *coup d'état*, because the proletariat had no means of influencing the army's educa-tion, training, recruitment and its entire mode of life. While Voro-shilov officially rejected these accusations, maintaining that the com-manding personnel was an entirely reliable revolutionary force with a substantial core of proletarian element, the whole policy of the army command clearly indicated that the government was none too pleased with the class origins of that personnel and was making every effort to build up the proletarian group within it, to make it less susceptible not only to the so-called kulak influences, but to those of the village as a whole.[153]

The policy of the recruiting of the military schools by drafting party and Komsomol members, trade-unionists and the army rank and file, speaks for itself. The Department of Military Schools called in its recruitment circulars for the following assignments of candi-dates: the Communist party was to supply 12.1 per cent of the stu-dents, the Komsomol 18.1 per cent, the trade-unions 3.2 per cent, the Red Army 44.3 per cent. This left only 22.3 per cent of the vacancies for candidates coming for the examinations on their own initiative.[154]

The acute political struggle within the party which ushered in the Five Year Plan was making an issue of the recruitment of the com-manding personnel. The same struggle had some effect on the internal cohesion and even the loyalty of the commanding personnel, even, indeed, of those belonging to the party. Voroshilov had openly admitted that in 1928 the Red Army had experienced difficulties caused by the general situation in the country at large. He spoke of the "considerable friction" between groups of the commanding personnel, although insisting that this was more true of the political personnel than of the commanders.[155]

Some of the non-party commanders were in some instances expressing their dissatisfaction with the taxation policy as it affected the village, and were voicing doubts as to the success of the rapid industrialization of the country.[156]

In one of the military schools a group of young Communists was conducting fractional nightly secret meetings and criticizing the party line as late as November 1929.[157]

Nevertheless, the results of the party purge of 1929 seem to indicate that the oppositional support within the army was not widespread among the commanding personnel. In the different districts, the percentage of those purged varied from 3 per cent to 5 per cent. Almost one-half (46.4 per cent) of those purged were expelled from the party because of ties with "alien elements"—plainly speaking, for being friendly with, and influenced by, middle class and kulak elements. The *Red Star* quoted E. Iaroslavskii's report that the results of the purge had shown that the commanding personnel of the army was satisfactory from the communist point of view.[158]

One is somewhat surprised to learn from the columns of the *Red Star* of the persistence of anti-semitism among the commanding personnel, including Communists among them. The army newspaper describes in detail the mockeries to which a Jewish platoon commander was subjected for a number of years. The so-called "Jewish stories" were frequently told by communist commanders in the presence of their Jewish colleagues. *Red Star* states that the regiment at the time went through a period of open anti-semitism. The communist cell of one of the companies was the spearhead of that movement. Commanders, members of the party, addressed their Jewish fellow-commander as "Jerusalem nobleman." The example set by the commanders spread among the men, and even on duty Jews were called "Yids." A similar situation was reported in another regiment.[159]

If one bears in mind the consistent policy of the Soviet Government against all forms of anti-semitism in the years since it took power, these survivals of crude forms of Jew-baiting are a strange phenomenon indeed. However, they are part of the record, and should be mentioned.

Reference was made in previous chapters to the deficient training of the reserve officers. The new problems set for the army by the industrialization of the country had made these deficiencies even more glaring than heretofore.

The statute of 1927 on obligatory military service set out to remedy the situation in making provision for the mass military training of the better educated youth of the country. It provided that in all colleges, workers' faculties, technical schools, secondary schools and other educational institutions of similar level, students had to undergo a pre-army military training within the walls of their respective schools and colleges.[160]

Graduates of these educational institutions were given the choice of entering military schools before the calling to the colors of their respective age groups, or of entering the ranks of the regular cadre Red Army, also ahead of their age groups, with the understanding that this service would be counted as a part of their obligatory military service. It was insisted that these graduates should enter cadre combat units only, and not serve in any clerical capacity. After two months on active service they were to go to the N.C.O.'s schools. After one year's service in the land forces and two years in naval units they were to pass an examination in military subjects to qualify as middle commanders of the reserve.[161]

Those passing the examination successfully were to be transferred to the transient command personnel of the territorial troops in the localities of their respective residences or places of employment.[162]

Military training in colleges consisted of a minimum of 180 hours and those physically fit had to spend two months in camp for tactical exercises.[163]

The program of these military studies aimed to produce reserve platoon commanders. At camp, the students were supposed to become acquainted with army life, get through a course of musketry, learn the rudiments of the tactics of their own arm, and obtain an understanding of tactics of the other arms. It was decreed that independent studies of military science by college students at the specially established military study rooms and musketry laboratories were not to be counted in the obligatory 180 hours.[164]

The examination of the infantry arm program shows that 34 hours were devoted to musketry, 110 hours to tactics and kindred studies,

16 hours to topography and only 16 hours to military statutes and regulations, with a mere 6 hours set aside for political studies. In other words, the program definitely aimed to train the student how to use the weapons of his arm and how to understand and apply elementary tactics.[165]

Military training in secondary schools did not actually get under way until the academic year 1929-1930, and even then it was introduced only at a limited number of schools in the guise of an experiment.[166]

That training was planned to offer elementary military knowledge, combined with fundamentals of military education and discipline, to enable the students to successfully continue their military studies in colleges. The courses at the secondary schools were interconnected with those at the colleges, in a measure forming a preparatory conditioning for the latter. Its end was to train a private of infantry, able to function within the framework of the section. The course consisted of physical hardening with a military slant to it, as well as of a study of military sciences. It was extended over three years, with 60 hours per annum, or 180 hours altogether, with an additional three weeks in camp.[167]

The teaching of military sciences at the secondary schools was entrusted to young pedagogues who had themselves gone through the advanced obligatory military training in their respective colleges. The main burden of training was in musketry, military topography and the elements of military hygiene. It was expected that graduates of secondary schools, should they be drafted into the army, would possess sufficient theoretical knowledge and practical experience to enable them to train successfully, while in the army, for the duties of junior, as well as middle commanders.[168]

As the air forces of the U.S.S.R. were rapidly expanding during the Five Year Plan, the methods of training of pilots and mechanics for these forces had assumed great importance. Four different types of schools were set up by 1929 for the education of the personnel of these forces.

The pilots were first trained in military theoretical schools of the Military Air Forces, which had two departments, one for land, the other for naval fliers. These schools gave theoretical training only, while the actual flying instruction was given in the Military Schools of Land and Naval Pilots. Graduates of the first type of schools were sent to pursue their studies in the schools of the second type. The program of the first included general educational as well as special subjects. The period of training lasted one year and six months for land, and two years and six months for naval fliers. In the Pilots' Schools the course extended for one year and six months for land, and one year for naval fliers. Thus, the total length of training was respectively three years for land, and three and a half years for naval pilots.[169]

The mechanics were trained in the Military Technical Schools of the Military Air Forces, which set as their goal the preparation of junior aviation mechanics. Their course lasted for two years.[170]

There were also United Military Schools of Pilots and Avio-mechanics, with separate departments following respectively the same programs as the Military Theoretical Schools and the Military Technical Schools.[171]

Such specialists as the radio operators, photogrammetrists, laboratory photography specialists, etc. were trained at the Military Schools of the Special Services of the Military Air Forces. The course varied from one year to one year and six months.[172]

The entrance requirements for the airmen schools were not high. Algebra and trigonometry, for instance, were not included. Candidates were accepted between the ages of eighteen and twenty-five.[173]

The difficulties in the path of the retraining of the commanding personnel both as to knowledge of the new military technical equipment, and understanding and development of new modes of tactics and strategy (these changes in armament and equipment postulated), was clearly realized by those at the head of the military organization of the U.S.S.R. As P. Dybenko wrote in one of the Soviet military periodicals in 1928, the army had to become in the methods of its training a technical school. He insisted that it was more important to become a narrow specialist thoroughly versed in some branch of military technical knowledge than to strive for encyclopedic dilettantism in the new techniques of warfare.[174]

This *entweder-oder* is typical of the lesser lights among the communist writers on military subjects of the time. The machine was an incomprehensible, almost mysterious deity. Better worship one at a time, rather than study the folklore of this new Olympus as a whole.

The question arises as to what extent the army was able to achieve mastery over its new equipment under the handicaps of accepting into military schools persons of inferior education.

C. Revinskii, writing in the *Red Star* in November 1929, answered that question in the negative, expressing the belief that the army personnel was not as yet sufficiently trained to serve well the rapidly growing technical means of the military forces.[175]

Even as late as 1935, Voroshilov admitted the danger that the commanding personnel might not be able to move ahead rapidly enough in knowledge and experience to meet the swift rise in the general cultural level of the men in the ranks who came from the expanding school system of Russia.[176]

Matters were made worse by the tendency to detail for teaching duties at the military schools, not the best commanders but rather those who, for some reason or other, were regarded as unsuitable for service in combat units. In 1929, N. Kuzmin advocated in the official army newspaper that the best of the commanders should be sent to teach in military schools after three or four years of service with the troops, and, after a period of pedagogical activity, be returned to duty in combat units again.[177]

The defect was not a new one in Russian armed forces. There was a tendency in the old Russian Army also for military pedagogues to become a group by themselves, isolated from the life of the troops. Even foreign observers were able to notice this defect quickly, as already referred to on page 57 above.

There was a tendency to introduce into army life the various features of the political and industrial life of the country at large, such as the so-called "self-criticism."

Pious hopes were expressed in official circles that self-criticism was gradually becoming in the hands of commanders and the political personnel, as well as party organs, a powerful weapon, helping them to improve the combat efficacy of the army. At the same time, it was noted that at least in some instances, self-criticism was applied without due consideration to the peculiar conditions of life in the army. Army orders were brought up for discussion and the commanding personnel discredited by destructive criticism.[178]

Mention has been made already, of the fear by non-partisan commanders of attacks upon them by Communists under the guise of self-criticism. This practice undoubtedly added considerably to making these commanders feel the lack of security of their positions and undermining their will-power.

Another feature of army life of the period was the introduction of the so-called socialist competitions, borrowed from the practice in industrial life. Apparently there was a great deal of confusion as to the manner in which this could be best applied in the army. In September of 1929, the Revolutionary Military Council issued a special instruction to concentrate in these competitions on problems of tactical training of troops.[179]

The instruction called attention to the lack of understanding of some of the commanders of the rôle and the significance of the socialist competition, even "bureaucratic resistance" to the practical application of that competition in army units. The opposition maintained that it was impossible to combine it with the specific conditions of army life. As the instruction stated, a part of the commanding personnel did not take any active part in the promotion of these competitions, regarding them as the concern of the political personnel only.

An *émigré* Russian military critic, Colonel A. Zaitsov, in summing up the results of the training of the Red Army commanders during the period under review, stated that the high standard of professional knowledge expected from a modern army officer could be acquired only on the basis of a sound general education. As the class policy of the Communist party forced it to sacrifice education to social origin, the general educational level of the graduates of the Soviet military schools made it impossible for them to become good commanders on the higher levels.[180]

This criticism was, in this writer's opinion, too categorical. Some of the most successful Russian military leaders in the first World War had come from the ranks of the graduates of the Junkers' Schools, which stood on a low level of general education. It is quite possible, by the same token, to visualize that, *in spite of* the deficiency of their general education, at least some of the graduates of the Soviet military schools of that period, because of their tenacity in the pursuit of military studies after graduation, might become excellent military leaders in the modern sense. It is impossible, however, to deny that the antithesis between education and political eligibility which had plagued the Red Army during the period of the first Five Year Plan was an important factor in lowering the standards of the commanding personnel.

Commissars

The most weighty issue affecting the political personnel of the army —that of the single command—was stabilized by the statute of 1928 and ceased to be an acute irritant, although even as late as in 1929, in the White Russian Military District, there were still noticeable the remnant of the so-called White Russia-Tolmachev opposition to the adoption in practice of the principles laid down in that respect.[181]

The Field Regulation of 1929 had clearly defined the rôle of the commissar. Paragraph 18 stated that both the commander and the commissar (or the political assistant) were to bear full responsibility for the condition and the combat efficacy of the unit. On the other hand, the commander was made solely responsible for operational direction of troops under his command.[182]

The comparison of the content of the paragraph with the original plans laid down by Frunze, shows plainly that, in so far as peacetime service was concerned, the commissars had won out in the contest and the commanders had obtained a mere shadow, leaving the substance of authority divided, and, in the case of the non-party commander, the lion's share going to the commissar in practice.

It was provided that the commissar had to supply the summary of the political situation necessary for reaching of an operative decision. He also was entrusted with the carrying out of the required political measures in connection with the combat activity of the troops.[183]

The commissars were to be fully posted as to the entire combat activity of the respective body of troops, as well as to the plans of the commander. Reciprocally, the latter was to be kept informed regarding political work within the unit.[184]

The commander was to make his final summation of a situation prior to arriving at a decision, in presence of the commissar (or the political assistant) and his chief of staff. It was stated, however, that the absence of the commissar should not delay the carrying out of the decision made, and that the commander was to arrive at the decision himself (i.e. the commissar had no voice in the matter).[185]

The general aim of the political work in the army was defined by the regulations as to the securing and strengthening of the combat efficacy of the troops, "as the armed support of the proletarian dictatorship." The principal task of the agitational-propaganda work in the army was set as educating the personnel in the sense of unlimited confidence, loyalty and unity with respect to the ideas and slogans of the Soviet Government. The inculcation of the correct understanding by the army masses of the leading rôle of the proletariat in the union of the workers and peasants, as well as the right appraisal of the class aims of war and the international interests of the working class and "all exploited" were set as goals for that activity, as well as the development of the revolutionary will to victory.[186]

The army thus remained a class army, in so far as the official view was concerned, and the class character of the future armed struggle was given a prominent place in the regulations.

The firm and consistent politico-moral condition of the troops was defined by the regulations as the most important foundation of the combat efficacy of the army.[187]

Political loyalty to the party was set, in this manner, ahead of any other condition. The army was to defend, not the land, but the minority group ruling it. To ensure this, it was carefully to regulate the "proletarian cementation" of the army personnel. An increase in the percentage of proletarians in a given unit was to be carried out, as a rule, through recruitment, although in special cases it was possible, in accord with the commanding personnel, to re-group party members of the respective army units.[188]

These provisions reflected the situation in the country: the party was still an armed camp in the midst of a recalcitrant peasantry.

Political work in the period immediately preceding military operations—before an offensive, for instance—was to be centered around the explanation of the importance of the operation, aimed at the creation of a definite political mood, and designed to concentrate the attention of the fighters on methods of combat.[189]

The commissars (as well as the Communists and the Komsomols) had to give a personal example of self-sacrifice and courage under fire. The regulations bluntly stated that such examples in action had a decisive significance.[190]

These detailed ordinances relating to the functions of the commissars were a striking contrast to the almost complete lack of reference to political work in the Field Regulations of 1925, which the new regulations had replaced.

The explanation of this, given in an editorial of the *Red Star* in a September 1929 issue, is an interesting confirmation of the already expressed thought that during the first years of the Five Year Plan the struggle of the commissars against the single command had borne fruit and that they had in practice, if not in theory, won the contest. The army newspaper underscored the fact that inclusion of detailed provisions relating to political work had discounted the changes which had taken place in organization, draft policy, training, upbuilding of cadres, as well as political work. As it stated editorially, the Red Army, in order to achieve victory, needed a high standard of political consciousness, as well as high qualifications in the military-technical sense. The army had to be led by men able to exploit to the best possible advantage all means of warfare.[191]

The final victories of the army of the proletarian dictatorship, ran the editorial, was possible only through combining these two elements: the military-technical efficiency and the high level of class consciousness.[192]

The particular attention of the readers was drawn to the part of the regulations stating that the Red Army was strong by reason of its class consciousness, and its unrestrained devotion to the cause of communism; also, that the disorganization of the military might of the enemy and the attraction to the proletarian revolution of the workers' and peasants' masses within the ranks of the enemy army (as well as of the toiling population of the theater of war) were the most important conditions of military operations.[193]

This was an entire program for a new form of warfare—through class-political means. It differed radically from Trotsky's ideas, and its inclusion in the Field Regulations, which made it a part of the accepted official military doctrine of the Red Army, was highly significant. With incorporation of this political strategy of war into the regulations, the important rôle of the commissar and the rest of the political personnel was greatly enhanced. It gave to that personnel a feeling of security and permanence, which they were lacking in the transitional period, when the unity of command formula was making rapid strides.

To what extent some of the political workers misunderstood their rôle in the field in the years preceding the publication of the new regulations is exemplified by the same editorial. It stated that in the preceding years some of the political workers called conferences of political instructors in the most crucial period of maneuvers, when the contending troops were in contact, thus making it impossible to follow the most important part of these maneuvers.[194]

The Internal Service Regulations of 1928 laid down the rule that the company political instructors were immediately subordinated to the regimental political commissar in so far as the political guidance was concerned, while in other respects they were placed under the battalion commander.[195]

In other words, the middle political personnel, of a regiment, for instance, was not subordinated to the commanding officer of the regiment (regardless of whether he was a Communist) in matters of political work.

Another paragraph of the same regulations entrusted the commissar, *on an even footing with the commander*, with the care of supervising the normal course of training of the unit in all branches and made him responsible for the maintenance of the standard of service in the unit, placing upon him the burden of the general supervision of the well-being and order in all spheres of the economic life and condition of the troops.[196]

These provisions of the Internal Service Regulations show even more clearly than those of the Field Service Regulations the large circle of activities reserved to the political personnel. They indicate to what extent, in the everyday life of the army, their influence was felt even in the aspects of service where one would expect the commander to be solely responsible (drill and technical military training in general).

The Statute of 1928 on the commanding personnel's service, decreed that the vacancies in the middle political personnel were to be filled from the ranks of the middle commanders who had passed through the military-political courses; also from among persons who had graduated from communist colleges and had satisfactorily passed the examination for reserve commander before completion of their obligatory military service. Platoon commanders, graduates of normal military schools, with at least two years' party standing, were the group from which students of the military political courses were supposed to be recruited.[197]

In other words, it was decided to recruit the political personnel from among persons with a sufficient military training to enable them to function with the same degree of military background and training as that of middle commanders. This was a definite break, not only with the tradition of the Civil War, but also with the practice of the NEP period, when the mass of the political personnel did not have technical military education or practical experience as commanders. The political worker was, at least in theory, becoming a kind of duplicate commander, specially trained for political duties, instead of being a civilian in military uniform, as was usually the case during the Civil War.

The general tendency toward the proletarization of the army found its expression, as was to be expected, also in the social origins of the political personnel. By January 1930 there were 46.5 per cent industrial workers among them (as against 29.9 per cent among the commanding personnel as a whole, including the political workers, and 36 per cent among platoon commanders).[198]

However, in practice, the plans for the recruitment of the military political courses from platoon commanders who had the normal military school education had remained for a time a dead letter. Thus, in 1929, not only non-commissioned officers, but even private soldiers were admitted to study in these courses. As the *Red Star* wrote, a new type of educational institution was coming into being, where students who did not graduate from normal military schools were trained (in one year) to become political instructors.[199]

Naturally enough, these students from the ranks did not have sufficient military training, and at least some of them had only a very meager general education, so that they were, both as military men and in general education, considerably below the level of the graduates of the military schools, with whom they were to share the responsibility for their respective units. Chances for a good career in the army were thus opened to Communists with a low educational background upon spending only one year in the military political courses.

The political advantage of this was clear: an outlet was given to ambitious but ignorant young Communists in the ranks of the army. The prospect of admission to these courses could be dangled before their eyes as a prize for conformity and zealous service. On the other side of the ledger was the inability of these young political workers to keep abreast even of their immediate task—that of political guidance and instruction.

That excellent source of case material for the study of the Soviet armed forces, the *Red Star*, printed in one of its September 1929 issues correspondence from Saratov to the effect that the purge had clearly shown the failure of a large part of the military Communists to give proof of a political education level corresponding to the high demands presented to party leadership. In one of the units 50 per cent of the political instructors examined were given reminders that their political knowledge was weak, although all questions asked were of a simple nature and dealt only with the day-to-day information on party line and policy.[200]

That conditions on the Volga were not exceptional was confirmed by a number of additional comments in the pages of the same newspaper. As Lukianovich wrote, a certain "disproportion" existed between the tempo in the rise of active interest on the part of the soldiers and the heightening of the level of theoretical knowledge among those who were called to provide political guidance and information to the army masses. He pointed to the low level of general education and even poor literacy of those in charge of political affairs of the army. The establishment of correspondence schools was advocated to help political personnel of the army improve their theoretical knowledge.[201]

In the face of these statements relating to the low level of general education of the political workers, one is not surprised to learn from a critique of the Bobruisk maneuvers of 1929 that the middle political personnel had not as yet succeeded in mastering even such rudimentary military tools of trade as regulations and map-reading.[202]

That the methods of checking on the social origins and the political past of the political workers was still far from perfection was intimated by the report on the expulsion from the party during the purge, of the regimental commissar of the 12th Rifle Regiment, who was found out to be a former officer of a White punitive detachment of Admiral Kolchak's army. Phenomena of social mimicry described in the previous chapter apparently were still in evidence even on the level of the higher political workers of the army.[203]

Examination of the available material seems to indicate that the same problem had arisen in the sphere of recruitment of the political workers as in the field of obtaining young commanders. The elements regarded as socially and politically desirable were lacking in sufficient education to enable them to carry out their work as political instructors and leaders to good advantage. Their opinion in matters purely military was apparently of small value and, under these circumstances, there was a wide gap between the task set for them by the Field and the Interior Service Regulations and their ability to carry it out satisfactorily. The wide powers given them were too heavy for their shoulders.

The appointment of Jan Gamarnik to the post of Chief of the Political Administration of the army, as well as to membership in the Revolutionary Military Council of the Union in October 1929 had inaugurated a new era in the field of army political work.[204] His work will be reviewed in the next chapter.

The acute political strife both within the party and in the country at large had set a tremendous task to the political personnel of the army. Whatever they may have lacked in theoretical political education and general cultural background, they certainly had proved themselves vigilant and of unflagging energy. That keen observer of the Soviet scene, W. H. Chamberlin, emphasizes the fact that the unremitting political agitation that the communist political apparatus carried out had averted any serious outbreaks within the Red Army, when news from home must have been often disquieting to the peasant soldier.[205]

And the political personnel of the army had been responsible for that work. They had kept the army loyal to the general party line.

Probably the keenest of the *émigré* Russian critics of the Red Army, Colonel Piatnitskii, wrote that the principle of mutual distrust was deeply imbedded in army life. People saw in every person they came in contact with, in their own colleagues even, possible traitors, stool-pigeons and *agents-provocateurs.*[206]

In Colonel Piatnitskii's opinion, the party-political organization had so strongly permeated the army masses and had attained such a stranglehold on its leadership that it would be extremely naïve to expect any serious explosion in the army. He thought that this could become possible only if the very machinery of the party should deteriorate or be dissolved in the flood of mobilized men during war. As he stated in 1931, such an explosion, regardless of the feelings of the masses of the Russian people, was possible only if war were to destroy all the calculations of the party with reference to the proletarian and "party cementation" of the respective arms. Outside of these two eventualities—disintegration of party leadership and war—Piatnitskii termed day-dreaming the hopes of the Russian *émigrés* abroad that the tide of the Red bayonets would turn upon the Kremlin.[207]

This diagnosis is quite significant, as it came at the time when in the Iron Age of Russia (as W. H. Chamberlin calls it) not less than two million Soviet citizens were deprived of liberty without anything that could plausibly be called "due process of law."[208]

The contrast with conditions during the Civil War was remarkable. As M. Kiselev, the author of reminiscences covering that period, reminds us, there were at that time even isolated instances of commissars inciting soldiers to disobey operational orders.[209]

That the Red Army had remained solidly loyal to the majority group of the party throughout the acute period of infra-party struggle which had reached new levels of bitterness, is a remarkable tribute to the efficiency of the army political administration. The days of the famous Circular No. 200 were past, and the leaders in the political administration of the army were free of oppositional influence, although during the period between January 1928 and June 1929 the party had expelled for various offenses, including "political heresy," 34,000 of its members.[210]

Voroshilov, in March 1929, accused the Trotskyist opposition of ceasing to be an opposition current within the party and turning into an anti-Soviet counter-revolutionary organization. He said that the height of the Trotskyist faction activity took place in the summer and toward the end of the year 1928, when a considerable amount of work was done by Trotskyists among industrial workers.[211]

One would expect that a man of Trotsky's prestige with the Soviet military would be able to bring to his side a large number of active partisans in the army, and to create, if not a serious threat of disruption to the armed forces, at least considerable disturbance. There is, however, no evidence to that effect, not even of an attempt in that direction, in the material examined. Voroshilov could write in February 1929 that the infra-party struggle did not divert the military workers from their task and that with the liquidation of the Trotskyist opposition, both the political education and the combat training of the troops were proceeding apace. He viewed with alarm, however, the movements of the rightist elements within the party, and feared that the infra-party struggle caused by the latter might divert the military leaders from their duties.[212]

At the same time, Voroshilov admitted that internal troubles in the country at large did not pass without some influence on the Red Army, and had created what he called a sequence of disease phenomena, not only among the rank and file soldiers, but among the commanding personnel as well, mainly among the political workers. He referred to the struggle between several groups within that personnel, singling out for special mention the supporters of the so-called White Russia resolution and those of the Tolmachev Military Communist College. These resolutions attacked the non-party commanders and cast doubt on the principle of unity of command as adopted in the Red Army, branding it as politically dangerous. These frictions, Voroshilov claimed, were liquidated by the Revolutionary Military Council with the assistance of the Central Committee of the party and army political party organizations "without any harm to the combat efficacy of the army and the upbuilding of the armed forces."[213]

Voroshilov added that the majority of the "erring comrades" had "sincerely and fully" acknowledged their mistake. In his opinion, this was the best possible guarantee of the loyal team-work of all elements in the army.[214]

During the previous serious infra-party conflict, the opposition elements in the army had control over the political administration; this time the intellectuals among the military Communists seemed to form the center for opposition tendencies. This was evidenced by the resolution adopted by the Tolmachev Military Political College. Voroshilov estimated that the Trotskyists had gathered about ten thousand partisans in the party and that the right opposition probably could muster support of their slogans among approximately the same number.[215]

One is inclined to think that Voroshilov's estimates fell far short of the real strength of the opposition elements within the party. There was a report made openly by a responsible party leader at the XVIth Party Congress in 1930 which could be interpreted to mean that the rightist opposition expected to obtain a majority in the Central Committee. E. Iaroslavskii had even referred, at the same Congress, to a discussion by a party clique of the possibility of effecting by force a change in the composition of the Central Executive Committee.[216]

The fact that the Red Army had maintained its discipline and retained a stanch allegiance to the Central Committee without a single serious incident seems to indicate clearly that the political personnel of the army had done yeoman service in eliminating sources of trouble and keeping the waverers in line. Whether that personnel was at the time an asset from the technical-military viewpoint is doubtful. But during the crisis of the first Five Year Plan, loyalty of the armed forces was a matter of paramount importance to the party majority. This consideration completely overshadowed all other problems of the upbuilding of the armed forces.

The material available does not lend itself to an analysis of how serious an effort, if any, was made by the opposition elements to provoke conflicts within the army, beyond discussions of resolutions and similar activities.

Communist Rank and File

The number of Communists in the Red Army grew very rapidly during the period under review. The following table shows the upward trend in the numbers of the party and party-affiliated groups between the years of 1927 and 1930:[217]

	No. of communist party members and candidates	No. of Komsomols	Total	Increase in a year	% of party-affiliated to the total personnel of the army
1927	78,200	119,800	198,000	28,000	36
1928	82,000	120,000	202,000	4,000	37
1929	93,200	140,000	233,000	31,000	42
Jan. 1, 1930	102,749	155,000	257,749	25,000	45
Apr. 1, 1930	119,000	177,000	296,000	....	..
July 1, 1930	140,944	183,272	324,216	66,667	58

The above table shows the tremendous change: the army had become, by the middle of 1930, an organization in which party-affiliated persons outnumbered in considerable measure the non-party element. There were about 325,000 party-affiliated persons in the army, as against a total of 562,000 of the total army personnel. The party members and candidates formed 57.2 per cent of the party-affiliated personnel, leaving thus to the Komsomol 42.8 per cent.[218]

The party members and candidates were distributed between the respective groups of the army hierarchy as follows:[219]

Commanding personnel (from the middle commanders up)	50.3%
Junior commanding personnel (N.C.O.'s)	27%
Rank and file soldiers	22.7%

Control of the party organization in the army was thus in the hands of the commanding personnel (the commanders *proprio dictu* and the political personnel). As far as the Komsomol was concerned, the soldiers and the N.C.O.'s formed 86.8 per cent of it.[220]

The higher standing groups in the military hierarchy were thus predominantly concerned with party membership and candidateship, while the Komsomol had the same position with respect to the soldiers in the ranks and the N.C.O.'s.

The rapid increase in party and Komsomol membership in the army during the year 1930 was in line with the effort of the Central Executive Committee of the party to bring in a large number of workers "from the bench" into party ranks. It was planned that these would form not less than one-half of the total party membership by the end of that year. It was also decided to accelerate the rate of bringing into the party of agricultural workers and kolkhoz peasants.

Party membership as a whole grew during the period from January 1928 to April 1930, and had increased in absolute figures from 1,302,854 in 1928 to 2,969,000 in 1930. It rose to about 3,500,000 in 1932. The proportion of workers "from the bench" had increased by the latter year to 45 per cent of the total enrollment. All workers, including agricultural, comprised 70 per cent.[221]

By 1933 party members and candidates in the army had reached 35 per cent of the total personnel, while the Komsomols stood at 24 per cent. In this manner the total for the party-affiliated groups had reached 59 per cent.[222]

The percentage of Communists among commanders in 1930 was higher than for the army as a whole:[223]

	Highest commanders	Senior commanders	Middle commanders
Party members:	76%	50%-52%	60%

The army itself was a fertile recruiting ground for the party as the table on the next page shows. It gives the number of persons inducted into the party within the year.[224]

| 1927 | 28,500 | 1929 | 37,142 |
| 1928 | 33,429 | 1930 | 85,771 |

The social origins of the military party organization had changed in the following manner :[225]

		Peasants	Workers	Employees	Others
1927	Army	35.2	39.7	22.5	2.6
	Party as a whole	19.	55.7	22.6	2.7
1928	Army	32.	41.	25.	2.
1930	Army		58.3		

For the party as a whole, the percentage of workers stood, by January 1, 1928, at 57.8 per cent and rose to 65.8 by January 1, 1930. Of these 46.9 per cent were workers "from the bench" in the latter year, as against 42.4 the year before.[226]

In 1934, following the purge and because of the standstill on new admissions to the party in 1933, the percentage of Communists in the army was somewhat lowered. By January 1, 1934, there were 25.6 per cent of Communists and candidates and 23.9 per cent of Komsomols, or a total of 49.5 per cent of party affiliated persons in the army.[227]

The results of the purge in 1933 in the army was considerably more favorable to the military Communists than was true of the members of the party at large. While in the army a mere 4.3 per cent were expelled from the party and 2.4 per cent transferred to the status of candidates and sympathizers, the figures for the party as a whole were 17 and 6.3 respectively.[228]

Voroshilov made a great deal of these figures, seeing in them a proof of loyalty of the military Communists to the general party line. Speaking in 1930 he made a similar comment with respect to the purge of 1929, when 5 per cent of the military Communists were compelled to leave the party, as against 11.7 for the party as a whole.[229]

It is however, legitimate to look for another explanation of the low percentage of purged party members in the army. Since such a large percentage of military Communists were of the commanding-political personnel, one may wonder whether the influence of the hierarchical relationship within the army, the daily association at work and in the Army Houses had possibly had an attenuating influence on the severity of the purge, as well as the desire of the party leadership to avoid the disruption of the army command by an extensive purge. One somehow gathers the impression that until the later period, the army party life had provided a fairly safe haven for adherents of heterodoxical views, provided these heretics did not show any activity in favor of the oppositional trends.

Whenever the small fry of the party—the Komsomols—were involved in oppositional activities they were dealt with ruthlessly. A report from the Caucasus published in the *Red Star* in October 1929 drew the reader's attention to the acute situation in the ranks of the military Komsomols with respect to the right oppositional trend among them. In the 82nd Rifle Regiment, one of the Komsomols, claiming to adhere to the party general line, expressed himself as opposed to the monopoly of the state in the field of foreign trade. Another Komsomol, sent to the village to work as an agitator for the party line, returned to the army imbued with the feeling, to which he proceeded to give voice, that the village was rapidly going downhill. "It is being pressed upon from all sides," he said. A third Komsomol, influenced by letters from his home village, advocated handling the kulak problem along the lines of the well-known Russian proverb: "Let the dog alone and he will not bite you."[230]

These falls from grace were explained by the correspondent of the army newspaper as the result of the influence of the village atmosphere and the lack of political education.[231]

There were, however, some party members who spoke out against the party agrarian policy. A report from the Urals mentioned a Communist who had criticized the scale of the grain requisitions, saying that in 1928 all grain was taken away not only from the middle peasants, but from the poor peasants as well.[232]

A correspondent from the Caucasus, commenting on the purge of 1929, stated that a number of military party cells did not sufficiently understand the general party line and had underestimated the importance of the decisive struggle with the existing tendency to tolerate the right opposition. That there were signs of attitudes among local Communists indicating an active disapproval of party leadership seems to be shown by an excerpt from the speech made at the time of the purge by a young Communist in the 2nd Georgian Division, to the effect that the difficulties experienced by the country were attributable to the lack of adequate leadership. He even went on to say that the revolution, obtained by force of arms, had proved itself premature: "A mistake had occurred at the time of the seizure of power."[233]

An incident at Kiev indicates that this was not an isolated case. A fairly recent recruit to party membership (1926 admission), a commander, had openly protested against the suppression of free speech and the persecution of those voicing critical opinions. "You have put the country on famine rations," said he.[234]

These episodes, taken at random from the pages of the army paper, may be considered as signs that at least a certain part of the military Communists was not immune to the influences of the political struggle within the party and shared the view that the village was treated too ruthlessly. Strangely enough, in spite of the wish of the party to lean on the urban proletariat in that hour of struggle with the village, in some districts workers formed a fairly large percentage of those purged from the ranks of the military Communists.

There seems to be sufficient evidence to show that even in 1929 disfranchised elements could enter not only the Red Army but the Communist party as well.

Another correspondent of the *Red Star* gave a summary of the purge in his locality, stating that 42.1 per cent of those expelled were "alien elements, who had hidden their past," or who had maintained relations with class aliens. Twenty-five per cent were purged because of "moral decay," 20.2 per cent for passive attitude in party life. It is interesting to note that in that locality the percentage of workers purged in the beginning of the investigation was inordinately high, but by the time the final results were reached, the percentage had dropped, so that 3 per cent of the workers in the group concerned were forced to give up their connection with the party, as against 9 per cent of the peasants and 7.3 per cent of the employees. Among those expelled, 0.1 per cent were persons with pre-revolutionary party standing; 22.9 per cent of 1917 standing, 20.5 per cent of 1924-1925, while the bulk (56.5 per cent) came from those who had joined the party during the period 1926-1929.[235]

This statement is open to several interpretations, one of which is that those in charge of the purge had become alarmed by the large percentage of workers expelled and began during the later stage of the purge to treat Communists of worker origin more leniently. This suggestion seems to find support in the reference to the large number of workers purged in the report by the Caucasian correspondent mentioned above; where an excuse was given that many among those purged were "pseudo-workers."

The change of policy with respect to the village had found its reflection in the class origins of the new members recruited into the party from among the Red Army personnel. Thus, in Kiev 388 candidates were inducted during six months of 1929. Among them were 84.2 per cent of workers, 9 per cent of agricultural workers and a mere 0.7 per cent of poor peasants, plus a lone "other." In 1928, during the same period, the newly inducted workers formed 69.1 per cent, agricultural workers 7.4 per cent, poor peasants were represented by 17 per cent, and middle peasants by 3.5 per cent, while "others" stood at 3 per cent.[236]

A summary from the important seaport town of Nikolaev stated that in the first quarter of 1929 in the 15th Rifle Division only 47 new members were inducted, in the second, 134. Of these 70 per cent were workers, about 27 per cent were poor peasants. There was only one employee among those taken into the party.[237]

In this manner the instructions of the Central Committee of the party and of the PUR on the proletarization of the Communist party in the army were carried out. One cannot fail to notice that the policy of the Central Committee had moved in the direction desired by the Left Opposition of 1927. At that time the opposition had pointed out that the influence of the proletariat in the army was on the decline and urged steps toward increasing that influence.[238]

I. S. Unschlicht, one of Voroshilov's principal collaborators, had voiced his apprehensions in 1928 regarding the military party personnel. He warned that the bulk of the army consisted of peasant youths, who shared, when entering the army, the political attitudes common to the rural younger generation; that letters from home kept these village trends alive among them. Unschlicht drew from this the conclusion that the pressure of what he called "the petty bourgeois element" on the party organization in the army was bound to be heavier than elsewhere. He traced to this the danger that the party organization in the army might be permeated by persons influenced by rightist opposition views, and thought that in the army the danger of this was greater than in the party at large.[239]

The party code, approved at the XIVth Party Congress in December 1925, provided that applicants for membership and candidateship in the party should be classified into: 1) workers and soldiers of worker and peasant descent; 2) peasants (other than soldiers), cottage artisans, who did not employ hired labor; and 3) others (employees, etc.). The first category was subdivided into: a) industrial workers and common laborers uninterruptedly occupied in physical work for hire; b) non-industrial workers, soldiers of worker and peasant origin and agricultural workers.[240]

For the group (a) of the first category, two references from party members of at least one year's standing were required; for (b) two references from party members of two years' standing; for the second category, three references from party members of at least two years' standing. The third category called for five references from party members of at least five years' standing.[241]

Under these regulations the peasant lads in the army were placed on an even footing with non-industrial workers at large and given preferred status, as against peasants outside the army. A good many of them had taken advantage of the chance to enter the party. As shown by the table on page 324 above, the army organization in 1927 had 35.2 per cent of peasants as against 19 per cent for the party as a whole. This state of affairs was ended by 1929. The XVth Party Congress had resolved that by the time the next congress was convened, the workers "from the bench" in the party should be brought up to 50 per cent.[242]

As illustrated by examples listed in the preceding pages, the middle peasant had disappeared altogether from the lists of admissions to party candidateship in the army, and even the poor peasant, the old standby of the party policy in the village, had as much chance of entering the military party organization at Kiev as had the biblical camel of passing through the needle's eye.

The army party organization had really become proletarian, with the worker element predominant.

Exclusion of the better educated elements from the party and the Komsomol because of the more rigid class-origin requirements led to the same difficulties in obtaining lower party leaders sufficiently informed to carry on their work adequately, as was the case in the sphere of recruitment of students for military schools. On the one hand, Voroshilov spoke at the XVIth Party Congress about the large percentage of the Komsomol draftees being rejected as unsatisfactory by the naval schools in 1931, on the other we have the evidence of the summary of the purge of 1929—where, for instance in the 32nd Rifle Division, 12 per cent of the Communists were found insufficiently trained in political matters. Among these there was a "large proportion" of the so-called "party-active" element, of those whom the party had entrusted with the education and indoctrination of the non-party personnel of the army.[243]

The party was recruited from elements with a low general culture without the leavening, as previously, from the better educated "others," at a time when the recruits for political leadership of the army were faced by the difficult task of pulling their weight in the reorganization and retraining of the armed forces caused by the changes in its technical equipment.

This lack of general education was compensated by the steadfastness of the military party organization in the face of the acute struggle in the village caused by the agrarian policy of the government and what Voroshilov had euphemistically called (following Stalin's lead) the "bending over" in some localities during the collectivization of the village—the excesses of zeal of the local party chieftains which had resulted in untold sufferings of the peasants affected. According to Voroshilov, this stormy experience in the village, as well as the efforts of the right opposition, were factors which made possible a thorough test of the political steadfastness and loyalty of the army. And the army had passed the test with flying colors. As Voroshilov stated it: "The army never faltered." He claimed that the right opposition was unable to cite a single instance proving political instability of the army as the armed might of the proletarian dictatorship.[244]

In keeping the army loyal, the rank and file of the communist military organization played an important rôle in that crucial period. They were the eyes and ears of the political machine in the army. It was through them that the soldiers and the lower commanders were vigilantly watched. The military Communists may have lacked general culture, but they certainly did not lack perseverance in their assigned task of acting as watchdogs of the Central Committee over the military forces of Russia.

The examples of the oppositional trends, particularly among the Komsomols, cited above, do not mean that the latter had become, even at the height of the party struggle, involved to any considerable extent in oppositional attitudes threatening the control of the Central Committee over the army. In so far as the party members were concerned, such trends were even less pronounced. At least there were no open demonstrations of support of the oppositional activities by substantial numbers of the military communists.

It is true that as late as 1926 the Komsomols in the army were predominantly a peasant-origin group. In that year only 37.7 per cent of them were registered as workers, against 58.3 per cent peasants and 9 per cent "others." In the navy in the same year, 55.1 per cent were workers and 35.6 per cent peasants. With this large percentage of peasants among them it is small wonder that groups of the Komsomol had become influenced by and became spokesmen for the peasant non-partisan soldiers, and had supported the latter in the sometimes excessive demands for improvements of the material conditions of army life and in dissatisfaction with the severity of the military discipline; or that they were inclined to disapprove of the party view as to the relationship between workers and peasants and were often involved in violations of army regulations. The conference of the military delegates at the VIIth Komsomol Congress, in considering the situation, had resolved to bring into the ranks of the komsomol organization in the military forces all the workers in the ranks and to strengthen the party leadership of the Komsomol.[245]

The loyal adherence of the bulk of the party affiliated personnel of the army to the Central Committee's line is the most remarkable as the "party enlightenment," the apparatus for the political indoctrination of the party membership and the Komsomol, was reorganized in 1928 and the new system, based largely on volunteer circles of study, did not work satisfactorily as yet. The *Red Star* wrote editorially that the party enlightenment machinery was not sufficiently exploited for the "ideological arming" of the party members against the right oppositional trend and the tendency to temporize with it. In some army units no effort whatsoever was made in this direction.[246]

In the light of the experience of the stormy period of the first Five Year Plan period, it is interesting to note to what extent Gusev's theses had been proved correct. In his paper on the reorganization of the army, prepared as part of the material for submission to the Xth Party Congress (March 1921), he had said that the only means of safeguarding the armed forces, then overwhelmingly peasant-recruited, from becoming involved in an anti-communist movement of a bonapartist type, was preservation of the political machinery of the army as it had developed during the years of the Civil War, and establishment of the necessary controls for guiding its work through a centralized control.[247]

It is beyond doubt that the firm grip of the political organs of the army, closely controlled in their turn by the Central Committee of the party, on the party organization in the armed forces and through them on the soldiers of the ranks, had kept the army in that period what it was intended to be—the faithful instrument of party dictatorship.

Soldiers

The progressive proletarization of the rank and file of the army was one of the outstanding traits of the period under review. While there was little change in the percentage of "cementation" of the army by proletarians in the period from 1918 to 1926, a rapid change was brought about during the first Five Year Plan. As the table below shows, the increase in the percentage of workers had changed between

1918 and 1926 only by 4 points, while between the years 1926 and 1932 it grew by 20.6 points.[248]

	1918	1920	1923	1925	1926	1929	1930	1932
Percentage of workers	14.1	14.8	15.7	17.7	18.1	24.3	26.9	38.7

Voroshilov, speaking at the XVIth Party Congress, stated that in 1927 there were in the army 23.8 per cent of industrial and agricultural workers, while by January 1930 their percentage had risen to 32.9, i.e. increased by 9.1 points in three years. He pointed to this increase as further proof that the proletarian influence in the army had been augmented.[249]

Nevertheless, the peasants continued to form the bulk of the soldiers. In 1927 they stood at 63.4 per cent and by January 1930 had declined to 57 per cent.[250]

The other groups of the population were represented by comparatively small numbers, as shown in the table immediately below:[251]

	Jan. 1, 1929	Jan. 1, 1930	Change
Workers	24.3%	26.9%	+2.6%
Peasants	60. %	57. %	—3. %
Employees	9. %	8.8%	—0.2%
Others	2.9%	2.2%	—0.7%

(The figures in this table are not comparable with those of Voroshilov quoted above, as they included agricultural workers as well.)

With the predominance of the peasantry in the ranks of the army, the events in the village during the period of collectivization of the rural economy were of the greatest importance to the state of mind of the soldiers.

As W. H. Chamberlin said, no one with first-hand knowledge of the Russian village could well believe that the average peasant left to his own free will would have given up his holding for membership in the new *kolkhozy*, or collective farms.[252]

In 1932 the state farms and the collective farms had produced together 84 per cent of the entire marketable supply of grain.[253]

The rapid reorganization of agriculture was achieved at the cost of a ferocious internal struggle, which, according to W. H. Chamberlin, assumed at certain times the aspect of a one-sided civil war and resulted in tremendous human and material losses.[254]

The Soviet Union, during the years 1929 to 1933, lost over half of its horses, almost half of its big-horned cattle, almost two-thirds of its sheep and goats, and over 40 per cent of its pigs.[255]

The loss in human life subsequent to the 1932-1933 famine, responsibility for which rests with the Soviet Government, was estimated by a careful observer, W. H. Chamberlin, to be no less than three to four million, this figure representing the excess of deaths over the normal mortality rate.[256]

The so-called "liquidation of the kulaks as a class" in 1929-1930 involved 4 to 5 per cent of the whole peasant population.[257]

The agrarian taxation policy laid heavy burdens not only upon the kulaks who were doomed, but on the middle peasants as well. Voroshilov, speaking in March 1930, said that in the spring of 1928, when difficulties were experienced in obtaining grain stocks, the conclusion was reached by the Central Committee of the party that the agricultural tax of 1927 was too light and that the peasants had accumulated large surpluses of money, for which they were unable to obtain manufactured goods in corresponding quantities. The 1928 tax was accordingly increased, apparently to a level which hit the middle peasants very hard. As Voroshilov stated it, 35 per cent of the poor and less wealthy peasants were freed of the tax, so that its burden had to be borne by 65 per cent of the peasants only. "The tax had proved too heavy for certain middle peasant groups," Voroshilov admitted.[258]

Under these circumstances, the class origins of the soldiers of the army could not fail to be of great concern to the ruling groups of the Communist party. Voroshilov underscored the fact that "under the conditions of acute internal class struggle, we are watching with particular zeal the purity of the class origins of the army." He admitted, however, that "because of the slipshod work of the draft commissions," sons of kulaks and near-kulaks had succeeded in entering the army. They were, later, found out and mercilessly thrown out of the armed forces.[259]

During that crisis in the relations between the party and the village, the activities of the right opposition presented a much greater danger to the hold on the soldiers by the Central Committee, than was the case of those of the left. The right group opposed the ruination of the better-off peasants, and, instead of confiscation of grain, advocated the raising of fixed prices at which it was purchased. It deprecated the rapid pace of industrialization and collectivization, and suggested that the individual farmer should be maintained and even helped.[260]

A program of this kind could easily have found support among the soldiers from middle peasant families. The importance of keeping these soldiers out of the party and also of reducing the number of their admissions into the military schools was obvious to the authorities, who made serious efforts to increase the number of workers in the ranks at the expense of the peasants.[261]

This change in the class policy had also affected very strongly the recruiting of junior commanding personnel—the N.C.O.'s. As the *Voennyi Vestnik* wrote in 1928, the percentage of the middle peasants and "others" in the regimental schools had gradually increased because of the desire to obtain for these schools young men of better physique and endowed with a certain degree of general education. This, of course, affected the class origins of those re-enlisting for the second term as junior commanders at the expense of the workers and poor peasants. To fill the regimental schools with politically desirable students, it was necessary to sacrifice both the physical and educational standards. And they were sacrificed to political expediency.[262]

The conflict between the political and purely military needs was again solved in favor of the political.

In July 1929 an increase in the percentage of workers in the regimental schools to 30 per cent was decreed, and an increase in the percentage of agricultural workers in these schools. These measures were combined with a further one aimed at bringing into these schools as many party and Komsomol members as possible. Execution of the provisions of that order was not always to the satisfaction of the authorities. The *Red Star* wrote that in some units a large number of agricultural laborers and poor peasants were unable to graduate from the regimental schools, because of insufficient knowledge shown by them at the examinations. The correspondent complained that the same requirements were applied to the middle peasants as to workers and poor peasants. As a result a considerable proportion of those belonging to the latter two categories had failed to pass the tests. They were, nevertheless, later promoted to the dignity of junior commanders by order of the commander of the division concerned.[263]

Simultaneously, complaints were heard that the principal shortcomings of the junior commanders lay in the insufficiently rapid growth of their cultural and political levels; that even with respect to the acquisition of new military knowledge, called for by the modern technical equipment of the army, the progress of the junior commanders was falling behind the strides made by the soldiers in the ranks. They were also criticized for their lack of responsibility for training their respective units, and for failing to maintain the proper distance between themselves and the private soldiers. They were even accused of failing to set a good example to the soldiers in matters of discipline.[264]

It was stated in the columns of the army newspaper in 1929 that the junior commanders had shown themselves utterly inadequate during the maneuvers of 1928. It was said that their cultural level and their political education differed but little from those of the privates, and that this circumstance impeded the successful training of the privates.[265]

The rate of improvement in the military education of the junior commanders as well as the level of their skill as instructors and leaders of men were deemed unsatisfactory. It was also stated that they lacked authority with the privates under their command in political matters.[266]

These criticisms were supplemented by a very curious, but not improbable remark, that, in many companies, the commanders were in the habit of sending to the regimental schools not the best among the private soldiers, but rather those they regarded as unsatisfactory. As will be recalled, similar instances had been reported during the Civil War period with respect to soldiers sent to Command Courses.[267]

The critics quoted above offered as a cure for the defects of the junior commanders a further "improvement in the social structure of the regimental schools," i.e. filling them with men of the type which had shown itself inferior in ability to acquire both the habits of command and the military and political knowledge requisite to middle peasant youths. One wonders to what extent the correspondents of the *Red Star* meant what they said, when they wrote: "We have broken the ice of mistrust in the ability of the agricultural laborer to become a good commander, although that laborer was insufficiently literate."[268]

The logic of the suggestion was poor, but the intent was clear. In spite of the disadvantages from the purely military viewpoint, the junior commanders had to be recruited from politically favored groups.

The lack of authority of the junior commanders with the rank and file was still further enhanced by the tendency of their immediate superiors (middle commanders) to interfere with the training of individual soldiers conducted by the former and to interrupt them rudely in the presence of their subordinates.[269]

The evidence of the newspapers' columns shows that the commanders were also inclined at times at least to abuse their disciplinary powers and to show off their importance to the men in the ranks.

The *Red Star*, under date of September 13, 1929, had informed its readers of the following incident: a commander had given an extra turn of duty to a private for talking in the ranks. The latter acknowledged the inflicted punishment by saying: "Aye, aye, an extra turn." For this talking in the ranks another turn of duty was added, and was accepted by the same conventional formula. Then a still further turn was given to the unlucky private. Another example was given: in a platoon disciplinary punishment was meted out to fifteen soldiers on the same day. The commander commented: "The regulations permit me to inflict five extra turns of duty. Well, I am giving these five turns. I do not recognize any social relationship. I am not a comrade, merely a superior."[270]

Another newspaper item reports a visit by a commanding officer to the mess room of his regiment. About a thousand-odd soldiers were sitting at tables awaiting dinner with impatience. When the commander entered the hall, the men were called to attention and had accordingly to stand up to greet their commander.[271]

The political personnel was also reported to treat soldiers severely during political studies. Thus a political instructor inflicted a five day arrest upon a soldier who had fallen asleep during the political studies' hour. Group leaders were apt to shout at soldiers, ordering them to tighten their belts, to set their caps at the prescribed angle, or to interrupt them rudely, whenever the soldiers asked for additional information.[272]

It is very likely that tendencies to abuse disciplinary powers were rather the exception than the rule, during the period reviewed. E. Wollenberg, who served in the Red Army at the time, claims that only in 1931-1933 had the international spirit and the socialistic basis of discipline and the "natural and free relations between officers and men" gone by the board. All the examples given above refer to occurrences in the years preceding the dividing line set up by Wollenberg. He himself reports for 1929 an interesting episode of an explanation given to a Reichswehr general by a young Red Army soldier of the relationship between commanders and men in the ranks of the Red Army, purporting to show that in the early years of the first Five Year Plan there still existed a very unusual degree of comradeship between the soldiers and their commanders.[273] Whether Wollenberg is right in his estimate of the relations between commanders and soldiers in the period preceding the dividing line he sets up, it is difficult to say positively, as there is a certain amount of evidence to the contrary.

For instance, a peculiar feature of army life of that period was the tendency to bring soldiers up for trial before military courts on relatively insignificant grounds. Instances of this given in an article of the *Red Star* include the case of a soldier sent up for trial for the loss of an old saw, valued at three rubles; another of a soldier who had refused to drink a solution of quinine at the ambulatory, and, finally, of two soldiers who had exchanged their boots, because the pair belonging to one of them was too tight. The author of the article states: "The enormous percentage of those conditionally condemned or condemned for insignificant terms shows that the courts are infringing on the sphere of disciplinary summary punishment. Sixty per cent of court cases in 1928 were brought to an end by the inquest judge, which is another indication of the insufficiency of reasons for sending men up for trial."[274]

This rashness in building up court cases certainly does not seem to confirm the picture of idyllic relations between commanders and men. Rather than proving a comradely spirit, which, as Wollenberg asserts, was in evidence at the time, this information may be regarded as a symptom of tension in the superior-subordinate relationship. Apparently punishments provided for by the none too mild Military Disciplinary Code were regarded by commanders as insufficient atonement for the insignificant peccadillos described above.

The Internal Service Regulations of 1928 stated that all members of the commanding personnel were superior officers with respect to all privates of the army and navy. The junior commanders and the corresponding levels of the political personnel were placed in the same relationship to privates of their own unit—the regiment or equivalent military formation.[275]

Another paragraph of the same regulations provided that the subordinate was to carry out all orders of his superiors (with the exception of those obviously criminal), directed to the good of the service or to the fulfillment of laws and military statutes. The orders were to be executed immediately, intelligently and punctually.[276]

The superiors were charged to admonish their subordinates or juniors in case of infringements of the rules of behavior or disturbance of public order in the streets or public places. The superiors were empowered, if necessary, to resort to measures other than mere admonition, and had the power of arrest of the subordinates misbehaving themselves outside the barracks.[277]

In other words, soldiers outside the barracks and off duty were under the supervision of the commanders and political personnel, and could be arrested by the latter for non-military offenses.

In theory, the soldier "off duty" had all the rights of a citizen and was subject only to the laws of the country, in so far as his behavior was concerned. In practice, there were very definite limitations of these rights.

To leave the barracks in off-duty hours, the soldier had to ask the permission of the sergeant-major of his company and had to return before the evening roll-call. Only the company commander could grant him permission to return later, or to absent himself from barracks in the hours set for training or studies.[278]

There was an additional difficulty, moreover, in these relations, caused by the low cultural level of the commanding personnel. The commanders, insisting on the cleanliness of the personal effects of the soldiers—canteens, for instance—did not bother to keep their own belongings in spotless condition. A soldier, punished for lack of attention in such matters, was at times able to observe, when making a service call on his commander, that the latter's room was in disorder, the bed unmade and the commander himself upon it fully clothed. The commander's own canteen was at times "moss-grown" with mildew.[279]

Aside from disciplinary pressure there was a concerted and consistent influence exercised on the soldiers through different means, controlled by the political personnel. One of the most striking features of this effort was the so-called wall-newspaper. It became known under that name by the end of 1921, although it is clear from the proceedings of the first conference of the publishers and editors of the Red Army press held in December 1921 that this form of publication, mostly hand-written, was already widespread in the Red Army prior to that date.[280]

In the period 1922-1924, the contents of the wall-newspapers was mainly centered on problems of day-to-day life of the respective regiments, battery, brigade, etc. As the author of a monograph dedicated to the wall-newspaper in the army states, it was the time of degeneration of that newspaper. It often occupied itself with criticism of the commanding personnel and destructive attacks upon its representatives. "The wall-newspapers were unable to trace a sharp dividing line between the insufficiencies which were rooted in causes of local character and those stemming from the national conditions; they had failed to move 'against the current,'" wrote N. Kudrin, the author of the above-mentioned monograph.[281]

The wall-newspaper was reflecting in this manner the general conditions of decay, of uncertainty and conflict, which had existed until the period of Frunze's reforms.

Simultaneously with Frunze's assumption of control over the armed forces, a new trend made its appearance in the editorial policy of the wall-newspapers. Their attention moved from problems of the economic life of the army to that of enhancing the combat efficiency of the troops, improvement of discipline and the building up of authority of the commanding personnel. However, the editors did not entirely shed the Old Adam of the period of decadence. Kudrin traces these survivals of the pre-reform period to the system of control and guidance of the wall-newspapers.[282]

At the conference of 1921 already mentioned, it was laid down that volunteers in any unit were to organize a literary circle, which, upon feeling itself competent, was to begin the publication of a handwritten newspaper or magazine. No method of control or guidance was established. Later on, in 1922-1924, the wall-newspaper became part of the activities of the soldiers' clubs. Those who edited it and wrote for it were not considered at the time as military correspondents. This designation was reserved for those who wrote for the columns of the newspapers published by the military districts. As a rule, a unit of a size corresponding to a regiment published a wall-newspaper as an adjunct to its regimental club. At the time the party organizations did not consistently guide the editorial policy of the newspaper, but interfered by censoring it and issuing peremptory orders to the editors.[283]

With the call to the colors of the age group of 1902 and the influx of fresh blood into the army, there was an upsurge of new wall-newspapers. They began to be published even by companies. At the same time, the decision of the second conference of the workers' rural and military correspondents, which met under the auspices of the Moscow *Pravda*, called for the abolition of the differentiation between the military correspondents and the contributors to the wall-newspapers. This gave a further impetus to the development and growth of the wall-newspapers, as the designation of military correspondent was a highly valued distinction.[284]

By the time of the third conference of the Red Army press—October 1925—the wall-newspapers had already attracted considerable attention of the authorities. Discussion of the utilization of these papers for the improvement of discipline became one of the most important subjects of the conference. By the fall of 1925 there were about 5,000 wall-newspapers in the army.[285]

The statute and instructions on wall-newspapers of the Red Army in peace time, published by the PUR's order No. 192, dated November 27, 1925, established rules for the control and guidance of these publications.[286]

It was decided that the activities of soldiers finding their outlet in the publication of the wall-newspaper should not remain on the voluntary basis as heretofore. On the contrary, they should be directed into a definite channel, so as to become a tool to influence the masses. The party was to use these papers to shape the opinion of the soldiers in accordance with party policy.[287]

The fate of the wall-newspapers is a good illustration of the growth and centralization of party control over the army, the political organs of the latter gradually taking for their province the vast field of political education and watching over all the phases of the soldier's life.

It was decided that the principal characteristic of the wall-newspaper was that it was a local organ, dealing with the life, the interests and the needs of the local collective. As to form, they were either hand-written on paper or multigraphed, or even printed. Sometimes they were thrown on a screen by means of a projector. The party cell was supposed to take the publication and the guidance of the editorial policy of these papers into its hands.[288]

In the units of the Territorial Militia these papers were not supposed to discuss problems concerning the village, unless these were in immediate and close connection with the life and activity of the unit concerned. Obviously, the detailed discussion of the agrarian policies and of the village reaction to them would hardly be welcomed by the party authorities at that time of acute crisis in their relationship with the peasantry.[289]

At first the exercise of control over the wall-newspaper did not proceed smoothly. N. Kudrin gives an illustration of that stage in its development. In one of the battalions of the 12th Rifle Regiment the military correspondents had decided to publish a wall-newspaper. The principal mover, a non-party teacher, collected the material for the first issue and went to the political instructor. The latter proceeded to cross out practically all of its contents, with the result that the teacher told him that under the circumstances the paper would not appear at all. The political instructor then said: "You are not a party member, you have no business to be a military correspondent," and decided to publish the paper himself. This had caused "general dissatisfaction" among the group of the military correspondents of the battalion.[290]

It was suggested that as long as the paper was the organ of the party, the commander should discuss all questions pertaining to it with the party organ, instead of giving any directions to the editorial board. Also, the political commissar and the political instructor were asked not to intervene directly in the publication of the paper, but to act through the same party organs. The managing editor of the paper was appointed by the party organization, while the editorial board was elected by the military correspondents of the unit from its own members. The board was then confirmed by the party organization.[291]

The presiding body of the party cell, or the bureau of the party collective, were to receive reports from the members of the editorial board who were party members, and to give them the "line" of their work as well as detailed instructions as to the editorial policy and the handling of the respective problems in the columns of the paper.[292]

The editors were discouraged from publishing critical items about the commanding personnel, as this was considered detrimental to discipline. On the other hand, items pertaining to party and Komsomol activities were encouraged and given preferential space.[293]

The principal means of indoctrination of the soldiers were the political studies. These had improved very considerably as against the level of 1924-1925 and were conducted "competently and without disfiguration of political perspectives," meaning that the "party line" was strictly adhered to. In the era of acute struggle in the village this was considered insufficient. It was suggested in the columns of the *Red Star* in 1929, that the political studies be turned into a "militant tribune."[294]

The program of political studies for soldiers, published in 1929, started with the explanation of the reasons of the existence of the Red Army. The soldiers were told that the conflict between the capitalist countries and the U.S.S.R. was irreconcilable because of class antagonisms, which prompted the inimical policy of the capitalists toward the land of the Soviets. An intervention was being prepared by the antagonistic world beyond the frontiers of Russia. The Shakhta trials and the attempts of the kulaks to oppose the agrarian policy of the government in 1928 were indicative that the internal foe had also refused to lay down arms. To meet these threats—at home and abroad—the workers and peasant youth were called into the army to safeguard the independence of the U.S.S.R. and the peaceful life of the toilers bent on the socialist building-up of the country.[295]

The importance of army discipline was emphasized. "Conscious" discipline was pointed to as the most important basis for the combat efficacy of the unit, as well as the Red Army as a whole. The difference between the "class character of discipline" in the Red Army and the discipline of the armed forces of the capitalist states, as well as that of the old Russia, was explained.[296]

Some space was devoted to the biography of the head of the army,

K. S. Voroshilov, and a brief sketch of the history of the Red Army during the Civil War was offered.[297]

One of the next items of the program is rather startling in the light of subsequent events. It called for the explanation to the soldiers that Britain was the imperialist state most inimical to Russia and the principal organizer of the intervention in the affairs of the U.S.S.R., preparing plans for an attack upon it. At the same time, Germany was singled out as a country which had suffered more than any other in the "imperialist" war; there existed between Germany and the U.S.S.R. treaty relations more normal than those with the other capitalist countries.[298] Apparently Marxian analysis proved no better for reading the future than the predictions of the vulgar bourgeois writers who foretold so often the collapse of the Soviet Government at the first attack from outside by a powerful enemy.

An internationalist note was sounded in the statement that the U.S.S.R. was the fatherland of the toilers and the humiliated of the world, and that it was also the stronghold of the proletarian revolution.[299]

An explanation of the "socialist reconstruction" of the village was included in the program.[300]

Apparently the latter point presented the greatest difficulty in practice. The peasant soldiers were directly affected by the reconstruction of rural life and were at times very critical of the explanations offered them. The *Red Star* wrote in November 1929, that one could often hear complaints from soldiers about political studies. In some units, the latter were even compared with the *slovesnost* of the old army (literally, "oral periods," i.e. studies relating to the duties of the soldier, general information about the army, elements of regulations and information about the imperial family and the superior officers). These complaints had mostly to do with the points of the program dealing with the agrarian policy of the government. The topic "how the party and the Soviet Government look upon the poor, the middle and the kulak peasants," handled by a group leader, reluctant at times to go into details and "falling back upon generalities," was not convincing to peasant soldiers. As the army paper wrote: "the middle peasant had kept his old convictions, felt jealous of the workers and retained a certain contempt for the poor peasant."[301]

The policy of getting soldiers to write letters home in support of the government's agrarian policy met at times with decided opposition on the part of the former. L. Degtiarev recorded instances when, during the grain procurement campaign of 1928, soldiers' letters would conclude: "do not believe this, it was written at the dictation of the political instructor."[302]

This difficulty was recognized by the program itself. The soldiers could not fail to see, it stated, the shortage of manufactured goods in the country and had themselves experienced deficiencies in a number of articles when living in the village. The peasant soldier believes that the peasant is paying too much for manufactured goods, and that this is "unjust." He may present to the government the program "to develop as widely as possible the light (consumers' goods) industry and to reduce the expenditures on capital construction . . . at any soldier conference we always have a considerable number of notes referring to shortage of goods and the disparity of prices."[303]

The answer to this was: only the industrialization of the country could guarantee the ability of the land to defend itself.[304] Apparently this argument had a good effect, as there is no evidence of peasant soldiers rising in arms to defend their way of living in the village.

What was deemed most important by the program was the inculcation of absolute confidence among the soldiers in the Communist party as the leader of toilers. This, stated the program, was "the main axial problem of our work." The work of "internationalizing" the outlook of the soldier was also considered of great importance. For this purpose he was to be given a full and vivid summary of the world revolutionary movement.[305]

The period from 1928 to March 1930 witnessed a renewal of direct religious persecution, coupled with intensification of anti-religious propaganda. From 1930 on, there was a restriction of direct persecution, accompanied by a still further increase in the intensity of anti-religious propaganda. As N. Klepinin states, in 1929 executions of the ecclesiastics had become common, believers were banished and imprisoned, churches were demolished in large numbers, or closed. This fate overtook even the famous national shrine of the Iberian Virgin in the Red Square of Moscow. Article 4 of the Soviet Constitution was amended to read that the Soviet law recognized freedom of belief and freedom of anti-religious propaganda, while the right of religious propaganda, previously conceded, was withdrawn. This policy was in full swing in 1929, although in July of the same year E. Iaroslavskii admitted that some 60 to 70 millions of the toiling population of the country had remained actively religious.[306]

The columns of the *Red Star* contained, in the period under review, a considerable number of items relating to the religious feelings of the soldiers and the pressure exercised upon them to suppress these feelings. As the paper stated, only the fear of being ridiculed had prevented some of the soldiers from wearing crosses. If asked directly: "Do you believe in God?," the average soldier would answer in the negative, because of the fear of hazing. The army paper correspondent had noticed a small ikon among the belongings of a soldier. "Is this yours?" he asked. The soldier answered: "No . . . yes . . . it's my wife's." "Possibly the fellow was concealing his religious feelings," comments the author of the item.[307]

The following statistics about religious convictions of soldiers of one of the cavalry regiments in 1928 may present some interest:

	Old Soldiers	Young Soldiers
Admitting religious beliefs	14%	24.5%
Vacillating	36%	45. %
Atheists	50%	30.5%

In the same year, in another regiment, 45 per cent had declared themselves as religious, 43 per cent as desiring to go to church; the same percentage insisted that they would go to church upon their return to the village.[308]

These religious feelings of the peasant soldiers during the period of intensified religious persecution, joined chronologically with the destruction of private rural economy, had no doubt added another difficulty for the party-political organs of the army to handle. Despite this, there is no reason to doubt the truth of the statement made by S. Kozhevnikov in the columns of the *Red Star* in 1929 that the soldier followed the party, had confidence in it and approved of its policy. Whether that approval was given freely is, of course, another question. Nevertheless, the absence of any serious upheavals in the army in that period seems to bear out the belief that at least a passive acquiescence was given by the peasant soldier to these policies.[309]

The same Kozhevnikov admitted that the soldiers had not understood the necessity of the decisive struggle with the kulaks. While the mass of the soldiers approved the effort to industrialize the country, they failed to comprehend that to bring about this industrialization it was necessary to overcome by "decisive means" the resistance of the "capitalist elements" of the village. At least this was true of those among the soldiers who were of middle peasant origin.[310]

One of the reasons for the insistence on a stricter discipline was the existence of these feelings among the soldiers. Even at a date when the relations between the state and the village had not as yet reached an acute stage it was thought that a certain deterioration of discipline could be traced to village influences. Serious attention given to the problem of enhancing discipline had resulted in considerable improvement.[311]

Speaking to a delegation of French workers in 1927, Voroshilov said that capital punishment was very rarely applied in the Red Army, that there were only isolated instances of shooting of soldiers and that other forms of punishment were identical with those imposed on the soldiers of the French army, i.e. reprimands, arrest and prison.[312]

In other words, Voroshilov claimed that the discipline of the Red Army was enforced by means not more drastic than those used by the armies of capitalist states.

As an interesting detail of Soviet thought on this subject, one could mention the attempts to apply the deductions of Pavlov's and Bekhterev's psychological studies to the training of soldiers. Such items as the methods of automatism were included in the themes recommended for study by the Central Committee of the Society for the furthering of Defense of the U.S.S.R. It was suggested that at the time of individual training of soldiers, it was particularly important to study whether automatism of action of the single fighter is desirable, or whether this automatism of action should be developed only during the subsequent stages of training. It was at the same time suggested that it would be important to inquire in what cases the fostering of automatism in the training of individual fighters might have a bad influence on the latter's initiative and ability to orient himself.[313]

This trend was not, however, carried through in the regulations, e.g. in the Infantry Combat Regulations of 1928 (republished in 1931). It was definitely stated that each fighter had to show initiative in carrying out combat tasks, whether singly or in a unit.[314]

From the viewpoint of material well-being and special privileges conferred upon soldiers, there was a definite progress. To counteract the lack of care of wearing apparel (a cavalryman was wearing out in two years five to six pairs of breeches, for instance, as against two pairs in the old army), it was advocated that uniforms be given to soldiers not for use only, but to remain in their possession after the expiration of their term of service under the colors. In 1928, it is true, cloth uniforms were not as yet issued to private soldiers, but it was suggested that, as soon as this was possible, one tunic and two blouses be given each soldier for two years.[315]

The feeding of soldiers had considerably improved. Many units had obtained individual tableware, instead of the common soup bowl from which formerly soldiers ladled out their food.

New iron bedsteads, hangers, stools began to make the barracks more livable. Hygiene had also improved. Soldiers took to brushing their teeth as a rule, and daily ablutions with cold water had come into vogue. All this was undoubtedly a step forward as against the unsanitary and unheated barracks of the early post-Civil War period.[316]

A number of special privileges were conferred upon the military and their families. These embraced special facilities for the soldiers' collective farms, as well as for members of collective farms called into the army. There were taxation alleviations and—particularly important under the crowded conditions of the Soviet city life—certain advantages as to obtaining living space and reduction in rent. Medical help, trips to health resorts, special rates on railways and waterways, advantages as to placement of children in schools and payment of tuition fees, were among the perquisites enjoyed by the military. These were extended to the family of a deceased soldier for a period of six months. Most of these privileges were more important to the commanding personnel than to private soldiers, although the collective farm and taxation privileges were of even greater significance to the privates.[317]

Transmigrant collective farms (mostly in the Far East) were given the status of Red Army farms, if they were organized by soldiers not later than one year after their leaving the army, and when not less than one-half of the males able to perform work were military. The plenipotentiaries of groups of soldiers wishing to settle on such farms were given special leave (not more than thirty days) and free transportation to the site of the prospective farm and back. The preferential right of obtaining land from the state land reserve was also extended to the military collective farms. These farms were able to obtain loans from the government exceeding by 15 per cent those granted to similar farms organized by civilians.[318]

Privates and junior commanders were authorized to send through the mails three ordinary letters and three postcards each month postage free. During the first year of service one postage-free parcel with personal effects not exceeding thirty-five kilograms was allowed. The family of the soldier, his relatives and even friends were permitted to write by letter and card, postage free, without any limitation as to number of communications.[319] This latter measure undoubtedly grew out of the interest of the government in having a check of the opinions of the soldiers' relatives and friends on the policy of the government, etc.

As a special inducement for re-enlistment of junior commanders, a relatively high supplementary pay was offered which varied from 35 to 50 rubles per month for section commanders to 85 to 120 rubles for chief boatswains of battleships.[320]

In theory the combat efficacy of the troops was placed ahead of all other considerations. In practice this was not always adhered to. There is considerable evidence of the frequent infringements on the time allocated for training by various activities under the auspices of the political personnel. For 1930 there is information about the 5th Rifle Corps, where, with the knowledge of and upon request of party organs, soldiers were temporarily taken off drill or even transferred from regimental schools to carry on clerical duties at the regimental bureau or to decorate "Lenin corners." The best students of these schools were frequently detailed for all kinds of clerical work. In one of the cavalry regiments a number of soldiers who had passed through the first term of their military training had sat on horseback but once in three months and had fired their rifles only three times. In another cavalry regiment a soldier was found who had never held a rifle in his hands during the entire period of his military service. Meetings of the party bureaus were called during drill hours, and the active part of the Communists as well as the commanding personnel were often called away from their work to attend meetings.[321]

There were also other tasks which infringed upon the time of the soldiers. For instance, in 1929, the Central Committee of the party had laid upon the PUR the task of training every year not less than 3,000 soldiers of worker and peasant origin for entering technical schools and colleges. The Red Army Houses had established special training courses for the training of such candidates.[322]

At the same time the army had to prepare not less than 75,000 workers able to guide the activities of collective farms or to take charge of departments on such farms.[323]

One should not, however, draw the conclusion from the above that on the average the soldier did not get a good training. The examples borrowed from the *Red Star* belong to the self-criticism category, that peculiar feature of Soviet life during certain periods, the tendency to give publicity to the shortcomings in order to attract attention to them and to spur those responsible to greater effort in improving conditions.

Nevertheless, it is impossible to deny that after the resolutions of the Revolutionary Military Council of January 31, 1930, about the training of a very large number of collective farm workers, these extraneous tasks imposed upon the army had become excessive. This was noticed by the authorities and the trend was reversed.

The regulations provided for a set limit for the daily training period. It was to be not more than eight hours a day. However, an additional hour could be assigned daily for cultural enlightenment studies and vocational training. As far as tactical exercises, maneuvers and target practice were concerned, the limitations did not apply.[324]

One of the important measures taken in 1929 was the transfer of the direction of the military training outside the ranks of the army to the commanders of the army corps and divisions. These were made responsible for the results of the training. The program of studies visualized three periods of instruction, each of 24 training days, or 540 training hours. It aimed to give to those instructed a "clear class understanding of their problems, as defenders of the proletarian revolution," also to implant discipline and initiative and to teach the use of weapons, as well as to acquaint the students with the modern technical means of warfare. The finished product of these training periods was envisaged as a private soldier fully able to function in a platoon. The instructors were selected among reserve commanders.[325]

In the same year, the Komsomol were directed to undergo obligatory military training, the supervision of which was entrusted jointly to the Central Committee of the Osoaviakhim and to that of the Komsomol. All youths born in the years 1906-1910 who had not as yet passed the examinations equivalent to those provided in the programs of military circles of the Osoaviakhim of the first degree were to undergo the training.[326]

It is quite probable that this measure was introduced not so much because of considerations of a military nature, but rather because of the desire to provide a reserve of party-affiliated fighters for an internal emergency.

Both these measures were steps in the direction of creating a large reservoir of men with elementary military training who could be rapidly absorbed in the organized reserves of the army in case of war.

The reference to discipline in the program of training is significant. It is the hall-mark of that period. The *Red Star* wrote in 1925 about the reasons for paying strict attention to matters of discipline. In the Civil War, the army newspaper said, the conscious warrior-revolutionary found the principal stimulus to discipline in the determination to defeat the class-enemy. With the defeat of that enemy the stimulus had disappeared. "We shall have to graft on and implant discipline in the process of the lengthy education of the young personnel not only during its service in the army, but outside it as well" —such was the conclusion.[327]

This quotation aptly illustrates the long way the Red Army had gone from the years of its birth to the days of the first Five Year Plan.

The accent was not on "revolutionary" any more, but on "discipline." The soldier's life was regulated in detail, and the Red warrior had become a regular soldier. In many aspects he differed radically from soldiers of other armies. The means by which he was held in line also differed. He was held not only by force alone, and the fear of punishment, but by a well-directed and constantly maintained stream of propaganda. It was the combination of these pressures upon him that shaped his consciousness and influenced his behavior.

In view of the growth of the U.S.O. Clubs in our own army, it is interesting to read items such as one that appeared in the Red Army paper in 1929 regarding the temporary club of one of the regiments of the Soviet armed forces in camp. It was housed in a well-built edifice. It had an outdoor amphitheater, fenced in, with a stage covered with an iron roof. It contained a library and a reading-room, a room for amateur artists and another for theatrical equipment "as in a good theater club," and an exhibit of wall-newspapers.[328] These clubs represented one of the most powerful means of influencing the morale of the soldiers, and went a long way toward making military life attractive.

In the light of the studies of the change in the Red Army life during the first Five Year Plan, S. I. Gusev's article in the *Politrabotnik* in 1921 makes interesting reading. Gusev wrote of opposing to the rapid growth of capitalism in the village with its fifteen millions of privately operated farms an even more rapid expansion of the nationalized heavy industry. He urged that the program of political education in the army should concentrate on showing to the peasant soldier that attempts at peasant restoration had inevitably led to the loss of the conquests of revolutions. That there was only one way to save the millions of peasants from pauperization—that of socializing the rural economy.[329]

Gusev's article reads almost like a blueprint of the Five Year Plan and the two-year political studies program thrown together.

Conclusions

The period under review saw the laying of the foundations of a truly formidable armed force in Soviet Russia. The various conflicts, both within the respective army groups, as well as between certain of them, had immensely complicated the problem of reorganization of the Red Army. There is no doubt that this antagonism retarded very substantially the growth in the efficacy of the armed forces of the U.S.S.R.

At the same time, certain features of that reorganization and of the program of the Five Year Plan had formed a framework for the future edifice of one of the greatest armies in the world. One of the most intelligent things about that reorganization was that the numerical strength of the army was not increased, and remained on the same level as heretofore. Because of this it was possible to furnish the existing units more quickly with modern weapons and to train them in the use of these. It was easier to improve the material well-being of the troops. It was also possible to maintain the upward trend of the proletarization and permeation of the army by the party-affiliated personnel, which was of great importance at the time for the stability of the régime.

The reform of secondary education effected by Bubnov, and the rapid expansion of the secondary school system, held great promise for the army, as it could look with confidence to a none too distant future when a reservoir of well-educated youngsters of politically acceptable classes would provide adequate candidates for command positions. It is very difficult to compare the army of 1924 with that of 1933 in terms of combat strength, expressed by some definite figure. It is quite clear, however, that the striking power of the army and its reserves of trained men and officers had increased at a great rate. Its serious weakness lay in the rebellious mood of the peasantry, millions of whom were to be called into the army in case of a major war. The conflict between country and city was at its height, and it is very doubtful whether in 1932 the Russian peasants would have taken the stand in the defense of their country that they are now taking.

In the subsequent period, which forms the subject of the next chapter, this serious danger was to a large extent eliminated.

TOWARD THE GREATEST ARMY IN
THE WORLD

THE growth of the striking power of the Red Army was so closely connected with the progress of industrialization under the several Five Year Plans that it is impossible to understand the fountainhead of its strength without some knowledge of the results of these plans in spheres more immediately connected with that of the armed forces of Russia.

One of the plausible explanations of the low estimate of the power of resistance of the Red Army which existed in some military circles, both in this country and in Great Britain, at the time of Hitler's attack upon Russia, is that it may have had roots in the lack of knowledge on the part of some of the military leaders of these countries of the outstanding facts as to the production of Soviet heavy industry and in their lack of faith in the information reaching them regarding the productivity of the military industry of the U.S.S.R.

H. R. Knickerbocker, in his *Is Tomorrow Hitler's?*, states that should one take the graph of Imperial Russian industrial production before the last war, and prolong it over the next twenty-three years at the same rate of increase as the years 1900-1914, one could show that czarist Russia would have produced more in 1940 than the Soviet industry under the Five Year Plans.[1]

This statement presupposes a very improbable circumstance: an uninterrupted upward trend of development, under a capitalist economic system, at the same rate throughout the period involved. It is, however, a striking reminder that before World War I Russian industry had developed at times at a very rapid tempo. The fact that Soviet industry continued to grow at a rapid pace during the years of depression in the western capitalist world no doubt enhanced very considerably the effect it made upon the imagination of that world.

V. Molotov stated at the XVIIIth Party Congress that the chief historical task assigned by the second Five Year Plan had been accomplished: all exploiting classes had been completely abolished and the causes giving rise to the exploitation of man by man and to the division of society into exploiters and exploited had been done away with "for all time." All these achievements were, according to Molotov, principally the result of the abolition of private ownership of the means of production.[2]

According to Molotov, the accomplishments of the first two Five Year Plans made it possible for the U.S.S.R. to enter upon a new phase of development: "the phase of the completion of the building of a classless, socialist society and the gradual transition from socialism to Communism."[3]

The results of the second Five Year Plan, in so far as industrial production was concerned, were very impressive indeed when considered from the viewpoint of the rate of development of industry. At the same time, Molotov was the first to point out that rates of development of industry should not be confused with the *level* of its development. In the latter aspect the U.S.S.R. was, and still is, lagging behind the more advanced capitalist countries.[4]

As Molotov said: "In the U.S.S.R., socialism has been built but only in the main. We have still a lot—a tremendous amount of work to do before we can really provide the U.S.S.R. with all it needs."[5] He cited some data as to per capita output of some of the principal products of industry in the U.S.S.R., as compared with those of some of the capitalist countries:[6]

Branch of Industry	USSR	USA	Germany	Great Britain	Japan
Electric power (kw. hours)	215	1,160	735	608	421
Pig Iron (kilograms)	86	292	234	183	30
Steel (kilograms)	105	397	291	279	62
Coal (kilograms)	757	3,429	3,313	5,165	643

(Figures for USSR represent 1937; those for other countries represent the latest published at the time of the Congress)

Per capita electric power consumption in Soviet Russia was in 1937 inferior not only to Germany but to Japan as well. In pig iron it was considerably ahead of that of Japan, but below that of Germany; and the same was true of steel. With respect to coal, Russia was also at a much lower level than Germany, while somewhat ahead of Japan. This was offset by the fact that in the field of oil industry the U.S.S.R., while very much behind the U.S.A., was far in advance of Germany and Japan.

Nevertheless, the levels reached in the fields vitally affecting national defense were substantial. Those set for the third Five Year Plan were very impressive indeed. The following table illustrates what had been achieved in some of these fields of production:[7]

Branch of Industry	1937	1913	1927-8	Planned for 1942
Coal (th. of tons)	127,300	28,900	35,400	230,000
Oil (th. of tons)	30,500	9,300	11,700	54,000
Peat (th. of tons)	23,800	1,600	11,700	49,000
Pig Iron (th. of tons)	14,500	4,200	3,300	22,000
Automobiles (units)	200,000	?	700	400,000

In order to surpass Great Britain in per capita output of pig iron, Russia had to increase the annual smelting to 25 million tons, which was somewhat more than the goal set by the third Five Year Plan. In order to surpass Germany in that respect, the U.S.S.R. had to increase the annual smelting of pig iron to 40-45 million tons. As Molotov pointed out: "this . . . is a much bigger task." To surpass the U.S.A. (at a depression level), production had to be increased to 50-60 million tons. Molotov called this "a gigantic task, a task which is far beyond the bounds of the third Five Year Plan."[8]

In the per capita consumption of electric power at the end of the third Five Year Plan period, the U.S.S.R. would outstrip the level of France in 1939, but would still have only two-thirds of Germany's consumption and slightly over one-third of the 1939 consumption of electric power in the U.S.A.[9]

One angle, stressed by the Soviet leaders themselves, should not be lost sight of—that on the eve of World War II Soviet Russia was acutely conscious that it had not succeeded as yet in "overtaking and surpassing" the levels of the more highly industrialized capitalist countries, notably Germany.

This meant that for a long war against Germany, or a combination of Germany and Japan, the U.S.S.R. was severely handicapped by its inability to produce essential sinews of war in the same quantities as its potential enemies. While it had accumulated a tremendous reservoir of military engines and weapons, its power to replenish this reservoir was still insufficient to enable it to wage successfully a long war *without importation of war materials in large quantities from abroad*. This fact alone should make for a great desire to postpone as long as possible the day of conflict with these formidable enemies, in order to gain time to increase further the productivity of Soviet industry and to lay in ever greater stocks of munitions.

These general considerations should not obscure the tremendous advances made in branches of industry particularly important in waging war on a modern scale. The budget appropriations for defense purposes were in themselves an indication of the great effort made by the U.S.S.R. to improve its military position. In 1937, approximately

23 billion rubles were spent on the army and navy. In 1938, the appropriation was nearly doubled and reached 40 billion rubles, with an additional appropriation of approximately 25 billion rubles. In 1939, the defense budget had reached 82 billion rubles and in 1940 the total provided for army, navy and defense industry had reached 105 billion rubles. As Ambassador Joseph E. Davies has stated in his *Mission to Moscow*: "These expenditures were tremendous. The outside world did not know or did not appreciate the huge preparedness campaign that was then being projected for the defense of Russia."[10]

In his report to the Secretary of State, Mr. Davies wrote on April 1, 1938, that one-fourth of the national revenues were appropriated in 1937 to war purposes, and that there were "indications of an almost feverish preparation for war." Immense stocks of food and supplies, including military equipment, tanks, submarine chasers, airplanes, trucks, etc., were reported by travelers as being en route to the Far East in an endless stream.[11]

As early as 1936, in his report at the meeting of the Central Executive Committee of the U.S.S.R., Molotov stated that the successes achieved by the railways had resulted in a considerable improvement in the supply of raw materials and fuel to industry. The railways had begun to cope successfully with the demands made upon them by the traffic offered. As Molotov said: "The railways have now ceased to hamper the growth of the national economy and are steadily becoming one of the decisive forces, a truly leading force in our development."[12]

Average daily loading had increased from 51,200 cars in 1933 to 88,000 cars in 1938, an increase of more than 70 per cent. The indices of utilization of rolling stock had improved very considerably during the same period, while the rolling stock itself was increased by the building of 6,000 new high-powered locomotives, as well as 186,000 cars, including 101,000 four-axle cars and over 5,000 passenger cars. Two hundred and sixteen new car repair shops were also built. They were characterized by L. Kaganovich as real factories.[13]

L. Kaganovich assured the XVIIIth Party Congress that "when need arises we shall also cope with military requirements. The railways will not be an obstacle. In case of necessity we shall supply all the requirements of the Red Army and transport everything promptly."[14]

This was a long way from conditions of the Soviet railways in 1933, which were described by Stalin at the XVIIth Party Congress in 1934 as "the weak spot which may act as a stumbling block, and is already acting as a stumbling block, to our whole economic life."[15]

True enough, the railways were working under strain and needed considerable further increase in equipment. However, in the five years elapsed since 1933, the railways had been improved sufficiently to cease to be one of the principal military handicaps of the Soviet Union.[16]

Mention should be made of the double-tracking of the railway from Murmansk to Soroka, and of the new line running transversely from Soroka to Plesetskaia to unite the two northern lines, both of which projects were included in the third Five Year Plan. This, combined with the double-tracking of the Archangel line, which was reported as begun in 1939, was an important step toward the increase in the traffic potentialities of Murmansk and Archangel, and offered new means of handling the import freight carried through these two ports —the only important outlets of European Russia on seas not blocked by potential enemies.[17]

The construction of the Baikal-Amur trunk line was started in 1939 and the line Karymskaia-Khabarovsk was double-tracked, which helped traffic in the Far East.[18]

Figures relating to the production of non-ferrous metals might be mentioned because of the great importance of these metals in war industry. As against that of 1933, the production of lead had increased by 571.6 per cent (the plan had provided for 85,000 tons in 1932-1933) ; of zinc by 506.1 per cent (the plan had provided for 77,000 tons in 1932-1933) ; of aluminum by 1,000 per cent (the plan had provided for 5,000 tons in 1932-1933) ; and the output of copper by 255.9 per cent (the plan had provided for 85,000 tons for 1932-1933).[19]

As Ambassador Davies officially reported to the Secretary of State on June 6, 1938, it was claimed that in European production (or rather as compared with the production of the European states) the Soviet Union held first place in total industrial output, in the manufacture of machine tools, tractors and motor trucks; second place in steel production and third place in coal output. By 1935, it had reached first place in oil and peat extraction, copper smelting, production of railroad freight cars and locomotives, and had taken second place in the generation of electric power and the manufacture of aluminum.[20]

The number of tractors employed in agriculture in the U.S.S.R. had increased from 210,000 in 1933, with 3,209,200 H.P. to 483,500 with 9,256,200 H.P. in 1938. The number of motor trucks employed in agriculture grew from 26,600 in 1933 to 195,800 in 1938. The total of machine and tractor stations rose from 2,900 in 1934 to

6,350 in 1938. This number was to be increased by a further 1,500, under the third Five Year Plan, by 1942.[21]

The number of automobiles in the Union had risen to 570,000 in 1939 and was expected to reach 1,700,000 by 1942, the plan calling for training of as many as 2,000,000 chauffeurs, mostly truck drivers. Over 90 per cent of the tractors in use in agriculture in 1939 were of Soviet manufacture.[22]

There was fairly reliable information on hand that the production of airplanes had reached a 400 per month level in 1938. Another source claimed that the production of airplanes had reached, as early as 1936, the 5,000 per annum level and that in 1939 the production of airplanes in Soviet Russia stood at 20,000 a year.[23]

The potential capacity for tank production in the Ural region alone was estimated by Ambassador Davies at 10,000 a year. In 1937 many factories already were converted to war uses and the introduction of caterpillar-tractor production was cited as one example of this.[24]

The redistribution of industry, taken in hand under the first Five Year Plan, continued to move apace.

Molotov stated in 1939 that the Far East had to produce locally all its requirements in fuel, and, as far as possible, metals, machinery, cement, lumber and building materials, also most of the bulk freight of the foods and "light" industries.[25]

In the Urals the third Five Year Plan called for the completion of the enormous Magnitogorsk iron and steel mills and the building between the Volga and the Urals of a "second Baku," which was expected to have an output of 7,000,000 tons of oil by 1942.[26] At Kuibyshev, on the Volga, two hydroelectric stations with an aggregate capacity of 3,400,000 kw. were under construction in 1939. Nickel works in the South Urals, Cheliabinsk Zinc Works, the Pribalkhash Works (partly) and Central Ural Copper Works (partly) were already put into operation by 1939. The output of the Ural coalfields had increased from 5,480,000 tons in 1934 to 8,060,000 in 1938 and the Siberian Kuznetsk coalfield output rose from 11,200,000 to 16,800,000 tons in the same period. It was expected that the output of the Ural coalfields would reach 25,900,000 tons in 1942, that of the Far Eastern territory 9,000,000, while those of Central Asia would produce 4,700,000 tons.[27]

These developments in the coalfields east of the Volga provided an important fuel base out of reach of enemy attacks from the west, as well as answering the needs of the armies defending the eastern extreme of the Union.

It may be added that the Soviet Union enjoyed 100 per cent sufficiency in coal, iron, petroleum, manganese, mica, chromite and potash; 90 per cent in sulphur and pyrites; 85 per cent in phosphates; 80 per cent in mercury and 60 per cent in zinc.[28]

The changes in the population were not less striking than those in the economic life of the country.[29]

Social Composition of the Population of the USSR

	1928	1937
Workers and employees	17%	35%
Collective farmers and handicraftsmen organized in producers' cooperatives	3%	55%
Individual peasants and handicraftsmen not organized in producers' cooperatives	73%	6%
Capitalist elements (private traders and kulaks)	5%	—
Miscellaneous (students, the armed forces, pensioners, etc.)	2%	4%

The decline in the number of non-organized individual peasants illustrates clearly what had occurred in Soviet agriculture. As Stalin mentioned at the XVIIIth Party Congress, the grain area of the collective farms had increased from 75,000,000 hectares in 1933 to 92,000,000 in 1938. The area cultivated by the individual peasants had decreased from 15,700,000 hectares to 600,000 hectares, or 0.6 per cent of the total grain area. More than 18,000,000 peasant households, or 93.5 per cent of all the peasant households, were united in collective farms.[30]

While it was not intended to stress communes in lieu of the agriculture *artel* type of collective farms, where a certain measure of subsidiary individualistic economic activity was retained, Molotov significantly added, in his speech replying to discussion at the XVIIIth Party Congress, that the government must see to it that the collective farmer's interest in his subsidiary husbandry did not conflict with his main duty—that of strengthening his collective farm and collective farm property. Also that the dimensions of the subsidiary plots of the collective farmers and the number of cattle owned by them individually must not exceed the maximum allowed.[31]

These remarks seem to indicate once more that the Old Adam of individualism was not yet entirely dead among the Russian peasantry and that only the strong arm of the government kept them to the collectivist line. Nevertheless, at the same time Stalin stressed the fact that Soviet society no longer contained antagonistic hostile classes; that the exploiting classes had been eliminated, while the workers, peasants and intellectuals who made up Soviet society were living and working in friendly collaboration.[32]

The policy of the party in internal affairs was in part revealed by Stalin as follows: "steadfastly to carry into effect our Socialist Constitution; to complete the democratization of the political life of the country; to strengthen the moral and political unity of Soviet society and fraternal collaboration among our workers, peasants and intellectuals; to promote the friendship of the peoples of the U.S.S.R. to the utmost, and to develop and cultivate Soviet patriotism."[33]

In the light of subsequent events, it seems justifiable to believe that the last part—the development and cultivation of Soviet patriotism—in the face of the thunderclouds rising both in the west and the east of the Soviet land, had a great deal to do with the changes in the official attitude of the party leaders toward the peasants and intellectuals. The army needed educated commanders as well as peasant youths in its ranks. Would intellectuals and peasants be entirely zealous in the Soviet cause if they continued to be treated as second-rate citizens or worse?

The expansion of the school and college system during the second Five Year Plan had offered the Red Army a remarkable opportunity to recruit youngsters fully able to operate the new equipment and to provide the leadership required by modern warfare.

The secondary schools grew particularly rapidly. There was a two-fold increase in attendance in the fifth, sixth and seventh grades and a fifteen-fold increase in the eighth, ninth and tenth grades during the years of the second Five Year Plan. The number of university and college students had reached a total of 550,000 and become greater than the combined total of those students in Germany, England, France, Italy and Japan.[34]

The libraries of Soviet Russia in 1939 contained seventy-five books for each one hundred inhabitants of the Union, which was over three times as many as Germany's libraries in 1934.[35]

The total number of students in all grades grew from 23,814,000 in 1933-1934 to 33,965,400 in 1938-1939. Of these the secondary school students increased from 5,482,200 to 12,076,000.[36]

What was particularly significant from the defense viewpoint was that the college-graduated technical specialists had also remarkably increased:[37]

	1933	*1938*
Engineers for industry and building (in thousands)	6.1	25.2
Engineers in transport and communications (in thousands)	1.8	6.1
	7.9	31.3

A radical change in the method of recruiting the ranks of the Communist party had also been made part of the rules of the party, adopted at the Party Congress. "The need for different categories of admission of new members and of varying probationary periods has disappeared. Accordingly, uniform conditions of admission and a uniform period of probation should be established for all new members, irrespective of whether they belong to the working class, the peasantry or the intelligentsia."[38] Thus ran the resolution of the Congress adopted on the report of A. Zhdanov.

These were momentous changes, and they could not fail to have a profound influence on the organization of personnel in the Red Army.

Organization

The Commissariat of the Army and Navy was renamed the Commissariat of Defense on March 15, 1934, and the Revolutionary Military Council was abolished. This reform made the People's Commissar for Defense the sole responsible head both of the Commissariat and of the armed forces on land. At the same time the collegiate principle was done away with throughout the whole military organization.[39]

These measures—radical departures from well established structure and principles in the Red Army—proved to be merely the starting point for even more revolutionary changes in the army structure.

The reorganization of the Commissariat and command was followed by a decree of the Central Executive Committee of the U.S.S.R., increasing the peacetime strength of the standing army from 562,000 to 940,000, starting the upward trend in the numerical strength of that army from the level at which it had stood since 1924.[40]

In 1935, the personnel of the standing army was still further increased—to 1,300,000 men. At that time, in addition to this armed land force, Soviet Russia had about 150,000 men in the troops of the Commissariat of the Interior (NKVD), which in June 1934 had absorbed the OGPU. (The latter's head had automatically become the head of the People's Commissariat of the Interior.) About 100,000 men made up the Frontier Guards, formed into seven divisions, all of which were entirely motorized.[41]

By January 1936, the number of divisions of the standing army had been increased so that they made up 77 per cent of all the divisions of the entire army, leaving for the territorial divisions only 23 per cent.[42] It will be recalled that it was mentioned on page 285 above, that the standing army, until the increase in its personnel, had consisted of 29 rifle and 12½ cavalry divisions, while the Territorial Militia had 42 rifle and 4 cavalry divisions, i.e. 41½ divisions of both arms in the standing army as against 46 in the Territorial Militia. The change effected by 1936 had thus reversed the ratio.

This trend had come to its logical conclusion in 1939, when, as Voroshilov announced at the XVIIIth Party Congress, the Territorial Militia system was abandoned altogether, and the whole Red Army was placed on the footing of a standing army.[43]

Voroshilov mentioned at the same Congress that the number of the standing rifle divisions had increased tenfold since the reorganization. Very likely Voroshilov had in mind the period prior to the first increase in the numbers of the standing army. If this be so, then the number of rifle divisions had risen by 1939 to 290. Since the strength of these divisions was increased from 13,000 to 18,000 men, as the establishments had provided before, it would appear that, on the basis of the above assumption, the Red Army in 1939 had in peacetime over five million men in its infantry alone.[44]

The total number of divisions was increased only gradually from 1934 on. At that time only a moderate proportion of the 67 per cent increase of the personnel went to the formation of new field units, as the number of the army rifle corps was increased only from 21 to 23 (3 to 4 Rifle divisions each).[45]

For 1935, the following distribution of forces between the respective military districts and separate armies (increased from ten to twelve) was given by a competent student:[46]

	1932		1935	
	Rifle Divisions	*Cavalry Divisions*	*Rifle Divisions*	*Cavalry Divisions*
Leningrad	6	1½	6	½
White Russia	10	2	12	3
Kiev ⎫ Kharkov ⎭	17	4	19	6
Central Asia	3	2	4	2½
Transcaucasia	7	½	6	1
Siberia	2	—	4	—
Far Eastern Army ⎫ Maritime Army Group ⎭	7	1	11	2½
Moscow	10	1½	10	½
Volga	5	1	8	1
N. Caucasus	5	3	5	2
Total	72	16½	85	19

Among the districts strengthened were those of White Russia and of the Ukraine, but the center of attention was on the Far Eastern armed forces and the districts forming the strategic reserve of these forces (Siberia, Central Asia, Volga). The proportion of the divisions belonging to the cadre army in 1935 is not clear from the material examined. Data available for 1936 make it probable that they were proportionally more numerous in 1935 than in 1933. It is very likely that this change was responsible for the absorption of the large part of the increase in the personnel of the standing army.

The Assistant Commissar of Defense, M. Tukhachevskii, had openly admitted in 1935 that the distribution of troops before the rise in tension in the Far East was no longer satisfactory. He stated the impossibility of imitating the German strategy in World War I and maneuvering between two fronts—the Far Eastern and the Western —because of colossal distances and the insufficiency of transport facilities. These made impossible the transfer of reserves from one front to the other. Under these circumstances it had become necessary to distribute forces so that security both in the West and the East was guaranteed by the forces assigned to the respective fronts. Accordingly, the Far Eastern military establishment was made independent of that in the West.[47]

In view of this, the increase in the personnel of the standing army had become unavoidable, and at the same time the tension in the Far East had made it advisable to transform as many as possible of the territorial divisions into standing divisions.

It is characteristic of the period that the Territorial Militia system was scrapped so rapidly and with so little opposition. The problem was approached in the tradition of Frunze, i.e. from the practical, and not from the theoretical, abstract viewpoint.

Voroshilov explained at the XVIIIth Party Congress in 1939 that the Territorial Militia system implied that upon mobilization the divisions would have numerically weak cadres. This predicated that in the first period after mobilization, the larger part of the rifle divisions and some units of other arms would be weakly organized and of limited combat value. He said: "The Territorial system was tolerable only while the armies of the capitalist countries were relatively small and had also to expand in wartime on the basis of weak cadres. The territorial system, as the foundation of our armed forces, came into contradiction with the requirements of the defense of the state, as soon as the principal imperialist countries began to increase their armies in size and to place them on a war footing even in peacetime."[48]

There was also another reason for scrapping the Territorial Militia system. Its methods of training troops did not correspond to the requirements of the new technical equipment of the army, and the new weapons it came to possess.[49]

The abandonment of the territorial system was accompanied by a thoroughgoing reorganization of the local organs of military administration. Instead of the army corps' and army divisions' mobilization districts, which had heretofore guided the activities of the county military commissariats, autonomous military commissariats were created in all autonomous republics, territories and provinces. The network of the county military commissariats was enlarged some three and a half times. This strengthening of the lower organs had made possible a better system of registration of persons subject to military service, and of organization of draft activities, and therefore laid a better groundwork for mobilization.[50]

Two additional military districts—Kalinin and Orel—were organized. Instead of the Far Eastern Red Banner Front, separate army administrations were installed, one for the Maritime Province, the other for the Amur.[51]

The national formations were disbanded and their personnel merged in the other army units. As Voroshilov stated: the Workers' and Peasants' Red Army was the sole army of the Soviet State and was recruited from citizens of the Soviet Union on a common and equal basis. The existence of separate small national military formations, permanently attached to their respective territories, was in contradiction to the fundamental principles of the Stalin constitution, and the principle of extraterritoriality in the recruitment of the army.[52]

In this manner, another peculiar feature of the Red Army was jettisoned. The army had become "one and indivisible," as in the days of the Empire. From the purely military viewpoint that undoubtedly had considerable advantages. It solved the problem of obtaining efficient commanders for the national units, who were at times difficult to secure. The political advantages were also obvious, particularly in view of efforts from abroad to utilize the national differences within the Union for fostering national dissension and embarrassing Soviet Russia in this manner in case of war.

The central administration of the army underwent a radical reorganization again in 1938, when the Supreme War Council came into being. The latter consisted of eleven members, including Joseph Stalin. The council took for its province the study and solution of all basic and important problems of the upbuilding of the Red Army.[53]

As already stated, the establishment of the rifle divisions was increased from 13,000 to 18,000. This increase in personnel was largely for the needs of the artillery of the divisions and to increase their machine-gun complement. However, the number of riflemen per platoon was also increased.[54]

The Rifle Corps were composed of three or, in exceptional cases, two rifle divisions. These corps averaged 60,000 men.

Another important innovation was the separation of the naval forces from the land army. A new commissariat—that of the navy— came into being on December 30, 1937.[55]

The general aim of the reorganization of the armed forces, as stated by Voroshilov in 1931 was: the U.S.S.R. must arrange its armed forces so as to obtain victory in the future war with as little loss to its army as possible, the war to be conducted on the territory of the enemy who attacked the land of the Soviets.[56]

This goal presupposed, of course, a high rate of efficiency of the armed forces. The logical sequel to it was Stalin's slogan coined in 1934—the Red Army must be stronger than any possible armed combination against the U.S.S.R.[57]

In 1939, Voroshilov officially announced at the XVIIIth Party Congress that the Red Army was better (meaning more efficient) than any other army, was well equipped technically, and that its training was excellent.[58]

This rapid transition from an army definitely backward in its technical equipment and armament (prior to the first Five Year Plan), through a period of complete re-equipment with the most modern machines and weapons which the army personnel, as Voroshilov admitted, had not entirely mastered, either technically or tactically, to an army aspiring to primacy among the armed forces of the world, is a startling development indeed. There is no parallel to this in modern history, with the exception of the rise of the armed might of Japan at the end of the nineteenth century, and at that, the development of the Nipponese modern armed might was spread over a considerably longer period.

The growth of the Soviet army in the 'thirties could be adequately described by the word "revolutionary." It was an answer in military terms to the equally revolutionary growth of the industrialization of the country, which was transforming Russia from an agricultural state into a land of highly developed industrial production. While from 1921 to 1924, from 1924 to 1929, and to some extent from 1930 to 1934, the process of change of the armed forces of the U.S.S.R. followed the slow rhythm of evolution, after 1934 the change was so rapid and radical that even persons paying close attention to Russian military problems often failed to grasp the import of the great change which was taking place.

The growth of combat efficacy of the army in the 'thirties will be examined later. In the meanwhile, attention must be given to the remarkable change in the attitude of the government to the problem of recruitment of the armed forces.

The new constitution adopted by the VIIIth Congress of the Soviets on December 5, 1936, provided that the organization of the defense of the U.S.S.R. and the direction of all its armed forces came within the jurisdiction of the U.S.S.R., as represented by its highest organs of power. The Supreme Council of the U.S.S.R. became the highest organ of state authority, and its Presidium was granted the power to appoint and replace the high command of the armed forces. In the intervals between the sessions of the Supreme Council of the U.S.S.R., the Presidium was authorized to declare a state of war in case of an armed attack upon the U.S.S.R., or in case of the need of fulfilling international treaty obligations of mutual defense against aggressors. It was also given the right to declare general or partial mobilization of the armed forces.[59]

The Council of People's Commissars was authorized to fix the annual contingent of citizens to be called for active military service and to direct the general organization of the armed forces of the country.[60]

Military service was made universal as well as obligatory by the constitution. "The defense of the fatherland is the sacred duty of every citizen of the U.S.S.R." it was stated in Article 133. Violation of the oath, desertion to the enemy, impairing the military might of the state, and espionage were made punishable "with the full severity of the law as the gravest crime," i.e. by capital punishment.[61]

The universal military service statute of 1939 was a consequence of the constitutional principles on the one hand and the new problems set to the armed forces of the U.S.S.R. by the international situation on the other.

Voroshilov's report made in August 1939 sheds light on the background of that remarkable statute, which in many ways was a startling departure from the principles of previous Soviet legislation governing obligatory military service.

The People's Commissar for Defense stated that the exploiting classes were definitely liquidated in Russia and that the workers, the collective farmers and the Soviet intellectuals were fused into a single front of labor. "Our country has turned from being a land of building up of socialism into a country of victorious socialism," said Voroshilov. The victory of socialism had made possible the complete equality of Soviet citizens confirmed by the new constitution.[62]

Radical changes had occurred, continued Voroshilov, in the organization and the recruitment of the armed forces. The numerical strength of the army and the navy had grown during the last nine years three and one-half times.[63]

A great deal of attention was paid by Voroshilov to the question of drawing into the army the graduates of secondary schools. He said that 145,000 graduates of such schools were called into the army in 1939. It was proposed to recruit from this contingent not only the regimental schools of the N.C.O.'s but the privates of the special arms as well. From the same group reserve commanders were also to be drawn.[64]

The statute had provided that secondary school graduates were to serve in the armed forces prior to admission to colleges. This had made immediately available for military service a much larger proportion of that group. Voroshilov explained that some secondary school students had in the past stayed there until the age of twenty-five; college students remained in colleges until the age of twenty-eight. Only upon reaching these ages, and, as a rule already burdened by a family of their own, college students, or college graduates, came before draft boards. They served only one year in the army under colors and were known as "one year men." The army was actually getting only a small part of that group. College graduates usually succeeded in obtaining positions in important non-military institutions and were often able to obtain further deferments, up to the age of thirty, when they were granted complete exemption from draft. As Voroshilov put it: "The state was spending means for the education of these citizens, while they were failing to perform even their civic duty to the state and did not serve in the army."[65]

The new statute authorized deferments on family grounds to sole wage earners who were maintaining by their labor not less than two members of their families incapable of work. Members of families thus recognized were: fathers older than 60 years of age; mothers, older than fifty-five; or fathers and mothers, invalids of the first and second group, regardless of age.[66]

The draft age had already been lowered from twenty-one to nineteen in 1936 by a decree of the Central Executive Committee. This age was retained by the statute; for the graduates of secondary schools it was lowered to eighteen.[67]

Another important and unusual departure was the increase in the term of obligatory service with the colors for junior commanders from two to three years, while the private soldiers, with the exception of those of the air forces and some auxiliary services, were to serve the same term as heretofore, i.e. two years.[68]

The People's Commissar for Defense pleaded in support of the extension of the term of service that the modern army had become a highly complex organization, involving various intricate machines and weapons, within which even a comparatively well-educated person had difficulty in functioning satisfactorily without a well-grounded and extensive training. Even privates of some of the specialized arms, like the signal corps, had to be trained systematically over a long period of time to be able to perform their duties satisfactorily. Under these circumstances privates of the air corps, as well as those of the frontier guard troops, were obligated to serve three years.[69]

The extension of the term of service of the junior commanders made possible the abolition of most of the second term service vacancies of these commanders, with such exceptions as those of the sergeant-major and of certain specialists. This measure in its turn had facilitated a more rapid accumulation of a large reserve of well-trained junior commanders. Voroshilov emphasized the rôle of the N.C.O.'s in the future war. "Junior commanders," he said, "will play the foremost and the most influential rôle in the future war."[70]

At the other end of the age-scale, ten years were added to the term of the obligatory reserve military service (from forty to fifty years of age). These ten oldest age groups were intended mostly for service in the rear.[71]

The details of the statute will be analyzed later under the respective subheadings. In the meanwhile, the principal object of that law could be summarized in this manner: it aimed at obtaining a large number of well-educated youths, secondary school graduates, regardless of their social origins. They were drawn into the army to serve as technical specialists and junior commanders. This measure paralleled the electoral system set-up of the new constitution of 1936, where every citizen who had reached the age of eighteen was entitled to vote, except the insane and those disfranchised by court sentence. To obtain rapidly a large reservoir of these trained young men, the draft age was lowered.

The top limits for reserve service age was raised to liberate for front duties as large a number of trained persons as possible. These steps, considered together, may be regarded as precautions taken in the face of an approaching major war.

Paragraph 3 of the statute symbolized the end of discrimination against certain classes of inhabitants of the U.S.S.R. with respect to military service: all male citizens of the country, regardless of race, nationality, creed, education, *social origin* and position were liable to military service in the *armed forces* of the U.S.S.R.[72]

Thus ended the attempt to recruit the armed forces of Soviet Russia from classes supposedly more loyal to the régime. There were, no doubt, many motives which led to the adoption of radical changes both of the franchise and of rules governing military service. It is impossible to examine here in detail the internal political motivation responsible for these changes. One of these motives, however, should be mentioned: in the face of the obviously impending attack by power-ful enemies from abroad, it was imperative to unite the entire popula-tion for the defense of the country and to satisfy at the same time the urgent need of the army for better educated N.C.O.'s and specialists.

The turn taken in the handling of recruitment of the rank and file, as well as of the officers' corps, was startling. The process reminds one of Lenin's famous draft of a paper for the *Granat Encyclopaedia,* written in 1914, where he gave his conception of the dialectic method: "Development along lines of repeating stages already passed . . . in a spiral, and not in a direct line, a jump-like development, catastrophic, revolutionary, 'interruption of graduality,' change of quantity into quality."

All these characteristics could be traced in the development of the structure of the Red Army in the 'thirties. The plan of building up the army officers' corps and even of recruiting its rank and file on a narrow class basis was carried to its extreme—and then completely abandoned. The army had become a truly national army, representing all classes of the community. The constantly growing contradictions and antagonisms of the straitjacket of class dictatorship, were swept away at one mighty stroke. Fresh forces were canalized into the army on a tremendous scale. The contradictions were solved and a truly modern army had become possible, instead of one setting a premium on mere political eligibility to the detriment of the better educated elements.

Commanders

The commanding personnel had undergone very considerable changes during the period 1934-1940. These changes were not all in the same direction. They succeeded each other rather in a spiral-like progression. At this stage, it is not always possible to trace clearly the reasons for some of these changes, particularly of those that had roots in the general course of development of the U.S.S.R. and were not the result of the process within the army itself. With the material available at present, all that is feasible is the tracing of the course of these changes, their outward shape, without attempting to probe the causal chain and to gauge the broader influences which had brought them about.

The typical characteristic of the highest and senior commanding personnel prior to the period examined was that practically all of them had taken part in the Civil War with the Red armed forces. In his speech at the XVIth Party Congress, Voroshilov stated that 96.6 per cent of commanders of rifle divisions and rifle regiments belonged to that category. In the cavalry the percentage was even higher— 97.5 per cent. Even among company commanders this element formed 70 per cent. Voroshilov was obviously proud of this fact: "All these commanders have traveled with us the road of Civil War. The proletarian revolution is as dear to them as to any worker and Communist." The former officers of the old army still formed 10.6 per cent of the total number of commanders. They were proportionally more numerous in the higher ranks; as among middle commanders they were represented by 6.7 per cent only. Voroshilov stressed the fact that most of these ex-czarist officers were at the time members of the party.[73]

The bulk of the commanding personnel consisted thus of former N.C.O.'s and privates of the old army, of workers, peasants and a small percentage of intellectuals, who had not served in the old army but had received their baptism of fire in the ranks of the Red Army. Most of these men were lacking in general education, although large proportions of them had received a considerable amount of technical military education and had acquired a great deal of command experience.

In discussing the ranking officers inherited by the Red Army from the old, Voroshilov stated in 1933 that there were very few large-scale organizers among them. He named S. Kamenev, Vatsetis, P. P. Lebedev, B. M. Shaposhnikov, S. A. Mezheninov, and N. N. Petin, adding that there were a score or so more of men coming into this category, of what he termed "real military specialists."[74] All rifle corps commanders were Communists. Ninety-three per cent of the rifle divisions' commanders and 95 per cent of the cavalry division commanders were party men. Rifle regimental commanders belonged to the party to the extent of 88 per cent. For the cavalry the figure was about the same. Battalion commanders had 72 per cent of Communists, while the middle commanders (company, platoon) included 69 per cent party members.[75]

The growth of the party personnel among senior commanders was very rapid. In the infantry 54 per cent, and in the artillery a mere 15 per cent, were Communists in 1928.[76]

There was a still further influx of workers into the ranks of commanders. By 1932, there were 40 per cent of workers for the commanding personnel as a whole, as against 28 per cent in 1928. This percentage rose to 42.3 per cent by July 1933.[77]

The levels of military education were distributed in the following manner:[78]

In 1933	War College Graduates	Abbreviated War College Course
Army Corps Commanders	33%	67%
Rifle Divisional Commanders	25%	75%
Cavalry Divisional Commanders	43%	57%
Regimental Commanders (rifle)	13%	87%

For 1934, Voroshilov gave another set of figures not actually comparable with those for 1933. Of all the highest commanding personnel, 78.9 per cent had graduated from military colleges (full or abbreviated course); of the senior commanders 48.2 per cent (42.7 per cent of these commanders were graduates of the normal military schools); of the middle commanders 81.4 per cent were graduates of the normal military schools. The chiefs of staff, it was stated, were in the vast majority War College (full course) graduates.[79]

The large percentage of corps, divisional, and regimental commanders who had attended the abbreviated courses of the War College meant that their general education was not high enough to permit them to attempt to go through the regular War College course, already made more elementary as against the programs of the old army days. Voroshilov stated that some of the commanders had passed twice through the abbreviated courses, which seems to indicate that it was not lack of zeal which had prevented them from taking the regular course.

As long as the soldiers in the ranks were drawn from poorly educated levels, the lack of general education among the large proportion of senior, or even highest commanders, did not lead to loss of prestige for the commanders. In later years, when, in 1938 for example, 32.8

per cent of the total draft had completed seven to ten grades of secondary schools, this circumstance led to peculiar situations, when commanders were not able to follow the cultural interest of the soldiers. There is a report of a discussion between a chief of staff of a unit and its commissar. The latter asked what had the former heard at the soldiers' political studies class he had just visited. "Who knows," replied the chief of staff, "they were discussing one or other of Peter's reforms!"[80]

The previous chapter contains references to the lowering of the educational standard of candidates for admission to military schools, which, of course, had reflected unfavorably upon the general educational level of the graduates of these schools. The situation was made worse by the shortening of the training period in these schools in 1930 by six to twelve months (depending on the arm concerned). This abbreviation of the period of studies was achieved largely at the expense of theoretical studies.[81]

The extreme practicalism in the training of future commanders led even to shaping the studies of the first year in these schools to the goal of training a section commander. Only in the second year was the student prepared for the command of a platoon.[82]

The deficiencies in the educational standards of graduates of military schools had attracted in 1933 the attention of the organ of the Red Army—the *Voennyi Vestnik*. S. A. Smirnov, commenting on the conditions prevailing at the military schools that year, wrote that these had not achieved as yet "in all spheres" results such as the army had a right to expect from them. "Our military schools," Smirnov commented, "are still markedly falling behind the stormy growth of our country." He analyzed the shortcomings of military education as stemming from the following roots: lack of individual responsibility on the part of students for the results of their work; lack of sufficient authority and responsibility on the part of the teaching staff; and, thirdly, insufficiency of theoretical information imparted to students.[83]

This lack of individual responsibility on the part of students was the result of the wide application of the so-called "brigade" method, where the head of the brigade was responsible for the work of his team, which in practice often led to his doing all the work. The military schools were not the only ones where this extreme form of teamwork in studies was encouraged. The reorganization of methods of study in these schools was in line with the decision of the Central Committee of the party of August 25, 1933, regarding secondary schools.[84]

The results of the pre-1933 system were described by Smirnov as tending to ignore the individuality of the student, encouraging collective solutions, "which in no way helps the development of a strong-willed, enterprising, firm and decisive commander, ready to assume responsibility, always and everywhere, in true bolshevik tradition."[85]

The new method prescribed that the theoretical side of any subject studied should be first outlined through lectures by the teaching staff, followed by individual study in the evening hours of materials suggested by that staff. Finally, this work was to be complemented by the imparting of practical acquaintance with the subject, through work on problems in class, in the field or on a plan.[86]

The new method of studies contrasted sharply with the previous one, where the theoretical discussion was almost entirely eliminated and the practical approach was carried to its extreme.[87]

Unfortunately, the introduction of the new methods of studies was followed by the overworking of students, who were given too much evening work. The students had only two hours every evening for this work. In the two five-day periods the students had eighty hours of class work with only sixteen hours of evening studies.

These eighty hours of class work consisted, in the first year, of studies at some of the schools, of:[88]

	Hours
Tactics	16
Drill and physical training	6
Russian	10
Political economy	12
Musketry	20
Mathematics	10
Auxiliary disciplines	6

After the reforms of 1933 a greater effort was made to improve the general cultural level of the students, and a number of additional subjects were introduced into the programs of military schools aiming to achieve that end. As Smirnov said, the growth of the modern military technique had made this imperative.[89]

A modern note was sounded by the introduction of motorization studies, as well as of those on the tactical use of armored units, anti-gas and anti-air-attack defenses. Fifty per cent of military schools were motorized by 1932. All infantry schools had developed artillery departments, while some had established tank departments, which made it possible to train commanders able to direct combinations of several arms in action.[90]

The extreme practicalism of the pre-1933 period was, quite possibly, the result of a violent swing from the ultra-theoretical method in military schools in the 'twenties, when the teaching staff were largely composed of former officers of the old army without Civil War experience, who had failed to provide the young commanders with sufficient practical knowledge. By 1933, the teaching staffs consisted of 90.5 per cent of the graduates of the normal military schools of the Red Army, had 65 per cent party members in their ranks, and 45 per cent of them had sprung from the workers' class. The comparison of these figures with those of 1925 shows that the old personnel was largely eliminated and replaced by young commanders of Soviet formation and proletarian origin. In 1925, 59 per cent of the teaching staff were former officers of the old army, and 50 per cent of its personnel belonged to the "others" class category. The new incumbents understood their task as moving in the opposite direction from the methods of their predecessors. They went to the other extreme, partly because of their weaker theoretical education. The reform of 1933 had levelled off the balance.[91]

An interesting editorial in the *Red Star* in 1935 confirmed the fact that these reforms had not sufficiently offset the basic shortcomings inherent in the methods of recruiting of military schools from elements without sufficient general education, "the not very high level of the general education of the students," as Smirnov mildly described it.

This editorial outlined the view that the new technical equipment of the army made it necessary for commanders to be on a high level of general culture, and possess "solid, firm knowledge in the field of general education in its several aspects." It developed the thesis that the use of modern military equipment in action calls for rapid and accurate calculations, which, necessarily, must be based on a thorough knowledge of mathematics, physics and chemistry. The editorial ends on the pessimistic note that commanders of some units did not appreciate sufficiently the extreme importance of improving the cultural level of their subordinate commanders and soldiers, and regarded studies in the field of general education as of no importance.[92]

Voroshilov spoke in November of the same year—1935—about the commanding personnel's failure to grow culturally as rapidly as the masses, and their inability at times to organize their work to suit the better-educated young soldiers. He stressed the fact, however, that every effort was made to re-train and re-educate that personnel, to help them to become better qualified for their work, to be able to meet the new demands upon them by the soldiers. Nevertheless, said he, "the danger of a breach between the tempo of the growth of the commanding personnel and that of the masses . . . existed in the Red Army."[93]

The need of obtaining better educated youngsters for the military schools had led to the temporary abandonment of the method of recruitment of these schools from the ranks of the army. The editorial in the *Red Star* in September 1935 pointed out that the work of educating the new commanders in that academic year had become more difficult because the candidates came mostly from civilian life. "Each new student had to be carefully studied from the first day of his admission to the schools," as these students had not passed through the filter of the political organs of the army before entering the military schools.[94]

The infusion of the student personnel by party and party-affiliated elements went on apace in the meanwhile. In 1933 there were 75 per cent of party members and candidates, also 19 per cent of Komsomols among the students, as against 30 per cent party members and 41 per cent of Komsomols in 1930. The total of 94 per cent of party-affiliated persons clearly indicates that the schools were practically closed to persons non-affiliated with the party or at least not desirous of becoming associated with it.[95]

The recruitment of military schools from the ranks of civilian youths continued until 1940. The *Red Star* wrote in January of that year: "The number of candidates from the ranks of the army was not large in the past." From 1940 on, junior commanders (both of first and second term service), junior reserve commanders not older than twenty-seven, privates of the age group called up in 1938, as well as privates of the reserve who had terminated their service with the colors during the two previous years, were invited to enter the military schools. These categories had to have certificates of completion of the seventh form, or better. Privates of the age group called into the army in 1939 were also permitted to enter the military schools provided they had completed their secondary school education.[96]

The last measure was obviously designed to take the fullest possible advantage of the large number of secondary school graduates who were drafted into the army in 1939.

There was a gradual improvement in the level of general education of candidates for admission to military schools. By 1935, 25 per cent of those admitted had education above the level of the seven grades of the secondary school; 60 per cent had completed the seventh grade, while 15 per cent (mostly former junior commanders) had education below the seventh grade norm. In 1936, 26 per cent of candidates had the seven grades' certificate, and 74 per cent those of eight or nine or had completed their secondary education. There was even a number of college students among them.[97]

By order of the People's Commissar of Defense of March 20, 1937, new rules of admission to military schools were introduced. Young men from seventeen to twenty-two years old with a certificate of completion of eight grades at least were to be admitted upon passing an examination in Russian and mathematics. Those with a completed secondary education, as well as college students, who had matriculated with the grade "good" in Russian and mathematics were admitted without these supplementary tests.[98]

From 1937, the duration of studies at the military schools was set at three years, with the exception of schools of ordnance and some technical schools, where the training lasted only two years. Graduates of secondary schools and college students remained for only two years in the infantry and cavalry schools. Prior to 1937 (since 1930) infantry and cavalry schools had three years' courses: artillery, engineers, etc., four years.[99]

Obligatory studies of general cultural subjects (foreign languages, literature, natural sciences, physics, mathematics, history and geography) were introduced for the commanders of the Red Army in 1935, with the program extending over two to three years. Voroshilov had commented in that connection that a commander is in his place only if he constantly works at his own education and strives to reach an ever higher level of knowledge.[100]

The *Red Star* published in 1935 some statistics regarding books read by students of the Kiev military schools "during the last few months": Pushkin was read by 617, Gogol by 244, Nekrasov by 240, Tolstoy by 146, Lermontov by 199, Gorky by 184, Turgenev by 280. It was stated that students had also read Dickens, Balzac, Romain Rolland and Barbusse, although no figures were quoted.[101]

This "back to the classics" trend is an interesting phenomenon, in line with a general tendency among the Soviet youth of the period. That Pushkin was so popular is not particularly surprising, but that Turgenev was read more than Gorky is astonishing.

The network of military schools had expanded in line with the general growth of the army personnel. In 1939 there were 63 military schools of the land forces and 32 special flying and technical aviation schools. Higher military education was taken care of by 14 military colleges and 6 special military faculties attached to civilian colleges.[102]

Exact numbers of students are not available, but Voroshilov spoke of "tens of thousands" of students in the land forces' schools and "more than twenty thousand Communists and Komsomols" who were trained in the aviation schools. The colleges also had "over a score of thousand" students.[103]

This educational effort was nothing short of gigantic. With the better educated human material available, schools were in a position to turn out thousands of young commanders with a good general education and special military training of the level of the Western European armies or even above that level. The numerous colleges provided ample means for the further improvement of that knowledge. The commanding personnel was thus rapidly changing from a backward and poorly educated group into a young, well-educated, well-trained, keen corps of modern officers.

There was no need to force the better educated Soviet youth into the military schools. The *Red Star* said in 1940 that scores of thousands of the young generation "were besieging" the portals of these schools.[104]

Colonel T. Makhin stated in his book on the Red Army that the popularity of the military schools among the educated Soviet youths had made great strides since 1935, particularly since the famous decree of September 22, 1935, which introduced personal ranks for the commanding personnel.[105]

This reform was caustically criticized by some of the military commentators in the socialist camp as restoring the "ranks and the gold-braided hierarchy of officers," giving "outward form to the army caste organization" and confirming the privileged position of the commanding personnel in the "classless" society of Soviet Russia.[106]

Nevertheless, it apparently had answered the wishes not only of the commanding personnel of the army, but of large sections of the Soviet educated young generation at large. Hence the great influx of that element into the military schools.

The motives for the reform were given in the statute itself. At the stage of development reached, the rôle of the commanding personnel had assumed first-rate importance. The party slogan: "the cadres decide all," in application to the Red Army meant first of all the creation of conditions guaranteeing the further growth and improvement of quality of the cadres and the commanding personnel as a whole. "For the entire mass" of commanders, political workers, military engineers, technicians, medical specialists, administrative personnel, etc., the service in the Red Army was decreed a lifelong profession.[107]

This word, so terrifying to the early political workers of the Red

Army, was openly pronounced by the government. The army became officially professionalized.

The introduction of military ranks, which were to reflect accurately the military as well as the special qualification of each member of the commanding personnel, their service career and merits "their power and authority," was made necessary, it was stated, by the particularly responsible tasks in educating and training of soldiers and the leading rôle of the commanders (in the narrower sense) in action.[108]

For the land and air forces the following ranks were introduced for commanders :[109] lieutenant, senior lieutenant, captain, major, colonel, brigadier (*Kombrig*), commander of division, commander of army corps, army commander of the 2nd rank, army commander of the 1st rank.

For the navy commanders the following ranks were decreed :[110] lieutenant, senior lieutenant, lieutenant commander (*Kapitan-Leitenant*), captain of the 3rd rank, captain of the 2nd rank, captain of the 1st rank, flagman of the 2nd rank, flagman of the 1st rank, flagman of the fleet of the 2nd rank, flagman of the fleet of the 1st rank.

In addition to these ranks a special one, that of the Marshal of the' Soviet Union, was also created. It was bestowed, in November 1935, on five of the ranking commanders: Voroshilov, Tukhachevskii, Egorov, Budenny and Bluecher.[111]

The rank terminology was a curious amalgam of ranks previously used in the armed forces of old Russia (particularly true of the navy) of the ranks previously used and later discarded (major and lieutenant commander) and the revolutionary ranks which had served since the Civil War for titles for the general officers and admirals of the Russian armed forces. The title of Marshal was an innovation, echoing the glories of the French revolution.

These rank gradations were supplemented by the ranks of junior lieutenant and the corresponding rank of junior military technician, introduced in 1937. These lower rungs of the military hierarchy were open to junior commanders graduated from special brief-term courses also to persons possessing better education who had completed their military service.[112]

This "table of ranks" did not introduce western General or Admiral ranks. Apparently the cumulative effect of the odium heaped on the czarist generals during 1917 and during the Civil War period was still weighing the balance against the introduction of ranks reminding of these much bedevilled old-army leaders.

However, even this step was taken. The decree of May 8, 1940, introduced for the land and air forces the ranks of: major general, lieutenant general, colonel general, general of the army. The last rank was reserved for commanders of armed forces composed of all arms. The first three had added to them the denomination of the arm the respective commander belonged to, such as Major General of Infantry, Lieutenant General of Artillery, etc.[113]

In the navy the ranks of rear admiral, vice admiral, admiral, admiral of the fleet were introduced. Naval engineers of admiral rank were to be known as engineer rear admirals, etc.[114]

The rank of colonel general did not exist in the old Russian army and was apparently borrowed from the *Reichswehr* terminology. Nor did the rank of admiral of the fleet exist in the old navy.

The statute of 1939 had in the meanwhile added the rank of lieutenant colonel.[115]

In defining the position of the commander in the narrow sense, the statute of 1935 had included the stipulation that persons of this category were to have a definite command standing and the military training. The division between the commanders *proprio dictu* and the balance of the commanding personnel was maintained. In the latter were included the political personnel, the military technical personnel and the medical specialists.[116]

Commanders removed from the rolls of the reserve because of age or illness were to keep their rank, adding to it the word "retired."[117]

The first rank was to be granted in accordance with regulations prescribed by the People's Commissar of Defense upon graduation from military schools or on passing certain examinations. Promotion was granted after a definite term of service in the ranks on condition of satisfactory attestation. These terms were fixed: for junior lieutenants, 2 years; for lieutenants, 3 years; for senior lieutenants, 3 years; for captains, 4 years; for majors, 4 years; for colonels, 8 years. There was a provision for promotion before the expiration of the decreed terms for distinguished service. For general ranks no terms of service were established. Promotion of commanders of these ranks was left to the discretion of the People's Commissar of Defense.[118]

The same Commissar was also granted the right of promoting to ranks higher than the next in the hierarchical order, in exception to the general rule of promotion to the next rank only. The rank was made alienable by decision of court only, otherwise the possession of a given rank was maintained for life. Appropriate rank insignia, consisting of squares, lozenges, etc. for the army, and braid stripes for the navy were made part of the uniform of the commanders.[119]

These insignia (with an additional special stripe) could be worn by the non-cadre commanders of the territorial troops, of the reserve, and those retired. In other words, the situation had reverted in this respect to the practice of the old army, and even went further than the latter's practice, as in that army reserve officers did not wear their uniforms off duty.[120]

The most important privilege was that conferred by Paragraph 50 of the Statute by which all commanders (except junior commanders) were freed from arrest by civil organs without a special authorization in each case by the People's Commissar of Defense. It was a peculiar *habeas corpus* which set the commanding personnel apart from the rest of the population.[121]

The age limits for active service underwent a sharp reduction again in 1939. They were lowered for lieutenants from 40 to 30, for senior lieutenants from 40 to 35, for majors from 45 to 40, for colonels to 45. For brigadiers they were established at 55, for commanders of divisions or higher ranks, at 60. The reason for this measure was given by Voroshilov as the desire to regulate better the promotion of the cadres of commanding personnel, as well as to permit more rapid accumulation of reserve commanders against a war emergency.[122]

One may see in it also the intention of clearing the ranks of senior and middle commanding personnel of the veterans of Civil War who were unfit, because of their educational level, to occupy the higher positions in the army.

As a measure of training men for reserve commanding personnel duties, the pre-army training of youths was reorganized. The primary military training was introduced in all secondary and incomplete secondary schools in grades 5, 6 and 7. The more advanced military training was to be given in grades 8, 9 and 10. In this manner, youngsters were given six years of obligatory military training while in the secondary schools. The primary training was allocated two hours in each six-day period, while the advanced instruction was to follow a "special program." Pre-army training of youths outside of schools was abandoned altogether as costly and unsatisfactory.[123]

This training was to be imparted by special military instructors carried on the faculties of the respective schools and drawn mostly from the ranks of the reserve commanders.[124]

The principle of unity of command underwent several radical changes in the period discussed, with the pendulum swinging first one way then another. The abolition of the collegiate system in the army in 1934 had carried the unity of command to the military districts and to the apex of the whole military system—the Commissar of Defense, freed from the collaboration of the Revolutionary Military Council. What were the subsequent changes will be considered under the next subheadings.

E. Wollenberg, in summing up the numerical strength of the army commanding personnel, wrote that between 1924 and 1937 some 100,000 persons had graduated from military schools. Of these about 60,000 had left the army for various reasons. By May 1937, when the great army purges began, the commanding personnel consisted of some 80,000 persons including about 20,000 Civil War veterans of the rank of major or higher.[125]

The decrease in numbers caused by the purge was rapidly made up by several means, which will also be stated under the next subheading.

It is characteristic that in addition to the various advantages offered to the commanders, another means of spurring the zeal of the military school students was introduced by a special law passed in modification of the 1939 Statute decreeing that in 1940 students of military and naval schools expelled for lack of success in their studies or for disciplinary shortcomings were obligated to serve their full terms of military service in the combat units of the armed forces, without any allowance for the time spent by them in schools.[126]

Such a threat must have served as a spur to the laggards. The *Red Star* explained that this measure was aimed at students still infested with the virus of "petty bourgeois habits." As the army newspaper said, a good many persons belonging to this category were openly gambling on being released from military service in case of expulsion from schools.[127]

As already stated, the level of commanders' standards, both as to general culture and as to special military knowledge, had very considerably increased during the last few years preceding this war. The judgment of the otherwise keen observer, Arthur W. Just, given in his book published in 1936, that the weakest spot in Soviet military power was to be found in the leaders and tacticians of the army, was not sound in 1941—at least in so far as the younger officers are concerned. The young men who had passed through the military schools during the period 1935-1940, were certainly, in the majority, as well educated and trained as any young officers in Western Europe.[128]

The picture drawn by the correspondent of the Moscow *Pravda* in May 1937 seems to give a truer picture of the cultural level of that young generation of Red Army commanders. The reporter talked to a commander at an advance post in the wilderness of the Far East.

The latter was well posted on the course of events in Spain, was able to discuss intelligently international affairs in general and his knowledge of Japanese politics was termed by the correspondent as nothing short of expert. The commander also followed closely economic development at home.[129]

This higher cultural level of the commanding personnel found a reflection in the well-organized life of the soldiers in the barracks, where even flowers, placed by commanders' wives, were not an incongruous touch.[130]

The description given by Just of the outward appearance of the commanders shows that they stood out in strong contrast to the drab mass of the general population. Well shaven, with a white collar under the collar of his tunic, the commander had at his disposal comfortable "even luxuriously furnished clubs." The best Crimean and other Black Sea resorts were available to him when on leave or recovering from an illness. While Just admits that the general standard of living of the commanders was well within that of the ordinary middle class in the West, despite such touches as interest in fashionable sports from polo to tennis, and even obligatory dancing lessons at the War College, the fact remains that in comparison with the average citizen the commanding personnel of the Army were very well off indeed.[131]

The lean and cold days of the early NEP were definitely over.

The pay also increased very considerably (by 286 per cent on the average) between 1934 and 1939. The table below gives the picture for 1939.[132]

	1934	*1939*	*Increase per cent*
Platoon Commander	260	625	240
Company Commander	285	750	263
Battalion Commander	335	850	254
Regimental Commander	400	1200	300
Division Commander	475	1600	337
Corps Commander	550	2000	364

The purchasing power of the ruble had declined during the period, but that decline had affected the commanders less than most of the citizens of the Union. The progressively larger increases in the pay of higher commanders were quite interesting. They make the difference in monetary income between the higher commander and those at the bottom of the ladder greater in 1939 than was true in 1934.

One of the reasons for the considerable improvement of the well-being of the commanding personnel was the organization of the military co-operative consumers' system which went a great deal toward making the commander's life more comfortable. This system had created retail shops, organized communal feeding, barber shops, laundries, and tailoring, and boot-making establishments. It grew into a huge enterprise with a turnover of one and a half billion rubles in 1935, maintaining 1,700 stores, about 1,000 industrial enterprises and 800 restaurants. Its work was a particular advantage to the commanders in the far-flung outposts of the Union, such as the Far East.[133]

The *Voentorg*, as the system became known, followed the commander into the encampments in the summer. It supplied camp furniture and equipment, as well as organized the feeding.[134]

True enough, general conditions in the country had affected, at certain periods, the stores of the *Voentorg* as well, and the *Red Star* of July 1937 voiced complaints of the Voronezh commanders whose families could not obtain kerosene for months. Women's stockings were unobtainable, there was a scarcity of cotton goods, leather footwear of certain types, china and ordinary thread. The fact remains, however, that on the whole the commanders had a considerable advantage in the use of the stores of this system.[135]

With the general scarcity of housing space in the urban centers, the commanding personnel again had a certain advantage in obtaining up-to-date apartments. There is, for instance, a report that in 1937 six new apartment houses containing 154 three-room units, would be completed in Moscow by New Year's for the use of the commanding personnel, and that in Leningrad a house with 30 three- and four-room apartments with all modern conveniences (hot water, gas, central heating and bathrooms) was completed for the use of the naval commanding personnel.[136]

This construction of apartment houses for the commanding personnel was conducted for years on a large scale. As early as 1935 there was a report of a whole "township" of military dwellings under construction in Moscow. Fourteen buildings, each of eighteen apartments, equipped with all modern conveniences surrounded by a garden with flower-beds, fountains, and even statuary, were part of this township. Children's playrooms, spotlessly clean, a communal restaurant with a roof-garden, and a mechanized steam laundry were additional features of the settlement.[137]

The rise in the level of bodily comfort and general culture led to certain complications in commanders' lives. E. Wollenberg states that this caused commanders to obtain divorces from wives of proletarian and peasant origin, "who were not up to 'society' standards," and to marry women belonging to the circles of the old aristocracy, the former bourgeoisie and the new bureaucracy. He claims that this was a mass phenomenon.[138]

That there was at least some ground for Wollenberg's assertion, items in the columns of the army newspaper seem to indicate. In July, 1937, for instance, the case of Senior Lieutenant Matveev was discussed. This commander was constantly nagging his wife for her lack of education, even telling her that she "did not deserve to live with a senior lieutenant." Matveev pointed out, as an example to be followed, the good manners of his former wife, who had come from "a decent family"—that of a merchant. Matveev's second wife applied for help to the commander of the regiment and to political workers, all to no avail.[139]

The *Red Star* conducted a campaign against the laxity of sexual morals of the commanding personnel (including Communists). It insisted upon energetic educational work among some of the wives of that personnel, who were loath to take any part in the social work and whose main occupations were sauntering along the main thoroughfare to show off their new dresses, and mild flirtations. Their motto was: "Since I am married, it is up to my husband to sweat, if need be, but to serve me my life on a china platter."[140]

Whether such attitudes were the rule or the exception, the material examined does not permit the writer to determine. There is, however, the assertion of the *Red Star* in 1935 that the behavior described was characteristic of a small minority only.[141]

The renewed great stress laid upon discipline in 1940 was a rather interesting phenomenon. It seemed to indicate a certain falling off of discipline among the soldiers, resulting from the purge of 1937, as well as the clear realization on the part of military authorities of the importance of enhancing the prestige of commanders, weakened by the reintroduction of the commissar control in consequence of that purge. The editorial in the *Red Star* in July 1940 was typical. Its very title was significant: "For the sharp increase of exigence on the part of commanders."

The commanders had no right to remain indifferent, wrote the army newspaper, even to the slightest infringement of the order imposing the obligation of the military salute upon subordinates.[142] This new feature of military courtesy had made its appearance in the Soviet army in June 1940,[143] introduced by order of Marshal Timoshenko, then Commissar of Defense. It was itself an outward manifestation of the effort to bolster up the authority of commanders.

Another editorial in the *Red Star* had emphasized that "without discipline there is no army. The more numerous the army, the more it is permeated with technical means, the stronger must be the discipline in all cells of the army organism." It insisted on the strictest order in all matters pertaining to barrack and garrison duties, and thundered against commanders inclined to pat the delinquent soldier on the shoulder. "For the commander to be exacting and strict fully coincides with the common patriotic task of fighters and commanders to strengthen the armed forces of the Soviet State."[144]

It went even further: "Those inclined to regard the insistence on a firm discipline and execution of orders, carried to the point of automatism, as standing in some pseudo-contradiction to the class affinity and the ideological proximity of commanders and soldiers, do not understand the substance of Soviet military discipline," wrote the newspaper.[145]

That all was not well in the field of disciplinary relations between commanders and soldiers is exemplified by a number of items that appeared in the columns of the Soviet army newspaper in 1940. For instance, it was reported in July of that year that the commanding officer of a battery had reprimanded one of the junior commanders. The latter objected: "Have you any right to give me directions? I am a Komsomol, while you are a non-party person." The commentary of the newspaper is even more significant: "Such a fact of unbridled conduct on the part of a Komsomol could have occurred only under conditions in which the party and Komsomol organizations interfere in the functions of commanders."[146]

The *Red Star* bluntly stated in July 1940 that in one of the army units recently endless criticism directed at commanders on various counts was in evidence at meetings not only of the party, but even of the Komsomol organizations. There was a tendency to issue orders indirectly to commanders by the party organizations. There was also a tendency to insist that commanders should report on their work to party collectives. The secretary of one such collective even had given directions to a commander, told off to present such a report, as to what it should contain.[147]

In the light of this information, the great effort made by Marshal Timoshenko to restore the authority of commanders, so badly affected by the purge, appears in its true light. It was an urgently needed measure and, as a major war was obviously threatening, every consistent step had to be taken to ensure this authority.

That this reappearance of direct party interference in the work of commanders was the direct result of the purge will become clear from discussion under the next subheading.

It is, however, only fair to say that there was ample evidence that the commanding personnel, despite its new ranks, gold braid and well-tailored clothes, continued to maintain close relationship with the soldiers in the ranks. A correspondence from the Kiev military district depicts, for instance, a commander of a group of batteries (*division*) chatting freely with the kitchen police detail, engaged in peeling potatoes, and discussing with them all kinds of topics from the technique of potato-peeling up. The same commander made it a point to address the meeting of his soldiers at least once a month on some important topic of current events.[148]

The tendency, so often in evidence in the western armies, to leave the task of training of soldiers to non-commissioned officers had also reared its head in the Soviet Union. "Commanders, appointed to conduct studies of soldiers, often hand over that work to their subordinates." In the company commanded by a junior lieutenant, regulations were studied under the guidance of soldiers insufficiently prepared for that task.[149] These are of course "self-criticism" items. How widespread the tendency actually was, it is impossible to judge from the material examined.

The opinion expressed by Ambassador Davies regarding the Red Army commanders is well worth quoting, as his adviser in military matters, Colonel Philip Faymonville, knew a great deal about the Red Army and did not permit any prejudice to stand in the way of his informed judgment. In his Brief on the Facts, Mr. Davies stated that the officers were considered to be of an excellent quality among the junior commanders,* and to be fair in capacity so far as higher command was concerned. Also that it was generally considered that the liquidation of the older and experienced generals during the purge had weakened the army "very materially." In his own view, as well as in that of Colonel Faymonville, this view, while "measurably true, is much exaggerated."[150]

In his Note on the Red Army, Ambassador Davies says that in 1937 the typical Red Army officer's military qualifications for the command of smaller units were considered excellent, but that "his qualifications for higher command were yet to be tested." The purge, the Ambassador was told, had resulted in the promotion of many of the younger officers who, while lacking in the experience of their predecessors, probably made up for it in greater energy and devo-

* This is not meant in the technical Red Army sense, but merely to indicate younger officers.

tion and loyalty to the government. "It was also said that these changes had resulted in a feeling of greater security on the part of the average soldier and the belief that his fate was now in the hands of more trustworthy and loyal officers than the 'Trotskyite traitors who had met a deserved fate.' "[151]

Even a cursory glance at the reports on the encounters with the Japanese troops during the so-called "border incidents" and on those of the Russo-Finnish War I, reveals the impressive record of devotion to duty and remarkable steadfastness under fire on the part of Soviet commanders. To mention only the instance of Junior Lieutenant Kuliagin, who, wounded in the throat and at the knee, got out of the burning tank its whole personnel, under violent machine-gun fire.[152]

With the conclusions recorded by Ambassador Davies regarding the younger commanders this writer has no quarrel. As to the greater security, etc. felt by the soldiers after the replacement of the commanders purged, one may remark that there is nothing on record to show that any apprehension had existed among them on that count before the purge. As to the higher commanders and their aptitude to lead large army units in the field, the situation does not seem to be so simple as to lend itself to this somewhat derogatory conclusion. In peacetime, it is exceedingly difficult for an outsider to establish whether the person concerned really possesses the necessary qualifications for troop leadership on a large scale. In the early days of the French Revolution, who was there to predict accurately whose names were to be written on the tablets recording the glory of France in those wars? By what standard is the ability of the Red generals to be measured?

Undoubtedly, the Red Army has among its generals many men of talent and sufficient military knowledge to provide highly successful leadership of the higher order. Whether the right persons will be chosen, only the future will tell.

The selection of Marshal Shaposhnikov for his important position seems to be an indication that personal merit expressed in military professional terms does guide the Soviet Government in the choice of the incumbents of the most important army posts, as does also the selection of Timoshenko and Zhukov.

The Great Army Purge

Mr. Walter Duranty in his *The Kremlin and the People* has recorded that he was told that the "Generals' " execution had struck the whole Soviet nation like a thunderbolt.[153] He also stated that the military abroad were shocked by the sudden ruthlessness of this affair, which had undoubtedly created the belief in their minds that the loyalty and the discipline of the Red Army must have been gravely impaired.[154]

Ambassador Davies did not share this latter view, and wrote to Mr. Early on July 4, 1937, that "it now looks as though the loyalty of the army to the Stalin government has not been weakened."[155]

The execution of eight high-ranking Soviet generals, which had made such a deep impression on public opinion both in Russia and abroad, was announced in the Moscow *Pravda* in its June 12, 1937, issue. The editorial, headed: "For Espionage and Treason to the Fatherland—Execution by Shooting," told the startled Muscovites that the Supreme Court in its Special Judiciary Session had rendered the verdict of guilty—of violating the military oath, of treason to the Red Army, and of treason to the Fatherland—in the cases of eight of the important leaders of the Soviet armed forces. All of them were condemned to loss of their military rank and the "highest measure of criminal punishment"—death by shooting. The sentence was carried out.[156]

These eight men were: the former Deputy People's Commissar of Defense, Marshal M. N. Tukhachevskii; the commanding generals of the military districts, I. E. Iakir and I. P. Uborevich; the head of the War College, A. I. Kork; the deputy commanding general of the military district, V. M. Primakov; the head of the Administration of Commanding Personnel, B. M. Feldman; the former Soviet Military Attaché to Great Britain, G. K. Putna; and the president of the Central Council of the Osoaviakhim, R. P. Eideman.[157]

Another former Deputy People's Commissar of Defense, Jan Gamarnik, who had headed the PUR, the organ charged with vigilance over the loyalty of the Red Army, had committed suicide, according to the official announcement, when faced with arrest. He was called by Voroshilov, whose deputy he was, "traitor and coward."[158]

The positions held by these generals in the army, particularly those of Tukhachevskii and Eideman, and the rôle of Gamarnik, as the party's trusted watch-dog over the army, made these executions and "suicide" of tremendous significance.

Voroshilov, in his order of June 12, 1937, stated that the Military Council attached to the People's Commissar of Defense had sat from June 1 to 4, jointly with members of the government, to hear and to discuss Voroshilov's report about the "treacherous, counter-revolutionary military fascist organization" which had secretly conspired to undermine the Red Army and had for a long time conducted "dastardly crippling, wrecking and espionage work in the Red Army."[159]

The ultimate aim of "that band" was to liquidate "at any cost and by any means" the Soviet order in Russia, to annihilate the Soviet Government and to restore in the U.S.S.R. the "yoke of the landowners and industrialists."[160]

Those executed were accused of preparing the murder of the leaders of the party and government, of conducting all kinds of sabotage activities in the field of national economy and national defense; also of attempts to injure the strength of the Red Army and of preparing its defeat in the future war. It was explained that through these activities, as well as the conduct of military operations in the war, the nine dead leaders were expecting to secure the defeat of the Red Army at the front and to bring about the downfall of the Soviet Government. In this work, they were looking for help from "their bosses," the military fascist circles of "one of the foreign states," and were ready to surrender the Soviet Ukraine in payment for that assistance, thus breaking asunder the U.S.S.R.[161]

The army magazine, specializing in party military matters, *The Communist of the Red Army* (*Kommunist RKKA*) had further elaborated these accusations by writing that the executed military leaders were in the service of the military intelligence of a foreign government and had supplied its "military circles" with information regarding the state of the Soviet military forces.[162]

It was explained that the group of convicted military leaders was able to conduct its work without being detected for many years because of "political carelessness" on the part of the political workers of the party and especially of those connected with the PUR, as well as the overlooking by these of the "laws of the class struggle." As a preventive measure, for the future, it was recommended that party organizations and the political workers of the army should inculcate all soldiers and commanders of the armed forces with "a revolutionary vigilance" of such a high level that they would be able to ferret out enemies regardless of protective coloring."[163]

"Criticism and self-criticism" at meetings, and the energetic correction of all shortcomings in party work which were revealed at party conferences were suggested as the best means to that end.[164]

The execution of the eight generals was merely the opening of the mass purge of the Soviet armed forces. The material examined does not permit one to state definitely how many members of the commanding personnel were executed or imprisoned during that purge. Among those who disappeared were: the Deputy Commissar of Defense, Marshal Egorov; head of the military aviation Army Commander Alksnis and the following commanders of military districts: Dybenko, Belov, Gailit, Garkavyi, Griaznov, Kuibyshev, Kashirin. The two leading naval commanders, Orlov and Viktorov, shared the same fate. The Commander of the Far Eastern Red Banner Front, Marshal Bluecher, perhaps the most popular, and one of the ablest of the high Commanders of the Red Army, who had risen from the ranks during the Civil War, also disappeared, and his fate is unknown.[165]

The People's Commissar of the Navy, Smirnov, also vanished. A fairly competent commentator stated that of the fifteen commanders of armies who were appointed in 1935, only one, S. Kamenev, died a natural death, one was still enjoying his high position, while all the others were declared "traitors" and "mad dogs," falling victims to the purge.[166]

Boris Souvarine, in his *Stalin*, stated that there had perished or disappeared without publicity in 1938 almost all the eighty members of the Council of War, formed in 1934 to assist the Commissar of Defense. He gives a long list of the highest army commanders who had disappeared, and wrote that it was estimated in the U.S.S.R. that more than thirty thousand of the commanding personnel of the army and navy fell under the scythe of the purge.[167]

E. Wollenberg, who is in a position to know a great deal about the causes of the army purge, asserts that throughout Soviet society and all its organizations there ran the ideological cleavage between the supporters of Soviet democracy and "those of the autocratic line" —between the internationalists, who were "seeking their allies among the workers of the world and the oppressed colonial races and the Soviet Union patriots who desire to yoke the U.S.S.R. to the wagon of a group of imperialist powers." Wollenberg went on to say: "This cleavage does not spare the Red Army."[168]

According to Wollenberg, Stalin "turned around and crushed the Soviet democratic internationalist opposition within the Red Army." He traced the roots of the immediate causes of the army purge to the Piatakov trial when "Radek purchased his own life by betraying the fact that Tuchachevsky, Gamarnik and their associates belonged to the Communist opposition." Moreover, Stalin and Voroshilov had a score to settle with Tukhachevskii, which dated from the days of the Civil War and the Polish campaign.[169]

Dr. Michael T. Florinsky, in his *Toward an Understanding of the U.S.S.R.*, estimates that for the Communist party as a whole (for the U.S.S.R. only), the purge involved the expulsion of some 466,000 members or almost 25 per cent of their total number in 1934, and of 516,000 candidates, or over 50 per cent of their total number in the same year.[170]

A fairly competent writer states that of the 71 members elected to the Central Committee of the party at the XVIIth party congress, nine were executed, twelve declared "enemies of the people" and probably executed, and twenty-four "disappeared." From 68 candidates for membership in the Central Committee, 14 were executed, two had committed suicide at the time of arrest, 9 were declared enemies of the people and 34 disappeared.[171]

In other words: What was going on in the Red Army was part and parcel of the general political situation within the Communist party in Russia. To understand the purge of the army one has to comprehend the roots of the general political crisis within the Communist party during that period.

Wollenberg says that "according to reliable sources of information" there actually was a plan for a "palace revolution" and the overthrow of Stalin dictatorship "by forcible means" and that the Red Army was assigned a decisive rôle in the execution of this plan, which was to be carried out under the leadership of Tukhachevskii and Gamarnik.[172]

Radek, at his trial, definitely mentioned Putna as one of the conspirators, but stated that Tukhachevskii had no idea of Putna's or his own "criminal rôle." Radek solemnly confirmed that he never had and would not have had "any dealings with Tukhachevsky connected with counter-revolutionary activities," because he knew Tukhachevskii's attitude to the party and the government to be that of an absolutely devoted man.[173]

Wollenberg states that these hints, however veiled, had influenced the conspirators to set the date of the "palace revolution" for the middle of May. Stalin, however, acted quickly and arrested not only Tukhachevskii but also "several hundred officers of high rank" in the early weeks of May. Some of those arrested, notably Petrovskii and Dubovoi, were promptly shot.[174]

What the actual plans and motives of the executed army leaders were, it is impossible to establish from the documents examined. Walter Duranty's *The Kremlin and the People*, and the volume by Ambassador Davies contain a great deal of interesting material on this matter. For the purposes of this study it will suffice to say that a conflict of major importance had arisen between a large section of the Red Army leaders and Stalin's group, and that the roots of this conflict were to be found not only in the army but in the Communist party at large. It is also important to note that the party machinery installed to insure the loyalty of the army to the régime had failed to function as was intended. The head of the PUR was apparently involved in the conflict on the side of the conspiring commanding personnel against the ruling Kremlin group. In other words, the situation of 1924, when the PUR had sided with the opposition against the majority of the Central Committee of the party, had, in a measure, repeated itself. In this manner, in the two major crises, the party control organ not only failed to perform its task, but actually was found on the opposite side.

One of the immediate consequences of the purge was the opening of numerous vacancies among the upper strata of command positions of the armed forces. This meant, of course, rapid promotion for those who had survived the purge and were not among the suspect.

As one of the outstanding examples, one might cite N. G. Kuznetsov, who was appointed to command the Pacific Fleet at the age of thirty-six. He was a graduate of the Naval School, Class of 1927.[175]

In the navy, 278 junior commanders were promoted to "leading command and political work" in the "three to four months" preceding February 1938. A lieutenant who had entered the Naval School in 1933, was given the command of a submarine. A senior lieutenant, graduated in 1933, was given the command of a submarine flotilla. A commander, graduated in 1938, was appointed to command another submarine. The chief-of-staff of the Baltic Fleet, Tributs, had graduated from the Naval School in 1930.[176]

In the army, among those promoted to the rank of brigadier early in 1939, there were three aviators, Rychagov, Proskurov and Eremenko, who in 1937 had the rank of senior lieutenant.[177]

Wollenberg wrote in 1939 that the purge had affected the higher levels of the commanding personnel much more severely than the lower groups of commanders, letting the latter off more leniently. As a result, the higher command posts and the army staffs were filled with "inexperienced youths." Companies were commanded by junior lieutenants, officers of the same ranks occupied the posts of the battalion chief-of-staff. To fill in the gaps, students of military schools (about 10,000) were in 1938 promoted in June, instead of at the usual October date.[178]

As the higher ranks were filled with the participants of the Civil War, the purge meant the elimination of a large number of commanders who had made their way up because of their revolutionary past and who had received only a scanty general education. In this respect, the purge had, partly at least, solved one of the fundamental contradictions of the Red Army—that between the requirements for educated military leaders set up by the mechanization of the army equipment and the modernization of its armaments, and the low general cultural level of a large part of its highest and senior commanding personnel.

The editorial of the periodical dedicated to party-political work in the army asserted in its February 1939 issue that in accordance with a directive of Stalin the Red Army leaders' posts in the command, political and administrative personnel were filled by "thousands of young, talented commanders and political workers."[179]

It seems that a deliberate attempt was made to set up the lower ranks of the commanding personnel and the N.C.O.'s against the higher, and to use this cleavage for the control of the army. Thus, the new head of the PUR, L. E. Mekhlis, speaking at the meeting of the party active workers of the Moscow Military District, accused his predecessor, Gamarnik, and his assistant, Bulin, of deliberately slowing up promotion of "a numerous army of junior and middle commanders and political personnel." He said that in the past "only a narrow circle of men" were rapidly promoted, and promised that under the direction of the Central Committee of the party and Marshal Voroshilov everything would be done "to lift that detachment to the height it deserves."[180]

The sharp reduction in the age limits for active service of commanding personnel, as mentioned above, accelerated still further the influx of younger men into the senior command ranks. The creation of the rank of junior lieutenant and its equivalents opened the officers' posts to the N.C.O.'s on a large scale, stimulating the latter's ambitions and making the purge a path for their advancement.

This process had affected the Civil War veterans in a way not unlike that which befell the ex-czarist officers during the post-Civil War reorganization of the army. They had ceased to be the most important element of the commanding personnel, although individual representatives of their group retained some of the most important positions in the armed forces.

The marshal's baton thus again came within the range of ambition of the young men of the army with the destruction of that upper crust of the Civil War veterans. This, no doubt, released tremendous new forces and precipitated a great struggle for advancement, as long as the established routine of promotion was broken up.

As Wollenberg claims, the purge had opened a golden era for careerists bent on making their way up. He says that the Soviet press contained expressions of disgust with commanders who had resorted to anonymous denunciations of their immediate superiors in order to move into their places.[181]

The incident of the commissar of the Leningrad Military Signal School, Rybkin, is typical. He was accused of having taken part in banquets with some of the purged commanders and of having occupied a place of honor at these functions. This was sufficient for the army newspaper to raise a hue and cry against Rybkin, accusing him of laxity in "liquidating the consequences of sabotage."[182]

The case of Lieutenant Kormstchikov is also characteristic. He was expelled from the party as "obviously unfit" because someone had unearthed the fact that a distant relative of his wife was formerly a clergyman.[183]

The mutual fear and suspicion which followed in the wake of the purge unfavorably affected discipline, and a great deal of ground was lost in this respect.

In some units the burden of maintaining discipline fell entirely upon the shoulders of the commissars. The army newspaper describes the situation in one of such units: the commander had made it a practice to report to the commissar every infraction of discipline in the unit. When discussing a misdemeanor in one of the sections, the commissar asked the junior commander in charge of it to explain why he permitted this to occur. The latter was astonished that anyone should hold him responsible for the maintenance of discipline in his section, and answered: "In what way does that concern me?"[184]

When three junior commanders of the same unit committed an infringement of discipline, the commander of the unit did not dare to inflict punishment and merely reported the matter to the commissar.[185]

A correspondent from the Ural Military District described the state of affairs in a unit where soldiers knew that they would escape punishment for disorderly conduct and infringements of discipline while on duty, that their company commander would overlook these infringements. Even at drill, after the command "Attention!" soldiers continued to laugh, talk and nudge each other, the sergeant-major looking on without making any attempt to stop this unmilitary behavior.[186]

These items, of course, belong to the "self-criticism" category. But they began to appear when those in charge of military affairs had clearly realized that it was impossible to permit things to continue the way they were going, since the purge, and that the prestige of the commanding personnel and army discipline had to be restored.

The reintroduction of the commissars, which had accompanied the purge, meant a complete reversal of the trend toward the unity of command. It placed the communist proletarian commanders in the position in which the ex-czarist officers found themselves during the Civil War. The details of this development will be examined under the next subheading. One instance, however, may be mentioned here to illustrate the situation in which commanders found themselves under the tutelage of the newly appointed commissars, who sometimes were utterly ignorant in military matters. During maneuvers in the Trans-Caucasian Military District one of the commanders had ordered his men to open fire upon the still invisible attacking "enemy." The commissar, upon hearing the command, immediately gave the order to cease firing "since it is impossible to fire upon an invisible target." Only the interference of one of the umpires, who happened to pass by, saved the commander from the accusation of being a saboteur.[187]

Speaking at the XVIIIth Party Congress, Voroshilov took notice of the opinion in the capitalist countries that the purge had greatly weakened the Red Army. He pointed to the achievements of the First Autonomous Red Banner Army in the Far East in action against the Japanese during the so-called "border incidents" (which really were battles on a large scale), as definite proof of the high combat efficacy of the Soviet armed forces and the excellent condition of the commanding and political personnel.[188]

The western world remained unconvinced, and the course of events during the first phase of the Russo-Finnish campaign served to strengthen still further the view that the purge had seriously weakened the Red Army.

It is exceedingly difficult to appraise the influence of the purge on the combat efficacy of the Soviet armed forces. The opinion of the U.S. Military Attaché in the U.S.S.R., then Colonel Faymonville, as reported by Ambassador Davies, was already mentioned above.[189]

In his letter to Mr. Sumner Welles of July 10, 1937, Ambassador Davies stated that there were many indications that France had lost faith in the power of her Russian ally and that he was impressed in England by the general feeling that England would be in a sad state if she had to rely on France with her internal weakness and on Russia "under the present conditions."[190]

To what extent, both in France and England, the news of the purge was seized upon, exaggerated and exploited by those bent on appeasement, is an open question. It would seem, however, that Ambassador Davies' conclusion, that the Red Army in 1937 was neither as strong as before the purge nor as weak after it as was supposed, comes near the mark.[191]

Marshal Timoshenko's energetic and intelligent work in rebuilding the discipline and improving the tactical training of the army in the months preceding Hitler's attack upon Soviet Russia had an excellent effect. Did it entirely compensate for the disruption caused by the purge and the loss of many talented military leaders? Was the decimated military intelligence service of Soviet Russia sufficiently rebuilt to render the same quality of service as before? These questions will have to be answered by future military historians who will find access to Soviet military archives. At present it is impossible to offer an evaluation based on sufficient authentic evidence.

Commissars

The political personnel of the armed forces shared with the commanders in the improvement of their material situation. Simultaneously with commanders, they were officially professionalized. The decree of September 22, 1935, established for them nine graduated ranks, corresponding to those of the commanders.

The lowest rung of the hierarchical ladder for the political workers of the army comprised within the commanding personnel was the *politruk* (political director). It was followed by the senior *politruk,* the battalion commissar and the regimental commissar, the division commissar, the army corps commissar, and the commissar of the army of the 2nd and that of the 1st rank.[192]

At the time the rank of the junior lieutenant was created, there was also established that of the junior *politruk*. It was provided that persons appointed to that rank were to be selected from the junior commanding and political personnel, as well as *from the Red Army private soldiers* not possessing an education equivalent to that given by the military political schools. These junior *politruks* were to remain for two years in their rank prior to promotion to that of *politruk*.[193]

The rank of junior *politruk* was established in order to fill the gaps among the political workers of the armed forces, thinned out by the purge. The fact that private soldiers, not possessing a high level of general education, could be appointed to that rank is well worth while noting. This opened a path to positions of power to active Communists who were not sufficiently educated to enter the ranks of commanders or political commanding personnel under normal circumstances.

The most important measure of the period which had radically affected the status and authority of the political personnel of the armed forces was introduced by the decree of May 10, 1937, which re-established the collegiate principle in the administration of the military districts and reintroduced the institute of military commissars in all units from regiment up, as well as in staffs, administrative offices, etc., regardless of whether the respective commanders were placed in the category of "single command" or not.[194]

The command of the military district (fleet or army) was entrusted to military councils, consisting of the commander of the troops of the district, and two members of the council. The commander of the troops was to preside at meetings of the council. All troops, administrative offices, etc., in the territory of the district were subordinated to the *council*, and not to the commander of the troops.[195]

The councils of the military districts were directly subordinated to the People's Commissar for Defense. Their province of activity was defined as comprising: the direction of the combat and political training of the troops of the district (fleet, army), mobilizational preparation of the troops, of the means of transport and the means of communication; the study and selection of the commanding personnel of the troops and administrative offices; the education of soldiers and the commanding personnel in the spirit of unrestrained loyalty to the fatherland and the Soviet Government, as well as "in the spirit of relentless struggle with the enemies of the people—with spies, diversionists and saboteurs"; supplies, sanitary and veterinary arrangements; anti-aircraft defenses, including the supervision of civil defense institutions and organizations; the directions of pre-army military training; of draft board activities, also the guidance of all defense construction work and of the civil participation in the work of strengthening the rear of the armed forces. In other words: all functions of direction and supervision of military activity, as well as civilian work pertaining to defense were placed again in the hands of a collegium of three persons, of whom only one was necessarily a trained military man.[196]

All orders emanating from the Council were to be signed by the commander of the troops, one of the other members of the Council and the chief-of-staff of the district. However, these orders were to be issued in the name of the commander of the troops of the district in the first person singular, "as he was the military superior of all the troops of the district and administrative offices in the territory of the district (fleet, army)."[197]

The statute of military commissars was approved by decree of August 15, 1937.

The first paragraph of this statute provided that the commissars were appointed for the direction and the immediate carrying out of party-political work in the units of the armed forces, military schools and administrative offices. The actual appointment of commissars to their posts was to be made by the People's Commissar for Defense upon recommendation of the PUR.[198]

Both the commissar and the commander were to share in the full responsibility for the education of the soldiers and members of the commanding personnel in the spirit of unrestrained loyalty to the fatherland and the Soviet Government and "the unmerciful struggle with the people's enemies." Jointly with the commander, the commissar was co-equally responsible for the politico-moral condition of his unit, for the strict carrying out of military duties by its personnel and the maintenance of military discipline by it; also for combat, operational and mobilizational readiness, and for the condition of the armament and military property belonging to the unit.[199]

The fourth paragraph is quite significant. It lays upon the commissar, jointly with the commander, the duty of protecting the unit from infiltration by the "people's enemies" (spies, diversionists, saboteurs), bringing "immediately and decisively" to a halt all actions that could harm the Red Army.[200]

The precise carrying out by members of the unit of all orders and instructions pertaining to the safeguarding of military secrets was made the duty of the commissar. He was to give personally an example in this respect and to use all possible means to heighten the feeling of responsibility by all members of the unit with regard to preservation of military secrets.[201]

The commissar was to study "every day and from every angle" the personnel of the unit, and was to know their moods, their needs and requirements.[202]

In the field of party-political work, the commissar was to direct the activities of the political organs, of the party and Komsomol organizations in line with instructions to that effect. He was to organize, as well as carry out, all party-political measures necessary for guaranteeing the "undeviating carrying out" of plans and tasks in the field of combat and political training of the unit, as well as of all forms of the soldiers' volunteer activity. The duty of maintaining contact with the local party organizations was also the province of the commissar.[203]

The commissar was instructed to strive to perfect his military knowledge "so that he could successfully execute his duties." At the same time it was ordained that the military training of the political personnel was the duty of the commissar jointly with the commander.[204]

The commissar was to keep the commander posted "systematically in accordance with regulations" as to the politico-moral conditions of the unit and of measures taken to combat "undesirable phenomena." The same task devolved upon him with respect to passing this information to the higher-standing commissar and the political organs.[205]

The attestation (the service record) of the commanding personnel was to be prepared by the commissar jointly with the commander of the unit, while the "detailed political characterization" of each member of the commanding personnel was left entirely to him. The attestation was to be signed by the commander and the commissar.[206]

Appointments and recommendations for promotion to the next rank, as well as the transfers of the commanding personnel, were to be executed by the commander and the commissar jointly.[207]

The commissar's activities were to be regulated by orders and instructions of the People's Commissar for Defense, by those of the PUR, as well as by orders and instructions of the military councils, military commissars and political organs to which they were subordinated.[208]

All orders were to be signed jointly by the commander and by the commissar.[209]

The Internal Service Regulations of 1937 provided that the regimental commissar was the superior officer for the entire personnel of the regiment, co-equally with the regimental commander. In the same manner, the company *politruk* (political director) was the superior officer for the entire personnel of his company co-equally with the company commander. He was made responsible for the politico-moral conditions as well as for combat training, discipline and the safekeeping of military secrets. The *politruk* was to prepare the attestations for the commanding personnel of the company jointly with its commander.[210]

On the rung of the hierarchical ladder below that of the *politruk* was placed the "platoon chief," who was subordinated immediately to the commissar and whose task was to organize the voluntary political and general cultural educational work centering around the regimental club. The care of the club premises and equipment was also entrusted to him.[211]

With the new important duties and responsibilities bestowed upon the political personnel, the need for a better general education of its members became even more urgent than heretofore. However, only as late as 1940 were the requirements for admission to military political schools raised to the eight to ten grades of secondary school education, with a military education requirement corresponding to that given by the regimental N.C.O.'s schools. This against the six grades required before.[212]

Strangely enough, even in 1940 the political reading requirements included only the *Brief History of the Russian Communist Party* and the *Red Army Man's Political Textbook*, plus a few of Lenin's writings such as *The State and the Revolution* and *Imperialism as the Highest Stage of Capitalism*, as well as Stalin's report at the XVIIIth party congress.[213]

In other words, not one writing of Marx or Engels was included in this obligatory reading list.

Admission requirements for the Military Political College were also changed. The candidates were to have general education equivalent to a full secondary school and a military training equal to that given by the normal military school. The political training was to be on the level supplied by the military political schools. Heretofore eight grades of general education were required and a merely elementary acquaintance with military matters, as well as a "comparatively restricted" political knowledge.[214]

To be admitted to the military political schools, the candidates from 1940 on had to have practical experience in party-political work equivalent to that of the *politruk* or the secretary of the unit's party bureau.[215]

The *Red Star*, in commenting on this reform of military political education, remarked editorially that some of the leaders of political organs took steps to prevent the ablest and best prepared from entering the political schools and colleges, sending instead those with the lesser education and inferior ability. These leaders were anxious to retain in their units the better men for work there. This was held up as an example of an "anti-state" attitude to be combatted energetically.[216]

The same trend, it will be recalled, made its first appearance in the Red Army as early as in the days of the Command Courses of the Civil War period. It had failed to disappear during the score of years that had passed since and had retained enough vitality to deserve to be singled out editorially by the leading army newspaper in 1940.

It is important to note that up to the very eve of Hitler's attack on Soviet Russia, the schools for the political personnel continued to be recruited from the ranks of persons with an inferior general and military education, although these persons were placed, upon graduation, in positions of what amounted to control over the actions of commanders. This feature of an insufficiently high cultural and military educational level of political personnel undoubtedly made for additional complications and difficulties in a situation already complex.

What was the cause of this deficiency? Either the better educated youths were not attracted to the political career in the army, or, perhaps, the government preferred to have during the crisis period persons without high educational qualifications in the army political personnel. Possibly it saw in the advancement of persons without high educational qualifications an instrument of control of the party organization in the army, distributing to the faithful plums in the political service according to their loyalty and not in accord with their military and general training.

Voroshilov, speaking at the XVIIIth Party Congress, remarked that the creation of the institution of military commissars, or rather, its universal reintroduction, was made necessary "by the constantly growing cultural and political demands of the fighters," as well as by the numerical increase and the growth of the technical equipment of the army.[217]

It is difficult to say in what way the poorly educated political personnel could better satisfy the needs of the soldiers whose education had advanced to a higher level. Further remarks by Voroshilov—that the commander and the commissar "are one whole" in the work of guiding combat and political training and education of their unit and are both responsible for its condition as well as "will lead the unit into action"[218]—made clear that the leadership in combat was also a part of the commissar's duties.

The reform amounted to the following: a person with an inferior military education and experience was given equal responsibility with the commander possessing a better military training and experience. That Voroshilov himself was aware of the cultural and military shortcomings of the political personnel was shown in the same speech. He stressed the fact that the commissar's duties include the care that "political workers correspond to their high commission" and that "their political literacy and general cultural level . . . should always be at the proper level."[219]

The growth in numbers of the political personnel was very rapid. In the period from 1934 to 1939 it had increased from about 15,000 to 34,000, or by 126 per cent.[220] During the Civil War, in November 1918 there were only 6,389 political workers in the army.[221]

As the rapid increase of the political personnel was particularly marked after 1937, one could possibly say that the purge had resulted in the doubling of its numbers.

As late as 1940, the *Red Star* wrote that it was of the greatest importance for the political leaders of the army to make a persistent effort to master military knowledge. "Political workers not possessing sufficient military training would not be able really to direct the combat training of the unit." It was suggested that each political worker, from the *politruk* up, should acquire military information "at least of the level provided for in the abbreviated program of the military schools."[222]

Apparently political workers were not even sufficiently acquainted with the army regulations; the leading army newspaper said that it was not sufficient merely to understand the regulations—the regulations must be well known.[223]

In spite of the apparent insufficiency of military knowledge, the interference of political workers in purely military matters was far-reaching. The *Red Star*, for instance, urged that whenever a unit was scheduled to proceed to the range for target practice, the *politruk's* duty was to check whether everything was in readiness for this. On the eve of tactical exercises, the commissar was supposed to check carefully all preparations and to correct immediately all shortcomings.[224]

In spite of the dual control, or perhaps because of it, instances had occurred of a company leaving for the range without being issued cartridges for the target practice.[225]

The political personnel included in 1940 about 15,000 acting *politruki* and assistant *politruki* who were not full-fledged party members. They were recruited from the Komsomols. One could, therefore, visualize a situation where a Komsomol acting as *politruk* would be placed in charge of political control of a company and would share equally with the company commander in the responsibility and control of the training of that company.[226]

Even in purely political matters, the guidance of the political personnel was not always on a very high level. To quote a few instances: a group leader conducting political training studies with soldiers, defined "class" as "exploitation of man above [sic] man," adding "of big over small."[227] The PUR had issued a special instruction regarding political studies for soldiers and junior commanders for the year 1939-1940. The *Red Star* cites the instance of a unit where even the Communists and Komsomols were not well acquainted with the contents of that instruction, which was not discussed at party and Komsomol meetings.[228]

Under these circumstances one is inclined to think that the desire to meet the demands of better educated soldiers had nothing at all to do with the reintroduction of military commissars.

A competent although not an impartial commentator, N. Garvi, wrote in 1937 that the return from the single command system to the collegiate form of command was dictated by the lack of confidence of Stalin in the political loyalty of the commanding personnel and by the necessity of strengthening the control of the party over the commanders and the "politico-moral" condition of the army masses. And the party, by that time, was being purged of opposition elements.[229]

Voroshilov himself spoke in 1939 of the task of the political organs of the armed forces being considerably increased in connection with the purging of "traitors" and "spies." The political personnel itself, said Voroshilov, was "considerably renewed" (purged) and thousands of "remarkable young men" were moved up to fill the various responsible positions. These young men, together with party organizations and *with the support of the honest non-party Red Army men,** commanders and other members of the commanding personnel "had, with an iron broom" cleansed the army of traitors.[230]

As the young junior commanders and the younger element among the commanders were set against the Civil War veterans, here also the Komsomol junior political workers and the younger Communists were made the bulwark of the government power and opposed to the old party members in the political service. This accent on youth of the lower ranks was characteristic of the period. That the new head of the PUR, Lev Mekhlis, was appointed to his position from the editorial chair of the *Pravda* and had had no connection with the army since

---

* The italics are the author's.

the days of the Civil War, is also typical of the reorganization of the political personnel. Mekhlis was promoted directly to the rank of Commissar of the Army of the 2nd rank. He removed from their posts the two Deputy Chiefs of the PUR—Bulin and Osepian—and, together with many other officials of the PUR, handed them over to the NKVD (Commissariat of Interior Affairs to which OGPU—the dreaded Soviet Secret Police—had been subordinated since 1934),[231] making a clean sweep of the directing personnel of the PUR.

The *Red Star* wrote in 1939 that Trotsky and his followers, who had for a long time occupied higher posts in the party and the government, had done a considerable amount of work "to weaken the army cadres, to demoralize them and to make them a political instrument of their counter-revolutionary work." Stalin was said to be giving a great deal of his time to the reorganization of the political machinery of the army, to repair the damage caused by these Trotskyists.[232]

These references seem to establish a definite link between the purging of opposition elements from the party and the shooting of the generals and the army purge in general. Chronologically, the destruction of the opposition elements in the party-political apparatus of the army had lagged somewhat behind the party purge.

The difficulties of the senior members of the political personnel, including the newly appointed military commissars themselves, *vis-à-vis* the lesser members of the same personnel during the purge period, were hinted at in the several "self-criticism" items in the army newspaper. One commissar was taken to task for his suggestion to an acting *politruk* to postpone the discussion of a matter raised by the latter until the political seminar period. Another was accused of neglect of the well-being of soldiers, with charges such as disorder in the dining-room, insufficient bathing arrangement, even the fact that the soldiers did not shave themselves regularly and did not cut their hair.[233] These items, very likely, came from the pen of the commissars' subordinates.

At the Military Political College, the basic subject studied was the fundamentals of Marxism-Leninism. Dialectic materialism and historic materialism, history of the U.S.S.R., general history, military history and the history of military art, political economy, history of foreign relations of the "epoch of imperialism," history of the military policy of the U.S.S.R., and world economics, were among the subjects included in the curriculum. The evening classes of the college were greatly expanded and offered courses to thousands of party members in the army. Branches of the college were established at Leningrad, Kiev, Minsk and even in the newly occupied Lemberg. The correspondence and evening courses had thus become effective means for the bettering of the political and general education for a large section of the commissars and other members of the political personnel of the army. The graduate studies at the college helped to prepare teachers for military colleges.[234]

The Russo-Finnish War was the first serious test of the reintroduced system of dual and collegiate control.

From an examination of the numerous items in the Soviet military press relating to the events of that war, one gets the impression that the commissars and the other members of the political personnel of the army actually took upon themselves the responsibilities for military matters in action. Thus one reads of a commissar who had stopped the regimental commander wanting to take a personal part in combat, telling him: "The commander has to direct his unit. I shall go to the firing line and figure out the situation myself." A *politruk* personally leads a company in attack. A commissar directs troops in action to rebuild a destroyed bridge and then leads a charge over it.[235]

The reforms undertaken by Marshal Timoshenko, who replaced Voroshilov at the post of the People's Commissar for Defense on May 8, 1940, were interpreted by quite a few students of Soviet military affairs as an indictment of the reintroduction of the institution of military commissars and of the subsequent weakening of army discipline and organization. The reintroduction of the single-command principle, the decree on generals' and admirals' ranks, the obligatory saluting of officers by soldiers and the new Disciplinary Code—all these are phenomena furnishing ground for such a view.[236]

Walter Duranty wrote, on January 28, 1941, that "precisely what rôle the Communist party, or civilian control, or the political department, as the Russians themselves call it, should play in army affairs" was questioned. While this rôle was important, because the army is the instrument of the State, its importance could not be carried "to the extent that you have divided authority and mixed orders. In such circumstances no army can function."[237]

These discussions had culminated in the decree abolishing the system of political commissars in the Soviet armed forces on August 12, 1940.[238]

The very recent changes in the Red Army organization do not come within the scope of this study. The sudden reintroduction of commissars after Hitler's attack upon the U.S.S.R. came as a considerable surprise to students of Soviet military affairs. Its previous abandonment was so recent and seemed to be based on results of practical war experience. At present the system of dual and collegiate control in military affairs is undergoing its severest test on the plains of Russia, and only future historians will be able to determine whether its reintroduction helped or hindered the operations of the Soviet armed forces. Such violent swings of the pendulum in organizational matters of armed forces do not usually pass without leaving disturbing influences in their wake. Whether the measure was justified on political grounds is impossible to determine at present.*

The period reviewed is characterized by the change of direction of the work of the political organs of the army. Their attention was redirected from the non-party peasant soldiers, from the supervision of the Komsomol and the rank and file party organizations, to the careful and searching supervision of the commanding personnel, the majority of whom were themselves Communists. This setting up of Communists to watch Communists in command positions was one of the anomalies brought about by the struggle within the party, and the purge.

It was not sufficient any more to be a Communist. It became necessary to be a stanch follower of Stalin. Not only those actively supporting the opposition, but the lukewarm as well, had become suspect. In this manner, a conflict situation between the commanders and the political personnel, which seemed to be brought to an end by the wide application of the principle of unity of command, was revived again.

Piatnitskii's analysis, written in 1931, that the influence of the party in the army and the knowledge by the party of what was going on within it is guaranteed fully by the functioning of the political organs, as long as the "pyramid of the party stands as a monolithic and unshaken mass" and "until the party does break up,"[239] reads now like a prophecy that in case of a serious infra-party struggle the political machinery of the army would not function as it should. It actually was deemed unsatisfactory by Stalin, and its personnel was largely eliminated and replaced by other men, more loyal to Stalin.

* *The New York Times* carried on October 11, 1942 a dispatch by Mr. Ralph Parker announcing the reintroduction of unity of command principle in the Red Army.

Rank and File Communists

Admission to the party was closed from 1933 to November 1, 1936. Between 1934 and March 1, 1939, the number of party members in the U.S.S.R. had declined by 286,000, and that of candidates by 46,000.[240]

Stalin's official explanation of this measure, offered at the XVIIIth Party Congress, was that between the XVIth and XVIIth Congresses the party had accepted about 600,000 new members and that such a mass influx, under the conditions prevailing in the years 1930-1933, meant "an unhealthy and undesirable enlargement of its membership." He stressed the fact that the party knew that not only the "honest and loyal" had entered its ranks, but also careerists, attempting to exploit the position of a party member for personal advancement ends. The party purge, begun in 1933, was continued to May 1935. Originally it was decided not to take in any new members until September 1936. In fact, new members were again accepted only beginning with November 1, 1936.[241]

The bold and timely promotion of new and young cadres was particularly important, said Stalin. He remarked that "the old cadres are sometimes inclined to keep a too persistent eye on the past, to cling to the past, to stay in the old rut and fail to observe the new in life," while the young cadres "possess in abundance the sense of the new, which is a valuable quality in every bolshevik worker." The solution he offered, after serving this notice on the old cadres, was a combination, the union of the old and the new, "in one common symphony of the party and the state guiding work."[242]

In practice that meant the end of the pre-eminence of the Old Guard of the party. Between the XVIIth and XVIIIth Congresses more than 500,000 young Bolsheviks were moved up to leading party and government posts.[243]

L. Mekhlis, speaking at the same Congress, mentioned that in 1937 the Central Committee of the party had decided to accept as party members 20,000 Komsomols, serving in the army. He claimed that not only the PUR but also a number of the political departments of the military districts had resisted the efforts of the party organizations to accept Komsomols into their ranks. As a result, only 7,000 Komsomols were accepted. The entire new party membership in the army during that year amounted only to 13,158 persons. This was contrasted by Mekhlis with 1938, when 101,310 persons were accepted as members or candidates. In the month of January 1939, 10,581 persons were so accepted. This led to the reappearance of rank and file soldiers in the military party organizations in considerable numbers, in contrast to the preceding years, when party membership in the army became practically restricted to the commanding personnel.[244]

Mekhlis admitted that a large number of military Communists expelled from the party were excluded on insufficient grounds. According to him, up to 50 per cent of those excluded were reinstated by the party commissions attached to the PUR. "We have to admit that the number of persons incorrectly expelled from the party was very large," said Mekhlis.[245]

The head of the PUR pointed out that members expelled in 1935, 1936 and 1937 when "enemies" were operating in the army "here and there" were complaining of having been expelled irregularly.[246]

What he further said was most enlightening as to the party *mores* during the purge. "It is time for all of us to regard the party member in the Stalin way, not to permit the expulsion of a man on grounds of whispers in corners, and to act only on the basis of documents and facts."[247]

The number of Komsomols in the army was more than doubled since 1937. Mekhlis ascribed this to the elimination of the "conspirators," who were blocking the admission of soldiers into the Komsomol. He said that in 1938 there was not a single political worker in the PUR assigned to look after the Komsomol affairs.[248]

The new brood of the Komsomols was quite different from the old one. It included more than 150,000 men with secondary or college education. From 1938 on, Komsomols began to be appointed to the positions of acting *politruki*. These were assigned to live in the barracks with the private soldiers (i.e. they did not share the quarters occupied by the commanding personnel). According to Mekhlis these young Komsomol members of the political personnel had acquired a "tremendous ascendancy" over the soldiers, whose life and interests they learned to know well.[249]

The leaders of the Komsomol were also purged—the party-political periodical of the army wrote in January, 1939, that Kosarev and some of the other secretaries of the Central Committee of the Komsomol had attempted to shield the "enemies." The latter and "their helpers" were blamed for encouraging moral laxness among the Komsomols. In 1938, wrote the periodical, there were instances of infringement of discipline and neglect of duty by the Komsomols in the army, without the Komsomol organizations taking any serious measures to counteract such tendencies.[250]

Some of the military Komsomol organizations were even accused of treating badly those of their members who were promoted to acting and assistant *politruki*.[251]

Until Stalin's promise at the XVIIIth Party Congress that mass purges would not be resorted to any more, the atmosphere of party and Komsomol life in the army was very tense. Even the top-ranking party committee members felt insecure. In 1937, the party conference of the Leningrad military district failed to re-elect one-third of the membership of the district party committee, and N. Garvi wrote in 1937 that in the military party organizations there were apparently strong groups of opposition elements and that in a number of military districts widespread arrests of Trotskyists and right oppositionists had taken place. He considered that at that time there still existed in the Red Army "revolutionary-internationalist traditions, connected with the name of the founder of the Red Army."*[252]

Garvi was apparently right, as an article in one of the Red Army periodicals said that in 1938 "the Red Army had accomplished an enormous work" in rooting out the surviving partisans of Gamarnik and Bulin, i.e. oppositional elements.[253]

In 1937, the purge was even fiercer in the army than in 1938. This seems to be indicated by the decision of the plenary meeting of the Central Committee of the party, published in the *Red Star* on January 20, 1938. This decision ordered all party organizations to "decisively bring to an end the mass, wholesale expulsions" from the party and to establish in fact an "individualized, differentiated approach" in arriving at decisions regarding expulsions from the party or readmission of those expelled.[254]

Walter Duranty, in his version of Voroshilov's report to Stalin in 1938 on the results of the purge, ascribed to Voroshilov the following commentary: "The foundations of discipline and comradeship are crumbling. No one dares to trust his fellow, either superior or subordinate. I hear it is the same in the navy. Both forces are demoralized."[255]

That party members in the armed forces were afraid to vouch for the candidates for admission to the party is confirmed by numerous items in the *Red Star*. In 1937, a member of the bureau of the Komsomol, Lieutenant Sokolov, asked a party member to recommend him for admission to the party. The latter answered: "I am afraid to recommend you. You work well, but, just the same, I am afraid to recommend you." The newspaper commented: "There are

* i.e. Trotsky.

manifestations of petty-bourgeois cowardice on the part of a number of Communists in the matter of deciding the question of giving recommendations for admission to the party."[256]

In the same year, a correspondent from Rostov-on-Don wrote: "Some Communists refuse without any reason to give recommendations to comrades desirous of entering the ranks of the party, not because the candidates are unworthy, but only on account of being afraid "of anything happening."[257]

For 1938 we have a report that during the entire year of 1937 not a single Komsomol was admitted into the party organization of the 89th Rifle Regiment.[258]

The reason for this desire not to incur any risks by giving recommendations is clear from the information published in the army newspapers regarding the transactions of the plenary meeting of the Central Committee of the party on March 5, 1937. It said that some of the party leaders did not give sufficient heed to party members, and acted as a rule without thought: either they praised "wholesale, or castigated them by the lot," expelled members from the party "by the thousand and by the tens of thousands without measure." As the result of such "soulless treatment," dissatisfaction and anger of one section of the party was aroused against the other. Under these circumstances "careerist-Communists" did not pay any attention to the fate of other party members and were ready to expel dozens of Communists from the party although they knew that there was no ground for this, simply in order to preserve their own reputation for vigilance.[259]

As the plenary meeting referred to above took place *before* the execution of the generals, one can well imagine the still further deterioration in the relationships between party members in the army after that time. The roots of the situation may be looked for in Stalin's directive of 1933 that "revolutionary vigilance is the very quality which is particularly indispensable to the Bolsheviki." It was stressed by the *Voennyi Vestnik* in that year that the crux of the situation was in the "attentive, daily studying of each party member and candidate."[260]

The resolution of the Central Committee of the party, which had started the 1933 purge, stressed that each Communist and candidate should be tested as to whether he was ready to struggle for the general party line, whether he was disciplined and politically prepared. "There cannot be a party member who does not carry on a decisive struggle with the opportunistic agents of the class enemies," first of all with the "right opportunists," and who does not give a "merciless repulse" to the "leftist" deviation from the party line, as well as every attempt at appeasement and opportunism.[261]

That the decision of the plenum of the Central Committees of March 5, 1937, did not bring entirely to an end the unsatisfactory situation within the party in the army, some evidence for later years seems to indicate. In January 1940, for instance, it was reported that a party member was expelled on grounds of "loss of class vigilance." The district party committee, upon investigating this case, found that the only reason for expulsion was that the member's father-in-law, who had died in 1920, had served in the White army. The expelled man had actually never seen him. Another party member was expelled, because of calumny that he had never served as a candidate and had obtained his candidate's card by fraud.[262]

There was, however, a very substantial difference in the treatment of these cases as against what very likely would have occurred in 1937. Both of the expelled men were reinstated, and publicity given to that reinstatement was clearly designed to discourage other expulsions for similar reasons.

To cite one more example of mutual mistrust among the military Communists: a certain Communist, Postolnyi, was rumored to have been seen at the Red Army House at the same table with a person later purged as an "enemy of the people." He was immediately hauled before the party organization meeting and cross-examined. Postolnyi admitted that this was true and that the "enemy" had also made a call upon him at his house, although Postolnyi was out at the time, so that they did not see each other. Postolnyi was reprimanded and accused of maintaining relations with the people's enemies. At the party bureau meeting this affair took a still odder turn: Postolnyi was proved guilty of entrusting the slaughtering of a suckling pig which he had purchased to a "person obviously not looked over." He was severely reprimanded and the question was raised of dismissing him from his work. He was actually expelled and it took three months for the district party committee to reinstate him. However, an "atmosphere of mistrust" continued to dog the hapless Postolnyi, even after that rehabilitation of his party status.[263]

It is clear that members of the party in the army had been living under a great deal of tension since 1933 and that this strain had become even more pronounced after the spring of 1937. Under these circumstances Stalin's promise at the XVIIIth Congress that there would not be any more mass party purges must have brought great relief to the military Communists. At the same time, should one remember that the party group occupying the more important posts in party organizations had treated the rank and file cavalierly during the purges, one has no reason to be surprised that the decimation of these leaders after the execution of the generals did not result in any attempt at active support of them by the party rank and file in the army. Stalin, too, had occasion to assume the rôle of protector of the humbler party members against the arbitrariness of the party aristocracy.

Living under this political pressure led to an overemphasis on political work in the army. Mekhlis referred to this phenomenon, ascribing it to the sabotage of the "enemies." He said that commanders were taken away from their military work for a month at a time even during the most important periods in the training of the troops, and were put to political studies at party schools. The work of the divisional party schools was so organized that commanders and Komsomols had to neglect their military work.[264]

The Komsomol leadership had shared in the general fate of persons of importance in the Union. It was stated by the party periodical of the army in 1937 that in a number of units the active workers in the Komsomol organizations were renewed to the extent of 60 to 70 per cent.[265]

There was apparently some relaxation of discipline among the Komsomol rank and file during the purge period, as they were in a preferred position, the government looking for their support at the time. By 1940 one sees again the reappearance of admonitions to the Komsomols to become the best soldiers, to carry out garrison duties, drill, etc., in a manner to set the example to the rest of the army.[266]

There was a tendency in some units for the leaders of the party organization to neglect keeping touch with purely military matters. Thus the *Red Star* referred to a case in which the secretary of the party collective of a cavalry regiment accompanied the squadrons on a practice march on horseback for only a few kilometers and then decamped in a car to the terminal point of the march. This instance was stated to be typical for the entire regimental bureau, members of which had seldom appeared on the range, in the field during tactical exercises, in camp, in the stables, or even in the accommodations of the men in the barracks.[267]

The reading of the new brief history of the party was made an important part of political studies. Nevertheless, even full-fledged Communists in some army units had made little progress in getting acquainted with that book. Thus in one regiment 65 Communists and commanders outside the party ranks were studying the work, but hardly any of them went beyond the first few chapters. Some of the Communists had not even made a start.[268]

That this was not an exceptional case is confirmed by another item stating that many Communists, after a year's study of party history, were still unable to go beyond the fourth chapter. The blame for this inability to master the book was placed at the door of the study circles formerly in vogue, which had insufficiently developed individual initiative in work.[269]

Even a relatively simple subject, such as the new universal military service law, was beyond the powers of comprehension of some of the Communists without the help of members of the political personnel.[270]

However, the new Communists recruited in 1939 and later were of a different educational level. As the army newspaper said: "It is not at all the same kind of people the army used to get two or three years ago." In the regimental school, for instance, 90 per cent of the new draft had a full secondary education and 9 per cent were college educated. It was pointed out that these better educated youths should be regarded as promising material for party bureau membership, in line with Stalin's program of sharing the leading positions between the young and the old cadres.[271]

Colonel Makhin drew attention in his book to Stalin's speech on May 2, 1935, upon the occasion of an army review. Stalin drank a toast to militant Bolsheviki "within and without the party." He defined the Bolshevik as a person devoted body and soul to the cause of the proletarian revolution, and said that often the non-party Bolsheviki were superior to party members, and, although outside of the party, remained faithful to it to the last breath.[272]

Voroshilov, speaking in 1939, practically repeated this statement. He said that the portion of the army which was outside the party and party-affiliated groups, consisted of truly non-party Bolsheviki, whose lives belonged entirely to the Red Army and the socialist fatherland.[273]

This new attitude toward the non-party element apparently was connected with the new trend toward "soviet patriotism," which was characterized by the party political periodical of the army as being indivisible from internationalism.[274]

In 1939, more than one-half of the entire personnel of the Red Army consisted of party members or Komsomols. This against 49.3 per cent in 1935.[275] Apparently there was a slight increase of the party element in proportion to the non-party, in spite of the tremendous expansion which the army personnel had undergone in these four years. And practically all of this increase came from the ranks of the youths who had entered the army as Komsomols or even non-party element.

To sum up: in party life in the army the same phenomenon was observable during the period under review as among commanders and the political personnel. There was an influx of better educated young element, and they occupied leading positions. The party veterans were decimated during the purge and had lost their monopoly on leadership. The great influx of youths made the whole party atmosphere one of buoyancy, and helped to erase the memory of the purge. The tendency to place party and non-party people within the same brackets with respect to loyalty made for the attenuation of the conflict which at times had become acute in the preceding period. The new members owed their advancement to Stalin's policies and had no reason to be disloyal to him.

Soldiers

A new note was sounded in the matter of the political education of the army. Instead of accentuating internationalism, the proletarian revolution and the solidarity of the working class of the world, the army newspaper of January 1939 asserted editorially that the defense of the fatherland was the most sacred, the most cherished duty of a "Soviet patriot"; that love for his native land, for the country which had nurtured him, should guide the thoughts and acts of Soviet patriots.[276]

The Universal Military Service Statute of 1939 solemnly enunciated the same thought: "The defense of the fatherland," ran its second paragraph, "is the sacred duty of every citizen of the U.S.S.R." The military service obligation was called the honorable duty of all citizens of the land.[277]

Walter Duranty gives a vivid description of the wide campaign, which, he says, "began in 1935 or thereabouts" and gained in strength from year to year. As he carefully explains, the idea of international socialism and universal brotherhood of workers was not wholly abandoned "but increasing stress was laid upon the duty of each Soviet citizen to love and work for his country and fight for it when the time came."[278]

The interview given by a Polish officer in 1940 to the reporter of the Riga *Handelsblatt* described the state of mind of the Red Army men. He was able to observe it among the Soviet troops of occupation in Galicia. "These men are convinced that Soviet Russia is the most civilized country in the world . . . their consciousness is entirely dominated by the idea of the overwhelming power of the U.S.S.R. . . . 'our Red Army is invincible' they kept repeating."[279]

Stalin's speech on November 7, 1941, included sentences typical of this new attitude of looking to Russia's past history for inspiration and example in the defense of the country: "Let manly images of our great ancestors—Alexander Nevsky, Dimitry Donsky, Kusma Minin, Dimitry Pozharsky, Alexander Suvoroff, Mikhail Kutuzoff—inspire you in this war."[280] Thus the *manes* of the ancient Dukes of Russia, of Catherine the Great's military leader, of the general who fought the battle of Borodino against Napoleon in 1812, were invoked. The allusions were easily understood by the Russian people, and were appealing to them. They had seen patriotic films devoted to the deeds of these traditional national heroes of Russia, had read novels describing their feats, and were taught at school a very different history from that contained in the books of the leading Soviet historian of the 'twenties, M. N. Pokrovskii.

In denouncing Hitler's program calling for "the destruction of the great Russian nation," and in enumerating the Russian men of genius who justified Russia's claim to greatness, Stalin had named only one Communist—Lenin, and one theoretician of Marxism—Plekhanov. All other names he brought up were either those of Russian writers (Belinskii, Gorky, Tolstoi, Pushkin), of musicians (Glinka and Tchaikovsky), of great scientists (Mechnikov and Pavlov), or of the general of the Napoleonic wars (Kutuzov).[281]

As the *New York Times* said editorially on December 10, 1940: "By this time it is no news that Joseph Stalin has been fostering Russian patriotism. He has knitted anew the ties with Russia's past severed in the first flush of communist victory."[282]

This work of mending the broken ties could be noticed even earlier than in 1935—the date indicated by Mr. Walter Duranty. Max Eastman, in his *Stalin's Russia*, gives a translation of extracts from the Moscow *Pravda* of June 9, 1934: "For the Fatherland! That cry kindles the flame of heroism, the flame of creative initiative in all fields in all the realms of our rich, our many-sided country. . . . The defense of the fatherland is the supreme law of life. . . . For the Fatherland, for its honor, glory, might and prosperity."[283]

The army newspaper wrote in 1937, commenting on the daring flight of Russian aviators to the United States, that the principal mainspring which had impelled them on their exploit was their love of their fatherland. This was followed by the statement that the wide masses of the people were always deeply patriotic and that many a time in the course of its history the Russian people had victoriously defended its country from various foreign invaders. The same newspaper defined Soviet patriotism as a sincere, selfless, unlimited love of their country, of its historic "progressive" past and beautiful present. This was coupled with internationalism: "the unrestrained loyalty to the interests of the toilers, to the great covenants of communism."[284]

The nearer the thundercloud of war drew to Russia, the more strongly was the first part of the definition accentuated and the second part subdued.

The cult of the Russian heroes of the war of 1812, and the revision of Pokrovskii's concepts of it, became the order of the day. The *Red Star* had published a brief summary of General Prince Bagration's military career on the day of the 175th anniversary of his birth, exclaiming that the Russian people had preserved Bagration's glory. On the 125th anniversary of the battle of Borodino, the *Voennaia Mysl* published an article by A. Baltiiskii, stressing the fact that Kutuzov had pursued moral-political aims in his strategy and that the battle was a decisive moral victory for the Russians, and had exercised influence on the final outcome of the entire campaign of 1812.[285]

The explanation of the reasons for this trend, besides the fact that it was a corollary of the plan for "socialism in one country," is probably to be found in a very practical military necessity—that of finding a common ground on which to unite the entire people of Russia for the defense of the country against the ever more probable onslaught of Hitlerite Germany.

An article in the *Red Star* in 1940 lifted the curtain somewhat and showed at least some of the reasons behind the fostering of this neo-patriotism. "History knows many instances when large nations and splendid armies fell to pieces, only because they were not supported by national unity, the unity of the country."[286]

The cement for this unity was Soviet patriotism, the revival of interest in Russian history and the making of the armed defense of the country a universal duty of all citizens of the U.S.S.R.

The comparison of these pronouncements of the late 'thirties and of 1940, with the contents of the "political literacy" primer published for the use of the Red Army soldiers in 1930 reveals clearly the long distance traversed during the decade. A. Kadyshev's *What Each Red Army Man Should Know* used the words: "Our army—the army of the international proletariat, the fighting vanguard of the world's socialist revolution." Even such an attentive and intelligent observer as S. Ivanovich concluded that the Red Army was an armed force without a fatherland—a view which could hardly be defended objectively at present.[287]

True enough, in speeches addressed to party members only, different notes were sounded. To cite an example: L. Mekhlis, the head of the PUR, said at the XVIIIth Party Congress in 1939 that should "the second imperialist war turn its point against the first socialist state in the world," the Red Army would, by carrying its military operations into the territory of the enemy, "fulfil its internationalist obligations and increase the number of Soviet republics"—a sentence that was received with applause by the audience. He added that the time was not distant when "our army, internationalist according to the ideology prevailing within it," would help the workers of the aggressor nations "to liberate themselves from the yoke of fascism, from the yoke of capitalist slavery and would liquidate the capitalist encirclement. . . ."[288]

There is, also, the testimony of the *Red Star* regarding a tank crew which took with them into battle in Poland a copy of the history of the Russian Communist party and read it at rest periods between actions.[289]

But these internationalist notes were drowned in the sound of patriotic music, directed at the country at large. The internationalist appeal in that period seemed to be aimed at the Communist party membership only. Apparently it was clear to Stalin and his group that an attempt to unite the peoples of the U.S.S.R. on the platform of an international revolutionary war would prove by no means as effective as that of the national war of defense of the land. Once this decision was made, the rest was a logical sequel to it, releasing the tremendous latent forces of Russian patriotism left dormant since the days of the Russian-Polish war of 1920, when an attempt was made to tap them.

This propaganda of patriotism was directed not toward a largely peasant army on a low educational level. The social composition of the Soviet armed forces had changed vastly since the days when Trotsky thought internationalist revolutionary ideas would not prove effective in rallying the Russian peasant soldier in a large-scale war. By 1937, 43 per cent of the soldiers were workers, as against 19.8 per cent in 1927. Among the junior commanders the percentage of proletarians had reached fifty.[290]

Non-collectivized peasants were represented in the army in 1937 by only 2.3 per cent. Among junior commanders this element formed 1.7 per cent.[291]

Three-quarters of the command personnel were former workers and peasants. There was therefore justification for the claim that commanders and soldiers had the same class interests, as contrasted with the Western European armies, where officers and soldiers, as a rule, came from different social strata. It presupposed, of course, that the collectivized peasant was not interested any more in farming on the individualistic basis; also that the old class interests were not replaced by new ones.[292]

Nevertheless, the fact that such an overwhelming majority of the soldiers came from the socialized sector of Soviet economic life had undoubtedly made a very substantial difference in their attitude to the state.

What, perhaps, had an equally important influence on their understanding of the task set to the Red Army was the fact that already in 1935 there were no illiterate recruits joining the army. As a correspondent wrote to the *Red Star*: "Three to four years ago my subunit was receiving 20-30 per cent of the semi-literate recruits. At the present time, the majority of the young soldiers have a solid education." The regimental schools of the N.C.O.'s were recruited from persons with a complete secondary education. A few years earlier, when the first Five Year Plan was already in full swing, the percentage completely illiterate was very considerable. Thus in one of the military districts in some of the territorial divisions the percentage of illiterates had reached eleven, while the semi-literates were reported as being present "in a large number." Even the units of the standing army of the same district had received among those recruits from the 1907 age-group more than two thousand completely illiterate youths.[293]

The draft centers were now filled with young men well developed physically, and, in the majority, with some military education. They included parachutists, Voroshilov's marksmen, qualified athletes and other youths who had benefited from the Osoaviakhim and other forms of pre-army training. A majority of the draft were thus already familiar with the elements of soldier's training and could be much more quickly assimilated into the army than the raw peasant recruits of the 'twenties.[294]

Very likely some of these reports were over-optimistic. Nevertheless, the change in the educational level of the recruits was very considerable, and found an immediate expression in the much wider cultural interests of the soldier masses.

In the late 'twenties the vast majority of soldiers (including a large proportion of the Communists among them) were unable to answer correctly the most elementary questions regarding the structure of the Soviet state and the basis of its power, even about the rôle of the company communist cell—to the extent that during psychological tests only 30 per cent of the *kolkhoz* peasants answered correctly such an elementary question as: To whom belongs the leading rôle in the union of workers and peasants in Soviet Russia?[295]

For 1940, on the other hand, we have descriptions of the activity of the soldiers' club in the Kalinin military district. A literary evening, devoted to the reading of the works of Pushkin, several others dedicated to other Russian classics, a musical circle, an amateur band —all these reflected the new interests of the soldiers, whose appetite for sports were catered to by gymnastic teams, ski clubs and other athletic voluntary organizations.[296]

Another interesting example: a company planned its rest day. Twenty-eight men went to take part in a ski competition; many went to the circus, as many went to see the patriotic film *Minin and Pozharskii*; however, an entire half of the company went to visit the different city museums, while a few remained in the barracks for a collective reading and discussion of newspapers.[297]

The pride of Soviet Russia in its soldiers seemed to have reached its apogee by 1940. In terms reminiscent of old Karamzin's "On Love for the Fatherland and National Pride," the *Red Star* wrote that the best characteristic of "men of our fatherland" were united in the collective image of the Red Army soldier—"the armed guardian of the untold wealth and happiness of the Soviet land." Each year, wrote the newspaper, was adding to these qualities still more majestic and noble traits. "Each year, like a surf of tremendous force, brings to the shield of our national glory still more heroic deeds of the sons of our Fatherland."[298]

Ambassador Davies' *Diary* quotes the opinion of the German military attaché, General von Koestrich, to the effect that "the human material—manpower—was excellent, physically strong, brave, and fine soldiers . . . that the Russian fliers were . . . superb—none better; that their parachute troops were excellent."[299]

The Universal Military Service Statute of 1939, as mentioned above, had increased the term of service for the junior commanders

of the land forces from two to three years. It also laid down a three
years' term of service both for privates and junior commanders, of
the air forces, the same for those serving in the land frontier guard
troops. For the navy, the term was set at five years both for rank
and file seamen and the junior commanders, while for the coast defense forces it was set at four years. On the same basis with these
were placed the crews of the frontier guard vessels.[300]

While the statute fixed the draft age at nineteen, it was lowered,
for those who had completed their secondary education, to eighteen.[301]

The age limit for the reservists was raised by ten years, from forty
to fifty. The ten oldest age groups were earmarked for auxiliary services in the rear only. According to this stipulation, the private soldiers
remained in the reserve for twenty-nine years. Of this period he was
to spend eighteen months in the ranks of the army during refresher
training periods. The junior commander was to remain in the reserve for twenty-eight years, including twenty-four months of refresher training periods.[302]

The age limit for the draft was actually lowered even further than
it would seem at the first glance. It was now counted not from January 1 of the year of draft as heretofore, but in the course of the entire
year. Therefore, in fact, youths from eighteen years and eight months
to nineteen years and eight months were to be called, as well as those
who had completed their secondary education, from seventeen years
and eight months to eighteen years and eight months.[303]

The unusual feature of the obligatory terms of service under colors
—that the junior commanders of the land forces had to serve one
year longer than the privates—was explained as being necessitated by
the fact that previously junior commanders upon graduation from
regimental schools served for only one year in their new capacity;
that this period was insufficient to permit them to acquire and retain
command habits.[304] Also that the lack of experience on the part of
junior commanders reacted unfavorably on the training of recruits
and had made it necessary to retain in the army a large number of second-term service junior commanders, who actually bore the brunt
of the training of soldiers. The abolition of the second-term service
engagements of junior commanders (with the exception of some
categories) made it possible to accumulate rapidly a reserve of well-
trained junior commanders. And this was regarded as exceedingly
important by the authorities in charge.[305]

There was nothing new in the reference to the shortcomings of the
regular term service junior commanders. This was a recurrent theme

in Soviet military literature. The *Voennyi Vestnik* wrote in 1930 that it was an undeniable fact that the section commander of the regular term service was "as yet far from adequate to the demands made upon him." Even the second-term junior commanders were not always satisfactory, and there was a shortage of them as against the establishment's provisions.[306]

As an illustration of the limitations of the ability of the junior commanders to cope with their duties, the *Voennyi Vestnik* published an item to the effect that a company sergeant-major, upon receiving the order to arrest a soldier and send him to the guard-house, had to come back three times to his company commander for additional instructions. Ultimately a platoon commander (an officer) was sent to supervise the procedure. "This is an example of the self-reliance and initiative of the company sergeant-major," concluded the article.[307]

Junior commanders of regular term service and privates were living in barracks. Married second-term junior commanders (and the corresponding ranks of the political personnel) were given accommodations outside of barracks. Bachelors of this group were either lodged in separate rooms in the barracks, or, by permission of the commander of the unit, accommodated outside of barracks.[308]

Both privates and junior commanders could leave barracks only on days set aside for this by the commander of the unit. From the end of the duty period to the evening roll-call, leave of absence was granted by the company sergeant-major. Absence after roll-call or liberation from duty was authorized by the company commander or the *politruk*.[309]

The young recruits were not sent to companies upon arrival. They were first assigned to special "receiving detachments," charge of which was given to some of the company commanders, in co-operation with *politruki*.[310]

Neither in line of duty, nor in personal matters, was the soldier permitted to address himself to the higher standing commanders, without authorization by his immediate superior. He could, however, address himself directly to the *politruk* and the commissar.[311]

A great deal of customary military pomp had become part of Red Army life. Giving an order or receiving it, persons in military service had to stand at attention and salute, unless uncovered. Addressing each other, all persons in military service had to stand at attention and salute (the latter whenever they had their headgear on). They had to address each other by their military rank. Whenever a direct superior visited barracks or any other place occupied by troops, he was greeted by the command "Attention!" or "Attention! Stand up!"[312]

Ralph Ingersoll witnessed, at the Moscow front in 1941, the smart bearing of the troops and their zeal in complying with the minutiae of drill and military courtesy.[313]

The firm insistence on traditional military deportment had called forth some exaggerated commentary as exemplified by the heading in the *Living Age* in May 1941 :* "The Red Army Turns Prussian." The article printed under that heading was a translation of one that had appeared in the *Molodaia Gvardiia* of Moscow, and depicted the reorganization of the system of discipline and training which had followed the appointment of Marshal Timoshenko to the post of People's Commissar of Defense.[314]

The new Disciplinary Code promulgated on October 12, 1940, replaced the code of 1925, when the experience of the Russo-Finnish campaign, which was interpreted in Soviet Russia as calling for a tightening up of discipline and a revamping of the military organization.[315]

Without knowing the adverse influence of the purge on army discipline, one cannot understand the reasons for the stern insistence of Timoshenko on the tightening of disciplinary relationships in the army. The sands were running low. The leaders of the Red Army could not fail to realize that they had a mere couple of years at best to get ready to face the mighty legions of the Nazis. There was no time left for a gradual improvement. Drastic and rapid changes, striking the imagination of the soldiers, had to be introduced forthwith in order speedily to restore the prestige of commanders, to make the rank and file forget the witch-hunt conducted in the army after the execution of the generals. The new Disciplinary Code was a link in that hastily forged chain.

Some of the principal differences of the new Disciplinary Code from that of 1925 were: previously the soldiers had to carry out all orders of their superiors except *criminal* ones; the superior officers had the right to use arms to obtain compliance with their orders only in the battle zone, and only with respect to battle orders. The new code, on the other hand, stated bluntly that the commander was not held responsible should he be compelled to use force or arms to enforce obedience or to restore discipline and order. It went even further: "A commander failing to exhibit firmness and decisiveness,

---

* This was written before the conviction of the editor of the *Living Age*.

stopping short of taking all possible measures to bring about compliance with his orders was subject to court-martial himself."[316]

A somewhat odd claim was made by Soviet military writers: that the discipline of the Red Army had to be firmer, and "must be characterized by demands more severe and more harsh," than was the case with discipline based solely on class subordination, i.e. in armies of capitalist states.[317]

Actually, this meant that Red Army discipline, on general principles, should be more severe than that in the armies of the bourgeois countries. "Insubordination must be punished by the most unmerciful measures." As the commander was responsible for the behavior of his subordinates, he had to be severe, demanding and just. "Every case of soft-heartedness and liberalism, even the smallest indulgence with respect to violation of discipline, results in great harm."[318]

"All those in the service of the Red Army, regardless of rank, must render complete obedience to their commanders and superiors." Exact fulfillment of orders "is the responsibility and the sacred duty of all soldiers and fighters of the Red Army." V. Osipov added that as a result of experience, the soldiers were convinced of the wisdom underlying the orders of their commanders and superiors.[319]

"The commander's order is the subordinates' law." In the words of the new code: "The strictest discipline is proper to the Red Army by its very nature."[320]

Severe punishments were listed. Besides reprimands and additional fatigue assignments, a soldier who disobeyed was liable to confinement to quarters up to six weeks, or could be placed under arrest in the guard-house for a period of ten to twenty days.[321]

The code provided also rewards, ranging from valuable gifts and cash bonuses to decorations and promotion in the service.[322]

The obligatory salute of commanders by soldiers, and of superiors by subordinates, was the outward symbol of this new, harsher, discipline.[323]

The junior commander's prestige was also enhanced. Even the Central Committee of the party added its authority and confirmed the instruction prepared by the chief of the PUR, Mekhlis, designed to establish the ascendancy of the junior commanders on a firm foundation. This instruction aimed to produce "strong-willed, exacting" junior commanders, "able to implant with a firm hand Soviet military discipline."[324]

As the overwhelming majority of the junior commanders were members of the Komsomol by 1940, it was said by the Soviet military writers of that period that the combination of command qualities with those required of a member of the Komsomol should result in a new source of strength for the army.[325]

One of the most interesting analyses of the new attitude toward discipline was contained in the article by Colonel A. A. Velikolutskii, which appeared in the *Voennaia Mysl* in 1940.

"In the army the superior must be independent from his subordinates," wrote Velikolutskii. The greater the dependence of the superior on the subordinate, the less the former would be able to exercise his functions of superior, the weaker will be the discipline. In support of this view, Velikolutskii quoted the first paragraph of the new disciplinary code: "Military discipline is the strict observance of the order established in the Red Army by the laws of Soviet government and military regulations, and maintained by orders and instructions of the superiors." The third paragraph of the same code laid upon all members of the military forces the duty to master and to abide by the military regulations, to "fulfil incontrovertibly" all orders and to preserve military secrets.[326]

Colonel Velikolutskii advanced the thought that during World War I victories were won by the armies which were superior in discipline to their antagonists. The German army was rich in victories, and one of the principal reasons for this should be looked for in its discipline, he wrote.[327]

Velikolutskii ascribed to Trotskyists and "other traitors" the attempt to educate the Red Army in the civil, rather than military spirit. He saw in this the proof that these "enemies of the people" knew that one of the surest ways to weaken the armed forces was to undermine their military discipline. The writer admitted that even at the time of his writing (1940), there were many persons, lacking in the sense of civic duty, in the U.S.S.R., who were inimical to military discipline. "Loud revolutionary phrases serve them as blinds for useless or saboteur activity." Such persons were, naturally, opposed to the strict fulfillment of demands of military regulations and derided drill.[328]

The author criticized those who shared in the "sufficiently well spread" opinion that "conscious" discipline was possible only within the framework of "some kind of democratic order," which would exclude elements of compulsion. He said that according to this concept the Red Army soldier, immediately upon joining the army, had to become "conscious," or one had to wait until the soldier became so. Only then would it be possible to exact from him all that is required by military discipline. In spite of the tremendous cultural-educational work performed in the U.S.S.R., the Red Army continued to receive, in addition to the mass of "conscious" young citizens and those "semi-conscious," also "non-conscious" people. As long as there were young recruits belonging to the second and third of these groups, order in the army had to be maintained not by suasion only, but by compulsion as well.[329]

This article reveals the new trend as well as the opposition to formal discipline still existing among the party members. "Self-criticism" items in the *Red Star* show that social pressure was added to the usual military sanctions to imbue the soldiers with the idea of discipline to make them comply strictly with the provisions of the military regulations.[330]

The comparison of Velikolutskii's reasoning with that of S. I. Gusev's in 1918 strikingly shows how differently the problem of discipline had developed in the Red Army from what its founders believed it would grow into. Gusev hoped for "free, voluntary, comradely discipline" which would render useless "strict" orders and summary punishment. Each transgressor of the military codes would be punished by means of the stern disapproval of his action by his comrades. Gusev thought that the guiding rôle of the officer would lose its decisive significance as soon as well-trained soldiers were able to orient themselves under battle conditions.[331]

Even a superficial attempt to compare the behavior of Red Army soldiers during the 1939 Polish campaign with that during the Civil War shows immediately the great improvement with respect to the treatment of the non-combatants. Such petty marauding as stealing of apples was apparently regarded as a serious offense.[332]

The material well-being of the soldiers had very considerably improved. The author of an article in the *Voennaia Mysl* in 1939 had flatly asserted that Soviet barracks were better than those of any army in the world, that the soldiers were better fed and better clothed than the rank and file of any capitalist army. It was emphasized that soldiers had a right to free sanatorium treatment and that all flyers were passed through sanatoria, regardless of their state of health.[333]

Voroshilov had made a statement at the XVIIIth party congress that the material well-being of the private soldier in the U.S.S.R. was on a high level, and that this was also true of the barracks, the food and the clothing.[334]

One can trace this improvement through items in the Soviet military press. Even in Siberia soldiers' dining-halls were serving a variety of dishes. The tables were covered with new oilcloth, the inventory included water jugs, mirrors, washstands and even artificial palms.[335] All these were luxuries undreamed of in the 'twenties.

In camp there were also improvements. Not only clean, smart tents, but also spotless bed-sheets and pillow-cases, clean towels and well-washed wooden floors.[336]

Recreation facilities for the soldiers had increased very considerably. As against 15,091 "Lenin corners" in 1934, there were 26,435 in 1939. The number of soldiers' clubs grew from 1,336 in 1934 to 1,900 in 1939. The larger army clubs, known as the Red Army Houses, had increased from 142 to 267. Army libraries included 25 million books.[337]

There is some information available regarding improvement in the physique of the soldiers. From 1927 to 1935 an increase of two centimeters in the chest measurement of the recruits was recorded. The average weight of the Soviet workers in 1935 was approximately five kilograms greater than that of the British workers of the same age.[338]

From time to time, however, complaints continued to crop up regarding the quality of food, lack of boiled water, etc., in the "self-criticism" items in the army press. Apparently there was still room for improvement, but the very fact of the appearance of these complaints in the press indicated that Red Army soldiers were expecting good food and comfortable barracks on a scale far above that of the early 'twenties.[339]

At the XVIIIth party congress, Voroshilov quoted extracts from diaries of Japanese officers killed in action during the so-called border incidents. One of these extracts tells of fourteen Soviet soldiers resisting for four hours the attack of an entire company of Japanese. They left their position only after a bayonet charge and hand-to-hand fighting. Another Japanese officer wrote that Russian soldiers were expert in the use of rifles and light and heavy machine guns, that Soviet snipers were adept at camouflage and using natural cover.[340]

Russian soldiers taken prisoner by the Japanese had exhibited, regardless of their party affiliation, high moral qualities, going on hunger strike rather than reveal military secrets to the enemy.[341]

During the period under review the soldier element had changed a great deal. A better educated youth found its way into the army. The soldier was well fed, well housed and decently clothed.

The purge period was undoubtedly harmful to discipline and interfered with training. Timoshenko's reforms, beyond doubt, set up a new barrier between the rank and file and the commanders. One must, however, remember what Willard Waller has recently written: "In some measure, the social distance between the officer and the men is functionally appropriate. It helps to make subordination bearable by preventing any real clash of personalities." Also that "In the army, carefully regulated unfamiliarity breeds respect."[342]

One question remains unanswered as far as this writer is concerned: Had the abrupt introduction of the new forms of discipline, however desirable in themselves, taken hold of the minds and the emotions of the soldiers sufficiently firmly by the time Hitler attacked Russia to stand up under the strain of the war? Did this new strain tend to develop a resentment directed against the commanders because of the unaccustomed and different forms of disciplinary relationship; and did this feeling make difficult, if not altogether impossible, the application of these new forms under war conditions? Was the reintroduction of the military commissars after the beginning of hostilities in any way connected with such feelings?

The task of adapting the human material to the new military technique, of training soldiers able to handle tanks, airplanes, motorized artillery and the complicated signal system was successfully accomplished during the decade of the 'thirties. The general growth of the Soviet educational system during the periods of the several Five Year Plans was the principal ally of the army in this work. Osoaviakhim's efforts also had an important influence. The collectivization of the rural life of Russia and the tractor stations, which had grown up with that change, also played a considerable rôle.

Only a country thoroughly industrialized, made machine-conscious in the highest degree, with a vastly expanded educational system, could supply a suitable soldier for the modern mechanized army on a scale commensurate with the historic task set to the armed forces of the U.S.S.R. The fate of these forces was closely linked to that of the advance in the industrial life of the country under the impulse of the several Five Year Plans. The Red Army's great achievements parallel the successes in the industrial and cultural fields. Its shortcomings are those arising from the rapid tempo of change and the insufficiencies of national economy and cultural life.

The soldier of the Red Army is a very different fighter from the poorly-educated peasant-soldier who fought so heroically in World War I—as different as Russian industrial development of 1914 from that of 1940.

All this is said with no intent to minimize the psychological preparation of the soldiers, the intensive propaganda of Soviet patriotism,
and of making national defense the universal duty of the entire population.

The rate of change in the development of the armed forces was
rapid. A few more years would have made a tremendous difference
for the further improvement in the quality of the human material in
the ranks of the armed forces. Just the same, one is inclined to think
that the private soldier of the Red Army as he stood, gun in hand,
facing the invader in 1941, was relatively more adequate to his task
than any other group in the army. The masses were growing faster
than the leadership.

Conclusions

The leaders of the Red Army have repeatedly asserted in the last
few years that the Soviet armed forces were in excellent condition and
fully able to cope with any foreign invader that would dare set foot
on Russian soil. The unfavorable comparisons of the efficiency and
mechanical equipment of the armed forces of the U.S.S.R. with those
of the capitalist countries of the West so prevalent in the 'twenties
had ceased in the 'thirties.

Thus in 1935 M. N. Tukhachevskii said: "Our Workers' and
Peasants' Red Army is strong. Its political might, its revolutionary
power, are insuperable. We must therefore know how to conduct war
in such a manner and to use technical means in such a way that in the
field also there should be no other army equal to our Red Army."[343]

At the XVIIIth party congress in 1939, Voroshilov exclaimed:
". . . that the enemy will be crushed and destroyed on short order is
pledged by the political and moral unity of the Red Army with the
entire Soviet people . . . another pledge is the fact that our Workers'
and Peasants' Red Army is a first-class army, better than any other
army, an army that is technically equipped and splendidly trained. . . .
Comrades, our army is invincible."[344]

I. Baz, writing in the *Voennaia Mysl* in 1939 said that the detrac-
tors of the Red Army were unable to name a force which could successfully resist the onslaught of the armed forces of the U.S.S.R.[345]

I. A. Khalepskii, a Soviet general prominently identified with the
development of the armored units of the Red Army, wrote in a book
dedicated to the Russian tank crews: "We, the tank men of the Red
Army, have advantages unknown to the tank men of the bourgeois

armies. Our excellent combat technique is in the hands of excellent men, who know what they are fighting for."[346]

Max Werner collected in his volume *Military Strength of the Powers* a great deal of information regarding the favorable estimates of the strength of the Red Army in the Western European press in the middle of the 'thirties. He put the Soviet air force in 1939 at between 10,000 and 12,000 planes with five trained reserve pilots for every active one. The Spanish Civil War experience was interpreted by some of the French observers as showing that Soviet airplanes had proved themselves far superior to all others.[347]

The second-in-command of the Red Army Force, Khripin, stated in 1936 that this force could stand comparison in numerical strength, in the quality of its equipment, and in the training of its personnel with those of all other countries.[348]

Max Werner estimated the number of tanks of the Red Army for 1938-1939 at 20,000. He quoted the German tank expert, General Guderian, to the effect that in 1935 the Russians already had produced their best and most modern motor vehicles in masses and had trained their troops excellently in the use of them, adapting also their tactical and operational aims excellently to the performance of these troops.[349]

The goal set by Soviet leaders at the beginning of the first Five Year Plan seemed to have been reached on the eve of World War II. As already mentioned, Voroshilov himself said at the XVIIIth party congress that the Soviet Union was in possession of the best army in the world. Contrary to this, there was a definite change in the trend of opinion of the western military experts after the army purge. The Russo-Finnish campaign marked the lowest ebb, although in Germany some of the military commentators continued to point to the unin-terrupted growth of the Red Army.

Objectively examined, the Red Army, it must be said, had come of age before the opening of the present hostilities. It is pertinent, there-fore, to examine the process of growth, isolate certain trends, and draw some theoretical as well as practical conclusions from that ex-amination.

One of the most persistent trends was that toward unity of com-mand, which was connected with the process of professionalization of the commanding personnel and its segregation from the rank and file soldiers. This development, as shown above, was not unin-ter-rupted. The infra-party struggle, which had heralded the introduction of the Five Year Plans, slowed up this process very considerably. The great army purge even reversed the trend. On the eve of the German attack upon the U.S.S.R. the principle of unity of command seemed to have reached its full development, and its application was established on a firm foundation. After the beginning of hostilities there was again an abrupt change toward the dual form of control of armed forces.

The persistence of that trend, its renascence even after the great army purge would seem to justify the conclusion that this trend had its roots in its functional effectiveness. Possibly, it was connected with the economy of effort growing out of the most adequate distribution of duties and functions called for by the modern army technique.

Apparently, on the present level of cultural development, there has to be a concentration of military authority in the hands of the specially trained persons to produce the best results both in peacetime and in the field during war. The recognition of this (not without the help of the military tradition via the old army and the examples of all Western armies) had apparently constantly helped this trend for almost a score of years.

On the other hand, the antithesis of the principle of single command had also survived that score and more of years. The institution of military commissars with its corollary development of army political organs continued to exist—in open or disguised form—from the early days of the Red Army almost right up to the present day. At times it retreated from positions already occupied, at others it advanced.

Its origin was in the practical necessity of watching over the politically suspect ex-czarist officers and the guerilla leaders who rose to command positions in the Red Army. From these early shoots there grew a mighty tree with roots deep in the masses of the Red Army. The later aim of the political organs was not to watch over the ex-czarist officers, but to supervise, from the political viewpoint, the entire army and its political indoctrination. At certain periods its activity went beyond that into the sphere of direction of operations.

At times of crises—1924 and 1937—the PUR had failed to function effectively. Nevertheless its ramified machinery was not scrapped. On the contrary, during the army purge it was amplified and given even greater powers after having been supplied with a new leadership and recruited from younger elements without close connections with the old bolshevik guard of the Civil War days.

Do the political organs owe their continued existence, even at the time when the entire upper strata of commanders had become members of the party, to the *divide et impera* policy? Or do they owe it to the fact of the dictatorship of a (relatively) numerically weak party group over a vast and populous country, supplying annually its army with hundreds of thousands of recruits?

It does not seem impossible that the gigantic task of converting every year huge masses of young soldiers into stanch supporters of the general party line, of turning them into disciplined loyal soldiers in the extremely difficult conditions of rapid economic and political change of the 'thirties, was of such magnitude as to prevent the effective combination in the hands of commanders alone of the functions connected with that problem together with those of the technical military leadership. That once given the party dictatorship, the presence of the political organs within the army was inevitable—this seems to be a plausible conclusion. The disadvantages of the political organs from the purely military standpoint (divided counsels, the weakening of the commanders' will-power, the undermining of their authority with the soldiers) were counterbalanced by political advantages to the extent that the choice had to favor these organs.

The continuous growth of *formal* discipline, with its outward symbols of respect for the superior, harsh, summary punishments, frequent instigation of judicial procedure against even minor offenders, the drawing further and further from the hopes of the founders of the Red Army for the conscious, comradely, forms of discipline, based on social pressure exercised of the soldiers' masses themselves on their less "conscious" comrades at arms—all this had paralleled the abandonment of the idea of the withering away of the state during the transition period. Nevertheless, the continued development of the element of compulsion in army life was unquestionably also influenced by the structural requirements of the army edifice. To be efficient, the army had to ensure obedience to commands and the unhesitating compliance with orders. On the level of the existing cultural development, this could not be attained by suasion alone. Hence discipline had to become harsh, particularly when political events had disturbed the army life—as had occurred in the 1937-1939 period.

The attempt to divert the army from its national character, both in personnel and doctrine, had to be abandoned in its original form. The army personnel had again become national even in theory after the publication of the Constitution of 1936 and the Universal Military Service Statute of 1939. Certain elements of internationalism were, however, retained, although the army had embraced the principle of the defense of the fatherland with great fervor. At the present stage of the armed struggle the element of patriotism is playing a decisive rôle in line with repeated emphasis of it by Soviet leaders in their speeches.

Whether later on the other part of the army credo, the internationalist one, will come again to the forefront is a matter for conjecture, but cannot be ruled out entirely. In case of a victory over the German Army and the moving of the battle-lines west, the Red Army would be able to draw considerable strength from the internationalist side of its doctrine, from its promise of liberation for the workers and the poor peasants from the fascist dictatorship. In the Balkans and in Central Europe, this aspect will be worth many divisions to the Red Army.

The continued existence of a separate party organization in the armed forces, independent of the local party machinery, had supplied the government with a remarkable instrument of control and intelligence not only with respect to commanders and non-party soldiers, but also in relation to the political organs of the armed forces as well. In both of the great crises the lower party collectives of the army were the powerful lever used by the government to overthrow the opposition and to frustrate the influence of the PUR. The communist cell had helped to win the Civil War. It has also done a great deal for the continued loyalty of the army to the majority group of the Central Committee of the party.

In this manner the complicated structure of the armed forces, with all its latent and open conflicts, checks and balances, had proved to be a very efficient guarantee of the faithfulness of the army in peacetime and also a source of a new form of army morale, which may prove extremely important should the Red armed forces carry the war west of the Soviet border.

The whole system is intimately interwoven with the principle and the practical application of party dictatorship. Should that principle be abandoned it would be improbable that the structure would continue to exist in its present form, as from the purely military viewpoint it has disadvantages.

NOTES

CHAPTER I

1. e.g. see *Soldatskie pis'ma 1917 goda,* Istpart, Moscow-Leningrad, 1927, pp. 8, 9. Also Fedotoff White, D. *Survival,* Philadelphia, 1939, University of Pennsylvania Press, pp. 66, 67, 68. For a comprehensive survey of this problem see Chernov, Viktor, *Rozhdenie revoliutsionnoi Rossii (Fevralskaia Revoliutsiia),* Paris-Prague-New York, 1934 (printed in Paris, 1934), pp. 255-283.

2. *1917 god v dokumentakh i materialakh,* edited by Pokrovskii, M. N. and Iakovlev, Ia. A. *Razlozhenie armii v 1917 godu,* prepared for publication by N. E. Kakurin, with a foreword by Ia. A. Iakovlev, Moscow-Leningrad, 1925, p. 7.

3. *ibid.,* pp. 10, 11.
4. *ibid.,* p. 13.
5. *ibid.,* p. 27.
6. *ibid.,* p. 30.
7. *ibid.,* pp. 31, 32.
8. *ibid.,* p. 34.
9. *ibid.,* p. 36.
10. *ibid.,* p. 52.
11. *ibid.,* pp. 90, 91.
12. *ibid.,* pp. 106, 107.
13. *ibid.,* pp. 112, 113.
14. *ibid.,* p. 138.
15. *ibid.,* p. 141.
16. *ibid.,* pp. 143, 144, 145.
17. Miliukov, P. *Rossiia na perelome,* v. I., Paris, 1927, p. 95.
18. *ibid.,* p. 96.
19. *Razlozhenie armii v 1917 godu,* Moscow-Leningrad, 1925, p. 175.
20. Denikin, A. I., General. *Staraia Armiia,* v. 2, Paris, 1931, pp. 37, 38.
21. Niessel, Général. *Le triomphe des bolshéviks et la paix de Brest-Litovsk,* Paris, Librairie Plon, 1940, pp. 29, 30. The figures include also those on leave.
22. *Razlozhenie armii v 1917 godu,* Moscow-Leningrad, 1925, pp. iv, vi.
23. *ibid.,* pp. vi, vii.
24. Niessel, Général. *op. cit.,* pp. 67, 70, 74.
25. Miliukov, P. *op. cit.,* v. I, p. 59.
26. Stankevich, V. B. *Vospominaniia 1914-1919 g.* Berlin, 1920, p. 99.
27. *ibid.,* p. 102. The Zimmerwald Conference was held in September 1915. Its more radical wing, headed by Lenin, issued a proclamation, calling on the armies to turn their weapons against their own bourgeoisie.
28. Miliukov, P. *op. cit.,* v. I, p. 69.
29. *ibid.*
30. Trotskii, L. *Kak vooruzhalas' revoliutsiia,* v. I, Moscow, 1923, p. 58.
31. *ibid.,* v. I, p. 118.
32. Blumenthal, F. *Politicheskaia rabota v voennoe vremia,* Moscow-Leningrad, 2nd ed., 1929, pp. 237, 238.

CHAPTER II

1. *Bolshaia Sovetskaia Entsikopediia,* v. 34, Moscow, 1937, p. 579. Petukhov, I. *Partiinaia organizatsiia i partinaia rabota v RKKA,* Moscow-Leningrad, 1928, p. 15.
2. Petukhov, I. *op. cit.,* p. 15.
3. Miliukov, P. *Rossiia na perelome,* v. I, Paris, 1927, p. 167. Information regarding the numerical strength of the Red Guards is merely an approximation. Another source (*Bolshaia Sovetskaia Etsiklopediia,* v. 34, p. 579) gives the figures for Petrograd as ten to twelve thousand in the middle of October 1917 and states that the same number had participated in the Gatchina and Pulkovo actions against General Krasnov's troops.
4. Bonch-Bruevich, V. *Na boevykh postakh Fevralskoi i Oktiabr'skoi revoliutsii,* Moscow, 1930, p. 146.
5. *ibid.,* p. 147.
6. *Bolshaia Sovetskaia Entsiklopediia,* v. 34, Moscow, 1937, p. 579.
7. Geronimus, A. *Partiia i Krasnaia Armiia,* Moscow-Leningrad, 1928, p. 10.
8. Rabinovich, S. E. *Vserossiiskaia voennaia konferentsiia bolshevikov 1917 goda,* Moscow, 1931, p. 26.
9. Dybenko, P. E. *Iz nedr tsarskogo flota k velikomu Oktiabriu,* Moscow, 1928, p. 151.
10. Pukhov, G. S. *Kak vooruzhalsia Petrograd,* Moscow, 1933, p. 39.
11. Bonch-Bruevich, V. *op. cit.,* p. 270.
12. Dybenko, P. E. *op. cit.,* pp. 63, 69.
13. Bonch-Bruevich, V. *op. cit.,* p. 270.
14. *ibid.,* p. 321.
15. *Grazhdanskaia Voina 1918-1921,* edited by Bubnov, A. S., Kamenev, S. S. and Eideman, R. P., v. 2, Moscow, 1928, p. 50.

16. Rabinovich, S. E. *op. cit.*, p. 7.

17. Miliukov, P. *op. cit.*, v. I, pp. 265, 266.

18. Rabinovich, S. E. *op. cit.*, p. 10.

19. *ibid.*, p. 11.

20. *ibid.*, p. 13.

21. *ibid.*

22. *ibid.*, pp. 16, 17, 18.

23. *ibid.*, pp. 18, 19.

24. *ibid.*, p. 27.

25. *ibid.*, pp. 41, 42, 43.

26. *ibid.*, p. 64.

27. *ibid.*, p. 70.

28. *ibid.*, p. 48.

29. *ibid.*, p. 49.

30. *ibid.*, p. 71.

31. *ibid.*, p. 53.

CHAPTER III

1. Dybenko, P. E. *Iz nedr tsarskogo flota k velikomu Oktiabriu*, Moscow, 1928, pp. 173, 174, 175, 176.

2. *ibid.*, p. 203.

3. *ibid.*, p. 177.

4. Bonch-Bruevich, V. *Na boevykh postakh Fevralskoi i Oktiabr'skoi revoliutsii*, Moscow, 1930, p. 154. *Bolshaia Sovetskaia Entsiklopediia*, v. 34, p. 579.

5. Dybenko, P. E. *op. cit.*, p. 69.

6. Bonch-Bruevich, V. *op. cit.*, pp. 288, 289.

7. *ibid.*, pp. 306, 307.

8. *ibid.*, p. 246.

9. *ibid.*, p. 324.

10. *ibid.*, p. 270.

11. Lenin, V. I. *Collected Works*, v. XX, book 1, New York, International Publishers, 1929, p. 50. Emphasis as used by translators.

12. *ibid.*, p. 52.

13. *ibid.*, p. 53.

14. For a more detailed description and analysis of Soviet philosophy of war see Fedotoff White, D. "Soviet Philosophy of War," *The Political Science Quarterly*, September 1936, pp. 321-353.

15. Lenin, V. I. *op. cit.*, v. XX, book 2, p. 14.

16. Wollenberg, E. *The Red Army*, London, 1938, Secker & Warburg, pp. 16, 19.

17. Rossiiskaia Kommunisticheskaia Partiia. VII S'ezd. *Stenograficheskii Otchet*, Moscow-Petrograd, 1923, p. 4.

18. *ibid.*, p. 12.

19. *ibid.*, p. 19.

20. *ibid.*, pp. 21, 22, 23, 26, 27.

21. *ibid.*, pp. 28, 29, 31.

22. *ibid.*, p. 131.

23. *ibid.*, p. 94.

24. *ibid.*, pp. 93, 105.

25. *ibid.*, p. 59.

26. *ibid.*, p. 75. Pukhov, G. S. *Kak vooruzhalsia Petrograd*, Moscow, 1933, p. 14.

27. Pukhov, G. S. *op. cit.*, pp. 12, 13.

28. Rossiiskaia Kommunisticheskaia Partiia. *op. cit.*, p. 66.

29. *ibid.*, pp. 67, 70.

30. Istpart. Komissiia po istorii Oktiabr'skoi revoliutsii i RKP(b). *Revoliutsiia i RKP(b) v materialakh i dokumentakh*, v. 7, Moscow, p. 209. Rossiiskaia Kommunisticheskaia Partiia (b). Statisticheskoe otd. Tsentr. Kom. RKP (b). *RKP (b) v tsifrakh*, Moscow, 1924, p. 3.

31. Rossiiskaia Kommunisticheskaia Partiia. VII S'ezd. *Stenograficheskii Otchet*, p. 205.

32. The author is of the opinion, for which he is unable to offer any documentary support, that Lenin was convinced at the time that the Allies were certain to win the war and that Germany and her satellites were faced with a certain defeat. Chicherin's information, which was placed before the People's Commissars upon the former's arrival from England, had strengthened Lenin in this view. The author was at Petrograd during the beginning of 1918 and had formed this hypothesis at the time, subsequent to conversations with Raskolnikov and E. Behrens, both of whom had access to Lenin and other members of the government. In other words, Lenin was convinced that the Brest-Litovsk treaty would be soon shattered by Germany's defeat in the West.

CHAPTER IV

1. Trotskii, L. *Kak vooruzhalas' Revoliutsiia*, v. I, Moscow, 1924, p. 101; also p. 406, footnote 36. Rymshan, M., Aleksinskii, K. and Karneev, B. *Revoliutsionnyi Voennyi Sovet S.S.S.R. za 10 let*, Moscow-Leningrad, 1928, pp. 9, 10, 14 give the following information: the Second All-Russian Congress of Soviets had issued on October 28 (old style), 1917 a decree establishing the Council of the People's Commissars and appointing a Committee on Military Affairs consisting

of Antonov-Ovseenko, Krylenko and Dybenko, thus founding the first central organ for the direction of military affairs of the Soviet state. On November 23, 1917 (old style) was founded the "All-Russian Collegium for the direction of the affairs of the military department," consisting of Podvoiskii, Sklianskii, Trotskii, Mekhonoshin, Antonov-Ovseenko, Iurenev and Lazimir. This collegium had replaced the above mentioned committee on Military Affairs.

2. Trotskii, L. *op. cit.*, v. 1, p. 102.

3. *ibid.*, v. 1, pp. 103, 105. The order of April 6, 1918 is quoted *ibid.*, v. 1, p. 406.

4. *ibid.*, v. 1, p. 121.

5. Decree on compulsory training in military art, published by the VTSIK of the Soviets on April 22, 1918 (quoted in Trotskii, L., *op. cit.*, v. 1, pp. 123, 124; see also p. 115).

6. *ibid.*, v. 1, p. 107.

7. Kakurin, N. *Kak srazhalas' revoliutsiia*, v. 1, Moscow-Leningrad, 1925, p. 134.

8. *ibid.*, p. 135.

9. *ibid.*

10. Pukhov, G. S. *Kak vooruzhalsia Petrograd*, Moscow, 1933, pp. 30, 31.

11. Kakurin, N. *op. cit.*, p. 135.

12. *Grazhdanskaia Voina 1918-1921*, edited by Bubnov, A. S., Kamenev, S. S. and Eideman, R. P., v. 2, Moscow, 1928, p. 95. The exact figure was given as 10,339.

13. Kakurin, N. *op. cit.*, v. 1, p. 136.

14. *ibid.*

15. *ibid.*, p. 137.

16. *Grazhdanskaia Voina 1918-1921*, v. 2, Moscow, 1928, pp. 53, 54.

17. *ibid.*, v. 1, p. 233.

18. *ibid.*, v. 2, p. 54.

19. *ibid.*, v. 2, p. 59.

20. Trotskii, L. *op. cit.*, v. 1, p. 314.

21. Thal, B. *Istoriia Krasnoi Armii*, Moscow-Leningrad, 6th ed., 1929, p. 64.

22. *ibid.*

23. Bunyan, James. *Intervention, Civil War, and Communism in Russia. April-December 1918. Documents and Materials*, Baltimore, The Johns Hopkins Press, 1936, p. 276.

24. *ibid.*, p. 275.

25. *ibid.*

26. Miliukov, P. *Rossiia na Perelome*, v. 1, Paris, 1927, p. 168.

27. *ibid.*

28. *ibid.*

29. Thal, B. *op. cit.*, p. 44.

30. *ibid.* The text of the decree quoted on p. 45. It was signed, among others, by N. Krylenko, as Supreme Commander in Chief and by the Commissars for Military and Naval Affairs, Dybenko and Podvoiskii.

31. *Grazhdanskaia Voina 1918-1921*, v. 2, Moscow, 1928, p. 51.

32. *ibid.*, v. 2, p. 52.

33. Thal, B. *op. cit.*, p. 53.

34. Kakurin, N. *op. cit.*, v. 1, p. 143.

35. *Grazhdanskaia Voina 1918-1921*, v. 2, p. 59. Thal, B. *op. cit.*, p. 53.

36. *ibid.*

37. Thal, B. *op. cit.*, p. 53. Petukhov, I. *Partiinaia organizatsiia i partiinaia rabota v RKKA*, Moscow-Leningrad, 1928, p. 33.

38. *ibid.*

39. *ibid.*, p. 52.

40. Denikin, A. I. *Staraia Armiia*, v. 1, Paris, 1929, p. 7.

41. *ibid.*, v. 1, p. 116.

42. Quoted in Petrovskii, D. A. *Voennaia shkola v gody Revoliutsii*, Moscow, 1924, p. 216.

43. Denikin, A. I. *op. cit.*, v. 1, p. 7.

44. *ibid.*, v. 1, p. 14.

45. *ibid.*, v. 1, p. 59.

46. *ibid.*, v. 2, Paris, 1931, pp. 9, 10.

47. *ibid.*, v. 2, pp. 10, 11.

48. *ibid.*, v. 2, pp. 12, 13.

49. *ibid.*, v. 2, pp. 25, 26.

50. *ibid.*, v. 1, pp. 69, 78, 79.

51. *ibid.*, v. 1, pp. 146, 147, 150.

52. *ibid.*, v. 1, p. 153.

53. *ibid.*, v. 2, p. 152.

54. *ibid.*, v. 2, p. 115.

55. *ibid.*, v. 2, p. 91.

56. Piatnitskii, N. V., Colonel. *Krasnaia Armiia SSSR*, v. 2, Paris, 1932, p. 14.

57. Denikin, A. I. *op. cit.*, v. 2, pp. 35, 36.

58. *1917 god v dokumentakh i materialakh*, edited by Pokrovskii, M. N. and Iakovlev, Ia. A. *Razlozhenie armii v 1917 godu*, prepared for publication by N. E. Kakurin, with a foreword by Ia. A. Iakovlev, Moscow-Leningrad, 1925, pp. 53, 54.

59. Graf, G. *Na "Novike,"* Munich, 1922, p. 327.

60. Trotskii, L. *op. cit.*, v. 1, p. 145.

61. Petrovskii, D. A. *op. cit.*, p. 161.

62. Niessel, Général. *op. cit.*, p. 21.

63. Miliukov, P. *op. cit.*, v. 1, pp. 34, 35.

64. *Grazhdanskaia Voina 1918-1921*, v. 2, pp. 93, 94, 95, 97.

65. *ibid.*

66. Trotskii, L. *op. cit.*, v. 1, p. 174.

67. *ibid.*, v. 1, p. 175.

68. *ibid.*, v. 1, p. 180.

69. *ibid.*, v. 1, pp. 154, 156, 410 (footnote 63).

70. *ibid.*, p. 172.

71. Voroshilov, K. *Stalin i Krasnaia Armiia*, 2nd ed., Moscow, 1937, p. 7.

72. Trotskii, L. *op. cit.*, v. 1, p. 225.

73. *Grazhdanskaia Voina 1918-1921*, v. 2, p. 104. Apparently this omits junior commanders, among whom former N.C. O. predominated.

74. Denikin, A. I. *op. cit.*, v. 2, pp. 163, 165.

75. Zaitzoff, A. *Die Rote Armee*, Berlin-Spandau, Obelisk-Verlag, 1934, p. 15. Trotskii, L. *op. cit.*, v. 2, book 1, p. 109.

76. *Krasnaia Zvezda*, No. 289 (4439), Dec. 20, 1939.

77. *Grazhdanskaia Voina 1918-1921*, v. 2, p. 168.

78. *ibid.*, p. 169.

79. Petrovskii, D. A. *op. cit.*, p. 12.

80. *ibid.*, p. 11.

81. *ibid.*, p. 12.

82. *ibid.*

83. *ibid.*

84. *ibid.*, p. 13. Trotskii, L. *op. cit.*, v. 2, book 1, p. 73.

85. Petrovskii, D. A. *op. cit.*, p. 17.

86. *ibid.*, p. 19.

87. *ibid.*, pp. 56, 57.

88. Niessel, Général. *op. cit.*, p. 21.

89. Petrovskii, D. A. *op. cit.*, p. 26.

90. *ibid.*

91. *ibid.*

92. *Grazhdanskaia Voina 1918-1921*, v. 2, p. 96. This figure includes 1897 graduates of the so-called "higher" (*vysshie*) schools.

93. *ibid.*

94. Petrovskii, D. A. *op. cit.*, p. 18.

95. *ibid.*, p. 16.

96. *ibid.*, p. 58.

97. *ibid.*, p. 12.

98. Trotskii, L. *op. cit.*, v. 2, book 1, p. 72.

99. *Grazhdanskaia Voina 1918-1921*, v. 2, pp. 107, 147, 148.

100. Petrovskii, D. A. *op. cit.*, pp. 228, 230.

101. *ibid.*, p. 230.

102. *ibid.*, p. 233.

103. *ibid.*, pp. 233, 234.

104. *ibid.*, p. 237.

105. Trotskii, L. *op. cit.*, v. 2, book 1, p. 109.

106. Petrovskii, D. A. *op. cit.*, pp. 110, 111.

107. *ibid.*, pp. 107, 115.

108. *ibid.*, p. 22.

109. *ibid.*, pp. 105, 111, 112.

110. *ibid.*, p. 20.

111. *ibid.*

112. *ibid.*, pp. 42, 112.

113. Trotskii, L. *op. cit.*, v. 2, book 1, pp. 353, 354.

114. *ibid.*, v. 2, book 1, p. 260.

115. *ibid.*, v. 2, book 1, pp. 252, 455 (footnote 47). *Grazhdanskaia Voina 1918-1921*, v. 1, p. 96.

116. Gul, R. *Voroshilov, Budennyi, Bluecher, Kotovskii*, Paris (year of publication not given), pp. 24, 25, 27, 28, 30, 32, 39, 42, 47.

117. *Grazhdanskaia Voina 1918-1921*, v. 1, p. 234.

118. *ibid.*, v. 1, p. 235.

119. Trotskii, L. *op. cit.*, v. 1, p. 17.

120. *ibid.*, v. 1, p. 152.

121. *ibid.*, v. 1, p. 146.

122. Blumenthal, F. *Politicheskaia rabota v voennoe vremia*, Moscow-Leningrad, 2nd ed., 1929, p. 23.

123. *Grazhdanskaia Voina 1918-1921*, v. 1, p. 215.

124. *ibid.*

125. *ibid.*

126. *Oktiabr'skaia Revoliutsiis i Grazhdanskaia Voina na Severe.* Compiled by A. I. Potylitsyn, v. 1, Archangel, 1933, p. 87.

127. *ibid.*, v. 2, pp. 38, 39.

128. *Grazhdanskaia Voina 1918-1921*, v. 1, pp. 20, 21.

129. Gul, R. *op. cit.*, pp. 25, 31.

130. Trotskii, L. *op. cit.*, v. 3, book 1, p. 318.

131. *ibid.*, v. 1, p. 409 (footnote 56).

132. *ibid.*, v. 1, p. 140.

133. *Kommunist RKKA*, No. 17-18, Sept. 1937, p. 42.

134. Trotskii, L. *op. cit.*, v. 1, p. 278.

135. Quoted in Trotskii, L. *op. cit.*, v. 1, p. 318.

136. Stankevich, V. B. *Vospominaniia 1914-1919 g.*, Berlin, 1920, p. 175.

137. *ibid.*, p. 165.

138. *ibid.*, pp. 239, 240.

139. Niessel, Général. *op. cit.*, p. 17.

140. *1917 god v dokumentakh i materailakh*, edited by Pokrovskii, M. N. and Iakovlev, Ia. A. *Razlozhenie armii v 1917 godu*, prepared for publication by

N. E. Kakurin, with a foreword by Ia. A. Iakovlev, Moscow-Leningrad, 1925, p. 173.

141. Quoted in Trotskii, L. *op. cit.*, v. 1, p. 406 (footnote 38).

142. *ibid.*, v. 1, p. 407.

143. *ibid.*

144. Niessel, Général. *op. cit.*, p. 202.

145. *Grazhdanskaia Voina 1918-1921*, v. 2, p. 112.

146. *ibid.*

147. *ibid.*, v. 2, p. 110.

148. Petukhov, I. *Partiinaia organizatsiia i partiinaia rabota v RKKA*, Moscow-Leningrad, 1928, pp. 31, 32.

149. Trotskii, L. *op. cit.*, v. 1, p. 28.

150. Petukhov, I. *op. cit.*, p. 32.

151. *ibid.*, pp. 32, 33.

152. *ibid.*, p. 33.

153. *Grazhdanskaia Voina 1918-1921*, v. 2, pp. 113, 132. Trotskii, L. *op. cit.*, v. 1, pp. 266, 267.

154. *ibid.*, v. 2, p. 114.

155. *ibid.*, v. 2, pp. 114, 115.

156. Petukhov, I. *op. cit.*, p. 33.

157. *Grazhdanskaia Voina 1918-1921*, v. 2, p. 64.

158. Trotskii, L. *op. cit.*, v. 1, pp. 183, 184.

159. *ibid.*, v. 2, book 1, p. 56.

160. Petukhov, I. *op. cit.*, pp. 34, 35.

161. *ibid.*, pp. 36, 51.

162. *ibid.*, p. 36.

163. *ibid.*, p. 39.

164. *ibid.*, p. 41.

165. *ibid.*

166. *Grazhdanskaia Voina 1918-1921*, v. 2, p. 117.

167. *ibid.*, v. 2, pp. 117, 118.

168. *ibid.*, p. 122.

169. *ibid.*, pp. 124, 125.

170. *ibid.*, p. 125.

171. Trotskii, L. *op. cit.*, v. 2, book 1, pp. 89, 90.

172. Petrovskii, D. A. *op. cit.*, pp. 86, 87, 102.

173. Trotskii, L. *op. cit.*, v. 2, book 1, p. 110.

174. *ibid.*, v. 2, book 1, p. 111.

175. *ibid.*

176. *ibid.*, v. 2, book 1, p. 112.

177. *ibid.*, v. 2, book 1, pp. 81, 82.

178. *ibid.*, v. 2, book 1, pp. 76, 453 (footnote 31).

179. *ibid.*, v. 2, book 1, p. 77.

180. *ibid.*

181. *ibid.*, v. 2, book 1, pp. 76, 77, 78.

182. *ibid.*, v. 1, p. 411 (footnote 69).

183. *ibid.*, v. 1, p. 267.

184. *Grazhdanskaia Voina 1918-1921*, v. 1, p. 168.

185. Trotskii, L. *op. cit.*, v. 1, p. 243.

186. Petukhov, I. *op. cit.*, p. 45.

187. *ibid.*, pp. 45, 46.

188. *ibid.*, p. 46.

189. *ibid.*, pp. 46, 47.

190. *ibid.*, p. 52.

191. *ibid.*, p. 55.

192. *ibid.*, p. 57.

193. *ibid.*, quoted on p. 61.

194. R.S.F.S.R. S'ezdy Sovetov Rabochikh, Krestianskikh, Krasnoarmeiskikh i Kazach'ikh Deputatov. VII S'ezd. *Stenograficheskii Otchet*, Moscow, 1920, p. 84.

195. *ibid.*, pp. 85, 86.

196. *Grazhdanskaia Voina 1918-1921*, v. 2, pp. 64, 126 (footnote 2).

197. *ibid.*, p. 86.

198. Petrovskii, D. A. *op. cit.*, p. 87.

199. *Grazhdanskaia Voina 1918-1921*, v. 2, pp. 67, 68.

200. *ibid.*, v. 2, p. 111.

201. Petukhov, I. *op. cit.*, p. 20.

202. *ibid.*

203. *ibid.*

204. *ibid.*, p. 21.

205. *Grazhdanskaia Voina 1918-1921*, v. 2, pp. 111, 112.

206. *ibid.*, v. 2, p. 116.

207. Petukhov, I. *op. cit.*, p. 22.

208. *ibid.*

209. *ibid.*

210. *ibid.*, p. 23.

211. *ibid.*

212. *Grazhdanskaia Voina 1918-1921*, v. 2, p. 117.

213. *ibid.*, v. 2, p. 119.

214. Petukhov, I. *op. cit.*, p. 24.

215. *ibid.*

216. *Resolution on Military Problem.* VIII Party Congress, Para XIV, subdiv. A. (quoted in *Grazhdanskaia Voina 1918-1921*, v. 2, p. 120).

217. *Grazhdanskaia Voina 1918-1921*, v. 2, p. 120.

218. Petukhov, I. *op. cit.*, pp. 25, 27.

219. *ibid.*

220. *Grazhdanskaia Voina 1918-1921*, v. 2, p. 123.

221. Quoted in Petukhov, I. *op. cit.*, p. 34.

222. *ibid.*

223. *Report of the Political Department of the First Army for the period from September 1918 to January 1919* (quoted in Petukhov, I. *op. cit.*, pp. 41, 42).

224. Petukhov, I. *op. cit.*, p. 42.
225. *ibid.*, pp. 43, 44.
226. *ibid.*, p. 44.
227. *ibid.*, p. 46.
228. *ibid.*, p. 24.
229. *ibid.*, pp. 55, 56.
230. Pukhov, G. S. *Kak vooruzhalsia Petrograd*, Moscow, 1933, p. 113.
231. *ibid.*, p. 114.
232. Trotskii, L. *op. cit.*, v. 2, book 2, p. 99.
233. Rossiiskaia Kommunisticheskaia Partiia (b). X S'ezd. *Stenograficheskii Otchet*, Petersburg, 1921, pp. 5, 6.
234. Trotskii, L. *op. cit.*, v. 2, book 2, p. 126.
235. *Grazhdanskaia Voina 1918-1921*, v. 2, p. 83.
236. *ibid.*
237. *ibid.*, p. 48.
238. Trotskii, L. *op. cit.*, v. 1, pp. 38, 39.
239. *ibid.*, v. 1, p. 116.
240. *Grazhdanskaia Voina 1918-1921*, v. 2, p. 85.
241. *ibid.*, v. 2, p. 83.
242. *ibid.*, v. 2, p. 87.
243. *ibid.*, v. 2, p. 17.
244. *ibid.*, v. 1, p. 203.
245. Pukhov, G. S. *Kak vooruzhalsia Petrograd*, pp. 79, 81, 103.
246. Coste, Charles. *La Psychologie Sociale de la Guerre*, Nancy, Imprimerie Berger-Levrault, 1928, p. 17.
247. *ibid.*, p. 18.
248. Pukhov, G. S. *op. cit.*, pp. 77, 78.
249. Trotskii, L. *op. cit.*, v. 2, book 2, p. 271.
250. *ibid.*, v. 2, book 2, p. 211.
251. *ibid.*, v. 2, book 2, p. 193.
252. Quoted in Piatnitskii, N. V. *op. cit.*, v. 1, pp. 14, 15.
253. Trotskii, L. *op. cit.*, v. 2, book 1, p. 138.
254. *ibid.*, v. 1, p. 243.
255. *ibid.*, v. 2, book 2, p. 228.
256. *ibid.*, v. 1, pp. 71, 72, 73.
257. *ibid.*, v. 2, book 2, pp. 231, 232.
258. *ibid.*, v. 2, book 2, p. 245.
259. *ibid.*, v. 1, pp. 416, 417 (footnote 99).
260. Costes, C. *op. cit.*, p. 2.
261. *ibid.*, pp. 11, 12.
262. *ibid.*, p. 12.
263. *ibid.*, pp. 53, 54. *L'Instruction sur le combat offensif des petites unités datée de 1919* and *Le réglement du 1er février 1920 sur les manoeuvres de l'infanterie.*

264. Trotskii, L. *op. cit.*, v. 3, book 1, p. 277.
265. R.S.F.S.R. *Distsiplinarnyi Ustav Raboche-Krestianskoi Krasnoi Armii*, Moscow, 1919, p. 8.
266. *ibid.*, pp. 5, 6.
267. *ibid.*, p. 9.
268. *ibid.*, pp. 11, 12.
269. *ibid.*, p. 12.
270. *ibid.*, p. 14.
271. *ibid.*, pp. 16, 17.
272. *ibid.*, p. 17.
273. *ibid.*, p. 19.
274. *ibid.*, pp. 20-24.
275. *ibid.*, p. 26.
276. *1917 god v dokumentakh i materialakh*, edited by Pokrovskii, M. N. and Iakovlev, Ia. A. *Razlozhenie armii v 1917 godu*, prepared for publication by N. E. Kakurin, with a foreword by Ia. A. Iakovlev, Moscow-Leningrad, 1925, p. 173 (no. 183).
277. R.S.F.S.R. *op. cit.*, pp. 27-30.
278. Blumenthal, F. *op. cit.*, p. 30.
279. *ibid.*
280. Kakurin, N. *op. cit.*, v. 1, p. 153.
281. *V ogne revoliutsii*, edited by L. Gurvich, Moscow, 1933, p. 47.
282. *ibid.*, p. 127.
283. *Grazhdanskaia Voina 1918-1921*, v. 1, p. 82.
284. *ibid.*
285. *ibid.*, v. 1, p. 289.
286. Trotskii, L. *op. cit.*, v. 2, book 1, p. 204.
287. *Grazhdanskaia Voina 1918-1921*, v. 2, p. 23.
288. *ibid.*, v. 1, p. 25.
289. Kakurin, N. *op. cit.*, v. 2, p. 12.
290. *Grazhdanskaia Voina 1918-1921*, v. 2, p. 21.
291. *ibid.*, v. 2, p. 22.
292. *ibid.*, v. 2, p. 24.
293. Miliukov, P. *Rossiia na perelome*, v. 1, Paris, 1927, pp. 174, 175.
294. Trotskii, L. *op. cit.*, v. 1, p. 28.
295. Bonch-Bruevich, Vlad. *Na boevykh postakh fevralskoi i oktiabr'skoi revoliutsii*, Moscow, 1930, p. 118.
296. *V ogne revoliutsii*, edited by L. Gurvich, pp. 112, 127.
297. Trotskii, L. *op. cit.*, v. 1, p. 237.
298. *ibid.*, v. 2, book 1, p. 110.
299. Kakurin, N. *op. cit.*, v. 1, pp. 123, 134.
300. *ibid.*, v. 1, p. 94.
301. *ibid.*, v. 1, p. 100.
302. *Oktiabr'skaia revoliutsiia i grazhdanskaia voina na Severe*, compiled by

A. I. Potylitsyn, v. 1, p. 47.

303. Pukhov, G. S. *op. cit.*, pp. 72, 73.

304. *ibid.*, pp. 106, 107.

305. *ibid.*, p. 107.

306. Trotskii, L. *op. cit.*, v. 2, book 1, p. 81.

307. *ibid.*, v. 3, book 1, pp. 188, 189.

308. *ibid.*, v. 2, book 1, pp. 84, 85, 86.

309. Babel, I. *Konarmiia*, Moscow-Leningrad, 1927, p. 103.

310. Miliukov, P. *op. cit.*, v. 1, pp. 177, 178.

311. *Grazhdanskaia Voina 1918-1921*, v. 1, p. 20.

312. Trotskii, L. *op. cit.*, v. 3, book 2, p. 7.

313. *ibid.*, v. 1, p. 21.

314. Agricola. *Der Rote Marschall*, Berlin, 1939, p. 72.

CHAPTER V

1. Rossiiskaia Kommunisticheskaia Partiia (b). X S'ezd. *Stenograficheskii Otchet* 8-16 Marta 1921. Petersburg, 1921, p. 21.

2. Trotskii, L. *Kak vooruzhalas' Revoliutsiia*, v. 3, part 1, Moscow, 1924, pp. 203, 204.

3. *Grazhdanskaia Voina 1918-1921*, v. 1, Moscow, 1928, p. 361.

4. *ibid.*, pp. 361, 362.

5. *ibid.*, p. 362.

6. *Kronshtadtskii Miatezh*, edited by N. Kornatovskii, Leningrad, 1931, p. 12.

7. *ibid.*, p. 24.

8. *Izvestiia Vremennogo Revoliutsionnogo Komiteta Matrosov, Krasnoarmeitsev i Rabochikh gor. Kronshtadta*, March 6, 1921 in *Pravda o Kronshtadte*, Prague, 1921, p. 62.

9. Miliukov, P. *Rossiia na perelome*, v. 1, Paris, 1927, p. 288.

10. Chamberlin, William Henry. *The Russian Revolution 1917-1921*, v. 2, The Macmillan Co., New York, 1935, p. 430.

11. *ibid.*, pp. 430, 431.

12. *Pravda*, Jan. 22, 1921 (quoted in Chamberlin, W. H. *op. cit.*, v. 2, p. 432).

13. Chamberlin, W. H. *op. cit.*, v. 2, p. 432.

14. *ibid.*

15. Rossiiskaia Kommunisticheskaia Partiia (b). X S'ezd. *Stenograficheskii Otchet* 8-16 Marta 1921. Petersburg, 1921, p. 25.

16. *ibid.*, p. 26.

17. *ibid.*, p. 27.

18. *Panama* was imported into the Russian language after the famous Panama Canal upheaval in France and came to denote any political scandal tinctured with dishonesty.

19. Rossiiskaia Kommunisticheskaia Partiia (b). *op. cit.*, pp. 30, 31.

20. *ibid.*, p. 32.

21. *ibid.*, pp. 41, 45.

22. *ibid.*, pp. 29, 30.

23. *ibid.*, p. 40.

24. *ibid.*, pp. 22, 23.

25. Rossiiskaia Kommunisticheskaia Partiia (b). IX S'ezd. *Stenograficheskii Otchet*. Moscow, 1920, pp. 44, 57, 68.

26. *ibid.*, pp. 57, 68.

27. *ibid.*, p. 67.

28. *Pravda*, January 21, Feb. 6, Feb. 12, 1921 (see Chamberlin, W. H. *op. cit.*, v. 2, p. 433).

29. Chamberlin, W. H. *op. cit.*, v. 2, p. 433.

30. *ibid.*

31. *ibid.*, pp. 433, 434.

32. *ibid.*, pp. 434, 435.

33. *ibid.*

34. *ibid.*, p. 435.

35. *ibid.*, p. 440.

36. Dybenko, P. E. *Iz nedr tsarskogo flota k velikomu Oktiabriu*, Moscow, 1928, pp. 199, 200.

37. Trotskii, L. *op. cit.*, v. 1, p. 140.

38. Dybenko, P. E. *op. cit.*, p. 143 (footnote 1).

39. *ibid.*, p. 78.

40. *Grazhdanskaia Voina 1918-1921*, v. 1, Moscow, 1928, p. 75.

41. *ibid.*, p. 85.

42. Bonch-Bruevich, Vlad. *Na boevykh postakh fevralskoi i oktiabr'skoi revoliutsii*, Moscow, 1930, p. 343.

43. Trotskii, L. *op. cit.*, v. 1, p. 278.

44. Pukhov, G. S. *Kak vooruzhalsia Petrograd*, Moscow, 1933, p. 36.

45. *Kronshtadtskii Miatezh*, edited by N. Kornatovskii, Leningrad, 1931, pp. 56, 57.

46. *ibid.*, p. 57.

47. *ibid.*, p. 60.

48. *ibid.*, p. 86.

49. Chamberlin, W. H. *op. cit.*, v. 2, pp. 436, 437.

50. e.g. see *Kronshtadtskii Miatezh*, edited by N. Kornatovskii, p. 55.

51. *ibid.*

52. *ibid.*

53. *ibid.*

54. *ibid.*, pp. 13, 14.

55. *ibid.*, p. 14.

56. *ibid.*, pp. 14, 15.

57. *ibid.*, p. 56.

58. *ibid.*

59. *Izvestiia Vremennogo Revoliutsionnogo Komiteta Matrosov, Krasnoarmeitsev i Rabochikh gor. Kronshtadta,* March 6, 1921 in *Pravda o Kronshtadte,* Prague, 1921, p. 66.

60. *ibid.,* March 7, 1921 in *op. cit.,* p. 76.

61. *ibid.,* March 9, 1921, in *op. cit.,* p. 99.

62. *ibid.,* March 10, 1921 in *op. cit.,* p. 110; March 12, 1921 in *op. cit.,* p. 134; March 16, 1921, in *op. cit.,* p. 181.

63. *ibid.,* March 13, 1921, in *op. cit.,* pp. 141, 142, 143.

64. Rossiiskaia Kommunisticheskaia Partiia (b). Statisticheskii Otdel Tsentralnogo Komiteta RKP (b). *RKP (b) v tsifrakh,* Moscow, 1924, pp. 5, 7.

65. Quoted in *Pravda o Kronshtadte,* pp. 13, 52.

66. *ibid.,* p. 62.

67. *Grazhdanskaia Voina 1918-1921,* v. 1, Moscow, 1928, p. 363.

68. *Pravda o Kronshtadte,* pp. 10, 11, 12.

69. *ibid.,* p. 14.

70. *ibid.,* p. 19.

71. *ibid.,* p. 15.

72. *Kronshtadtskii Miatezh,* edited by N. Kornatovskii, p. 33.

73. *Pravda o Kronshtadte,* p. 38.

74. Chamberlin, W. H. *op. cit.,* v. 2, p. 441.

75. *Pravda o Kronshtadte,* p. 9.

76. *ibid.*

77. *ibid.,* pp. 9, 10.

78. *ibid.,* p. 9.

79. *ibid.,* pp. 9, 10.

80. *Izvestiia Vremennogo Revoliutsionnogo Komiteta* etc., March 8, 1921 in *Pravda o Kronshtadte,* pp. 82, 83.

81. *ibid.,* March 11, 1921 in *op. cit.,* p. 120.

82. *ibid.,* March 16, 1921 in *op. cit.,* pp. 172, 173.

83. Chamberlin, W. H. *op. cit.,* v. 2, pp. 442, 445.

84. *Pravda o Kronshtadte,* p. 40.

85. Wollenberg, E. *The Red Army,* Secker & Warburg, London, 1938, pp. 114, 116. *V ogne revoliutsii,* edited by L. Gurvich, Moscow, 1933, p. 58.

86. *Kronshtadtskii Miatezh.* ALIIP. "*Svodki po raionam o nastroenii rabochikh na fabrikakh i zavodakh, fevral-mart 1921,*" p. 130.

87. *ibid.,* p. 131.

88. *ibid.,* p. 132.

89. *ibid.*

90. *ibid.,* p. 133.

91. *ibid.,* pp. 133, 134.

92. *Kronshtadtskii Miatezh,* p. 247.

93. *ibid.,* pp. 93, 94, 100.

94. *ibid.,* pp. 100, 101.

95. *ibid.,* pp. 67, 68.

96. *ibid.,* p. 32.

97. *ibid.,* p. 80.

98. Dybenko, P. E. *op. cit.,* p. 38.

99. Agricola. *Der Rote Marschall,* Berlin, 1939, p. 78. *Kronshtatdskii Miatezh,* p. 95.

CHAPTER VI

1. *Voina i voennoe iskusstvo v svete istoricheskogo materialisma,* Moscow, 1927, p. 173.

2. For Marxian views on military dogma see Fedotoff White, D. "Soviet Philosophy of War," *The Political Science Quarterly,* Sept. 1936, pp. 334-337.

3. *Voina i voennoe iskusstvo v svete istoricheskogo materialisma,* pp. 156, 157.

4. *ibid.,* p. 157.

5. *ibid.,* p. 142.

6. See page 189 above.

7. Trotskii, L. *Kak vooruzhalas' Revoliutsiia,* v. 2, book 1, Moscow, 1924, pp. 59, 452 (footnote 26).

8. *ibid.,* v. 2, book 1, p. 59.

9. *ibid.,* v. 2, part 1, p. 454 (footnote 37).

10. Frunze, M. *Izbrannye Proizvedeniia,* Moscow, 1934, p. 7.

11. Frunze, M. *Sobranie Sochinenii,* v. 1, Moscow, 1929. A. Bubnov's *Preface,* p. xxvi.

12. Trotskii, L. *op. cit.,* v. 3, book 2, p. 201.

13. *ibid.,* v. 3, book 2, p. 202.

14. Fedotoff White, D. "Soviet Naval Doctrine," *Journal of the Royal United Service Institution,* August 1935, p. 610, gives an idea of the spirit in which the discussion of the naval doctrine was conducted.

15. Trotskii, L. *op. cit.,* v. 3, book 2, p. 203.

16. *ibid.*

17. Frunze, M. *Izbrannye Proizvedeniia,* p. 552 (footnote 18).

18. *ibid.,* p. 551 (footnote 18).

19. Svechin, A. *Strategiia,* 2nd ed., Moscow, 1927, pp. 8, 9.

20. Trotskii, L. *op. cit.,* v. 3, book 2, p. 207.

21. *ibid.*, p. 208.
22. *ibid.*, v. 3, book 2, pp. 212, 213.
23. *ibid.*, v. 3, book 2, pp. 215, 216, 218.
24. *ibid.*, v. 3, book 2, p. 168.
25. *ibid.*, v. 3, book 2, p. 230.
26. *ibid.*, v. 3, book 2, pp. 268, 269.
27. *ibid.*, v. 3, book 2, p. 270.
28. *ibid.*, v. 3, book 2, pp. 272, 273.
29. Frunze, M. *Izbrannye Proizvedeniia*, Moscow, 1934, p. 7.
30. *ibid.*, pp. 12, 14.
31. *ibid.*, p. 17.
32. *ibid.*
33. *ibid.*, p. 451.
34. Trotskii, L. *op. cit.*, v. 3, book 2, pp. 242, 243.
35. *ibid.*
36. *ibid.*, v. 3, book 2, pp. 249, 250.
37. *ibid.*, v. 3, book 2, p. 254.
38. *ibid.*, v. 3, book 2, p. 267.
39. *ibid.*, v. 3, book 2, pp. 205, 206.
40. *ibid.*, v. 3, book 2, p. 213.
41. Frunze, M. *Izbrannye Proizvedeniia*, Moscow, 1934, pp. 22, 23.
42. *ibid.*, pp. 63, 66.
43. Trotskii, L. *op. cit.*, v. 3, book 2, p. 205.
44. Tukhachevskii, M. P. *Voina kak problema vooruzhennoi bor'by*, in *Bolshaia Sovetskaia Entsiklopediia*, Moscow, 1928, v. XII, pp. 577, 596.
45. *ibid.*, pp. 584, 585, 590, 597.
46. Svechin, A. *Strategiia*, 2nd ed., Moscow, 1927, pp. 178 (footnote 2), 179.
47. *ibid.*, p. 183.
48. Trotskii, L. *op. cit.*, v. 3, book 2, p. 205.
49. *ibid.*, v. 3, book 2, pp. 251, 253.
50. *ibid.*, v. 3, book 2, pp. 254, 256.
51. *ibid.*, v. 3, book 2, p. 264.
52. *ibid.*, v. 3, book 2, pp. 225, 226.
53. *ibid.*, v. 3, book 2, p. 226.
54. *ibid.*, v. 3, book 2, p. 224.
55. *ibid.*, v. 3, book 2, p. 247.
56. *ibid.*, v. 3, book 2, p. 248.
57. *ibid.*, v. 3, book 2, p. 235.
58. *ibid.*, v. 3, book 1, pp. 18, 19, 20.
59. *ibid.*, v. 3, book 1, p. 59.
60. *ibid.*, v. 3, book 2, p. 239.
61. *Grazhdanskaia Voina 1918-1921*, v. 2, Moscow, 1928, pp. 33, 34, 39.
62. Trotskii, L. *op. cit.*, v. 2, book 1, pp. 149, 151.
63. *ibid.*, v. 2, book 2, p. 153.
64. Pukhov, G. S. *Kak vooruzhalsia Petrograd*, Moscow, 1933, p. 24.
65. Trotskii, L. *op. cit.*, v. 3, book 2, p. 204.

CHAPTER VII

1. R.S.F.S.R. IX S'ezd Sovetov Rabochikh, Krest'ianskikh, Kazach'ikh i Krasnoarmeiskikh Deputatov. *Stenograficheskii Otchet*, Moscow, 1922, p. 187.
2. *ibid.*
3. *ibid.*, p. 188.
4. *ibid.*
5. Trotskii, L. *Kak vooruzhalas' Revoliutsiia*, v. 2, book 1, Moscow, 1924, pp. 83, 86.
6. Frunze, M. *Izbrannye Proizvedeniia*, Moscow, 1934, p. 49.
7. *ibid.*, p. 78.
8. Rossiiskii Leninskii Kommunisticheskii Soiuz Molodezhi. Shestoi S'ezd. *Stenograficheskii Otchet*, Moscow-Leningrad, 1924, pp. 306, 307.
9. Rosiiskaia Kommunisticheskaia Partiia (b), XI S'ezd. *Stenograficheskii Otchet*, Moscow, 1922, pp. 253, 254.
10. *ibid.*
11. Rossiiskii Leninskii Kommunisticheskii Soiuz Molodezhi. *op. cit.*, p. 309.
12. Petukhov, I. *Partiinaia organizatsiia i partiinaia rabota v RKKA*, Moscow-Leningrad, 1928, p. 59.
13. Frunze, M. *op. cit.*, p. 79.
14. Geronimus, A. A. *Partiia i Krasnaia Armiia*, Moscow-Leningrad, 1928, p. 121.
15. Petrovskii, D. A. *Voennaia shkola v gody revoliutsii*, Moscow, 1924, pp. 29, 51, 54.
16. *ibid.*, p. 160.
17. Frunze, M. *op. cit.*, p. 401.
18. Petrovskii, D. A. *op. cit.*, p. 115.
19. *ibid.*, p. 160.
20. *ibid.*, p. 78.
21. Geronimus, A. A. *op. cit.*, pp. 113, 125, 148.
22. *ibid.*, p. 135.
23. *Voennaia Mysl*, No. 12, 1939, p. 52. Voroshilov, K. E. *Stat'i i Rechi*, Moscow, 1936, p. 563.
24. Geronimus, A. A. *op. cit.*, p. 148.
25. *ibid.*, p. 122.
26. *ibid.*, pp. 122, 123.
27. *ibid.*, p. 123.
28. *ibid.*
29. Rossiiskaia Kommunisticheskaia Partiia (b). IX S'ezd. *Stenograficheskii Otchet*, Moscow, 1920, pp. 350, 351.
30. *ibid.*, pp. 353, 354.
31. *ibid.*, pp. 356, 357.
32. *ibid.*, pp. 358, 359.
33. *ibid.*, pp. 360, 361, 394, 395.
34. *ibid.*, pp. 361, 395.

35. Trotskii, L. *op. cit.*, v. 2, book 1, pp. 115-121.

36. *ibid.*, v. 3, book 2, pp. ix, x.

37. Frunze, M. *op. cit.*, p. 84.

38. *Voennoe Delo*, No. 40 (see Trotskii, L. *op. cit.*, v. 2, book 1, p. 115).

39. Trotskii, L. *op. cit.*, v. 2, book 1, pp. 118, 121.

40. Piatnitskii, N. V., Colonel. *Krasnaia Armiia*, v. 2, Paris, 1932, p. 84.

41. Frunze, M. *op. cit.*, p. 84.

42. *ibid.*, p. 485.

43. *ibid.*, pp. 378, 379.

44. *ibid.*, p. 382.

45. *ibid.*, p. 474.

46. Trotskii, L. *op. cit.*, v. 3, book 2, p. 162.

47. *ibid.*, v. 3, book 2, p. 163.

48. *ibid.*, v. 3, book 2, p. 164.

49. *ibid.*, v. 3, book 2, p. ix.

50. *ibid.*, v. 3, book 2, p. vii.

51. *ibid.*, v. 3, book 1, p. 8.

52. Tuchatschevsky, M. *Die Rote Armee und Die Miliz*, Kleine Bibliothek der Russischen Korrespondenz, No. 51, Leipzig, 1921, pp. 4, 5.

53. *ibid.*, p. 5.

54. *ibid.*, pp. 6 to 16.

55. Makhine, Théodore H., Colonel. *L'Armée Rouge*, Payot, Paris, 1938, pp. 21, 176.

CHAPTER VIII

1. Frunze, M. *Izbrannye Proizvedeniia*, Moscow, 1934, p. 164.

2. Rossiiskii Leninskii Kommunisticheskii Soiuz Molodezhi. Shestoi S'ezd. *Stenograficheskii Otchet*. Moscow, 1924, p. 308.

3. *ibid.*, p. 309.

4. *ibid.*, p. 310.

5. *ibid.*, pp. 312, 314, 315.

6. *ibid.*, p. 320.

7. *ibid.*, p. 322.

8. Frunze, M. *op. cit.*, p. 409.

9. *ibid.*, pp. 407, 409, 436.

10. Rossiiskii Leninskii Kommunisticheskii Soiuz Molodezhi. *op. cit.*, p. 311.

11. Frunze, M. *op. cit.*, p. 483.

12. *Krasnaia Zvezda*, No. 297, Jan. 1, 1925.

13. Frunze, M. *op. cit.*, p. 403.

14. Petrovskii, D. A. *Voennaia shkola v gody revoliutsii*, Moscow, 1924, pp. 25, 26, 27.

15. Voroshilov, K. *Oborona SSSR*, Moscow, 1927, pp. 26, 65.

16. Zaitzoff, A. *Die Rote Armee*, Obelisk-Verlag, Berlin-Spandau, 1934, pp. 20, 21. *Bolshaia Sovetskaia Entsyklopediia*, v. 39, Moscow, 1938, p. 400.

17. *Bolshaia Sovetskaia Entsyklopediia*, v. 59, Moscow, 1935, p. 264. Voroshilov, K. *op. cit.*, p. 29.

18. *Bolshaia Sovetskaia Entsyklopediia*, v. 59, p. 264.

19. Trotskii, L. *Kak vooruzhalas' Revoliutsiia*, Moscow, 1924, v. 3, book 1, pp. 275, 276.

20. *ibid.*, v. 3, book 1, p. 276.

21. *ibid.*, v. 3, book 1, p. 277.

22. *ibid.*, v. 3, book 1, pp. 277, 279.

23. *Grazhdanskaia Voina 1918-1921*, v. 2, Moscow, 1928, pp. 97, 98.

24. *ibid.*, v. 2, p. 98.

25. *ibid.*, v. 2, pp. 101, 103.

26. *ibid.*, v. 2, p. 107.

27. *ibid.*, v. 2, pp. 105, 109.

28. *ibid.*, v. 2, p. 105.

29. *ibid.*, v. 2, p. 108.

30. *ibid.*, v. 2, p. 106.

31. Trotskii, L. *op. cit.*, v. 3, book 2, pp. 202, 203.

32. Frunze, M. *Izbrannye Proizvedeniia*, p. 433.

33. *Grazhdanskaia Voina 1918-1921*, v. 2, pp. 106, 107, 147, 148.

34. Voroshilov, K. E. *Stat'i i Rechi*, Moscow, 1936, p. 50.

35. *Krasnaia Zvezda*, No. 297, Jan. 1, 1925.

36. Frunze, M. *op. cit.*, p. 159.

37. *ibid.*, pp. 56, 68, 69.

38. *ibid.*, p. 185.

39. Wollenberg, E. *The Red Army*, Secker & Warburg, London, 1938, pp. 65, 66.

40. Trotskii, L. *op. cit.*, v. 2, book 1, pp. 106, 107.

41. *ibid.*, v. 2, book 1, p. 100.

42. *ibid.*, v. 2, book 2, pp. 115 (footnote 25), 308.

43. Wollenberg, E. *op. cit.*, pp. 62, 63.

44. Maiskii, I. *Demokraticheskaia kontr-revoliutsiia*, Petrograd, 1923, p. 46.

45. Frunze, M. V. *Sobranie Sochinenii*, v. 2, Moscow, 1926, p. 171.

46. *ibid.*, v. 2, p. 151.

47. *ibid.*, v. 2, p. 36.

48. Trotskii, L. *Moia Zhizn'*, Riga, 1930, v. 2, p. 253.

49. *ibid.*, v. 2, pp. 253, 254.

50. Frunze, M. V. *op. cit.*, v. 2, p. 37.

51. Piatnitskii, N. V., Colonel. *Krasnaia Armiia SSSR*, v. 2, Paris, 1932, p. 115.

52. *ibid.*, v. 2, p. 116.

53. Voroshilov, K. *Oborona SSSR,* Moscow, 1927, p. 75.

54. *ibid.,* p. 76.

55. *ibid.,* p. 73.

56. *ibid.,* p. 66.

57. Petrovskii, D. A. *op. cit.,* p. 158.

58. *ibid.,* p. 159.

59. *ibid.,* pp. 159, 164.

60. *ibid.,* p. 164.

61. *ibid.,* p. 166.

62. *ibid.,* p. 54.

63. *Krasnaia Zvezda,* No. 147 (443), July 1, 1925.

64. Trotskii, L. *Novyi Kurs,* Moscow, 1924, p. 91.

65. *ibid.,* p. 92.

66. Petrovskii, D. A. *op. cit.,* p. 26. Voroshilov, K. *Oborona SSSR,* p. 105.

67. *Grazhdanskaia Voina 1918-1921,* v. 2, pp. 67, 68. Voroshilov, K. *Oborona SSSR,* p. 105.

68. Piatnitskii, N. V. *op. cit.,* v. 2, p. 117.

69. Petrovskii, D. A. *op. cit.,* p. 26.

70. Piatnitskii, N. V. *op. cit.,* v. 2, p. 102.

71. Makhine, Théodore H., Colonel. *L'Armée Rouge,* Payot, Paris, 1938, pp. 114, 115.

72 Petrovskii, D. A. *op. cit.,* pp. 54, 78.

73. Smilga, I. *K voprosu o stroitelstve Krasnoi Armii,* Moscow, 1920, pp. 22, 23.

74. Frunze, M. V. *Sobranie Sochinenii,* v. 2, p. 182.

75. *ibid.,* v. 2, p. 183.

76. *ibid.,* v. 2, pp. 183, 184.

77. Voroshilov, K. *op. cit.,* pp. 24, 25.

78. Voroshilov, K. E. *Stat'i i Rechi,* Moscow, 1936, pp. 76, 77.

79. Frunze, M. *Izbrannye Proizvedeniia,* Moscow, 1934, pp. 407, 408.

80. *ibid.,* p. 408.

81. *ibid.,* p. 233.

82. *ibid.,* p. 189.

83. Voroshilov, K. E. *op. cit.,* p. 77.

84. Wollenberg, E. *op. cit.,* pp. 182, 183.

85. *Krasnaia Zvezda,* No. 297, Jan. 1, 1925; No. 15 (311), Jan. 18, 1925.

86. Wollenberg, E. *op. cit.,* p. 183.

87. *Voennyi Kalendar',* Petersburg, 1924, p. 225.

88. *ibid.*

89. Frunze, M. *Izbrannye Proizvedeniia,* p. 431.

90. Wollenberg, E. *op. cit.,* p. 183.

91. Voroshilov, K. E. *Stat'i i Rechi,* p. 27. Frunze, M. *op. cit.,* p. 430.

92. Voroshilov, K. E. *op. cit.,* p. 27.

93. Frunze, M. *op. cit.,* p. 430.

94. *ibid.,* p. 431.

95. *Krasnaia Zvezda,* No. 297, Jan. 1, 1925.

96. Frunze, M. *op. cit.,* p. 403.

97. *ibid.,* pp. 156, 404.

98. *ibid.,* p. 401.

99. *ibid.,* p. 236. Piatnitskii, N. V. *op. cit.,* v. 1, p. 44.

100. *Krasnaia Zvezda,* No. 147 (443), July 1, 1925.

101. Trotskii, L. *Kak vooruzhalas' Revoliutsiia,* v. 3, book 1, pp. 188, 189. Voroshilov, K. E. *Stat'i i Rechi,* p. 75.

102. Petrovskii, D. A. *op. cit.,* pp. 113, 114.

103. Frunze, M. *op. cit.,* pp. 363, 364.

104. *ibid.,* p. 233.

105. *ibid.,* p. 234.

106. *Krasnaia Zvezda,* No. 297, Jan. 1, 1925.

107. Frunze, M. *op. cit.,* p. 405.

108. Petrovskii, D. A. *op. cit.,* p. 116.

109. *ibid.,* p. 30.

110. Steinmetz, S. Rudolf. *Die Philosophie des Krieges,* Johan Ambrosius Barth, Leipzig, 1907, p. 146.

111. *ibid.,* p. 147.

112. Wollenberg, E. *op. cit.,* pp. 181, 182.

113. Blumenthal, F. *Politicheskaia rabota v voennoe vremia,* Moscow-Leningrad, 1929, Smilga, I. *K voprosu o stroitelstve Krasnoi Armii,* pp. 12, 13. Voroshilov, K. E. *Stat'i i Rechi,* p. 553.

114. Smilga, I. *op. cit.,* p. 19.

115. Petukhov, I. *Partiinaia organizatsiia i partiinaia rabota v RKKA,* Moscow-Leningrad, 1928, p. 49.

116. *ibid.,* p. 54.

117. Smilga, I. *op. cit.,* p. 20.

118. Petukhov, I. *op. cit.,* pp. 57, 58.

119. *ibid.,* p. 59.

120. *ibid.,* pp. 61, 65.

121. *ibid.,* pp. 68, 69.

122. Savko, N. *Ocherki po istorii partiinoi organizatsii v Krasnoi Armii. 1918-1923 gg.* Moscow-Leningrad, 1928, p. 71.

123. Petukhov, I. *op. cit.,* pp. 72, 73.

124. *ibid.,* p. 73. Savko, N., *op. cit.,* pp. 71, 72.

125. *ibid.,* p. 77.

126. *ibid.*

127. *ibid.*

128. *ibid.,* pp. 78-80. Smilga, I., *op. cit.,* pp. 20, 21.

129. Vishniakov, N. P. and Arkhipov, F. I. *Ustroistvo vooruzhennykh sil SSSR,* 2nd ed., Moscow, 1926, p. 94.

130. *ibid.*

131. *ibid.*, pp. 93, 94.

132. *ibid.*, p. 93.

133. *ibid.*, p. 95.

134. Frunze, M. *Izbrannye Proizve-deniia*, p. 409. *Sobranie Sochinenii*, v. 3, p. 358.

135. Petukhov, I. *op. cit.*, pp. 81, 82.

136. *ibid.*, p. 120.

137. *ibid.*, p. 104.

138. Gusev, S. I. *Grazhdanskaia Voina i Krasnaia Armiia (1918-1924)*, Moscow-Leningrad, 1925, p. 215.

139. Petukhov, I. *op. cit.*, pp. 186, 187.

140. *ibid.*, p. 187.

141. *Sbornik tsirkuliarov PUR'a*, No. 39, Nov. 13, 1924 (quoted in Petukhov, I., *op. cit.*, p. 95).

142. Petukhov, I. *op. cit.*, p. 95.

143. *ibid.*

144. *ibid.*, p. 103.

145. Gusev, S. I. *op. cit.*, pp. 5, 6.

146. Rossiiskaia Kommunisticheskaia Partiia. X S'ezd. *Stenograficheskii Otchet*, Petersburg, 1921, pp. 74, 75, 76.

147. Voroshilov, K. E. *Stat'i i Rechi*, p. 236.

148. *Krasnaia Zvezda*, No. 147 (443), July 1, 1925.

149. Vishniakov, N. P. and Arkhipov, F. I. *op. cit.*, p. 91.

150. Frunze, M. *Izbrannye Proizve-deniia*, p. 235.

151. *Krasnaia Zvezda*, No. 149 (445), July 3, 1925.

152. *Voennyi Kalendar'*, Petersburg, 1924, p. 332.

153. *ibid.*

154. *ibid.*

155. Ivanovich, St. *Krasnaia Armiia*, Paris, 1931, p. 51.

156. Kharitonov, N. *Politicheskii apparat Krasnoi Armii*, Moscow, 1929, pp. 30-32 (quoted in Ivanovich, St., *op. cit.*, pp. 50, 51).

157. Vishniakov, N. P. and Arkhipov, F. I. *op. cit.*, p. 93.

158. Voroshilov, K. *Oborona SSSR*, 2nd ed., p. 79.

159. *ibid.*, p. 80.

160. Blumenthal, F. *op. cit.*, pp. 13, 14.

161. Bubnov, A. *Boevaia podgotovka i politicheskaia rabota*, Moscow, 1927 (quoted in Blumenthal, F., *op. cit.*, p. 50).

162. Geronimus, A. A. *Partiia i Krasnaia Armiia*, Moscow-Leningrad, 1928, p. 157.

163. *ibid.*, pp. 157, 158.

164. Vishniakov, N. P. and Arkhipov, F. I. *op. cit.*, p. 91.

165. *ibid.*

166. Ivanovich, St. *op. cit.*, pp. 47, 48, 49.

167. Kharitonov, I. *op. cit.*, pp. 21, 22, 23 (quoted in Ivanovich, St., *op. cit.*, p. 50).

168. Savko, N. *Ocherki po istorii partiinoi organizatsii v Krasnoi Armii 1918-1923 gg.*, Moscow-Leningrad, 1928, p. 70.

169. Geronimus, A. A. *op. cit.*, pp. 157, 158, 159.

170. Savko, N. *op. cit.*, p. 67.

171. Gusev, S. I. *op. cit.*, p. 98.

172. Rossiiskaia Kommunisticheskaia Partiia (b). XI S'ezd. *Stenograficheskii Otchet*, Moscow, 1936, p. 303.

173. *ibid.*, pp. 303, 304.

174. *ibid.*, p. 307.

175. Trotskii, L. *Novyi Kurs*, Moscow, 1924, pp. 11, 15.

176. *ibid.*, p. 16.

177. Ivanovich, St. *op. cit.*, p. 74.

178. *ibid.*, p. 49.

179. Savko, N. *op. cit.*, p. 66.

180. Rossiiskii Leninskii Soiuz Molodezhi. Shestoi S'ezd. *op. cit.*, p. 305.

181. *Krasnaia Zvezda*, No. 151 (437), July 5, 1925.

182. Rossiiskii Leninskii Soiuz Molodezhi. Shestoi S'ezd. *op. cit.*, p. 320.

183. *ibid.*

184. *ibid.*, p. 322.

185. *ibid.*, pp. 322, 323.

186. *ibid.*, p. 324.

187. *ibid.*, p. 325.

188. *ibid.*, p. 322.

189. *ibid.*

190. *ibid.*, p. 321.

191. Voroshilov, K. *Oborona SSSR*, pp. 131, 132.

192. Rossiiskii Leninskii Soiuz Molodezhi, Shestoi S'ezd. *op. cit.*, p. 324.

193. *ibid.*, p. 316.

194. *ibid.*, p. 317.

195. *ibid.*, p. 318.

196. Voroshilov, K. *op. cit.*, pp. 147, 148.

197. *ibid.*, pp. 149, 150.

198. *ibid.*, pp. 148, 151.

199. *Voennyi Vestnik*, No. 30, Oct. 25, 1930 (quoted in Piatnitskii, N. V., *op. cit.*, v. 1, p. 21). In the third column in the source used there are obvious typographical errors, which were corrected.

200. *ibid.*, v. 1, p. 53.

201. *Voennyi Vestnik*, No. 3, Jan. 21,

1928 (quoted in Piatnitskii, N. V., *op. cit.*, v. 1, p. 54).

202. Ivanovich, St. *op. cit.*, p. 92.

203. Trotskii, L. *Novyi Kurs*, p. 36.

204. *Krasnaia Zvezda*, No. 297, Jan. 1, 1925.

205. *Svodka PURKKA o perevyborakh rukovod. Part. Organov osen'iu 1926 g.-Aprelia 1927 g. Moskva* (quoted in Piatnitskii, N. V., *op. cit.*, v. 1, p. 40).

206. Piatnitskii, N. V. *op. cit.*, v. 1, p. 23.

207. Ivanovich, St. *op. cit.*, p. 91.

208. Savko, N. *op. cit.*, pp. 69, 70.

209. Petukhov, I. *op. cit.*, p. 66.

210. *ibid.*, pp. 68, 69.

211. Bukharin, N. *Partiia i oppozitsiia na poroge XV parts'ezda*, Moscow-Leningrad, 1927, pp. 110, 111.

212. *Krasnaia Zvezda*, No. 2 (298), Jan. 3, 1925.

213. Petukhov, I. *op. cit.*, pp. 72 (footnote 1), 73. Geronimus, A. A., *op. cit.*, pp. 179 (footnote 4), 185.

214. Geronimus, A. A. *op. cit.*, p. 157.

215. *ibid.*

216. *ibid.*, p. 158.

217. Rossiiskii Leninskii Kommunisticheskii Soiuz Molodezhi. *op. cit.*, p. 315.

218. *ibid.*, pp. 315, 316.

219. Ivanovich, St. *op. cit.*, p. 93.

220. Rossiiskaia Kommunisticheskaia Partiia (b). XI S'ezd. *Stenograficheskii Otchet*, Moscow, 1936, p. 305.

221. *ibid.*, p. 306.

222. Voroshilov, K. E. *Stat'i i Rechi*, p. 45.

223. Voroshilov, K. *Oborona SSSR*, Moscow, 1927, p. 23.

224. *ibid.*

225. *Krasnaia Zvezda*, No. 297, Jan. 1, 1925.

226. *ibid.*

227. *ibid.*

228. Gusev, S. I. *op. cit.*, p. 196.

229. *Voennyi Kalendar'*, Petersburg, 1924, p. 224.

230. Denikin, A. I. *Staraia Armiia*, v. 2, Paris, 1931, pp. 160, 165.

231. Geronimus, A. A. *op. cit.*, p. 167.

232. *ibid.* Frunze, M. *Izbrannye Proizvedeniia*, p. 181.

233. Geronimus, A. A. *op. cit.*, p. 167.

234. Gusev, S. I. *op. cit.*, p. 174.

235. Frunze, M. V. *Sobranie Sochinenii*, v. 3, Moscow, 1927, p. 312.

236. Blumenthal, F. *op. cit.*, pp. 155, 166.

237. Gusev, S. I. *op. cit.*, p. 137.

238. *ibid.*, p. 142.

239. Geronimus, A. and Orlov, V. *VKP i voennoe delo v rezoliutsiiakh s'ezdov i konferentsii*, 2nd ed., 1928, pp. 99, 102 (quoted in Ivanovich, St., *op. cit.*, p. 100).

240. *Instruktsiia o poriadke raspredeleniia grazhdan po rodam i chastiam voisk*, Aug. 10, 1925, No. 107 (quoted in Piatnitskii, N. V., *op. cit.*, v. 1, p. 18).

241. Frunze, M. *Izbrannye Proizvedeniia*, p. 90.

242. Frunze, M. V. *Sobranie Sochinenii*, v. 3, p. 188.

243. *Krasnaia Zvezda*, No. 2 (293), Jan. 3, 1925.

244. Kamenev, L. *Polozhenie v strane i partii*, Moscow, 1923, pp. 17, 18.

245. Ivanovich, St. *op. cit.*, pp. 68, 69.

246. Piatnitskii, N. V. *op. cit.*, v. 1, pp. 13, 14.

247. *ibid.*, v. 1, p. 14.

248. Ivanovich, St. *op. cit.*, pp. 67, 68.

249. *ibid.*, pp. 65, 66.

250. *ibid.*, pp. 66, 67.

251. Frunze, M. *Izbrannye Proizvedeniia*, p. 436.

252. Voroshilov, K. *Oborona SSSR*, pp. 134, 135.

253. Frunze, M. V. *Sobranie Sochinenii*, v. 2, Moscow, 1926, p. 5.

254. Frunze, M. *Izbrannye Proizvedeniia*, p. 429. Voroshilov, K. *Oborona SSSR*, p. 139.

255. Voroshilov, K. *Oborona SSSR*, pp. 140, 144.

256. *ibid.*, pp. 141.

257. Trotskii, L. *Kak vooruzhalas' Revoliutsüa*, v. 3, book 1, pp. 322, 323. Geronimus, A. A., *op. cit.*, p. 148.

258. Ivanovich, St. *op. cit.*, p. 88.

259. Voroshilov, K. *op. cit.*, pp. 153, 154.

260. *Krasnaia Zvezda*, Feb. 4, 1927, May 10, 1928, June 12, 1928 (quoted in Ivanovich, St., *op. cit.*, p. 117).

261. Frunze, M. V. *Sobranie Sochinenii*, v. 2, pp. 6, 286 (footnote 5).

262. *ibid.*, p. 286 (footnote 5).

263. Movchin, N. *Komplektovanie Krasnoi Armii*, Moscow, 1926, pp. 248, 250, 251.

264. Voroshilov, K. *Oborona SSSR*, p. 113.

265. *ibid.*, p. 109.

266. Piatnitskii, N. V. *op. cit.*, v. 2, p. 47.

267. *ibid.*, v. 2, p. 79.

268. *ibid.*, v. 2, p. 76.

269. Movchin, V. *op. cit.*, pp. 204, 205.
270. Piatnitskii, N. V. *op. cit.*, v. 2, p. 69.
271. *ibid.*, v. 2, p. 70. Voroshilov, K., *op. cit.*, pp. 111, 112.
272. Piatnitskii, N. V. *op. cit.*, v. 2, p. 20.
273. Frunze, M. *Izbrannye Proizvedeniia*, p. 425.
274. Zaitzoff, A. *Die Rote Armee*, p. 21.
275. Frunze, M. *op. cit.*, pp. 426, 427.
276. Frunze, M. V. *Sobranie Sochinenii*, v. 3, p. 359.
277. *ibid.*, v. 2, pp. 52, 53.
278. Frunze, M. V. *Stat'i i Rechi*, Moscow, 1934, p. 320 (quoted in Velikolutskii, A. A. "Nekotorye mysli o voennoi distsipline," *Voennaia Mysl*, No. 6, 1940, p. 9).
279. *Voennyi Kalendar'*, Petersburg, 1924, pp. 345, 346.
280. *ibid.*, pp. 346, 347.
281. *ibid.*, p. 347.
282. *ibid.*, p. 370.
283. *Krasnaia Zvezda*, No. 17 (313), Jan. 21, 1925. *ibid.*, Feb. 26, 1927 (quoted in Piatnitskii, N. V., *op. cit.*, v. 1, p. 49).
284. Vishniakov, N. P. and Arkhipov, F. I. *op. cit.*, p. 96.
285. *ibid.*
286. Frunze, M. V. *Sobranie Sochinenii*, v. 2, p. 190.
287. Movchin, V. *op. cit.*, p. 242. The total adds to more than 100. Apparently a typographical error in the source used.
288. *Grazhdanskaia Voina 1918-1921*, v. 2, p. 73.
289. Rabinovich, S. E. *Vserossiiskaia voennaia konferentsiia bolshevikov 1917 goda*, Moscow, 1931, pp. 35, 36, 37, 38.
290. Voroshilov, K. E. *Stat'i i Rechi*, p. 339.
291. Geronimus, A. A. *op. cit.*, p. 175. Geronimus, A. and Orlov, V., *op. cit.*, p. 305 (quoted in Ivanovich, St., *op. cit.*, p. 99).
292. Geronimus, A. and Orlov, V. *op. cit.*, pp. 99, 102. *Krasnaia Zvezda*, May 14, 1929 (quoted in Ivanovich, St., *op. cit.*, pp. 101, 102).
293. Wells, H. G. *The New World Order*, Alfred A. Knopf, New York, 1940, p. 60.
294. Frunze, M. *Izbrannye Proizvedeniia*, p. 164.
295. Ivanovich, St. *op. cit.*, p. 72.
296. Voroshilov, K. *Oborona SSSR*, pp. 76, 77.
297. Frunze, M. *Izbrannye Proizvedeniia*, pp. 405, 406.
298. Voroshilov, K. *Oborona SSSR*, p. 25.
299. Voroshilov, K. E. *Stat'i i Rechi*, pp. 281, 282, 563, 564.
300. Trotskii, L. *Moia Zhizn'*, Riga, 1930, v. 2, pp. 253, 254, 261, 282.

CHAPTER IX

1. Chamberlin, William Henry. *Russia's Iron Age*, Little, Brown & Co., Boston, 1934, p. 41.
2. *ibid.*, p. 48.
3. *ibid.*, p. 63.
4. Frunze, M. V. *Sobranie Sochinenii*, 1927, v. 3, pp. 92, 267, 168.
5. Makhine, Théodore H., Colonel. *L'Armée Rouge*, Payot, Paris, 1938, p. 24.
6. Voroshilov, K. *Oborona SSSR*, Moscow, 1927, pp. 22, 35, 48, 125.
7. Voroshilov, K. E. *Stat'i i Rechi*, Moscow, 1936, p. 196.
8. *ibid.*
9. *ibid.*, pp. 199, 200, 201, 202.
10. *ibid.*, pp. 202, 203.
11. *ibid.*, pp. 205, 206.
12. *ibid.*, pp. 207, 208.
13. *ibid.*, pp. 208, 209.
14. *ibid.*, p. 210.
15. *ibid.*, p. 211.
16. *ibid.*
17. *ibid.*, p. 246.
18. *ibid.*, pp. 605, 609.
19. *ibid.*, p. 609.
20. *ibid.*
21. U.S.S.R. Gosplan SSSR. *Piatiletnii plan narodno-khoziastvennogo-stroitelstva SSSR*, v. 1, Moscow, 1930, 3rd ed., pp. 6, 7.
22. *ibid.*, pp. 10, 11.
23. *ibid.*, p. 11.
24. *ibid.*, p. 13.
25. Zaitzov, A. *Armed Forces* in *Russia/U.S.S.R. a complete handbook*, edited by P. Malevsky-Malevitch, William Farquhar Payson, New York, 1933, p. 255.
26. *ibid.*
27. U.S.S.R. Gosplan SSSR. *op. cit.*, v. 1, p. 15.
28. *ibid.* p. 16.
29. *ibid.*, p. 40.
30. *ibid.*, p. 44.
31. *ibid.*, p. 33.
32. *ibid.*, p. 94.

33. *ibid.*
34. *ibid.*, p. 159.
35. *ibid.*
36. *The Soviet Union Today,* edited by P. Malevsky-Malevitch, a Payson book, from the Paisley Press, New York, 1936, pp. S-48, S-49.
37. Florinsky, Michael T. *Toward an understanding of the U.S.S.R.,* The Macmillan Co., New York, 1939, pp. 162, 163.
38. *ibid.*, pp. 161, 162.
39. *ibid.*, pp. 159, 160.
40. U.S.S.R. Gosplan SSSR. *op. cit.,* v. 3, p. 37.
41. Adamheit, Th. *Rote Armee Rote Weltrevolution Roter Imperialismus,* Nibelungen-Verlag, Berlin-Leipzig, 1935, p. 143.
42. Just, Arthur W. *The Red Army,* Figurehead, London, 1936, p. 75.
43. Zaitsov, A. *op. cit.,* p. 262. K. L. von Oertzen in *Abruestung oder Kriegsvorbereitung,* Zentralverlag G.m.b.H., Berlin, 1931 (p. 44) gives the number of divisions as 28 infantry and 10 cavalry in the standing army, 43 infantry and 3 cavalry in the Territorial Militia. The number of army corps given by him is the same as indicated in the text of this work (21 infantry and 4 cavalry). He also gives the following figures as to armament : 1,700 airplanes, 250 tanks, 675 heavy guns, 3,837 field guns, 12,530 heavy machine guns, 13,880 light machine guns. D. Heinrici in *"Die Rote Arbeiter und Bauern Armee,"* Osteuropa, Heft 9, June 1932 (p. 696) gives the same number of divisions as von Oetzen.
44. *ibid.*, p. 262.
45. *ibid.*, pp. 262, 263.
46. *ibid.*, p. 263.
47. *ibid.*, p. 252.
48. *ibid.*, p. 260.
49. *ibid.*, p. 261. Also Piatnitskii, N. V., Colonel, *Krasnaia Armiia SSSR,* v. 2, Paris, 1932, p. 50..
50. U.S.S.R. *Zakon ob obiazatelnoi voennoi sluzhbe,* Moscow, 1927, subdivision I, paras 4, 5.
51. *ibid.*, subdivision I, paras 6, 7.
52. *ibid.*, subdivision I, para 7.
53. *ibid.*
54. *ibid.*
55. *ibid.*, subdivision I, paras 9, 11.
56. *ibid.*, subdivision I, paras 17, 18.
57. *ibid.*, subdivision I, para 19.
58. Ivanovich, St., *Krasnaia Armiia,* Paris, 1931, p. 42.
59. Zaitsov, A. *op. cit.,* p. 261.
60. *ibid.*
61. U.S.S.R. *Zakon ob obiazatelnoi voennoi sluzhbe,* Moscow, 1927, subdivision XVI, paras 196, 199.
62. *ibid.*, subdivision XVII, para 210.
63. Soiuz Osoaviakhim SSSR. *Pervoe vsesoiuznoe sovestchanie revisionnykh komissii soiuza Osoaviakhim,* Moscow, 1931, pp. 15, 16.
64. *ibid.*, pp. 8, 9.
65. *ibid.*, pp. 20, 21.
66. Tsentralnyi Sovet Soiuza Osoaviakhim SSSR. *Osoaviakhim na novom etape,* Moscow, 1931, pp. 4, 10.
67. *ibid.*, pp. 10, 18.
68. *ibid.*, p. 10.
69. Piatnitskii, N. V. *op. cit.,* v. 2, p. 28. Soiuz Osoaviakhim SSSR, *op. cit.,* p. 7.
70. Piatnitskii, N. V. *op. cit.,* v. 2, p. 29. Soiuz Osoaviakhim SSSR, *op. cit.,* p. 21.
71. Piatnitskii, N. V. *op. cit.,* p. 31.
72. *ibid.*, pp. 28, 29.
73. Soiuz Osoaviakhim SSSR, *op. cit.,* p. 21.
74. *ibid.*, p. 41.
75. Soiuz Osoaviakhim SSSR i Osoaviakhim RSFSR. *Usloviia i programmy dlia postupaiustchikh v shkoly voenno-vozdushnykh sil RKKA,* 2nd ed., Moscow, 1929, pp. 3, 4.
76. Tsentralnyi Sovet Soiuza Osoaviakhim SSSR, *op. cit.,* p. 11.
77. Soiuz Osoaviakhim SSSR i Osoaviakhim RSFSR. *Primernaia programma kruzhka voennykh znanii nachalnogo tipa.,* 2nd ed., Moscow, 1928, p. 3.
78. *ibid.*, p. 4.
79. *ibid.*
80. *ibid.*, pp. 6, 9.
81. Voroshilov, K. E. *Stat'i i Rechi,* Moscow, 1936, p. 230.
82. *ibid.*, pp. 230, 231.
83. *ibid.*, p. 233.
84. *Pravda,* May 13, 1928; *Izvestiia,* Jan. 27, 1929 (quoted in Ivanovich, St., *op. cit.,* p. 77).
85. *Krasnaia Zvezda,* April 23, 1929 (quoted in Ivanovich, St., *op. cit.,* pp. 77, 78).
86. *Krasnaia Zvezda,* April 23, 1929 (quoted in Ivanovich, St., *op. cit.,* p. 78).
87. *ibid.*, p. 79.
88. *ibid.*, p. 80.
89. *ibid.*
90. *ibid.*
91. *Krasnaia Zvezda,* No. 212 (1711), Sept. 14, 1929.

92. *ibid.*

93. *ibid.*, No. 216 (1715), Sept. 19, 1929.

94. *ibid.*, No. 212 (1711), Sept. 14, 1929.

95. *ibid.*, No. 274 (1773), Nov. 28, 1929.

96. *ibid.*

97. *ibid.*

98. *ibid.*

99. *ibid.*, No. 227 (1726), Oct. 2, 1929.

100. *ibid.*, No. 226 (1725), Oct. 1, 1929.

101. *ibid.*, No. 242 (1725), Oct. 19, 1929.

102. Ivanovich, St. *op. cit.*, p. 83.

103. Piatnitskii, N. V. *op. cit.*, v. 1, p. 25.

104. Voroshilov, K. E. *Stat'i i Rechi*, Moscow, 1936, p. 230.

105. *ibid.*, p. 230, also Piatnitskii, N. V., *op. cit.*, v. 1, p. 15.

106. Ignatiev, P., Count. *Education in Russia/U.S.S.R.*, New York, 1933, pp. 673, 674.

107. *Krasnaia Zvezda*, No. 240 (1739), Oct. 17, 1939.

108. Ignatiev, P., Count. *op. cit.*, p. 675.

109. *ibid.*, p. 674.

110. Chamberlin, William Henry. *op. cit.*, pp. 288, 289.

111. *ibid.*, pp. 289, 290.

112. *ibid.*, p. 291.

113. Zaitsov, A. *op. cit.*, p. 270.

114. *ibid.*, p. 269.

115. *ibid.*, p. 270.

116. *Voina i Revoliutsiia*, No. 9, 1929 (quoted in Ivanovich, St., *op. cit.*, p. 33).

117. *ibid.*

118. *ibid.*, p. 76. *Krasnaia Zvezda*, No. 209 (1708), Sept. 11, 1929.

119. U.S.S.R. *Polozhenie o prokhozhdenii sluzhby srednim, starshim i vysshim nachalstvuiustchim sostavom v mirnoe vremia.* Moscow-Leningrad, 1928, pp. 3, 5.

120. *ibid.*, subdivision 1, para 1.

121. *ibid.*, subdivision 1, paras 13, 15.

122. *ibid.*, subdivision 1, para 14.

123. *ibid.*, subdivision 1, para 24.

124. *ibid.*, subdivision 1, paras 27, 33. Also Piatnitskii, N. V., *op. cit.*, v. 2, p. 98.

125. *ibid.*, subdivision 1, para 22. Also Piatnitskii, N. V., *op. cit.*, v. 2, p. 98.

126. U.S.S.R. *op. cit.*, subdivision 1, para 26.

127. *ibid.*, subdivision 1, paras 34, 35.

128. Piatnitskii, N. V. *op. cit.*, v. 2, p. 94, table 22.

129. *ibid.*, v. 2, pp. 99, 100.

130. *ibid.*, v. 2, pp. 93, 96.

131. U.S.S.R. Tsentralnyi Sovet OSO SSSR, *Polozhenie i plan raboty.* Sektsiia obucheniia i vospitaniia nauchno-izsledovatelskoi komissii TsS OSO SSSR, Moscow, 1927, p. 25.

132. *ibid.*

133. U.S.S.R. *Polozhenie o prokhozhdenii sluzhby*, etc., Moscow-Leningrad, 1928, subdivision 1, para 49.

134. Ivanovich, St. *op. cit.*, p. 86.

135. Wollenberg, E. *The Red Army*, London, 1938, p. 188.

136. U.S.S.R. *op. cit.*, subdivision 1, para 49, footnote.

137. *ibid.*, subdivision 1, para 64.

138. *ibid.*, subdivision 1, para 293.

139. *ibid.*, subdivision 1, paras 426, 429, 436.

140. *ibid.*, subdivision 1, paras 441, 465, 466.

141. Piatnitskii, N. V. *op. cit.*, v. 2, p. 101.

142. *ibid.*

143. *ibid.*, v. 2, p. 100.

144. *ibid.*, v. 2, pp. 113, 114. In 1926 the commanding personnel was reduced by 16,000 (Voroshilov, K. E. *Stat'i i Rechi*, Moscow, 1936, p. 99).

145. *Krasnaia Zvezda*, No. 233 (1732), Oct. 9, 1929.

146. Gusev, S. I. *Grazhdanskaia voina i Krasnaia Armiia*, Moscow-Leningrad, 1925, p. 190 (footnote 1).

147. *Krasnaia Zvezda*, No. 221 (1720), Sept. 25, 1929.

148. *ibid.*, No. 252 (1751), Oct. 31, 1929.

149. *ibid.*, No. 235 (1734), Oct. 11, 1929.

150. *ibid.*, No. 277 (1776), Dec. 1, 1929.

151. *ibid.*

152. The Communist Party of the U.S.S.R. *Stenograficheskii Otchet XVI S'ezda Vsesoinznoi Kommunisticheskoi Partii (b)*, Moscow, 1930, p. 442.

153. Voroshilov, K. E. *Stat'i i Rechi*, Moscow, 1936, pp. 443, 444, 445.

154. Berezkin. "Itogi ukomplektovaniia VUZov," *Voennyi Sbornik*, No. 12 (quoted in Piatnitskii, N.V., *op. cit.*, v. 2, p. 104).

155. Voroshilov, K. E. *op. cit.*, p. 152, 285.

156. *Krasnaia Zvezda*, No. 252 (1751), Oct. 31, 1929.

157. *ibid.*, No. 277 (1776), Dec. 1, 1929.

158. *ibid.*, No. 224 (1723), Sept. 28, 1929, also No. 223 (1722), Sept. 27, 1929.

159. *ibid.*, No. 275 (1774), Nov. 29, 1929.

160. U.S.S.R. *Zakon ob obiazatelnoi voennoi sluzhbe*, Moscow, 1927, subdivision XIII, para 142.

161. *ibid.*, subdivision XIII, paras 143, 144, 147.

162. *ibid.*, subdivision XIII, para 148.

163. Piatnitskii, *op. cit.*, v. 2, p. 75.

164. U.S.S.R. Upravlenie v.-u. zavedenii GURKKA. *Programmy po vysshei doprizyvnoi podgotovke v grazhdanskikh vysshikh uchebnykh zavedeniiakh*. v. 1. Infantry, Moscow, 1928, pp. 5, 6.

165. *ibid.*, p. 8.

166. *Krasnaia Zvezda*, No. 210 (1709), Sept. 12, 1929.

167. *ibid.*

168. *ibid.*

169. Soiuz Osoaviakhim SSSR i Osoaviakhim RSFSR. *Usloviia i programmy dlia postupaiustchikh v shkoly voennykh vozdushnykh sil RKKA*, 2nd ed., Moscow, 1929, pp. 5, 6.

170. *ibid.*, p. 6.

171. *ibid.*

172. *ibid.*

173. *ibid.*, pp. 21, 22.

174. Dybenko, P. "Organizatsiia snabzheniia," *Voina i Tekhnika*, No. 2/3, 1928, p. 5.

175. *Krasnaia Zvezda*, No. 255 (1754), Nov. 3, 1929.

176. Voroshilov, K. E. *op. cit.*, pp. 638, 639.

177. *Krasnaia Zvezda*, No. 264 (1767), Nov. 16, 1929.

178. *ibid.*, No. 252 (1751), Oct, 31, 1929.

179. *ibid.*, No. 213 (1712), Sept. 15, 1929.

180. Zaitsov, A. *op. cit.*, p. 269.

181. *Krasnaia Zvezda*, No. 252 (1751), Oct. 31, 1929. Also Bubnov, A. *Preface* to Frunze, M. V. *Sobranie Sochinenii*, v. 1, Moscow, 1929.

182. U.S.S.R. *Polevoi Ustav 1929 g*, Moscow, 1929, para 18.

183. *ibid.*

184. *ibid.*

185. *ibid.*, para 23.

186. *ibid.*, paras 63, 64.

187. *ibid.*, para 68.

188. *ibid.*, para 72.

189. *ibid.*, para 76.

190. *ibid.*, para 75.

191. *Krasnaia Zvezda*, No. 209 (1708), Sept. 11, 1929.

192. *ibid.*

193. *ibid.*

194. *ibid.*

195. U.S.S.R. *Vremennyi Ustav Vnutrennei Sluzhby RKKA*, Moscow, 1928, para 122.

196. *ibid.*, para 145.

197. U.S.S.R. *Polozhenie o prokhozhdenii sluzhby srednim, starshim i vysshim nachalstvuiustchim sostavom v mirnoe vremia*, Moscow-Leningrad, 1928, para 70 (footnote 1 to the same para).

198. *Krasnaia Zvezda*, No. 110, 1930 (quoted in Piatnitskii, N. V., *op. cit.*, v. 1, p. 15).

199. *Krasnaia Zvezda*, No. 230 (1729), Oct. 5, 1929.

200. *ibid.*, No. 223 (1722), Sept. 27, 1929.

201. *ibid.*, No. 209 (1708), Sept. 11, 1929.

202. *ibid.*, No. 215 (1714), Sept. 18, 1929.

203. *ibid.*, No. 214 (1713), Sept. 17, 1929.

204. *ibid.*, No. 240 (1739), Oct. 17, 1929.

205. Chamberlin, W. H. *op. cit.*, pp. 141, 142. N. N. Alexeyev had estimated that in 1931 about 1,800,000 persons were imprisoned or deported. (*Russia/USSR*, New York, 1933, p. 206.)

206. Piatnitskii, N. V. *op. cit.*, v. 1, p. 60.

207. *ibid.*

208. Chamberlin, W. H. *op. cit.*, p. 157.

209. Kiselev, Mikhail. *Agitpoezd*, Moscow, 1933, p. 5.

210. Alexeyev, N. N. in *Political Structure, Russia/U.S.S.R.*, New York, 1933, p. 216.

211. Voroshilov, K. E. *op. cit.*, p. 331.

212. *ibid.*, p. 282.

213. *ibid.*, p. 285.

214. *ibid.*

215. *ibid.*, p. 334.

216. Alexeyev, N. N. *op. cit.*, pp. 216, 217.

217. Piatnitskii, N. V. *op. cit.*, v. 1, p. 21.

218. *ibid.*, v. 1, pp. 21, 22.

219. *ibid.*, v. 1, p. 24.

220. *ibid.*, v. 1, p. 23.

221. Alexeyev, N. N. *op. cit.*, pp. 214, 215.

222. Voroshilov, K. E. *op. cit.*, p. 574.

223. Piatnitskii, N. V. *op. cit.*, v. I, p. 25.

224. *ibid.*, v. I, p. 53.

225. *ibid.*, v. I, p. 54. Voroshilov, K. E., *op. cit.*, p. 446.

226. Voroshilov, K. E. *op. cit.*, p. 423.

227. *ibid.*, p. 611.

228. *ibid.*

229. *ibid.*, pp. 423, 424.

230. *Krasnaia Zvezda*, No. 231 (1730), Oct. 6, 1929.

231. *ibid.*

232. *ibid.*

233. *ibid.*, No. 205 (1704), Sept. 6, 1929.

234. *ibid.*

235. *ibid.*, No. 241 (1740), Oct. 18, 1929.

236. *ibid.*, No. 215 (1714), Sept. 18, 1929.

237. *ibid.*

238. Voroshilov, K. E. *op. cit.*, pp. 443, 444.

239. *Krasnaia Zvezda*, Sept. 15, 1928 (quoted in Piatnitskii, N. V., *op. cit.*, v. I, p. 17).

240. Geronimus, A. and Orlov, V. *VKP(b) i Voennoe delo*, 2nd ed., Moscow, 1928, p. 105.

241. *ibid.*

242. Voroshilov, K. E. *op. cit.*, p. 423.

243. *ibid.*, p. 468. *Krasnaia Zvezda*, No. 223 (1722), Sept. 27, 1929.

244. *ibid.*, pp. 442, 443.

245. Geronimus, A. and Orlov, V. *op. cit.*, pp. 327, 328.

246. *Krasnaia Zvezda*, No. 209 (1708), Sept. 11, 1929.

247. Gusev, S. I. *op. cit.*, p. 94.

248. Piatnitskii, N. V. *op. cit.*, v. I, p. 15. *Russia/U.S.S.R.*, p. 268.

249. Voroshilov, K. E. *op. cit.*, p. 444.

250. *ibid.*

251. Piatnitskii, N. V. *op. cit.*, v. I, p. 18.

252. Chamberlin, W. H. *op. cit.*, p. 66.

253. Florinsky, Michael T. *op. cit.*, p. 160.

254. Chamberlin, W. H. *op. cit.*, p. 73.

255. *ibid.*, p. 74.

256. *ibid.*, p. 88.

257. *ibid.*, p. 80.

258. Voroshilov, K. E. *op. cit.*, p. 327.

259. *ibid.*, p. 283.

260. Savitzky, N. *Agriculture in Russia/U.S.S.R.*, p. 419.

261. Zaitzov, A. *op. cit.*, pp. 267, 268.

262. *Voennyi Vestnik*, No. 32, 1928 (quoted in Ivanovich, St., *op. cit.*, p. 81).

263. *Krasnaia Zvezda*, No. 260 (1759), Nov. 12, 1929.

264. *ibid.*, No. 273 (1772), Nov. 27, 1929.

265. *ibid.*, No. 213 (1712), Sept. 15, 1929.

266. *ibid.*

267. *ibid.*

268. *ibid.*, also No. 273 (1772), Nov. 27, 1929.

269. *ibid.*, No. 213 (1712), Sept. 15, 1929.

270. *ibid.*, No. 211 (1710), Sept. 13, 1929.

271. *ibid.*, No. 203 (1702), Sept. 1, 1929.

272. *Krasnaia Zvezda*, July 10, 1928, Feb. 7, 1928 (quoted in Ivanovich, St., *op. cit.*, pp. 111, 112).

273. Wollenberg, E. *op. cit.*, pp. 187, 188.

274. *Krasnaia Zvezda*, No. 264 (1763), Nov. 16, 1929.

275. U.S.S.R. *Vremennyi Ustav Vnitrennei Sluzhby*, Moscow, 1928, para 28.

276. *ibid.*, para 31.

277. *ibid.*, para 36.

278. *ibid.*, paras 244, 245.

279. Kudrin, N. *Krasnoarmeiskaia stennaia gazeta*, Moscow-Leningrad, 1927, p. 65.

280. *ibid.*, p. 6.

281. *ibid.*, pp. 12, 13.

282. *ibid.*, p. 13.

283. *ibid.*, pp. 13, 14.

284. *ibid.*, p. 14.

285. *ibid.*, pp. 14, 15.

286. *ibid.*, p. 4.

287. *ibid.*, p. 16.

288. *ibid.*, pp. 17, 20.

289. *ibid.*, p. 27.

290. *ibid.*, p. 30.

291. *ibid.*, pp. 32, 33, 35.

292. *ibid.*, pp. 36, 38.

293. *ibid.*, pp. 66, 69.

294. *Krasnaia Zvezda*, No. 272 (1771), Nov. 26, 1929.

295. U.S.S.R. Politicheskoe Upravlenie RKKA SSSR. *Sbornik prikazov i tsirkuliarov*, No. 16, 1929. *Dvukhletniia programma politzaniatii s krasnoarmeitsami*, pp. 9, 11.

296. *ibid.*, p. 17.

297. *ibid.*, pp. 32, 67.

298. *ibid.*, pp. 105, 114.

299. *ibid.*, p. 132.

300. *ibid.*, p. 166.

301. *Krasnaia Zvezda*, No. 272 (1711), Nov. 26, 1929.

302. Degtiarev, L. *Politrabota v Krasnoi Armii v mirnoe vremia.* 3rd ed., p. 50 (quoted in Ivanovich, St., *op. cit.*, p. 104).

303. U.S.S.R. Politicheskoe Upravlenie RKKA SSSR, *op. cit.*, p. 235.

304. *ibid.*, p. 236.

305. *ibid.*, p. 238.

306. Klepinin, N. *Religion in Russia/U.S.S.R.*, pp. 632, 633, 636, 643, 644, 645.

307. *Krasnaia Zvezda*, August 15, 1928 (quoted in Ivanovich, St., *op. cit.*, p. 105).

308. *ibid.*, June 1, 1928 (quoted in Ivanovich, St., *op. cit.*, p. 106).

309. *ibid.*, No. 201 (1700), Sept. 1, 1929.

310. *ibid.*

311. Kudrin, N. *op. cit.*, pp. 60, 64.

312. Voroshilov, K. E., *op. cit.*, p. 175.

313. Tsentralnyi Sovet OSO SSSR. *Polozhenie i plan rabot sektsii obucheniia i vospitaniia nauchno-izsledovatelskoi komissii*, Moscow, 1927, p. 20.

314. U.S.S.R. *Boevoi Ustav Pekhoty*, part 1 (1928), Moscow, 1931, para 12.

315. Kazanskii i Liatti. "Ocherednaia zadacha v vestchevom dovolstvii Krasnoi Armii," *Voina i Tekhnika*, No. 1, 1928, pp. 9, 11.

316. *Krasnaia Zvezda*, No. 206 (1705), Sept. 7, 1929.

317. Solntsev, V. I. *L'goty voennosluzhastchim, voennoobiazannym i ikh sem'iam*, 2nd ed., Moscow, 1931, pp. 6, 14, 15.

318. *ibid.*, pp. 24, 26, 30.

319. *ibid.*, p. 76.

320. *ibid.*, p. 131.

321. *Krasnaia Zvezda*, Feb. 22, 1930, Feb. 9, Feb. 12, 1930 (quoted in Ivanovich, St., *op. cit.*, pp. 54, 55).

322. *ibid.*, No. 278 (1777), Dec. 3, 1929.

323. Solntsev, V. I. *op. cit.*, p. 24.

324. U.S.S.R. *Vremennyi Ustav Vnutrennei Sluzhby RKKA*, 1929, para 209.

325. *Krasnaia Zvezda*, No. 241 (1740), Oct. 18, 1929.

326. *ibid.*, No. 242 (1741), Oct. 19, 1929.

327. *ibid.*, No. 16 (312), Jan. 20, 1925.

328. *ibid.*, No. 201 (1700), Sept. 1, 1929.

329. Gusev, S. I. *op. cit.*, p. 155.

CHAPTER X

1. Knickerbocker, H. R. *Is Tomorrow Hitler's?*, Reynal & Hitchcock, New York, 1941, p. 123.

2. Molotov, V. *The Soviet Union in 1942.* Report made to the Eighteenth Congress of the Communist Party of the Soviet Union (Bolsheviks) and reply to the discussion. March 14 and 17, 1939, Workers Library Publishers, New York, 1939, pp. 5, 6.

3. *ibid.*, p. 5.

4. *ibid.*, p. 19.

5. *ibid.*

6. *ibid.*, p. 20.

7. *ibid.*, pp. 31, 32.

8. *ibid.*, p. 25.

9. *ibid.*, pp. 25, 26.

10. Davies, Joseph E. *Mission to Moscow*, Simon and Schuster, New York, 1941, p. 484.

11. *ibid.*, pp. 303, 304.

12. Molotov, V. M. *The Plan of Construction and Peace. Report on the Plan of National Economy for 1936*, delivered Jan. 10, 1936 at the Second Session of the meeting of the Central Executive Committee of the U.S.S.R., Workers Library Publishers, New York, 1936, pp. 10, 11.

13. *The Land of Socialism Today and Tomorrow.* Reports and speeches at the Eighteenth Congress of the Communist Party of Soviet Russia (Bolsheviks), March 10-21, 1939, Moscow, 1939, pp. 331, 332.

14. *ibid.*, p. 336.

15. *ibid.*, p. 330.

16. *ibid.*, p. 332.

17. *ibid.*, p. 334. Also Molotov, V. *The Soviet Union in 1942*, p. 91.

18. *The Land of Socialism Today and Tomorrow*, pp. 332, 334.

19. *ibid.*, pp. 306, 307.

20. Davies, Joseph E. *op. cit.*, p. 392.

21. *The Land of Socialism Today and Tomorrow*, pp. 25, 26. Molotov, V. *The Soviet Union in 1942*, p. 46.

22. Molotov, V. *op. cit.*, p. 43.

23. Davies, Joseph E. *op. cit.*, p. 326. Werner, Max. *Military strength of the powers*, Modern Age Books, Inc., New York, 1939, pp. 59, 60.

24. Davies, Joseph E. *op. cit.*, pp. 102, 103, 506.

25. Molotov, V. *The Soviet Union in 1942*, p. 47.

26. *ibid.*, pp. 45, 46.

27. *The Land of Socialism Today and Tomorrow*, pp. 306, 318, 320.
28. Davies, Joseph E. *op. cit.*, p. 387.
29. Molotov, V. *The Soviet Union in 1942*, pp. 6, 7.
30. *The Land of Socialism Today and Tomorrow*, p. 24.
31. Molotov, V. *The Soviet Union in 1942*, pp. 90, 91.
32. *The Land of Socialism Today and Tomorrow*, p. 33.
33. *ibid.*, p. 35.
34. Molotov, V. *The Soviet Union in 1942*, p. 13.
35. *ibid.*
36. *The Land of Socialism Today and Tomorrow*, p. 31.
37. *ibid.*, p. 32.
38. *ibid.*, p. 448.
39. *The Soviet Union Today*, edited by P. Malevsky-Malevitch, a Payson book, from the Paisley Press, New York, 1936, p. S-16.
40. *ibid.*
41. Makhine, Théodore H., Colonel. *L'Armée Rouge*, Payot, Paris, 1938, p. 176. *The Soviet Union Today*, p. S-2.
42. *ibid.*, p. 179.
43. Voroshilov, K. E. *Rech na XVIII S'ezde VKP (b)*. March 13, 1939, Moscow, 1939, p. 11.
44. *ibid.*, p. 12. Compare Max Werner's estimate in *Military Strength of the Powers*, p. 38, where a considerably lower number of divisions is given.
45. *The Soviet Union Today*, pp. S-16, S-17.
46. *ibid.*, p. S-17.
47. *Izvestiia*, Feb. 28, 1938, quoted in *ibid.*, p. S-18.
48. Voroshilov, K. E. *op. cit.*, p. 10.
49. *ibid.*, pp. 10, 11.
50. *ibid.*, p. 11.
51. *ibid.*
52. *ibid.*
53. *ibid.*, p. 12.
54. *ibid.*
55. *ibid.* Also Makhine, Th., *op. cit.*, p. 209.
56. Voroshilov, K. E. *Stat'i i Rechi.* Moscow, 1936, p. 459.
57. *The Soviet Union Today*, p. S-16.
58. Voroshilov, K. E. *Rech' na XVIII S'ezde*, p. 32.
59. Strong, Anna Louise. *The New Soviet Constitution.* A study in Socialist Democracy, Henry Holt & Co., New York, 1937, pp. 125, 126, 129, 134, 135.
60. *ibid.*, Article 68 (e), p. 140.

61. *ibid.*, Article 133, p. 157.
62. Voroshilov, K. E. "O proekte zakona o vseobstchei voinskoi povinnosti." *Voennaia Mysl*, No. 9, Sept. 1939, p. 5.
63. *ibid.*, p. 5.
64. *ibid.*, p. 10.
65. *ibid.*
66. *ibid.*, p. 11.
67. U.S.S.R. *Vedomosti Verkhovnogo Soveta SSSR*, No. 32 (55), Sept. 23, 1939. *Zakon o vseobstchei voinskoi obiazannosti.* Chapter 11, para 14. Voroshilov, K. E., *op. cit.*, p. 7.
68. Voroshilov, K. E. *op. cit.*, p. 7.
69. *ibid.*, p. 8.
70. *ibid.*
71. *ibid.*, p. 11.
72. U.S.S.R. *Vedomosti Verkhovnogo Soveta SSSR*, No. 32 (55), Chapter 1, para 3.
73. Voroshilov, K. E. *Stat'i i Rechi*, p. 445.
74. *ibid.*, pp. 556, 575.
75. *ibid.*
76. *ibid.*, p. 521.
77. *ibid.*, pp. 521, 613.
78. *ibid.*, pp. 575, 576.
79. *ibid.*, p. 613.
80. *Partiino Politicheskaia Rabota v RKKA*, No. 1, 1939, p. 28.
81. *Voennyi Vestnik*, Feb. 1933, No. 2, p. 39. Smirnov, S. A. "Komandnye kadry RKKA."
82. *Voennyi Vestnik*, Jan. 1933, No. 1, p. 78. Smirnov, S. A. "Vuzy v novom uchebnom godu."
83. *ibid.*, p. 76.
84. *ibid.*
85. *ibid.*, p. 77.
86. *ibid.*
87. *ibid.*, p. 76.
88. *ibid.*, p. 78.
89. *ibid.*, p. 79.
90. *Voennyi Vestnik*, Feb. 1933, No. 2, pp. 39, 40. Smirnov, S. A. "Komandnye kadry RKKA."
91. *ibid.*, p. 39.
92. *Krasnaia Zvezda*, No. 172 (3117), July 28, 1935.
93. *Krasnaia Zvezda*, No. 267 (3212), Nov. 20, 1935.
94. *Krasnaia Zvezda*, No. 218 (3163), Sept. 20, 1935.
95. Vsesoiuznaia Kommunisticheskaia Partiia (b), XVII S'ezd, Jan. 26-Feb. 10, 1934. *Stenograficheskii Otchet.* Moscow, 1934, p. 233.
96. *Krasnaia Zvezda*, No. 14 (4463), Jan. 17, 1940.

97. Makhine, Th. *L'Armée Rouge*, p. 115.

98. *ibid.*

99. *ibid.*, p. 116.

100. *ibid.*, pp. 118, 119.

101. *Krasnaia Zvezda*, No. 242 (3187), Oct. 18, 1935.

102. Voroshilov, K. E. *Rech' na XVIII S'ezde*. 1939, p. 21.

103. *ibid.*

104. *Krasnaia Zvezda*, No. 156, July 6, 1940.

105. Makhine, Th. *op. cit.*, p. 115.

106. *Sotsialisticheskii Vestnik*, No. 10, 1937, p. 6. Garvi, P. "Krasnaia Armiia na novom etape."

107. U.S.S.R. *Sobranie Zakonov i Rasporiazhenii Raboche-Krestianskogo Pravitelstva SSSR*. No. 57, Nov. 23, 1935, *Otdel* 1, p. 822.

108. *ibid.*

109. *ibid.*

110. *ibid.*, p. 823.

111. *Krasnaia Zvezda*, No. 268 (3213), Nov. 21, 1935.

112. U.S.S.R. *op. cit.*, No. 51. *Otdel* 1, Aug. 17, 1937, pp. 486, 487.

113. *Novoye Russkoye Slovo*, New York, June 25, 1940.

114. *ibid.*

115. Voroshilov, K. E. "O proekte zakona o vseobstchei voinskoi povinnosti." *Voennaia Mysl*, No. 9, 1939, p. 13.

116. U.S.S.R. *op. cit.*, No. 57, *Otdel* 1, Nov. 23, 1935, pp. 828, 829.

117. *ibid.*, p. 826.

118. *ibid.*, p. 828. Also No. 51, *Otdel* 1, Aug. 17, 1937, p. 487.

119. *ibid.*, pp. 829, 830, 831.

120. *ibid.*, p. 833.

121. *ibid.*, p. 836.

122. Voroshilov, K. E. *op. cit.*, pp. 12, 13.

123. *ibid.*, p. 14.

124. *ibid.*

125. Wollenberg, E. "Krasnaia Armiia posle 'chistki,'" *Russkiia Zapiski*, Paris, Jan. 1939, p. 77.

126. *Krasnaia Zvezda*, No. 155, July 5, 1940.

127. *ibid.*, No. 156, July 6, 1940.

128. Just, Arthur W. *The Red Army*. Figurehead, London, 1936, p. 22.

129. *Geroicheskie Budni*, Leningrad, 1938, p. 5.

130. *ibid.*, p. 6.

131. Just, Arthur W. *op. cit.*, pp. 27, 28.

132. Voroshilov, K. E. *Rech' na XVIII S'ezde*, 1939, pp. 22, 23.

133. *Krasnaia Zvezda*, No. 233 (3178), Oct. 8, 1935.

134. *ibid.*, No. 150 (3698), July 2, 1937.

135. *ibid.*

136. *ibid.*, No. 254 (3802), Nov. 3, 1937.

137. *ibid.*, No. 188 (3133), Aug. 16, 1935.

138. Wollenberg, E. *The Red Army*, Secker & Warburg, London, 1938, pp. 188, 189.

139. *Krasnaia Zvezda*, No. 163 (3711), July 17, 1937.

140. *ibid.*, No. 161 (3106), July 15, 1935.

141. *ibid.*

142. *ibid.*, No. 155 (4604), July 5, 1940.

143. *Novoye Russkoye Slovo*, New York, June 25, 1940.

144. *Krasnaia Zvezda*, No. 155, July 5, 1940.

145. *ibid.*

146. *Krasnaia Zvezda*, No. 158, July 9, 1940. Also No. 43 (4492), Feb. 22, 1940.

147. *ibid.*, No. 158, July 9, 1940.

148. *ibid.*, No. 299 (4449), Dec. 31, 1939.

149. *ibid.*, No. 23 (4472), Jan. 29, 1940.

150. Davies, Joseph E. *op. cit.*, p. 409.

151. *ibid.*, pp. 480, 481.

152. *Krasnaia Zvezda*, No. 13 (4482), Jan. 16, 1940.

153. Duranty, Walter. *The Kremlin and the People*, Reynal & Hitchcock, New York, 1941, p. 66.

154. *ibid.*, p. 68.

155. Davies, Joseph E. *op. cit.*, p. 168.

156. *Pravda*, June 12, 1937.

157. *ibid.*

158. *Prikaz Komissara Oborony SSSR*, No. 96, June 12, 1937, *Kommunist RKKA*, No. 9-10, May 1937, p. 2.

159. *ibid.*, p. 1.

160. *ibid.*, p. 2.

161. *ibid.*

162. *ibid.*, p. 4.

163. *ibid.*, pp. 5, 6.

164. *ibid.*, p. 7.

165. Uralskii, V. "Sud'ba Bluechera." *Chasovoi*, Nov. 1, 1938, pp. 8, 9.

166. Nikolskii, V. "Nagrady i peremestcheniia v Krasnoi Armii." *Chasovoi*, March 10, 1939, p. 5.

167. Souvarine, Boris. *Stalin*, Alliance

Book Corporation, Longmans, Green & Co., New York, 1939, p. 635.

168. Wollenberg, E. *The Red Army,* London, 1938, p. 209.

169. *ibid.,* p. 214.

170. Florinsky, Michael T. *Toward an Understanding of the U.S.S.R.,* New York, 1939, p. 111.

171. Nikolskii, V. "Velikii Razgrom," *Chasovoi,* Feb. 1, 1939.

172. Wollenberg, E. *op. cit.,* pp. 241, 242.

173. U.S.S.R. People's Commissariat of Justice. *Report of Court Proceedings in the case of the Anti-Soviet Trotskyite Centre.* Verbatim Report, Moscow, 1937, pp. 105, 109, 146.

174. Wollenberg, E. *op. cit.,* p. 242.

175. Nikolskii, V. "Krasnye 'admiraly.' " *Chasovoi,* Sept. 1, 1938, p. 12.

176. Nikolskii, V. "Nagrady i peremestcheniia v Krasnoi Armii." *Chasovoi,* March 10, 1939, p. 9.

177. Varnek, P. "Itogi chistki," etc. *Chasovoi.* Oct. 1, 1938, p. 9.

178. Wollenberg, E. "Krasnaia Armiia posle 'chistki.' " *Russkiia Zapiski,* Paris, January, 1939, p. 179.

179. *Partiino Politicheskaia Rabota v RKKA,* No. 3, February 1939, p. 5.

180. *Krasnaia Zvezda,* No. 18 (3868), Jan. 22, 1938.

181. Wollenberg, E. *op. cit.,* p. 179.

182. *Krasnaia Zvezda,* No. 8 (4158), Jan. 10, 1939.

183. *ibid.,* No. 27 (2877), Feb. 3, 1938.

184. *ibid.,* No. 3 (4153), Jan. 4, 1939.

185. *ibid.*

186. *ibid.,* No. 20 (4170), Jan. 26, 1939.

187. Wollenberg, E. *op. cit.,* p. 181.

188. Voroshilov, K. E. *Rech' na XVIII S'ezde VKP (b),* Moscow, 1939, p. 19.

189. Davies, Joseph E. *op. cit.,* p. 409.

190. *ibid.,* p. 172.

191. *ibid.,* p. 173.

192. U.S.S.R. *Sobranie Zakonov i Rasporiazhenii Raboche-Krestianskogo Pravitelstva SSSR. Otdel Pervyi.* Aug. 17, 1937, No. 51, Aug. 27, 1937, No. 55.

193. U.S.S.R. *op. cit., Otdel Pervyi,* Aug. 17, 1937, No. 51.

194. U.S.S.R. *op. cit., Otdel Pervyi,* May 27, 1937, No. 31.

195. *ibid.*

196. *ibid.*

197. *ibid.*

198. U.S.S.R. *op. cit., Otdel Pervyi,* Aug. 27, 1937, No. 55.

199. *ibid.*

200. *ibid.*

201. *ibid.*

202. *ibid.*

203. *ibid.*

204. *ibid.*

205. *ibid.*

206. *ibid.*

207. *ibid.*

208. *ibid.*

209. *ibid.*

210. U.S.S.R. *Narodnyi Komissariat Oborony Soiuza SSR. Ustav Vnutrennei Sluzhby RKKA,* 1937, Moscow, 1938, pp. 21, 22, 26, 27.

211. *ibid.,* p. 35.

212. *Krasnaia Zvezda,* No. 160, July 11, 1940.

213. *ibid.*

214. *ibid.*

215. *ibid.*

216. *ibid.*

217. Voroshilov, K. E. *Rech' na XVIII S'ezde VKP (b),* Moscow, 1939, pp. 11, 12.

218. *ibid.,* p. 26.

219. *ibid.,* p. 25.

220. *ibid.,* p. 26.

221. Movchin, N. *Komplektovanie Krasnoi Armii,* Moscow, 1926, p. 74.

222. *Krasnaia Zvezda,* No. 331 (4482), Feb. 10, 1940.

223. *ibid.*

224. *ibid.*

225. *ibid.*

226. *ibid.,* No. 41 (4490), Feb. 20, 1940.

227. *ibid.,* No. 137 (3082), June 16, 1935.

228. *ibid.,* No. 3, Jan. 4, 1940.

229. Garvi, N. "Krasnaia Armiia na novom etape," *Sotsialisticheskii Vestnik,* No. 10, 1937, p. 9.

230. Voroshilov, K. E. *Rech' na XVIII S'ezde VKP (b),* Moscow, 1939, p. 26.

231. Nikolskii, V. "Novye rukovoditeli Krasnoi Armii," *Chasovoi,* Sept. 1, 1938, p. 7.

232. *Krasnaia Zvezda,* No. 290 (4440), Dec. 21, 1939.

233. *ibid.,* No. 20 (4469), Jan. 26, 1940, No. 5, (4454), Jan. 6, 1940.

234. *ibid.,* No. 284 (4434), Dec. 14, 1939.

235. *ibid.,* No. 2 (4451), Jan. 3, 1940, No. 30 (4479), Feb. 6, 1940, No. 26 (4475), Feb. 2, 1940.

236. Dalin, D. "Reorganizatsiia Krasnoi Armii." *Sotsialisticheskii Vestnik,* Feb. 25, 1941, pp. 47-49. *Novoye Russkoye Slovo,* New York, May 11, 1940, October 17, 1940.

237. *New York Times,* January 28, 1941.

238. *Philadelphia Inquirer,* Aug. 13, 1940.

239. Piatnitskii, N. V. *op. cit.,* v. 1, pp. 55, 56.

240. Florinsky, Michael T. *op. cit.,* pp. 110, 111.

241. Stalin, Io. *Otchetnyi doklad na XVIII S'ezde Partii o rabote Ts.K. VKP (b),* Moscow, 1939, pp. 41, 42.

242. *ibid.,* pp. 44, 45.

243. *ibid.,* p. 46.

244. Mekhlis, L. *Rech' na XVIII S'ezde VKP (b),* Moscow, 1939, p. 10.

245. *ibid.*

246. *ibid.,* p. 11.

247. *ibid.*

248. *ibid.*

249. *ibid.,* pp. 11, 12.

250. *Partiino-Politicheskaia Rabota v RKKA.* No. 1, 1939, pp. 41, 42.

251. *ibid.*

252. Garvi, N. "Krasnaia Armiia na novom etape," *Sotsialisticheskii Vestnik,* No. 10, 1937, p. 8.

253. *Partiino-Politicheskaia Rabota v RKKA,* No. 3, Feb. 1939, p. 5.

254. *Krasnaia Zvezda,* No. 16 (3866), Jan. 20, 1938.

255. Duranty, W. *op. cit.,* p. 127.

256. *Krasnaia Zvezda,* No. 168 (3716), July 23, 1937.

257. *ibid.,* No. 171 (3719), July 27, 1937.

258. *ibid.,* No. 2 (3852), Jan. 3, 1938.

259. *ibid.,* No. 16 (3866), Jan. 20, 1938.

260. B. V. "Voprosy vnutripartiinoi raboty," *Voennyi Vestnik,* No. 3, March 1933, pp. 73, 74.

261. "Vsemirno istoricheskaia pobeda," *Voennyi Vestnik,* No. 1, 1933, p. 4.

262. *Krasnaia Zvezda,* No. 2 (4451), Jan. 3, 1940.

263. *ibid.,* No. 27 (3877), Feb. 3, 1938.

264. Mekhlis, L. *op. cit.,* p. 10.

265. Chernelevskii, N. "Vyshe bolshevistskuiu bditelnost' komsomoltsev," *Kommunist RKKA,* No. 17-18, Sept. 1937, pp. 42, 43.

266. *Krasnaia Zvezda,* No. 15 (4464), Jan. 18, 1940.

267. *ibid.,* No. 160, July 11, 1940.

268. *ibid.,* No. 31 (4480), Feb. 8, 1940.

269. *ibid.,* No. 25 (4474), Feb. 1, 1940.

270. *ibid.,* No. 280 (4430), Dec. 9, 1939.

271. *ibid.,* No. 282 (4432), Dec. 11, 1939.

272. Makhine, Th. H. *L'Armée Rouge,* Paris, 1938, pp. 154, 155.

273. Voroshilov, K. E. *op. cit.,* p. 31.

274. *Partiino-Politicheskaia Rabota v RKKA,* No. 3, Feb. 1939, p. 7.

275. Voroshilov, K. E. *op. cit.,* p. 31.

276. *Krasnaia Zvezda,* No. 4 (4154), Jan. 5, 1939.

277. U.S.S.R. *Verkhovnyi Sovet. Vedomosti Verkhovnogo Soveta SSSR,* No. 32 (55), Sept. 23, 1939, paras 1, 2.

278. Duranty, W. *op. cit.,* pp. 201, 202.

279. *Novoye Russkoye Slovo,* New York, Feb. 4, 1940.

280. *New York Times,* Nov. 8, 1941.

281. *ibid.,* Nov. 7, 1941.

282. *ibid.,* Dec. 10, 1940.

283. Eastman, Max. *Stalin's Russia,* W. W. Norton & Co., New York, 1940, p. 26.

284. *Krasnaia Zvezda,* No. 231 (3779), Oct. 6, 1937.

285. *ibid.,* No. 159, July 10, 1940. Baltiiskii, A. "Borodino," *Voennaia Mysl,* No. 89, 1937, pp. 10, 41.

286. *ibid.,* No. 1, Jan. 1, 1940.

287. Ivanovich, St. *Krasnaia Armiia,* Paris, 1931, pp. 11, 12.

288. Mekhlis, L. *op. cit.,* pp. 6, 16.

289. *Krasnaia Zvezda,* No. 1, Jan. 1, 1940.

290. *Kommunist RKKA,* No. 19-20, 1937, p. 71.

291. *ibid.*

292. *ibid.,* p. 72.

293. *Krasnaia Zvezda,* No. 234 (3179), Oct. 9, 1935. Puchkov, "Ob obstcheobrazovatelnoi rabote s krasnoarmeitsami i mladshim nachsostavom," *Voennyi Vestnik,* No. 18, June 25, 1930, p. 42.

294. *Krasnaia Zvezda,* No. 254 (3199), Nov. 2, 1935.

295. Rubtsov, V. "Marksistskaia Psikhologiia i puti ee ispolzoraniia v boevoi podgotovke i politrabote Krasnoi Armii," *Voina i Revoliutsiia,* v. 2, 1930, pp. 63, 64.

296. *Krasnaia Zvezda,* No. 52 (4501), March 4, 1940.

297. *ibid.,* No. 41 (4490), Feb. 20, 1940.

298. *ibid.,* No. 1 (4450), Jan. 1, 1940.

299. Davies, Joseph E. *op. cit.,* p. 83.

300. U.S.S.R. Verkhovnyi Sovet. *Ve-*

domosti Verkhovnogo Soveta SSR, No. 32 (55), Sept. 23, 1939, para 7.

301. *ibid.*, para 14.

302. Voroshilov, K. E. "Doklad 31 Avgusta 1939," *Voennaia Mysl*, No. 9, 1939, p. 12.

303. *ibid.*, p. 8.

304. *ibid.*

305. *ibid.*

306. Kuibyshev, N. "Problema kadrov i sverkhsrochnikov," *Voennyi Vestnik*, No. 17, June 15, 1930, p. 4.

307. P-nyi, "O nekotorykh prichinakh peregruzki nachsostava v lageriakh," *Voennyi Vestnik*, No. 16, June 5, 1930, pp. 61, 62.

308. U.S.S.R. Narodnyi Komissariat Oborony Soiuza SSR. *Ustav Vnutrennei Sluzhby RKKA*, 1937, Moscow, 1938, paras 99, 100.

309. *ibid.*, para 147.

310. *ibid.*, paras 291, 292.

311. *ibid.*, para 22.

312. *ibid.*, paras 23, 25, 32.

313. Ingersoll, Ralph. "Powerful Moscow Battery Manned by Snappy Crew," *The Evening Bulletin*, Philadelphia, Pa., Nov. 7, 1941.

314. Ossipov, V. "The Red Army Turns Prussian," *The Living Age*, May 1941, p. 210.

315. Dalin, D. "Reorganizatsiia Krasnoi Armii," *Sotsialisticheskii Vestnik*, No. 4 (469), Feb. 25, 1941, p. 47.

316. *ibid.*, p. 48.

317. Ossipov, V. *op. cit.*, p. 211.

318. Dalin, D. *op. cit.*, p. 48.

319. Ossipov, V. *op. cit.*, p. 211.

320. *ibid.*, pp. 211, 212.

321. *ibid.*, p. 212.

322. *ibid.*

323. Dalin, D. *op. cit.*, p. 48.

324. *Krasnaia Zvezda*, No. 162, July 13, 1940.

325. *ibid.*

326. Velikolutskii, A. A., Colonel. "Nekotorye mysli o voinskoi distsipline," *Voennaia Mysl*, No. 6, June 1940, pp. 3, 4.

327. *ibid.*, p. 7.

328. *ibid.*, pp. 7, 8.

329. *ibid.*, pp. 8, 9.

330. *Krasnaia Zvezda*, No. 22 (4471), Jan. 28, 1940.

331. Gusev, S. I. *Grazhdanskaia Voina i Krasnaia Armiia*, Moscow-Leningrad, 1925, pp. 10, 11, 12.

332. *Krasnaia Zvezda*, No. 1, Jan. 1, 1940.

333. Nozdrunov, M. K., Kombrig. "Stalin-sozdatel boevoi mostchi Krasnoi Armii," *Voennaia Mysl*, No. 12, 1939, p. 55.

334. Voroshilov, K. E. *Rech' na XVIII S'ezde VKP (b)*, Moscow, 1939, p. 22.

335. *Krasnaia Zvezda*, No. 6 (4455), Jan. 8, 1940.

336. *ibid.*, No. 157 (3102), July 10, 1935.

337. Voroshilov, K. E. *op. cit.*, p. 23.

338. Makhine, Th. H. *op. cit.*, p. 58.

339. *Krasnaia Zvezda*, No. 4 (4453), Jan. 5, 1940.

340. Voroshilov, K. E. *op. cit.*, pp. 28, 29.

341. *Geroicheskie Budni*, Leningrad, 1938, pp. 35, 36.

342. Waller, Willard. *The War in the Twentieth Century*, Random House, New York, 1940, pp. 517, 518.

343. *Sowjetunion 1935. Reden und Berichte von J. Stalin, W. M. Molotow*, etc., Moscow-Leningrad, 1935, p. 233.

344. *The Land of Socialism Today and Tomorrow*, Moscow, 1939, p. 298, has a translation of these remarks. See Voroshilov, K. E., *op. cit.*, p. 32.

345. Baz', I. "Zakony pervostepennoi gosudarstvennoi vazhnosti," *Voennaia Mysl*, No. 10, 1939, p. 16.

346. Landa, M. M., editor. *Tankisty*, Moscow, 1936, p. 11.

347. Werner, Max. *The Military Strength of the Powers*, Modern Age Books, New York, 1939, pp. 60, 61, 63.

348. *ibid.*, pp. 58, 59.

349. *ibid.*, pp. 71, 72.

INDEX

A

Adamheit, T., German writer on military subjects, views of, on results of first Five Year Plan, 285

Adlerberg, General Imperial Russian Army, memorandum on wartime officers by, 50

Agitation, among soldiers for equalization of material conditions, 187; for abolition of political departments and Special Departments, 187

Agricultural production (of U.S.S.R.), of 1913 compared to 1927/28, 282; expansion of agricultural labor under Five Year Plans, 283; deviation from Five Year Plans in agriculture, 284

Alexander Nevsky, medieval Russian Duke, 412

Alexis Military School, cadets' social origins analyzed, 43, 44, 45

Alksnis, Ia. I., former head of Soviet military aviation, disappears during purge, 387

All-Army Conference, concerned with demobilization of old army, 39

All-Russian Bureau of Military Commissars, organized, 78; replaced by Political Department of the Revolutionary Military Council, 78; concentrates on agitation and training of military commissars, 81; most important departments of: Agitation-Enlightenment and Schools for Military Commissars, 81

All-Russian Central Committee, adopts resolution on obligatory military service, 41

All-Russian Executive Committee, resolution of on obligatory military service, 41

Altvater, V. M., Rear Admiral Imperial Russian Navy, conference of, with Lenin and Trotsky, 28; patriotism of, 211

Anarchists, at the Second Congress of Baltic Fleet Delegates, 136; freedom of press and speech for, advocated by Kronstadt insurgents, 147; associations of, with seamen, 155

Anti-Semitism, in the 27th Rifle Division, 153; among commanders, 308

Antonov, A. S., Socialist Revolutionary, guerillas of, viii

Antonov-Ovseenko, V. A. Oppositionist (Communist), arrival of, at Helsing-

fors, 18, 19; replaced as head of PUR by Bubnov, 241

Archangel (city of), traffic possibilities between Murmansk and, 354

Armiia i Revoliutsiia, 168, 193

"Army opposition of 1921," causes for, 88; agitation of, for subordination of commissars to party collectives condemned by party, 89; advocates curtailment of army political organs, 230; suggestions rejected by party, 230

Army syndicalism, elements favoring "democratic" methods of control dubbed, 82; traditions echoed by 1923 Trotskyist opposition, 254

Artel, type collective farms, 356

Atamans, elements of, in Ukrainian Red Army units, 64, 65

Attestation *see* Service Record

Automobile production (in U.S.S.R.), needs of the army in, 278; infancy of, 279; increase in, 283; produced in 1932, 284; produced in 1937, 352; motor-truck production in 1933 and 1934, 354; number of automobiles in U.S.S.R., 355

Aviation (Soviet), increase in industry production, 278; Osoaviakhim's role in development of, 290; rapid expansion of, during Five Year Plans, 310; types of schools for, set up, 310; duration of courses in these schools, 311; entrance requirements, 311; production of planes in 1937 and 1939, 355; network of military aviation schools expanded, 373; rapid promotion of aviators after purge, 389; fliers passed through sanatoria, 422; Max Werner's opinion of, 426; Khripin's opinion of, 426

B

Babel, I. Soviet writer, describes Red cavalry, 55; *Cavalry Army*, 122

"Bag-pipe" (volynka), slang for strike in Petrograd in 1921, 127, 128

Bagration, P. I., Prince, hero of 1812 War, *Red Star's* article on, 413

Baikal-Amur trunk line, beginning of construction of, 354

Balkans, value of international aspects of Red Army in, 429

Baltic Fleet (Soviet), deterioration of personnel of, claimed by Trotsky, 127; influence of seamen's social origins on Kronstadt rebellion, 128, 129,

ical workers' reluctance, 232; Bubnov's project of transition to, approved, 232; reasons for slow rate of introduction of, 234; percentage of commanders with plenary powers, 234; Party circular on, 235; plenary form of, 236; introduction of, postponed in national units and navy, 236; trend to subordination of political organs to military, 239; opposition to, continues, 239; regulated by Rev. Milit. Council, 239; political personnel win struggle about, 240; suffers setback on eve of Five Year Plan, 240; stabilized by statute, 313; remnants of opposition to, in 1929, 313, 314; Field Regulations (1929) indicate commissars had won over commanders, 314; changes in application of, 377, 378; trend on, reversed, 392, 426; purge places communist commanders in position of ex-Imperial officers during Civil War, 392; collegiate principle in military districts reestablished, 394; dual control detrimental, 399; reasons for abolition of, 398, 400; Russo-Finnish War tests dual and collegiate control, 402; reintroduction of unity of command, 402, 428; abolition of, after Hitler's attack, 402, 403, 427; crucial test of dual control during current war, 402, 403; a persistent trend for, 426, 427; reasons for persistence, 427

Command Courses (Red Army), begin functioning, 55; post of Commissar in Chief of Military Educational Institutions created, 55, 56; old régime inheritance, 56, 57; self-governing bodies, 56; cadets' political education, 56; cadets' social origins, 56, 59; relationship between directors and commissars of, 56, 57; number of courses opened, 57; instructors in, 57; their disregard of Civil War experience, 57, 58; types of military educational institutions planned, 58; number of graduates, 58, 59; higher type of, opened, 59; cadets' party affiliation, 59, 62; graduates merely well-trained privates, 59; role of commissars of, 59, *esprit de corps* of, 60; methods of recruitment of, 61, 62, 334, 398; cadets' educational level, 61, 62; percentage of graduates of in Red Army in 1923, 1924, 62, 63; graduates as commanders, 63, 200; cadets abused by populace, 152, 153; conspiracy among Peterhof cadets, 153; deserters during Kronstadt rebellion, 153; enthusiasm and discipline acquired at, 154; dispensed with, 201; graduates of, urged to enter Military Schools, 215; admission requirements into Military Political Schools at the level of, 238; number of graduates of in army in 1928, 292

Commander in Chief (Red Army), entrusted with command of Soviet armed forces at the head of Field Staff, 38; member of the Bureau of the Rev. Milit. Council, 39; independent in strategic-operational matters, 39; Svechin advocates wide powers for, 160

Commanders of Workers', and Peasants' Army (Soviet name for officers), Red Commanders and ex-officers become known as, 60; professional revolutionaries among, 64; guerilla leaders included, 64; lack of homogeneity, 66; conflicts among, during Civil War, 66; antagonistic to subordinates, 66; dissatisfied with their position, 79, 80; conflicts with commissars, 80; execution of, 86; given wide coercive powers, 112; differentiation between junior and other commanders, 113; take advantage of position, 121; level of training of middle and junior commanders criticized by Trotsky, 174; position during NEP not enviable, 187; material improvements in, advocated, 187; "anti-Soviet" tendencies among, 187; professionalization of, 201; evolution of, 203; composition of, in 1921, 204; deserters among, 204; purge of 1921, 204; percentage of communists, 204; purge of 1924, 204, 205; social origins of, 205; ex-officers predominate during Civil War, 206; party affiliation of, 206; education of, 206; Trotsky on low educational level of, 206, 207; reserve commanders' deficiencies, 207; represented during NEP as homogeneous, 207; age limits aimed at ex-officers, 208; staff officers indispensable, 208; advantages of Party affiliation, 209; Frunze on promotions, 211, 213; Piatnitskii's classification of, 213; lack of fusion of, 213, 214; unification of command makes for cleavage among, 218, 228; overburdened by political work, 219, 220; low level of discipline, 220, 221; Wollenberg on "democratic" tendencies among, 220, 221; questionnaire on ethics of, 221; absence of special clubs for, 221; Red Army and Red Navy Houses' functions, 222; poor material conditions of, 222, 223; pay, 222, 223; material

M

Magnitogorsk, 277, 355
Makhin, Theodore, Colonel Imperial
    Russian Army, defection of, 53, 374,
    410
Makhno, Nestor, Ukrainian guerilla
    leader, viii; as Red Army command-
    er, 64, 65; endeavored to find support
    in united village, 104, 128
Markin, N. G., Commissar of Volga Red
    Armed Flotilla, 118
Marx, Karl, contribution of, to military
    doctrine, 158, 397
Mekhlis, L. E., chief of the PUR, 390;
    appointed from editorial chair of
    Pravda, 400, 401, 404, 405, 409; on in-
    ternationalist aims of Red Army, 414,
    420
Mensheviki (former) among staff of De-
    partments of Party Building, 243
Metallurgy, 279, 281, 282, 283, 284,
    351, 352, 354; expanse of, under third
    Five Year Plan, 355, 356
Mezheninov, S. A., ex-General Imperial
    Russian Army, 367
"Middle" peasants, 100, 106; promised by
    Trotsky that no change to communistic
    form of economy will be forced on
    them, 106, 119, 328, 332; admission of,
    to Military Schools restricted, 332, 333,
    341
Mikeladze, Military Commissar, killed
    by Dumenko, 65
Military Calendar (Voennyi Kalendar),
    222, 258
Military Colleges (Red Army), gradu-
    ates of, 201; number of, in 1927, 201,
    226, 227; lowering of intellectual re-
    quirement for admission to, 227, 292,
    299, 303, 368, 374
Military Commissars, reintroduction of,
    in 1937, viii; functions of, 34, 73, 74;
    All-Russian Bureau of, 41, 42, 56, 57,
    59, 60; Provisional Government Front
    Commissars, 73, 74, 75, 76, 77, 78, 79;
    relations of, with commanders, 79;
    type of "good" commissar, 80; con-
    flicts of, with commanders, 80; agita-
    tion for abolition of, 80, 82, 83, 84, 85;
    conflicts with soldiers of, 86; demarca-
    tion of functions from Political De-
    partments, 86, 87; evolution of, 88,
    89, 90, 93, 95, 96; conflicts of, with
    Communist cells, 98; given wide dis-
    ciplinary powers, 112, 121, 140, 141,
    154, 200; relations of, with non-Party
    commanders, 209, 219, 220, 225; trend
    to command duties among, 229, 230,

238; violation of Party discipline by,
230, 231; reorganization of political
organs suggested, 231, 232; lack of
unanimity among on unity of command,
232; functions defined, 233, 234, 235,
237, 238; low cultural level of, 238,
239; control commanders' promotion,
242; non-proletarian elements among,
242; victory of, over rank and file party
organizations in army, 255; disciplinary powers of, 271, 308, 314, 315;
misunderstand their role, 316; political
directors subordinated to, 316, 317;
social mimicry among, 319; energy of,
319; keep Red Army loyal, 320, 322,
330, 386; advancement of young political workers after purge, 390, 391, 392,
393; graduated ranks introduced for,
393; statute of, 395, 396; reasons for
reintroduction of, 398, 399; purge of,
400, 401, 402; assume guidance in action, 402; abolition of, and reintroduction after Hitler's attack, 402, 403, 424,
427; party dictatorship makes army
political organs inevitable, 428
Military Communism (War Commu-
    nism), brought to an end by Kron-
    stadt rebellion, 126, 183, 199, 202
Military co-operatives *(Voentorg)*, 379,
    380
Military correspondents, collaborators of
    wall-newspapers not included among,
    338; difference between military cor-
    respondents and those of wall-news-
    papers abolished, 338, 339
Military Council, 385, 386; of the mil-
    itary districts established, 394, 395
Military Courts, *see* Court-martials
Military Districts (of Red Army), 285;
    distribution of forces between, 359,
    360; new districts added, 361; unity
    of command introduced in, 377, 378;
    collegiate principle reestablished in,
    394
Military doctrine (Soviet), formulated,
    157, 158, 159, 160, 161; Frunze's and
    Gusev's outline of, 161; Lenin not in
    favor of advocates of proletarian mil-
    itary doctrine, 161, 162; discussions
    on, reflect dissatisfaction on part of
    military with Trotsky, 163; Trotsky's
    views on, 162, 163, 164, 165, 166, 167,
    168, 169; theses submitted by Frunze
    and Voroshilov on, 169, 170, 171;
    Frunze's viewpoint modified, 171; Tu-
    khachevskii's position on, 171, 172;
    Svechin's theories, 172, 173; Trotsky's
    views on position warfare in the West,
    174, 176; impossibility to unite peas-

Army officers' viewpoint, 209; growth of professional military class, 228; commanding personnel officially professionalized, 374, 375

Proletarians, percentage of workers in the Red Army in 1920, 105; change in attitude of, in 1921, 130; among Communists in Red Army, 245; young proletarians in the navy, 246, 247; percentage of Communists in the army, as against Party as a whole, 257; percentage of, among soldiers, 257, 258; percentage of, in different arms, 260; numerical expansion of, during Five Year Plans, 277, 278; planned increase of, according to Five Year Plans, 277, 278; proletarization of army during Five Year Plans, 278, 283, 284; increase in percentage of, in Military Schools, 293, 294; percentage of, among commanders in 1929-1930, 296; aim of army political work defined as "armed support of proletarian dictatorship," 314; army's "proletarian cementation," 315; percentage of, among army political workers, 317; among military Communists, 324; large percentage of, among purged, 326; predominate among recruits for party membership in armed forces, 326, 327; favored by Party Code, 327; XVth Party Congress on increasing percentage of "workers from the bench" in the Party, 328; rapid increase of, among soldiers, 330, 331; increase of percentage of, in regimental schools, decreed, 333; increase in number of workers 1928-1937, 356; increase of, among commanders, 368; percentage of, among soldiers and junior commanders, in 1937, 414, 415; among commanders, 415

Proletariat, Russian, lacks in numerical strength during Civil War, 66; percentage of, in the army, 90; without it "army would have fallen to dust," 90; interests of, not identical with those of the "middle" peasants, during Civil War, 106; does not want return of capitalists, 109; common bond with peasantry, 109; dissatisfied with army's privileges, 184; disinclined to enter Military Schools during NEP, 186; numerical weakness of, obstacle to introduction of militia system, 189; IXth Party Congress plans armed camps of, 191; in secondary schools, 292

Propaganda, slogans used for workers, 106; for "middle" peasants, 106; love for socialist fatherland substituted for

patriotism, 109; influence of, on outcome of Civil War, 124; Trotsky's theses for propaganda among soldiers, 255, 256; watchword "Communist Party is the leader and organizer of victory," 257; discussion of rural problems barred, 257; trend to regard political work as part of "cultural enlightenment," 257, 258; systematic political indoctrination of soldiers a novelty, 258; propaganda under fire, 259, 260; to overcome kulak trends, 259; S. Gusev's views on political enlightenment, 260; Osoaviakhim's activities in the field of, 289, 290; aim of political work in the army defined as "armed support of the proletarian dictatorship," 314; task of agitational-propaganda work set as education in unlimited loyalty to the Soviet Government, 314; "Party Enlightenment's" shortcomings, 330; program of political studies (1929), 340; emphasis on importance of discipline, 340; Voroshilov's biography expounded to soldiers, 340, 341; on Great Britain and Germany, 341; internationalist note sounded in, 341; soldiers critical of some arts of, 341; on industrialization, 342; on Communist Party and internationalism, 342; low level of political studies' guidance, 400; little progress made in study of Party's history, 409, 410; defense of fatherland, trend in, 411, 412; patriotic films, novels, and history teaching, 412; role of, in preparedness, 425; value of internationalist aspects of, 429

Provisional Government (of Russia), failure of, to reorganize army, 3; inability to improve army supplies, 8; policy of, increasing the rate of degeneration of armed forces, 15

Pukhov, G., Soviet writer on military subjects, on peasant volunteers in 1918, 31; on desertions in the Petrograd Military District, 103

PUR (Political Administration of the Republic), calls Congress of Political Workers of the Red Army, 87; replaces Political Department of the Revolutionary Military Council of the Republic, 87; prepares statutes governing political departments, 87; A. S. Bubnov, head of, 199; N. Glagolev, an employee of, 231; circular No. 200, issued by, 231; large number of leaders of, on opposition's platform, 231; new head appointed, 231; to guide party and political work, 236; liaison with civilian Party organizations to be maintained by local organs of, 236; control bureau of soldiers' letters attached to, 237; members of, belong to Trotskyite opposition, 241; personnel of, replaced, 241; activity of, regulated by Party's Central Committee, 241; activities' scope defined, 241, 243; Conflict Commission attached to, 241, 242; Permanent Political Council presided over, by PUR's chief, 241, 242, 251, 252, 253, 254; head of (A. S. Bubnov), made People's Commissar of Education, 297, 299; Gamarnik appointed head of, 319; responsible for army's loyalty during the first Five Year Plan, 320; circular of, on proletarization of Party military organization, 327, 338, 346; accused of laxity, 386; head of, involved in conflict, 389; L. E. Mekhlis made head of, 390, 395, 400; Deputy Chiefs of, removed, 401, 404, 405, 414, 420; failure of, during crises, 427, 429

Purge, 1920-1922 "cleansing" affects percentage of Communists in military schools, 186; army purge of 1921, 204; army purge of 1924, 204, 205, 212; of party affiliated elements of the navy, 248, 249; mass expulsions of military Communists, 253; results of 1929 purge in the army, 308; 1929 purge shows low political educational level, 318, 328; regimental commissar expelled during, 319; 1933 purge lowers percentage of Communists in the army, 324; results of 1929 and 1933 purges favor military Communists, 324; large percentage of workers among those purged, 326; decline in number of commanding personnel, caused by, 378; renewed stress on discipline after, 381; effect of, on commanding personnel, 383, 384; W. Duranty's opinion of, 384, 385; effect of, on military abroad, 385; Davies' view on, 385; execution of generals, 385; Voroshilov's report on military conspiracy, 385, 386; linking those executed with foreign military intelligence, 386, 387; roots of the army purge in the Party crisis, 388; vacancies made by purge in higher command positions, 389; rapid promotion of younger commanders following purge, 389, 390; elimination of Civil War veterans' predominance among commanders, 390; opens mass promotion of junior commanders to middle commanders' ranks, 390; opens golden

era for careerists, 391; has adverse effect on discipline, 391; general reintroduction of military commissars follows, 392; results in influx of ignorant men into commissars' ranks, 392; foreign opinion of the results of, 392, 393; junior *politruk* rank created to fill gaps caused by, 383, 394; reverses trend toward unity of command, 394, 395; numerical growth of political personnel after, 399, 400; Party purge 1933-1935, 404; expulsion from Party on insufficient grounds, 405; party *mores* during, 405; Komsomol leaders purged, 405; tense atmosphere in Party and Komsomol during, 406; decision to end mass purging, 406; mistrust sown by, 406, 407, 408; Stalin's directive at the root of, 407; purge of leaders leaves rank and file cold, 409; mass removal of Komsomol's active workers, 409; adverse influence of, on army discipline, 419, 423, 424; interferes with training, 423, 424; PUR strengthened during, 427

Pushkin, A. S., Russian poet, read by Military Schools' students, 373; reference to, in a speech by Stalin, 412; a soldiers' club devotes evening to reading of works of, 416

Putilov Works, tractor-building at, 283

Putna, G. K., ex-Soviet Military Attaché to Great Britain, execution of, 385

R

Rabichev, N. N., collaboration of, with Trotsky on theses on propaganda among soldiers, 255

Rabinovich, S. E., Soviet writer on politico-military subjects, 305

Radek, Karl, leading Soviet publicist, betrays Tukhachevskii, 387

Rafail, M. A., Communist Oppositionist, takes issue with Lenin, 132

Ranchevskii, Socialist Revolutionary of the Left, opposes regular army, 178, 179

Ranks (personal, of commanding personnel), introduction of, stimulates applications for Military Schools' vacancies, 374; introduction of, criticized, 374; reasons for introduction of, 374, 375, 376; for political workers also, 393; introduction of generals' and admirals' ranks, 402

Raskolnikov, F., Communist naval leader, 50; accused for role in Kronstadt rebellion, 128

Rations (for Red Army soldiers), improvement in, 263, 264; for pre-draft trainees, 268, 269, 344; better than any other army, 422; complaints on quality of, 423

Rear Militia, unfit socially for the Red Army to serve in, 107; statute of, 107, 287

Rebellions, *see also* Kronstadt rebellion, of Volsk Division, 105; of Nikolaevsk Division, 105; peasant insurrections, 119, 120; army units joint Tambov insurgents, 187; introduction of militia system hindered by peasant rebellions, 188, 191; of the Bessarabian Division, 195

Receiving Detachments (of the Red Army, for training recruits), 418

Red Army, combining defense of "socialist Fatherland" with liberation of working class world over, x; morale of, x; inheritance from Imperial Army, xi, 4; origins of, 4; proletarian volunteers for, 30, 31, 32; organization of, 33, 35, 36, 37, 40; first regular units of, organized, 40; early discipline of, 40, 41; transition to draft system of, 41, 42, 52, 53; kulaks and sons of bourgeoisie not admitted to, 107; in practice these classes represented in, 108; will to victory of, 109, 116, 117, 118, 121; advantages of, over White armies, 122, 123, 124; party discipline factor in victories of, 125; personality of leaders important, 125, 126, 172; accepted by peasants as means of national defense, 175, 176, 177, 178, 179, 183, 184; lack of well-defined plan for reorganization after Civil War, 185, 186; percentage of Communists in, 187; Party committee's low valuation of, in 1924, 187, 188; anti-Communist trends in, 188; numerical strength from 1924 on, 197, 201; 198; Frunze's concept of, 199, 200; length of service in, 201; likeness of to western armies, 203; remains instrument of class control, 203, 204, 207, 216, 227; application of democratic methods within Party organizations is limited, 231, 239, 240; non-partisan elements continue to predominate numerically, 249, 250; becomes Red not only in ideology, 250, 251, 259; school for communism, 260; percentage of proletarians allocated to different arms of, 260, 261, 262; service in army becomes attrac-

tive to peasants, 263; improvements in material conditions of, 263, 264; hours of work in, 264, 265, 267; cadres of the Territorial Militia, 268, 269; numerical preponderance of Russians in, 272, 273, 274; deficient in combat efficacy during NEP, 275, 276; impact of Five Year Plans on, 277, 278, 280, 281; privileged position of, under Five Year Plans, 285; national formations of, 285, 286, 287, 288; Party view of combat efficiency being function of political consciousness, 292; technical means acquired by, during Five Year Plans, 292, 295, 304, 305; difficulties within caused by general conditions of the U.S.S.R., 308, 312, 313; remains officially a class army, 314, 315, 319; loyalty of, during infra-party struggle, 320, 321, 322, 329; internal troubles, influence on, 321; party-affiliated elements begin to predominate numerically in, 322, 323, 324; haven for heterodoxical views, 324, 325, 329; increase in workers' percentage in, 330, 331; efforts to reduce percentage of peasants in, 332, 344, 345, 346, 347; foundations for a formidable armed force laid, 349; importance of reorganization of secondary schools' system for, 349, 357; 350; collegiate principle done away with, 358; increase in numerical strength of, 358, 359; abandonment of Territorial Militia plan, 359, 360, 361; national formations disbanded, 361; aim of reorganization of, 362; claims to front place among armies of the world, 362; "revolutionary" growth of, 362; service in, made universal and obligatory, 363, 366; 364; becomes a truly national army, 366; effect of the purge on, 385, 386, 387-393; harm done by the oppositionists to, 401; overemphasis of political work in, 409; party affiliated elements in 1939 in, 410; internationalist aims of the Red Army, 413, 414; German favorable opinion of, 416; customary military pomp revived in, 418; discipline in, more strict than in other armies, 420; Japanese opinion of, 423; barrier between commanders and soldiers set, 423, 424; growth of educational system ally of, 424; fate of, linked with industrialization, 424, 425, 426; political organs in, made inevitable by party dictatorship, 428, 429

Red Army and Navy Houses, *see* Houses of

perial Russian Navy, trial of, 53; author's conversation with, 72; accuses Bolsheviki of being German agents, 72; accused by Trotsky of supporting Lisanevich's attempt at rebellion, 72

Stcherbachev, D. G., General Imperial Russian Army, 5

Steinmetz, S. R., German military sociologist, on penalty of giving preference for class reasons, 227

Stepanov, N. A., military Communist, on mood of Petrograd's inhabitants during Kronstadt rebellion, 152, 153; on conspiracy among Peterhof cadets, 153

Strategy, during Civil War influenced by material deficiencies, 116; Tarasov-Rodionov's views on, 159, 160; maneuver character of Civil War, 169, 170; Budenny's vulgarization, 170; suggestion of adapting Red Army's structure to maneuver strategy, 170; offensive strategy advocated, 170, 171; A. Svechin's views on, 172; political offensive aim may be combined with strategic defense, 172, 173; Trotsky denies Red Army was first to adapt maneuver strategy, 173; Frunze's views on, 278; Red Army's political strategy, 316

Strikes, during Kronstadt rebellion, 151, 152, 154

Supply Services (of Red Army), deficiencies of, during Civil War, 115, 116; feeding of soldiers during Civil War, 116, 117; inadequate supplies in 1921, 184, 185; change in methods of supply during NEP, 185, 186; improvement of, under Frunze, 201, 263, 264; Territorial Militia still deficient in uniforms and equipment, 266; imports from abroad during World War I, 281, 282; improvement in soldiers' material well being, 344; further improvements in, 422

Supreme Council of National Economy (VSNKH), office of industrial mobilization added to, 279

Supreme Council of the U.S.S.R., Presidium of, granted power to appoint armed forces' high command, 363; to declare war, 363

Supreme Military Council (of Soviet Russia), established, 36; appoints commissars of District and Regional Councils, 75

Supreme Staff (All-Russian), replaces the All-Russian Collegium for the Organization of the Workers' and Peasants' Red Army, 33

Suvoroff, Alexander, Generalissimo, Prince, 412

Svechin, A. A., ex-General Imperial Russian Army, professor Soviet War College, enters Soviet service, 37; advances ideal of national army, 160, 161; for freedom of military thought, 162; connects revolutionary era with empiricism in military affairs, 162, 163; his debate with Velichko, 173, 180; opposes militia plan, 191, 192; events prove him right, 192

Svechin, M. A., General Imperial Russian Army, commanded army cavalry corps, 76

Sventitskii, Colonel Imperial Russian Army, analysis by, of social origins of Alexis Military School cadets, 43, 44, 45

Sverdlov, Iakov, formerly President of All-Russian Soviet Central Committee, 28, 30; on lack of desire on the part of proletarians to continue fight with Germans, 30

Sympathizers (with Communist Party tenets), cells formed of, 93; method of recruitment of, 93, 104, 105

Syrtsov, S. M., Oppositionist (Communist), criticizes mass recruitment of Communists in Red Army, 133; opposed by Trotsky, 133, 134

T

Tactics, influenced during Civil War by material deficiencies, 116; Tarasov-Rodionov's views on, 160; active character of Red Army tactics during Civil War, 170; tendency in Red Army to improvise, 177; tactical thought in Red Army molded by Imperial Field Service Regulations, 177; Frunze's view on connection of new tactics with application of internal combustion engine in warfare, 278, 291

Tambov rebellion, army units join rebels, 187; shatters militia plans, 191, 192

Tanks, Voroshilov on importance of, 279; tractor-building under Five Year Plans, 283, 284, 354; potential capacity of production, 355; General Khalepskii's opinion of Soviet tank forces, 425, 426; Max Werner's views, 426; other foreign views on Soviet tank forces, 426

Tarasov-Rodionov, A. I., Soviet writer, views of, on military doctrine, 159; on dependence of strategy and tactics on

DESCRIPTIVE PHONETICS

DONALD R. CALVERT, Ph.D.

Director
Central Institute for the Deaf
St. Louis, Missouri

Thieme-Stratton, Inc., New York 1980
Georg Thieme Verlag Stuttgart • New York

Publisher: Thieme–Stratton Inc.
381 Park Avenue South
New York, New York 10016

Library of Congress Cataloging in Publication Data

Calvert, Donald R
  Descriptive phonetics.

  Bibliography: p.
  Includes index.
  1. Phonetics. 2. Speech. I. Title.
P221.C25   414   79-27737
ISBN 0-913258-70-9

Medical Illustration: Leona Allison
Design: Ivy Fleck Strickler
Composition: Composing Room of Michigan

DESCRIPTIVE PHONETICS   ISBN 0-913258-70-9
Library of Congress Catalog card number 79-27737

Last digit is the print number: 9 8 7 6 5 4

CONTENTS

DEDICATION

To Ruth,
whose generation taught me,
and to Clay,
whose generation I now gladly teach.

PREFACE

Descriptive Phonetics was written to present the features of American-English speech that will be most useful to a broad spectrum of readers. It was developed especially with those in mind who are preparing to be "modifiers" of the speech of others—speech/language pathologists, teachers of speech for children with language and hearing impairment, instructors in English as a second language, and coaches of dramatics and elocution. Such persons need not only to "know about" speech but to develop the rare skill of analysis that is essential for successfully undertaking to change the speech of another person. In this endeavor, they will share the lineage of a long historical continuum of English and American phoneticians and teachers of speech.

The early British phoneticians honed to a fine edge the ability to describe speech as they heard it and to figure out how it was produced. Their most important instruments in this intimate art were their own ears and their essential skills—the facility to analyze and to interpret on the spot. Some admitted to the use of Edison's recording device after its invention in 1877, but only to confirm the observation of their senses. Although collectively immortalized by the irascible Henry Higgins of Shaw's "Pygmalion," they were individualists, working parallel but apart. It was a major achievement of compromise to form the International Phonetic Association near the end of the 19th century and for its members to promulgate an acceptable set of phonetic symbols, the International Phonetic Alphabet, still in use today. Of course, that apparent show of agreement has never deterred phoneticians—notable recently, Trager and Smith—from using other symbols they believed superior for their particular purpose. Neither has there been unanimity in respect to the proper segmentation of speech, the number of phonemes in the language, or the way speech sounds should be described.

Among those early phoneticians were some who considered themselves "teachers of speech." Alexander Melville Bell (1819–1905) of Edinburgh, like his father before him, was one of these who used his talent to change the speech of his students to more acceptable patterns. For such teachers, the scope of analysis required determination of how changes could be made, and their repertory included techniques to effect these changes. But the foundation for their teaching remained a critical ear and the capability of instantaneous analysis.

The prime importance of the individual's cultivated ear, and the talent for what may be called the "power of analysis," are often overlooked in our understandable urge to be scientific. Experimental or instrumental phonetics transfers reliance from the ear to the eye, and from broad analysis to the studied measurement of single parameters. Intuitive individual perception, suspect as a means to derive immutable fact, has sometimes been rejected as a worthy means to achieve a number of applied purposes. This is not to denigrate the contribution of the laboratory approach to phonetics. It has been, and will in the future be, immense. But the abundance of elegant instruments with lights, needles, scopes, dials, screens, or printouts of the speech investigator in his laboratory are no substitute for the clinician or teacher on the spot with a discriminating ear, a nervous system trained for analysis of what he hears, and a selection of strategies for changing speech behavior.

With this in mind, *Descriptive Phonetics* emphasizes the detailed analysis of, and understanding for, how our speech units are formed, in the same sense that "descriptive linguistics" examines a language in terms of its internal structure. Chapters I and II provide the reader with important tools of analysis—a phonetic transcription system and an understanding of the speech mechanism and processes. Exercises at the end of each chapter provide opportunity for developing transcription skill and gaining familiarity with useful vocabulary. Chapters III and IV examine the formation of each of the primary American-English phonemes, with notes on coarticulation effects that are then amplified in Chapter V. Exercises direct the student in analyzing the actions essential for forming various speech units. Further complexity in the task of analysis is added in Chapter VI with speech rhythm and supra-segmental features of speech. Variable pronunciations are presented for analysis in Chapter VII, which deals with standard and non-standard speech and the dialectical differences thereof. Finally, Chapter VIII describes the products of speech production available for our sensory perception—acoustic, visual, tactile, and kinesthetic.

This book is designed primarily as a text for students beginning the study of phonetics. More is said about its use as a supplement to course lectures in the Foreword To The Instructor that follows. Chapters II and VIII introduce the fields of physiologic and acoustic phonetics, respectively, preparing the student for further study in either area. However, the book may also serve as a resource for the advanced student who wishes to review the detailed descriptions of phonemes in Chapters III and IV, or for the professional clinician and teacher who makes use of the analysis of spellings, and of the list of words, sentences, and contrast pairs that accompany the description of each phoneme in those chapters.

Not all phoneticians will be happy with what I have written. One may feel that there is not enough detail on acoustic phonetics, whereas another may lament the omission of neurology in dealing with physiologic phonetics.

Others may object to my categorization of phonemes, perhaps disappointed that /h/ does not follow the traditional classification as a "glottal" fricative, or they may miss the semantic flatulence of calling /l/ a "liquid" of either a "light" or a "dark" character. Still others may observe that the text does not share the currently popular enthusiasm for the concept of distinctive features, or does not carry heavy documentation for all its statements. One can scarcely put to paper his thoughts about phonetics without offending a phonetician somewhere who will become provoked enough to respond with a treatise on the subject. So be it! Descriptive phonetics is not an exact science, and efforts to develop a consistent nomenclature are well overdue.

The pronunciations in this book reflect my personal linguistic heritage. Born and reared within 100 miles of Omaha, Nebraska, I have lived for significant periods in Portland, Oregon, the San Francisco Bay Area, Arlington, Virginia, and St. Louis, Missouri, always with my ears unstopped. I speak my own peculiar dialect of "traveled" General American-English.

I acknowledge with gratitude the advice and suggestions of my colleagues at Central Institute, especially Randall Monsen, S. Richard Silverman, Ira Hirsh, and Carol DeFilippo, and the invaluable editorial assistance of Helen Roberts. The comments of Elizabeth Carr Holmes of Honolulu and of Akiro Honda of Sapporo, Japan, were extremely helpful.

D.R.C.

FOREWORD TO THE INSTRUCTOR

This text follows sequences designed to help college-level students learn from its contents. No previous knowledge of phonetics, and only rudimentary knowledge of anatomy, physiology, and physics, is prerequisite. Its general pedagogic path begins with introduction of material in the chapter text associated with relevant illustrations and examples, followed by exercises at the end of chapters for practice and familiarity, and then reinforcement here and there in the book through application in some practical context or related to something the student is likely to know well already. The chapters follow an order the author has found advantageous in presenting a semester's course of three credits (about 45 lecture hours). Although *Descriptive Phonetics* may help the student as a course of study for self-instruction, its best use is as a supplement to lectures that include presentation of a generous sampling of live speech or recordings for students to transcribe and analyze.

The primary purpose of this book is to present to the student an opportunity to develop listening and analytic skills, to gain knowledge and understanding of speech, to be introduced to some of the special areas of phonetics, and to have access to resource materials that may be helpful for future application. These objectives are outlined below with chapter designations:

SKILLS

1. Phonetic transcription, broad and narrow IPA (I through VII)
2. Use of common symbols to indicate speech rhythm features (VI)
3. Analysis of how speech units are produced (II through VI)

KNOWLEDGE AND UNDERSTANDING

4. Development and purposes of orthographic systems (I)
5. Anatomy and physiologic processes of speech production (II)
6. Categorization of consonants by place and manner of production (II, III)

7. Categorization of vowels by place and height of tongue elevation (II, IV)
8. Influences of phonetic context and coarticulation (III, IV, V)
9. Nature of tongue twisters and difficult articulations (V)
10. Relation of speech rhythm and pronunciation (IV, VI)
11. Relation among standards, dialects, and defects of speech (VII)
12. Historical perspective on speech and phonetics (I, VII)
13. Sensory products of speech—acoustic, visual, tactile, kinesthetic (II, VIII)
14. Relation of acoustic parameters to oral positions (II, III, IV, VIII)
15. Vocabulary associated with phonetics (I through VIII)

INTRODUCTION TO AREAS OF PHONETICS

16. Physiologic phonetics (II, III, IV, V)
17. American-English pronunciation (I, III, IV, V, VII)
18. Dialects (VII)
19. Acoustic phonetics (II, VIII)

RESOURCE MATERIAL FOR REFERENCE

20. Formation of primary American-English phonemes (III, IV)
21. Spellings for primary phonemes (I, III, IV)
22. Word examples of phonemes—initial, medial, and final positions (III, IV)
23. Examples of phonemes in sentence units (III, IV)
24. Sets of words contrasting similar or often confused phonemes (III, IV)
25. The Northampton symbol system for reading and spelling use (I)

Each of these objectives, which collectively form a basis for examination of the student, is pursued in various parts of the book. For example, skill in phonetic transcription is developed over the course of several chapters. First, the International Phonetic Alphabet (IPA) is put into perspective with other orthographic systems, as the difference between alphabet spelling and the sounds of speech is emphasized in Chapter I. Exercises at the end of the chapter proceed from distinguishing phonemes common to groups of words having varied spellings through transcription tasks of gradually increasing difficulty, to word transcription using broad IPA symbols for all common American-English phonemes. In Chapter II, the newly learned IPA symbols are immediately applied in the text to indicate pronunciation of possibly unfamiliar terms for anatomy of the speech mechanism and speech processes. The task is then reversed at the end of the chapter with exercises requiring the student to sound out the new vocabulary, using the increasingly familiar IPA symbols before spelling the words in Roman alphabet letters. In Chapters III and IV, the student is again required to review knowledge of the IPA in order to understand the production of consonants and vowels. Exercises at the end of Chapter IV require the student to sound out nonsense speech units written in IPA symbols, and then transliterate them into alphabet symbols he believes most appropriate. Chapter V directly instructs the student in transcribing connected speech units with suggestions and illustrations in the text, followed by exercises in using some narrow transcription symbols. By now the student should be learning to transcribe connected speech the way it is actually spoken, including numerous coarticulation effects, rather than simply the more typical word transcription. Chapter VI helps prepare the student to use basic symbols for stress, intonation, and phrasing, again reinforced by exercises at the end of the chapter. Then IPA symbols are used extensively to define non-standard speech and to compare dialects in Chapter VII, with exercises now requiring finer phonetic distinctions.

Of course, the written text cannot replace the spoken word for developing careful listening and transcription skills. The instructor may wish to develop his own material or may deliver the exercises, graded for difficulty such as those in Chapter I, by live voice. Dictation of nonsense units is especially valuable to help the student with careful listening to speech sounds, since no semantic context will be available to depend upon.

A similar sequence is followed to help the student learn to analyze how units of speech are produced. Phonetic transcription is just the beginning of this sequence. Prepared with IPA symbols, and with the vocabulary and understanding of speech production processes from the first two chapters, the student is presented with direct descriptions of the articulatory sequences involved in producing phonemes in Chapters III and IV. From these simple sequences for individual phonemes, Chapter V presents step-by-step, detailed descriptions of connected units of speech, taking into account important effects of coarticulation. The student participates in the process by pursuing exercises at the end of these chapters. Features of speech rhythm are added to the analysis of coarticulated phonemes in Chapter VI. Again, the text may be supplemental to live presentations by the instructor in leading the student to analyze speech units as they are actually spoken.

Important vocabulary is defined within the text, and selected words and phrases are emphasized in bold type with definitions reviewed at the end of each chapter. Important words and concepts related to phonetics are cross referenced in the index. Words likely to be unfamiliar when introduced in one chapter are used again for reinforcement in later chapters whenever possible. Annotated references for suggested reading are presented at the end of each chapter to provide the student with direction for a next step in learning, should his interest or that of the instructor suggest it.

To the skills, knowledge, introductions, and resource materials, which are the main objectives of the book, may be added an **attitude** about speech. This is concerned with the student's sensitivity to variations in speech. A growing child naturally adopts the speech patterns of the people around him, especially his immediate family, and does not question whether the patterns are good or bad, right or wrong, better or poorer than that of others. They are his and his family's, and of course they are good. When he encounters a pattern markedly different from his, such as a major dialect variation, it is to be expected that he may judge that such people "talk funny," and may even judge them inferior because of this. Those around him may voice agreement, reinforcing his belief. Such secure beliefs associated with self-image die hard. For some, this pleasant myth persists throughout a lifetime. On the other hand, if he moves or expands his activities, the growing child may find himself in a group, a school, or even a society in which his speech pattern is considered "funny" and inferior by the majority of his new peers. His response of rebellion or adaptation may be devastating, reflecting confusion and uncertainty. Whatever has been the student's experience with speech variations, he is likely to be ready to develop his own philosophy and attitudes about them and his own speech.

Chapter VII leads the student through some of the thinking about standards, non-standard speech patterns, and the variations of dialects so that he may reach some of his own conclusions. Arbitrary standards and value judgments are de-emphasized, and the dialects of American-English are given historical perspective. The intention is to prepare the student to accept his own dialect as the result of where he happened to be born and grow up, and to accept the dialect of others on the same basis rather than consider either on a scale of value. However, it is unrealistic to leave the student thinking that no value judgments about speech are made, and the subject of non-standard speech is examined with some care.

A common use students make of a course in phonetics is improvement of their own speech. This is not unlike students who study psychology in order to gain an understanding of or a solution to their own emotional problems. Students' speech patterns are among their most important personal attributes, probably second only to physical appearance, in shaping self-image and influencing those around them. At high school and college age especially, students will wish to improve their speech. In *Descriptive Phonetics,* opportunity to practice pronunciations are abundant in the word and sentence lists of Chapters III and IV, and Chapter VII presents a sequence of exercises for improving enunciation. Future speech/language pathologists and teachers, of course, will be interested in developing speech patterns that will be good models for their clients or students.

In this book, I have attempted to present to the student a prose style that will directly convey ideas and information and yet be fairly lively and interesting. Historical sequences have been included in association with phonetic concepts. References to English literature have included some works of Lewis Carroll, Bernard Shaw, Joel Chandler Harris, E.B. White, H.L. Mencken, and the King James version of the Old Testament. I have avoided the heavy documentation style of theses and research papers in favor of a more smoothly flowing narrative that I hope will lend some pleasure to reading and learning about *Descriptive Phonetics*.

Chapter I

ORTHOGRAPHIC SYSTEMS

Systems of written language symbols are as old as civilization. In fact, they are the mark of a civilized society that senses the need to place in a more permanent form the spoken thoughts and experiences that constitute its culture. Early man used **pictograms** to express his ideas simply and directly. Drawings of a man hunting a deer commemorated a successful deer hunt. The Chinese and Japanese reduced their pictograms to simplified lines representing the form of the object. Over many generations, they developed highly stylized characters or **logograms,** with each symbol representing an entire word (Figure I–1). Egyptian hieroglyphics included pictograms and some **ideograms** with characters expressing a symbolic idea associated with the object. The ostrich feather, for example, was a common symbol for truth. Hieroglyphics also included a few characters that represented either a speech sound or a syllable. A simplified drawing of an owl represented the [m] sound as in *man,* the shape of a loaf of bread the [t] as in *too,* and a lion the [l] as in *lip.* The Phoenicians went further in developing a set of **phonograms,** written symbols unrelated to objects to represent all the various sounds of their speech. Our **alphabet** of written symbols comes by this route; from the Greeks, who named their first two symbols "alpha" and "beta," to

1

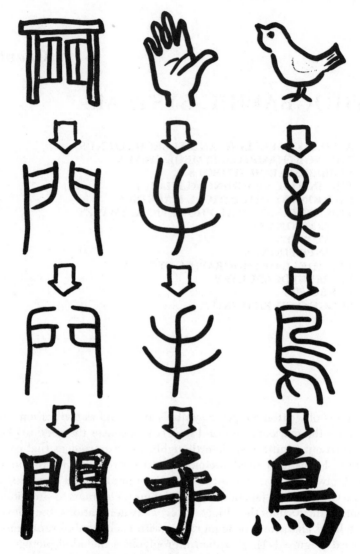

Figure I-1.   Evolution of Japanese logograms from pictograms.

the Romans, from whom we have the *Roman Alphabet* that English and several other languages use (Figure I–2).

   Orthography refers to the accurate or accepted spelling of words using the symbols of an alphabet. Most orthographic systems relate written language to spoken language, using alphabet letters as phonograms. Ideally, an orthographic system would have one written symbol for each spoken sound, and every time that symbol appeared, it would always be given that same

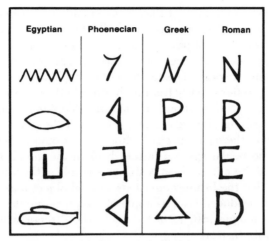

Figure 1-2. Evolution of alphabet symbols from Egyptian to Roman alphabets.

sound. This would enable us to "sound out" any new word we read so that we could pronounce it correctly. Conversely, if we knew how to pronounce a word, we should also be able to spell it correctly. Such an ideal one-to-one sound/symbol correspondence seldom occurs, unfortunately.

ALPHABET SPELLING AND SPEECH SOUNDS

As spoken language grows and changes, written language follows, but at a slower pace and sometimes at a great distance. English developed from a mixture of the language of Europe. Anglo-Saxon, derived primarily from Germanic dialects, was influenced by the Scandinavian languages of northern Europe, French, the Romance languages of southern Europe, and classic Greek and Latin. A word has been borrowed here and there from Arabic, East Indian, and American Indian languages. American-English is still growing, absorbing new words from languages around the world and adopting words from its own ethnic groups. While this richness of origins enhances our facility in expressing ourselves, it has left spelling and pronunciation in some cases far apart.

By listening carefully to the way speech is pronounced, we become aware that our American-English speech consists of a number of sounds that recur in words and phrases so that we recognize them in connected speech. For example, we hear a highly similar sound at the beginning of the word *cab* and at the end of the word *tack*. We also hear this sound in such words as *ski, occur, ache,* and *liquor,* and we note that although the spelling changes the common sound is essentially the same. Each of these similar sounds is actually produced in a slightly different manner because of the different speech sounds around them. Yet they have enough in common to be considered as examples of a class of sounds we will later see is written as /k/. Such classes of sounds are called **phonemes.** Phonemes are abstractions derived by generalizing from a number of similar sounds that actually occur in speech. Variations among the sounds within a phoneme class are called **allophones.** They differ slightly from each other both in the way we produce them and in the way they sound to our ear. Allophonic variations do not influence the meaning of words. However, when the phoneme changes to another phoneme, the meaning also changes. For example, if the *k* in *key* is produced by a particular speaker farther back in the mouth than usual—as might happen for the *c* in *cool*—it is still an example of the phoneme /k/, and *key* is heard so that the listener envisions a metal object that unlocks doors. But if the sound produced is an example of the phoneme /t/, produced with the front of the tongue instead of the back, the listener will hear *tea* and think of the drink, instead.

One major problem of orthography is that the Roman alphabet does not contain enough symbols to represent all the different speech sound classes, or phonemes, of American-English. We have only 26 alphabet letters to represent 43 basic phonemes. The five letters that we call vowels (*a, e, i, o, u*) must represent 18 different vowel and diphthong phonemes. The 21 consonant letters represent 25 different consonant phonemes. There is, for example, no special letter that represents the medial consonant in the words *leisure* and *pleasure.* A number of other phonemes have to be represented by a combination of two letters such as *sh, th, wh, ch,* and *ng.*

A second related irregularity of American-English is that the letters are not always pronounced the same way each time they appear. Whereas most consonant letters represent a single sound, none of the vowel letters does so exclusively. Note how pronunciation of the letter *o* changes in these words: *ton, top, told, tomb, woman, women.* A third inconsistency of our orthography is that a single speech sound may be represented by a number of different letters or combinations. The sound of /f/, for example, may be spelled *f (fir), ff (differ), ph (phone),* or *gh (rough).* Still a fourth irregularity is that we have a number of letters in spelling that sometimes represent no sound. These silent letters include the *p* in *pneumonia,* the *l* in *half,* the *k* in *knife,* the *t* in *listen,* the *b* in *debt,* and the *gh* in *through.* If these variants were not enough, we have words that are spelled the same but are pronounced differently (*read/read, bow/bow, live/live, uses/uses, tear/tear*), and those that are spelled differently but pronounced the same (*him/hymn, bare/bear, mince/mints,* and *rite/right/write/wright*).

These inconsistencies and irregularities, which most Americans take for granted and learn in stride, cause immense problems for non-English speakers and for children who have a reading disability. Just when a rule of spelling or pronunciation seems to be emerging, a number of important exceptions appear. We could hardly have made the spelling and pronunciation more difficult if we had set out to do so. As the English dramatist George Bernard Shaw said in the preface to his play, *Pygmalion,*

> The English have no respect for their language, and will not teach their children to speak it. They cannot spell it because they have nothing to spell it with but an old foreign alphabet of which only the consonants— and not all of them—have any agreed speech value. Consequently no man can teach himself what it should sound like from reading it. . . . Most European languages are now accessible in black and white to foreigners: English and French are not thus accessible even to Englishmen and Frenchmen.

Despite these obvious problems of our system of orthography, attempts at spelling reform have been largely unsuccessful. Benjamin Franklin and Noah Webster made some early attempts in this country. Notable among more recent efforts was the 40-year experiment by the *Chicago Tribune.* Beginning in 1934, the *Tribune* published lists of words that were to be simplified when spelled in that newspaper. These included such changes as *catalog* for *catalogue, fantom* for *phantom, burocracy* for *bureaucracy,* and *iland* for *island.* New words were added to the list such as *frate* for *freight,* and others that had not been well accepted, such as *sodder* for *solder,* were dropped. Teachers, writers of spelling books, and scholars of language complained persistently, and the new spellings just did not catch on with the public. With an editorial entitled "Thru is through and so is tho," the experiment was abandoned in 1975.

Even though our conventional spelling has a less-than-perfect relation to the sounds of all our words, the relation is often useful. We can and do "sound out" new words when reading. **Phonics** is an application of the alphabet symbol-to-speech sound relation organized into a tool for teaching beginners to read. Cartoonists rely on our knowledge of the symbol/sound relation when they spell the sounds of noises such as *pow* and *zap,* or have a dog bark *arf* or *woof woof.* Similarly, when a foreign language does not use the Roman alphabet and we wish to spell its words for English pronunciation, we judge which of our letters would most closely reflect the sound of the words. This process is called **transliteration.** Languages such as Russian, Chinese, and Japanese, which are in occasional use by people with Roman alphabet languages, are often transliterated by journalists, or by those who make maps and must spell place names. An example is the Russian word for *no,* which is written нет in the Russian Cyrillic alphabet. It has the sound roughly of our word *net,* but with the vowel *e* corresponding to the first two sounds in *yes* so that the word is commonly transliterated "*nyet.*" At times, native speakers seek to correct transliteration that they believe misrepresents their pronunciation. For example, in 1978, the government of the People's Republic of China decreed that all publications printed in that country in English, French, German, Spanish, and other Roman alphabet languages be transliterated into its standard Pinyin phonetic system, developed in 1958. *Peking* is to be written *Beijing* and *Chunking* as *Zhongquing* to approximate better their native pronunciation.

THE NORTHAMPTON SYMBOL SYSTEM

Many people have tried to analyze our spelling and pronunciation in order to determine its intrinsic system and rules and to make these available to help children and foreigners who wish to learn our language. Alice Worcester, a teacher of deaf children at the Clarke School in Northampton, Massachusetts, published in 1885 a set of symbols taken from the Roman alphabet that she found beneficial in teaching speech and reading. These **Northampton symbols** were revised and organized into systematic charts (Figures I–3 and I–4) in 1925 by Caroline Yale*, and they are still useful in teaching deaf children today.

The principle of the Northampton symbol system is to use as primary symbols either the alphabet letters that most frequently occur for particular speech sounds or letters that almost invariably represent the sound. To handle the many irregularities, secondary and even tertiary symbols are also used. For example, the letter *k* is the primary symbol for the /k/ phoneme, as in *kind*, because it almost always represents that sound when it appears in spelling. But the letter *c* is written for that sound in the spelling of such common words as *car, cat, can, come, could,* and *cup,* and it actually occurs more frequently in common usage than *k* to represent the /k/ phoneme. Unfortunately, the letter *c* also frequently has the sound that is associated with *s*, as it does in *city*, or that associated with *sh*, as occurs in *ocean*. The letter *c* was therefore designated a secondary spelling for the /k/ sound, and it is also used as a secondary spelling for the /s/ sound (see Figure I–3).

A special contribution of this system is its handling of vowels. It was noted, for example, that when the letter *a* is followed by a consonant and then the letter *e*, the combination has the sound of *a* as in *make*. Note this sound and spelling in such words as *cake, fame, sane, bale, take,* and *safe*. Note also how adding the *e* in the following words changes pronunciation of the vowel sound:

mad	made
at	ate
dam	dame
hat	hate
man	mane
pal	pale

---

*Yale, Caroline: *Formation and Development of English Elementary Sounds*. Northampton, Massachusetts, Gazette Printing Company 1925.

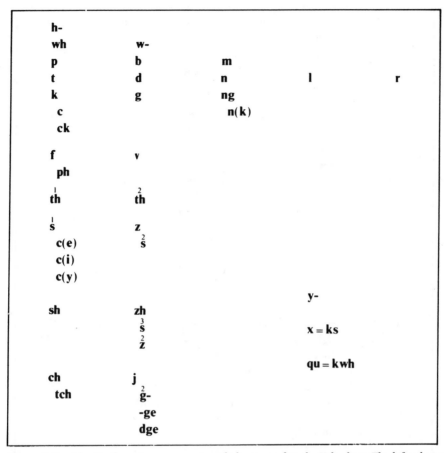

Figure I–3. The Northampton consonant symbols arranged in the Yale chart. The left column is occupied by voiceless sounds, the second column by the voiced forms of the same sound, and the third column by nasal resonant sounds. Horizontally, the consonants are arranged by place of articulation. Secondary symbols are indented. See Table I–2 for guide to pronunciation. Courtesy, The Clarke School.

To represent the vowel sound in the first column, the written symbol -a- is used. For the vowel sound in the second column, the written symbol a-e is used, the dash indicating an intervening or adjoining consonant. Similarly, the symbol i-e is used for the vowel in *kite, time,* and *dine,* and the symbol o-e is used for the vowel in *hole, bone,* and *phone* (see Figure I–4). Table I–1 shows the regularity with which the written symbol for vowel sounds in common words corresponds to the speech sound they are to represent. It is apparent that some vowel symbols, such as the a-e, the u-e, and the i-e, are very regular, whereas other symbols, such as the *ow* and o-e, represent more than one sound most of the time.

The Northampton system is best used as a teaching medium. It may

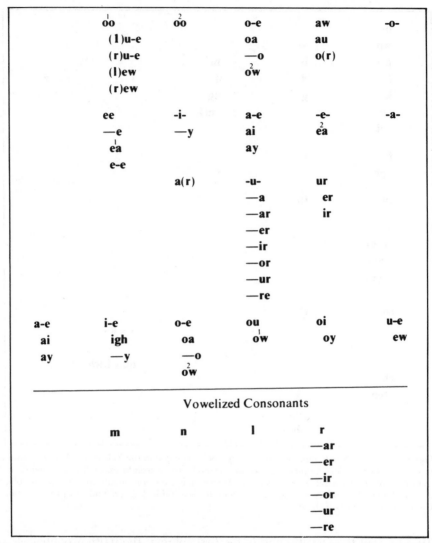

Figure 1-4. The Northampton vowel symbols arranged in the Yale chart. The upper line contains the back round vowels, the second the front vowels, and the third line the mid vowels. The lowest line contains the diphthong sounds, and the very bottom line contains the vowelized consonants that perform the function of a vowel in some words. Secondary symbols are indented. See Table I-3 for guide to pronunciation. Courtesy, The Clarke School.

serve to give the young child who has speech or language delay written symbols to associate with the speech units upon which he is working, coincidentally providing a written record of his progress for him and his parents to see. It also has served, with the aid of a skillful teacher, to help poor readers establish a link between their own speech production and our orthography,

TABLE I-1 THE PROPORTION OF TIMES EACH OF 20 NORTHAMPTON SYMBOLS REPRESENTS THE DESIGNATED VOWEL SOUNDS IN 7500 COMMON WORDS

NORTHAMPTON VOWEL SYMBOLS	VOWEL SOUND IN SAMPLE WORD	PROPORTION OF TIME SYMBOL OCCURS TO REPRESENT THAT VOWEL SOUND (%)	NORTHAMPTON VOWEL SYMBOLS	VOWEL SOUND IN SAMPLE WORD	PROPORTION OF TIME SYMBOL OCCURS TO REPRESENT THAT VOWEL SOUND (%)
a-e	make	100	-u-	cup	73
u-e	cute	100		unite	24
aw	law	100	ea	meat	74
i-e	kite	99		head	24
oi	boil	99	-e-	bet	70
oa	boat	98		be	30
ee	beet	96	ou	out	60
-i-	pin	91		rough	35
	child	9	oo	boot	59
ai	bait	90		cook	41
au	caught	88	-o-	top	53
-a-	cat	83		told	40
	table	13	ow	low	52
				cow	48
			o-e	home	34
				come	66

9

providing a phonic system for sounding-out unfamiliar words. Adaptations of the system have been used similarly to help foreign students pronounce English words.*

VISIBLE SPEECH SYMBOLS

A number of attempts have been made to produce written symbols related to articulatory positions so that the reader would have cues to aid in producing the associated speech sounds. Francis Mercurius Van Helmont† in 1667 promoted the belief that letters of the Hebrew alphabet were based on the configuration of the speech organs in producing certain sounds (Figure I–5). In the 19th century, Alexander Melville Bell‡ devised a system of written symbols with curves and lines roughly corresponding to a profile view of the organs of speech: the nose, the lower lip, the point of the tongue, the throat, etc. The symbols were essentially directions to do something with the mouth. The /n/, for example, was represented by the symbol illustrated in Figure I–6. The direction of the opening at the top of the crescent in that symbol indicated the tongue tip was upward. Closure of the tongue against the upper gum ridge was shown by closure of the character by lines at the top. Voicing was suggested by the vertical line, and open nasal resonance was shown by the sigmoid line completing the closing at the top. With such symbols, the speech sounds of any language could be represented. For a time, the Bell symbols were used in teaching speech to deaf children, but these were eventually abandoned because of their complexity and unfamiliarity to most teachers and the inevitable need to transform them to the symbols of the Roman alphabet.

THE INITIAL TEACHING ALPHABET

Sir James Pitman introduced his Initial Teaching Alphabet to the United States in the 1960's.§ He attempted to eliminate ambiguity by having only one symbol for each spoken sound. The symbols he used were either regular alphabet letters or were made to look like alphabet letters, augmenting the Roman alphabet for a total of 44 symbols (Figure I–7). The intention was that the young child might learn this system of reading first, then transfer easily to our usual system of orthography for reading and writing. It

---

*Laubach, Frank C. et al.: *The New Streamlined English Series.* Syracuse, N.Y., New Readers
    Press, Revised 1971.
†abHelmont, F.M.B.: *Alphabeti vere Naturalis Hebraici Brevissima Delineatio,* 1667.
‡Bell, A. M., *The Mechanism of Speech.* New York, Funk & Wagnalls Co., 1916.
§Pitman, Sir James K.B.E.: Can i.t.a. Help the Deaf Child? *Proceedings: International Conf.
    on Oral Educ. of the Deaf.* Wash. D.C., A. G. Bell Assn, 1967, Vol. I, pp. 514–542.

Figure I-5. Diagrams by F. M. B. abHelmont (1667) to illustrate relation between Hebrew alphabet symbols and the speech mechanism.

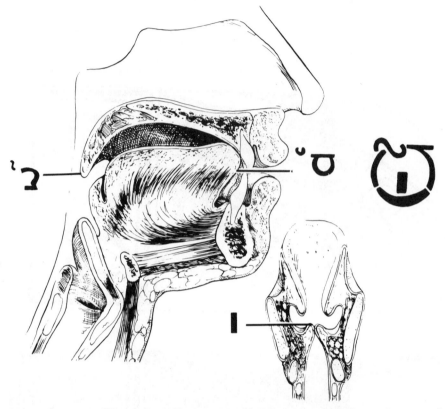

Figure 1-6. Alexander Melville Bell's phonetic symbol for /n/ based on place and manner of production.

would be necessary for many children's books to be printed in these symbols. Although there was a flurry of interest in the 1960's, the Initial Teaching Alphabet has not found common use in the United States.

DICTIONARY DIACRITICAL MARKINGS

Pronouncing dictionaries have had to develop systems to indicate how words are commonly pronounced. They use modifying symbols, attached to letters, which are called **diacritical markings.** Pronunciation of the letters with attached markings are suggested by key words. These systems constitute the most available and constant references to pronunciation for most people. However, they assume some knowledge of the language for pronunciation of the key words, the symbols vary from dictionary to dictionary, and they are not available in general reading without a dictionary as ready reference. A teacher may effectively use the diacritical markings to indicate pro-

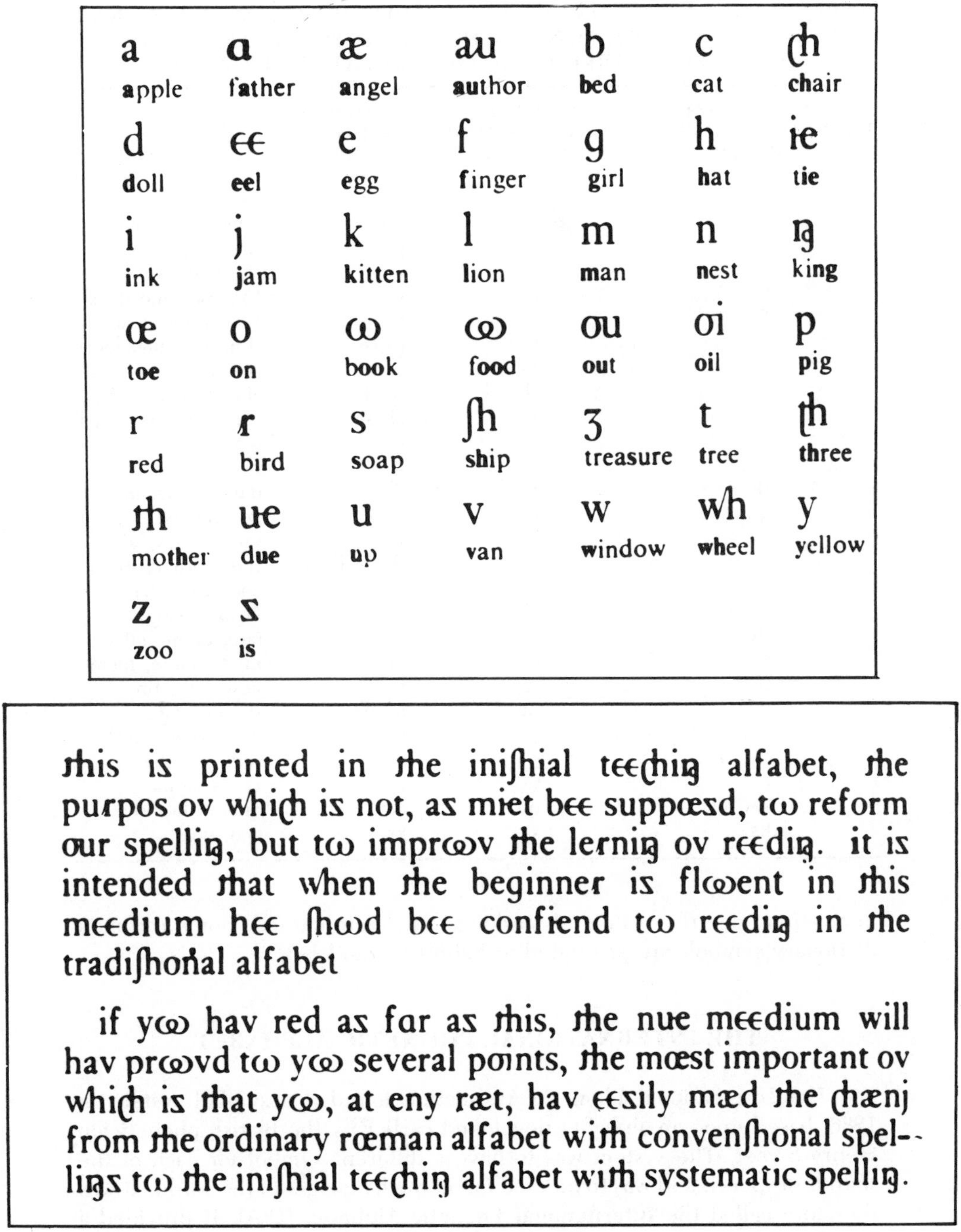

a apple	ɑ father	æ angel	au author	b bed	c cat	ch chair
d doll	ee eel	e egg	f finger	g girl	h hat	ie tie
i ink	j jam	k kitten	l lion	m man	n nest	ŋ king
œ toe	o on	ω book	ω food	ou out	oi oil	p pig
r red	ɾ bird	s soap	ʃh ship	ʒ treasure	t tree	th three
th mother	ue due	u up	v van	w window	wh wheel	y yellow
z zoo	ʒ is					

ᚦhis is printed in ᚦhe iniʃhial teeᚲhiŋ alfabet, ᚦhe purpos ov whiᚲh is not, as miet bee suppœsd, tω reform our spelliŋ, but tω imprωv ᚦhe lerniŋ ov reediŋ. it is intended ᚦhat when ᚦhe beginner is flωent in ᚦhis meedium hee ʃhωd bee confiend tω reediŋ in ᚦhe tradiʃhoñal alfabet

if yω hav red as far as ᚦhis, ᚦhe nue meedium will hav prωvd tω yω several points, ᚦhe mœst important ov whiᚲh is ᚦhat yω, at eny ræt, hav eesily mæd ᚦhe ᚲhænj from ᚦhe ordinary rœman alfabet wiᚦh convenʃhonal spel--liŋs tω ᚦhe iniʃhial teeᚲhiŋ alfabet wiᚦh systematic spelliŋ.

Figure 1-7. The Initial Teaching Alphabet (i.t.a.) of Sir James Pitman. At top, symbols arranged alphabetically with key words. At bottom, example of spelling using the i.t.a. symbols.

TABLE I-2 PRIMARY CONSONANT SYMBOLS OF THE INTERNATIONAL PHONETIC ALPHABET, THE NORTHAMPTON SYSTEM, AND COMMON DICTIONARY MARKINGS, WITH ASSOCIATED KEY WORDS

INTERNATIONAL PHONETIC ALPHABET SYMBOLS	PRIMARY NORTHAMPTON SYMBOLS	COMMON DICTIONARY SYMBOLS	KEY WORDS
h	h-	h	he, ahead
ʍ	wh	hw	when, everywhere
p	p	p	pie, stopped, sip
t	t	t	tie, later, sit
k	k	k	key, become, back
f	f	f	fan, coffee, leaf
θ	th	th th	thin, nothing, tooth
s	s	s	see, upset, makes
ʃ	sh	sh sh	she, sunshine, fish
tʃ	ch	ch ch	chair, teacher, such
w	w-	w	we, awake
b	b	b	boy, rabbit, cab
d	d	d	day, fading, mud
g	g	g	go, begged, log
v	v	v	vine, every, give
ð	th	th th th TH	the, bother, smooth
z	z	z	zoo, lazy, size
ʒ	zh	zh	vision, beige
dʒ	j	j	jam, enjoy, edge
m	m	m	my, camera, team
n	n	n	new, any, tin
ŋ	ng	ng ng	singer, song
l	l	l	low, color, bowl
r	r	r	red, oral, bar
j	y-	y	yes, canyon
kʍ	qu	kw	queen, liquid
ks	x	ks	taxi, box

nunciation once the system of markings has been learned. Some common dictionary symbols are presented in Tables I–2 and I–3.

THE INTERNATIONAL PHONETIC ALPHABET

The International Phonetic Association founded a symbol system in 1886, based upon an alphabet developed earlier by the British phonetician Henry Sweet. The system was to have a different symbol for each of the sounds of speech and was to be used for all the languages of the world. It was therefore called the **International Phonetic Alphabet** (IPA). It provided a way for phoneticians from different languages to communicate with each other and a common system for scholars of language to use in the literature.

TABLE I-3 PRIMARY VOWEL SYMBOLS IN THE INTERNATIONAL PHONETIC ALPHABET, THE NORTHAMPTON SYSTEM AND COMMON DICTIONARY MARKINGS, WITH ASSOCIATED KEY WORDS

INTERNATIONAL PHONETIC ALPHABET SYMBOLS	PRIMARY NORTHAMPTON SYMBOLS	COMMON DICTIONARY SYMBOLS	KEY WORDS
i	ee	ē	east, beet, me
ɪ	-i-	ĭ	if, bit
ε	-e-	ĕ	end, bet
æ	-a-	ă	at, bat
ɑ	a(r)	ŏ ä	odd, father, pa
a	-o-	ŏ	hot, Boston, car (Eastern U.S.)
ʌ	-u-	ŭ u	up; cub (stressed)
ə	-u-	ŭ ə ə	upon, nation, cobra (unstressed)
u	oo	ōō	ooze, boot, too
ʊ	oo	ŏŏ oo	book, could
ɔ	aw	ô aw	awful, caught, law
ɝ	ur	ûr ur	urn, burn, fur (General U.S.)
ɜ	ur	ûr	urn, burn, fur (Eastern and Southern U.S.)
ɚ	ur	ēr er	urbane, obliterate, burner (unstressed)
eɪ	a-e	ā	able, made, may
e	a-e	ā	vibrate (unstressed)
oʊ	o-e	ō	own, boat, no
o	o-e	ō	obey, rotation (unstressed)
aɪ	i-e	ī	ice, mine, my
aʊ	ou	ou	out, loud, now
ɔɪ	oi	oi	oil, coin, boy
ju	u-e	ū	use, cute, few

With a few modifications, this system continues to be the most widely used for phonetic notation.

The IPA is not intended to be used as a system of spelling for any language but as a system to symbolize visually any speech sound. The symbols *p*, *b*, *t*, *d*, *k*, *g*, *l*, *m*, *n*, *r*, *f*, *v*, *s*, *z*, *h*, and *w* come directly from the Roman alphabet (see Table I-2). Other symbols are from Greek or were especially created for the purpose. When one wishes to designate a phoneme, the IPA symbol is traditionally placed in virgules, or slash marks, as in /k/ for the phoneme that is common to *key, coo, class, bark, account,* and *ski.* To designate a particular sound that was spoken or a group of connected speech sounds, the symbol is placed in squared brackets as in [k] for the sound in the unit [ki] for pronunciation of the word *key.*

There are two levels of transcription. **Broad transcription** uses the primary symbols of the IPA to designate phonemes and the speech sounds as they are usually produced. **Narrow transcription** uses symbols, somewhat like the diacritical markings of dictionaries, to indicate something special about the way the sound has been produced. For example, the symbol [ˌ] indicates the sound was made on the teeth. Thus, a /t/ phoneme written as [t̪] was made with the tongue tip closing against the upper front teeth rather than the gum ridge. Note how this narrow transcription can be useful in describing how the [d̪] sound in *width* [wɪd̪θ] is produced, or how the Russian [n̪] is made.

Symbols of the International Phonetic Alphabet will be used to designate speech sounds throughout this book. Broad transcription symbols are presented in Tables I-2 and I-3. Exercises are presented at the end of this chapter to help the reader learn to use these symbols. Some useful symbols of narrow transcription are presented in Table I-4.

Consonants. In addition to the familiar symbols of the Roman alphabet, the IPA uses the Greek capital Theta /θ/ to represent the voiceless sound written *th* as in *thin, thank,* and *thumb,* and it uses the /ð/ to

TABLE I-4 SOME SYMBOLS OF IPA NARROW TRANSCRIPTION USEFUL IN DESCRIBING VARIATIONS IN AMERICAN-ENGLISH ARTICULATION

SYMBOL	MEANING	EXAMPLES		COMMENTS
ˌ	dentalized	[wɪd̪θ]	*width*	Made against upper front teeth
˜	nasalized	[mĩn]	*mean*	Made with excess nasality
°	voiceless	[pl̥eɪ]	*play*	Made without usual voicing
ˇ	voiced	[ə̌hed]	*ahead*	Made with some voicing
ˌ	syllabized	[bɑtl̩]	*bottle*	Given duration of a syllable without a vowel present
ː	lengthened	[tɛnːaɪts]	*ten nights*	Sound held longer than usual
┴	tongue raised	[mɛ̝t]	*met*	Tongue slightly higher than usual
┬	tongue lowered	[mɛ̞t]	*met*	Tongue slightly lower than usual
ʻ	aspirated	[læpʻ]	*lap*	Stop consonant exploded where not necessary or usual

represent the voiced *th* as in *this, that,* and *those.* A printed *w* turned upside down, /ʍ/, is used for the voiceless *wh* as in *why, which, when,* and *where.* A lengthened sigmoid /ʃ/ is written for the voiceless *sh* as in *shoe, bush,* and *ocean.* A symbol like a cursive *z* is produced as /ʒ/ for the middle consonant in *vision* and *measure.* The symbol /ŋ/, written like an *n* with one side lengthened and hooked to suggest the *g* is used for the final sound written as *ng* as in *song, wing,* and *bang.* The letter *j* is used for the brief glide sound found initially in *yes* [jɛs].

The two affricate phonemes that combine a stopping of breath and then release with friction at the same point of contact are commonly written as two symbols touching each other to indicate that they are produced with a single impulse. For example, the *ch* sound in *chew, chin,* and *church* is written with the /t/ and /ʃ/ symbols combined as /tʃ/. Note that this sound, produced as a single impulse as in *why chew* [ʍaɪtʃu], is more compact than the simple combination of [t] and [ʃ] in *white shoe* [ʍaɪt ʃu]. Similarly, the initial sound in *John, jam,* and *jaw* is written [dʒ].

Vowels. Vowel symbols combine various kinds of common script with a few invented symbols. The /u/ and /i/ are typical lower case letters, whereas the /ʊ/ and /ɪ/ are capital letters reduced to the size of lower case. The /e/ and /ɛ/ use two kinds of script for writing the letter *e,* and the /a/ and /ɑ/ are different ways to write the letter *a.* The /æ/ is a combination of *a* and *e,* a symbol once used in English orthography. The /ɔ/ is like a reversed *c,* the /ʌ/ an inverted *v,* and the /ə/ is an *e* written upside down and reversed. The /ɜ/ and /ɝ/ is like a number 3 with a hook on the latter one to show [r] quality. The diphthongs, which move from one position to another in a single syllable, are written as combinations of the simple vowel symbols, but they are not attached.

The International Phonetic Alphabet attempts to provide symbols for differences in stress, or the force with which a sound is produced. Very useful is the /ʌ/ for the stressed vowel in *up, cut,* and *bump,* and the /ə/ for essentially same vowel when it is unstressed as the first sound in *above* [əbʌv]. The /ə/, which is called the "schwa" vowel from the German "schwach" meaning weak, is softer and of shorter duration than the /ʌ/. Many vowels when unstressed become the /ə/. For example, notice what happens to the written *a* in *table* [teˈɪbl̩] when it is unstressed in *vegetable* [vɛdʒətəbl̩]. The /ə/ can occur as the unstressed sound for any of the vowel letters in connected speech, for example the *o* in *command* [kəmænd], the *a* in *above* [əbʌv], the *u* in *upon* [əpɑn], the *e* in *release* [rəlis], and the *i* in *attic* [ætək].

IPA representation for stressing and unstressing is more ambiguous for other vowel sounds. The /i/ is often written as /ɪ/ when unstressed. By convention, the final *y,* unstressed in such words as *many, very, happy,* and *baby,* is written as [ɪ]. To the ear, the American-English sound is closer to /i/ but of shorter duration and of less intensity. The convention of transcribing the final *y* as /ɪ/ stems from the British-English pronunciation, which was thought desirable for "good speech," but it seems ill suited for transcribing common American-English speech. Compare the two vowels in *easy* [izɪ], which actually sound more similar than the vowels in *busy* [bɪzɪ]. A completely different symbol for the unstressed /i/ might be helpful. The reader may wish to use for accuracy an accompanying narrow transcription symbol (see Table I–4) for [ɪ̣], which indicates the tongue is raised in producing this sound. This accounts for the tongue position closer to the high position for /i/ but also for the unstressed condition of reduced duration and intensity with the conventional /ɪ/ transcription.

Diphthongs. Diphthongs [dɪfθɔŋz] are combinations of two vowel sounds in a single syllable. One of the vowels, called the **nucleus**, is longer and more intense, whereas the other vowel, called the **glide**, is shorter and weaker. The stronger nucleus is written with its own symbol; the unstressed glide is written with a symbol for the vowel of slightly lower tongue position than its sound to the ear would suggest. For example, the [aɪ] as in *pie* has [a] written for its nucleus and [ɪ] written for its unstressed glide, even though the unstressed glide sounds more like [i]. Similarly, the diphthong [oʊ] as in *go* has its glide written [ʊ] despite its sound heard closer to the [u]. This transcription of the diphthong glide follows in the [aʊ] as in *cow*, the [eɪ] as in *bay*, and the [ɔɪ] in *boy*.

When the diphthongs [oʊ] and [eɪ] occur in unstressed syllables, they are written with the single symbols [o] and [e]. Examples of the unstressed [o] are in the words *obey* and *donation*. Examples of the unstressed [e] are in the words *vacation* and *fatality*. By convention, the other diphthongs /aɪ/, /aʊ/ and /ɔɪ/ are transcribed the same in stressed and unstressed syllables.

THE IDEAL ORTHOGRAPHIC SYSTEM

Several systems of orthography have been described in this chapter, none of which seems to be ideal for all uses. Perhaps no single system could meet all our needs for written language symbols, but the ideal system should meet the following criteria:

1. It should have a consistent one-to-one sound/symbol correspondence. That is, each time a symbol appears, it should always have the same speech sound, and each speech sound should be written by only one symbol.
2. There should be symbols to correspond to all the different speech sounds of our language. Different symbols should be available for all the important sounds, including those that are different in stressed and in unstressed syllables. If possible, additional symbols, rather than modifying markings, should be included in the systems to correspond to all the sounds of all the world's spoken languages.

3. The symbols should be those familiar to the culture. Symbols needed for English should be symbols that English speaking people commonly use. The Roman alphabet letters are most common, but other common symbols, such as those on a typewriter (#, &, @, %, *) or numerals would have to be added to cover all the English speech sounds.

4. The symbols should be sufficiently simple so that persons of all ages could write them. The symbols would need to be within the capability of writing by almost all the people in the culture. Ideally, too, the symbols should be so simple that one might use them to transcribe connected speech at the rate it is spoken, much as we use shorthand writing systems.

5. The symbols should be distinctive enough to avoid visual confusion. Such similiarities as the IPA has in the groupings /ɜ/, /ɝ/, /ɛ/, and /e/, /ə/, /ɚ/, for example, may cause visual confusions to the reader or transcriber.

6. The system should have internal consistency. The method for showing that some vowels are unstressed, for example, should apply to all vowels. When a sound changes its characteristics because of coarticulation, the notation should be consistent for all similar changes. Perhaps symbols for a group of sounds of similar manner or place of articulation could have common characteristics.

7. The symbols should, if possible, tell the reader something about the manner and place of articulation. The Bell Visible Speech symbols were an attempt at this.

Analysis of these several criteria suggest that some may be conflicting. It would be difficult to develop symbols that suggested manner and place of articulation and yet be familiar symbols of the culture, or to account for all the sounds of spoken language and yet have only symbols that could be simply written. The ideal orthographic system may, therefore, be that which is best for a specific purpose, with a number of systems available for various uses.

REVIEW VOCABULARY

Allophones—examples of variations within a phoneme class resulting from different phonetic environments.

Alphabet—the system of written symbols common to a language.

Broad transcription—in IPA, transcribing in phoneme symbols only, without modifying markings to indicate allophonic or other phonetic differences.

Diacritical markings—symbols used to modify alphabet letters or phonetic symbols to indicate differences in pronunciation.

Diphthong—a sequence of two vowel sounds produced in a single syllable with one sound dominant.

Glide—the shorter, less stressed vowel of a diphthong.

Ideograms—written symbols representing symbolic ideas.

Logograms—written symbols representing entire words.

Narrow transcription—in IPA, transcribing in phoneme symbols plus modifying markings to indicate variation in production.

Nucleus—the longer dominant vowel of a diphthong.

Orthography—the commonly accepted spelling using alphabet symbols.

Phoneme—an abstract class of speech sounds containing common elements and influencing the meaning of speech.

Phonics—an application of the relation between alphabet letters or groups of letters and speech sounds as an aid to improving reading.

Phonograms—written symbols representing speech sounds.

Pictograms—drawings that represent only the objects or events depicted.

Roman alphabet—the system of written symbols used in English and several other European languages, transmitted from the Romans.

Transliteration—the process of selecting alphabet letters to represent a group of speech sounds.

EXERCISES

1. Determine the IPA symbol for the consonant phoneme common in each of the following lists of words. Note the differences in spelling.

(a)	(b)	(c)	(d)
stay	speed	malt	then
washed	city	plan	bother
two	science	sleep	bathe
hot	kiss	ballot	the
try	psychology	pillow	other
better	assume	clear	teethe
wasted	desks	elbow	that
twice	splice	blue	leather

(e)	(f)	(g)
laugh	legend	who
phone	judge	high
half	giant	ahead
coffee	edge	hers
off	agile	behold
after	orange	whole
Philip	jazz	anyhow
often	ledge	hen

2. Determine the IPA symbol for the vowel or diphthong phoneme common in each of the following lists of words. Note the differences in spelling.

(a)	(b)	(c)	(d)
seek	about	credit	land
easy	south	enter	amble
streaks	our	feather	and
evil	bound	bend	tan
we	cow	said	rack
being	clown	leopard	fast
teams	power	get	manual
chic	towel	nest	attack

(e)	(f)	(g)
tomb	book	find
soon	put	time
chew	should	by
rule	shook	cried
group	wouldn't	higher
fruit	full	type
lose	woman	height
boost	foot	ride

Transcribe in IPA symbols only the consonants as you would say them (or from another's dictation) in the following words:

3. /p, b, t, d, k, g, l, m, n, r, f, v, s, z, h, w/

goat	cave	soap	maybe
hog	mount	sleep	gained
walk	race	balloon	bottom
who	waffle	vacate	roof
doze	half	favors	license

4. /ʍ, θ, ʃ, ð, ʒ, ŋ, j/

why	thin	shoe
the	vision	think
sing	yes	when
this	sure	pleasure
healthy	mirage	you
washing	those	ink
usual	singing	wealth
where	yellow	show

5. /ʧ, ʤ/

jam	chew	church
judge	watch	edge
enjoy	adjust	hatchet
exchange	change	gauge

6. All consonants.   Review Table   I-2.

public	famine	was	hash
tag	which	sling	judge
quiet	church	splice	traverse
devotion	machine	heather	yours
wig	gin	quill	pave
vision	thong	erosion	both
fad	thick	their	match
leisure	disks	streak	yesterday
frenzy	transient	snooping	splashes

Transcribe in IPA symbols all consonants and vowels as you would say them (or from another's dictation) in the following words:

7. /u, ʊ, ɔ/

book	caught	all	moon
law	boots	tools	balls
put	shook	thought	could
choose	June	good	tomb

8. /i, ɪ, ɛ/

beet	mean	when	zen
dim	quenched	these	sing
quick	sheet	yet	geese
then	jig	whip	pin

9. /æ, ɑ, ʌ/

at	chants	arm	bunk
mom	much	thus	an
tuck	bomb	Tom	palm
lack	judge	thank	back

10. /ə, ɝ, ɚ/ plus previously practiced vowels

butter	third	furnace	burner
bird	girl ·	zebra	Adam
above	upon	fern	evil
banner	turning	better	liquor

11. All pure vowels. Review Table I–3.

ahead	whose	under	yawn
foot	each	youth	went
learning	imagine	doctor	should
turn	bath	son	whim
fought	cause	watch	spurn

Transcribe in IPA symbols all consonants, vowels, and diphthongs as you would say them (or from another's dictation) in the following words:

12. /eɪ, oʊ, aɪ, aʊ, ɔɪ/

eight	own	time	foil
load	cold	boys	around
stain	mile	date	choice
light	now	rain	spoil
tried	toasts	drown	clown

13. All consonants, vowels, and diphthongs. Review Tables I–2 and I–3.

looks	them	hawk	about
quickly	watched	temper	leisure
branch	tomatoes	whimper	filing
weaves	thirst	gusher	yesterday
omen	wonder	tuba	just

14. All consonants, vowels, and diphthongs. Review Tables I–2 and I–3.

yeast	chalk	Utah	girl
occasion	hinder	method	voices
allow	whose	father	badge
why	put	wish	once
changes	wrong	queen	supper

SUGGESTED READING

Albright, Robert W.: The International Phonetic Alphabet: Its Backgrounds and Development, *International Journal of American Linguistics.* Volume 24, #1, Part III, January, 1958.

This scholarly work traces the International Phonetic Alphabet from phoneticians of 16th Century England to development of the first IPA in 1888, and through its various modifications. It is based on Albright's doctoral dissertation at Stanford University and also appears as a 78-page monograph, Publication #7, of the Indiana University Research Center in Anthropology, Folklore and Linguistics. It includes descriptions of a number of early orthographic systems.

Yale, Caroline A.: *Formation and Development of Elementary English Sounds.* Northampton, Mass., Clarke School, 1946.

This 46-page paperback contains the original organization of the Northampton symbols by Yale, with a description of formation of the phonemes and some aids to their development for teachers of deaf children. The updated material is currently embodied in a longer treatise on teaching speech to deaf children, called *Speech Development,* and published at the Clarke School in 1971, as part of their school curriculum series.

Chapter II

THE SPEECH PRODUCTION MECHANISM AND PROCESSES

- **THE SPEECH MECHANISM**
  - **LIPS**
  - **TEETH**
  - **ALVEOLAR RIDGE**
  - **PALATE**
  - **VELUM**
  - **TONGUE**
  - **MANDIBLE**
  - **ORAL CAVITY**
  - **NASAL CAVITY**
  - **PHARYNX**
  - **LARYNX**
  - **SUB-LARYNGEAL STRUCTURES**
- **SPEECH PROCESSES**
  - **RESPIRATION**
  - **PHONATION**
  - **RESONATION**
  - **ARTICULATION**
- **REVIEW VOCABULARY**
- **EXERCISES**
- **SUGGESTED READING**

Among the creatures of Earth, only man has achieved speech. All species of animals communicate, many by vocal noises, but none has approached the complexity and sophistication of our spoken language. Yet the body parts we use to produce speech do not appear to be greatly different from those of other animals with teeth, tongues, and palates. And we, as they, regularly use these oral structures for more basic bodily functions, especially breathing and eating. However, we know that a healthy human baby has the innate potential to speak, a potential that apparently is specific to our species. This suggests a unique nervous system capable of abstracting, associating, memorizing, recognizing, recalling, and formulating—a nervous system that has evolved to make use of our given body parts for the production of speech.

THE SPEECH MECHANISM

The term "speech mechanism" should not appear to imply a simple mechanical system of pulleys and levers, or even an electronic system of transistors and capacitors. Our anatomy and physiology are too complex for that. But "speech mechanism" is a useful term to refer collectively to the body parts used in producing speech. This chapter aims to present those anatomic and physiologic concepts that will contribute most to the study of descriptive phonetics, rather than an exhaustive exposition of the subject. Where possible, we will use the common Anglicized terms along with Latinized names, prefixes, and suffixes that commonly describe place of articulation and manner of speech production. The typical General-American pronunciation will be indicated with symbols of the International Phonetic Alphabet, aided by accent marks to show the stressed syllable. We begin with the most obvious part of the speech mechanism, the lips.

Lips (Prefix *labio*- [leíbɪo], suffix -*labial* [leɪbɪəl])

The lips are a complex of muscles and other tissues. Running vertically in the center of the upper lip, just below the nose, is a grooved indentation called the **philtrum** [fɪltrəm]. At the lip border, the skin changes to form the characteristic reddish **vermilion** [vɝˈmíljən], which is an adaptation of the mucous membrane that lines the mouth. Inside both the upper and lower lips at the midline is a thin flexible membrane called the labial **frenum** [frinəm] that connects the lip to the alveolar [ælvíolɚ] processes between the central incisors. These can be felt with the tongue tip. The lips have a great capacity for varied movements, and much of their range of movements is utilized in producing our speech sounds.

The versatility of the lips results from a complex system of muscles. Of central importance is the **orbicularis oris** [orbɪkjulɑ́rɪs órɪs] muscle with its fibers in a circular pattern around the periphery of the mouth. It can contract to round the lips with a wide to small opening, even closing the rounded lips and protruding them. The orbicularis oris is actually a layer of muscle fibers coming from other muscles that are inserted into the lips, rather than having an origin and insertion of its own. These other facial muscles contribute greatly to lip movement and versatility. From the upper jaw or **maxilla** [mæksílə] come muscles that raise and lower the upper lip and draw up and back the corners of the mouth. From the lower jaw or mandible [mǽndɪbəl] come muscles that raise and lower the lower lip, protrude it, and draw down and back the corners of the mouth. From the cheeks or **bucca** [bʌ́kə] comes the wide, flat **buccinator** [bʌ́ksɪneɪtɚ] muscle, mingling its fibers in the orbicularis oris and controlling the corners of the mouth. From the neck come muscles that can pull down the corners of the mouth. These varied muscles also affect the facial expressions (frown, grin, smile, sneer, pout) we use in association with speech and to communicate non-speech information.

Although the primary bodily function of the lips is to help receive and contain food and fluids in the oral cavity, they perform a number of actions in speech production. The lips can be closed passively by elevating the lower jaw, or mandible, until the teeth close together. However, the closures of speech articulation require variability in firmness and rapid motions of short duration, and they are usually made with the teeth apart. This action requires active muscular closure by the upper and lower lips moving simultaneously to the center of the mouth. In most speakers, the lower lip is the more mobile in rapid connected speech, and in some speakers, the upper lip may move very little. The lips close by muscular action to stop the breath stream, as in articulating /p/, /b/, and /m/, the **bilabial** [baɪleɪ́bɪəl] consonant sounds. Closure for the /p/ requires the greatest bilabial firmness to contain the air pressure built up in the oral cavity. Less firmness is required for /b/, and still less for /m/, which has nasal emission of air flow. By bringing the lower lip close to the upper front teeth, the breath stream can be constricted to create friction for the /f/ and /v/, the **labio-dental** consonant sounds. This articulation requires that the lower lip be moved upward without simultaneous lowering of the upper lip, while the teeth remain open. Many speakers pull the lower lip slightly inward toward the upper teeth, also. Then too, the lower lip must be held briefly close to the upper front teeth, just far enough away to permit air to escape between them, but close enough to constrict air flow for audible friction. This position of closeness is called **approximation** [əprʌ́ksəmeɪʃən]. Rounding the lips with varying degrees of opening contributes to the production of the bilabial consonants /w/ and /ʍ/, the vowels /u/, /ʊ/, and /ɔ/, and the diphthongs [dɪfθɔŋz] /ou/, /ɔɪ/, and /au/. Some lip rounding is also present in fricative [frɪ́kətɪv] consonants /ʃ/ and /ʒ/, and in affricates [ǽfrɪkəts] /ʧ/ and /ʤ/.

Teeth (Prefix *dento-*, suffix *-dental*)

The teeth play a passive but important role in speech production. Their primary function is to cut and grind in chewing food. For the growing child, dentition undergoes significant changes (Figure II-1) that influence speech. The **deciduous** [disídjuəs] teeth, sometimes called the primary or "baby" teeth, erupt during a period of from six months to two years of age to include

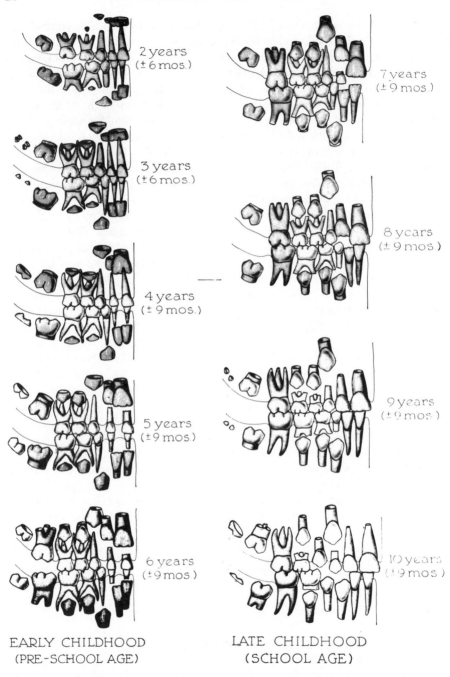

Figure II-1. Stages of children's dentition. Deciduous teeth are shown in dark tint, permanent teeth in white. From the chart, "Development of the Human Dentition," I. Schour & M. Massler, American Dental Association, 211 East Chicago Avenue. Chicago, Illinois 60611.

20 teeth—10 in the maxilla and 10 in the mandible. They are arranged in symmetrical sets of five teeth on each side, beginning from the midline: **central incisor** [ɪnsáɪzɚ], **lateral incisor, canine** [keínaɪn] (or eye tooth), **first molar** [moʊlɚ], and **second molar.** Starting at about age six, the deciduous teeth are gradually replaced by 32 **permanent** teeth—16 in the maxilla and 16 in the mandible—arranged in symmetrical sets of eight teeth on each side. Beginning from the midline, these are as follows: **central incisor, lateral incisor, canine, first bicuspid** [baɪkʌ́spɪd] (having two sharp points, or cusps, and sometimes called a "premolar"), **second bicuspid, first molar, second molar,** and variably in the teens or early twenties, the **third molar** or "wisdom" tooth. No further development occurs into adulthood, but with decay or damage, teeth may be altered by extraction or repair, or the set may have to be partially or completely replaced with dentures.

When the teeth are closed, the maxillary and mandibular molars and the bicuspids rest intermeshed with each other, normally with the inner **cusps** or points of the maxillary teeth against the midline of their mandibular counterparts. The maxillary canines and incisors overlap the outer surface of their mandibular opposites. This fitting together or "bite" when closed is called the dental **occlusion** [oklúʒən], and an abnormality of the bite is referred to as a **malocclusion** [mæ̀lokl úʒən].

The sides of the tongue pressed against the molars help direct the breath stream toward the front of the mouth as in /ʃ/ and /ʒ/. The lower lip approximates the maxillary incisors to constrict the breath stream for the labio-dental consonants /f/ and /v/. The tongue tip similarly approximates the maxillary incisors for production of the lingua-dental /θ/ and /ð/. The slightly opened maxillary and mandibular incisors provide friction surfaces for the /s/, /z/, /ʃ/, and /ʒ/. When the incisors are absent, as they are for a time between deciduous and permanent dentition at about age seven (see Figure II-1), sounds that require friction against the teeth cannot be produced well. Similarly, when decayed teeth must be replaced, or when there is a malocclusion, production of these consonants is adversely affected.

Alveolar Ridge (Prefix *alveolo-* [ælvíolo], suffix *-alveolar* [ælvíolɚ]

In both the maxilla and the mandible, the teeth are contained in alveolar processes or sockets, commonly called the "gum ridges." The alveolar processes behind the maxillary incisors and canine teeth form a rather pronounced ridge that figures prominently in consonant articulation. The tongue presses against this alveolar ridge to stop the breath stream for the /t/, /d/, and /n/, and just behind the ridge for /tʃ/ and /dʒ/. Pressing the narrow point of the tongue against the center of the ridge permits the breath stream to escape around both sides of the tongue for the /l/ sound. The tongue tip

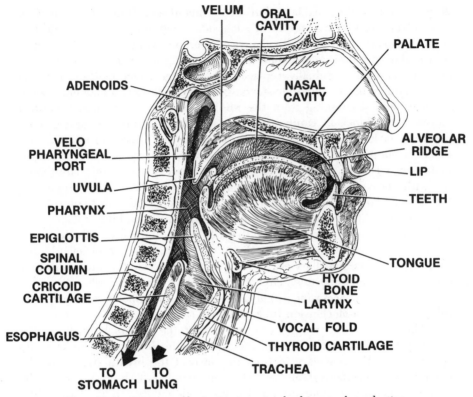

VELUM
ORAL CAVITY
PALATE
ADENOIDS
NASAL CAVITY
ALVEOLAR RIDGE
VELO PHARYNGEAL PORT
LIP
UVULA
TEETH
PHARYNX
EPIGLOTTIS
TONGUE
SPINAL COLUMN
HYOID BONE
CRICOID CARTILAGE
LARYNX
ESOPHAGUS
VOCAL FOLD
THYROID CARTILAGE
TO STOMACH
TO LUNG
TRACHEA

Figure II-2.   Diagram of basic structures involved in speech production.

approximates the alveolar ridge in the most common formation of the /s/ and /z/. The front of the tongue, at a greater distance from the ridge, forms constriction of the breath stream to produce the /ʃ/ and /ʒ/ sounds.

Palate (Prefix *palato-* [pǽlətou], suffix *-palatal* [pǽlətəl] and *palatine* [pǽlətin])

Farther inside the mouth, just beyond the alveolar ridge of the maxilla, is the **palate,** commonly called the "bony" or "hard" palate. It forms part of the roof of the mouth, but it is both a roof and a floor, as it separates the nasal cavity from the oral cavity. Its primary bodily functions are to help contain food in the oral cavity and to provide a hard upper surface for the action of swallowing. From the alveolar processes of the maxillary teeth, the palate arches upward. The height and narrowness of the arch, sometimes called the palatal "vault," varies greatly with facial structure. Evidence of the palate's embryologic manner of development from the two sides is apparent by feeling the midline suture running from between the central incisors the length of the palate to disappear at the juncture of the hard and soft palates. As the superior (upper) surface of the oral cavity, the palate contributes to vowel resonance by determining the shape of the cavity. It helps to direct the breath stream toward the front of the mouth for consonant articulation. The back of the tongue presses against the back of the palate or the velum in the production of /k/, /g/, and /ŋ/. The tip of the tongue is lifted toward the palate, just behind the alveolar ridge, to help form the /r/ sound.

Velum (Prefix *velo*- [víloʊ], suffix -*velar* [vilɚ])

Farther back on the roof of the mouth, posterior to and adjoining the palate, is the **velum** [viləm], commonly called the "soft palate." It consists of muscle and connective tissue covered by a continuation of the mucous membrane of the palate. Its primary purpose is to help keep food and fluids from entering the nasal cavity. The velum is very flexible and mobile, opening to permit air to flow through the nasal cavity to and from the throat. To achieve this control, the velum participates in opening and closing the **velopharyngeal** [viloferíndʒəl] **port,** the aperture that connects the nasal cavity and the oral cavity. It is sometimes referred to as the "nasopharyngeal" port (Figure II-2). At the midline of the posterior border of the velum is the **uvula** [júvjulə], from the Latin meaning "little grape," an appendage that apparently serves little function in man.

The mobility of the velum derives from having muscles coming from above, below, and behind it. The paired **levator** [livéɪtɚ] muscles enter the velum at the midline and contract to raise it toward the posterior wall of the throat. The **tensor** [tɛnsɚ] muscles contract to make the velum taut, especially during swallowing, and they influence the opening and closing of the orifice of the **Eustachian** [justéɪkɪən] **tube,** which lies near the origin of these muscles in the throat (see Figure II-3). The **glossopalatine** [gláso-pǽlətin] muscles pass from the undersurface of the tongue to the palate along each side of the oral cavity, making noticeable bundles called the **anterior pillars of the fauces** [fɔsiz]. When the glossopalatines contract, they draw down the sides of the velum and at the same time, draw up and back the sides of the tongue. The **pharyngopalatine** [feríŋgopǽlətin] muscles rise from the larynx and pass along each side of the oral cavity, forming another pair of prominent bundles called the **posterior pillars of the fauces,** and then they insert into the midline of the velum. They act to depress the velum while elevating the throat and larynx [lɛ́rɪŋks].

By helping to close the velopharyngeal port, the velum helps direct the breath stream to the oral cavity for articulation and for primarily oral reso-

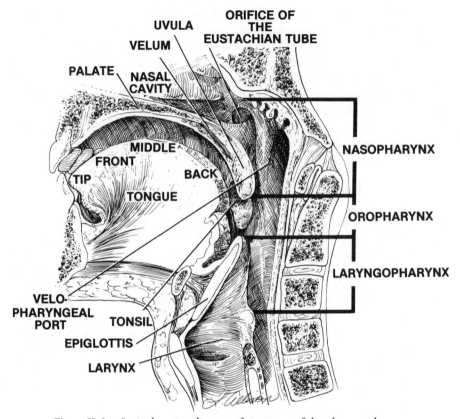

Figure II–3.   Sagittal section diagram of structures of the pharyngeal area.

nance as in vowel sounds. When the velum is relaxed and the port is opened, the breath stream can enter the nasal cavity for predominantly nasal resonance as in /m/, /n/, and /ŋ/.

Tongue (Prefixes *lingua-* [lɪŋgwə] and *glossa-* [glasə], suffixes *-lingual* [lɪŋgwəl] and *-glossal* [glasəl])

    The Latin root *lingua,* the same for "tongue" and for "language," reflects the historic importance ascribed to the tongue as the vehicle for spoken language. We commonly speak of "foreign tongues" or of the "mother tongue" when we mean the spoken language. Without a doubt, the tongue is of very great importance in producing speech. Its exceptional mobility permits it to shape the oral cavity almost infinitely. Its primary bodily purpose is to direct food to the back of the oral cavity during swallowing. This highly mobile muscular organ arising from the floor of the oral cavity derives its remarkable versatility from dual control by **intrinsic** [ɪntrɪ́nsɪk] muscles that change its shape and **extrinsic** [ɛkstrɪ́nsɪk] muscles that are largely responsible for its movement within the oral cavity.

The intrinsic muscles are named for their direction within the tongue: the **vertical,** which widens and flattens the tongue tip; the **inferior longitudinal** (from base to apex), which widens and shortens the tongue, depresses the tip, and makes the upper surface convex; the **superior longitudinal,** which widens, thickens, and shortens the tongue, raises its tip and edge, and makes the upper surface grooved or concave; and the **transverse** (from midline to both sides), which elongates, narrows, and thickens the tongue, and can lift its sides. The extrinsic muscles connect the tongue to the temporal bone of the skull, the mandible, the **hyoid** [haɪ́ɔɪd] bone, and the velum. They include the following: the **styloglossus** [staɪ́loglɑ́səs], running forward and downward from the styloid process of the temporal bone to enter the sides of the tongue, which elevates the rear of the tongue and retracts it when protruded; the **genioglossus** [ʤɪ́nɪoglɑ́səs], running upward from the mandible as a great fan-shaped muscle, forming a large part of the tongue's bulk and providing for the majority of its activity, which depresses, retracts, and protrudes the tongue; and the **hyoglossus** [haɪ́oglɑ́səs], extending upward from the hyoid bone into the posterior half of the sides of the tongue, which helps retract the tongue and depresses its sides. These extrinsic muscles interweave with the intrinsic muscle fibers to form a very complex pattern.

The anatomic landmarks of the tongue include its **root** or posterior portion connecting with the hyoid bone and epiglottis, the **apex** [eɪ́pɛks] at the anterior end, its **dorsum** [dorsəm] or superior surface, and the septum [sɛptəm] or midline structure of connective tissue. The surface under the front of the tongue is connected with the mandible centrally by the lingual **frenum** [frinəm]. For describing speech, it is convenient to label positions on the dorsum that figure prominently in articulatory activity. These positions are the **back,** the **middle,** the **front** (sometimes called the "blade"), the **tip,** and the **point,** which is derived when the tongue is narrowed and pointed (Figure II–4).

The tongue can narrow and point, as it does for the /l/, or it can present a broad front as in producing /ʃ/ and /ʒ/, where there is no tip or point evident. It can close off the oral cavity and quickly release compressed breath as it does for /t/, with the tongue tip against the alveolar ridge, and for /k/, with the back of the tongue against the velum or palate. With somewhat reduced closure pressure, the same action is involved in producing /d/ and /g/. The tongue can close the oral cavity at the alveolar ridge for /n/ and at the velum for /ŋ/, with nasal emission of voice. It can form a central groove to direct the breath stream as it does for /s/, or the tip can be elevated and drawn back (retroflexed) toward the back of the oral cavity as in /r/. The front and back of the tongue can be raised and lowered by subtle degrees in order to alter the

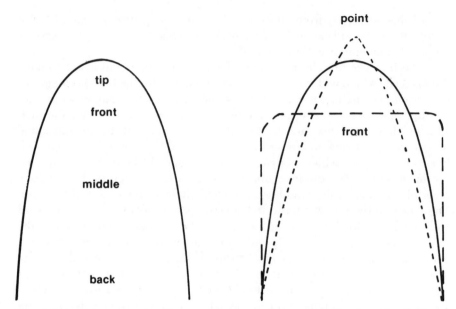

Figure II–4. Top or superview diagram of the tongue in its normal relaxed position (left), and in positions of a narrow point (as in /l/) and a broad front (as in /ʃ/).

oral cavity for vowel resonance. All the vowel sounds are influenced by tongue action, and the only consonants in English that do not have direct tongue involvement are the following: /m/, /p/, /b/, /v/, and /f/.

Mandible (Prefixes *mandibulo-* and *genio-*, suffixes *-mandibular* and *-genial*)

The mandible, or lower jaw, plays both a passive and an active role in articulation. It serves as a foundation for the large genioglossus muscle of the tongue and it houses the mandibular teeth. It can be elevated to close and lowered to open the jaw for vowel articulation. This movement is accomplished by four muscles, the primary muscles of mastication (Figure II–5). These are as follows: the **temporal** muscle, originating over a large fan-shaped area of the temporal bone of the skull and converging downward and forward to form a tendon inserted into the mandible, which elevates and retracts the mandible to close the jaw; the **masseter** [mǽsətɚ], which also closes the jaw and runs downward from the **zygomatic** [zaɪɡomǽtɪk] arch or "cheek bone" to insert into the lateral surface and angle of the mandible; the **internal pterygoid** [tέrəɡɔɪd] muscle, which arises from the pterygoid (wing-like) plate at the base of the skull and runs downward and backward to

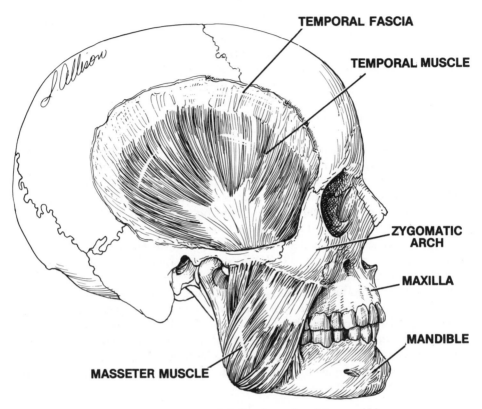

TEMPORAL FASCIA

TEMPORAL MUSCLE

ZYGOMATIC ARCH

MAXILLA

MANDIBLE

MASSETER MUSCLE

Figure II–5.   Diagram of skull and muscles of the mandible.

insert onto the medial surface of the posterior vertical portion and angle of the mandible, assisting in closing the jaw and protruding the mandible; and the **external pterygoid** muscle, which also arises from the base of the skull but runs horizontally to insert into the top of the posterior portion of the mandible, permitting it to assist gravity in depressing the mandible as well as giving it lateral movement needed in chewing.

Oral Cavity (Prefix *oro-*, suffix *-oral*)

This cavity extends from the oral aperture or mouth in front to the posterior wall of the pharynx or throat, from the palate and velum above to the base of the tongue, and laterally between the teeth or the cheeks if the jaws are open. Its primary purpose is to contain food for chewing and swallowing. For speech, it changes size and shape for vowels and resonant consonants through action of the mandible, tongue, velum, and lips. It also channels the breath stream out of the mouth for other than nasal sounds to be articulated by the tongue, lips, and mandible.

For vowel production, one end of the oral resonating cavity is opened at the mouth while the velopharyngeal port is closed for primarily oral resonance. Then the combined action of the tongue and mandible alters the size and shape of the cavity to determine its resonant characteristics, and the lips relax, round, or protrude to influence resonance of the cavity further. For the nasal consonants /m/, /n/, and /ŋ/, the oral cavity is closed off at the lips, alveolar ridge, or velum, respectively, whereas the back of the oral cavity is opened to the nasal cavity through the open velopharyngeal port. In producing /n/ and /ŋ/, the lips are apart to form an open front oral cavity, which contributes to the resonant characteristics of these sounds. If the lips were to be closed, even though the tongue might be in position for /n/ or /ŋ/, the sound would be perceived as sounding closer to /m/.

The oral cavity provides various surfaces between which the breath stream can be constricted and turbulence can be created. The /h/ is the least constricted of the fricative consonants and, accordingly, requires the greatest breath effort to produce turbulence. Positioning for resonation of surrounding vowels forces the breath stream across the velum and palate above and the tongue below to make /h/ a **lingua-palatal** or **lingua-velar** fricative, depending on the adjoining vowels. When the lips are rounded with a small aperture to constrict breath, the /ʍ/ is produced as a **bilabial** fricative. The tongue, lips, teeth, palate, and alveolar ridge participate in constricting breath for other fricative consonants.

Nasal Cavity (Prefix *naso-*, suffix *-nasal*)

The nasal cavity extends from the nostrils or **nares** [nériz] in the front to the posterior wall of the pharynx, and from the base of the skull above to the palate and velum below. It is primarily designed to receive inhaled air and to filter it, warm it, and direct it toward the **trachea** [treıkıə] or "windpipe." An ample blood supply in the mucous membrane lining of the nasal cavity warms the inhaled air before it travels into the lungs. This soft moist lining contributes to the distinctive resonance characteristics of the cavity.

The nasal cavity participates in speech resonance with either closure or opening of the velopharyngeal port. It is always open at the nostrils unless blocked by mucous or infection. With the velopharyngeal port closed, the nasal cavity resonates voice vibration in conjunction with the oral cavity for the overall quality of voice that is distinctive for a particular speaker. While vocalizing /ɑ/, the speaker can noticeably influence vocal resonance characteristics by pinching the nostrils closed, making the nasal cavity closed at both ends. With the velopharyngeal port open, the nasal cavity has open resonance characteristic of /m/, /n/, and /ŋ/.

Pharynx (Prefix *pharyngo-*, suffix *-pharyngeal*)

The **pharynx** [fɛ́rɪŋks], throat, or pharyngeal cavity extends from the posterior portion of the nasal cavity downward through the back of the oral cavity to the larynx [lɛ́rɪŋks]* (see Figure II–3). The anatomic functions of the pharynx are (1) to receive food from swallowing and move it toward the esophagus and stomach and (2) to channel air from respiration between the nose and the mouth and the trachea and lungs. The pharynx is a vertical tube with three parts: the **nasopharynx** [neízofɛ́rɪŋks], a continuation of the nasal cavity; the **oropharynx** [órofɛ́rɪŋks], a continuation of the oral cavity, and the **laryngopharynx** [lɛrɪ́ŋgofɛ́rɪŋks], the area just above the larynx. The tube is lined with mucous membrane over a number of muscles. The nasopharynx houses the funnel-shaped orifice of the **Eustachian** tube, which permits ventilation of the middle ear.

The nasopharynx can be closed off from the oropharynx where they join at the **velopharyngeal port.** Closure is achieved by a complex muscular action involving the levator muscle of the velum (described earlier) that raises the velum and uvula toward the posterior pharyngeal wall. The **velopharyngeal sphincter** [sfɪŋktɚ], which runs from the midline of the velum around the sides of the pharynx to insert into the midline of the back of the pharynx, protrudes and elevates the pharyngeal wall and also aids in pulling the velum posteriorly. The **superior constrictor** muscle contracts the pharynx in the nasopharyngeal region, aiding further with a raising and circular closing action of the velopharyngeal port.

For speech production, the pharynx acts as a resonating chamber for voice. Its primary alteration is the velopharyngeal closure that not only directs voice into the oral cavity but reduces the length of the pharyngeal tube. The pharynx can also be altered in its circumference throughout its length, first by the action of three pharyngeal constrictor muscles that can contract the pharynx—primarily as an aid to moving food toward the esophagus—and then by two pharyngeal levator muscles that elevate and widen the pharynx. The changes can alter the resonating characteristics of the pharynx and thus the sound of the voice.

Larynx (Prefix *laryngo-*, suffix *-laryngeal*)

The **larynx** [lɛ́rɪŋks] is a structure of cartilage and muscles situated atop the trachea. Its primary bodily purpose is to protect the lungs by preventing food particles and fluids from entering the trachea through the **glottis** [glɑtəs], its port or opening to the pharynx (see Figure II–3). Directly above the glottis and posterior to the root of the tongue is the leaf-shaped and

---

*The pronunciation [fɜ́rɪŋks] and [lɛ́rɪŋks] is also common.

flexible **epiglottis** [ɛ́pɪglɑ́təs], a cartilaginous structure that is moved downward and backward with the tongue during swallowing to cover the glottis, thus channeling food and fluids to the esophagus [isɑ́fəgəs] and stomach (see Figure II–7). Food materials that accidently enter the larynx are expelled by coughing. A secondary bodily purpose of the larynx is to close the trachea at the glottis so that air in the lungs keeps the **thoracic** [θorǽsɪk] or chest cavity rigid as a help in such action as elimination, childbirth, and heavy lifting.

The larynx may be viewed as an extension and specialized adaptation of the cartilaginous rings that form most of the circumference of the trachea (Figures II–6 and II–7). The bottom ring of the larynx is the **cricoid** [kraɪkɔɪd] cartilage, which completely encircles the trachea as a foundation for the larynx. Its name, cricoid, comes from its resemblance to a signet ring. From its narrowest part in the front, the cricoid widens upward as it extends

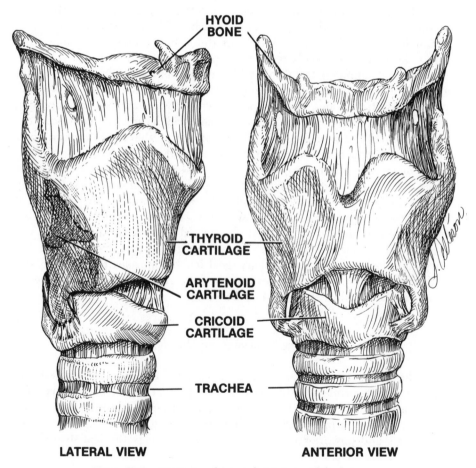

HYOID
BONE

THYROID
CARTILAGE

ARYTENOID
CARTILAGE

CRICOID
CARTILAGE

TRACHEA

LATERAL VIEW   ANTERIOR VIEW

Figure II–6.　Diagrams of external structures of the larynx.

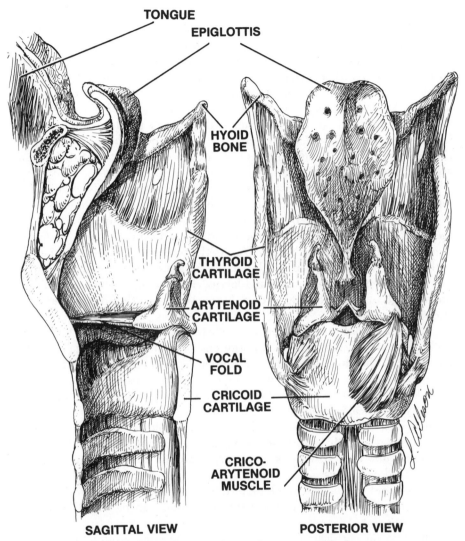

TONGUE

EPIGLOTTIS

HYOID
BONE

THYROID
CARTILAGE

ARYTENOID
CARTILAGE

VOCAL
FOLD

CRICOID
CARTILAGE

CRICO-
ARYTENOID
MUSCLE

SAGITTAL VIEW   POSTERIOR VIEW

Figure II-7.   Diagrams of internal structures of the larynx.

backward into its tall, broad signet portion. Upon this posterior shelf of the cricoid rests the paired **arytenoid** [ɛrətínɔɪd] cartilages. The forward angle of these highly mobile, pyramidal-shaped cartilages aids in attachment of the **vocal folds,** commonly but inaccurately called the "vocal cords." The vocal folds attach anteriorly inside the angle of the largest structure of the larynx, the **thyroid** [θaɪrɔɪd] cartilage, named for its shape resembling a shield. The thyroid cartilage is prominent in the neck, especially in post-adolescent males, as the "Adam's apple." It overlaps the sides of the cricoid cartilage but does not complete the circumference of the larynx in the back (see Figure II–7). The two sides of the thyroid meet in a sharp angle in the front with a V-shaped notch at the top and extend backward on both sides, widening both downward and upward at its posterior borders into inferior and superior **cornua** [kornúə] or horns (see Figure II–6). The inferior horns of the thyroid cartilage form joints in contact with the lateral surfaces of the cricoid cartilage, which lies below and inside the thyroid. The superior horns are connected by ligaments to the posterior extensions of the horseshoe-shaped **hyoid** [haíɔɪd] bone, which lies horizontally just above them. The front of the hyoid's "U" may be felt in the neck, just above the notch at the frontal angle of the thyroid cartilage.

The **hyoid** bone plays a prominent role as attachment and foundation for muscles and ligaments involved in swallowing and phonation. Uniquely, it is not articulated with other bones of the body but gets its support from ligaments and muscles coming from the mandible and skull. It sits in an intermediate position at the back of the base of the tongue and directly at the top of the larynx. Their common attachment to this bone brings about a muscular interaction between the tongue and larynx. For example, when raising the tongue high, as in producing a tense /i/, one may feel the thyroid cartilage rise simultaneously.

The **vocal folds** are like horizontal curtains protruding from the lateral walls of the larynx, joined at the anterior end of their common attachment to the angle of the thyroid cartilage and open (at rest) at the posterior end, where each fold attaches to one of the arytenoid cartilages (see Figure II–11). Each fold is lined with mucous membrane, which encloses a vocal ligament medially and vocal muscles at the sides. Just above each vocal fold, and lying beneath a pair or protrusions called "ventricular" folds or "false" vocal folds, are mucous glands that lubricate the vocal folds during their rapid action.

The important structures that participate in laryngeal function are summarized as follows:
1. The **cricoid** cartilage at the base of the larynx and atop the trachea
2. The paired **arytenoid** cartilages sitting on the high back of the cricoid cartilage ring
3. The **thyroid** cartilage with its two sides wrapping around the cricoid cartilage and open in the back
4. The **hyoid** bone, which lies horizontally just above the thyroid cartilage and at the back of the base of the tongue
5. The two **vocal folds,** which attach separately to an arytenoid cartilage in the back of the larynx and come together in the front to attach inside the angle of the thyroid cartilage.

These structures interact to produce phonation in a complex relationship under the control of extrinsic muscles, those having attachment to structures outside the larynx, and of intrinsic muscles, with both attachments within the larynx.

The **extrinsic muscles** of the larynx have attachments to the mandible in front and above, to the skull above, and to the thorax below. Together they act as a sling that can move the larynx up, down, forward, or backward, or combinations of these. Most of these extrinsic muscles affect the position of the hyoid bone with its resulting movement directly influencing the movement of the laryngeal structures. The **hyoglossus** muscle, mentioned earlier in relation to the tongue, extends downward from the posterior half of the sides of the tongue, attaching to the rear horns of the hyoid bone. The **geniohyoid** muscle arises from the internal surface of the mandible to attach to the front of the hyoid bone, working with the hyoglossus to draw the hyoid bone forward. The **mylohyoid** [maɪlohaɪɔɪd] muscle, which forms the floor of the mouth, also comes from the mandible to raise the hyoid. The **digastric** [daɪgæstrɪk] muscle, which arises both from the mandible and the temporal bone, and the **stylohyoid** [staɪlohaɪɔɪd] from the temporal bone help elevate and draw the hyoid backward. Three other extrinsic muscles that fill out the neck along side the larynx have origins below the hyoid and act to depress the larynx. These include the **sternohyoid** [stɜ'nohaɪɔɪd], which attaches to the clavicle and the sternum, and the **omohyoid** [oʊmohaɪɔɪd], which is attached to the superior edge of the scapula. The **sternothyroid** muscle arises from the sternum and uppermost ribs, attaching directly to the thyroid cartilage to depress it. A continuation of this muscle, the **thyrohyoid,** travels from the thyroid cartilage upward to the hyoid bone and can depress the hyoid bone or elevate the larynx.

Although the extrinsic muscles influence phonation to some extent, it is a group of intrinsic laryngeal muscles that contributes primarily to producing the sound (see Figures II–8, II–10, and II–11). The **cricothyroid** muscle originates at the narrow front of the cricoid cartilage, with one portion rising vertically to insert into the lower surface of the front of the thyroid and the other portion rising at an angle backward to attach on the outside of the lower portion of the thyroid at its lower horn (see Figure II–8). This muscle pulls the cricoid and thyroid cartilages closer together, resulting in a lengthening and tensing of the vocal folds. The **lateral cricoarytenoid** muscle arises from the narrow anterior area of the cricoid cartilage and is inserted onto the base of each arytenoid cartilage, along with the **posterior cricoarytenoid,** which arises below from the broad posterior surface of the cricoid (see Figure II–10). These muscles act as antagonists in adducting (closing) and abducting (opening) the vocal folds and the glottis (Figure II–9). The lateral cricoarytenoids contract to rock the arytenoid cartilages medially, approximating and slightly tensing the vocal folds. The posterior cricoarytenoids contract to rock the arytenoids laterally, separating and relaxing the folds (Figure II–10). A set of **interarytenoid** muscles, one transverse and one oblique, join the posterior surfaces of the arytenoids to contract and adduct them for approximation of the vocal folds (see Figure II–10). The **thyroarytenoid** muscles form a large part of the vocal folds and the

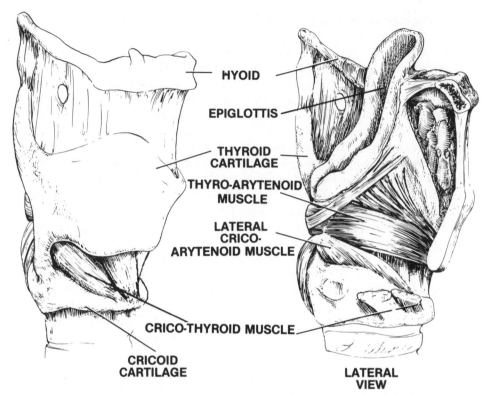

HYOID

EPIGLOTTIS

THYROID
CARTILAGE

THYRO-ARYTENOID
MUSCLE

LATERAL
CRICO-
ARYTENOID MUSCLE

CRICO-THYROID MUSCLE

CRICOID
CARTILAGE

LATERAL
VIEW

Figure II–8.   Lateral view diagrams of structures and intrinsic muscles of the larynx.

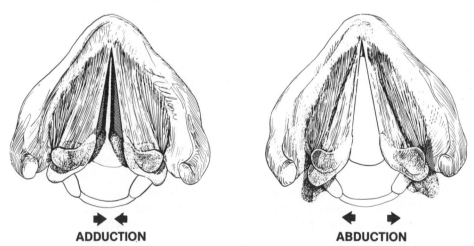

ADDUCTION

ABDUCTION

Figure II–9.   Superior view diagram of actions involved in abduction (opening) and adduction (closing) of the glottis.

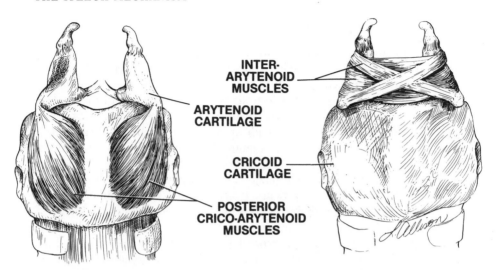

Figure II–10. Posterior view diagrams of cricoid and arytenoid cartilages, and intrinsic muscles of the larynx.

lateral walls bounding them (Figure II–11). They arise from the angle of the thyroid cartilage, inserting into the arytenoid cartilages on either side. When the **thyromuscularis** [θaíromʌ́skjulɛ́rɪs] portions of these muscles contract, they move the arytenoid cartilages forward, shortening and relaxing the vocal folds. The **vocalis** [vokǽlɪs] portions of the thyroarytenoid muscles are attached similarly but have fibers that also insert along the entire length of the vocal ligament. With contraction of its parts, this muscle can tense portions of the vocal fold differentially, resulting in subtle pitch differences.

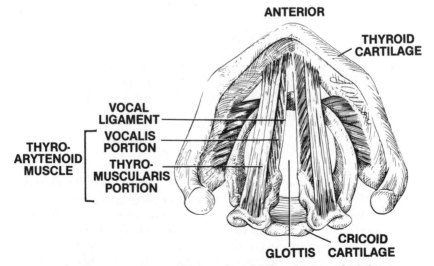

Figure II–11. Superior view diagram of vocal folds and arytenoid cartilages.

Sub-Laryngeal Structures

Beneath the larynx are the organs of respiration that provide breath flow, the basic material of speech. Immediately below the cricoid cartilage of the larynx is the **trachea,** consisting of a tube of 16 to 20 irregular cartilage rings descending downward just in front of the esophagus until the trachea divides into smaller tubes. These paired tubes, the **bronchi** [bráŋkɪ], enter the lungs and further subdivide into small **bronchioles** [bráŋkɪolz], which house numerous air sacs containing the minute **alveoli** [ælvíolɪ]. In the alveoli, oxygen is exchanged for carbon dioxide in the blood of the tiny capillaries of the cell walls. The major muscle influencing the lungs is the large, broad **diaphragm** [daíəfræm]. It arises around the circumference of the lower thoracic cavity to form two semi-circular domes upon which rest the base of the lungs. When they contract, the domes flatten and pull downward, with the soft lung tissue expanding and following. The reduced air pressure inside the expanded lungs forces air from the greater atmospheric pressure outside the body to flow through the respiratory tract and into the lungs. The diaphragm is assisted in this **inhalation** or "inspiration" phase of respiration by expansion and upward movement of the rib cage with contraction of other muscles of the thorax and neck. These include the **external intercostals** [ɪntɚkástəlz] between the ribs, the triangular shaped **scalenes** [skelínz], and the **pectoral** [péktɚəl] muscles, which help elevate the ribs. The **exhalation** or "expiration" of air is achieved by a combination of the (1) effect of gravity, (2) elastic reaction of cartilage and lung tissue, (3) relaxation of the muscles of inhalation, (4) contraction of the **internal intercostal** muscles, and (5) contraction of a group of muscles of the abdominal region that anchor the ribs and compress the abdominal viscera to reduce thoracic volume.

SPEECH PROCESSES

Speech is the end product of four processes or actions occurring simultaneously and cooperatively. These are respiration, phonation, resonation, and articulation, which together are responsible for the variety of sounds we use to transmit spoken language.

Respiration

Respiration is accomplished by a complex interaction of the aforementioned structures and muscles. The exhalation phase provides the flow of breath for speech. Air, which is elastic and occupies space, is forced from the large cavity of the lungs through the bronchi and into the narrow tube of the trachea. Since air pressure increases inversely with tube diameter, the exhaled breath is under considerable pressure as it reaches the trachea below the glottis, and it will expand upward through the vocal tract to equalize pressure on the outside. This positive pressure is essential to pro-duce speech. If allowed to escape through the open glottis during normal respiration, breath may flow into the pharynx and outside through the un-obstructed nasal or oral cavity without necessarily being audible to listeners. By taking a "deep breath" and letting it escape rapidly, however, exhalation pressure increases and turbulence with audible friction is created in the open respiratory tract as the breath is forced across surfaces of the tract.

Inhalation while talking occurs at some of the pauses between speech phrases with fairly rapid and brief expansion of the lungs. Outside air usually flows in through the oral cavity during speech, whereas in regular breathing it typically is received by the nasal cavity where it may be filtered, warmed, and moistened. Some speakers habitually, or in excitement, make inhalation audible, resulting from friction in the vocal tract when air pressure is too great. Speakers may practice silent inhalation during speech by balancing the volume and rate of inhaled air with vocal tract openness.

In normal breathing, the relative duration of inhalation and exhalation is about the same. But when speaking, the duration of exhalation in a single respiratory cycle is usually about 10 times as long as that of inhalation and may be as much as 50 times as long for practiced speakers. Since no more breath is used in speaking than in regular breathing exhalation, the extended duration of exhalation during speech reflects a remarkable control and econ-omy in using the breath stream in order to sustain connected speech. This efficiency, realized by the synergistic [sɪnɚ-ʤístɪk] functioning of the respira-tory muscles, larynx, and articulatory mechanism, apparently is learned. Think of the difference in control, for example, between the baby crying violently and always "running out of breath," and the trained singer or speaker who can easily sustain voice for long periods.

The sounds of friction, created when air flow passes against the various surfaces of the vocal tract, can transmit very limited speech information. For example, in whispering, the vocal folds are closed but a chink between the arytenoid cartilages allows the escape of subglottal air under great pressure into the vocal tract. Considerable friction and turbulence is set up at the glottis as the primary sound source to be amplified and shaped by the re-sonating cavities above, forming the resonant consonants and vowels. The articulators of the oral cavity narrow or stop the breath flow for other conson-ants such as /f/, /s/, and /t/. Speech can thus be transmitted, but the range of distance is extremely limited, since such friction sounds are of low acoustic intensity, audible only to the listeners close at hand.

Phonation

In order to transmit speech over a distance, **phonation** [foneíʃən] or voicing is required. Phonation is accomplished by rapid rhythmic closing and opening of the glottis with the vocal folds. The muscles described earlier help close the glottis by adducting the arytenoid cartilages and steadily approximating the vocal folds, but lightly enough so that they can be parted by accumulated subglottal air pressure. Once they are parted, the subglottal pressure is released and the folds again approximate through a combination of muscular tension and aerodynamic effect. For phonation to occur, subglottal pressure must be greater than supraglottal [súprəglátl] pressure and greater than glottal resistance. During phonation, the vocal folds follow this rhythmic cycle:

1. Closing of the glottis
2. Increasing of air pressure beneath the glottis
3. Bursting apart of the folds from air pressure with release of a puff of compressed breath
4. Closing of the folds again under constant muscle tension, with temporarily decreased air pressure at the glottis "sucking" the folds back together.

Air pressure beneath the glottis increases as air continues to flow from the lungs and trachea, and the pattern is repeated. Viewed by high-speed motion picture photography, it is apparent that the phonation cycle is not a simple opening and closing, like two sliding doors abutting over their length on a horizontal plane. Rather, there is usually a greater opening centrally, and the adduction and abduction occur with undulating, aerodynamically influenced waves of the vocal folds in both vertical and horizontal dimensions. The subglottal portions of the vocal folds, increasing in thickness as they approach the glottis, also show upward wave-like movements during phonation.

The periodic puffs of breath that occur during phonation form a string of pulses of **compression** and **rarefaction** [rɛrəfækʃən] of air molecules that constitute **sound waves.** When sufficiently amplified by the resonant cavities of the vocal tract above, the sound of phonation is easily audible to listeners. The rate or frequency at which the glottis is forced open so that puffs of compressed breath result determines the **fundamental frequency,** or F_0, of the resulting voice sound. If, for example, the glottis completes 125 of the closing-opening phonation cycles in a second, the fundamental frequency, or F_0, of the resulting sound will be 125 cycles-per-second, written in physical terms as 125 Hertz (Hz). As the rate of opening-closing cycles increases or decreases, the F_0 increases and decreases accordingly, and listeners judge that the pitch of the voice rises or falls.

Changes in fundamental frequency come about through interaction of the lungs and the larynx. The size and mass of the vocal folds determine the range of frequencies possible for a speaker. Adult males with larger, heavier larynges [lɛrínʤiz] typically have a lower average F_0 (about 100 to 125 Hz) than do adult females (about 180 to 220 Hz), and the developing larynx of a pre-adolescent child may have an even higher fundamental. Changes in F_0 of a given speaker occur through a combination of alterations in (1) tension of the vocal folds and (2) subglottal air pressure. The folds are lengthened and thus tensed by the muscles influencing the airflow of exhalation. When F_0 is to rise, as for a question requiring a yes-or-no answer or to give stress to a syllable, the principal mechanism is tensing of the folds with some increase in subglottal pressure. When F_0 drops, as it might at the end of a declarative sentence, a reduction of subglottal pressure appears to be the primary mechanism. In rapid connected speech, changes in vocal fold tension and in subglottal pressure are involved in combination.

An increase in **intensity** of voice, heard by listeners as increased loudness, occurs when the amplitude of horizontal vocal fold movement is increased so that the glottis is opened wider, permitting a larger volume of compressed breath to be released. This comes about by a complex interaction of (1) increased subglottal pressure, (2) control of the vocal folds for firm closure and long closure periods so that no breath flow is wasted, and (3) expansion of the vocal tract for reduced supraglottal pressure. One or more of these mechanisms is involved when voice intensity is increased during speech. For a decrease in intensity, the opposite of these conditions is applicable. Of course, overall intensity of speech may be increased or decreased by alteration of the resonating cavities of the vocal tract as well. Surprisingly, instrumental studies have shown that loud speech (less than shouting) may require no more breath than quiet speech, and that stressed vowels consume no more air than unstressed vowels. This suggests an efficiency and economy of air flow at the glottis when loud speech is produced. It is apparently possible to reduce the intensity of a sound by only partially closing the glottis in such a manner as to permit some of the non-vibrating air to escape.

In their rhythmic opening and closing of the glottis to produce the fundamental frequency of voice, the vocal folds actually create a complex sound with secondary vibrations of air molecules resulting from wave-like motions as the folds gradually open and close. The resulting sound thus includes **overtones** that are higher in frequency than the fundamental. The overtones of voice are whole number multiples of the fundamental frequency called **harmonics** [harmánıks]. Harmonics are numbered so that the fundamental is considered the first harmonic. The second harmonic has twice the frequency of the fundamental, the third three times, the fourth four times, etc. If the fundamental frequency were 125 Hz, for example, the second and successive harmonics would be 250 Hz, 375 Hz, 500 Hz, 625 Hz, and so on. The lower the fundamental frequency, the greater the number of harmonics possible within the range of hearing. Since the harmonics result from vibrations of parts of the vocal folds, each successive harmonic is less intense than the previous one, until the highest ones cannot be heard at all. Considering the combinations of fundamental frequency and harmonics occurring in unison, the sound produced by the larynx is a complex one resulting from a complex sound wave.

Resonation

The complex sound produced by the larynx itself is not loud, but it can be amplified for easy audibility by the cavities above the larynx through the process of **resonation.** A similar kind of amplification occurs when we speak through a megaphone, shout into a cave, sing in a shower enclosure, or pass a vibrating tuning fork over a glass partly filled with water. Many kinds of objects, including a cavity filled with air, will tend to vibrate when struck or when another vibrating body is placed near them. The frequency of their vibration depends upon various factors such as the size of the object or cavity and the shape of the cavity and its openings. As we fill a glass with water while occasionally tapping it with a spoon, the pinging sound will rise in frequency as we pour more water in, reducing the volume of air in the glass. If we sing or play a musical note of the same frequency near the glass, the glass and the air in it will "ring" with sympathetic vibration, resulting in an increased loudness of the sound. The frequency at which an object or cavity of air can be set to ringing loudest is called its **natural frequency.** We say it is "tuned" to that frequency. A resonating cavity will respond not only to a simple sound such as tapping with a spoon or playing a musical note but also to a complex sound like that which results from phonation—the fundamental frequency of voice plus its overtones. The resonator will respond to and amplify the overtones to which it is tuned or "in tune." The closer the cavity's natural frequency is to the original sound. the greater the resonation. But if the original sound and the resonating cavity are greatly out of tune, there can be little resonation and may even be a reduction of the sound. Thus, resonating cavities selectively amplify parts of the complex vocal sound.

The vocal tract above the glottis acts as a resonator for the sound produced by phonation. While the tract was previously described as three cavities (oral cavity, nasal cavity, and pharynx), it may be treated as a single resonating cavity, with coupling of its component cavities, that is capable of a great variety of adjustment to alter the sounds it will resonate. Figure II–12 shows a schematic diagram of the vocal tract viewed as a resonating system with mechanisms for some of these alterations.

The distinctive sound of an individual's voice, referred to as its **quality** or "timbre" [tɪmbɚ], is produced primarily by a combination of the person's habitual range of fundamental frequency blended with the overtones that are amplified or subdued through resonation. The manner in which a person's vocal folds habitually perform may also contribute to quality—for example, a sound of "breathiness" is heard resulting from frequent incomplete closure of the glottis during adduction of the vocal folds. Influences of resonation on voice quality include:
1. The overall size of the vocal tract
2. The relative size of the three major cavities

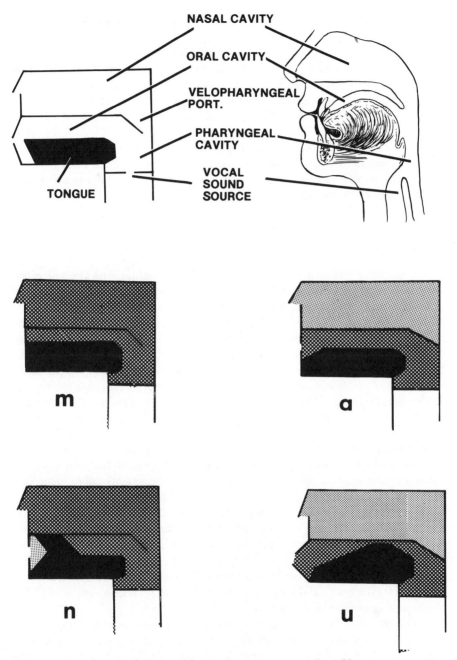

Figure II–12. Schematic diagrams of the vocal tract as a system of variable resonating cavities for speech sounds.

3. Habitual muscle tensing that may raise the larynx and change the size and shape of the pharynx
4. The size of the tongue in relation to the oral cavity
5. The moistness and softness of the cavity walls, which reduce resonation and "damp" some components of voice
6. The relative openness of the jaw and lips during speaking
7. The relative openness of the velopharyngeal port during production of vowels and oral resonant consonants.

Accumulations of mucous during upper respiratory infections or abnormal growth of adenoid tissue influence nasal resonance. General bodily factors such as the weight of bones and other tissue and size of the chest cavity may also contribute to overall voice quality.

Articulation

Resonance not only contributes to speech by amplifying the voice and determining its quality, but it participates importantly in articulation. **Articulation** may be defined as shaping the breath stream that flows from the glottis, voiced or unvoiced, to form the sounds of speech. The vowels and resonant consonants are articulated primarily by adjustments in resonance (see Figure II-12). The nasal resonant consonants /m/, /n/, and /ŋ/ derive their distinctive character from openness of the velopharyngeal port, while the oral cavity is closed off at the lips for /m/, at the alveolar ridge for /n/, and at the velum for /ŋ/. The resonance for /l/ and /r/ is produced by partially blocking the oral cavity and reducing its air volume by intruding the tongue into it. The /w/ and /j/ are produced with resonance similar to /u/ and /i/, respectively, but with shorter duration. Differences among American-English vowels are produced entirely by adjustment in the oral cavity to influence resonance. For vowels and resonant consonants other than /m/, /n/, and /ŋ/, the velopharyngeal port is closed off but air in the nasal cavity is set into resonant vibration by the palate, which vibrates with the oral cavity. Except for the small openings at the nostrils, the nasal cavity operates for vowels as a nearly closed resonating cavity. If one closes off the nostrils during vowel production, though, the change in sound can be noticeable. The primary determiners of oral resonance for producing different vowels are (1) the height of the tongue, (2) the place at which the tongue is elevated, and (3) the shape and openness of the lips (see Figure II-12).

For consonants other than the resonant consonants, the tongue, jaw, and lips act as shapers of the breath stream. They may constrict the flow of the stream, acting like a valve system, to cause audible friction against the velum, palate, alveolar ridge, or teeth, as in /h̃/, /f/, and /s/, or they may constrict it by themselves as the lips do for /ʍ/. The other primary action of articulation is to stop the flow of breath suddenly, sometimes releasing it with an audible explosion for /p/, /t/, and /k/. A detailed description of articulation is presented in Chapters III, IV, and V.

REVIEW VOCABULARY

Abducting—moving apart as in the vocal folds abducting to open the glottis. (See Figure II-9.)

Adducting—drawing together as in the vocal folds adducting to close the glottis. (See Figure II-9.)

Alveolo-, -alveolar—referring to the prominent alveolar ridge just behind the maxillary incisors and canine teeth. Example: lingua-alveolar, involving the tongue and alveolar ridge.

Approximation—position of closeness of speech organs that permits a constricted flow of air.

Articulation—shaping the breath stream to form the sounds of speech.

Bronchi—cartilaginous ringed tubes leading downward from the trachea to each lobe of the lungs.

Cusps—sharp points of the teeth.

Deciduous—in reference to teeth, the first and temporary set.

Dento-, -dental—referring to the teeth. Example: labio-dental, involving the lips and teeth.

Epiglottis—a cartilaginous structure at the base of the tongue and directly above the glottis.

Eustachian tubes—tubes connecting the nasopharynx with the middle ear cavity, permitting ventilation of the middle ear.

Extrinsic muscles—having an attachment to structures outside of an organ such as the tongue or larynx.

Frenum—a thin, flexible connecting membrane. Examples: labial frenums, lingual frenum.

Fundamental frequency—in reference to voice, rate at which glottis opens and closes during phonation. Written F_0. Heard by listener as pitch of the voice.

Genio-, -genial—referring to the mandible, especially the chin, Example: genioglossus muscle, involving the mandible and tongue.

Glosso-, -glossal—referring to the tongue. Example: the glossopalatine muscle, connecting the tongue and palate.

Glottis—opening that connects the trachea and laryngopharynx. Space between the vocal folds.

Harmonics—overtones that are whole number multiples of the fundamental frequency.

Intensity—in reference to voice, volume of the voice increasing with amplitude of glottal opening. Heard by the listener as loudness of the voice.

Intrinsic muscles—having both attachments within an organ such as the tongue or larynx.

Labio-, -labial—referring to the lips. Example: bilabial, involving both lips.

Laryngo-, -laryngeal—referring to the larynx. Example: laryngopharynx, the portion of the pharynx just above the larynx.

Lingua-, -lingual—referring to the tongue. Example: lingua-alveolar, involving the tongue and alveolar ridge.

Malocclusion—an abnormal or atypical fit of the maxillary and mandibular teeth in relation to each other.

mandible—the lower jaw.

Mandibulo-, -mandibular—referring to the mandible or lower jaw. Example: mandibular incisors, front teeth of the lower jaw.

Maxilla—the upper jaw.

Naso-, -nasal—referring to the nasal cavity. Example: nasopharynx, the portion of the pharynx at the back of the nasal cavity.

Occlusion—intermeshing and overlapping of the maxillary and mandibular teeth.

Oro-, -oral—referring to the oral cavity. Example: oropharynx, the portion of the pharynx at the back of the oral cavity.

Overtones—tones of a complex sound that are of a higher frequency than the fundamental.

Palato-, -palatal, -palatine—referring to the bony or hard palate that separates the oral and nasal cavities. Example: lingua-palatal, involving the tongue and palate.

Pharyngo-, -pharyngeal—referring to the pharynx or throat. Example: pharyngopalatine, involving the pharynx and palate.

Philtrum—indentation in skin between nose and center of upper lip.

Phonation—the process of creating voice at the larynx.

Quality—in reference to voice, the distinctive sound resulting from a combination of habitual range of F_0 blended with overtones amplified or subdued through resonation.

Resonation—the process of modifying a sound by passing it through a cavity of air or by placing a vibrating object against another object capable of vibrating.

Sound waves—a series of pulses of compression and rarefaction of air molecules within the range of hearing.

Sympathetic vibration—the resonant vibration of an object or a cavity of air with its natural frequency the same as that of the sound source.

Trachea—the windpipe or cartilage rings leading downward from the larynx to the bronchi and the lungs.

Velo-, -velar—referring to the velum or soft palate. Example: lingua-velar, involving the tongue and velum.

Velopharyngeal port—the aperture that connects the nasopharynx and oropharynx, sometimes called the nasopharyngeal port.

Vermilion—the reddish skin of the outside surface of the lips.

EXERCISES

Transcribe in Roman alphabet orthography the words that correspond to the following phonetic units:

1. Parts of the speech mechanism

tʌŋ	frinəm	haiɔid
viləm	θairɔid	mændɪbəl
fɛrɪŋks	treɪkɪə	keɪnaɪn
pælət	juvjulə	daɪəfræm

2. General phonetic terminology

neɪzəl	dɛntḷ	ædʌkʃən
spitʃ	ɪntrɪnsɪk	kʌɑlətɪ
voukəl	fənɛtɪks	ɛkstrɪnsɪk
okluʒən	ʍɪspɚ	foneɪʃən

3. Parts of the speech mechanism

kraɪkɔɪd	pɛktɚəl	vokælɪs
mæksɪlə	ɛpɪglɑtəs	sfɪŋktɚ
ɪnsaɪzɚ	baɪkʌspəd	kɑrtɪlədʒ
kævətɪ	justeɪkɪən	ælviolɚ

4. General phonetic terminology

hɑrmɑnɪks	kəmprɛʃən
tɜ·bjulənts	fʌndəmɛntl̩
ɪntɛnsətɪ	rɛspɚeɪʃən
vaɪbreɪʃən	frikʍənsɪ

SUGGESTED READING

Zemlin, Willard R.: *Speech & Hearing Science: Anatomy and Physiology.* Englewood Cliffs, N.J., Prentice-Hall, Inc. 1968

An exceptionally fine text on anatomy and physiology directed to knowledge a serious student of phonetics will need. Includes valuable sections on the ear and the nervous system.

Fink, Raymond B., and Demarest, Robert J.: *Laryngeal Biomechanics.* Cambridge, Mass., Harvard University Press, 1978

This volume includes descriptions and illustrations to help understand the actions of the larynx. It was created by the combined talents of a physician (Fink) and a medical illustrator (Demarest). It uses excellent drawings, X-ray photographs, and schematic diagrams to illustrate the complex relations and actions associated with phonation.

Palmer, John M.: *Anatomy for Speech and Hearing,* 2nd ed. New York, Harper & Row, 1972

This paperback manual features large drawings that simplify anatomic relations. Tables present clear descriptions of structures, muscles, and nerves, and their functions related to respiration, phonation, and articulation.

Chapter III

CONSONANT PRODUCTION

- **ANALYSIS OF CONSONANTS**
  - **STOP CONSONANTS**
  - **FRICATIVES**
  - **AFFRICATES**
  - **ORAL RESONANTS**
  - **NASAL RESONANTS**
- **REVIEW VOCABULARY**
- **EXERCISES**
- **SUGGESTED READING**

Speech sounds have traditionally been divided into **consonants** and **vowels,** with **diphthongs** [dɪfθɔŋz] considered a special kind of vowel. However, the distinction between consonants and vowels is not as sharp as popular usage might suggest. The division is hard to justify on a purely phonetic basis, since many consonants are nearly indistinguishable from vowels, either in the way they are produced or in their resulting acoustic properties. The /w/ and /j/ are very similar to the /u/ and /i/, respectively. There seems little difference between the [r] at the end of *far* [fɑr], which is usually considered a consonant, and the same sound at the end of *fir* [fɝ], where it is treated as part of a vowel sound. However, some differences are apparent. As a group, American-English vowels are all voiced and oral resonant sounds, whereas consonants are more variable. Some consonants, like /p/ and /f/, are voiceless. Some are made with a combination of voicing and friction noise, like /v/ and /ð/. Others, particularly the /m/, /n, and /ŋ/, are voiced with open nasal resonance. Several, like the /r/, /l/, and /w/ are voiced resonants similar to vowels.

One reasonable definition of a vowel is "a speech sound which may constitute a syllable or the nucleus of a syllable," whereas a consonant is considered "a speech sound which is used marginally with a vowel or diphthong to constitute a syllable."* A few consonants can take the place of

---

*Wise, Claude M. *Applied Phonetics*. Englewood Cliffs, N.J., Prentice Hall, 1957.

vowels, like the [n̩] in the final unaccented syllable of *button* [bʌtn̩]. However, in a single syllable word like *ton* [tʌn] or in a stressed syllable as in *tonnage* [tʌnɪdʒ], the consonant cannot serve the syllable function of a vowel. It is also interesting to observe that some vowels and diphthongs can stand alone as isolated words, although none of the consonants can do so. Note, for example, /aɪ/ as *I* and /eɪ/ or /ə/ as *a*. Even though we cannot formulate a final and entirely consistent distinction with a single dividing characteristic, the dichotomy of consonant and vowel will serve us here to divide the sounds of speech for description in this and the next chapter.

Consonant phonemes have traditionally been described by their place of articulation, their condition of voicing, and by their manner of production. **Place of articulation** refers to those parts of the speech mechanism involved most prominently in production of the sound. Consonants may be classified by their place of articulation using the structures outlined in Chapter II. For example, the /t/ may be described as a "lingua-alveolar" sound (the tongue touches the alveolar ridge), the /f/ as a "labio-dental" sound (the lip approximates the teeth), and the /θ/ as a "lingua-dental" sound (the tongue touches the teeth). Consonants involving phonation, such as /b/, /m/, /v/, and /l/, are called **voiced** sounds. Those without phonation, such as /p/, /t/, /f/, and /h/, are called **voiceless** sounds. Sometimes these are referred to as "unvoiced" or "breath" sounds. **Manner of production** refers to the way the speech mechanism modifies the voiced or voiceless air stream. Although the actual variety of modifications is wide, consonants may be conveniently grouped by five primary classes: **stops, fricatives, affricates, oral resonants**, and **nasal resonants**.

Consonants are conventionally categorized in brief descriptive terms by their distinctive features of place of articulation, voicing, and manner of

MANNER OF PRODUCTION	PLACE OF ARTICULATION					
	Lingua-Dental	Lingua-Alveolar	Lingua-Palatal	Lingua-Velar	Bibabial	Labio-Dental
Stops		t d		k g	p b	
Fricatives	θ ð	s z	ʃ ʒ	h ʍ		f v
Affricates		tʃ ⟶ tʃ dʒ ⟶ dʒ				
Oral Resonants		l	r j	w		
Nasal Resonants		n		ŋ	m	

Figure III–1. Consonant sounds of American-English ordered by their place of articulation and manner of production.

production. For example, the /t/ is called a "lingua-alveolar, voiceless stop" sound; the /v/ a "labio-dental, voiced fricative," and the /l/ a "lingua-alveolar, oral resonant." Figure III–1 orders consonant sounds by these descriptive terms.

ANALYSIS OF CONSONANTS

The consonant phonemes of American-English speech are described individually in this chapter. Their written symbols, as used in the International Phonetic Alphabet (IPA), in dictionaries, and in the Northampton symbol system are listed, along with key words to assist in pronunciation. A typical place of articulation and manner of production is outlined, using both the conventional descriptive terms and a step-by-step analysis of their production. Then the most common American-English spellings associated with the phoneme are presented, along with some irregular spellings. This is followed by words, sentences, and contrast discrimination exercises for each consonant phoneme. Notes are added about some phonemes.

A word of caution to the reader. These descriptions of the phonemes of our language may suggest there is a single or standard way of producing each sound. This is not the case! The descriptions are generalizations of how most people produce speech sounds. Each of us makes accommodations for our unique anatomy and for our skill in moving the speech mechanism rapidly about. We did not learn speech by carefully watching and copying how someone else moved his tongue and lips, or made closure of the velopharyngeal port. We learned speech by listening, and, by trial-and-error, moving our speech mechanism this way and that until the sound we produced was similar to that which we heard from others. Since there is more than one possible way to produce the same sound, it is to be expected that there will be individual differences in the particular way people habitually produce speech.

Individual analysis begins with the stop consonants, then moves to the fricatives, the affricates, and the resonants. Exercises are included at the end of the chapter.

Stop Consonants

The stop consonant phonemes of General American-English speech are /p/, /t/, /k/, /b/, /d/, and /g/. These consonants are sometimes called "plosives" or "aspirates." The essential action in their production is an interruption of the air stream, whether voiced or voiceless, by a closure within the oral cavity. The interrupting action has two possible phases: first, the necessary **stop** phase with its rapid closure, and second, the more variable **aspira-**

tion or "plosive" phase, when impounded air is released. Some allophones of these stop phonemes are made without aspiration or are made with varying degrees of diminished aspiration. For example, whereas the [p] in *pot* is both stopped and aspirated, the [p] in *spot* is stopped but not aspirated. The differences can be verified by placing the back of the hand just in front of the lips while producing the two words alternately.

IPA   p
Dictionary   p Key Words: *pie, tap, happy*
Northampton p

/p/ PRODUCTION—Bilabial Voiceless Stop

The /p/ is made with the velopharyngeal port closed and without voice. There are two phases possible: first, the necessary **stop** phase, with its rapid closure, and second, the **aspiration** or plosive phase, with variable release.

Stop: the lips close and the breath is held and compressed in the oral cavity. Closure is more tense and of greater duration than for /b/.

Aspiration: the breath compressed in the oral cavity is released suddenly as an audible explosion of air between the lips.

In connected speech, the /p/ may or may not be released with aspiration. It is usually released with audible aspiration in these situations:

1. As the initial consonant in a syllable as in *pie, report, bypass.*
2. As the final consonant following /m/, which is **homorganic**, that is, made at the same place of articulation, as in *lamp, blimp, bump.*
3. As the final consonant following /s/ as in *lisp, hasp, cusp.*
4. In the medial position, but somewhat softer, as in *apple, apron, carpet, upon.*

The /p/ is usually released without audible aspiration in these situations:

1. As the final consonant following vowels and most voiced consonants as in *up, harp, hop, stop.*
2. Following /s/ in the same syllable as in *spy, spear, sport, despair* (compare the soft release of the [p] in *spy* with the exploded release in *pie.* The /p/ is released with explosion when it initiates a syllable (compare the soft release in *the sport* with the exploded release in *this port*).

The /p/ is released into the position of the following voiceless consonant in such combinations as *kept, hips, stop sign, sheep shears, hop farm.*

/p/ SPELLING—*p* is Primary Spelling

-*pp*- in medial positions in words such as *apple, happy, pepper, oppose* is given a single [p] sound. When two [p] sounds abut at the end of one word and the beginning of another, as in *stop pushing*, the closure period is held longer for [stɑp:uʃɪŋ].

-*m( )th* results in an intruded [p] sound, not included in spelling, between an [m] and a following breath sound as in *warmth* [wɔrmpθ], *comfort* [kʌmpfɚt], dreamt [drɛmpt], and *something* [sʌmpθɪŋ]. Note that /m/ and /p/ are homorganic.

/p/ WORDS

Initial		*Medial*		*Final*		*Clusters*
pack	pool	upon	paper	up	shop	spy
pie	pun	apple	rapid	cap	cape	spring
peas	peak	approve	repair	chop	deep	split
pill	pot	apply	happy	jump	sharp	carps
pry	place	stopping	keeper	lamp	help	kept
pride	plunge	stupid	oppose	camp	clasp	grasps

/p/ SENTENCES

1. Polly takes pride in preparing apple pie.
2. Please provide a pleasant place to play.
3. The pine wood you chopped is kept upon the pile.
4. The spines on that sponge are spaced apart.
5. Pack the spare parts in the portable package.
6. Purple pleases particular people.

/p/ CONTRASTS

/p/—/b/		/p/—/t/		/p/—/k/	
pack	back	pie	tie	pear	care
pill	bill	pan	tan	pan	can
peas	bees	pin	tin	peep	keep
peak	beak	pop	top	Pope	cope
tap	tab	lip	lit	pain	cane
rope	robe	pop	pot	part	cart
cap	cab	rap	rat	lap	lack
rapid	rabid	sipping	sitting	seeping	seeking

Note: the /p/ is developed early by children and is seldom misarticulated.

IPA   t
Dictionary   t Key Words: *tie, sit, later*
Northampton   t

/t/ PRODUCTION—Lingua-alveolar Voiceless Stop

The /t/ is made with the velopharyngeal port closed and without voice. There are two phases possible: first, the necessary **stop** phase, with its rapid closure, and second, the **aspiration** or plosive phase, with variable release.

Stop: the tip of the tongue closes against the alveolar ridge with the sides of the tongue against the molars, and the breath is held and compressed in the oral cavity. Closure is more tense and of greater duration than for /d/.

Aspiration: the breath compressed in the oral cavity behind the tongue is released suddenly as an audible explosion between the alveolar ridge and tip of the tongue through slightly open teeth and lips.

In connected speech, the /t/ may or may not be released with aspiration. It is usually released with audible aspiration in these situations:
1. As the initial consonant is a stressed syllable as in *tie, retire, until, attest.*
2. As the final consonant following consonants that are **homorganic**, having the same or nearly the same place of articulation, as in *want, salt, cart.*
3. Following voiceless consonants in the final position as in *kept, act, fished, watched, laughed,* or when a medial consonant as in *after, luster, sitting.*
4. The /t/ is released into the position of the following voiceless consonant in such combinations as *pats, that sign, that part, what for, white car, what thing,* and *that ship.*

The /t/ is usually released without audible aspiration in these situations:
1. As the final consonant following vowels as in *at, but, hot, let, sit.*
2. Following /s/ in the same syllable in *stop, stove, steam, restore* (compare the soft release of the [t] in *stop* with the exploded release in *top*). However, the /t/ is released with aspiration when it initiates a syllable (compare the soft release (in *the store* with the exploded release in *this tore*).

The /t/ between vowels, especially in an unstressed syllable, is sometimes produced as a brief, voiced "flap" of the tongue, rather than a voiceless stop, as in *better, butter, pity, waiting, beautiful.*

/t/ SPELLING—*t* is Primary Spelling

-tt- in medial positions in words such as *lettuce, pretty, better, motto, kitten* is given a single [t] sound. When two [t] sounds abut at the end of one

word and beginning of another, as in *hot time*, the closure period if held longer for [hɑt:aɪm].

-ed following breath consonants as in *fished, watched, laughed, taped, backed, fixed, laced,* except following [t] as in *skated, waited.*

Th- as in *Thomas, Thames, Theresa, Thompson, thyme* may be said as /t/.

-n( )s results in an intruded [t] sound, not included in spelling, between [n] and [s] as in *chance, fence, tense, dance, cancel, stencil.*

Rare Spellings: *yacht, indict, debt, doubt, receipt, eighth, ptomaine, two.* The *t* is silent in *listen, soften, often, castle, thistle, bristle, whistle.*

/t/ WORDS

Initial		Medial		Final		Clusters
too	try	after	potato	at	act	eighth
take	train	into	until	cut	waked	stream
tube	tree	pretty	city	gate	touched	lets
toe	trust	letter	motto	west	dropped	acts
time	twin	sister	shouting	lent	washed	guests
team	twelve	chapter	rotate	salt	next	gifts

/t/ SENTENCES

1. Tom walked two miles to get that hat.
2. Ted can't touch the tip of his tongue.
3. The train will cart the tools to town.
4. Twin trolleys travel twelve times.
5. As we watched, he fished and caught twenty trout.
6. Yesterday Theresa bought a beautiful valentine.

/t/ CONTRASTS

/t/—/d/		/t/—/θ/		/ /—/t/	
tie	die	tin	thin	lass	last
ton	done	tick	thick	necks	next
try	dry	tree	three	pass	past
metal	medal	tinker	thinker	Bess	best
writing	riding	taught	thought	mass	mast
unto	undo	bat	bath	slip	slipped
mat	mad	boat	both	guess	guests
coat	code	fateful	faithful	wash	washed

Note: Europeans may make the /t/ with insufficient aspiration in the initial and the final positions, and they may make closure with the tip of the tongue on the inside surface of the upper front teeth rather than on the alveolar ridge. The /t/ is one of the most frequently occurring consonants in American-English speech.

IPA   k
Dictionary   k Key Words: *key, back, become*
Northampton k (c, ck)

/k/ PRODUCTION—Lingua-velar Voiceless Stop

The /k/ is made with the velopharyngeal port closed and without voice. There are two phases possible: first, the necessary **stop** phase, with its rapid closure, and second, the **aspiration** or plosive phase, with a variable release.

Stop: the back of the tongue closes against the front of the velum or back portion of the palate, and the breath is held and compressed in the back of the oral cavity and in the oropharynx.

Aspiration: the breath compressed in the oral cavity and oropharynx is released suddenly as an audible explosion of air between the tongue and roof of the mouth.

In connected speech, the /k/ may be released with variable aspiration. The /k/ is released with a strong aspiration in these situations:

1. As the initial consonant in a syllable as in *key, come, kite.*
2. As the final consonant following the homorganic sound [ŋ] as in *sink, tank, trunk, drink.*

The /k/ is released with a light aspiration in these situations:

1. As the final sound of most words as in *back, take, thick*, the final /k/ closure producing less acoustic information than either final /p/ or /t/.
2. In the medial position as in *stocking, across, pocket.*

The /k/ is released without audible aspiration in these situations:

1. As the final consonant of a syllable, followed by a voiced consonant that begins the next syllable, as in *backdoor, blackball, like new, bookmark.*
2. Following /s/ in the same syllable in *scold, ski, scare* (compare the soft release of the [k] in *scare* with the strongly aspirated release in *care*). However, the /k/ is released with aspiration when /k/ initiates a syllable (compare the soft release in *the ski* with the aspirated release in *this key*).

The /k/ is released into the position of the following voiceless consonant in such combinations as *backed, black tie, bake pies, backfire, backside, milk shake.*

/k/ SPELLING—*k* is Primary Spelling

-*ck* always has the /k/ sound as in *back, clock, buck, brick, neck.*

c (a, o, u) has the /k/ sound as in *cake, because; core, decorate; cut, biscuit.* The *c* before *l* as in *clerk* and before *r* as in *craft* also has the /k/ sound.

-*c* as in *tic, chic, talc* has the /k/ sound.

-*cc*- as in *occur, accord, staccato* takes the /k/ sound, following the *c* before *a, o,* and *u* pronunciation just described, and is given as a single /k/ sound. When two /k/ sounds abut at the end of one word and beginning of another as in *black cat*, they are given as a single [k] sound but the closure period is held longer for [blæk:æt].

ch in some words has the /k/ sound as in *ache, echo, chorus, chemist, technique, chasm, conch.*

-*que* as in *technique, Basque, pique, baroque* has the /k/ sound.

qu in some words has the /k/ sound as in *liquor, conquer, quay, queue.*

kh- is a rare spelling for /k/ as in *Khan, khaki.*

-*ng( )th* results in an intruded [k] sound, not included in spelling, between [ŋ] and a final [θ] as in *length* [lɛŋkθ] and *strength* [stɹɛŋkθ].

/k/ WORDS

Initial		Medial		Final		Clusters
key	clay	monkey	picture	book	oak	milks
cat	close	basket	stocking	rock	stick	scream
count	cloud	across	jacket	wake	tick	asks
coal	cry	became	pocket	cake	duck	looked
caught	crown	bucket	likeable	park	ink	desks
kite	cream	pumpkin	accident	thank	work	thinks

/k/ SENTENCES

1. Kate could carry the kitten carefully.
2. Carl's book was in his jacket pocket.
3. By accident, the kite caught on the oak.
4. For breakfast at eight o'clock we had cocoa and biscuits.
5. Ask about the desks and the ink on those books.
6. Carol looked like a monkey running across the park.

/k/ CONTRASTS

/k/—/g/		/k/—/t/		/k/—/p/	
cap	gap	kite	tight	care	pear
rack	rag	key	tea	can	pan

tack	tag	back	bat	scare	spare
come	gum	cry	try	lack	lap
could	good	scream	stream	ache	ape
curl	girl	stark	start	cart	part
meeker	meager	scare	stare	cry	pry
bicker	bigger	caught	taught	keep	peek

Note: the /k/ is developed early by children and is seldom misarticulated by those with normal hearing. It is one of the most frequently occurring consonants in American-English speech.

IPA   b
Dictionary   b Key Words: *be, cab, rabbit*
Northampton b

/b/ PRODUCTION—Bilabial Voiced Stop

The /b/ is made with the velopharyngeal port closed and with voice. There are two phases possible: first, the necessary stop or **closure** phase, and second, the **release** phase, which is variable.

Closure: the lips close as voicing begins or continues, and the air is held briefly in the oral cavity. Closure is usually less tense and of shorter duration than for /p/.

Release: the lips are opened as voicing continues. Voicing begins with the lips closed and the /b/ is released into the following voiced sound when it is the initial sound of an utterance, as in *boy,* or immediately following a breath consonant, as in *this boy*. Between two voiced sounds as in *about,* the /b/ is a brief closure and release with continued voicing. Immediately before a voiceless consonant, as in *lab coat,* the /b/ is closed but not released with voicing. As the final sound of an utterance, as in *lab,* the /b/ is either held without release or is released lightly.

/b/ SPELLING—*b* is Primary Spelling

-bb- in medial positions in words such as *rabbit, cabbage, rubber, pebble, ribbon* is given a single /b/ sound. When two /b/ sounds abut at the end of one word and beginning of another as in *tub brush*, the closure period is held longer for [tʌb:rʌʃ].

-pb- occurs rarely as [b] in *cupboard, clapboard.*

/b/ WORDS

Initial		Medial		Final		Clusters
be	blue	baby	maybe	tub	orb	absorbed
by	blow	robin	nobody	crab	curb	table
bad	block	number	about	globe	herb	bulbs
bed	bread	rabbit	October	cube	bulb	arbor
boy	brave	pebble	bluebird	sob	cob	number
book	broom	ribbon	remember	bib	crab	tumbler

/b/ SENTENCES

1. The rubber ball absorbed the bounce.
2. Both October and November have bright blue weather.
3. Bring Ben the big brown book by' the table.
4. Robins, bluebirds, and blackbirds are above the boat.
5. Maybe somebody will buy Bob's big globe.
6. Rabbits have been breaking into the cabbage.

/b/ CONTRASTS

/b/—/p/		/b/—/v/		/b/—/m/	
back	pack	berry	very	be	me
bill	pill	best	vest	bay	may
bees	peas	boat	vote	by	my
beak	peak	gibbon	given	bear	mare
tab	tap	saber	saver	bath	math
robe	rope	bow	vow	lab	lamb
cab	cap	cabs	calves	Bob	bomb
rabid	rapid	Serb	serve	crab	cram

Note: the /b/ is mastered early by children and is seldom misarticulated. Spanish speakers may not make the sound with firm lip closure, substituting the bilabial fricative /β/, which sounds like /v/, to American-English listeners. Germans and Russians may produce the final /b/ as /p/.

IPA   d
Dictionary   d Key Words: *day, mud, fading*
Northampton d

/d/ PRODUCTION—Lingua-alveolar Voiced Stop

The /d/ is made with the velopharyngeal port closed and with voice. There are two phases possible: first, the necessary **closure** or stop phase, and second, the **release** phase, which is variable.

Closure: the tip of the tongue closes against the alveolar ridge with the sides of the tongue against the molars, the breath is held briefly in the oral cavity. Closure is usually less tense and of shorter duration than for /t/.

Release: closure of the tip of the tongue on the alveolar ridge is released as voicing continues.

Voicing begins with the closed position, and the /d/ is released into the following voiced sound when it is the initial sound of an utterance as in *day*, or immediately following a breath consonant as in *this day*. Between two voiced sounds as in *eddy*, the /d/ is a brief lingua-alveolar closure and release with continued voicing. Immediately before a voiceless consonant, as in *red car*, the /d/ is closed but not released with voicing. As the final sound of an utterance, as in *bad,* the /d/ is either held without release or is released lightly. As the final consonant following consonants that have the same or nearly the same lingua-alveolar place of articulation (*held, hand, hard*), the /d/ is audibly released.

/d/ SPELLING—*d* is Primary Spelling

-*dd*- in medial positions in words such as *ladder, ridden, sadder, middle,* and final as in *odd* and *add* is given a single /d/ sound. When two /d/ sounds abut at the end of one word and beginning of another as in *bad day,* the closure period is held longer for [bæd:eɪ].

-*ed* has the sound of /d/ following vowels, as in *bowed, stayed,* and voiced consonants, as in *saved, bathed, buzzed, judged, opened, steamed, rubbed, begged,* other than after the /d/.

-*ld* occurs with a silent *l* in *could, should, would.*

-*ed* has the sound of [əd] following a /d/ as in *waded* [weɪdəd], *molded, deeded,* and after /t/ as in *waited* [weɪtəd], *batted, rated.*

/d/ WORDS

Initial		Medial		Final		Clusters
do	draw	ladder	jaded	did	used	cards
day	dream	lady	handed	dead	loved	bonded

dog	dry	wonder	condition	hand	clothed	molds
dish	drop	somebody	abdicate	bold	stoned	laden
duck	dwarf	children	meadow	bird	changed	hoarding
down	dwell	hardy	nobody	head	dreamed	address

/d/ SENTENCES

1. The lady did dry the dog's dish.
2. The Indian children played under cliff dwellings.
3. Daddy changed the damp diaper.
4. Reindeer are herded down to the sandy meadow.
5. Somebody handled the caged bird.
6. Dwight wondered if anybody could find a hundred dollars.

/d/ CONTRASTS

/d/—/t/		/d/—/ð/		/d/—/n/	
die	tie	den	then	dough	no
done	ton	doze	those	dear	near
dry	try	day	they	done	none
medal	metal	dough	though	down	noun
riding	writing	dare	there	dead	den
undo	unto	fodder	father	bad	ban
mad	mat	ladder	lather	bid	bin
code	coat	reed	wreathe	mad	man

Note: the /d/ is mastered fairly early by children but is often misarticulated. It is one of the most frequently occurring consonants in American-English speech.

IPA   g
Dictionary   g Key Words: *go, log, begged*
Northampton   g

/g/ PRODUCTION—Lingua-velar Voiced Stop

The /g/ is made with the velopharyngeal port closed and with voice. There are two phases possible: first, the necessary **closure** or stop phase, and second, the **release** phase, which is variable.

Closure: the back of the tongue closes against the front of the velum or back portion of the palate as voicing begins or continues, and air is held briefly in the back of the oral cavity and in the oropharynx. Closure is less tense and of shorter duration than for /k/.

Release: closure of the back of the tongue and the velum—palate is released as voicing continues.

As the initial sound of an utterance (*girl*) or immediately following a breath consonant (*this girl*), voicing begins with the lingua-velar closure, and the /g/ is released into the following voiced sound. Between two voiced sounds (*again*), /g/ is a brief closure and release with continued voicing. Immediately before a voiceless consonant (*big coat*), the /g/ is closed but not released with voicing. As the final sound of an utterance (*big*), the /g/ is closed and released lightly.

/g/ SPELLING—*g* is Primary Spelling

-gg- in medial positions in words such as *buggy, stagger, trigger, wriggle*, and in the final position as in *egg* is given a single /g/ sound. An exception is the word *suggest* [sʌgdʒɛst]. When two /g/ sounds abut at the end of one word and beginning of another as in *big girl*, the closure period is held longer for [bɪg:ɝl].

g(a, o, u) has the /g/ sound as in *game, began; gone, forgot; gun, begun*. The *g* before *l* as in *glass* and before *r* as in *grow* also has the /g/ sound.

-*gue* has the /g/ sound as in *vague, rogue, vogue, intrigue, brogue*.

gu- has the /g/ sound as in *guest, guilty, guess, guile, guard, guarantee*.

gh- has the /g/ sound with silent *h* as in *ghost, gherkin, ghoul, ghastly*.

(e)x- in such words as *exam, exact, exist, exhibit, example* has the sound of [gz].

-*ng* has the [ŋ] sound as in *sing, singer, ring, wrong, lung, ringing, hanger* except for *finger* [fɪŋgɝ], *linger* [lɪŋgɝ], *longer* [lɔŋgɝ] and *hunger* [hʌŋgɝ].

/g/ WORDS

Initial		Medial		Final		Clusters
go	glad	again	buggy	egg	vague	single
gate	glove	begin	bigger	dog	rogue	angled
gun	glow	ago	stagger	tug	intrigue	tangled
good	grow	forgave	trigger	bag	bag	finger
gone	green	angry	wriggle	dig	big	suggest
guess	ghost	hungry	logger	leg	beg	giggle

/g/ SENTENCES

1. The big gray goose is gone.
2. August has begun and the green bugs are bigger.

3. Greg forgot the grapes on the garden gate.
4. The big girls giggled again.
5. He got his gloves together on the log.
6. We guessed that the single flag was gone.

/g/ CONTRASTS

/g/—/k/		/g/—/d/		/g/—/ŋ/	
gap	cap	go	dough	rug	rung
rag	rack	gate	date	sag	sang
tag	tack	lag	lad	log	long
gab	cab	rig	rid	big	bing
gum	come	goes	doze	hug	hung
good	could	got	dot	bag	bang
girl	curl	gun	done	rig	ring
meager	meeker	bigger	bidder	wig	wing

Note: the /g/ is mastered by children at about age four and is seldom misarticulated.

Fricatives

The fricative [frɪkətɪv] consonants of American-English are /h/, /ʍ/, /f/, /θ/, /s/, /ʃ/, /v/, /ð/, /z/, and /ʒ/. These sounds, sometimes called "spirates," require turbulence heard as audible friction. Some turbulence occurs as air flows through the glottis and pharynx. However, the primary sources of audible friction for consonants are the structures of the oral cavity: the lips, teeth, tongue, alveolar ridge, palate, and velum. Audible friction may occur either with the voiceless breath stream as in /h/, /ʍ/, /f/, /θ/, /s/, and /ʃ/, or combined with voicing as in /v/, /ð/, /z/, and /ʒ/. Several other speech sounds include some degree of friction in their production but are not dependent upon audible friction for their perception.

IPA   h
Dictionary   h Key Words: *he, ahead*
Northampton h-

/h/ PRODUCTION—Lingua-velar, Lingua-palatal Voiceless Fricative

With the velopharyngeal port closed, breath is directed through the oral cavity, which assumes the configuration of the adjacent vowel, with sufficient force to produce audible friction. The /h/ has no special formation of its own but changes with the vowels that surround it. In the initial position as in *he*, /h/ is produced as a voiceless fricative. In the intervocalic position, as in *ahead*, /h/ is usually produced as a voiced fricative [ḥ]. The /h/ is always followed by a vowel in English and is sometimes considered a glide because of its short duration. The relative lack of constriction in most vowel positions requires that breath be emitted with greater force than for other fricatives in order to make /h/ audible.

/h/ SPELLING—*h* is Primary Spelling

wh- in words *who, whose, whom, whole, whoop* has the [h] sound.
-gh- has the sound of /h/ in Celtic names such as *Callaghan, Caragher, Monoghan*, and is silent in the final position as in *Hugh*.
-h is not pronounced as a final consonant in exclamations *oh* and *ah*.
h- is silent in the words *honor, honest, honesty, honorary, hour, herb, heir*.

/h/ WORDS (The /h/ does not occur in the final position)

Initial		*Medial*	
he	high	ahead	unhook
his	how	behind	mahogany
hat	her	perhaps	anyhow
hoe	hen	rehearse	behold
hail	home	mohair	lighthouse
who	hook	behave	inhuman

/h/ SENTENCES

1. Perhaps he has a home ahead.
2. Unhitch Harold's heavy horse.
3. Who has a house on the highway?
4. Helen hoes her hollyhocks.
5. He hides behind the lighthouse.
6. How can he help the whole of humanity?

/h/ CONTRASTS

/ /—/h/		/h/—/ʍ/		/h/—/θ/	
eat	heat	hen	when	hatch	thatch
it	hit	high	why	high	thigh
ate	hate	heat	wheat	hum	thumb

air	hair	hay	whey	heard	third
you	hew	height	white	hick	thick
Ed	head	hitch	which	hump	thump
add	had	heather	whether	Hank	thank
ooze	whose	heel	wheel	heft	theft

Note: /h/ never occurs as a final sound in English. The cockney dialect pattern of intrusion and omission of /h/, associated with the East End of London, is not apparent in American-English. However, the omission of /h/ before [ju] is found among some speakers in such words as *humid, huge, human,* and *humor.* /h/ is mastered early by children and is seldom misarticulated.

In some phonetic literature, the /h/ is described as a "glottal" fricative, assuming that the source of audible friction is at the glottis. In other than whispered speech, the site of friction is primarily the velum and palate above and the tongue surface below. One can observe the difference between glottal friction and oral friction by alternately whispering [hi̯] and then producing [h] as it would be before a regular oral production of [hi]. In some speakers, part of the turbulence contributing to audible friction for /h/ may be produced at the glottis.

IPA   ʍ
Dictionary   hw, wh Key Words: *when, everywhere*
Northampton   wh

/ʍ/ PRODUCTION—Lingua-velar, Bilabial Voiceless Fricative

With the velopharyngeal post closed, the lips are rounded with a small aperture as for the vowel /u/ and may be slightly protruded, and the back of the tongue is raised toward the velum. Breath is directed through the oral cavity and through the constricted opening of the lips with sufficient force to produce audible friction. The /ʍ/ is sometimes considered a glide because of its brief duration. In the intervocalic position, as in *nowhere,* the /ʍ/ usually becomes a voiced fricative [ʍ̬].

/ʍ/ SPELLING—*wh*- is Primary Spelling

-*w*- following *s* as in *swim, swat, sway;* following *t* as in *twin, twirl, twenty,* and following *th* as in *thwart* has the /ʍ/ sound.

(s)u- produces a [ʍ] glide for *u* between [s] and another vowel as in *suede* [sʍeɪd], *persuade* [pɚsʍeɪd], *assuage* [əsʍeɪʒ].

/ʍ/ WORDS (The /ʍ/ does not occur in the final position)

Initial		*Medial*		*Clusters*	
where	while	anywhere	meanwhile	twelve	sweet
what	which	somewhere	erstwhile	twenty	swing
why	wheat	everywhere	afterwhile	twin	swag
when	wheel	elsewhere	worthwhile	twig	sway
whisper	whine	nowhere	somewhat	twinkle	sweat
whip	whale	overwhelm	horsewhip	thwart	schwa

/ʍ/ SENTENCES

1. Some*wh*ere the *wh*ite *wh*ale *s*wims.
2. *Wh*y do the t*w*enty t*w*in *wh*eels *wh*ine?
3. *Wh*at does *wh*eat sell for, mean*wh*ile?
4. The bob*wh*ite's *wh*istle continued a*wh*ile.
5. *Wh*ere is the *wh*ip *wh*en we need it?
6. *Wh*eeler goes no*wh*ere *wh*ile White goes every*wh*ere.

/ʍ/ CONTRASTS

/ʍ/—/w/		/ʍ/—/v/		/ʍ/—/h/	
where	wear	whine	vine	where	hair
whet	wet	why	vie	when	hen
what	watt	while	vile	what	hot
whine	wine	whale	veil	white	height
which	witch	wheel	veal	whale	hail
whey	way	whet	vet	wheat	heat
while	wile	where	very	wheel	heel
whether	weather	whence	vents	whim	him

Note: some American-English speakers habitually omit or reduce the friction and add voicing to the /ʍ/ so that it is closer to /ʍ/ or /w/, as in [wɛn] for [ʍɛn], or [waɪt] for [ʍaɪt]. In combinations such as *swim* and *twin*, some speakers may make the sound closer to [ʍ] for [sʍɪm] and [tʍɪn]. Continental Europeans frequently have difficulty learning this sound, often substituting the /v/ as in [vɛn] for [ʍɛn], or [vaɪt] for [ʍaɪt]. The /ʍ/ is one of the last sounds mastered by children and is among the most frequently misarticulated consonants.

IPA   f
Dictionary   f Key Words: *fan, leaf, coffee*
Northampton f (ph)

/f/ PRODUCTION—Labio-dental Voiceless Fricative

With the velopharyngeal port closed, the lower lip approximates the upper front teeth, and breath is continuously emitted between the teeth and lower lip as audible friction. The /f/ is usually of greater duration and produced with more force than /v/.

/f/ SPELLING—*f* is Primary Spelling

-ff- as in *off, coffee, waffle, office, staff, cuff* is given as a single [f]. When two /f/ sounds combine at the end of one word and beginning of another as in *half free*, the duration of the resulting single fricative is extended for [hæf:ri].

-gh as in *rough, laugh, enough, cough, trough* has the /f/ sound.

ph- as in *phone, philosophy, phonetics, aphasia, diphthong* has the /f/ sound.

-lf occurs rarely as /f/ with silent *l* as in *calf* and *half.*

/f/ WORDS

Initial		Medial		Final		Clusters
fun	fly	after	refer	if	beef	soft
feet	float	before	effort	off	cough	sifts
fast	flower	elephant	fifteen	wife	tough	reflect
field	free	coffee	office	puff	staff	laughs
four	frost	softly	different	laugh	loaf	surfed
five	friend	coughing	prophet	calf	safe	turfs

/f/ SENTENCES

1. Frank found a knife in the field.
2. The staff had coffee and waffles before flying to the office.
3. Francis studies phonetics and philosophy on Friday.
4. The flowers from the field float on the surf.
5. Four or five flags flew freely.
6. Fifteen different elephants followed his friend.

/f/ CONTRASTS

/f/—/v/		/f/—/θ/		/f/—/p/	
fine	vine	fought	thought	fast	past
safe	save	Fred	thread	fool	pool
belief	believe	fin	thin	fry	pry
surface	service	fret	threat	flee	plea
fat	vat	free	three	pheasant	peasant
file	vile	laugh	lath	laughed	lapped
feel	veal	first	thirst	leaf	leap
proof	prove	reef	wreath	from	prom

IPA   θ
Dictionary   th, th Key Words: *thin, tooth, nothing*
Northampton th

/θ/ PRODUCTION—Lingua-dental Voiceless Fricative

With the velopharyngeal port closed and the sides of the tongue against the molars, the tip of the tongue, spread wide and thin, approximates the edge or inner surface of the upper front teeth, and breath is continuously emitted between the front teeth and tongue to create audible friction. The /θ/ is of greater duration and produced with more force than /ð/.

/θ/ SPELLING—*th* is Only Spelling

-th as in *bath, teeth, birth, health, width, month,* and in compound words as in *bathtub, birthday, earthquake, faithful, healthy.*
    th(r) as in *three, through, throw, thread, threat.*
    th- as in *thin, think, thumb, thought,* and in compound words as in *something, anything, nothing.*
    -th- as in *author, arithmetic, athlete, ether.*

/θ/ WORDS

Initial		Medial		Final	
thin	three	arithmetic	anything	teeth	north
thaw	through	pathetic	birthday	oath	fourth
thank	threat	cathedral	faithful	growth	month

theater	theme	ether	earthquake	cloth	length
theft	third	ethics	something	booth	width
thud	thief	pathos	nothing	path	wealth

/θ/ SENTENCES

1. *Three thin* men came *through* our *theater*.
2. Every*thing* nor*th* or sou*th* will *thaw Thursday*.
3. We *think* some *thief* stole a *thousand things*.
4. A fai*thful* au*thor thinks through* his *theme*.
5. Great mon*thly* grow*th* of his mou*th* is a *threat* to heal*thy* tee*th*.
6. No*thing* is so pa*thetic* as a *thirsty athletic youth*.

/θ/ CONTRASTS

/θ/—/ð/		/θ/—/t/		/θ/—/s/	
thin	this	thin	tin	thin	sin
theme	these	thick	tick	thank	sank
throw	though	three	tree	thaw	saw
ether	either	thinker	tinker	theme	seem
booth	booths	thought	taught	path	pass
teeth	teethe	bath	bat	growth	gross
wreath	wreathe	both	boat	lath	lass
thigh	thy	faithful	fateful	faith	face

Note: the /θ/ is acoustically one of the weakest speech sounds. It is one of the last sounds mastered by children and is among the most frequently misarticulated consonants. The /θ/ is very difficult for most foreign born speakers to learn, present only in English, Gaelic, Greek, and Spanish among European languages. The /t/ or /s/ are frequent substitutions by foreign speakers.

IPA   s
Dictionary   s Key Words: *see, makes, upset*
Northampton   s (c before i, e, y)

/s/ PRODUCTION

There are two prevalent formations for American-English /s/. The lingua-alveolar position is more common than is the lingua-dental formation.

Alveolar /s/—Lingua-alveolar Voiceless Fricative (tongue tip up position)

With the velopharyngeal port closed and the sides of the tongue against the upper molars, the tip of the tongue, narrowly grooved, approximates the alveolar ridge just behind the upper incisors, and breath is continuously directed through the narrow aperture between the alveolar ridge and the grooved tip of the tongue against the closely approximated front teeth with audible friction.

Dental /s/—Lingua-dental Voiceless Fricative (tongue tip down position)

With the velopharyngeal port closed and the sides of the tongue against the upper molars, the tip of the tongue approximates the lower incisors near the gum ridge, and the front of the tongue, slightly grooved, is raised toward the alveolar ridge and forms a narrow aperture through which breath is continuously directed against the closely approximated front teeth with audible friction.

/s/ SPELLING—s is Primary Spelling (Extremely variable, sometimes pronounced /z/ as in *business*, /ʒ/ as in *leisure*, and /ʃ/ as in *sugar*)

-*ss* as in *assess, kiss, lass, message, cross, assume* has a single /s/ sound.

-*s* as a plural form, past tense or possessive is /s/ after voiceless consonants (other than *s*) as in *apes, cats, lasts, laughs, cat's, Jack's.*

c-(*i, e, y*) has the /s/ sound as in *city, excite, pencil; fence, cent, accent; cycle, cytology, mercy.*

ps- with a silent *p* is /s/ in *psychology, pseudo-,* and *psalm.*

sc-(*i, e, y*) has the /s/ sound as in *science, scissors; scent, scene, scythe.*

-*st*- with a silent *t* is /s/ in *hasten, listen, fasten, Christmas.*

Less frequently, the /s/ occurs for -*z* as in *waltz* and *quartz*, and as *sch*- in *schism.*

-*x*- forms a derived affricate [ks] in such words as *tax, six, box, taxi, hexagon,* and *rex.*

/s/ WORDS

Initial		Medial		Final		Clusters
see	skin	basket	lesson	us	bats	wasps
swim	spring	Christmas	missile	boss	tops	gasps
slow	splash	fasten	possible	miss	beaks	mists
small	straw	history	basin	this	laughs	beasts
speak	scream	recent	gasoline	horse	else	asks
stay	square	license	asleep	peace	once	risks

/s/ SENTENCES

1. Six boats sped outside the limits.
2. Some nests would soon be destroyed.
3. The message crossed the sea swiftly.
4. Sarah signed for a gasoline license.
5. Psychology may be a science associated with excitement.
6. Jack's cats scooted against the fence.

/s/ CONTRASTS

/s/—/z/		/s/—/θ/		/s/—/ʃ/	
sue	zoo	sin	thin	seat	sheet
seal	zeal	sank	thank	sock	shock
racer	razor	saw	thaw	seep	sheep
lacer	laser	seem	theme	cast	cashed
fleece	flees	pass	path	fasten	fashion
price	prize	gross	growth	gas	gash
bus	buzz	lass	lath	mass	mash
loose	lose	face	faith	Swiss	swish

Note: the /s/ is among the most frequently misarticulated consonants, produced variously toward /θ/ (lisping) or toward /ʃ/. It is degraded by abnormal dentition and often with dentures, and is one of the first sounds affected by hearing loss. The /s/ is one of the most frequently occurring consonants in American-English speech.

IPA ʃ
Dictionary sh, sh Key Words: *she, fish, sunshine*
Northampton sh

/ʃ/ PRODUCTION—Lingua-palatal Voiceless Fricative

With the velopharyngeal port closed and without voice, the sides of the tongue are against the upper molars, the broad front surface of the tongue is raised toward the palate just back of the alveolar ridge, forming a central aperture slightly broader and farther back than for /s/, to direct the breath stream continuously through and against the slightly open front teeth as audible friction. The lips are usually slightly rounded and protruded, approximating the position for /ʊ/.

/ʃ/ SPELLING—*sh* is Primary Spelling

s as in *sure, sugar, sumac, insurance.*
-*c*- as in *ocean, specie, facial, special, racial, social.*
-*ss*- as in *assure, fissure, issue, mission, Russian.*
ch as in *machine, chic, crochet, mustache, creche.*
-*t(ion)* as in *nation, action, relation, phonation.*

Less frequently as *sch*- in *schist, schwa, schnapps*; -*sc*- as in *fascist, fascia,* and *conscience*; -*chs*- as in *fuchsia,* and -*x*- as in *anxious.*

In the following adjectival suffixes: -*c(ious)* as in *precious, delicious;* -*t(ious)* as in *facetious, fractious*; -*c(eous)* as in *sebaceous*; -*s(eous)* as in *nauseous,* and -*sc(ious)* as in *conscious.*

/ʃ/ WORDS

Initial		Medial		Final	
sheep	shop	fashion	wishes	mash	radish
shall	shake	bushel	fished	harsh	English
should	shed	ashamed	rushing	wish	splash
shoe	shower	ocean	pusher	push	foolish
shut	shrink	assure	insure	fresh	establish
ship	shrub	nation	machine	crush	relish

/ʃ/ SENTENCES

1. She washed the shirt in the shower.
2. The nations gave assurance to shed racial persecution.
3. Her facial expressions should show emotion.
4. The English shining brush kept his shoes shipshape.
5. Bashful Shirley shrank from social relations.
6. Washing machines are precious in Russian shops.

/ʃ/ CONTRASTS

/ʃ/—/ʒ/		/ʃ/—/s/		/ʃ/—/tʃ/	
glacier	glazier	sheet	seat	sheep	cheap
Aleutian	allusion	shock	sock	ship	chip
assure	azure	sheep	seep	chic	cheek
pressure	pleasure	cashed	cast	marsh	march
vacation	occasion	fashion	fasten	wash	watch
fuchsia	fusion	gash	gas	wish	witch

vicious	vision	mash	mass	dishes	ditches
dilution	delusion	swish	Swiss	washed	watched

Note: the /ʃ/ is degraded by abnormal dentition and often with dentures. Spanish speakers are likely to substitute /tʃ/. Some Europeans may make the /ʃ/ too far back on the palate, or may round and protrude the lips to a greater degree than for the American-English /ʃ/.

IPA   v
Dictionary   v Key Words: *vine, have, ever*
Northampton v

/v/ PRODUCTION—Labio-dental Voiced Fricative

With the velopharyngeal port closed, the lower lip approximates the upper front teeth, and voice is continuously emitted between the teeth and lip with enough force to create audible friction combined with voicing. The /v/ is shorter in duration and usually produced with less force than /f/. In termination of an utterance, the /v/ has a breath finish.

/v/ SPELLING—*v* is Only Spelling (With the exception of *-f* in *of* and variable voicing of *-ph* in **Stephen**)

Rare spelling of *-vv-* occurs in the slang words *flivver* and *savvy*. The *-lv* occurs with the *l* silent in *salve, halves, calves*. Intervocalic *-w-* is /v/ for most Hawaiian words (see Chapter VII).

/v/ WORDS

Initial		*Medial*		*Final*	
vine	vowel	ever	servant	have	believe
very	vault	over	fervor	gave	weave
view	vice	river	velvet	live	twelve
vote	vain	divide	envisage	glove	delve
vow	value	heavy	invite	groove	serve
visit	voice	knives	advantage	move	carve

/v/ SENTENCES

1. The river divides the village we visited.
2. Have you voted in the seventy-seventh district?

3. A *v*ariety *of* ele*v*en *v*egetables gi*v*es a *v*ery hea*v*y flavor.
4. He car*v*ed the *v*eal and ser*v*ed the gra*v*y.
5. Di*v*ide ele*v*en by fi*v*e and twel*v*e by se*v*en.
6. The bra*v*e ser*v*ant do*v*e o*v*er the wa*v*es.

/v/ CONTRASTS

/v/—/f/

van	fan
vine	fine
save	safe
prove	proof
vile	file
live	life
veal	feel
service	surface

/v/—/ð/

van	than
vat	that
veil	they'll
lave	lathe
cave	scathe
ever	weather
glover	brother
fever	either

/v/—/b/

very	berry
vest	best
vote	boat
given	gibbon
saver	saber
vow	bow
calves	cabs
serve	Serb

/v/—/w/

vane	wane
very	wary
vest	west
vent	went
vee	we
vail	wail
vet	wet
vaults	waltz

Note: the /v/ is mastered late by children, much later than /f/, and is misarticulated with moderate frequency. Spanish speakers may substitute /b/ for initial /v/ and produce the voiced bilabial fricative /β/ in medial positions.

IPA   ð
Dictionary   ~~th~~, <u>th</u>, t̶h̶ Key Words: *the, bathe, bother*
Northampton ẗh

/ð/ PRODUCTION—Lingua-dental Voiced Fricative

With the velopharyngeal port closed and the sides of the tongue against the molars, the tip of the tongue approximates the edge or inner surface of the upper front teeth, and voice is continuously emitted between the teeth and tongue with enough force to create audible friction combined with voicing. The /ð/ is usually shorter in duration and produced with less force than /θ/. In termination of an utterance, the /ð/ has a breath finish.

/ð/ SPELLING—*th* is Only Spelling (Frequently has the sound of /θ/)

th- occurs as /ð/ in a few words that are used frequently as in *the, this, that, they, them, then, there, these, those, their.*
-*th* rarely occurs as /ð/ as it does in *smooth* and *with*.
-*th(e)* as in *bathe, teethe, soothe, loathe, scythe, breathe*.
-*th(er)* as in *bother, either, mother, father, feather, another*.
-*th(ing)* as in *breathing, bathing, clothing, mouthing, soothing*.
-*th(s)* has the /ð/ sound when a final /θ/ is pluralized by *s* as in *moth–moths, mouth–mouths, booth–booths*.

/ð/ WORDS

Initial		Medial		Final	
the	these	bother	other	soothe	smooth
this	though	weather	lather	bathe	with
that	those	rather	feather	tithe	breathe
they	there	either	bathing	clothe	loathe
them	thus	father	soothing	lathe	wreathe
than	then	mother	although	teethe	seethe

/ð/ SENTENCES

1. *These* fea*th*ers bo*th*er *th*em.
2. *They* buy *th*is lea*th*er in *th*ose boo*th*s.
3. Fa*th*er and mo*th*er are *th*ere.
4. *They* ba*th*e wi*th* soo*th*ing la*th*er.
5. O*th*er ba*th*ers swim wi*th* smoo*th* brea*th*ing.
6. *The* mo*th*s fly ei*th*er *th*is way or *th*at.

/ð/ CONTRASTS

/ð/—/θ/		/ð/—/d/		/ð/—/v/	
this	thin	then	den	than	van
these	theme	those	doze	that	vat
though	throw	they	day	they'll	veil
either	ether	though	dough	either	fever
booths	booth	wreathe	reed	lathe	lave
teethe	teeth	father	fodder	scathe	cave

wreathe	wreath	lather	ladder	brother	glover
thy	thigh	there	dare	weather	ever

Note: the /ð/ is one of the last sounds mastered by children and is among the most frequently misarticulated consonants. /ð/ occurs very frequently in speech and *the* is among the most common words spoken. The /ð/ is very difficult for most foreign born speakers to learn, present only in English, Spanish, and Danish among European languages.

IPA   z
Dictionary z Key Words: *zoo, size, lazy*
Northampton z

/z/ PRODUCTION

There are two prevalent formations for American-English /z/. The lingua-alveolar position is more common than the lingua-dental formation. In termination of an utterance, the /z/ has a breath finish.

Alveolar /z/—Lingua-alveolar Voiced Fricative (tongue tip up position)

With the velopharyngeal port closed and the sides of the tongue against the upper molars, the tip of the tongue, narrowly grooved, approximates the alveolar ridge just behind the upper incisors, and combined voice and breath are continuously directed through the narrow aperture between the alveolar ridge and the grooved tip of the tongue against the closely approximated front teeth with audible friction. Duration and breath pressure is usually less than for /s/.

Dental /z/—Lingua-dental Voiced Fricative (tongue tip down position)

With the velopharyngeal port closed and the sides of the tongue against the upper molars, the tip of the tongue approximates the lower incisors near the gum ridge; the front of the tongue, slightly grooved, is raised toward the alveolar ridge and forms a narrow aperture through which combined voice and breath are continuously directed against the closely approximated front teeth with audible friction. Duration and breath pressure are usually less than for /s/.

/z/ SPELLING—z Is Most Consistent Spelling (s occurs more frequently for /z/)

z as in *zoo, zebra, hazel, lazy, glaze, breeze.*

-zz- as in *dazzle, muzzle, buzz, jazz* has a single /z/ sound.

s as in *close, rise, chasm, is, was, his, bruise*; and in plural forms, past tense, or possessives after voiced consonants, vowels, /s/, /ʃ/, or /tʃ/ as in *dogs, runs, man's, boy's, kisses, washes,* and *matches.*

Less frequently, the /z/ occurs as -ss- in *scissors*, -sth- in *asthma*, and as initial x in such words as *xylophone, Xavier,* and *Xanadau.*

-x- forms a secondary affricate [gz] in such words as *exit, exist,* and *examine.*

/z/ WORDS

Initial		Medial		Final		
zoo	zebra	easy	visit	buzz	is	webs
zipper	zinc	dozen	nozzle	jazz	was	adds
zeal	zenith	music	dazzle	breeze	these	eggs
zephyr	zany	hazard	puzzle	use	those	dolls
zone	zen	rosin	dozed	eyes	songs	homes
zero	zodiac	weasel	busy	nose	gives	pans

/z/ SENTENCES

1. These eyes are the eyes of a weasel.
2. Zen and the zodiac are at their zenith these days.
3. A dozen zoo zebras graze lazily.
4. Music dazzled those busy boys.
5. His zipper was used easily.
6. The poison posed a hazard to these trees.

/z/ CONTRASTS

/z/—/s/		/z/—/ð/		/z/—/ʒ/	
zoo	sue	bays	bathe	bays	beige
zeal	seal	breeze	breathe	lows	loge
razor	racer	close	clothe	rues	rouge
laser	lacer	tease	teethe	Caesar	seizure
flees	fleece	lays	lathe	tease	prestige
prize	price	seas	seethe	reason	lesion
buzz	bus	rise	writhe	hazard	azure
lose	loose	ties	tithe	desert	measure

Note: the /z/ is one of the last consonants mastered by children and is among the most frequently misarticulated consonants, produced variously toward /ð/ (lisping) or toward /ʒ/. Some Europeans, particularly Spanish and Swedish speakers, may substitute /s/ regularly. The /z/ is degraded by abnormal dentition and often with dentures.

IPA   ʒ
Dictionary   zh, zh Key Words: *vision, beige*
Northampton zh

/ʒ/ PRODUCTION—Lingua-palatal Voiced Fricative

With the velopharyngeal port closed and the sides of the tongue against the upper molars, the broad front surface of the tongue is raised toward the palate just back of the alveolar ridge, forming a central aperture slightly broader and farther back than for /z/, to direct voice continuously through and against the slightly open front teeth with enough force to create audible friction combined with voicing.

/ʒ/ SPELLING

There is no alphabet symbol consistently and especially associated with /ʒ/. The most frequent symbol is *s*.

-s- as in *vision, occasion, usual, casual, measure, lesion, usury, aphasia, Asia*.

-g(e) as in *beige, loge, garage, regime, rouge, menage, assuage, prestige*.

-z- as in *azure, brazier, seizure*.

/ʒ/ WORDS—Does not occur initially in English

Medial		*Final*	
vision	aphasia	beige	corsage
usual	usury	loge	menage
occasion	treasure	garage	prestige
casual	division	rouge	montage
measure	seizure	assuage	persiflage
lesion	regime	camouflage	collage

/ʒ/ SENTENCES

1. His leisure brought unusual pleasure.
2. The envisioned Persian treasure was a delusion.
3. Occasionally decisions lead to confusion.
4. The garage was camouflaged in beige.
5. The collision and explosion caused a lesion affecting his vision.
6. The treasurer measured usury rates.

/ʒ/ CONTRASTS

/ʒ/—/ʃ/		/ʒ/—/ʤ/	
glazier	glacier	pleasure	pledger
allusion	Aleutian	lesion	legion
azure	assure	prestige	vestige
pleasure	pressure	vision	pidgeon
occasion	vacation	Asia	aged
fusion	fuchsia	assuage	cage
vision	vicious	rouge	huge
delusion	dilution	collision	religion

Note: the /ʒ/ is one of the last developed and mastered consonants, and one of the least frequently occurring sounds in English.

Affricates

The affricate [ǽfrɪkət] sounds are sometimes called "stop-fricatives" because they combine a stop immediately followed by a fricative on the same impulse. During the stop phase, the fricative position is anticipated by tongue and lip movement so that the air stream is aspirated directly and immediately into the position of the fricative. The affricate phonemes of American-English are /ʧ/ and /ʤ/. Connecting the stop and the fricative symbols into a single written symbol emphasizes that the affricate is a phoneme and is made on a single impulse. The stop and fricative portions of each of these phonemes are **homorganic**, that is, they are produced at the same place of articulation. These two affricates can also initiate an utterance in American-English as, for example, in *chin* and *just*. An affricate, to be considered a phoneme in our speech, must be homorganic and able to initiate an utterance. A number of other affricates occur in speech, which are derived from **coarticulation**—that is, from producing two sounds in sequence so that they influence how each other is produced. Such derived affricates are considered a cluster of consonants rather than a phoneme. For

example, the commonly derived affricate of [ts] as in *bits,* although the stop
and fricative portions are homorganic, is not a combination that can begin an
utterance in American-English (as it does in *tsetse* [tsɛ́tsi] of Bantu origin).
Other examples of derived affricates are the [kʍ] as in *queen* and the [ks] in
box. They are not articulated in a homorganic position, and even though they
are associated with alphabet symbols *qu* and *x,* respectively, they are not
considered phonemes. The derived affricates are written with separated IPA
symbols.

IPA   ʧ
Dictionary   ch, c̪h Key Words: *chair, such, teacher*
Northampton ch (tch)

/ʧ/ PRODUCTION—Lingua-alveolar, Lingua-palatal Voiceless Affricate

With the velopharyngeal port closed and the sides of the tongue against
the upper molars, the tip of the tongue closes on or just behind the alveolar
ridge; air held and compressed in the oral cavity is exploded as audible
breath through the broad aperture between the alveolar ridge and front of
the tongue, directing the breath stream through and against the slightly
open front teeth as audible friction. The position is essentially that for the /ʃ/
except that instead of the steady flow of breath for friction, breath is compressed by the tongue closure slightly farther back on the alveolar ridge than
for the /t/, and breath is released more slowly but with greater pressure than
for the /t/. This affricate is produced with a single impulse of breath, even
though it includes components of both the /t/ and the /ʃ/ sounds.

/ʧ/ SPELLING—*ch* is Primary Spelling

-*tch* as in *watch, match, catch, crutch, kitchen.*
-*t(ure)* as in *fracture, nature, furniture, lecture.*
-*t(ion)* as in *bastion, mention, convention, question.*
-*(n)s(ion)* with an intruded /t/ for [nʧ] as in *mansion, tension, scansion,
pension.*
-*t(u)-* as in *virtue, factual, obituary, natural, mortuary.*
Infrequently with *c-* as in *cello; -t(eous)* as in *righteous.*

/ʧ/ WORDS

	Initial		Medial		Final
chop	cherry	kitchen	bachelor	watch	each
choose	cheese	nature	fatuous	march	such

change	chase	mention	natural	church	rich
chin	children	mansion	election	branch	latch
chair	check	virtue	capture	lunch	coach
child	chapter	riches	peaches	which	wretch

/tʃ/ SENTENCES

1. The *ch*ildren *ch*ose pea*ch*es for lun*ch*.
2. Whi*ch* vir*t*ue ma*tch*es his ri*ch*es?
3. With a ma*tch*, he sear*ch*ed for the bu*tch*er's *ch*airs.
4. Na*t*ure's man*s*ions are tha*tch*ed by her bran*ch*es.
5. The ba*ch*elor's ki*tch*en was *ch*eerful.
6. The *ch*urch mouse sear*ch*ed for *ch*eese.

/tʃ/ CONTRASTS

/tʃ/—/dʒ/		/tʃ/—/ʃ/		/tʃ/—/t/	
cheap	jeep	cheap	sheep	chime	time
batches	badges	chip	ship	chin	tin
lunch	lunge	cheek	chic	chew	too
chain	Jane	march	marsh	beach	beat
chin	gin	watch	wash	each	eat
chunk	junk	witch	wish	pitch	pit
choke	joke	ditches	dishes	match	mat
chug	jug	watched	washed	kitchen	kitten

Note: the /tʃ/ is among consonants frequently misarticulated. French speakers are likely to substitute /ʃ/.

IPA   dʒ
Dictionary   j Key Words: *jam, edge, enjoy*
Northampton   j

/dʒ/ PRODUCTION—Lingua-alveolar, Lingua-palatal Voiced Affricate

With the velopharyngeal port closed and the sides of the tongue against the upper molars, the tip of the tongue closes on or just behind the alveolar ridge; with accompanying voice, air held and compressed in the oral cavity is released through the broad aperture between the alveolar ridge and front of the tongue, directing the breath stream through and against the slightly open front teeth as combined voice and audible friction. The position is essentially that for /tʃ/ except that the production is accompanied by voice and given with slightly less force. The affricate is produced with a single impulse of breath, even though it includes components of both the /d/ and the /ʒ/ sounds.

/dʒ/ SPELLING

j is the most common spelling in the initial position with a variety of spellings in the intervocalic and final positions.

j- as in *judge, jail, jealous, jewel, juice.*
-dg(e) as in *edge, lodge, ridge, judge, badger.*
g(*i, e, y*) as in *tragic, engine; gem, gauge; gypsy, gymnasium.*
-dj- as in *adjust, adjourn, adjoin.*
-d- as in *cordial, gradual, soldier.*
-gg- as in *exaggerate.*

/dʒ/ WORDS

Initial		*Medial*		*Final*	
jam	giant	lodges	adjourn	age	village
jaw	gem	badger	soldier	edge	bridge
joy	gentle	tragic	exaggerate	gauge	cottage
jump	general	agent	gradual	ledge	college
jelly	gene	agitate	enjoy	orange	judge
Jim	gyrate	adjust	angel	urge	strange

/dʒ/ SENTENCES

1. The *ju*d*ge* and *j*ury *g*au*g*ed the lo*g*ic of his ple*dge.*
2. *J*ohn asked *J*ames for *j*uice and *j*am with his oran*g*e.
3. The mana*g*er said the lar*g*e *j*et en*g*ine was of avera*g*e *age.*
4. Hu*g*e pa*g*es of lan*g*uage *g*ave an ima*g*e of ma*j*estic le*g*ends.
5. *J*ack lo*dg*ed in the re*g*ion of the sol*d*iers.
6. *G*inger and *J*ane *j*ust *j*oked about the *g*iant cabba*g*e.

/dʒ/ CONTRASTS

/dʒ/—/tʃ/		/dʒ/—/j/		/dʒ/—[dz]	
jeep	cheap	juice	use	budge	buds
badges	batches	joke	yoke	rage	raids
lunge	lunch	Jack	yak	siege	seeds
Jane	chain	Jello	yellow	wage	wades

gin	chin	jail	Yale	wedge	weds
junk	chunk	jam	yam	age	aids
joke	choke	jet	yet	hedge	heads
jug	chug	Jew	you	ridge	rids

Oral Resonants

These consonants depend primarily upon alterations of resonating cavities for their production, rather than upon friction or interruption of the air stream. The process of resonation was described in Chapter II. By dropping or raising the mandible, elevating or lowering the tongue, and varying the opening and rounding of the lips while the velopharyngeal port is closed, the sound of phonation produced at the glottis is selectively changed to amplify certain bands of acoustic energy while reducing others. All vowels are resonant sounds, and a number of resonant consonant sounds are sometimes called "semi-vowels," or "vowelized" consonants, because of their similarity. The oral resonant consonant phonemes of American English are /w/, /j/, /l/, and /r/. These consonants are often given a second order designation, based on variations in their manner of production, to distinguish them from vowel sounds. The /w/ and /j/ are referred to as **glides** because of their rapid movement into a following vowel sound. The /l/ is called a **lateral** sound, since its position with the narrowed point of the tongue closed against the alveolar ridge forces emission of the voice laterally around both sides of the tongue. The /r/ may be called a **retroflex** sound when it is produced so that the tongue tip flexes toward the back of the oral cavity.

IPA   w
Dictionary   w Key Words: *we, awake*
Northampton w-

/w/ PRODUCTION—Lingua-velar Bilabial Oral Resonant Glide

With the velopharyngeal port closed, the lips are rounded for an aperture slightly smaller than for the vowel /u/ and may be slightly protruded. The tongue is elevated in the back of the mouth as for /u/. Voice is directed through the oral cavity and the rounded lips for a brief period, gliding into the position of the vowel that follows. No audible friction is created so that /w/ is not simply the voiced cognate of /ʍ/. Size of the /w/ lip aperture can be sensed in the syllable [wu]. The /w/ is of short duration and is always released into a vowel.

/w/ SPELLING—*w* is Primary Spelling

o- as in *one, once, everyone, anyone,* and *someone.*

-(ng)u- A [w] glide occurs for *u* in *language* [læŋgwɪʤ], *linguist,* [lɪŋgwɪst], *languish* [læŋgwɪʃ]. The [w] intrusion also occurs in *memoirs* [mɛmwɑrz].

-u- A [w] glide may intrude between the rounded high back vowels [u] or [ʊ], and following vowels in connected speech, as in *you all* [juwɔl], *no easy* [nouwizɪ], *now it* [nauwɪt].

w is silent in *who, whole, write, wrinkle, sword, answer.*

/w/ WORDS (The /w/ does not occur in the final position)

Initial		Medial		Clusters
we	wash	away	unwind	dwell
way	weed	always	seaweed	dwarf
were	won	anyone	jewel	dwelling
wet	one	forward	backward	dwindle
wood	would	inkwell	sandwich	Dwight
winter	wise	reward	otherwise	Gwendolyn

/w/ SENTENCES

1. We went away last week.
2. William awoke wet in the windy warm weather.
3. We went wading in the water anyway.
4. The west window was washed for the winter.
5. Everyone always works well on the wagon.
6. Warren dwells west of the woods.

/w/ CONTRASTS

/w/—/ʍ/		/w/—/r/		/w/—/v/	
wear	where	wed	red	wane	vane
wet	whet	wake	rake	wary	very
watt	what	wade	raid	west	vest
wine	whine	wise	rise	went	vent
witch	which	one	run	we	vee
way	whey	wave	rave	wail	veil
wile	while	witch	rich	wet	vet
weather	whether	wove	rove	waltz	vaults

Note: the /w/ is mastered early by children and is seldom misarticulated.

IPA   j
Dictionary   y Key Words: *yes, canyon*
Northampton y-

/j/ PRODUCTION—Lingua-palatal Oral Resonant Glide

With the velopharyngeal port closed and the tip of the tongue behind the lower front teeth, the front of the tongue is raised high toward the palate and voice is directed through the oral cavity for a brief period as the tongue and lips take the position of the following vowel sound with continued voicing. The lips may be slightly pulled back with the raised tongue. Tongue-palate aperture is slightly smaller and farther back than for the vowel /i/. Note the difference in *ye* [ji]. The /j/ is of short duration and is always released into a vowel.

/j/ SPELLING—*y* is Primary Spelling

-i- as in *onion, pinion, William, union, million, stallion, familiar, view.*
u- blending with [u] for *use* [juz], *union, utilize, cute.*
ew blending with [u] for *few* [fju], *ewe, pew.*
ue blending with [u] for *fuel* [fjul], and *eu* as in *feud.*
Rarely as *-j-* in *hallelujah, -g(n)-* as in *poignant.*
The /j/ is often intrusive between words ending in /i/ or /ɪ/ and those beginning with a vowel as in *see it* [sijɪt], *die out* [daɪjaʊt], and *stay in* [steɪjɪn].

/j/ WORDS (The /j/ does not occur in the final position)

Initial		*Medial*	
yard	young	onion	barnyard
year	yacht	loyal	familiar
yes	yield	minion	canyon
yet	yellow	bullion	few
yolk	use	beyond	cute
yarn	unit	million	William

/j/ SENTENCES

1. The *y*oung *y*eoman from *Y*ork was lo*y*al.
2. The can*y*ons be*y*ond are famil*i*ar.

3. Daniel *y*earned to have a *y*ellow *y*acht.
4. *Y*our opin*i*on is pecul*i*ar.
5. *Y*esterday the *y*oungsters were compan*i*ons.
6. Will*i*am's on*i*ons are mixed with *y*east and egg *y*olks.

/j/ CONTRASTS

/j/—/w/		/j/—/ /		/j/—/ʤ/	
yet	wet	yam	am	yam	jam
yoke	woke	year	ear	yell	jell
yield	wield	yearn	earn	yacht	jot
yell	well	Yale	ale	yet	jet
yes	Wes	yoke	oak	yak	jack
yaks	wax	yeast	east	yawn	John
Yale	wail	yawning	awning	yoke	joke
yacht	watt	canyon	cannon	year	jeer

Note: the /j/, when released into /u/, is sometimes considered to form a glide-vowel combination or diphthong [ju], as in *use, cute, you,* and *few.*

IPA   l
Dictionary   l Key Words: *low, bowl, color*
Northampton l

/l/ PRODUCTION—Lingua-alveolar Lateral Oral Resonant

With the velopharyngeal port closed, the point of the tongue (see Figure II–4) closes with slight pressure against the alveolar ridge with opening on both sides, as voice escapes around the tongue and out the oral cavity. The mouth opening is that for the preceding or following vowels. The /l/ is voiced when it initiates a syllable and when it is preceded by a voiced consonant ([bl], [gl]) in the same syllable. It is given partially without voice, especially near the point of juncture, when it is preceded by a voiceless consonant in the same syllable ([pl̥], [kl̥], [sl̥], [fl̥]) except in *s-l* clusters (*splash, sclerosis*) where the stop is unreleased.

When /l/ follows homorganic consonants /t/, /d/, or /n/, the tongue tip remains on the alveolar ridge, narrowing to a point as the sides of the tongue pull to center for lateral emission of voice, as in *handle* [hændl̩]. When /l/ is the final consonant following another consonant (*cable* [keɪbl̩], *angle* [æŋgl̩], *bottle* [bɑtl̩], *gavel* [gævl̩]), the /l/ may become a semi-vowel and be produced with the duration of a syllable. As the initial consonant (*lay*) or in a consonant blend (*play*), the /l/ has the very brief duration of a glide.

/l/ SPELLING—*l* is Primary Spelling

ll as in *all, fall, follow, million, llama, Lloyd* has a single /l/ sound.
-le as in *bottle, valuable, little, middle, table, people.*
-el as in *pommel, funnel, gavel, kennel.*
-sl- with silent *s* as in *island, isle, aisle, Carlisle.*
-ln with silent *n* as in *kiln.*
The *l* is silent in *palm, balm, talk, walking, calf, halves.*

/l/ WORDS

Initial		*Medial*		*Final*	
lay	loose	tulip	dollar	oil	bell
leaf	lunch	eleven	William	owl	fall
low	lamb	family	yellow	hole	able
like	leg	lily	fellow	school	uncle
lion	lift	always	selling	all	gavel
loud	log	along	teller	mill	motel

/l/ SENTENCES

1. While flying, he will have a cool bottle of milk.
2. Eagles fly aloft easily in glorious splendor.
3. Ronald's dollars were obligated for clothes and blankets.
4. The class wrote well in the middle of the school blackboard.
5. Twelve healthy girls helped build Uncle William's wall.
6. The child sold old pencils as cold bleak snowflakes fell.

/l/ CONTRASTS

/l/—/w/		/l/—/r/		/l/—/n/	
leap	weep	lies	rise	line	nine
leak	week	lair	rare	low	no
led	wed	late	rate	let	net
let	wet	blew	brew	bowl	bone
lake	wake	glow	grow	slow	snow
sleep	sweep	flank	frank	willing	winning
slim	swim	cloud	crowd	towel	town
sleet	sweet	play	pray	tell	ten

Note: the /l/ is mastered late by children, with /w/ substitution common, but it is seldom misarticulated later in life. Europeans may articulate /l/ forward off the upper teeth rather than farther back off the alveolar ridge. Orientals produce a sound [l] with the tongue point touching behind the alveolar ridge giving impression of an /r/ substitution.

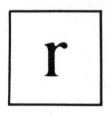

IPA   r
Dictionary   r   Key Words: *red, bar, oral*
Northampton r

/r/ PRODUCTION—Lingua-palatal Oral Resonant

The essence of /r/ is intrusion of the tongue high in the oral cavity without contacting the roof of the mouth. There are two prevalent formations for American-English /r/. The tongue tip up position is more common than the tongue tip down position.

Tongue tip up position: with the velopharyngeal port closed and the sides of the tongue against the upper molars, the tongue tip is raised toward the palate just behind the alveolar ridge but without contact; voice escapes between the tongue and palate-alveolar ridge and out the oral cavity. The lips may be slightly protruded similar to /ʊ/ but usually take the position of the surrounding vowels. If the tongue tip is curled back toward the palate, it is referred to as a "retroflex" /r/.

Tongue tip down position: with the velopharyngeal port closed and the sides of the tongue against the upper molars, the front of the tongue is raised toward the palate with the tip neutral or pointing downward; voice escapes between the tongue and palate-alveolar ridge and out the oral cavity. The lips may be slightly protruded similar to /ʊ/ but usually take the position of the surrounding vowels.

The /r/ is voiced when it initiates a syllable and when it is preceded by a voiced consonant ([br], [gr], [dr]) in the same syllable. It is given partially without voice, especially near the point of juncture, when it is preceded by a voiceless consonant in the same syllable ([pr̥], [tr̥], [kr̥], [fr̥], [ʃr̥], [θr̥]) except in *s-r* clusters (*scratch, spring, string*) where the stop is unreleased. Following lingua-alveolar consonants /t/ and /d/ as in *try* and *dry*, the /r/ is produced as a fricative.

/r/ SPELLING—*r* is Primary Spelling

rr as in *barrel, ferry, horrible, burr, whirr, purr* has a single /r/ sound.
wr- as in *write, wrecker, wring, wrought, wren, wrist.*

rh- as in *rhinocerous, rhinology, rhyme, rhythmic, Rhesus.*
Rarely as *-rrh* in *catarrh*, *-rt-* in *mortgage*, *-rps* in *corps.*

/r/ WORDS

Initial		Medial		Final	
ran	write	very	marry	car	or
red	wrist	around	terrible	air	dear
rock	wren	orange	berry	four	chair
rub	rhyme	story	arrow	near	are
rake	right	bedroom	carrot	fire	dare
rose	room	already	sorry	hair	bar

/r/ SENTENCES

1. Around the rugged rock the ragged rascal ran.
2. Mary and George are crying.
3. The barbecued ribs brought forth hungry truck drivers.
4. April's strong threatening rains shrank their garments.
5. Three chairs are in the orange room.
6. Sarah wrote for radio about tomorrow's race.

/r/ CONTRASTS

/r/—/w/		/r/—/l/		/r/—/ɜ˞/ or /ɚ/	
reap	weep	rise	lies	train	terrain
run	won	rare	lair	bray	beret
red	wed	rate	late	dress	duress
rate	wait	brew	blew	crest	caressed
rail	wail	grow	glow	broke	baroque
reek	week	frank	flank	throw	thorough
train	twain	crowd	cloud	creed	curried
trig	twig	pray	play	crowed	corrode

Note: during development of /r/, a /w/ substitution is common among children and may persist as sub-standard speech into adulthood. Some foreign speakers may use a trilled [r̃], or the one-tap trill of British inter-vocalic [ɾ], which may make *very* [vɛrɪ] sound like [vɛdɪ]. Orientals produce a sound /l/ with the tongue point touching behind the alveolar ridge, giving the impression of an /l/ substitution. General American preconsonantal /r/ as in *park* or *first* and final /r/ as in *bar* or *more* are either omitted or replaced by a vowel in New England and Southern speech.

There are two American-English vowels with /r/ quality. They are the accented /ɜ˞/ as in *fur* and *certain*, and the unaccented /ɚ/ as in *maker* and *caller* (see Chapter IV). These vowels differ from the consonant /r/ (1) by their greater duration, (2) by constituting a syllable, and (3) by tongue movement toward rather than away from the /r/ tongue position.

Nasal Resonants

The nasal resonant consonants of American-English are /m/, /n/, and /ŋ/. Like the oral resonants, they are produced by alteration of the resonating cavities of the vocal tract, but with two important differences. First, the velopharyngeal port is open, permitting open resonation in the nasal cavity. Second, the oral cavity is completely closed off at some point, forcing the flow of breath through the nasal cavity (see Figure II-12). For production of /m/, the resonating tube includes the oral cavity occluded at the lips as well as the open nasal cavity. For /n/, the resonating tube includes the oral cavity behind the lingua-alveolar closure. In addition, there is a resonating cavity in front of the lingua-alveolar closure and between the open lips. Vibration of the hard structures of the oral cavity causes resonation in this supplemental cavity, helping to differentiate /n/ from /m/. Similarly, the oral cavity with open lips in front of the lingua-velar closure for /ŋ/ contributes resonance that helps distinguish it from /m/ or /n/. Figure III-2 shows a schematic diagram of the resonating cavities for the nasal resonant consonants.

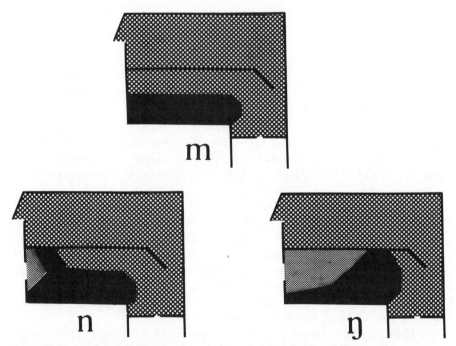

Figure III-2.   Schematic diagram of the resonating cavities for the nasal resonant consonants.

IPA   m
Dictionary   m Key Words: *my, team, camera*
Northampton m

/m/ PRODUCTION—Bilabial Nasal Resonant

With the lips closed, voice is directed through the open velopharyngeal port to the nasal cavity and out the nostrils. The tongue lies flat in the mouth or is prepared for the following vowel, providing opening for resonation of the voice in the entire oral cavity closed off by the lips, as well as resonation in the open nasal cavity. The teeth are slightly open. (See Figure III–2.)

/m/ SPELLING—*m* is Primary Spelling

-*mm*- as in *hammer, summer, command, immobile, accommodate* has a single /m/ sound.
  -*mb* with silent *b* as in *lamb, comb, dumb, bomb, clamber, climber.*
  -*mn* with silent *n* as in *hymn, damned, column.*
  -*lm* with silent *l* as in *calm, palm, psalm, balm, salmon.*
  -*gm* with silent *g* as in *phlegm, diaphragm.*

/m/ WORDS

Initial		Medial		Final	
me	men	summer	coming	am	storm
may	mount	hammer	camera	whom	realm
meat	might	animal	fireman	time	heroism
miss	mat	among	remember	lamb	diaphragm
more	moon	family	somewhere	hymn	team
must	malt	lamp	smell	palm	roam

/m/ SENTENCES

1. Remember them at Christmas in December.
2. He smiled as his dream of heroism came true.
3. Some animals from the farm may harm him.
4. Mary combed the mother lamb.
5. Firemen have more time at home in summer.
6. My room may not accommodate them.

Note: the /m/ is one of the most frequently occurring consonants in American-English speech.

/m/ CONTRASTS

/m/—/b/		/m/—/n/		/m/—/ŋ/	
mean	bean	mob	knob	sum	sung
make	bake	mow	no	hum	hung
mat	bat	met	net	dumb	dung
match	batch	sum	sun	ram	rang
rum	rub	rum	run	Sam	sang
roam	robe	ram	ran	Kim	king
lambs	labs	coming	cunning	swim	swing
lamer	labor	terms	turns	bomb	bong

Note: the /m/ is one of the first sounds mastered by children and is seldom misarticulated.

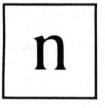

IPA   n
Dictionary   n Key Words: *new, tin, any*
Northampton n

/n/ PRODUCTION—Lingua-alveolar Nasal Resonant

With the tip of the tongue closed against the alveolar ridge and the sides of the tongue against the upper molars, voice is directed through the open velopharyngeal port to the nasal cavity and out the nostrils. The back of the tongue is down and open to the oropharynx for resonation of voice in the oral cavity behind the lingua-alveolar closure as well as for resonation in the open nasal cavity. In addition, the teeth and lips are open, forming a resonating cavity in front of the lingua-alveolar closure. Tongue pressure at the alveolar ridge is less than for either /t/ or /d/. (See Figure III-2.)

/n/ SPELLING—n is Primary Spelling

-nn- as in *inn, cunning, cannot, running, spanned, funny* has a single /n/ sound.

    kn- with silent *k* as in *knife, know, knee, knob, knit, knight.*
    gn- with silent *g* as in *gnat, gnome, gnu, gnash, gnaw, gnarled.*
    -gn with silent *g* as in *align, malign, sign, reign, feign, deign.*
    pn- with silent *p* as in *pneumatic, pneumonia.*
    mn- with silent *m* in *mnemonic.*

/n/ WORDS

Initial		Medial		Final	
not	nut	banana	snow	can	ripen
knife	north	annotate	snake	align	cotton
gnarled	new	funny	any	sign	kitten
pneumonia	neck	connote	tiny	inn	burn
know	nap	peanut	under	on	learn
name	nice	Indian	only	been	listen

/n/ SENTENCES

1. Nancy knelt with her bananas on the napkin.
2. He knew that nine knives were near the window.
3. The sign next to the barn was gnarled.
4. The knight's knee needed pneumatic panels.
5. Can you run down the green lawn?
6. The queen's reign spanned seven generations.

/n/ CONTRASTS

/n/—/d/		/n/—/m/		/n/—/ŋ/	
no	dough	knob	mob	ban	bang
near	dear	no	mow	fan	fang
none	done	net	met	ran	rang
noun	down	sun	sum	win	wing
den	dead	run	rum	kin	king
ban	bad	ran	ram	pin	ping
bin	bid	cunning	coming	thin	thing
man	mad	turns	terms	sun	sung

Note: the /n/ is one of the first sounds mastered by children and is seldom misarticulated. Foreign speakers may need to learn to make the American-English /n/ off the alveolar ridge rather than off the upper front teeth. The /n/ is one of the most frequently occurring sounds of American-English speech.

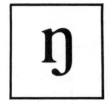

IPA   ŋ
Dictionary   ng, n͡g Key Words: *song, singer*
Northampton ng

/ŋ/ PRODUCTION—Lingua-velar Nasal Resonant

With the back of the tongue closed against the front portion of the velum or back of the palate, voice is directed through the open velopharyngeal port to the nasal cavity and out the nostrils. The teeth and lips are open and the tip of the tongue rests just behind the lower front teeth, forming a resonating cavity in front of the tongue-palate closure. Tongue pressure at the velum or palate is less than for the /k/ or /g/. (See Figure III–2.)

/ŋ/ SPELLING—-*ng* is Primary Spelling

-n(k) as in *ink, sink, think, bank* in the same syllable; often in adjoining syllables through assimilation as in *income, include, Concord.*
   -n(g) as in *single, angry, mingle, bangle, jungle, hunger.*
   -n(x) as in *lynx, phalanx, minx, anxious, jinx.*
   -ngue as in *tongue, harangue, meringue.*

/ŋ/ WORDS (/ŋ/ does not occur in the initial position)

Medial		Final	
singer	finger	sing	along
hanger	longer	long	hang
swinger	younger	sang	singing
donkey	strongest	lung	running
drinks	anger	among	working
thanks	lengthen	bring	thinking

/ŋ/ SENTENCES

1. Among the young donkeys were angry wranglers.
2. Frank thinks playing ping-pong makes him hungry.
3. He sang a song in a lilting language.
4. He sings strongest on spring evenings.
5. I think Hank drank some writing ink.
6. He spent the long evening drinking with swinging singles.

/ŋ/ CONTRASTS

/ŋ/—/g/		/ŋ/—/n/		/ŋ/—/m	
wing	wig	bang	ban	sung	sum
ding	dig	fang	fan	hung	hum
tong	tog	rang	ran	dung	dumb
tongue	tug	wing	win	rang	ram
ringer	rigger	king	kin	sang	Sam
dinger	digger	ping	pin	king	Kim
banging	bagging	thing	thin	swing	swim
longing	logging	sung	sun	bong	bomb

Note: the /ŋ/ is one of the first sounds mastered by children and is seldom misarticulated. In informal speech, the *-ing* ending is frequently pronounced as [ɪn] as in *singing* [sɪŋɪn] and *walking* [wɔkɪn].

REVIEW VOCABULARY

Affricate consonant—a stop released into a fricative position as a single speech sound. Affricate phonemes are /ʧ/ and /ʤ/.

Aspiration—audible release of breath as with the [p] in *pot*.

Closure—oral cavity stop action of voiced consonants /b/, /d/, and /g/.

Coarticulation—influence of one speech sound on the adjacent sound in connected speech.

Consonant—a speech sound used marginally with a vowel to constitute a syllable.

Diphthong—a sequence of two vowel positions taken in a single syllable with one of the vowel positions dominant.

Fricative consonant—a speech sound with audible friction as its primary perceptual feature. Fricatives are /h/, /ʍ/, /f/, /θ/, /s/, /ʃ/, /v/, /ð/, /z/, and /ʒ/.

Glide—referring to a consonant, a very brief sound rapidly blending into the following vowel sound. Glides include /w/, /j/, and, sometimes, /l/ and /r/.

Homorganic—made in the same or very nearly the same place of articulation.

Intruded sound—a sound resulting from coarticulation, as the intruded [t] in *chance* [ʧænts].

Lateral—a sound in which air escapes around the sides of the tongue. The /l/ is the lateral sound of American-English.

Manner of production—the way the speech mechanism modifies the voiced or voiceless air stream in articulation.

Nasal resonant consonant—produced with open velopharyngeal port. The nasal resonant consonants are /m/, /n/, and /ŋ/.

Oral resonant consonant—produced with closed velopharyngeal port. The oral resonant consonants are /w/, /j/, /l/, and /r/.

Place of articulation—those parts of the speech mechanism involved most prominently in production of speech sounds.

Release—opening of voiced stop consonants /b/, /d/, and /g/.

Retroflex—bending backward, as in the tongue position for a retroflex /r/.

Stop consonant—a speech sound with closure or stopping of the air stream as its primary perceptual feature. The /p/, /t/, /k/, /b/, /d/, and /g/ are stop consonants.

Vowel—a speech sound that may constitute a syllable or the nucleus of a syllable.

EXERCISES

1. Write the IPA symbol that matches each of the following brief descriptions.

   (a) Bilabial Nasal Resonant
   (b) Lingua-alveolar Voiceless Stop
   (c) Lingua-palatal Voiceless Fricative
   (d) Lingua-velar Voiced Stop
   (e) Lingua-dental Voiceless Fricative
   (f) Lingua-palatal Oral Resonant Glide
   (g) Labio-dental Voiceless Fricative
   (h) Lingua-alveolar, Lingua-palatal Voiceless Affricate
   (i) Lingua-velar Bilabial Oral Resonant Glide
   (j) Lingua-dental Voiced Fricative
   (k) Lingua-velar Voiced Stop

    (l) Lingua-velar Nasal Resonant

   (m) Lingua-palatal Voiced Fricative

   (n) Bilabial Voiced Stop

   (o) Labio-dental Voiced Fricative

   (p) Lingua-alveolar Lateral Oral Resonant

   (q) Bilabial Voiceless Stop

   (r) Lingua-palatal, Lingua-velar Voiceless Fricative

   (s) Lingua-alveolar Nasal Resonant

   (t) Lingua-alveolar Voiced Stop

   (u) Lingua-velar, Bilabial Voiceless Fricative

   (v) Lingua-velar Voiceless Stop

   (w) Lingua-alveolar, Lingua-palatal Voiced Affricate

   (x) Lingua-palatal Oral Resonant

2. Write the brief descriptive terms for the features of place, voicing, and manner of production associated with each of the following consonants. Example: /p/—Bilabial Voiceless Stop.

   (a) /v/   /r/   /ʧ/   /m/   /d/   /w/

   (b) /n/   /j/   /ʍ/   /l/   /h/   /dʒ/

   (c) /b/   /k/   /ð/   /g/   /ŋ/   /z/

   (d) /f/   /s/   /t/   /ʃ/   /ʒ/   /θ/

3. Write the IPA symbol that matches each of the following descriptions of speech sound production.

   (a) With the velopharyngeal port closed and without voice, the lips close and breath is held and compressed in the oral cavity. Breath is released suddenly as audible aspiration between the lips.

   (b) With the velopharyngeal port closed and without voice, the sides of the tongue are against the upper molars, the broad front surface of the tongue is raised toward the palate just back of the alveolar ridge, forming a central aperture slightly broader and farther back than for /s/, to direct the breath stream continuously through and against the slightly open front teeth as audible friction.

   (c) With the tip of the tongue closed against the alveolar ridge and the sides of the tongue against the upper molars, voice is directed through the open velopharyngeal port to the nasal cavity and out the nostrils. The back of the tongue is down and open to the oropharynx. The teeth and lips are slightly open.

    (d) With the velopharyngeal port closed and with voice, the back of the tongue closes against the front of the velum or back portion of the palate as voicing begins or continues, and air is held briefly in the back of the oral cavity and in the oropharynx. Closure of the back of the tongue and the velum-palate is released as voicing continues.

    (e) With the velopharyngeal port closed, the point of the tongue closes with slight pressure against the alveolar ridge with opening on both sides, as voice escapes around the tongue and out the oral cavity.

4. Describe a detailed sequence of voicing, resonance, and articulatory actions for the generalized and isolated production of each of the following speech sounds.

    (a) Voiceless fricatives /f/, /θ/, and /ʍ/.
    (b) Nasal resonants /m/, /n/, and /ŋ/.
    (c) Voiced stops /b/, /d/, and /g/.
    (d) Voiced fricatives /v/, /ð/, and /ʒ/.
    (e) Affricates /tʃ/ and /dʒ/.
    (f) Oral resonants /w/, /j/, and /l/.
    (g) Voiceless stops /p/, /t/, and /k/.

SUGGESTED READING

Bronstein, Arthur J.: *The Pronunciation of American English.* Englewood Cliffs, N.J., Prentice-Hall, Inc., 1960.

    Chapters 4, 5, and 6 (pp. 59–130) survey the consonants of American English with numerous diagrams to show positions in the oral cavity.

Griffith, Jerry, and Miner, Lynn E.: *Phonetic Context Drillbook.* Englewood Cliffs, N.J., Prentice-Hall, Inc., 1979.

    This paperback provides for each of the American-English consonants a variety of phonetic contexts in words, phrases and sentences that are used in everyday language. The practice words are selected from among those most commonly used.

Chapter IV

VOWEL AND DIPHTHONG PRODUCTION

- **ANALYSIS OF VOWELS AND DIPHTHONGS**
  - **FRONT VOWELS**
  - **BACK VOWELS**
  - **MIXED VOWELS**
  - **DIPHTHONGS**
- **REVIEW VOCABULARY**
- **EXERCISES**
- **SUGGESTED READING**

Vowels are not classified in the same way as are consonants. American-English vowels, as pointed out in Chapter III, are all made with essentially the same manner of production. They are voiced and are oral resonant sounds. The different sound quality of vowels depends upon variations in the shape of the oral cavity. Shaping for the most part is achieved by the tongue, with important differences also made by jaw opening and lip rounding. Therefore, categorization has traditionally been by place and by height of tongue elevation, with supplementary notation of lip rounding. Tongue height, considered in relation to the palate and velum above it, is measured in tongue-to-palate or tongue-to-velum distance. This measure accounts for the jaw opening as well as for movement of the tongue, since the entire tongue must follow the vertical movement of the mandible.

The three primary classes of vowels, grouped by place of tongue elevation, are **front vowels, back vowels,** and a group usually termed **mixed vowels** which consists of those with central tongue elevation or those that do not fit easily into the first two groups. **Diphthongs** are considered to be a special kind of vowel sound. The front and back vowels, together with the mixed vowels and the two unique positions taken for diphthongs (the /e/ and /o/), may be schematically viewed on the vowel diagram of Figure IV–1. Of course, during actual production, the positions and degrees of tongue elevation are not so neatly symmetrical, especially when one considers individual variability and the influence of adjoining sounds during connected speech.

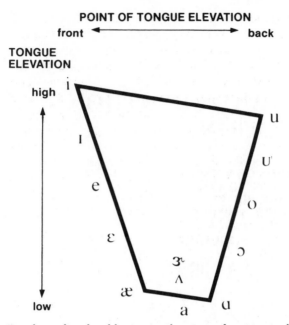

Figure IV–1.   Vowel sounds ordered by tongue elevation and position in the oral cavity.

However, the diagram does serve to relate, visually, one vowel to another for tongue height and the point of highest tongue elevation. Note the shift of the point of tongue elevation toward the center as the tongue is lowered.

Some of the IPA symbols for vowels, as mentioned in Chapter I, can indicate the presence or absence of stress on a syllable. **Stress** refers to the pointing up or drawing special attention to a unit of speech. It is accomplished by a number of speech actions discussed in Chapter VI, including making the selected unit louder or longer. When the stress is on a syllable within a word, we refer to it as **accent**. The /ʌ/ and /ɝ/ symbols are used for accented syllables, as in *utmost* [ʌtmost] and *hurting* [hɝtɪŋ], respectively. The unaccented or reduced counterpart of /ʌ/, made at the same place of articulation, is /ə/ as in *upon* [əpán]. The unaccented counterpart of /ɝ/ is /ɚ/ as in *butter* [bʌtɚ]. Diphthongs /eɪ/ and /oʊ/ also have unaccented counterparts written as [e] and [o], respectively. They are used in transcribing accenting in such words as *rotate* [roútet] and *rotation* [roteíʃən].

ANALYSIS OF VOWELS AND DIPHTHONGS

The vowel and diphthong phonemes of American-English speech are described individually in this chapter. Their written symbols as used in the International Phonetic Alphabet (IPA), in dictionaries, and in the Northampton symbol system are listed, along with key words to assist in pronunciation. A typical place of articulation is outlined, using both the conventional descriptors and a step-by-step analysis of their production. Then the most common American-English spellings of the phoneme are presented, along with some irregular spellings. This is followed by words, sentences, and contrast discrimination exercises for each vowel and diphthong phoneme. Notes are added about some of the phonemes.

As with the consonants of Chapter III, the reader should heed this word of caution. These descriptions of the phonemes of our language may suggest there is a single or standard way of producing each sound. This is not the case! The descriptions are generalizations of how most people produce speech sounds. Individual differences are significant.

The individual analysis begins with front vowels, then moves to the back vowels, the mixed vowels, and finally to the diphthongs. Exercises are included at the end of the chapter.

Front Vowels

The front vowels of American-English, in order of their tongue height, are /i/, /ɪ/, /ɛ/, and /æ/. With the tip of the tongue lying just behind and usually touching the inner surface of the mandibular incisors, the front of the tongue is raised toward the palate without touching it, and without approximating it closely enough to cause turbulence resulting in audible friction (Figure IV–2). The tongue-to-palate distance appropriate for each front vowel may be achieved either by differentially elevating the front of the tongue from its base of the stationary mandible or by raising and lowering the mandible while the front of the tongue is steadily posed high. The reader can demonstrate these alternative ways to achieve the same acoustic results by producing the front vowels—/i/, /ɪ/, /ɛ/, and /æ/—in front of a mirror.

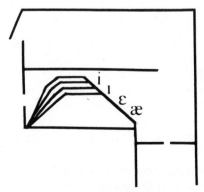

Figure IV–2. Schematic diagram of relative tongue positions for front vowels.

First, place a pencil eraser between the front teeth to maintain a constant jaw opening and produce the front vowels in the foregoing order. One may feel the tongue height dropping. Next, begin with the tongue and jaw opening for producing /i/, then drop the jaw in observable steps to produce /ɪ/, /ɛ/, and /æ/, keeping the tongue posed in the same position. Repeat the sequence several times in order both to feel and see the changes in positions. Note that as the tongue elevation decreases, the point of elevation is also slightly farther back in the mouth. The reader may also examine his pattern of producing front vowels by watching in a mirror as he says the following series of words:

	[i]	[ɪ]	[ɛ]	[æ]
1.	beat	bit	bet	bat
2.	meet	mit	met	mat
3.	peat	pit	pet	pat
4.	lead	lid	led	lad
5.	dean	din	den	Dan
6.	keen	kin	Ken	can

In connected speech, the tongue height for front vowels may be achieved by a combination of tongue and mandible adjustments. Some speakers use one kind of adjustment more regularly than the other. When the front of the tongue is elevated, as the mandible remains steady, there is a tendency for the lips to be pulled back, or retracted, at the corners. For some speakers, front of the tongue raising is accompanied by lip retraction along with an increased separation of the lips. This may be especially marked for the highest front vowel, /i/. The associated lip separation may expose mandibular front teeth or maxillary front teeth or both. This action can provide readily observable visual information for speech reading, a topic discussed in Chapter VIII.

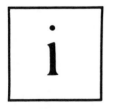

IPA   i
Dictionary   ē Key Words: *eat, seed, be*
Northampton   ee (ea, e-e, -e)

/i/ PRODUCTION—High Front Vowel

With the velopharyngeal port closed and the sides of the back of the tongue closed against the upper molars, the middle to front portion of the tongue is raised high, nearly touching the palate and alveolar ridge, while the tip of the tongue touches lightly behind the lower front teeth, and voice is given. The upper and lower front teeth are slightly open. The lips are not directly involved but are slightly open and tend to retract at the corners as the front of the tongue is raised.

/i/ SPELLING

-e occurs most frequently as in *be, me, she, he, we*.

ee is very consistent for /i/ as in *eel, agree, see, feet, seed, three.*

ea may take other sounds but occurs frequently as /i/ as in *eat, tea, teach, leave, please, east.*

Less frequently and irregular spellings include ey as in *key; e-e* as in *eve; ei* as in *either; -i* as in *ski; ie* as in *chief; i-e* as in *marine; eo* as in *people; ae* as in *aeon; oe* as in *Phoenix; -is* as in *debris; e-* as in *equal; -i-* as in *chic.*

/i/ WORDS

Initial		Medial		Final	
eat	either	seed	read	be	trustee
eve	Easter	leave	feet	he	free
eel	equal	believe	green	key	knee
east	eager	teach	bead	agree	flee
each	enough	these	chief	plea	tea
even	eagle	lease	sheep	three	see

/i/ SENTENCES

1. These teams seem even.
2. We believe he needs these keys.
3. Jean Green sees three bees.
4. He receives Steve's fees.
5. We'll eat Lee's green beans.
6. She pleases these Eastern trustees.

/i/ CONTRASTS

/i/—/ɪ/		/i/—/ɛ/	
deep	dip	meat	met
deed	did	bead	bed
beat	bit	neat	net
peak	pick	seat	set
bean	bin	mean	men
peach	pitch	teen	ten
eat	it	we'll	well
eel	ill	keep	kept

Note: /i/ has the highest tongue position of the front vowels.

Alternative Pronunciation

-y when unstressed is pronounced either /i/ or /ɪ/ in General American as in *candy, lobby, only, very, army, baby, hardly*. This unstressed final sound is also spelled *-ie* as in *cookie*, *-ey* as in *monkey*, and *-i* as in *taxi*. The IPA symbol [ɪ] may be used for transcription.

/i/ immediately before /r/ is frequently modified in General American to become /ɪ/ as in *beer, here, near, year, rear, peer*.

IPA   ɪ
Dictionary   ĭ, i Key Words: *if, bit*
Northampton   -i- (-y)

/ɪ/ PRODUCTION—High Front Vowel

With the velopharyngeal port closed and the sides of the back of the tongue closed against the upper molars, the middle to front portion of the tongue is raised toward the palate and alveolar ridge, slightly lower and farther back than for the /i/, while the tip of the tongue touches lightly behind the lower front teeth, and voice is given. The upper and lower front teeth are open, slightly wider than for /i/. The tongue is less tense than for /i/ and the corners of the mouth retract little with tongue elevation.

/ɪ/ SPELLING

i- occurs most frequently as in *it, in, if, bit, sick, lift, fish, mirror*.

-y- is frequently /ɪ/ as in *gypsy, syrup, gypsum, myth, gym, hymn*.

ea(r), ee(r), ei(r), and *e(r)e* usually have the /ɪ/ sound as in *hear, sheer, weird*, and *here*, respectively.

Less frequent and irregular spellings include *-ee-* as in *been*, *-u-* as in *busy*, *-ui-* as in *built*, *-ie-* as in *sieve*, *-o-* as in *women*, *-e-* as in *pretty*, and i-e as in *give*.

Unstressing of several vowels, especially in New England and Southern speech, leads to /ɪ/ as in *courage, devote, kitchen, character, Dallas, relate*.

-y when unstressed is pronounced either /i/ or /ɪ/ in General American, but more often /ɪ/ in New England and Southern as in *candy, lobby, only, very, army, baby, hardly*.

/ɪ/ WORDS

The /ɪ/ does not occur in final position except for unstressed final -y in New England and Southern speech.

Initial		*Medial*		*Final -y*	
in	into	his	pill	only	city
it	ignorant	busy	quill	busy	any
if	interest	kitten	written	ready	heavy
id	insect	limb	sit	hilly	bury
ill	idiot	mit	tin	kitty	curry
is	invert	nick	victor	pretty	duty

/ɪ/ SENTENCES

1. The little kitten is pretty.
2. Will the insect sit still?
3. Give him a pill in the gym.
4. The pink crystal is thin.
5. Is it in this tin?
6. Bill spilled his liquor.

/ɪ/ CONTRASTS

/ɪ/—/i/		/ɪ/—/ɛ/	
dip	deep	mit	met
did	deed	bid	bed
bit	beat	knit	net
pick	peak	sit	set
bin	bean	tin	ten
pitch	peach	will	well
it	eat	lid	led
ill	eel	hid	head

Note: the /ɪ/ is one the most frequently occurring sounds in American-English speech.

IPA   ɛ
Dictionary   ĕ, e Key Words: *end, bet*
Northampton -e- (ea)

/ɛ/ PRODUCTION—Front Vowel

With the velopharyngeal port closed and the sides of the back of the tongue closed against the upper molars, the middle to front portion of the tongue is raised slightly toward the palate and alveolar ridge, lower and farther back than for the /ɪ/ or /e/, while the tip of the tongue touches lightly behind the lower front teeth, and voice is given. The upper and lower front teeth are open slightly wider than for /ɪ/. The corners of the mouth do not retract with the slight tongue elevation.

/ɛ/ SPELLING

e- occurs most frequently as in *end, ebb, estimate, ten, lent.*

-ea- is frequently /ɛ/ as in *head, meant, bread, dread, steady, breakfast.*

Several vowel combinations associated with /r/ have the /ɛ/ sound including -e(r)e as in *there* and *where*, -eir as in *their* and *heir*, ai(r) as in *air* and *fair*, -ea(r) as in *pear* and *bear*, -a(r)e as in *bare* and *care*, and ae(r)- as in *aerial.*

Less frequent and irregular spellings include a- as in *any*, -ay- as in *says*, ae- as in *aesthetic*, -ai- as in *said*, -ei- as in *heifer*, -ie- as in *friend*, -ue- as in *guest*, -u- as in *bury*, and -eo- as in *leopard.*

/ɛ/ WORDS

The /ɛ/ does not occur in final position

Initial		Medial	
edge	extra	men	head
end	elephant	bed	said
egg	else	get	many
elm	engine	them	friend
every	excel	beg	guest
any	effort	neck	bear

/ɛ/ SENTENCES

1. Many men said Fred would wed.
2. Tell Ben's friend about the ten bears.
3. The pet hen would not be fed any bread. ·
4. Let their bed and chairs stay there.
5. Where was the tent sent Wednesday?
6. Their eggs compare fairly well.

/ɛ/ CONTRASTS

/ɛ/—/ɪ/		/ɛ/—/æ/	
met	mit	bet	bat
bed	bid	net	gnat

net	knit	set	sat
set	sit	ten	tan
ten	tin	head	had
well	will	send	sand
led	lid	end	and
pair	peer	led	lad

Note: the /ɛ/ is one of the most frequently occurring speech sounds in American-English speech.

IPA   æ
Dictionary   ă, a Key Words: *at, bat*
Northampton -a-

/æ/ PRODUCTION—Low Front Vowel

With the velopharyngeal port closed and the mouth open wider than for the other front vowels, the middle to front portion of the tongue is raised farther back than the other front vowels, while voice is given. The sides of the back of the tongue may move away from the upper molars and the tongue tip may move slightly behind the lower front teeth.

/æ/ SPELLING

a- occurs most frequently as in *at, and, an, bat, rabbit, black.*
Less frequent and irregular spellings include *-ai-* as in *plaid, -au-* as in *laugh, -i-* in *meringue,* and *-a-e* as in *have.*

/æ/ WORDS

The /æ/ does not occur in final position.

Initial		*Medial*	
at	after	cat	salmon
an	aunt	ham	rather
and	Adam	sand	example
add	absolute	dad	grant
amp	answer	sang	dance
ask	atom	that	laugh

/æ/ SENTENCES

1. Ask the man at that stand.
2. That stamp is an example of bad planning.
3. Dad has had the answer after all.
4. The black cat sat in the grass.
5. The half-back can catch that pass.
6. Master the answer by half past nine.

/æ/ CONTRASTS

/æ/—/ɛ/		/æ/—/ɑ/	
bat	bet	cat	cot
gnat	net	pad	pod
sat	set	Dan	Don
tan	ten	cad	cod
had	head	shack	shock
sand	send	cap	cop
and	end	pat	pot
lad	led	gnat	not

Note: the /æ/ is usually in an accented syllable of a polysyllabic word. A common non-standard production, particularly before nasal consonants, involves raising of the back of the tongue sides to touch the back molars with a resulting [ɛ̃] sound from tongue elevation and restriction of voice for oral resonance, noticeable in such words as *chance* [ʧɛ̃nts], *camp* [kɛ̃mp], and *can't* [kɛ̃nt].

[ær] is a common alternate pronunciation for [ɛr] in such words as *chair, fare, rare, air,* and *bear.*

[a] is a common alternate pronunciation for [æ] in New England speech for such words as *bath, and, hat, man, tack,* and *laugh.*

Back Vowels

The back vowels of American-English, in order of their tongue height, are /u/, /ʊ/, /ɔ/, and /ɑ/. With the tip of the tongue behind and slightly below the mandibular incisors, or lightly touching the lower gum ridge, the back of the tongue is raised toward the velum near its juncture with the palate (Figure IV–3). The high point of the tongue neither touches the velum nor approximates it closely enough to cause turbulence and audible friction. Like the front vowels, the tongue-to-velum distance appropriate for each back

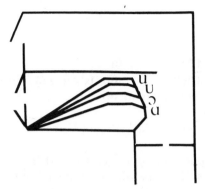

Figure IV–3.   Schematic diagram of relative tongue positions for back vowels.

vowel is achieved by a combination of lingual and mandibular adjustments. As the tongue elevation decreases, the point of elevation is slightly farther forward in the mouth. When the back of the tongue is raised, the lips tend to round. The highest back tongue position for /u/ is accompanied by the tightest rounding and the smallest lip aperture. The /ʊ/ and /ɔ/ have lower tongue positions and wider lip openings. Back tongue elevation and lip rounding are reciprocal. As the lips are rounded even for /w/ or /ʍ/, the back of the tongue also tends to rise so that tongue position influences the sound of both these consonants. The degree of lip rounding for back vowels is variable from speaker to speaker. Some speakers use very little lip rounding for /u/, /ʊ/, and /ɔ/, compensating by tongue positioning. The reader may experience this compensatory tongue action by observing in a mirror as he purposely attempts to produce /ʊ/ with the lips open, unrounded, and relaxed. As with lip retraction for front vowels, lip rounding for the back vowels /u/, /ʊ/, and /ɔ/ can assist the observer in speech reading. The /ɑ/ is also a back vowel, but the lips are not rounded for this sound. This vowel has the greatest jaw opening of all American-English vowel sounds and is formed by slightly raising the back of the tongue and moving it slightly backward into the oropharynx.

The following series of words provide examples of the steps of tongue elevation and lip rounding for the back vowels:

	/u/	/ʊ/	/ɔ/	/ɑ/
1.	cooed	could	cawed	cod
2.	shoe	should	Shaw	shod
3.	who	hook	hawk	hock
4.	Lew	look	law	lock
5.	rue	rook	raw	rock
6.	noon	nook	naught	not

IPA   u
Dictionary   ōō, ü, o͝o Key Words: *ooze, boot, too*
Northampton o͝o

/u/ PRODUCTION—High Back Round Vowel

With the velopharyngeal port closed and the sides of the back of the tongue closed against the upper molars, the back of the tongue is raised high and tense, nearly touching the palate, the lips are rounded and may be slightly protruded for a small aperture, and voice is given. The tongue tip is just behind the lower front teeth, and the upper and lower teeth are slightly open. The aperture of the rounded lips is smaller than for any other vowel and is almost imperceptibly wider than for /w/ (compare in the syllable *woo*).

/u/ SPELLING

-oo occurs most frequently as in *boot, cool, mood, loose, noon, too;* however, the *oo* may often have the sound of /ʊ/.

-o as in *do, who, to, tomb, whom.*
-ew as in *blew, crew, chew, grew, drew, brew.*
-u-e as in *rude, rule, crude, Luke, presume.*
-ou as in *you, group, troup, soup, ghoul, wound.*
-ui- as in *fruit, cruise, bruise, recruit.*

Irregularly and infrequently as *-o-e* as in *lose, whose, move; -oe* as in *shoe, canoe; -ue* as in *true, blue, sue; -iue-* as in *lieu, lieutenant; -ioux* as in *Sioux; -au-* as in *Sault; -ough* as in *through* and *slough; -u* as in *flu, gnu, tulip; -wo* as in *two; -eu-* as in *rheumatism* and *-eue* as in *queue.*

/u/ WORDS

The /u/ seldom occurs as an initial vowel except in slang and in Hawaiian words.

Initial	Medial		Final	
ooze	boot	moon	too	do
oodles	crew	move	who	drew
oops	doom	rude	queue	blew
	fruit	tomb	shoe	through
	group	school	you	flu
	lose	whom	true	canoe

/u/ SENTENCES

1. R*u*th's s*ou*p s*oo*n gr*ew* c*oo*l.
2. The ripe fr*ui*t *oo*zed thr*ough* the bamb*oo*.
3. D*o* y*ou* appr*o*veof the m*o*ve?
4. T*wo* gr*ou*ps from sch*oo*l went thr*ough* the z*oo*.
5. He cleaned the b*oo*th in the r*oo*m with a bl*ue* br*oo*m.
6. Wh*ose* t*oo*th was l*oo*sened by a sp*oo*n?

/u/ CONTRASTS

/u/—/ʊ/		/u/—/ju/	
pool	pull	boot	butte
fool	full	ooze	use
wooed	would	coot	cute
stewed	stood	booty	beauty
Luke	look	coo	cue
cooed	could	moot	mute
shooed	should	food	feud
kook	cook	whose	hues

Note: a few words are variable in pronunciation by choice with either /u/ or /ʊ/, including *roof, coop, hoof, root,* and *hoop.* Some words are variably pronounced with either /u/ or /ju/, including *new, tune, duke, due, nude, suit,* and *resume.*

IPA	ʊ
Dictionary	o͝o, u Key Words: b*oo*k, *could*
Northampton	o͝o²

/ʊ/ PRODUCTION—High Back Round Vowel

With the velopharyngeal port closed and the sides of the back of the tongue closed lightly against the upper molars, the back of the tongue is raised high, but lower and with less tension than for /u/, the lips are rounded and may be very slightly protruded for an aperture larger than for /u/, and voice is given. The tongue tip touches behind the lower front teeth, and the upper and lower teeth are slightly open.

/ʊ/ SPELLING

-oo(k) is almost invariably /ʊ/ as in *look, book, hook, cook.*
-oo- as in *good, wool, wood, hood, stood.*
-u- as in *put, bush, pull, sugar, full, bull.*
-ou- as in *would, should, could.*
Rarely as -o- as in *wolf* and *bosom;* -or- as in *worsted.*

/ʊ/ WORDS

The /ʊ/ does not occur in initial or final positions of words.

	Medial	
cook	hood	pull
look	woolen	bush
book	wooden	could
shook	full	should
good	put	would
stood	push	wolf

/ʊ/ SENTENCES

1. He took a cook book from the butcher.
2. He looked at the brook in the woods.
3. The bushel basket was full of cookies.
4. Pull up the woolen hood.
5. He could be good if he would.
6. He should push and pull the wooden cart.

/ʊ/ CONTRASTS

/ʊ/—/u/		/ʊ/—/ou/	
pull	pool	pull	pole
full	fool	bull	bowl
would	wooed	could	code
stood	stewed	should	showed
look	Luke	stood	stowed
could	cooed	good	goad
should	shooed	brook	broke
cook	kook	cook	coke

Note: a few words are variable in pronunciation by choice with either /ʊ/ or /u/, including *roof, coop, hoof, root,* and *hoop.*

IPA   ɔ
Dictionary   ô, aw Key Words: *awful, caught, law*
Northampton aw (au)

/ɔ/ PRODUCTION—Back Round Vowel

With the velopharyngeal port closed, the back and middle portion of the tongue is slightly raised with elevation similar to /o/ but the mouth is open wider than for /o/, the lips are rounded and slightly protruded for an aperture larger than for /o/, and voice is given. The tongue tip touches behind the lower front teeth. Tense lip rounding and wide mouth opening is the essence of /ɔ/.

/ɔ/ SPELLING

au- occurs most frequently for /ɔ/ as in *auto, audio, taut, applause, vault, haunt, laundry.*
aw occurs very consistently for /ɔ/ as in *awe, awful, yawn, lawn, law, saw, jaw.*
Less frequently but consistently *-augh(t)* as in *caught, fraught, taught, naught;* and *ough(t)* as in *bought, thought, brought, ought.*
Less regularly but frequently *o-* as in *off, loft, wrong, cloth, strong,* and *a(1)-* as in *ball, all, call, talk, altogether, small, already.*
Infrequent and irregular -oa- as in *broad, abroad; -o-e* as in *gone;* and *-ou-* as in *cough, trough.*

/ɔ/ WORDS

Initial		Medial		Final	
awful	always	taut	caught	saw	straw
awning	all	applaud	taught	raw	craw
awl	almost	vault	thought	law	draw
auto	off	yawn	bought	paw	thaw
audio	often	talk	cloth	caw	gnaw
auction	ought	walk	wrong	jaw	slaw

/ɔ/ SENTENCES

1. They all thought they saw him yawn.
2. We bought almost all the cloth at the auction.
3. He was taught always to call the law.

4. *They sought* the wr*o*ng *law* officer.
5. The *faw*n *o*ften w*a*lked on the str*aw.*
6. *We* th*ough*t he would f*a*ll *o*ff the *au*tomobile.

/ɔ/ CONTRASTS

/ɔ/—/ɑ/		/ɔ/—/ou/	
caught	cot	fawn	phone
hawk	hock	bought	boat
naught	not	caught	coat
taught	tot	paws	pose
caller	collar	taught	tote
auto	Otto	bawl	bowl
wrought	rot	call	coal
pawed	pod	fall	foal

Note: the /ɔ/ is one of the most inconsistently used vowels in American-English speech. Its acoustic distinctiveness depends upon lip rounding and protrusion, which, with some tongue elevation, is its primary difference from /ɑ/. Speaker variability in the tenseness of lip shaping and dialectic differences in usage lead to a continuum of lip rounding and protusion ranging from speakers using a strongly lip-shaped /ɔ/ in many words to others with almost total absence of the vowel and universal substitution of /ɑ/. The *aw, au-,* and *-augh(t)* spellings are most consistently pronounced /ɔ/, but at the extreme of omission for some General American speakers, even these spellings are produced as /ɑ/ so that *awful* becomes [ɑfəl], *law* becomes [lɑ:], *taut* is said [tɑt], *haunt* is said [hɑnt], and *caught* is [kɑt]. Apparently the /ɑ/ for /ɔ/ substitution, and the degree of lip shaping, is not phonemically critical for speech intelligibility.

The *o-* spelling is highly variable so that some speakers who say [lɔ:] for *law* may say [klɑθ] for *cloth* and [kɑst] for *cost*. *On* is most frequently pronounced [ɔn] in Southern speech but [ɑn] by most General American speakers and [an] by many in New England. The *-og* words, such as *log* and *dog*, are given a strong /ɔ/ in Southern speech but /ɑ/ throughout the rest of the country. The /ɑ/ for /ɔ/ variability holds for *a(1)* words such as *ball, call,* and *all*, with varying degrees of lip rounding and protrusion tension used.

The *o(r)* spelling has very high variability even within a dialect group. In words such as *or, for, born,* and *origin,* the vowel may be heard as /ɔ/, /o/, /ou/, or /ɑ/. In New England and Southern speech, the *o-* before intervocalic /r/ is often /ɑ/ as in *origin* [ɑrɪdʒən] and *forest* [fɑrɪst], even though *for* is likely to be [fɔə] or [fɔr]. In St Louis, although *coffee* is said [kɔfɪ], *cork* is said [kɑrk], and *born* is said [bɑrn]. Of course, the New England and Southern omission of the preconsonantal and final /r/ adds further variability to *o(r)* pronunciation.

Principally in New England, and following British pronunciation, a slightly rounded /ɔ/ or /ɑ/ of rather short duration is used for some -o-spellings. Written /ɒ/, it is especially prominent before voiceless stop consonants as in *hot, not, rock, top,* and *spot.* It may also be heard in New England *coffee, cost, long, lost,* and *song.*

IPA   ɑ
Dictionary   ŏ, ä Key Words: *odd, father, pa, ah*
Northampton a(r)

/ɑ/ PRODUCTION—Low Mid-back Vowel

With the velopharyngeal port closed, the tongue is relaxed and slightly raised in the back with the tip touching behind the lower front teeth, the mouth is opened wider than for any other vowel as voice is given. The lips are not rounded or protruded, differing from /ɔ/ primarily in this characteristic. The /ɑ/ differs from /ʌ/ in having a wider mouth opening and lower back-of-tongue elevation.

/ɑ/ SPELLING

-o- occurs most frequently as in *fog, top, bother, common, bomb, rod, borrow.*

a(r) occurs frequently whether or not the -r is pronounced as in *car, part, barn, bark, yard, arm, are, army.*

-al(m) with silent -l- as in *palm, calm, psalm, balm, alms.*

The /ɑ/ occurs infrequently and irregularly as -a in *father, mamma, pa, was, watch;* as -ea(r)- in *heart* and hearth; -ua(r)- in *guard;* -ow- in *knowledge;* -e- in *sergeant;* -aa(r) in *bazaar;* and ho- with silent h- as in *honest.*

The /ɑ/ is popularly written *ah* as an exclamation or to indicate the /ɑ/ in a character's speech pattern.

/ɑ/ WORDS

The /ɑ/ occurs in final position only in slang as *pa, ma,* and *ha.*

Initial		*Medial*	
art	honest	father	Tom
arm	olive	heart	beyond
are	ominous	bomb	bar
ark	onset	palm	car

army	oxen	calm	doll
honor	onyx	don	psalm

/ɑ/ SENTENCES

1. Father's car is parked in the barn.
2. Palm trees are arched toward the ark.
3. Mom was calm despite the ominous army.
4. Honesty is the policy for Olive to observe.
5. Tom's honor is beyond need of bonding.
6. The bazaar and arcade are not far.

/ɑ/ CONTRASTS

/ɑ/—/ɔ/		/ɑ/—/ʌ/		/ɑ/—/æ/	
cot	caught	bomb	bum	not	gnat
hock	hawk	calm	come	shock	shack
not	naught	cot	cut	cop	cap
tot	taught	psalm	some	psalm	Sam
collar	caller	pop	pup	knock	knack
Otto	auto	shot	shut	rot	rat
rot	wrought	cop	cup	pot	pat
pod	pawed	dock	duck	cot	cat

Note: the /ɑ/ is quite variable in American-English, often interchanged with /ɔ/ and /æ/. See the discussion of /ɑ/ - /ɔ/ usage as notation in the /ɔ/ section of this chapter. The "broad *a*" of some Eastern speakers makes *aunt* pronounced [ɑnt], *ask* [ɑsk], and *bath* [bɑθ]. New England speakers may use /ɒ/ for -o-, particularly followed by a voiceless stop as in *top, hot,* and *lock,* and may use [a] for *a(r)* in *park* [paːk], *arm* [aːm], and *car* [kaː].

Mixed Vowels

In the center of the vowel diagram of Figure IV–1 are **mixed vowels** with more central tongue elevation or without any special point of elevation. The /ʌ/ is produced with a relaxed tongue, lying fairly flat in the oral cavity, and is thus called the "natural" vowel. The jaw opening for the natural vowel is minimal so that the tongue-to-palate velum distance is small, and tongue height on the diagram is greater than for the /æ/ and /ɑ/, which have the greatest jaw opening. To gauge the extremes of tongue and jaw positions for American-English vowels, the reader might carry out the following exercises, moving from the natural vowel position to the position for each vowel at the corners of the vowel diagram:

$$[ʌ] \rightarrow [i]$$
$$[ʌ] \rightarrow [u]$$
$$[ʌ] \rightarrow [æ]$$
$$[ʌ] \rightarrow [ɑ]$$

The exercise may be conducted with a brief pause between the vowels or with the vowels smoothed together for [ʌi], [ʌu], [ʌæ], and [ʌɑ], with vocalization or without.

At the bottom center of the diagram is the /a/, a sound limited primarily to New England in the United States. It occurs in New England dialect as described in Chapter VII, with a wide jaw opening and middle tongue elevation in words like *Boston* [bastən], *Harvard* [havəd], *park* [pak], and *car* [ka:]. In stage pronunciation, the [a] is preferred over either [æ] or [ɑ] in such words as *path, ask,* and *bath.*

Inside the vowel diagram is another sound considered a mixed vowel—the /ɝ/. This sound differs from all other vowels in one important aspect of production. Whereas the other vowels are produced with the tongue tip against the lower front teeth or just behind the teeth, the /ɝ/ requires that the tip be raised or pulled back to form a broad front similar to that formed for /ʃ/. Positioning of the tongue tip can be observed in shifting from another vowel to /ɝ/ as in [ɑɝ] and [uɝ]. Note in producing [sɝ] that the tongue tip pulls back considerably for the [ɝ] but that less movement is needed in making [ʃɝ].

IPA ʌ
Dictionary ŭ, u Key Words: *up, cub*
Northampton -u-

/ʌ/ PRODUCTION—Low Mid Vowel

With the velopharyngeal port closed, the tongue lies relaxed in the mouth with slight elevation in the middle to back portion, the upper and lower front teeth are separated similar to the degree of opening for /ɛ/, and voice is given. The tip of the tongue touches lightly behind the lower front teeth. With the relaxed tongue, the /ʌ/ is called the "natural" or "neutral" vowel.

/ʌ/ SPELLING

u- is most frequent and consistent as in *cup, but, up, abut, hundred, under.*

-o-e is frequent but not consistent as in *come, done, above, money, hover.*

-ou- as in *rough, trouble, couple, enough, touch, tough, double.*

-o- as in *ton, son, month, won, tongue, color, compass.*

Infrequently –oe- as in *does.*

/ʌ/ WORDS

The /ʌ/ does not occur in the final position of words.

Initial		*Medial*	
upper	usher	cup	flood
upward	utter	tub	blood
under	utmost	hunt	rough
ultimate	oven	but	couple
uncle	ultra-	some	nothing
other	ugly	done	mother

/ʌ/ SENTENCES

1. Some other mothers were at the hunt.
2. The usher led the young couple upward.
3. The buns in the sun oven are done.
4. Come hunt the ugly bug.
5. The bunny jumped in the mud puddle.
6. His son must run through the flood.

/ʌ/ CONTRASTS

/ʌ/—/ɑ/		/ʌ/—/ʊ/		/ʌ/—/ɛ/	
bum	bomb	luck	look	bun	Ben
come	calm	tuck	took	nut	net
gun	gone	stud	stood	but	bet
nut	not	shuck	shook	hull	hell
putt	pot	putt	put	lug	leg
duck	dock	buck	book	mutt	met
cut	cot	cud	could	pun	pen
sum	psalm	crux	crooks	money	many

Note: the American-English /ʌ/ occurs in few other languages and is produced close to /ɑ/ in British-English. It is used for stressed vowels with
primary or secondary accent in polysyllabic words. Primary stressing is apparent in such words as *upper, couple, ultimate, nothing, begun,* and *en-
compass.* Secondary stressing of /ʌ/ occurs with a change in word form when
the syllable of the root word would take a primary accent /ʌ/, as in *conduct*
(n.) [kɑ́ndʌkt] and *upset* [ʌpsɛ́t] and in words with clear secondary accent on
the first syllable as in *úmbrélla, únléss, úntíl,* and *últérior.* Or it may reflect
the stressing of a particular speaker, as when in formal speech the word
nation might be said [neɪ́ʃʌn].

   The unstressed counterpart of /ʌ/ is /ə/, called the "schwa" vowel. For
/ə/, the tongue is more relaxed, and duration is considerably shorter. It is
used for very lightly stressed syllables as in the following words:

Initial	*Medial*	*Final*
*a*bóve [əbʌv]	lém*o*n [lɛmən]	sóf*a* [soufə]
*a*gáin [əgɛn]	tábl*e* [teɪbəl]	cóbr*a* [koubrə]
*a*wáy [əweɪ]	nát*io*n [neɪʃən]	banán*a* [bənænə]

Medial Syllables
tél*e*phóne [tɛləfoun]
púrp*o*sefúl [pɝpəsfʊl]
fúnd*a*méntal [fʌndəmɛntl̩]

   The /ə/ is used especially for vowels that are so reduced in stressing that
pronunciation is changed to the schwa as in the following words:

	Lightly stressed	*Unstressed*
*pá*vement	[peɪvmɛnt]	[peɪvmənt]
amḗnd	[æmɛnd]	[əmɛnd]
crísis	[kraɪsɪs]	[kraɪsəs]
authórity	[əθorɪtɪ]	[əθorɪtɪ]
befóre	]bifor]	[bəfor]

   The /ə/ can be spelled with any vowel alphabet letter (*a, alone; e,
moment, i, pencil; o, comply; u, circus*) and with many combinations (*ae,
Michael; ai, fountain; au, authority; eo, pigeon; ea, sergeant; ie, conscience;
io, religion; ous, dangerous,* etc.)
   Frequently used, short linking words are often reduced to /ə/ in connected speech so that their former or "dictionary" pronunciations are almost
forgotten. Especially noticeable are *was* [wɑz], *from* [frɑm], *of* [ɑv], *a* [eɪ],
and *the* [ði]. For emphasis, these typically unstressed words are often "restressed" with /ʌ/ as in "a government *of* [ʌv] the people," or "that's the way
it *was* [wʌz]."

/ə/ WORDS

Initial		Medial		Final	
about	appeal	alphabet	relative	sofa	vanilla
above	arouse	chocolate	syllable	soda	camera
another	attach	company	emphasis	tuba	gorilla
away	abate	buffalo	accident	zebra	cinema
awhile	allow	elephant	parasol	quota	arena
alive	amaze	parachute	cinnamon	drama	stamina

Note: the /ə/ is one of the most frequently occurring sounds in American-English speech.

IPA   ɝ
Dictionary   ûr, er Key Words: *urn, burn, fur*
Northampton ur (er, ir)

/ɝ/ PRODUCTION—High Mid Vowel

With the velopharyngeal port closed and the sides of the tongue closed against the upper molars, the tongue is slightly retracted. As voicing begins, the tip or front of the tongue is raised toward the palate just behind the alveolar ridge but without contact. The /ɝ/ differs from the consonantal /r/ (see Chapter III) in the following ways: (1) /ɝ/ has greater duration, (2) it constitutes a syllable, (3) it has tongue movement toward rather than away from the /r/ tongue position, and (4) it is never given voiceless following voiceless consonants as the /r/ is. The /ɝ/ is the only vowel for which the tongue tip is necessarily raised from just behind the lower front teeth.

/ɝ/ SPELLING

-*er* most frequently as in *her, herd, stern, merchant, kernel, fern.*
ur very often as in *urn, burn, fur, recur, turtle, curd, murmur.*
-*ir* frequently as in *fir, bird, first, firm, girl, squirm, girdle.*
ear- as in *earth, pearl, search, earnest, earn, learn.*

Less frequently and irregularly as follows: -*or* as in *worm, word;* -*urr* as in *purr, burr;* -*our-* as in *journey;* -*aur-* as in *restaurant;* and -*yr* as in *myrtle.*

/ɝ/ WORDS

Initial		Medial		Final	
earn	erstwhile	turn	dirt	fir	purr
urn	early	curl	bird	sir	burr
irk	ermine	hurt	first	stir	cur
Ernest	urban	turf	girl	fur	infer
earnest	urge	work	learn	blur	her
earth	herb	worm	heard	spur	recur

/ɝ/ SENTENCES

1. Her bird heard the cat purr.
2. The merchant burned the ermine curtain.
3. Earl learned to do dirty work.
4. The early bird deserves the worm.
5. He turned the earth to grow turf and herbs.
6. The first girl stirred the burning soup.

/ɝ/ CONTRASTS

/ɝ/—/ʊ/		/ɝ/—/ʌ/		/ɝ/ or /ɚ/—/r/	
shirk	shook	hurt	hut	terrain	train
stirred	stood	lurk	luck	beret	bray
curd	could	shirk	shuck	duress	dress
lurk	look	shirt	shut	corrode	crowed
word	wood	pert	putt	caressed	crest
furl	full	burn	bun	baroque	broke
gird	good	curt	cut	thorough	throw
Turk	took	burrs	buzz	curried	creed

Note: the unstressed counterpart of /ɝ/ is written /ɚ/. For /ɚ/, the tongue is more relaxed and duration is considerably shorter. It is used in very lightly stressed or unstressed syllables as in the following words:

móther	múrmur	revérberate
lábor	terráin	pervért
mártyr	urbáne	fermént

The /ɚ/ is spelled by a number of vowels combined with r, including any combination that spells /ɝ/.

Diphthongs

Diphthongs are considered single phonemes, each having a sequence of two different vowel positions. One of the positions is the dominant **nucleus** (sometimes called the "radical") with greater duration; the other position, the **glide** (or "vanish"), is of reduced duration and stress. Both positions are taken in a single syllable. The diphthongs of American-English are /eɪ/, /oʊ/, /aɪ/, /aʊ/, and /ɔɪ/. Rather than the static plot of the steady or "pure" vowels shown in Figure IV–1, diphthongs should be represented by movement of the tongue within the oral cavity. Figure IV–4 uses the outline of the vowel diagram to show the direction of movement for the two positions of each diphthong. All diphthong phonemes of American-English move from the nucleus to the glide position. From Figure IV–4, it may also be seen that the diphthongs move from a lower tongue elevation to a higher elevation.

IPA   eɪ
Dictionary   ā Key Words: *able, made, may*
Northampton a-e (ai, ay)

/eɪ/ PRODUCTION—Front Diphthong

With the velopharyngeal port closed and the sides of the back of the tongue closed against the upper molars, the middle and front portion of the tongue is raised toward the palate and alveolar ridge, slightly lower and farther back than for the /ɪ/ as voice is given; then the tongue briefly rises toward the /ɪ/ height as voice continues. The tip of the tongue touches lightly behind the lower front teeth. The upper and lower front teeth are open and may move from the /e/ to the /ɪ/ opening. The [e] portion is the longer nucleus and the [ɪ] portion is the shorter glide. For many speakers, the glide portion may have a tongue-mouth position close to /i/ but of short duration.

/eɪ/ SPELLING

a-e occurs most frequently as in *ate, cake, able, paper, grateful, makeshift.*

ai- is frequently /eɪ/ as in *aim, braid, rain, main, braille.*

-ay is also frequently /eɪ/ as in *may, say, pray, maybe, delay, tray.*

Less frequently *-a-(y)* is /eɪ/ as in *baby, lady, shady, navy, wavy.*

When *a-e* is changed to *a-(ing)*, the pronunciation remains /eɪ/ as in *saving, making, bathing, wading, baking.*

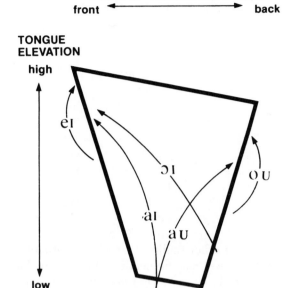

POINT OF TONGUE ELEVATION
front ←————————————→ back

TONGUE
ELEVATION
high

low

Figure IV-4. Movement of diphthongs by tongue elevation and position in the oral cavity.

Initial stressed *a-* in some polysyllabic words has the /eɪ/ sound as in *amiable, aviary, atrium, atheist, Abraham.*

Irregular spellings include *ei-* as in *eight, weigh, freight,* and *neighbor;* *-ea-* as in *steak* and *great;* *-ey* a in *prey* and *they;* *-au-* as in *gauge;* *-e-e* as in *fete;* *-ee* as in *matinee* and *melee,* and *-et* as in *sachet* and *ballet.*

/eɪ/ WORDS

Initial		Medial		Final	
age	apex	bake	label	may	neigh
ache	eight	came	baby	bay	weigh
aid	aviary	date	making	say	decay
aim	alien	face	placed	spray	away
able	apron	steak	taper	they	matinee
ape	acre	gain	relation	prey	ballet

/eɪ/ SENTENCES

1. They say the paper may decay.
2. The ape weighed eight hundred and eighty pounds.
3. James and Kate came to play today.
4. The agent placed the tapes on the tray.

5. Label the baby's play pail and clay.
6. The amiable whale sprayed his neighbor.

/eɪ/ CONTRASTS

/eɪ/—/ɛ/		/eɪ/—/ɪ/	
mate	met	mate	mit
date	debt	late	lit
bait	bet	tame	Tim
rake	wreck	weight	wit
main	men	bait	bit
gate	get	hate	hit
laid	led	chain	chin
fade	fed	fate	fit

Note: when *ai-*, *a-e*, or other spellings associated with /eɪ/ occur with /r/, as in *air* and *bare*, the vowel may be heard and transcribed as /eɪ/, /e/, or /ɛ/. The *ai-* or *a-e* before /l/, as in *ail* and *bale*, may be transcribed as /eɪ/ or without the glide as /e/, according to listener judgment.

In American-English, the /eɪ/ occurs usually with primary accent in words such as *átrium*, *máking*, and *matinée*. It also occurs with secondary accent as in polysyllabic words with the *-ate* endings of *lúbricáte*, *incórporáte*, and *mítigáte*. But when unaccented, it is produced and transcribed as a pure or monothong vowel /e/. This usually occurs when the sound is in the syllable next to the accented syllable, as can be seen in the form changes of the following pairs of words:

/eɪ/	/e/
nátive	natívity
fátal	fatálity
vácate	vacátion
cháos	chaótic

Note that the unaccented /e/ may also be pronounced /ə/ in some of these words. The unaccented /e/ also occurs in bisyllabic words ending in an unaccented *-ate* such as *dónate*, *órate*, *víbrate*, and *rébate*, immediately following the accented syllable. As the last sound of an utterance, it is usually transcribed as /eɪ/.

European speakers should observe that American-English /eɪ/ is a diphthong and not the monothong /e/ they are used to producing as in the French *les* [le] and the Spanish *se* [se].

IPA   ou
Dictionary   ō Key Words: *own, boat, no*
Northampton o-e (oa, -o, ow)

/ou/ PRODUCTION—Back Round Diphthong

With the velopharyngeal port closed, the middle and back portion of the tongue is raised toward the palate, slightly lower than for /ʊ/, the lips are rounded and may be slightly protruded for an aperture larger than for /ʊ/ as voice is given; then the tongue briefly rises toward the /ʊ/ height and the rounded lip aperture decreases in size as voice continues. The tip of the tongue touches lightly behind the lower front teeth. The [o] portion is the longer nucleus and the [ʊ] is the shorter glide. For many speakers, the glide portion may have a tongue-lip position close to /u/ but of short duration.

/ou/ SPELLING

o occurs most frequently as in *hold, both, old, go, no, so.*
-o-e is very consistently /ou/ as in *home, note, mole, rose, hope,* and *smoke.*
ow as in *blow, crow, row, owe, own, throw.*
oa- as in *road, boat, moan, oats, oak, whoa.*
-oe as in *toe, hoe, doe, sloe, woe, roe.*
Irregular spellings include *-au-* as in *chauffer, -eau* as in *beau, -ew* as in *sew, -ough* as in *though* and *dough, -eo-* as in *yeoman, -oo-* as in *brooch,* and *-ou-* as in *soul.*

/ou/ WORDS

Initial		*Medial*		*Final*	
oak	ocean	boat	toes	go	toe
oats	over	pole	thrown	no	hoe
only	oaf	code	both	so	woe
opal	odor	showed	rose	row	sew
own	omen	broke	hope	low	dough
open	oval	road	smoke	bow	though

/ou/ SENTENCES

1. The cr*ow* was sl*ow*ly going h*ome*.
2. *The b*oa*t goes* ov*er the* ocean.

3. Joe wrote the note in code.
4. The doe's bones won't grow.
5. Don't throw snow at the pony.
6. Those roses have their own odor.

/ou/ CONTRASTS

/ou/—/u/		/ou/—/ɔ/	
pole	pull	phone	fawn
bowl	bull	boat	bought
code	could	coat	caught
showed	should	pose	paws
stowed	stood	tote	taught
goad	good	bowl	bawl
broke	brook	coal	call
coke	cook	foal	fall

Note: when o, oa-, o-e, or other spellings associated with /ou/ occur with /r/, as in for, oar, and bore, the vowel may be heard and transcribed as /ou/, /o/, or /ɔ/, and dialectically as /ɑ/. The o, oa-, o-e, and other spellings before /l/, as in cold, coal, and hole, may be transcribed as /ou/ or without the glide as /o/, according to listener judgment.

In American-English, the /ou/ occurs usually with primary accent in words such as only, emotion, and below. It also occurs with secondary accent in polysyllabic words such as telephone, monotone, and chromosome. When unaccented, it is traditionally transcribed as a pure or monothong vowel /o/. This usually occurs when the sound is in the syllable next to the accented syllable as can be seen in the form changes of the following pairs of words:

/ou/	/o/
rótate	rotátion
lócate	locátion
dónate	donátion
prórate	prorátion

The unaccented /o/ also occurs in words just before the accented syllable as in obey, opinion, omission, and obese, and after the accented syllable as in geode. As the final unaccented syllable in window, polo, pillow, elbow, and potato, the sound may be transcribed either /o/ or /ou/, according to listener judgment. As the last sound of an utterance, it is usually transcribed as /ou/, even when unstressed.

IPA   aɪ
Dictionary   ī Key Words: *ice, mine, my*
Northampton i-e (igh, -y)

/aɪ/ PRODUCTION—Low Back to High Front Diphthong

With the velopharyngeal port closed and the mouth open as for /æ/, the middle and front portion of the tongue is raised more than for /ʌ/ but less than for /æ/ while voice is given; then the tongue briefly rises in front toward the /ɪ/ height and the mouth opening is slightly decreased as voice continues. The tip of the tongue touches lightly behind the lower front teeth. The [a] portion is the longer nucleus and the [ɪ] portion is the shorter glide. For some speakers, the nucleus may be closer to the /ɑ/ position and the glide close to /i/ but of short duration.

/aɪ/ SPELLING

i occurs most frequently but inconsistently as /aɪ/ as in *child, mild, find, wild, mind, idol, idea, alibi, I.*

i-e occurs less frequently but more consistently as in *ice, ride, file, bike, time, kite, chide.*

-y as in *by, why, my, cry, deny, nylon, psychology, ply, fry.*

-ie as in *die, vie, pie, tie, cried, lie.*

-igh as in *high, fight, light, might, night, right.*

Less frequently and irregularly *-y-e* as in *type, style, Clyde; -ui-* as in *guide, beguile; -ye* as in *rye, dye, lye; -uy* as in *buy, guy; -ei-* as in *height, sleight; -oi-* as in *choir;* and spelled *eye* or *aye.*

/aɪ/ WORDS

Initial		Medial		Final	
ice	item	find	light	by	die
ivy	idea	child	psyche	my	lie
idle	icicle	wild	shine	guy	sigh
iris	eyes	kind	fright	deny	bye
aisle	eyed	pine	type	thigh	buy
ivory	island	hide	height	sky	rye

/aɪ/ SENTENCES

1. *I* tr*i*ed to fl*y* the k*i*te.
2. M*y* g*ui*de l*i*kes *i*ce cream.
3. The ch*i*ld's b*i*ke is the r*i*ght s*i*ze.
4. T*i*me has been m*igh*ty k*i*nd to Cl*y*de.
5. Wh*y* does the br*i*de wish to b*uy* a f*i*le?
6. M*y* *eye*s are t*i*red from cr*y*ing.

/aɪ/ CONTRASTS

/aɪ/—/ɑ/		/aɪ/—/ɪ/		/aɪ/—/aʊ/	
type	top	ride	rid	dine	down
ride	rod	fine	fin	mice	mouse
pipe	pop	like	lick	nine	noun
like	lock	type	tip	lied	loud
light	lot	sign	sin	by	bow
fire	far	hide	hid	high	how
side	sod	light	lit	file	fowl
hide	hod	bite	bit	spite	spout

Note: the /aɪ/ occurs in stressed syllables and does not have an unstressed transcription as do /eɪ/ and /oʊ/. When a speaker strongly downgrades stress for an /aɪ/ spelling, the unstressed sound may become either /ɪ/ or /ə/. Note the following possible pronunciations in these stress situations:

	Stressed /aɪ/	Unstressed to /ɪ/	Unstressed to /ə/
psychólogy	[saɪkɑlədʒɪ]	[sɪkɑlədʒɪ]	[səkɑlədʒɪ]
critéria	[kraɪtɪrɪə]	[krɪtɪrɪə]	[krətɪrɪə]
gigántic	[dʒaɪgæntɪk]	[dʒɪgæntɪk]	[dʒəgæntɪk]

The /a/ occurs alone in American-English primarily in New England dialect and in some stage speech, taking the mouth position for /æ/ with the tongue height between /æ/ and /ʌ/, in such words as the following:

	General American	New England
ask	[æsk]	[ask]
path	[pæθ]	[paθ]
park	[pɑrk]	[pak]
car	[kɑr]	[kaː]

IPA   aʊ
Dictionary   ou Key Words: *out, loud, now*
Northampton ou (ow)

/aʊ/ PRODUCTION—Low Back to High Back Round Diphthong

With the velopharyngeal port closed and the mouth opened as for /æ/, the middle and front portion of the tongue is raised more than for /ʌ/ but less than for /æ/ while voice is given; then the tongue briefly rises in the back toward the /ʊ/ height, the mouth opening is slightly decreased and the lips are round as for /ʊ/ as voice continues. The tip of the tongue touches lightly behind the lower front teeth and may move back slightly for the /ʊ/ portion. The [a] portion is the longer nucleus and the [ʊ] portion is the shorter glide. For some speakers, the nucleus may be closer to the /ɑ/ position and the glide close to /u/ but of short duration.

/aʊ/ SPELLING

ou- occurs frequently and consistently as in *out, mouse, found, mouth, shout, ground, ouch.*
ow occurs frequently as in *owl, fowl, cow, town, plow, howl, allow.*
Irregularly and infrequently *-ough* as in *bough, drought; -au-* as in *Faust, kraut; hou-* with silent *h* as in *hour.*

/aʊ/ WORDS

Initial		*Medial*		*Final*	
out	outlaw	count	town	now	vow
ouch	outline	found	fowl	cow	endow
ounce	outfit	mouse	gown	sow	allow
oust	output	doubt	dowel	prow	somehow
ours	outlet	noun	towel	how	eyebrow
owl	hour	about	brown	bough	thou

/aʊ/ SENTENCES

1. I doubt that the trout is now out of the water.
2. Count us out for about an hour.
3. Our brown cow has been found.
4. The mouth is rounded for the /aʊ/ sound.
5. The scouts are around the outside of the house.
6. A loud shout left no doubt about the cow.

/aʊ/ CONTRASTS

/aʊ/—/ɑ/		/aʊ/—/ʌ/		/aʊ/—/aɪ/	
shout	shot	town	ton	down	dine
spout	spot	down	done	mouse	mice
down	don	gown	gun	noun	nine
cowed	cod	bout	butt	loud	lied
scout	Scott	found	fund	bow	by
gout	got	cowl	cull	how	high
pout	pot	noun	nun	fowl	file
tout	tot	pout	putt	spout	spite

Note: the /aʊ/ occurs in stressed syllables and does not have an unstressed transcription as do /eɪ/ and /oʊ/. The /a/ occurs alone in American-English primarily in New England dialect and in some stage speech, taking the mouth position for /æ/ with tongue height between /æ/ and /ʌ/, in such words as the following:

	General American	*New England*
ask	[æsk]	[ask]
path	[pæθ]	[paθ]
park	[pɑrk]	[pak]
car	[kɑr]	[ka:]

IPA   ɔɪ
Dictionary   oi Key Words: *oil, coin, boy*
Northampton oi (oy)

/ɔɪ/ PRODUCTION—Back Round to High Front Diphthong

With the velopharyngeal port closed, the back and middle portion of the tongue is slightly raised with elevation as for /ɔ/, the mouth is open for /ɔ/ with lips rounded and slightly protruded as voice is given; then the lip rounding relaxes and the tongue briefly rises toward the /ɪ/ height as voice continues. The lower jaw may move upward from the opening of /ɔ/ to the smaller opening of /ɪ/. The [ɔ] portion is the longer nucleus and the [ɪ] portion is the shorter glide. For many speakers, the glide portion may have a tongue-mouth position close to /i/ but for short duration.

/ɔɪ/ SPELLING

oi- most frequently as in *oil, ointment, voice, coin, foil, Detroit.*
oy frequently as in *oyster, soy, coy, loyal, boycott, boy, toy.*

/ɔɪ/ WORDS

Initial	Medial		Final	
oil	foil	boycott	boy	toy
oiler	coin	royal	soy	deploy
ointment	voice	mastoid	coy	cloy
oyster	join	appoint	joy	enjoy
	soil	goiter	Roy	destroy
	loin	thyroid	poi	Troy

/ɔɪ/ SENTENCES

1. The royal boy enjoyed his toys.
2. Oysters help avoid thyroid goiters.
3. The ploy was poised to destroy Troy.
4. Roy's noise annoyed the envoy.
5. Boiling oil will foil the spoilers.
6. They deployed a destroyer as decoy for the convoy.

/ɔɪ/ CONTRASTS

/ɔɪ/—/aɪ/		/ɔɪ/—/ɔ/		/ɔɪ/—/ɝ/	
toil	tile	coil	call	oil	earl
poise	pies	foil	fall	loin	learn
toys	ties	toil	tall	voice	verse
loin	line	boil	ball	boil	burl
foil	file	joy	jaw	poise	purrs
boy	buy	cloy	claw	boys	burrs
voice	vice	noise	gnaws	royal	rural
oil	aisle	soy	saw	coil	curl

Note: an /ɔɪ/ for /ɝ/, and an /ɝ/ for /ɔɪ/ substitution occurs in non-standard urban New York pronunciation as in [gɔɪl] for *girl* and [ɝl] for *oil.*

REVIEW VOCABULARY

Accent—stress on a syllable within a word.

Back vowels—vowels with resonance influenced by raising of the back of the tongue (include /u/, /ʊ/, /ɔ/, and /ɑ/).

Front vowels—vowels with resonance influenced by raising of the front of the tongue (include /i/, /ɪ/, /ɛ/, and /æ/).

Mixed vowels—vowels with resonance influenced by raising the middle of the tongue or with no tongue elevation (include /a/, /ʌ/, and /ɝ/.

Round vowels—vowels with resonance influenced by rounding and slightly protruding the lips (include /u/, /ʊ/, and /ɔ/).

Stress—pointing up or drawing special attention to a unit of speech.

EXERCISES

1. Place the following front vowels in order of tongue elevation:

   /ɛ/   /e/   /i/   /æ/   /ɪ/

2. Place the following back vowels in order of tongue elevation:

   /ʊ/   /o/   /ɑ/   /u/   /ɔ/

3. From memory, draw the vowel diagram and fill in static vowel phonemes. Be sure to label the two dimensions. Check Figure IV–1.

4. Pronounce and transliterate into Roman alphabet symbols the following nonsense monosyllabic units:

[gɪf]	[ʌik]	[θɔk]	[stɔɪp]
[mɛŋ]	[saʊp]	[kʌut]	[kɪb]
[ʃɑlt]	[ðæd]	[vɛbz]	[fiʒ]
[zuθ]	[bɑv]	[heɪm]	[æŋk]

5. Pronounce and transliterate into Roman alphabet symbols the following nonsense bisyllabic units, being sure to observe accent where vowel transcriptions indicate:

[teɪdəs]   [haɪskɚ]   [splinod]
[jɚmæb]   [frɔɪθəʃ]   [hɝ·slɪg]
[wɑvlʌt]   [ðautn̩]   [kʌmoʤub]
[ʧoumbet]   [bekɪz]   [prɪŋed]

SUGGESTED READING

Bronstein, Arthur J.: *The Pronunciation of American English*. Englewood Cliffs, N.J., Prentice-Hall, Inc., 1960

Chapters 7, 8, 9, and 10 survey the vowels and diphthongs of American English (pp. 131–204) with numerous diagrams to show tongue height and positioning.

Griffith, Jerry, and Miner, Lynn E.: *Phonetic Context Drillbook*. Englewood Cliffs, N.J., Prentice-Hall, Inc., 1979

This paperback provides for each of the American-English vowels and diphthongs a wide variety of phonetic contexts in words, phrases and sentences that are used in everyday language. The practice words are selected from among those most commonly used.

CONNECTED SPEECH AND THE INFLUENCE OF CONTEXT

The previous chapters have analyzed the elements of our speech, treating them as segments to be described and considered individually. This has been necessary to understand the make-up of speech. At the same time, we have warned that such analysis is somewhat artificial, since speech does not actually occur in discrete segments. In normal speech—i.e., real connected speech—speech sounds do not follow one another as separate and distinct units like beads on a string. Rather, the necessary movements of the articulators from the place and manner of one sound to those of the next influence the way each phoneme is produced. The influence of adjoining sounds upon each other is called **coarticulation**. Coarticulation occurs for any unit of connected speech so that even in a simple word like *pin*, the influence of the [ɪ] in the nucleus of the syllable is apparent in both the [p] and the [n] sounds, in how they are formed as well as how they sound. A vowel such as the low front /æ/, with a fairly wide mouth opening. can influence the way two or three or even four other sounds before it are produced.

In some cases, vowels in context do not actually reach the target production described for them in the analyses of Chapter IV, but merely head for that target before merging into the following sound. In instrumental analysis, either physiologic or acoustic, it is often impossible to mark an exact place where one sound ends and the next begins. Since we have over 40 phonemes in American-English and thousands of words, the possible variations caused by phonetic context can be extensive. Here we point out a few of the most significant effects of the context of connected speech, some of which influence phonetic transcription.

INFLUENCES OF CONTEXT

Place of Articulation

The place of articulation of a consonant or a vowel varies with the vowels or consonants that precede or follow it. The specific place where the tongue touches the roof of the mouth to produce /k/, for example, differs depending upon whether the adjoining vowel is made by elevating the front of the tongue (as for /i/) or the back of the tongue (as for /u/). Figure V-1 illustrates these different points of contact for the /k/ phoneme on the palate and on the velum, respectively. This slight difference in place of tongue contact on syllables [kik] and [kuk] results in predictable changes in the acoustic characteristics of /k/. Even though both [k] allophones are recognized as

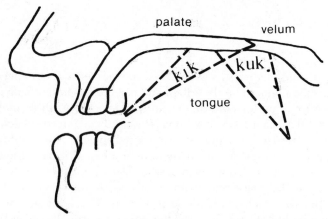

Figure V-1.   Relative positions for contact of the tongue for the stop portion of /k/ associated with the front vowel /i/ and with the back vowel /u/.

representing the phoneme /k/, coarticulation with vowels has made them different acoustically. This slight acoustic difference in the [k] may provide important cues for the listener in distinguishing whether the adjoining vowel sound was [i] or [u]. Similarly, when the consonant sound is different, as in syllables [ik] and [it], the relative position of the tongue contact to produce [k] (on the palate) and to produce [t] (on the alveolar ridge) influences the sound of the adjoining vowel [i] so that it is slightly different in the two syllables.

Voicing

Although phonemes have previously been described as being either voiceless or voiced sounds, the presence of voicing in their allophones is markedly influenced by coarticulation. When a breath sound like /t/ is produced in rapid speech between two voiced sounds (the intervocalic position) as in the word *butter*, it tends to be partially voiced as [bʌt̬ɚ], falling between the sounds of /t/ and /d/. The allophone of /t/ in such a word may be heard with voicing ranging from [bʌtʻɚ] with full aspiration, to [bʌt̬ɚ] with very light aspiration and some voicing, to [bʌdɚ], which is voiced and not aspirated. Similarly, the /r/ and /l/, though usually considered voiced consonants, when blended with a preceding voiceless consonant are produced almost without voicing, especially where they join the preceding voiceless consonant. Note in the following pairs of words that the /r/ and /l/ are produced in the first word with voice and in the second almost without voice:

ray [reɪ]—pray [pr̥eɪ]	lie [laɪ]—ply [pl̥aɪ]
rue [ru]—true [tr̥u]	lay [leɪ]—clay [kl̥eɪ]
rye [raɪ]—fry [fr̥aɪ]	low [loʊ]—slow [sl̥oʊ]
row [roʊ]—crow [kr̥oʊ]	lee [li]—flee [fl̥i]

The narrow transcription symbols (see Table I–4) of [̬] for voicing and [̥] for indicating voiceless breath are useful when careful transcription of these subtle differences is important.

Duration

Length of vowel sounds is influenced by the manner of articulation of the consonant that follows them. Vowels are typically shorter before a stop consonant or affricate than before a fricative or resonant consonant.

Note that the vowel is of greater duration in the first word of these pairs:

ease	— eat
if	— it
us	— up
tame	— take

The vowel is also of shorter duration before a voiceless stop or affricate than before its voiced counterpart, made in the same position. Note the difference in vowel duration in the following pairs of words:

edge	— etch	sub	— sup
ad	— at	bag	— back
lab	— lap	sued	— suit

Notice how the vowel duration differs in these sets of words even though the consonant has the same place of articulation:

ad — an   — at
cub — come — cup
lug — lung — luck

Double letters in the same syllable as in *butter* and *summer* are produced as a single consonant sound. However, when the same consonants join at the end of one word and the beginning of the other, they are produced as one sound but the duration is usually extended. Compare *summer* [sʌmɚ] with *some more* [sʌm:or], *falling* [fɔlɪŋ] with *fall line* [fɔl:aɪn]. The stop phase of similarly combined stop consonants is also held longer as in *hot time* [hɑt:aɪm], *top pair* [tɑp:ɛr], and *black cat* [blæk:æt].

Release of Stops

Stop consonants have the possibility of both a stop or closure and an aspiration or release action. An initial voiceless stop followed by a vowel is both stopped and audibly aspirated as in *pie*. But when the stop is preceded by /s/, as in *spy*, it is unaspirated but the breath pressure is released to begin voicing for the vowel that follows. The sound of the [p] in the *sp-* combination may be heard as sounding very close to the /b/ sound but of somewhat greater duration. Compare [spɑ] with [sbɑ], [stu] with [sdu], and [ski] with [sgi]. In considering the similarity of these sounds, it is noteworthy that English does not have [sb], [sd], or [sg] combinations in words, so that the confusion does not influence meaning.

Stop consonants at the end of utterances are frequently not released or are released so gently that they are not audible. In the word *up*, for example, the [p] need not be released because the influence of lip closure on the termination of the [ʌ] vowel presents the listener with sufficient acoustic information about the place of articulation of the final sound to know that the /p/ phoneme was present. If the place of articulation of the adjoining sound is similar, however, the final stop must be aspirated to be distinguished. In the word *amp*, the [m] and [p'] are both articulated at the lips. The final [p'] must be exploded in order to be heard. Similarly, if the manner of articulation of the last two sounds is the same, that is if they are both stops, the final stop must be exploded to be distinguished. Note that in *at*, the [t] can be unreleased but in *apt* or *act*, it must be released with an audible explosion.

Consonant Blends

When two consonants adjoin within a syllable and the first uses part of the speech mechanism not necessary to produce the second, the position of the two consonants may be taken simultaneously so that they are produced in very rapid succession as a **consonant blend**. For example, in the word *blue*, the position for the [l] with the tongue point against the alveolar ridge can be taken while the lips are still closed for the [b]. When they are released, the [l] is of very brief duration, a glide, between the [b] and [u]. If the [l] position is not taken simultaneously with the [b] position, an /ə/ sound is likely to intrude between [b] and [l]. The combinations of [br] as in *breeze*, [pɹ] as in *pray*, and [pl] as in *play* are other examples of such blends. The [kl] combination as in *clay* can also be a blend as the back of the tongue can make a closure on the palate for the [k] position, while the point of the tongue simultaneously touches the alveolar ridge in anticipation of the [l]. The [gl], [kɹ], and [gr] combinations are other examples of this kind of consonant blend.

Abutting Consonants

When two stops occur successively but in separate syllables, as the [tp] in *footpath* or the [db] in *hardball*, instead of closures and releases for each of the stops, there is a lingua-alveolar closure, followed immediately by a bilabial closure, and a single release from the latter position. Note the closures and single release in *woodcraft, black tie, football,* and *lab coat.* When the stops are made in the same position, as in *hotdog, hip bone,* and *black gown*, only a single closure and release is needed with an appropriate change in voicing and aspiration. When the same stops abut as in *black cat, mad dog,* and *big girl*, a single stop is closed and released but the closure period is usually held for a longer time, as in *black key* [blæk:i].

When a stop is followed immediately by a fricative, an affricate-like sound is derived. Note, however, that the secondary affricate formed in producing *white shoe* [ʌaɪtʃu] is different from the primary affricate in *why chew* [ʌaɪtʃu], in that the closure of [t] in *white shoe* is held longer to give it identity, whereas the [tʃ] in *why chew* is produced on a single impulse. Other secondary affricates may be formed as [kʃ] in *makeshift*, [ts] in *hot stove*, [pf] in *hop farm*, [df] in *headfirst*, and [ks] in *backside*. Among these, only [ks] and [kʌ] have associated alphabet letters, the *x* and the *qu*, respectively.

Syllabic Consonants

Resonant consonants in the final position may take the full durational value of a syllable, without an associated vowel, when they follow a consonant made in essentially the same position, or in positions that permit a consonant blend. In the word *kitten* [kɪtn̩], the homorganic [t] and [n] have a common lingua-alveolar place of articulation so that the tongue need not move when the /t/ stop is released as a nasal /n/. Note the syllabic final consonant in *ridden* [rɪdn̩], *stop 'em* [stɑpm̩], and *bottle* [bɑtl̩]. In the blends of *uncle* [ʌŋkl̩] and *eagle* [igl̩], the syllabic /l/ can also be formed.

Intrusion

When nasal resonant consonants /m/, /n/, and /ŋ/ immediately precede a voiceless fricative such as /s/ or /θ/, a voiceless stop sound with closure in the same position as the nasal consonant is likely to intrude. Note that in the word *chance*, a [t] stop is produced between the [n] and [s] sounds to form [ʧænts], as though the word were spelled *chants*. During the closure of the [n], some breath pressure is necessarily built up in preparation for the fricative [s] that follows. Release of that pressure into the [s] creates the sound of the aspiration of a lingua-alveolar voiceless stop, or /t/. In the word *length*, the intruding stop takes the lingua-palatal position for /k/ to produce [lɛŋkθ]. A [p] may similarly be created at the juncture of [m] and [θ] in *something*.

The glides [w] and [j] are sometimes intruded in order to separate vowels that end one word and begin another. Following /u/ as in *to eat*, a glide [w] may bridge between [u] and the following [i] to form [tuwit]. Note the same intrusion after lip rounded vowels as in *go on* [gouwɑn], *New England* [nuwɪŋglənd], and *bow out* [bauwaut]. Following the high front vowels /i/ or /ɪ/, a [j] sound may intrude as in *see it* [sijɪt], *die out* [daɪjaut], and *stay in* [steɪjɪn].

Assimilation

To simplify the motions of articulation, one adjoining consonant may partially or completely conform to the manner or place of articulation of the other. Nasal resonant consonants are especially susceptible to accommodation or partial assimilation, taking the place of articulation of the following sound. For example, the /n/ before a /k/ sound takes the place of articulation of the /k/, that is, the back of the tongue against the palate or velum, changing the nasal from /n/ to /ŋ/ as in the words *ink, thank, think, bank, sunk, income,* and *pancake.* The /n/ also changes to an /ŋ/ position before /g/ as in *single* or *finger.* The /m/ may change, too, toward the /k/ and /g/ position as in the word *pumpkin,* often becoming [pʌŋkɪn]. Note the assimilation as *handkerchief* becomes [hæŋkɚʧɪf].

Complete assimilation may take place when the manner and place of articulation of adjoining sounds are very similar, as is shown in dropping the [s] in *this show* [ðɪʃoʊ] and *horseshoe* [horʃu], while producing the dominant [ʃ] sound. The words *cupboard* and *kiln* are examples of equalization or complete assimilation, where omission of the /p/ before /b/ and the /n/ following /l/ are so common as to have become standard pronunciation.

Omission

A number of speech sounds are omitted in connected speech. The most apparent of these is the vowel sound in *not* when that word is unstressed. The omission from speech of this sound in *can't, wouldn't, didn't,* and *haven't* is marked by an apostrophe in writing. The /h/ and /ð/ are also frequently dropped in rapid connected speech as *Where is he?* becomes [ʍɛrɪzi], and *Stop them!* becomes [stɑpm̩]. Final consonants of words are occasionally omitted during rapid speech as *Let me go!* becomes [lɛ mi goʊ]. Whole syllables may be omitted in the phenomenon called "haplology" when two very similar syllables occur in close succession. *Mississippi,* for example, is often pronounced [mɪsɪpi] by natives of that state rather than [mɪsəsɪpi]. *Coca Cola* may similarly become [koʊ koʊlə]. When a different sound occurs between two sounds that are essentially the same to cause a difficult articulation, as in *-sts,* the intervening sound may be omitted and the first sound is elongated. Examples are the *-sts* in *guests,* which is often pronounced [gɛs:], or the *-sks* in *asks,* which may become [æs:]. Similarly, when a final /ɚ/ follows an /r/ as in *mirror* or *bearer,* the words may be said as [mɪr:] or [bɛr:]. To say "5/6," one encounters [sɪksθs] in the last syllable, which regularly becomes [sɪks] or [sɪkts].

The Glottal Stop

In addition to the voiceless stops /p/, /t/, and /k/, produced by the lips, tongue, and palate in the oral cavity, an abrupt hiatus of voicing can be produced at the glottis by closing the vocal folds tightly and then releasing them to continue voicing. This **glottal stop** is written as /ʔ/ in the IPA. It is often used in General American to separate two words when the first ends and the next begins with a vowel. The glottal stop is especially needed to separate /ə/ or /ʌ/ and any following vowel as in *the uncle* [ðəʔʌŋkl̩], *the only* [ðəʔoʊnlɪ], and *the apple* [ðəʔæpl̩]. In the phrase *he eats,* two [i] sounds adjoin and when produced together might be confused with the word *heats.* The simple elongation of [i:] leaves the meaning ambiguous so that it is helpful to stop voicing very briefly between the words for them to be distinguished as in [hiʔ its] and *we even* [wiʔ ivən]. Of course the speaker may, instead, insert a [j] glide to separate the vowels as in *he eats* [hijits], described previously in the section on intrusion. The glottal stop also occurs in [i] and [ɪŋ] sequences such as in *being* [biʔɪŋ].

In conversational General American speech, the glottal stop is sometimes substituted for /t/ between the homorganic /n/ and /n/ as in *mountain* [maunˀn̩], *sentence* [sɛnˀn̩ts], *Denton* [dɛnˀn̩], *Scranton* [skrænˀn̩], and *Benton* [bɛnˀn̩]. A similar substitution may be made between /l/ and /n/ as in *Hilton* [hɪlˀn̩] and Skelton [skɛlˀn̩]. Some New York City speakers habitually substitute the /ˀ/ for /t/ in such words as *bottle* [bɑˀl̩] and *little* [lɪˀl̩]. Hawaiian words, with their heavy use of vowels, make extensive use of the glottal stop for separation as in *nuuanu* [nuˀuɑnu] and *Hawaii* [hɑwɑiˀi].

Influence of /r/ and /l/ Sounds

The /r/ and /l/ have very strong influence on adjoining speech sounds. As resonant sounds, they are like vowels but with the tongue intruding more into the oral cavity. Following a pure or monothong vowel, movement of the tongue toward the point-upward /r/ or /l/ position during continued voicing creates a diphthong sound. The word *eel*, which appears to have just the two sounds [i] and [l], actually sounds like [iəl], [iɪl], or [ijl]. Similarly, in *school* and *poor*, movement of the tongue creates an /ə/ following the vowel. By convention, this /ə/ sound between the vowel and the /r/ or /l/ is not transcribed unless very prominent. It is an understood influence of the /r/ and the /l/ sounds.

When spelling suggests the /i/ before /r/ as in such words as *beer, here, year, peer,* and *rear*, positioning of the tongue in anticipation of the /r/ makes the vowel much closer to /ɪ/. Even though *bean* would be transcribed [bin], *beer* would be transcribed [bɪr], unless the vowel were especially emphasized as [i]. Similarly, the /eɪ/ before /r/ is difficult to distinguish. Although the vowel in *bake* is clearly /eɪ/, the vowel in *bare* may be heard as either /ɛ/ for a transcription of [bɛr], as /e/ for a transcription of [ber], or as /eɪ/ for a transcription of [beɪr]. If the /e/ is diphthongized for a full /eɪ/, the word *bare* might sound like [beɪjɚ], suggesting two syllables and the name *Bayer*. The words *care, dare, fair, hair, pear, heir,* and *mare* offer similar difficulty. Again, the /ou/ before /r/, articulated as a diphthong, would create a triphthong sound for *ore* to become [ouɚ] or [ouwɚ]. It is more appropriately transcribed as [or], but it may be pronounced [or], [ɔr], [ɑr], or [ouɚ] in the United States. The same would be true for the words *core, for, door, port, course, court, four, forest,* and *orange*. For General American, the following transcriptions are recommended:

beer [bɪr]
bare [bɛr]
bore [bor]

The listener should use the alternative transcriptions to indicate subtle differences in pronunciation by a speaker or group of speakers.

The diphthongs /eɪ/ and /ou/, when they immediately precede an /l/ sound, may similarly be transcribed without their glide, unless the speaker emphasizes the glide portion. The words *pale* and *bail* may be written [pel] and [bel] unless the speaker gives obvious emphasis to the glides for [peɪl] and [beɪl]. Similarly, the words *bowl* and *hole* may be transcribed [bol] and [hol] unless heard as [boul] or [bouwəl], and [houl], respectively.

DIFFICULT ARTICULATIONS

Articulating speech sounds is a skill. Some speech sounds require greater skill and are more difficult to master than others as we are learning speech. Certain sequences and clusters of speech sounds in words also seem more difficult to articulate than others. Consonants (C) separated by vowels (V) seem easiest, as in words like *bee* (CV), *cap* (CVC), *above* (VCVC), and *relate* (CVCVC). Consonants in clusters are more difficult in words like *desks* (CVCCC), *scream* (CCCVC), *spliced* (CCCVCC), *pharynx* (CVCVCCC), and *sixths* (CVCCCC). People with otherwise accurate articulation occasionally stumble over difficult or unfamiliar words with clusters of consonants. Many words with such clusters are habitually mispronounced by a large portion of American-English speakers. Among these are the following:

Word	Desirable Pronunciation	Common Mispronunciation	Articulation Change
library	[laɪbrerɪ]	[laɪberɪ]	omit second consonant
arctic	[ɑrktɪk]	[ɑrtɪk]	omit third consonant
athlete	[æθlit]	[æθəlit]	insert vowel
diphthong	[dɪfθɔŋ]	[dɪpθɔŋ]	change consonant
realtor	[riltɚ]	[rilətɚ]	insert vowel
nuclear	[nukliɚ]	[nukjulɚ]	insert vowel
asterisk	[æstɚɪsk]	[æstɚɪk]	omit second consonant
guests	[gɛsts]	[gɛs:]	omit medial consonant
mirror	[mɪrɚ]	[mɪr:]	omit syllable

Other words commonly mispronounced include *chimney, larynx, ophthalmologist, subsidiary, exorbitant, liaison, jeopardy, recognize, suggest,* and *temperature.*

Especially difficult sequences of words are called "tongue-twisters." Children verbally wrestling with "she says she sells sea shells" is a common part of American-English culture. Peter Piper and his proverbial "peck of pickled peppers" has been traced to an English grammar* published in London in 1674, but it was probably around by word of mouth much earlier. Rapid repetition of the apparently simple name "Peggy Babcock" is reputed to be one of the most difficult tongue-twisters in the language.

What makes these particular sequences so difficult? Seldom are the words difficult by themselves. There are no difficult clusters of consonants in a phrase like *she says she sells*. It is apparent that the problem comes from the sequence of consonants that are highly similar in some aspects of articulation but different in another. The difficulty is in our ability to control the anticipation of sequences to come, or our "feed forward" mechanism. For example, two fricatives made with turbulence against the front teeth, but with the slight difference in tongue position of /s/ and /ʃ/, are placed in a sequence of /ʃ/-/s/, /ʃ/-/s/ (*she says she sells*) and then reversed /s/-/ʃ/ (*sea shells*), changing the pattern slightly but apparently beyond the ability of our physiologic speech mechanism to manage with rapid repetitions. To test this, the reader should try repeating the following sequence rapidly without vowels: [ʃsʃssʃ], [ʃsʃssʃ], [ʃsʃssʃ]. *Peggy Babcock* is loaded with stop consonants (/p, g, b/) made at different places of articulation and in clusters. The simple combination of *Greek grapes* loads the system with lingua-velar stops (/g, k/) and throws a bilabial stop (/p/) into the sequence to break the rhythm. The word *lemon* can be repeated rapidly with little trouble and *linament* can be repeated with only a little more difficulty. But combine the two and repeat *lemon linament* rapidly, and the best articulator will be helpless. Here are a few other twisters, notable for their brevity and simplicity, for the reader to say or repeat rapidly and to analyze:

> We surely shall see the sun shine soon.
> Which wristwatches are Swiss wristwatches?
> Toy Boat
> Unique New York
> His shirt soon shrank in the suds.
> Shave a cedar shingle thin.
> A cup of coffee in a copper coffee pot.
> Thirty-three free throws.
> Soldiers' shoulders.

ANALYSIS OF CONNECTED SPEECH

Speech can be analyzed and described at a variety of phonetic levels. The important effects of coarticulation, just pointed out, make it clear that a static phoneme-by-phoneme view of speech is a great over-simplification. It is a useful starting place, but stopping at that level of analysis would overlook the important allophonic differences as well as the transitions from one

---

*Wallis, John: *Grammatica Linguae Anglicanae*. Oxford, 1674.

sound to another. We speak only in connected coarticulated speech and we apparently depend upon the normal flow of speech in order to understand it. On the other hand, because of the immense complexity of speech—the neurologic innervation, the sequences of muscular action, the movements of structures, and the aerodynamic variations that must occur—some very sophisticated equipment and hours of careful measurement would be required to delineate exhaustively all that occurs in producing a simple utterance like [kæt]. Instrumental physiologic phonetics is concerned with the study of just such phenomena.

However, it is also possible to describe the actions that occur more briefly and in general terms. Such descriptions of the sequences involved in connected speech may serve both as an introduction to further study of speech dynamics and for the immediate uses of practical or applied descriptive phonetics. We can begin to describe units of connected speech using the tools we have at hand: phonetic symbols (Chapter I), basic knowledge of the speech mechanism and processes (Chapter II), vocabulary and understanding about the place of articulation and manner of producing consonant and vowel sounds (Chapters III and IV), our personal ability to analyze the tactile (touch) and kinesthetic (muscle stretching) information fed back to us as we produce speech, and perhaps the assistance of such homey apparatus as a mirror and flashlight. Certainly the literature of instrumental phonetics provides a continuing, invaluable resource for clarification, correction, and confirmation of our judgments.

We begin with simple units that form familiar words, first briefly describing the sequence of actions, then analyzing the movements and conditions in more detail. Then, for further analysis, we consider some of the errors that might have a high probability of occurrence during production. Bracketed numerals relate sections of these descriptions.

Analysis of meat [mit]

Description

With the velopharyngeal port open and the oral cavity closed at the lips, voicing begins (1). As voicing continues, the front of the tongue elevates (2) with the tip against the lower front teeth, and almost simultaneously (3), the lips open slightly and the velopharyngeal port closes. The front of the tongue is very high, nearly touching the palate (4). The tip of the tongue begins to move upward, voice terminates abruptly (5), and the tip of the tongue moves upward rapidly from behind the lower front teeth to press against the front (6) of the alveolar ridge, closing off the flow of air (7). The tongue front and tip relax, and the air held and compressed in the oral cavity is released as breath flow ceases (8).

Analysis

1. Resonance for [m] involves the nasal cavity open at both ends and the oral cavity open at the pharynx but closed at the lips.
2. The tongue begins to move toward the [i] position during the production of [m].
3. Opening of the lips and closure of the velopharyngeal port must be almost simultaneous for the transition from [m] to [i].*
4. Resonance for [i] involves the nasal cavity closed at the velopharyngeal port and the oral cavity open at both ends, but the size of the oral cavity is reduced by the high front tongue position, and the opening at the lips is narrow.
5. Before voicing terminates, the tongue tip is already moving upward, influencing the acoustic characteristics of the end of the [i] sound.
6. Closure for the [t] is forward on the alveolar ridge, almost to the upper front teeth, because of the front tongue position for the preceding [i]. Compare to the position of the [t] closure back on the alveolar ridge following [u] as in [mut].
7. As voicing terminated, the glottis remained open and breath continued to flow into the oral cavity, closed off at the tongue and alveolar ridge, and compressing air in the oral cavity.
8. Depending upon the situation, the release can be very soft and almost silent, or it can be produced with an audible explosion or aspiration.

Error Implications

Consider the misarticulations that might have taken place during production of [mit] at each of the moments numbered above:

1. Had the velopharyngeal port been closed, a sound like /b/ would have been produced, changing the meaning of the word to *beat.*
2. If the tongue does not begin moving toward the [i] position before oral resonance begins, an [ə] sound may intrude for [məit].
3. If the lip opening and velopharyngeal port closure do not occur almost simultaneously, the [i] will be hypernasal and have the sound of [ĩ].†
4. If the front of the tongue is not high enough, the vowel resonance may sound like [ɪ] or [ɛ], so that the word would be heard as *mit* or *met.*
5. Had the voicing continued too long while the tongue tip was moving upward, an [ə] might have intruded to form [miət].
6. Closure farther back on the alveolar ridge might have permitted intrusion of [ə] or a lingua-alveolar fricative between [i] and [t].

---

*Instrumental studies reveal that the velopharyngeal area moves more slowly than the tongue and lips so that closure may actually follow lip opening slightly.

†The usual lag in velopharyngeal closure does make the beginning of the vowel somewhat more nasal than the same vowel would be in a syllable such as [pit].

7. If the flow of air had not continued to produce an abrupt closure, the final consonant might have been heard as the less tense [d].
8. If the [t] is aspirated and breath flow continues with the tip of the tongue opened only slightly and grooved, the final sound may be heard as [s] so that the word becomes [mits].

It is obvious from this analysis and description of articulation that the simple speech unit we produce for the word *meat* is really very complex. It involves changes in resonance from primarily nasal to primarily oral, changes from voicing to voiceless breath, fine tongue adjustments within the oral cavity to create just the right resonance for a particular vowel sound, and a stoppage and release of the breath stream. Positions for any subsequent speech sound are anticipated during production of preceding sounds, and positioning of the tongue for closure of the breath stream is influenced by tongue position of the previous sound. A number of misarticulations are possible in producing this short but complicated speech unit.

Next, we analyze an utterance that forms the word *fence*. Note that this speech unit has an intruded [t] sound, which is not reflected in its spelling.

Analysis of fence [fɛnts]

Description

With the velopharyngeal port closed, breath is forced through the oral cavity (1), and the lower lip approximates the maxillary front teeth so that air flow is constricted through the narrow opening (2) to cause turbulence and audible friction. During the friction (3), the front-to-mid part of the tongue moves up slightly toward a position between /e/ and /æ/ (4). Simultaneously (5), voicing begins and the lower lip is dropped (6). Voicing continues (7) as the tip of the tongue closes against the middle (8) of the alveolar ridge, closing off the flow of air through the oral cavity, and almost simultaneously (9), the velopharyngeal port opens (10). The tongue remains in the lingua-alveolar position but increases muscular tension, as simultaneously (11), voicing ceases and the velopharyngeal port closes. Breath pressure (12) is built up briefly behind the tongue. The tongue releases the breath pressure as it pulls rapidly (13) but slightly away from the alveolar ridge and forms a narrow groove. The breath stream is directed through the narrow aperture between the alveolar ridge and the grooved tip of the tongue (14) against the closely approximated front teeth (15) to form turbulence with audible friction, as breath flow ceases.

Analysis

1. Sufficient breath pressure must come from the lungs to force the stream of air through the oral cavity.

2. The slight separation or approximation of the lower lip and upper front teeth is critical to form a narrow opening for developing turbulence with audible friction.
3. While the friction for [f] is being produced, the tongue is already advancing toward the position of [ɛ].
4. The position for [ɛ] involves raising the front of the tongue to the exact position that will create the resonant formants for this vowel.
5. The beginning of voicing and moving away of the lower lip is simultaneous.
6. The moving away of the lower lip is achieved by relaxation of lip muscles; the lower jaw need not move for the following [ɛ] position.
7. Resonance for the [ɛ] involves the nasal cavity closed at the velopharyngeal port,* and the oral cavity open at both ends but restricted at the mid-to-front by the elevated tongue.
8. The point of [n] closure is determined by the tongue position of the preceding vowel [ɛ], farther back than that for the [i] and farther forward than for the [u].
9. Opening of the velopharyngeal port to the nasal cavity is almost simultaneous with closure of the oral cavity by the tongue.*
10. Resonance for the [n] involves the nasal cavity open at both ends, and the oral cavity closed by the tongue at the alveolar ridge. Another resonance cavity is formed in front of the tongue and between the lips, which must be open for this sound.
11. Termination of voice and closure of the velopharyngeal port must be simultaneous.
12. Breath pressure sufficient for the fricative [s] must be built up behind the tongue which has previously (10)–(11) increased muscular tension in order to hold and compress the breath.
13. Lingua-velar closure and rapid release of the breath pressure creates an aspirated [t‘] sound before the [s], like a fricative [ts].
14. Grooving narrows the aperture necessary for the fricative sound specific to [s].
15. Breath turbulence around the front teeth is necessary for the friction sound of [s].

Error Implications

Consider the misarticulations that might take place at each of the moments numbered above:

1. Insufficient sub-glottal breath pressure will not create audible friction so that the initial sound may be perceived as a weak [v].

---

*Instrumental studies reveal that the velopharyngeal port actually opens during the last portion of the vowel [ɛ], anticipating the nasal resonant [n], and begins its gradual closure as the tongue tip begins to close on the alveolar ridge.

2. If the opening is too wide, friction will not be created at the labio-dental position so that the initial sound may be heard as [h] or may seem to have been omitted.

3. If the tongue does not advance toward the [ɛ] position until friction terminates, an [ə] sound may intrude between [f] and [ɛ] to form [fəɛnts].

4. Positioning of the tongue too high or too low will create a vowel near /e/ or /æ/, respectively.

5. If voicing begins before the lip is dropped, a [v] sound may intrude between [f] and [ɛ] for [fvɛnts].

6. If the jaw is dropped to pull the lower lip away, the tongue will have to compensate by rising higher to form [ɛ]. Its rise during voicing may cause intrusion of a [ə] sound before the [ɛ] position is achieved for [fəɛnts], giving the impression of a two-syllable word.

7. If the velopharyngeal port should open too soon, the vowel will be a nasal [ɛ̃] sound.

8. The position of the front of the tongue for [ɛ] places the tip of the tongue just below the middle of the alveolar ridge. In order to make closure of the oral cavity almost simultaneous with opening of the velopharyngeal port, the tongue tip must close at the closest position on the alveolar ridge. Otherwise, the ending of the [ɛ] may have excessive open nasal resonance.

9. If the velopharyngeal port should be delayed in opening, the voiced stop [d], homorganic with [n], may intrude for [fɛdnts].

10. Resonating cavities to produce [n] require that the lips be open in front of the lingua-velar closure. If not, the bilabial nasal resonant [m] will be heard instead.

11. Should the velopharyngeal port remain open as voicing ceases, breath would escape from the nasal cavity, leaving insufficient oral breath pressure for the [s].

12. Unless the breath is compressed briefly behind the tongue, not enough pressure will be built up for the [s].

13. If the tongue were to move too slowly or too far away, breath pressure necessary for [s] would be dissipated, possibly giving the listener perception of a final [z].

14. If the front of the tongue were too broad, a [ʃ] sound would replace the intended [s].

15. The teeth must be fairly close together to create necessary turbulence for audible friction.

It is readily apparent that the simple one-syllable word *fence* involves a number of very complex articulatory movements. For example, voicing and resonance change from the first breath sound to the vowel with oral resonance, to the nasal resonant [n], to the voiceless sounds that terminate it. The position of the tongue for the vowel sound must be anticipated during production of the initial fricative consonant. Position of the tongue on the alveolar ridge for [n] was determined by the vowel [ɛ] that preceded it. The first three phonemes are continuants that flow easily into each other, but the intruded [t] stops the flow of breath briefly. This stop is necessary to give a clear [s] sound or the unit might sound like *fens* [fɛnz]. Note that nearly simultaneous articulatory movements are required at three moments, numbered 5, 9, and 11 in the analysis.

Other units of connected speech may be analyzed with descriptions such as those used for [mit] and [fɛnts], considering coarticulation effects noted earlier in this chapter. The reader may begin with the unit of *spoon* [spun]. Consider how the [p] would be different were it not preceded by [s], and how the [n] would differ if the vowel before it were [i] instead of [u]. What would probably happen to the *n* if it were followed by a [k]? Other suggested words to analyze are listed in the exercises at the end of this chapter.

TRANSCRIPTION OF CONNECTED SPEECH

Accurate phonetic transcription of how another person says a speech unit requires a good deal of skill and discipline. We not only need to know the IPA symbols well and to listen carefully, but we need to inhibit some of our habitual thinking about speech, spelling, and language. We must guard against thinking of how we believe it should be said "correctly," how we might have said it, how it is spelled, how we would typically segment language into units of words, phrases and sentences, and what the speech unit means. Our auditory-perceptual system is tuned to ignore subtle phonetic differences, such as allophonic or speaker variations, in favor of focusing on the meaning of spoken language. Because we cannot always hear all speech sounds well, we have developed effective use of a mental catalogue of probabilities based on other perceptual cues. These cues are available from **redundant** phonetic, linguistic, and contextual information. Redundancy refers to the presence of more information than is absolutely necessary for understanding. Redundancy permits us to use other available cues to guess what an unheard or poorly heard speech sound most probably was. We have developed the habit of hearing only enough speech to get the meaning and of ignoring the rest.

To retrain the auditory perceptual system, we may begin by attending to spoken nonsense syllables or larger nonsense units. In a bisyllabic unit such as [spruʧɪŋ], we do not have the meaning of the word to help us fill in or remember sounds. However, the consonant cluster of [spr] is a familiar one in American-English and the [ɪŋ] ending makes the unit sound like a word, so that it is fairly easy to hear and transcribe. If we create a bisyllabic unit like [tsɝhtuʍ], which contains the same number of phonemes as [sprutʃɪŋ], we encounter difficulty because of some unfamiliar sequences. The [ts] affricate does not occur except in compound words, the [ʍ] does not occur at the end of a word, and the [h] is always followed by a vowel in American-English. Here, our well learned catalogue of probabilities can give us misinformation. There is little phonetic information available except by listening to each sound in the sequence. The student may wish to have a friend create similar nonsense units or use unfamiliar foreign words, and read them to him for practice in transcription. Unfamiliar American-English words may also be helpful.

A second step in retraining our auditory-perceptual system is to transcribe speech in connected units just as it is spoken. We do not speak with a string of separated words anymore than we say words with distinct and separate phonemes. In the printed phrase, *he wore a white tie*, we see the words as distinct linguistic units, each contributing something special to the thought conveyed by the sentence. But when the sentence is spoken in normal conversational speech, it is usually a single phonetic unit, [hiworəʍaɪtːaɪ]. The temptation to transcribe this sentence [hi wor ə ʍaɪt taɪ] is strong, but note how this would overlook that only a single [t] sound was produced at the end of *white* and beginning of *tie*. Compare a word-by-word transcription of the phrase, *this surely evened Dick's score*, with that of a connected transcription:

Word-by-Word   [ðɪs ʃurlɪ ivənd dɪks skor]
Connected   [ðɪʃurlɪʔivəndɪksːkor]

The "word" transcription above ignored many coarticulation effects: the assimilation of the [s] in *this* before the [ʃ] sound of *surely*, the glottal stop between vowels, the single [d] joining *evened* and *Dick's*, and the single lengthened [sː] between *Dick's* and *score*. To practice connected transcription, the reader may have a friend say short phrases in a natural, conversational manner. If necessary, the speaker may repeat the phrase but must do so exactly as said the first time. The transcriber should then read the phrase back aloud from his transcription to see if the original speaker agrees that it matches his production. The following phrases may be helpful practice transcribed as single units of speech:

around the rock	*say it isn't so*
not that time	*pick up a couple of bucks*
play it again	*you lost your chance*
nobody knows him	*let me at him*

For increased familiarity with connected transcription, the student may read aloud this passage from *Charlotte's Web* by E. B. White:

[əspaɪdɚzwɛb ɪztrɔŋgɚðænətlʊks].
[ɔlðouɪtsmeɪdəv θɪn],
[dɛləkətstrændz], [ðəwɛbɪz
nɑtizəlɪbroukən]. [hauwɛvɚ],
[əwɛbgɛtstorn ɛvrɪdeɪ baɪðəʔɪnsɛks
ðætkɪkəraundɪnət], [ændəspaɪdɚ
mʌstribɪldɪt ʍɛnətgɛtsfuləholz].
[ʃɑrlət laɪktəduɚwivɪŋ
dɝɪŋðəleɪtæftɚnun],
[ændfɝn laɪktəsɪtnɪrbaɪŋwɑʧ].

Theŕe are a number of ways the listener can help himself with the difficult task of phonetic transcription. When confronted by unfamiliar words or nonsense units, the transcriber will unconsciously seek additional speech information through lipreading. This supplementary visual information, discussed in Chapter VIII, can be very helpful in discriminating slight differences within speech units. The rate of transcribing speech is considerably slower than the rate of producing speech, so that the listener will have to remember a number of sounds in a particular sequence. He will need to "record" the live signal in his auditory perceptual memory system and possibly "play it back" several times as he completes the transcription. This process is called **re-auditorizing**—that is, listening by memory to something over and over again. The strength of the recalled auditory signal will fade quickly unless reinforced by the motor memory of producing the speech unit. In listening to difficult words, the transcriber may find himself unconsciously moving his tongue or lips as he re-auditorizes, "getting his tongue around the word," so to speak. If developed with care, so as not to substitute the transcriber's pronunciation for that of the speaker, this motor memory for perceived speech can help the transcriber both discriminate the sounds and remember them. Motor aspects of speech perception are discussed in Chapter VIII.

Of course, for units of speech of several phrases or paragraphs, the transcriber will need a magnetic tape or other recording device. An audiotape recording provides long-term storage and the possibility of playing a unit of speech back as often as needed. A video-tape recording can provide lipreading information as well as the acoustic signal. An important consideration in recordings and in live listening is the acoustic environment. Of special concern is high background noise, which may establish a disadvantageous signal-to-noise ratio. Keeping the recording microphone close to the speaker's lips will help, but care must be taken to see that air flow of speech against the microphone does not distort the acoustic signal.

As we move to longer units of speech, we shall see in the next chapter that features of speech rhythm also influence the production of speech sounds and their coarticulation.

REVIEW VOCABULARY

Abutting Consonants—consonants joined in coarticulation but in separate syllables. The [tb] in *football* is an example.

Assimilation—conforming of one sound to the manner of production or place of articulation of a neighboring sound. The *n* in *ink*, for example, takes the same place of articulation as the final [k], to be pronounced [ŋ] for [ɪŋk].

Coarticulation—any influence of one speech sound upon the manner of production or the place of articulation of a neighboring sound.

Consonant blend—a sequential combination of consonants within a syllable in which the positions of the two may be taken simultaneously. The [bl] in *blue* is an example.

Glottal stop—an abrupt hiatus of air at the glottis during connected speech as in *he eats* [hiʔits].

Intruded consonant—a consonant not included in spelling but phonetically present with coarticulation as the [t] in *chance*.

Re-auditorize—to recall the sound of a unit of speech.

Redundant—having more information that is absolutely necessary for intelligibility.

Syllabic consonant—a consonant that serves the function of a vowel as the nucleus of an unaccented syllable. The [l̩] in *bottle* [bɑtl̩] is an example.

EXERCISES

Using the narrow transcription symbols of Table I–4, transcribe the following speech units as you would say them in conversational speech.

1. Voicing [̥], [̬]

three	crew	behind	somewhere
pray	splash	sitting	little
slim	clean	butter	scratch
please	fry	ahead	thrill

2. Lengthening [:]

soon know	about time	bad days
some men	big girl	cub bears
full load	black car	ripe pears
spare ribs	tap pins	this service

3. Syllabic consonants [ˌ]

little	ridden	bread 'n butter
kitten	bottle	riddle
cattle	Eden	cuddle
digging	slap 'em	eaten

4. Intrusion [t], [p], [k], [w], [j]

chance	something	go out	we each
Samson	transcribe	no older	the east
length	fancy	two hours	panther
suspense	comfort	to eat	else

5. Follow the sequence of production below and transcribe, with three IPA symbols, the speech unit that matches the description.

> With the velopharyngeal port closed and without voicing, the lips are closed and the teeth slightly open. As breath flow begins, the front of the tongue begins moving upward in anticipation of the next sound as air held and compressed in the oral cavity is audibly exploded between the lips, and as the mandible drops slightly. Voicing begins, after lip opening and aspiration, as the front tongue height just lower than that for [ɛ] is achieved (resonation condition—oral cavity open at lips, nasal cavity closed at velopharyngeal port). Voicing is continued as the tip of the tongue begins moving upward and forward, anticipating the next sound. Then voicing ceases as breath is directed between the broad, thin tip of the tongue and the maxillary incisors, where they are closely approximated to cause turbulence and audible friction. Breath flow ceases.

6. Describe what went wrong if a speaker, intending to produce the word, *plunk* [pl̩ʌŋk], instead produced each of the following units:

[pl̩ʌnt]	[pl̩ʌk]
[blæŋk]	[pʌŋk]
[blʌŋk]	[pəlʌŋk]

7. Write out descriptions of the sequences involved in producing each of the following words as you would say them.

better	glass	smooth
twist	pleasure	mixed
whole	gentle	catch

8. Transcribe each of the following phrases in connected IPA transcription as you would say them in conversational speech. Each is a single phrase.

    a. the easy way out
    b. this seems okay
    c. big girls don't cry
    d. under the yumyum tree
    e. better safe than sorry
    f. the days of wine and roses

SUGGESTED READING

Dew, Donald, and Jensen, Paul: *Phonetic Processing: The Dynamics of Speech*. Columbus, Ohio, Chas. E. Merrill Publishing Co., 1977.

Chapter 5, "Coarticulation," emphasizes the coordination of various parts of the speech mechanism in producing speech sounds and the influence of context upon the production of neighboring sounds (pp. 109–130).

Malmberg, Bertil: *Phonetics*. New York, Dover Publications, Inc., 1963.

Chapter VII, "Combinatory Phonetics," deals clearly with some of the important influences of context and coarticulation (pp. 56–73). The syllable is described as it relates to several languages. This book, by a famous Swedish phonetician, is good basic reading for the beginning student.

Chapter VI

SPEECH RHYTHM AND SUPRA-SEGMENTAL FEATURES

- **ACCENT**
- **EMPHASIS**
- **PHRASING**
- **INTONATION**
- **RATE**
- **REVIEW VOCABULARY**
- **EXERCISES**
- **SUGGESTED READING**

One of the first things we notice when hearing a foreign language is a kind of "melody" or rhythmic variation in the flow of speech. This is especially apparent when we do not understand the language and listen just for its sound pattern. We refer to the "lilt" of Irish speech, we note the constant falling and rising pitch and the long resonant consonants of Scandinavian languages, and we are conscious of a regular cadence in Spanish. But we are often surprised when foreign speakers comment on the rhythm of American-English. Listening as we usually do primarily for the meaning, we are often unaware of the rhythmic patterning in the sound of our own speech. Of course, individuals and dialect groups develop differences in their speech patterns, but in this chapter we are interested in those features general to American-English, and those influencing meaning and understanding rather than contributing primarily to aesthetic effect.

The general term used here for this phenomenon is **speech rhythm.** One also finds in the phonetic and linguistic literature such terms as speech "melody" or "patterning," "prosodemes," and the "prosodic" or "temporal" features of speech. Because these features occur in longer connected units, as compared to the segments of phonemes or individual speech sounds, they are often called the **supra-segmental features** of speech. The word "rhythm" has musical and poetic connotations that may be somewhat misleading, since the rhythm of natural connected speech bears only distant resemblance to the more orderly rhythmic structures of music and poetry, but it is nevertheless a serviceable generic term for our use.

The basic unit of speech rhythm is the **syllable**. It is usually described as a cluster of coarticulated sounds produced on a single speech impulse. We recognize in speaking the following words, for example, single impulses or syllables in *go, cat,* and *stretch;* two syllables in *apple, going,* and *pleasant;* three syllables in *terminate, radio,* and *microphone;* and four syllables in *America, tabulation,* and *celebrating.* Our intuitive judgment about how many syllables are present, and thus our notion of what constitutes a syllable, has not satisfactorily been confirmed by instrumental studies. This is true for both physiologic studies of the production of syllables and for acoustic studies of the results of their production. A continuing problem has been in determining spoken syllable boundaries. The spoken or phonetic syllable is not necessarily the same as the written syllable and does not always follow the written segmentation recommended by dictionaries and writing guides. This is primarily because our connected speech does not observe word boundaries. Note that in writing, we would segment the syllables in the phrase, "not even an apple," as *not-ev-en-an-app-le,* whereas for natural connected speech, we might recognize the syllables as [nɑ-ti-və-nə-næ-pl̩].

The syllable is a cluster of coarticulated sounds usually with consonants bordering a vowel. Syllables terminating in a vowel are called "open" syllables, and those ending with an arresting consonant are called "closed." The essential nucleus or central element of the syllable is a vowel or diphthong sound. Consonants may either initiate or terminate a syllable but cannot function as its nucleus, except for the syllabic consonants mentioned in Chapter V. A syllable may consist entirely of a vowel, as in the case of the *a* in "find a boat." In American-English, the most common syllable cluster is a consonant-vowel (CV) combination as in the *-ly* of *lovely.* Almost as common is the consonant-vowel-consonant (CVC) as in the *-ton* of *Washington.* A VC pattern as in the *up-* of *upset* is less common. (Refer to the section on Difficult Articulations in Chapter V for other syllable patterns.) Consonants may be compounded in a single syllable, as in the CCVCC cluster of *stems,* but different vowels do not cluster in a syllable. Each pure vowel or diphthong forms its own syllable nucleus. In the word *being,* for example, the syllables are *be-* (CV) and *-ing* (VC), compared to the single syllable of the word *bing* (CVC). Note that *being* and *bing* would sound very similar were it not for the bisyllable-unisyllable distinction. Speakers verbally mark the syllable boundary in words such as *being* in a number of ways. A /j/ may be intruded to separate the two vowels for [bijɪŋ], the duration of [i] may be extended to point up its difference as in [bi:ɪŋ], a very brief hiatus or glottal stop may separate the vowels for [biʔɪŋ], or a sudden change in fundamental voice pitch may accompany the slight change in tongue position to distinguish the two vowels. Note similar verbal markings for the short but bisyllabic words *eon* and *boa*. Such verbal markings contribute to the listener's discrimination of the number of syllables and thus the intended word.

Syllable clusters influence coarticulation and relate to the timing of speech. American-English syllables average about two-tenths of a second with variations according to individual speaker differences and patterns of stressing. When given equal stress by a speaker, syllables are of roughly equal duration, regardless of their phonetic complexity. Thus *ram* and *scram* may be produced in about the same period. Similarly, *buy* and *bite* may be forced into the same time frame, primarily by reducing the duration of the [aɪ] in *bite*. The compression of a number of phonemes into the single, brief speech impulse of a syllable forces the compact or intrinsic coarticulation of those sounds within the syllable. Phonemes are thus presented to the listener not haphazardly but coarticulated in syllable clusters. Such clusters help in our recognition of each phoneme because of the transitional characteristics of consonant-vowel and vowel-consonant junctures, which give listeners important perceptual information. Of course, coarticulation effects also extend beyond or are extrinsic to syllable boundaries, as pointed out in Chapter V. We shall see in the following pages how the syllable also contributes to speech rhythm.

The sound of American-English speech rhythm results from a very complex combination of **accent, emphasis, phrasing, intonation,** and **rate.** What we hear is the interaction of variations in loudness, pitch, and duration of syllables, occurring in series of connected phrases and pauses. The product provides the listener with information that influences meaning, assists in listening and understanding, and may give aesthetic interest to speech.

ACCENT

Accent is one form of speech stress. **Stress** points out, sets apart, focuses on, or otherwise gives vocal prominence to a unit of speech. Accent refers to the stress given a syllable within a word compared with its other syllables. For example, the *work-* syllable in *working* is given greater stress than the *-ing* syllable, and the *-cause* in *because* is stressed above the *be-*. It is characteristic of English that every word of more than one syllable have a syllable stressed above the others, and that stressed syllables be audibly different from those of lesser stress. English is, therefore, called a "stress-timed" language. Many other languages, which do not observe this variable stressing pattern but have a more regular beat, are referred to as "syllable-timed." American-English uses less difference between heavily stressed and unstressed syllables than does British-English (see Chapter VII).

American-English observes three basic levels of accent with "primarily accented," "secondarily accented," and "unaccented" syllables. The levels differ relative to each other for a particular speaker, in a specific word at a given moment, and they have no absolute acoustic values that can be specified. It is generally the nuclear vowel of the syllable that undergoes change for accent rather than its consonants. The accentéd syllable is made with greater physiologic force, resulting in (1) greater loudness, (2) greater duration, and (3) a rise in pitch. The accented-unaccented ratio can and often is achieved by reducing force of production on the unstressed or de-accented syllable, giving it reduced loudness, reduced duration, and a lowered pitch in relation to the standard syllable, which now seems to be stressed by virtue of not having been reduced. In connected speech, most persons use a combination of expansion of the stressed syllable and reduction of the unstressed to produce accenting. Because of the resulting acoustic variability, the unreliability of listener judgments, and the vagary of specifying absolute levels of stress, it is possible to argue for four, five, or even more levels of accent. However, it is unlikely that such proliferation of levels beyond the basic three would serve any but the phonetician bent upon the study of fine accent differences.

There are several ways to indicate accent graphically. The International Phonetic Association uses a vertical mark /'/ above and before the syllable with primary accent, a mark of the same size and shape /ˌ/ below and before the syllable with secondary accent, and no mark for unaccented syllables. Thus the word *above* is marked [ə'bʌv], *hotdog* is marked ['hɑt,dɔg] to show secondary accent, and *absolute* is marked [ˌæbsə'lut] with no mark before the unaccented middle syllable, [sə]. These marks have the advantage of international usage in the literature but the disadvantage of suggesting a separation of phonemes: in ['hɑt,dɔg], the secondary accent mark intrudes between the [t] and [d], which are actually closely coarticulated. Dictionaries frequently use a heavy mark (ʹ) above and just after the syllable of primary stress, and a lighter mark of the same position and length (ʹ) just after the syllable with secondary stress. Another system places directly above the vowel nucleus an acute accent mark (ʹ) for strong or heavy stress, a caret [kɛrət] (ˆ) for secondary stress, a grave [greɪv] accent mark (ˋ) for tertiary stress, and a breve [briv] mark (˘) for the unstressed syllable. A simpler demonstrative system frequently used in teaching or improving speech is the use of a strong acute mark (ʹ) directly above the vowel nucleus of the syllable with primary accent, a weaker and shorter mark (ʹ)directly above the nucleus of the syllable with secondary accent, and no mark above an unaccented syllable.

This latter system has some advantages where teaching or improving speech are concerned. It is visually simple with no angles or positioning to learn. The intensity and durational differences between stronger and weaker stressing are readily apparent, illustrated through the visual analogy of combined darkness (or thickness) and length of the accent marks. The marks placed directly above the syllable nucleus focus attention upon the vowel as the primary phoneme of change, and the succession of letters or phonetic

symbols are not interrupted by intervening marks. Still another advantage is
that the therapist, teacher, or transcriber may indicate several levels of stress
if he wishes to by making the accent marks relatively longer or darker by
degrees. This simple system of accent marking will be used throughout this
book.

Which syllable should be given strong or weak accent? In American-
English, there is a strong tendency for bisyllabic words to have their accent
on the first syllable, especially for the vocabulary used in reading books of
young children. The accented syllable usually precedes suffixes such as *-ing*,
-er, -est, -cious, -y, and *-tion*, which are rarely stressed themselves. But the
accented syllable frequently follows unaccented prefixes such as *a-, be-, re-,
de-, ad-*, and *ex-*. Note the following words:

máking	háppy	replý
fáster	nátion	detáin
quíckest	abóve	admíre
delícious	bewáre	extént

It is difficult to establish hard and fast rules for applying accent in
American-English words. Deciding which syllable to accent is largely a matter of following conventional usage. Our listening, in expectancy of hearing
the conventional stressing patterns, is so attuned that we may actually not
understand familiar words when the accent is transposed. Pronounce the
following words, strongly accented as indicated, and note how unfamiliar
they sound:

América	enérgetic	dependént
sylláble	emotiónal	intensíty
intéresting	intónation	catégorize
foundatión	secretarý	cónsider

One reason these words seem to sound so unfamiliar is that pronunciation changes almost automatically as we change accenting. Unstressed syllables tend to have a /ə/ nucleus. Note how the *-i-* in *America* becomes [ə] in
América, and [ɪ] or [i] when it is stressed in *Ameríca*. In the word *syllable*,
the *-a-* changes from [ə] to [eɪ] or [ɑ] when it is given unconventional stress.
Accented syllables are likely to follow their usual vowel spelling pronunciation, as described in Chapter IV, whereas those unaccented often change.
Diphthongs /eɪ/ and /oʊ/ become pure vowels /e/ and /o/ when unstressed,
except in final open syllables. The /i/, /æ/, /u/, and /ɑ/ tend to become /ɪ/, /ɛ/,
/ʊ/, and /ʌ/, respectively, when reduced, and, if deaccented further, become
/ə/. This change in pronunciation with accent is reflected in the spelling of
some words as in *pronounce-pronunciation, maintain–maintenance*, and
sustain-sustenance.

For some pairs of words that have the same spelling, differences in accent and the resulting changes in pronunciation give information that influences meaning. Accent in this regard may be considered to be **phonemic.** Note how the syllable accented determines meaning in the following pairs of words:

pérfect	(adjective)	—	perféct	(verb)
prógress	(noun)	—	progréss	(verb)
rébel	(noun)	—	rebél	(verb)
cónflict	(noun)	—	conflíct	(verb)
ábstract	(adjective)	—	abstráct	(verb)
cómplex	(noun)	—	compléx	(adjective)

Note the change in meaning with movement of the primary accent from the first to last syllable in the following words: *survey, suspect, torment, transport, subject, reject, produce, digest, escort, insult, exile, content, recess.* Although there are standards of conventional accent usage for most words, some words are produced with alternative accented syllables without influencing meaning. For example, *adult* is said both as *ádult* and as *adúlt.* Compare accenting patterns with friends on the following words: *automobile, cigarette, concrete, contrary, defense, dictator, gasoline, illustrate,* and *locate.* For such words, accent is not **phonemic.**

The presence or absence of secondary accent also changes the meaning of a number of words, especially those with an *-ate* suffix. Compare the following and note also that the *-a(t)e* in these words changes pronunciation with stressing from /ə/ to /eɪ/.

No Secondary Accent		**Secondary Accent Present**	
delíberate	(adjective)	delíberáte	(verb)
affíliate	(noun)	affíliáte	(verb)
délegate	(noun)	délegáte	(verb)
gráduate	(noun)	gráduáte	(verb)
móderate	(adjective)	móderáte	(verb)

Secondary accent is usually present in words compounded from two other words. *Aírpláne, hótdóg, cówbóy,* and *básebáll* are examples in which the second syllable is almost never reduced to /ə/.

In some phonetic contexts, reduction of the unstressed syllable may lead to omission of the /ə/ when a following resonant consonant is homorganic with the previous consonant. In *cattle,* for example, both the [t] and [l] have a lingua-alveolar place of production. The final syllable may be reduced from [kǽtəl] to use of the syllabic [l̩] in [kǽtl̩] when the tongue does not move from the alveolar ridge in coarticulation. This reflects a great reduction of stress in which the resonant consonant /l/ takes the function of a syllable nucleus, as [ļ]. Note similar reduction in *kitten, button,* and *little.* The ultimate extreme of stress reduction is complete omission of the unstressed syllable. The British have a particular tendency to omit and telescope unstressed syllables, as noted in Chapter VII. In American-English, there are a number of words that commonly have syllables omitted in conversational speech. Note the following examples:

	Formal	**Conversational**
annual	[ǽnjuəl]	[ǽnjul]
evening	[ivənɪŋ]	[ivnɪŋ]
family	[fǽməlɪ]	[fǽmlɪ]
miniature	[mɪ́nɪətʃɚ]	[mɪ́nɪtʃɚ]

Other words that frequently have omitted syllables include *reference, several, temperature, toward, valuable, veteran, difference, diamond, favorable,* and *interest.*

EMPHASIS

Emphasis refers to the stressing of a word or words within a phrase or sentence. Like accent, emphasis is produced primarily by greater physiologic force resulting in increased loudness and duration of syllables within the stressed word, with an accompanying change in pitch. Some words may be de-emphasized by reduction in force, thus making other words stand out. Emphasis may also be achieved by pauses surrounding words or by unusual elongation of duration of a selected syllable. Levels of emphasis are even more variable and difficult to specify than levels of accent. Graphic marking of emphasis should ideally be separate from and not interfere with accent markings. The simple expedient of underlining the stressed words will accomplish this, reserving double underlining for very heavy emphasis. Single and double emphasis underlining may be translated into printed material as *italics* and **bold type,** respectively.

Unlike accent, emphasis is not applied according to recurring patterns or conventional usage. Its application is personal and relates to a speaker's intent. Of course, emotional state may be transmitted by exaggerated emphasis on exclamations, but here we are more interested in how language information is transmitted. Each speaker includes a pattern of emphasis in his formulation of phrases, which adds information over and above the string of phoneme segments, their grouping into syllables, and the syllable accent pattern. For example, he may choose to label something, as in "The next to the last syllable is called the penultimate syllable," drawing special attention to the label word. He may wish to reiterate or stress a fact such as, "I say we can't make it." He may seek to compare or contrast parallel thoughts, as "We

<u>drove</u> home but they <u>walked</u> home." A common use of emphasis is in response to situational context. As an example, try saying the sentence *My house is five miles down the road* several times with each of the words given emphasis in turn. Imagine the context in which emphasizing a particular word might be relevant. For example, emphasizing *my* would indicate "I don't mean your house or his house." Emphasizing *miles* could suggest, "and that's a long distance, possibly too far to go." Try the same exercise for the sentence *That baby is crying again.*

Emphasis may also serve to distinguish in speech a single compound word from an adjective and noun word combination. Compounds such as *hotdog, cowboy, airplane, baseball,* and *blackbird* usually have their primary accent on the first syllable, the modifier portion, with secondary accent on the second noun portion. In some situations, it is useful to clarify that two separate words are intended, for example, to differentiate "a blackbird" from "a black bird." The difference, designated by a physical separation in script, is marked in speech by reversing the stress, placing emphasis on the second word—"bláckbírd" compared with "black <u>bird</u>." Note how this is useful in such pairs as *highchair—high chair, greenhouse—green house, bearskin— bare skin, hotdot—hot dog.*

De-emphasis creates phonetic changes similar to reduction of unaccented syllables. Frequently used short connective words are almost never emphasized and tend to be reduced toward /ə/. Such words as *was, of, the,* and *a,* are so commonly produced in connected speech with /ə/ that, when restressed for special emphasis, they are usually produced with /ʌ/ rather than their original pronunciations. Words like *to, you,* and *my* may also be reduced to /ə/ but usually return to their original vowel when given special emphasis.

PHRASING

A speech **phrase** is defined phonetically as a continuous utterance bounded by silent intervals. In the phrase, syllables, which themselves are clusters of segmental phonemes, are linked together in coarticulated clusters. The intervals between phrases are called **pauses.** Speech **phrasing** is related to breathing but does not necessarily reflect breathing patterns. All inhalations during connected speech occur between phrases, that is, during pauses, but inhalation does not always occur with each pause. A speaker may say two or three or more phrases on the same breath. Note in the familiar quotation "I came, I saw, I conquered" that the three phrases can easily be said with a single breath. Figure VI–1 illustrates some relations between phrasing and breathing.

Some pauses are marked in writing by such punctuation marks as commas, periods, semi-colons, colons, question marks, and exclamation marks.

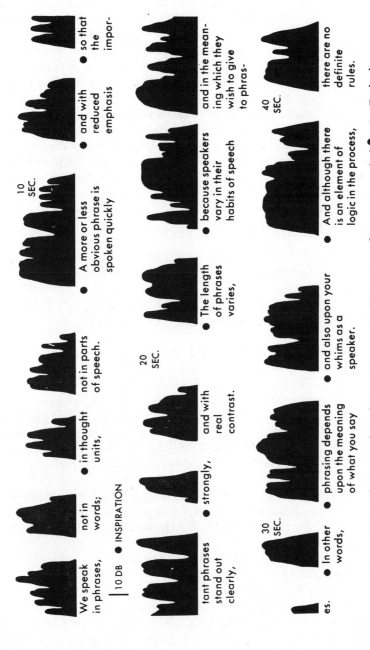

We speak in phrases, ● not in words; ● in thought units, ● not in parts of speech.

|10 DB ● INSPIRATION

A more or less obvious phrase is spoken quickly ● strongly, ● and with real contrast.

tant phrases stand out clearly, ● and with reduced emphasis ● so that the impor-

The length of phrases varies, ● and also upon your whims as a speaker.

because speakers vary in their habits of speech ● and in the meaning which they wish to give to phras-

phrasing depends upon the meaning of what you say ● In other words, ● es.

And although there is an element of logic in the process, ● there are no definite rules.

10 SEC.

20 SEC.

30 SEC.

40 SEC.

Figure VI–1. Phrasing as shown by intensity variation. Note points of inspiration marked ● . After Fairbanks.

However, speech phrasing and written punctuation do not correlate exactly. Note that in the phrase "the red, white and blue," although a comma is present, the speaker may say the passage as a single phrase [ðəredʍaɪtn̩blu]. Conversely, the speaker may use a pause for emphasis where no punctuation exists as in "today (pause) is the last day (pause) of vacation." A conventional visual marking for speech phrasing that points up the grouping of words into a phrase is a ligature [lɪgətɚ] or a curved underlining, as for example in "today is the last day of vacation." This marking has the drawback of possible interference with underlining for emphasis and does not give any indication of the relative length of pauses. Another helpful system of visual marking is the use of vertical lines at pauses, using more lines for longer pauses. Usually one, two, or three lines are sufficient to mark the range of pauses used in speech. For example, in *I'll go* ||| *but I expect to return* | *sooner or later,* the vertical lines mark the boundaries of phrases and indicate the relative duration of pauses. This system may be used with regular spelling or IPA symbols. Note the following:

I think	|||	*therefore*	||	*I am*
[aɪθɪŋk]	|||	[ðɛrfor]	||	[aɪæm]

knife			*fork*			*and spoon*
[naɪf]			[fork]			[ændspun]

In transcribing with IPA symbols, accurate phonetic transcription requires that a phrase be written with consecutive symbols, without interruption for word boundaries. This indicates junctures that are coarticulated. The large spaces between symbols, therefore, mark phrase boundaries so that vertical line markers are not necessary unless the transcriber wishes to show the relative duration of a pause. Some transcribers prefer to transcribe word-by-word with spaces left between words to facilitate reading from transcription. In this case, the vertical markers are essential, not only to show duration but to mark phrase boundaries.

The speaker determines which and how many words to link together in a phrase, and the duration of pauses, in order to facilitate the listener's understanding of the intended message. He may use phrasing patterns for the following purposes:
1. To group the words of a thought into a unit
2. To create emphasis
3. For parenthetical comments
4. To accommodate to difficult listening situations
A very important use of phrasing is in presenting units of meaning to the listener. In the sentence "We went to the store | because we were hungry," two different but related thoughts are presented to the listener in two phrase units. Note how an inappropriate phrasing would interfere with meaning if

we said the sentence as "we went to the | store because we | were hungry."
Series items may also be separated with pauses as in "knives | forks | and
spoons." Emphasis is created by setting apart the word or phrase to be
emphasized; for example, "I want to go ||| now || without delay." Such pause
emphasis is usually accompanied by loudness and pitch rise to indicate stress
further. An aside or parenthetical comment, sometimes referred to as an
"apostrophe," is set apart with pauses as in "The weather | I believe | is going
to get better." The aside phrase is usually de-emphasized with lowered
loudness and pitch. The sensitive speaker takes into account difficulties his
listeners might have in understanding speech. He may use shorter phrases
and longer pauses when his subject matter is complex or unfamiliar to the
listener, when the listener is very young or may have a disability in understanding, or when speaking in a noisy background or to large audiences.

A speaker uses some pauses for formulating the next phrase or future
phrases during extemporaneous speech, especially in explanatory discourse.
Although we do not fully understand the process of rapidly formulating
speech as in fluent conversation, pauses may figure very prominently. Some
speakers use extensive pauses associated with "filler words," while appar-
ently formulating what they will say next. Such patterns as "Well, ||| uh ||| I
suppose ||| that || all things considered, || you know, | uh . . ." give the
speaker considerable time to think and to formulate phrases that carry real
meaning. Listeners can note the irregularity of phrasing and pause duration
in conversational or extemporaneous speech, compared with the more regular pattern of oral reading. It is indeed amazing that speech can be formulated so rapidly when one considers that the speaker must accomplish the
following:
1. Select the appropriate words
2. Place them in an appropriate order
3. Change their forms and endings to agree with the conventions of
   American-English syntax
4. Select segmental phonemes to produce the words orally
5. Prepare the pattern of syllables and coarticulation
6. Apply accent, emphasis, intonation, and phrasing patterns.
All these tasks and more are accomplished at an average conversational rate
of 200 words per minute or more.

INTONATION

Whereas accent reflects changes in the syllables within a word, and
emphasis reflects changes in the words in a phrase, **intonation** involves
changes over an entire phrase. The nature of the change is primarily in the
rising and falling of pitch. These pitch inflections provide audible **intonation
contours,** which can give a level of meaning over and above the string of

phonemes, the pattern of accent, and the application of emphasis. This is an added meaning rather than a change in meaning. In several languages, notably Chinese, the pitch of syllables does actually change meaning so that a single CVC syllable may have several different meanings, depending upon pitch level.

Important in describing intonation contours are (1) the degree of pitch change, (2) the direction of change, and (3) the rate of change. Varying as we do in fundamental voice pitch, speakers do not seek a target of absolute pitch levels for intonation but use contrast of relative levels. Four relative pitch levels are conventionally recognized in American-English intonation. Level 2 is a standard or baseline for a phrase from which the speaker drops to 1 or rises to 3. Level 4 is reserved for expressions of surprise or high emotional outburst. The levels may be shown by using the respective numbers for each word or syllable, as in the following:

(3)   (3)

Hurry up! He's coming.

(2)   (2)

(1)

With this system, one can refer to "He's coming" as having here a 2-3-1 intonation contour. Levels may be more graphically marked by lines drawn under and over parts of the phrase at the relative heights as follows:

Hurry up! He's coming.

Direction of pitch change can be inferred from left-to-right positions, and the rate of change may be illustrated by connecting the pitch levels with slanting lines at varied angles. Note the following markings:

Hurry up!   He's coming

My goodness!

For most purposes, these connected contour lines, observing target levels of 1, 2, 3, or 4, with the lines sloping to show rate of change, will be sufficient for marking intonation. At best, they or any system will correlate only roughly with measured variations in fundamental voice frequency.

Many intonation patterns result, in part, from pitch changes caused by application of accent and emphasis. For example, note the following sentence:

I lost my ruler.

The word *ruler* is a key word to be emphasized above the rest of the sentence by greater intensity and duration, and by a rise in fundamental voice frequency. Normally, the **accent** pattern of *ruler* would be *rúler,* with the second syllable unaccented. As a final word of this phrase, *ruler* has the final syllable greatly de-accented, not only with intensity and duration reduction but with an unusual audible drop in pitch to relative level 1, below the rest of the phrase. **Emphasis,** in order to aid meaning, determines that intonation will change primarily on *ruler,* the emphasized word. These parts of the intonation contour are dictated by accent and emphasis. The unusual drop in pitch on the final syllable, however, is a product of **intonation** that tells the listener something new. Here, it says "the utterance is completed." Compare the intonation contours in these sentences:

I lost my ruler.

I lost my ruler, my pen and my pencil.

In the second sentence, the rising intonation on ruler, with the help of appropriate phrasing, tells the listener "keep listening, there's more to come." In a sentence such as "We brought knives, forks, dishes, and spoons," note how the rising pitch on *knives, forks,* and *dishes* signals the listener that there is more to come in a series, whereas the dropping pitch on *spoons* indicates the end of the series and the utterance. In this case, the end of the series is also marked by the word *and,* occurring just before the last word, so that *and* and the intonation contour provide complementary and redundant information to aid the listener. Try this sentence again without *and* but with the appropriate intonation, and then again with *and* but with the same intonation rise on *knives, forks, dishes,* and *spoons.* Note that the meaning can be carried by either *and* or the intonation contour, but that the sentence is more easily understood with both.

Indication of a series and of termination of an utterance are just two uses of intonation. Signalling a question is another important use. The phrase "they will," for example, is declarative-interrogative ambiguous. That is, it could be a statement, "They will," or a question, "They will?" Whereas in writing we differentiate with punctuation marks, in speech the difference is marked by intonation contour. The rising intonation here is that which is associated with a question, telling the listener that a response is expected of him. In this case, the intonation contour strongly influences meaning and may be considered to be **phonemic.** If the order of the words in the phrase were reversed for "will they," the word order itself indicates a question so that intonation of "Will they?" provides redundant information.

The purest form of phonemic intonation in American-English is with the expression "oh" [ou]. The syllable does not have a meaning of its own but can serve as a vehicle for conveying meaning through intonation. Note these common intonation messages:

Carrier	Intonation Message
oh	"I'm still listening to you."
oh\	"I understand."
oh\	"Now I finally understand it."
oh/	"Really, are you sure?"
oh oh	"Now you're in trouble."

Some speakers use many intonation carriers in conversation, especially when they wish to signal another speaker that they are listening and do not want to interrupt the speaker's flow of discourse. Such carriers as *uh huh* [ʌhʌ], *mmm* [m:], and *yeah* [jɛə] are common. The signaller may use a nasalized form of *uh huh* [m:ɦm:] to avoid opening his mouth during listening. Note how intonation contours carry information with these carriers:

Carrier	Information
uh huh	"I'm still listening."
uh huh	"I understand."
uh huh	"I didn't know that," or "That's really interesting."

Carrier	Information
mmmmmm	"I'm still listening."
mmmmmm	"Is that so?"
mmmmmm	"I didn't know that." or "That's really interesting."

Note also how the standard greeting of "hello" can convey a message with intonation:

	Intonation Message
hello	"I am pleased to meet you"
hello\	"I am very pleased to meet you"

he̶l̶l̶o̶   "What do you want with me?"
                                       (telephone)

A great variety of intonation contours may be identified, influenced by accent and intonation patterns, length of the phrase, linguistic intent of the message, and emotional affect of the speaker. Three contours recur that may be considered conventional usage of American-English intonation. These are as follows:

Falling Intonation (2 or 3 to 1)

A falling intonation pattern signals the termination or completion of an utterance, suggesting that no verbal response is required of the listener. It is most often found at the end of a phrase, and it is accompanied by decreased intensity and syllable duration, with vowels reduced to their unaccented pronuciation or to /ə/. Note the falling intonation in the phrases, "That's all" and "its over."

Rising Intonation (2 to 3)

A rising intonation pattern signals an unfinished situation in which something is needed from the listener or something more is to come from the speaker. It marks a series of items as in "the knife, fork, dishes, and spoon." It indicates a question that is likely to take a "yes" or "no" answer as in "Are you coming home?" or "Is that all there is?"

Rising-Falling Intonation (2 to 3 to 1)

A pattern that first rises and then falls is one of the most common intonation contours, the one commonly used when making a simple statement of fact, or giving a command. Note the contour in "The store is closed now" and in "Come here." This pattern is also used for questions that require an answer of information other than "yes" or "no." Note the pattern in "What's the trouble?" and "Where are you going?" These questions usually begin with *where, when, how, why,* or *what.*

A special use of intonation is to indicate saracasm by using a declarative statement word order with the intonation pattern of a question. Note the conflicting pattern in the following:

That's a good idea.

Here the speaker tries to convey "you may think that is a good idea but I really doubt it, myself," without saying so in words.

RATE

The **rate** at which speech is produced is usually measured in the number of words or syllables per unit of time. An average syllable's duration is 0.18 seconds, yielding about 5 to 5.5 syllables/second. Most adults read orally from 150 to 180 words/minute and produce 200 or more words/minute in conversational speech. Individuals vary, of course, in the rate at which they talk. Maximum rate of producing speech appears to be limited by articulatory control. With simple repetitive articulatory movements, speakers reach maximum rates of about 8 syllables/second but cannot exceed this even with practice. Although the time it takes to produce different speech sounds varies greatly, it is interesting to note that speakers average a rate of 10 sounds/second in conversation. At faster rates, it is difficult to coordinate articulation and errors begin to occur. At the rate of 15 sounds/second, errors are frequent and speech is distorted. Comprehending speech, on the other hand, occurs much faster, as does silent reading and thinking in general. While we typically produce speech at 10 sounds/second, we can understand it at as much as 30 sounds/second when paying careful attention.

A speaker's rate is influenced by a number of factors. The duration of pauses and the number of pauses contribute to rate, as does the use of extended vowel duration for stressing accented syllables and emphasized words. Of course, stressed syllables have greater duration than unstressed syllables so that either habitual heavy stressing or great reduction on unstressed syllables influences overall rate of speech. In normal conversation, the number of syllables in a phrase influences rate. A speaker who says "My name is John" as a single phrase is likely to say "My name is John Brown" in the same time period, cramming in an additional syllable. The other syllables must be spoken more rapidly to accomplish this. As was pointed out in the discussion of phrasing, in difficult listening situations, speakers are likely to reduce rate by using more and longer pauses. They may also articulate more accurately, slowing down the rate of syllable production within a phrase, particularly in public speaking. Emotion or mood is also indicated by rate. For example, "The lawn is green and soft and cool" invites the speaker to slow the rate so that the listener can see and feel the situation as the speaker does. Excitement, on the other hand, is indicated by rapid rate with syllables crammed together in short phrases.

There is no conventional way to mark rate visually. Some writers bunch words such as "sonofagun" to indicate rapid production as though the phrase were a single word. When using IPA symbols, the curved underlined ligature may be used to show unusually rapid production as in [sʌnəvəgʌn]. Compare the phrase "Let's pick up a couple of bucks" when said at a normal rate and then very rapidly.

normal rate   [lɛts pɪkʌpəkʌpələvbʌks]

rapid rate   [ləts pɪkəpəkəpl̩əbʌks]

Combined simultaneous transcription of broad and narrow IPA symbols, together with the markings of accent, emphasis, phrasing, intonation, and rate of connected speech would be a formidable task. It is likely that repeated listening to recordings would be necessary for complete and accurate description of a passage of speech. Even if a trained listener could recognize, recall, and transcribe all these aspects of descriptive phonetics during an extended utterance, the resulting composite of markings would make difficult reading. Fortunately, the usual task of transcribing and marking would require only one or two dimensions of speech description. Whether used singly or in combinations, though, the markings for phonemes and for aspects of speech rhythm are especially useful to describe nonstandard and dialectic speech, as described in the next chapter.

REVIEW VOCABULARY

Accent—stress applied to a syllable in a word.

Emphasis—stress applied to a word in a phrase.

Intonation—pitch variations within a phrase.

Intonation contours—the pattern of pitch variations of intonation, including the degree, direction, and rate of pitch change.

Pause—silent intervals between phrases.

Phonemic—having the characteristic of a phoneme, influencing the meaning of speech.

Phrase—a continuous utterance bounded by silent intervals.

Phrasing—organizing flowing speech into phrases.

Rate—the number of syllables or words per unit of time.

Speech rhythm—the general term referring to the combined aspects of accent, emphasis, phrasing, intonation, and rate.

Stress—pointing up or drawing special attention to a unit of speech.

Supra-segmental features—features of speech over and above phoneme segments, especially aspects of speech rhythm.

Syllable—a cluster of coarticulated sounds with a single vowel or diphthong nucleus, with or without surrounding consonants.

EXERCISES

1. Transcribe the following words in IPA symbols as you would say them, and mark the primary accent in each word:

revolver	suspect (verb)	radio
inflation	suspect (noun)	reward
obese	insult (verb)	tedious
natural	insult (noun)	consenting

2. Say the following sentence seven times, emphasizing a different word each time. Describe the context in which the emphasis would be appropriate.

   > "I am the captain of my fate."

3. Transcribe the following speech units in connected IPA symbols as you (or another speaker working with you) would say them, observing coarticulation effects, and marking phrasing and pause duration using |, ||, and ||| symbols.

   a. I don't believe it. I got an A.
   b. Well, sure enough. It's time to go.
   c. No longer, my friends, can we sustain this hard, difficult effort.
   d. My God, what terrible thing have you done?
   e. 'Tis the East and Juliet is the sun.

4. Mark the following paragraph from "The Bathtub Hoax" by H. L. Mencken as you would read it, using markings for accent, emphasis, and phrasing with relative duration of pauses.

   > On December 20 there flitted past us absolutely without public notice one of the most important profane anniversaries in American history to wit: the seventy-fifth anniversary of the introduction of the bathtub into these states. Not a plumber fired a salute or hung out a flag. Not a governor proclaimed a day of prayer. Not a newspaper called attention to the day.

5. Transcribe in IPA symbols the following section from "Jabberwocky" by Lewis Carroll as you would say it. Observe coarticulation effects of phrasing and mark relative duration of pauses.

   > 'Twas brillig and the slithy toves
   > Did gyre and gimble in the wabe:

All mimsy were the borogoves,
And the mome raths outgrabe.
Beware the Jabberwock, my son!
The jaws that bite, the claws that catch!
Beware the jubjub bird, and shun
The frumious Bandersnatch!

SUGGESTED READING

Lehiste, Ilse: *Suprasegmentals*. Cambridge, Mass., The MIT Press, 1970.

A well written basic book on speech rhythm with numerous references to research in the field.

MacKay, Ian R. A.: *Introducing Practical Phonetics*. Boston, Little, Brown & Co., 1978.

Chapter 9, "Word Stress," and Chapter 13, "Sentence Stress, Timing and Intonation," give a brief but good overview of some aspects of speech rhythm.

STANDARDS, DIALECTS, AND DEFECTIVE SPEECH

There are many variations in speech among those who speak American-English. Some of the differences in pronunciation have been pointed out in previous chapters. These and other variations have been the subject of considerable study and description by phoneticians and have prompted numerous attempts to establish standards for speech. However, standards suggest arbitrary value judgments, and controversy always erupts when we judge one way of speaking to be better than another. So personal is speech that even the suggestion that our speech may not be "good," may not be "correct," or may sound "funny" to someone else can cause great embarrassment and even threaten self- or group-image. This causes us to view the variability of speech in different ways, as reflected here in describing deviations from suggested **standards** and **dialects** held in common by groups of speakers, and how these variations differ from **defects** of disordered speech, which call for professional intervention. It is especially relevant for persons who seek to change or influence the speech of others (classroom teachers, speech/language pathologists, and instructors of public address, elocution or drama) to have a frame of reference for considering, first, whether a speech variation merits change, and second, whether direct intervention is appropriate.

STANDARDS

Standards are concerned with what speech ought to be. What is correct pronunciation? What is good speech? Who sets the standards? These questions have plagued phoneticians, teachers, and those who strive for propriety, elegance, and a systematic order of things. A number of the criteria that have been suggested for standards of pronunciation are presented here.

Criteria for Standard Pronunciation

What Most People Say

This criterion of the popular mode suggests that the standard pronunciation should be that which is used most. In other words, the speech pattern that calls least attention to itself is best because it is so common. Without attention called to habits of speech, there is little interference with transmission of the content or message to be conveyed. Television and radio commercials appear to respect this reasoning with their predominance of General American announcers and performers. It has at least the appearance of a democratic solution to the problem of standards but is not entirely consistent with our traditional respect for minority rights and differences.

What Educated People Say

The standard called "The King's English" has been accepted throughout most of England. Sometimes called "Received (accepted) Pronunciation," it is defined as the English spoken by graduates of the large private schools (Eton, Harrow, Rugby) of England; that is, by the Royal family, Members of Parliament, British professionals, industrialists, and bankers. Accordingly, it is strongly associated with an elite social class. It is this style of pronunciation that Henry Higgins taught the cockney girl, Liza Doolittle, in Bernard Shaw's *Pygmalion*, in order to pass her off as an English "lady." It has become the Standard English adopted for the British and often the American stage.

In the United States, however, educated persons in Boston, Atlanta, and Omaha are likely to speak quite differently. But in our mobile society, since "educated" increasingly means "traveled," the speech of well educated persons is becoming more alike, regardless of native dialect. Another "elite" standard in America is the speech of famous, popular, or highly respected persons—folk heroes, athletes, and adventurers—regardless of their social class or education.

What the Media Say

National network broadcasting of radio and television presents a fairly uniform speech pattern to millions of listeners. Reports on listening and viewing habits suggest that these media have an important influence on speech, especially on developing a national standard of pronunciation. They present predominantly a General American pattern of what people throughout most of America speak. Moving pictures present a wider variety of dialects to represent different locales, but blending of the American television and cinema industries is a move toward more unified pronunciation. Live stage speech, particularly in the East, is still likely to reflect "Standard English" (southern British) pronunciation used on the British stage.

What Dictionaries Say

The chicken or the egg, the pronunciation or the dictionary, which came first? Of course, dictionaries are intended to reflect speech as it is commonly used. Webster's Unabridged Dictionary reports that its standard of pronunciation is "the usage that now prevails among the educated and cultured people to whom the language is **vernacular.**" However, dictionary pronunciation has also become the common American "school standard" for correctness, a written static record of the educated pronunciation of one generation to be learned in turn by successive generations. In this sense, dictionaries may act as a conservative and stabilizing influence, actually retarding changes in pronunciation. To account for obvious dialect differences, American-English dictionaries often present more than one possible pronunciation with the most frequent (or preferred) given first. Common variations in pronunciation associated with different patterns of stressing, however, are often overlooked so that *of* is to be pronounced [ɑv] when it is most often pronounced [ʌv] or [əv], and *was* is typically listed as [wɑz] even though it is usually said as [wʌz] or [wəz].

How Words Are Spelled

Chapter I describes the disparate relationship between spelling and pronunciation. Yet spelling has a strong influence upon pronunciation in our culture in which reading is important. Until the 17th and 18th centuries, for example, the initial *h-* was rarely pronounced in English. But with popular

availability of printed books and periodicals, and the influence of Latin pronunciation, the initial *h-* became pronounced as /h/ more frequently in a
process that still continues. Note the use of /h/ in the following words:

Silent h-	*Inconsistent*	*h- pronounced*
heir	herb	hospital
honest	homage	heretic
hour	humble	host

A more recently developed word that is likely to be encountered first in
print, *herbicide,* is almost universally pronounced with the initial /h/, even
though its root word *herb* is mixed in its pronunciation. The attraction of
spelling pronunciation can also be seen in the mixed pronunciation of *often*
as [ɑfən] or [ɑftən].

Historical Precedence

This criterion, like dictionary pronunciation and spelling pronunciation,
suggests a static standard. Correctness would be based on the origin of the
word. The standard pronunciation of foreign words, such as the Latin *data*
and *ad hoc,* would be the way Romans pronounced the words centuries ago.
Place names, such as *Los Angeles* and *New Orleans,* would also be pronounced as they would have been in the country of their origin. Except
among scholars of languages, this criterion seems not to be well observed. In
fact, some areas of the country seem to delight in pronouncing names in their
own contrary style. In the Missouri-Illinois area, for example, there are the
towns of New *Athens,* pronounced [eíθənz]; New *Madrid,* said as [mǽdrɪd];
Cairo, commonly pronounced [keírou], and *Nevada,* which is pronounced
[nəveɪdə].

The historical criterion is too static to survive a dynamic language. It
does not permit the many changes in pronunciation that have taken place
and will continue to take place. Then too, new words are being added to our
language every day. It is estimated that there are now over 600,000 different
words in English, compared with about only 140,000 in Shakespearean
times.

The Situation

This criterion recognizes, realistically, that we do not speak the same
way in all situations. In addition to stage speech, three levels of speech are
often considered. The first is a "formal" or literary level, in which we speak
in sentence structure as we write, pronouncing words with great care. It is
sometimes referred to as "careful" or "citation" form. Vowels are usually
given their full stressed spelling value. For example, *what* would be pro-

nounced [ʍɑt] instead of the more common [ʍʌt]. The endings of words would be clearly enunciated, with stop consonants often audibly released so that *lap* would be said as [læpʻ] with full aspiration rather than [læp] without release. In its extreme, some politicians, attorneys, and other public speakers lend formality to their speech by over-emphasizing the endings of words so that *end* becomes [ɛndə]. Even continuant consonants may be released as though they were stops. For example, as the final words of phrases, *dollars* may be said [dɑlɚzʌ], *some* pronounced as [sʌmʌ], and *due* given as [duʌ] or [djuʌ].

The second level is called "cultivated **colloquial**," a level of "well educated ease." Pronunciations are in the **vernacular,** that is, the native common usage of educated persons who have learned them as children. Such speech would be suitable for a wide range of situations from academic seminars to business transactions to everyday commerce with persons both familiar and unfamiliar. Here the speaker would use the dialect of his region.

The third level is often called "everyday informal." It reflects somewhat less distinct enunciation, more rapid speech, and the influence of unstressing on vowels in connected strings of words. Running words together and occasionally omitting some syllables is characteristic. This level is usually reserved for "small talk," speaking to a very familiar person or to a younger person in an informal situation when one's linguistic "hair is down." Indistinctness of enunciation is compensated for by familiarity, which enhances intelligibility.

Intelligibility

Here the criterion is whether speech is understood, regardless of how words are pronounced. However, speech **intelligibility** is likely to vary considerably with such factors as familiarity with the speaker, dialect of the listener, noise background, complexity of subject content, level of message redundancy (phonetic, linguistic, and environmental), and rate of message transmission. The standard would need to change with each situation. This criterion by itself also overlooks the important impressions listeners infer about the speaker in addition to receiving the message.

Beauty

Pronunciation and speech habits that are most pleasing to our ear are best. Such a criterion creates two major problems: first, it overlooks the importance of intelligibility, and second, the desirable aesthetic standard is very difficult to describe. We cannot deny that some people have speech patterns that are particularly pleasing, hold our interest, or seem to lend importance to themselves and their messages. Voice quality and intonation patterns are heavy contributors to such impressions. Unfortunately, our judgments about what is impressive and pleasant are very subjective, and a universal standard based on aesthetic qualities of speech is almost futile to define.

None of the Above

One might reach the conclusion that since no single criterion is completely satisfactory, there should be no standards of pronunciation at all. This reasoning is individualistically and democratically appealing, but it is unrealistic. So long as people strive for something better, standards will be developed as practical targets. While we as Americans may reject the concept of a single universal standard, we probably have in the back of our minds a number of the criteria just cited when we seek to improve our speech. We may shift somewhat from one criterion to another as the situation changes, but we are likely to fall back upon one or more criteria when we seek correctness.

Non-Standard Speech

Even though absolute standards are difficult to identify and describe, we recognize that some speech habits are so divergent as to be considered "non-standard" or far outside the range of acceptable American-English speech. The following types of non-standard speech are common.

Non-English Speakers

What is commonly referred to as a foreign "accent" is made up of a number of variations in intonation patterns, stressing differences, and pronunciations. For example, notable among many continental Europeans is difficulty in pronunciation of the lingua-dental consonants /θ/ and /ð/. Either /t/ or /s/ is frequently substituted for the breath /θ/, so that *thing* becomes [tɪŋ] and *something* may become [sʌmpsɪŋ]. Treatment of the /θ/ in Chapter III includes lists of words for contrasts of /θ/-/t/ and /θ/-/s/ for practicing the difference in articulation. Substitution for the voiced /ð/ may be either /d/ or /z/ so that *these* may be said as [diz] and *this* may be pronounced [zɪs]. Chapter III compares words with such /ð/-/d/ differences. In addition, the foreign student may profit from a comparative exercise such as the following:

	Standard	Non-Standard	
the	[ðʌ]	[dʌ]	[zʌ]
this	[ðɪs]	[dɪs]	[zɪs]
that	[ðæt]	[dæt]	[zæt]
those	[ðouz]	[douz]	[zouz]
then	[ðɛn]	[dɛn]	[zɛn]

Another especially difficult pronunciation, particularly for Spanish and Italian speakers, is the English vowel /ɪ/ which falls between the /i/ and /ɛ/. The substitution is likely to be /i/ so that *this* becomes [ðis] or [zis] and *it* may be said [it] to be confused with *eat*. In the section on /ɪ/ in Chapter IV, there are lists of words contrasting the /i/-/ɪ/ sounds. The foreign student may also profit from exercises that compare vowels adjoining on the vowel diagram of Figure IV–1 as follows:

Practice saying speech units from left to right, then right to left.

[i]	[ɪ]	[e]	[ɛ]	[æ]
[mi]	[mɪ]	[me]	[mɛ]	[mæ]
[ki]	[kɪ]	[ke]	[kɛ]	[kæ]
[di]	[dɪ]	[de]	[dɛ]	[dæ]
[bit]	[bɪt]	[beɪt]	[bɛt]	[bæt]
[mit]	[mɪt]	[meɪt]	[mɛt]	[mæt]

Many Europeans do not produce voiceless stops with as much force or aspiration as do Americans. This results in reduced duration and different acoustic frequency characteristics so that the voiceless stops sound like their voiced cognates to the American listener. The student may be helped by first practicing exaggerated production of voiceless syllables [pʌ], [tʌ], [kʌ]; [pl̥ʌ], [kl̥ʌ]; and [pr̥ʌ], [tr̥ʌ], [kr̥ʌ], and then practicing comparison of /p/-/b/, /t/-/d/, and /k/-/g/ words listed for these phonemes in Chapter III. A common non-standard pronunciation for Germans is the substitution of the labio-dental /v/ for both /w/ and /ʍ/. *We* may be heard as [vi] and *water* as [vɑtɚ], and *what* becomes [vɑt] while *when* becomes [vɛn]. This substitution is especially noticeable because the /w/ and /ʍ/ occur so frequently in American-English speech. Sections treating /w/ and /ʍ/ in Chapter III include lists of words contrasting these phonemes with the substituted /v/.

Many Europeans produce the /eɪ/ in all words as a pure vowel [e], whereas in English it is usually a diphthong, /eɪ/, especially in stressed and final open syllables. The foreign student might begin by practicing production of the diphthong as [ei], with equal stress and duration of the two familiar components, and then reduce stress on the second component as [i], rather than try to produce [ɪ] as the second component. Reduced stress on the [i] glide will achieve the same result. Practice in comparing the following pairs of syllables may be helpful:

A	[eɪ]	[e]
take	[teɪk]	[tek]
name	[neɪm]	[nem]
late	[leɪt]	[let]
safe	[seɪf]	[sef]

Japanese has a speech sound similar to both American-English /l/ and /r/. The sound, written as /ɭ/ in IPA script, is produced with the tongue point briefly touching the roof of the mouth on the palate just behind the alveolar ridge. The tongue shaping is similar to /l/ with manner of production like a brief flap (such as the [t] in *city*), while the place of articulation is farther back on the palate and close to the place of articulating /r/. As a result, when an American listener expects to hear /r/, acoustic information from the tongue touching the palate with lateral emission suggests the lingua-alveolar /l/, making *rice* sound like *lice*. Similarly, when one expects to hear /l/, information from the tongue position well behind the teeth and alveolar ridge suggests the lingua-palatal /r/, so that *low* sounds like *row*. The non-standard production is not a simple /l/–/r/ substitution, as our hearing suggests, but substitution of a single sound, native to Japanese, for either.

After studying the positions of American-English /l/ and /r/ as described in Chapter III, the Japanese student might practice vocalizing while moving the tongue from the /l/ position (well forward on the alveolar ridge) back and not touching the palate for the /r/, then back to /l/, alternating positions as voicing continues. Practice on word lists and sentences with /l/ and /r/ in Chapter III might also be helpful.

Immature Speech

Immature speech consists of those patterns, different from the prevalent speech patterns of adults within a dialect group, that an individual uses because of lack of experience and/or maturation. Such speech in children is normal and not considered to be defective or to require special intervention for improvement. With normal opportunity, the immature patterns will fade and be replaced by more adult ones. Improvement toward mature speech comes with (1) the natural process of physical, mental, and social maturation, (2) adequate exposure to the adult speech patterns of the dialect group, and (3) satisfactory experience in using spoken language.

Psychologists, linguists, and speech pathologists have studied progressions from the absence of speech in the baby through the developing speech of the young child to the achievement of mature speech patterns in the older child and young adult. The articulation of English consonants and vowels in connected speech is mastered early, usually by the eighth or ninth year of life. Some learning of sophisticated speech rhythm patterns and, of course, new vocabulary continues into later life, but speech is expected to mature within the first decade. If it does not, some special attention is indicated to direct the person toward more mature speech patterns or to determine the cause of the persistent immature pattern.

An example of a common speech phenomenon encountered in young children is the /f/ for /θ/ substitution. These dental, voiceless fricative consonants differ only in the labial/lingual place of production. They are acoustically very similar. The /f/ is mastered early, usually by age 3 or 4 years, whereas /θ/ is seldom mastered before 6 or 7. By his third birthday, the child, now somewhat aware of numbers, will likely respond to a question about his age as [fri] for *three*. The /f/ will usually occur whenever /θ/ is expected so that *thin* becomes [fɪn] and *thank you* is [fæŋk ju]. As the child grows older, /θ/ will begin to appear, at first inconsistently alternating with /f/, and then more regularly, except in seductive phrases such as *free throw*, which is likely to persist for some time as [fri frou], and *forty-three* as [fortɪ fri]. Finally, the older child will master the appropriate use of these two consonants, so very similar in manner (voiceless fricative) and place (dental) of articulation.

The /l/ and /r/ sounds are notoriously difficult for some children to develop, and their non-standard productions sometimes persist into adult speech. A frequent pattern is substitution toward /w/, /j/, or /ʊ/ in place of /l/ in the intervocalic, preconsonantal, or final positions, so that *dollars* becomes [dɑwɚz], *William* becomes [wɪjəm], *million* may become [mɪjən], *salt* may be [sɑʊt], and *tell* may become [tɛʊ]. The /w/ for /l/ in the initial position is more obvious and likely to be treated as an adult speech defect. The /r/ shares a similar pattern of lip-rounding substitutions with some dialect variations camouflaging preconsonantal and final non-standard articulations.

Mispronunciations

Some mispronunciations occur from reading words we have never heard spoken, making our best guess from the spelling. It is unlikely, for example, that many young readers will know how to pronounce *chic* as [ʃik], *bade* as [bæd], or *brooch* as [broutʃ] the first time they are read. Their spellings contradict the pronunciation rules they have subconsciously learned.

A source of frequent mispronunciation comes from reference to a simpler, more familiar form. The [aʊ] in *pronounce* [pronaʊ́nts], for example, is likely to lead to *pronunciation* being said [pronaʊntsieíʃən] rather than [pronəntsieíʃən]. The [eɪ] in *nation* [neɪʃən] may influence *national* to be said as [neɪʃənl̩] rather than [næʃənl̩]. A reference mispronunciation may occur even when the familiar form is more complex, as, for example, the verb *orient* being said [orɪəntet], influenced by the more familiar noun *orientation*.

Another frequent cause of mispronunciation is avoidance of a difficult articulation cluster. *Picture* [pɪktʃɚ] may be simplified to [pɪtʃɚ], undifferentiated from *pitcher*. *Arctic* [arktɪk] is frequently simplified to [artɪk], and *sentence* [sɛntənts] may be said [sɛnəts] or [sɛnənz]. Note the reduction of articulatory complexity in the following pronunciations:

	Non-standard pronunciation	Complex cluster
government	[gʌvɚmənt]	[ɚnm]
surprise	[səpraɪz]	[ɚpr]
governor	[gʌvənɚ]	[vɚn]
library	[laɪbɛrɪ]	[brer]

Akin to simplification of a cluster by omission is the insertion of a vowel to separate a difficult cluster. The following are common mispronunciations:

	Non-standard pronunciation	Complex cluster
athlete	[æθəlit]	[θl]
realtor	[rilətɚ]	[lt]
chimney	[ʧɪmənɪ]	[mn]
poplar	[pɑpələ˞]	[plɚ]

Omission of unstressed syllables in connected speech has also been considered less than standard for careful articulation. Note the very common mispronunciations of these words:

	Careful preferred	Common non-standard
every	[ɛvɚɪ]	[ɛvrɪ]
separate (adj.)	[sɛpɚɪt]	[sɛprɪt]
chocolate	[ʧakolət]	[ʧaklət]
vegetable	[vɛʤətəbəl]	[vɛʤtəbəl]
interested	[ɪntɚɛstəd]	[ɪntrəstəd]
federal	[fɛdɚəl]	[fɛdrəl]
national	[næʃənl̩]	[næʃnl̩]
reasonable	[rizənəbl̩]	[riznəbl̩]

Yet the non-standard usage is so prevalent, even among well-educated people, that for such words, either pronunciation has become acceptable. What has been "non-standard" has become, or is becoming, "standard," and the former standard will begin to sound awkward and pretentious, or perhaps be limited to more formal, literary style.

Still another form of mispronunciation is reversal of consonant order, a phenomenon called **metathasis** [mətǽθəsɪs]. Note these changes in /r/ and /ɚ/:

	Standard	Reversal
perspiration	[pɚspɚeɪʃən]	[prɛspɚeɪʃən]
hundred	[hʌndrɛd]	[hʌndɚd]
children	[ʧɪldrɛn]	[ʧɪldɚn]
pronounce	[pronaʊnts]	[pɚnaʊnts]
professor	[profɛsɚ]	[pɚfɛsɚ]

Such reversals also occur for /v/ and /l/ as in [rɛvələnt] for *relevant* and [kælvɚɪ] for *cavalry*.

Omission of the final consonant of a cluster of either breath consonants or of voiced consonants is generally considered non-standard even though it is a characteristic of Black American-English dialect. Note the following examples:

	Standard	*Non-standard*
last	[læst]	[læs]
next	[nɛkst]	[nɛks]
end	[ɛnd]	[ɛn]

Sometimes the omission is of a medial consonant or vowel with compensatory extension of duration, as in the following:

	Standard	*Non-standard*
lists	[lɪsts]	[lɪs:]
nests	[nɛsts]	[nɛs:]
mirror	[mɪrɚ]	[mɪr:]
error	[ɛrɚ]	[ɛr:]

These omissions are especially noticeable when they influence syntax, as in the following words:

	Standard	*Non-standard*
cracked	[krækt]	[kræk]
shaved	[ʃeɪvd]	[ʃeɪv]

The /r/ is a non-standard intrusive sound for some speakers as in [wɑrʃ] or [wɔrʃ] for *wash*. Some New Englanders intrude /r/ between words ending and beginning with vowels in connected speech. Note the following phrases:

	Intrusive /r/
law in	[lɔrɪn]
saw at	[sɔræt]
Canada as	[kænədɚ æz]
area of	[ɛriɚ əv]

The habit persists in some final words of phrases such as idea as [aɪdiɚ] and *data* as [deɪtɚ].

The [iə] or [ɪə] sound after /d/ in connected speech may degenerate to [djə] or further with friction to [ʤə] in such words as the following:

	Standard	[djə]	[ʤə]
medium	[midiəm]	[midjəm]	[miʤəm]
Indian	[ɪndiən]	[ɪndjən]	[ɪnʤən]
tedious	[tidiəs]	[tidjəs]	[tiʤəs]
Canadian	[kəneɪdiən]	[kəneɪdjən]	[kəneɪʤən]

This common degeneration led to calling Arcadians [arkeídiənz] in Louisiana "Cajuns" [keídʒənz].

Imprecise Enunciation

In addition to standards for pronunciation, we have standards for the clarity of speech, referred to as **enunciation** or diction. As our articulators move from position to position in coarticulated running speech, they achieve more or less accurately the formations necessary to produce each phoneme. The range of accuracy can vary from careful, crisp, and sharp enunciation to approximated, sloppy productions. When enunciation is so casual, slurred, and imprecise that it affects **intelligibility**, it is considered non-standard. Enunciation also suggests personal attitudes, abilities, and intelligence, and it may be considered non-standard if it evokes negative impressions about the speaker. We are familiar with the obviously non-standard enunciation that we exhibit after dental anesthesia, and with the slurred barely intelligible speech of the drunken person. At the other extreme is the professional speaker, actor, or announcer who seems to form, effortlessly, each vowel and consonant so accurately that there is little or no ambiguity. Between these extremes there is a range of precision influenced by the following factors: (1) physiologic control over the articulators, (2) the model from which one has learned speech, (3) attitudes toward the speaking situation, and (4) the speaker's awareness of the value of good enunciation for either speech intelligibility or a favorable impression.

Unless one has significant impairment of physiologic control, it is possible to improve one's enunciation by a conscious effort. Demosthenes (384–322 B.C.) placed pebbles in his mouth to improve his speech. These impediments forced him to articulate speech sounds consciously and with great care. When the pebbles were removed, his deliberate practice apparently improved his natural speech. It is not necessary to speak with a mouth full of pebbles, but the principle of making oneself consciously aware of the mechanics of speech production is as sound today as it was in ancient Greece. Relearning habitual motor skills, such as is involved in improving the precision of one's speech enunciation or diction, is generally facilitated by a sequence beginning with analysis of component parts of the action to effect more precise production and to bring them to the level of consciousness. Then the components are placed into increasingly larger and more complex action units, while the speed of production is gradually increased with practice, maintaining the precision of the relearned components. Feedback about the success of relearning completes the sequence.

For the reader who wishes to improve his enunciation, the following exercises are based on the Demosthenean principle:

1. Review formation of individual speech sounds in Chapters III and IV.

Follow slowly with your own speech mechanism the sequence of articulatory movements for each phoneme.
2. Produce each phoneme in syllables of CV (Consonant-Vowel), VC, CVC, and VCV, taking care to produce each phoneme slowly and consciously.
3. Read aloud the words listed for each phoneme in Chapters III and IV with phonemes in the initial, medial, and final positions, and in clusters where appropriate. Produce each speech sound clearly and carefully.
4. Read aloud the pairs of contrast words as listed for phonemes in Chapters III and IV, taking care to feel and hear the difference in producing the key phonemes.
5. Read aloud the following section from Lewis Carroll's "Jabberwocky," reading slowly at first and taking care to produce all sounds accurately, including giving full value to all vowels, stressed or unstressed:

> Twas brillig, and the slithy toves
>> Did gyre and gimble in the wabe:
> All mimsy were the borogoves,
>> And the mome raths outgrabe.
> 'Beware the Jabberwock, my son!
>> The jaws that bite, the claws that catch!
> Beware the Jubjub bird, and shun
>> The frumious Bandersnatch!'
> He took his vorpal sword in hand;
>> Long time the manxome foe he sought-
> So rested he by the Tumtum tree,
>> And stood awhile in thought.

6. Now, reread at a faster pace but be careful to maintain clear enunciation of all words. Read more rapidly until you reach a comfortable and natural pace but with crisp and accurate enunciation. Use a listener to help judge progress.
7. Select familiar prose passages to read aloud, following the sequences of steps 5 and 6.
8. Extemporaneously, describe pictures to a listener, maintaining improved enunciation as much as possible.
9. These exercises, which may take several weeks to complete, may be recorded to provide self-feedback, or they may be monitored by a critical listener for external feedback.

Irregular Voice and Rhythm

We observe a very broad latitude for acceptable speaking voice. The processes of phonation and resonation, described in Chapter II, create a remarkable variety of fundamental frequency and overtone relationships we call **voice quality.** Without pathology of the vocal tract, some persons unconsciously develop voices that are habitually nasal, breathy, or harsh. They encounter a range of listener reactions from acceptance to repulsion.

Greater open nasal resonance in vowels, sometimes referred to as "nasal twang," is generally present in the northern Midwest more than in other parts of the country. Hypernasality is also prevalent in some rural areas of the Midwest and Southwest and in some urban centers of the West Coast. Newsboys [ĕkstrɔ̄], [ĕkstrɔ̄], [ĕkstrɔ̄] and carnival barkers [hɔ̃ɪ], [hɔ̃ɪ], [hɔ̃ɪ] habitually relax the velum and increase nasal resonance. Other talkers with hypernasal voice quality often have habits of speaking with the tongue raised in the back of the mouth, with a very relaxed velum, or with little movement of the jaw and lips. Any of these habits may contribute to the perception of undesirable nasality. A change to more oral resonance may be achieved by taking steps to change such habits. For example, in producing vowel sounds, the bunching of the back of the tongue may be avoided by care in touching the tongue tip against the back of the mandibular incisors during production.

Breathy voices result from excess air escaping from the glottis during phonation. Breathiness occurs naturally during excitement or exertion, and some people effect a breathy voice to evoke interest. If persistent breathiness affects speech intelligibility or fluency, the speaker may want to consult a laryngologist or a speech/language pathologist. For moderate breathiness, the student may benefit from such exercises as extending duration of vowels to gain efficient use of breath pressure at the glottis, then practicing syllables first with voiced consonants adjoining a vowel and later with voiceless consonants. This may be followed by slowly counting aloud ("one-and-two-and-three-and . . .") with continuous voicing, maintaining sufficient volume for a listener six feet away, and extending the count longer with each trial.

"Harsh" voices suggest the negative impression they give listeners. Descriptive adjectives such as "rough, strident, metallic, and grating" reflect common attitudes of listeners. In the absence of apparent pathology, muscular tension or vocal abuse may be the cause. Reference to a laryngologist or speech/language pathologist is suggested if harshness persists.

A Summary View of Speech Standards

It is clear that we do observe some standards for speech. They are implicit and generalized from usage rather than explicitly stated in order to shape usage. The standards are based on several criteria, which change with the situation. Non-standard speech is easier to define than is the standard. When intelligibility is reduced or when the listener receives a negative impression of the speaker, the speech pattern is generally considered to be non-standard.

DIALECTS

"Then said they unto him, 'Say now *Shibboleth*': and he said 'Sibboleth': for he could not frame to pronounce it right" (Judges xii–6). The unfortunate Ephraimite whose language did not include the /ʃ/ sound revealed his nationality by his speech when he pronounced it [sɪbolɛθ], for then the Gileadites of the Old Testament "took him, and slew him at the passages of Jordan." Though the consequences are not always so drastic, we are each marked by how we speak—where we grew up, where our parents were born, how we were educated, what religious or racial groups we represent, how extensively we have traveled, where we have lived, our occupations, even our ambitions. Phoneticians have *shibboleths,* or key words that can identify important things about us. For while our written language may be fairly uniform, our speech is variable and idiomatic.

Dialects are the words, language forms, pronunciations, and speech habits peculiar to people of a specific geographic region who are part of a larger group using the same language. American-English, for example, is a dialect of the English language, as is Australian-English, Canadian-English, South African-English, and that of other countries in which the people are native speakers of English. Even though there are recognized differences in the speech of these various countries, a person from one English speaking country can understand persons from another. In popular usage, dialect has also come to mean the speech patterns associated with any ethnic or other group with different language habits. Thus, Black American-English is considered a dialect of American-English, identified by certain habits of language usage and speech. Dialects occur because of ethnocentric convergence of a group for a common cause, or because of isolation—either geographic or social, either forced or by choice. Easy and rapid transportation, migrations, and pervasive mass media reduce dialect differences, but so long as groups of people have special common interests or are isolated, dialects are likely to persist.

American-English

For our purposes, American-English is that English spoken within the United States. Although some have argued as early as the Revolutionary War that "American" should be considered a different language, there is too much in common with the language used by the natives of the British Isles and of other English dialects in far flung parts of the world to accept this argument, except on political or patriotic grounds. American-English is different from the language of England because of the great distance by which the countries are separated, and because of different patterns of migration and expansion. The differences include vocabulary (truck—lorry, elevator—lift, vacation—holiday), spelling (generalization—generalisation, spelled—spelt), and pronunciation ([bɪn]—[bin], [nu]—[nju], [læf]—[laf]). Another major difference is in rhythm, especially the pattern of stressing and unstressing. American-English is spoken at a slower rate with less varied intonation, and a secondary stress is given to syllables of long words. British-English is more animated with greater intonation variations. The British give heavy stress to the selected syllable, obscuring or even telescoping unaccented vowels. Thus *Worcestershire* becomes [wʊstəʃɪə] and *waistcoat* becomes [wɛskət]. Such telescoping is historically responsible for "Bedlam," derived as the familiar name for London's famous Bethlehem Hospital. This pattern of stressing is especially noticeable on words with *-ary* suffixes so that British *dictionary* becomes [dɪkʃənrɪ], *secretary* is said [sɛkrətrɪ], and *ordinary* is pronounced [ɔrdnrɪ]. This habit gave rise to the story that a British gentleman visiting the United States referred to Niagara Falls when he returned home as "Niffles."

Within the major dialect of American-English, there are numerous sub-dialects. Here, "sub-" is used in the sense of smaller, rather than inferior. Dialect areas are not distinct, sharply defined entities with patterns consistently different from their neighbors. Rather, there is considerable overlapping, and one small dialect area may be part of one or more larger areas. For example, the pronunciation of the ice cream sundae as [sʌndə] is peculiar to natives of a very small area centered in the city of St. Louis, whereas the St. Louis area is part of a larger dialect area of the Mid-West in which *born* is commonly pronounced [bɑrn], and this larger area in turn is part of a still larger Southern dialect area in which the word *greasy* is pronounced [grizɪ] and *on* is said [ɔn]. Yet, St. Louis is borderline for

Figure VII-1.   The three major dialect areas of the United States.

pronunciation of the word *drought* where some people pronounce it [draʊt] and others pronounce it [draʊθ]. As one moves north toward Chicago, [draʊθ] is prevalent, but if one moves west or south, [draʊt] is more common.

American-English is conventionally divided into three major geographic areas of marked dialect differences. These are New England, Southern American and General American (Figure VII–1). If we were to consider slight dialect differences, such as the pronunciation of *sundae* around St. Louis, we could divide the country into literally hundreds of minor dialect areas with extensive overlapping of boundaries. But here we are interested primarily in major variations, particularly in different pronunciations that are systematic and common to more than a few words. In addition to the three major areas, two of the smaller dialect areas, a state and a city, as well as the cultural-racial dialect of Black-English, will be described as examples of less general dialects.

New England

This dialect area includes the states of Maine, New Hampshire, and Rhode Island, and the eastern portions of Connecticut, Massachusetts, and Vermont (see Figure VII–1). The early colonists who settled this area came from the South of England and brought with them dialects of the area around London. Many were well educated and emigrated for reasons of religious freedom. In the new world, they resumed their livelihood as artisans and merchants, creating the character of the Yankee trader who was to be active in the shipping trade of the world. Their commerce and their location on the seaboard kept the colonists in frequent contact with England, so that their speech patterns changed essentially as those of England changed. The area was aptly named "New England."

So successful were the early colonists in dominating the economy that when later settlers with different English dialects came from the northern parts of England and from Scotland and Ireland, they found it necessary to move on to seek their fortune, and they went westward into upper New York and Ohio and toward Iowa and the great plains.

The most common characteristic pronunciation of Southern England that persists in the New England dialect area is omission of /r/ in the final position of words and just before consonants. With -r in the final position, the preceding stressed vowel is either elongated or is diphthongized with a /ə/ off-glide. Note the following examples:

	General American	New England
car	[kɑr]	[kaː]
were	[wɝ]	[wɜː]

poor	[pʊr]	[pʊə]
fear	[fɪr]	[fɪə]
bear	[bɛr]	[bɛə]
four	[for]	[foə]

With the final unstressed /ɚ/, the /r/ quality is omitted so that *after* becomes [æftə] and *better* becomes [bɛtə]. In the preconsonantal position, the *-r-* is similarly treated as in the following examples:

	General American	New England
third	[θɝd]	[θɜːd]
cursed	[kɝst]	[kɜːst]
farm	[fɑrm]	[faːm]
park	[pɑrk]	[paːk]
fort	[fort]	[foət]
fired	[faɪɚd]	[faɪəd]

The initial *r-*, and the *-r-* between vowels in such words as *arrow, borrow, around*, and *erase* are given full /r/ quality however.

A second pronunciation persisting from its southern English origin and attributed to New England is that called the "broad *a*." In some words, the /æ/ of General American is pronounced /ɑ/ so that *ask* becomes [ɑsk] and *bath* becomes [bɑθ]. The broad *a* as /ɑ/ is especially prevalent in and around the city of Boston, but in much of New England the /a/ is more often used for General American /æ/. Note the following pronunciations:

	General American	New England /a/	Broad a /ɑ/
class	[klæs]	[klas]	[klɑs]
ask	[æsk]	[ask]	[ɑsk]
path	[pæθ]	[paθ]	[pɑθ]
rather	[ræðɚ]	[raðə]	[rɑðə]

The broad *a* pronunciation is sometimes used in other parts of the United States on the stage, for pedantic or fashionable purposes, or by Anglophiles.

Another pronunciation more typical of New England than of General American is the use of [ju], or sometimes [ɪu], in such words as *new, duty, student, tune*, and *duke*. This residual of Southern England compares with the General American use of /uː/ or /u/. New Englanders also use a slightly rounded /ɑ/ of brief duration in words such as *hot, not, rock, top*, and *spot*. This sound, written phonetically as /ɒ/, is close to a partially rounded /ɔ/ but of shorter duration, used in such words as *coffee, cost, long, lost*, and *song*. Still another typical New England pronunciation is [aɪðə] and [naɪðə] for *either* and *neither*.

These characteristic pronunciations are becoming less common now in

New England, for although the early seaboard colonists could avert the waves of new immigrants from abroad, present day New Englanders can hardly resist infiltration from the rest of the United States, nor can they control the speech of network radio and TV performers that influences their pronunciation inexorably toward General American.

Southern American

The Southern American-English dialect area is designated roughly as the area south of a broad border line that could be drawn from east to west through the southern half of Maryland; northern West Virginia; the southern parts of Ohio, Indiana and Illinois; through southeastern Missouri and the northwest corner of Arkansas, curving southward through the eastern quarter of Texas to the Gulf of Mexico (see Figure VII–1). The dialect is most prevalent in the "deep South" states of North Carolina, South Carolina, Georgia, Florida, Alabama, Mississippi, and Louisiana. It is variable in the border states, including Kentucky and Tennessee.

Early settlers of Virginia came from southern England at about the same time (1607) as New England was being colonized (1620). Although the Massachusetts and the Virginia colonies had a common linguistic origin, there was a virgin wilderness and often hostile Indians between them. This permitted less exchange with each other than with their common mother country, England. The Virginia colonists, with a plantation economy, had less commerce with England, and thus tended to change their speech less to parallel the changes taking place in England. In order to have enough land for their plantation crops, the families and descendents of the planters of tidewater Virginia moved southward and westward into the Florida peninsula and to the Gulf of Mexico. They took their early southern England dialect inland with them, further separating it and themselves from the influences of changes taking place in England. The Southerners who moved into the remote mountain regions of Kentucky, Tennessee, and West Virginia were even more isolated, and retained some of their Shakespearean English well into the 20th century.

Later immigrants to the South found much of the land already occupied by large plantation holdings and accordingly moved westward to find land of their own. An exception is the southern part of Louisiana, which was dominated by French influence and received immigration of the Arcadians (Cajuns) of Canada. A major group of immigrants into the South in the latter part of the 18th century were the Black slaves brought from Africa. They learned and adapted the Southern dialect, and shaped it by "Africanisms" of their own.

Southern dialect reflects its common heritage with New England in the characteristic omission of final and preconsonantal /r/. The vowel before -r or

-*r*- is often elongated and sometimes simplified, rather than diphthongized as is common in New England. Note the following examples:

	General American	New England	Southern
four	[for]	[foə]	[foː]
fort	[fort]	[foət]	[foːt]
fired	[faɪɚd]	[faɪəd]	[fɑːd]
flowers	[flauɚz]	[flauəz]	[flɑːz]

However, *fear* becomes [fɪə], and *four* sometimes is pronounced [foə]. The broad *a* is commonly used in place of the New England /a/ before -*r*- as in these examples:

	General American	New England	Southern
car	[kar]	[kaː]	[kɑː]
farm	[farm]	[faːm]	[fɑːm]
large	[lardʒ]	[laːdʒ]	[lɑːdʒ]
park	[park]	[paːk]	[pɑːk]

Stressed /ɝ/ and unstressed /ɚ/ of General American are pronounced /ɜ/ and /ə/ in words like *third* [θɜːd] and *sister* [sɪstə], as they are in New England.

Simplification of diphthongs can also occur in Southern Speech without -*r*- as in the following words with /aɪ/:

	General American and New England	Southern
I	[aɪ]	[ɑː]
my	[maɪ]	[mɑː]
nice	[naɪs]	[nɑːs]
time	[taɪm]	[tɑːm]

Southern pronunciation favors [ju] or [ɪu] in other words as *new, tune,* and *student.* There is a tendency toward use of /ɔ/, for example in *on* as [ɔn] compared with [ɑn] farther north. The South pronounces -*og* words as a well rounded /ɔ/ in such words as *log, frog,* and *dog,* compared with a less rounded /ɔ/ in General American and /ɑ/ or /a/ in New England

The "drawl" that is attributed to Southern speakers is not universal but is characteristic of some speakers. The rate of articulation, contrary to popular belief, is not slower than in General American. Rather, it is the result of a combination of an increased range of pitch change for intonation and diphthongization of some simple vowels. Characteristic of the drawl is the intrusion of /j/ and /w/ glides followed by the /ə/. The following pronunciations of words are examples that contribute to the drawl sound.

sit	[sɪjət]	*cord*	[kɔwəd]
less	[lɛjəs]	*board*	[bouwəd]
class	[klæjəs]	*good*	[guwəd]

A special pronunciation of Southern speech is the use of /ɪ/ rather than /ə/ in some unstressed syllables, as in the following words:

salad	[sælɪd]	*respect*	[rɪspɛkt]
kitchen	[kɪtʃɪn]	*believe*	[bɪliv]
palate	[pælɪt]	*dispose*	[dɪspouz]
bracket	[brækɪt]	*predict*	[prɪdɪkt]
lettuce	[lɛtɪs]	*debate*	[dɪbeɪt]
wanted	[wɔntɪd]	*relate*	[rɪleɪt]

A peculiar single word pronunciation throughout the South is [grizɪ] for *greasy*, compared with [grisɪ] in most of the rest of the country. The /ɛ/ sound is frequently replaced with other vowels or diphthongs as *cent* may become [sɪnt] and *ten* becomes [tɪn], *bed* becomes [bɛəd] or [bɛjəd], and *get* becomes [gɛət]. Before intervocalic /r/, the [ɛ] in General American *dairy* [dɛrɪ] is frequently said [eɪ] as [deɪrɪ], and *Mary* is pronounced [meɪrɪ].

Industrialization, migrations, and easy travel, as well as pervasive public media, are influencing Southern American-English dialect toward General American pronunciation. In such major cities as Atlanta, Birmingham, Charleston, and Houston, one is likely to hear General American almost as commonly as Southern dialect. This is especially true in colleges, universities, and the headquarters of national businesses. However, because of the greater portion of rural area in the South, its dialect is likely to change more slowly than is that of New England.

General American

The second and successive waves of English settlers came from northern England, Scotland, and northern Ireland. Their dialects were different from those colonists who emigrated earlier from southern England and had settled on the seaboard. The southern English colonists so dominated both the Massachusetts and the Virginia areas that the later immigrants felt compelled to move beyond the coast in order to realize their dream of owning their own land and making their fortune. The settlers of western New England moved into upper New York state and westward by the Great Lakes to Ohio, Indiana, Illinois, and Iowa. Those Scottish and Scotch-Irish immigrants who first settled in western Pennsylvania and southern New Jersey migrated south into the Shenandoah valley, the southern mountains, and on to Texas and the cattle country of the northern plains. Those who could not find land in Maryland and Virginia moved westward through the Cumberland Gap into Kentucky and Tennessee and north into Illinois, Missouri, and Kansas. Their dialects moved with them as they migrated westward through the Ohio Valley, across the Mississippi, on to the Great Plains and eventually to the Pacific Coast. These immigrants came in great numbers, fanned out over a broad area into the central and western United States, and established their prevalent speech habits as the basis of today's General American dialect.

The word lists and exercises of Chapters III and IV and the pronunciations in this book reflect the author's General American dialect. General American is marked by pronunciation of *r* wherever it is included in spelling. Not only the initial glide as in *red* and the cluster glide as in *green*, but the intervocalic *-r-* in *very*, the final *-r* in *bar*, the preconsonantal *-r-* in *barn*, and the unstressed *-er* in *farmer* are produced with /r/ quality. The *a* in such words as *ask*, *last*, *bath*, *can't*, and *rather* is pronounced /æ/, compared with the New England /a/ or /ɑ/. In nearly all unstressed suffixes, vowels reduce to /ə/ as in the following words:

surface	[sɜˑfəs]
salad	[sæləd]
pocket	[pɑkət]
bunches	[bʌntʃəz]

Either and *neither* are pronounced [iðɚ] and [niðɚ], compared with the New England [aɪðə] and [naɪðə].

Other vowel sounds are somewhat variable over the vast area of General American. The *-o-* vowel, for example, varies with the consonant that follows. General American *on* is usually pronounced [ɑn] compared with [ɔn] in Southern, and sometimes [an] in New England. *Doll* is pronounced [dɑl] compared with the New England [dɔl], and *-og* words such as *log*, *dog*, and *frog* are usually pronounced [ɔg] in General American and Southern, compared with [ag] or [ɑg] in New England. The *-or* words such as *for*, *more*, and *horse* vary with [ɔr], [or] and [ɑr] pronunciations heard.

Comparison of the Major Dialects

For comparison of the three major dialect areas of the United States, the following short passage is word transcribed in each dialect:

"Give your doll her bath," Aunt Mary said, placing a bar of soap on the stand near the sink. "Her hair is dirty and greasy." Neither the older woman nor the little girl noticed the new kitchen curtain blowing as the first sign of the rising storm.

**General
American:** [gɪv jɚ dɑl hɚ bæθ], [ænt mɛrɪ sɛd], [pĮeɪsɪŋ ə bɑr əv soup ɑn
ðə stænd nɪr ðə sɪŋk]. [hɚ her ɪz dɚtɪ ænd grisɪ]. [nɪðɚ ðə
ouldɚ wumən nor ðə lɪtĮ gɚl noutəst ðə nu kɪtʃən kɚtn̩
blouɪŋ æz ðə fɚst saɪn əv ðə raɪzɪŋ storm].

**New
England:** [gɪv jɜə dɔl hɜː baθ], [ant mærɪ sɛd], [pĮeɪsɪŋ ə baː əv soup ɑn
ðə stand nɪə ðə sɪŋk]. [hɜː hɛə ɪz dɜtɪ and grisɪ]. [naɪðə ðə
ouldə wumən nɔə ðə lɪtĮ gɜl noutəst ðə nju kɪtʃən kɜtn̩ blouɪŋ
az ðə fɜːst saɪn əv ðə raɪzɪŋ stɔəm].

Southern: [gɪv jɜː dɑl hɜː bæjəθ], [ænt meɪrɪ sɛjəd], [pĮeɪsɪŋ ə baː əv
soup ɔn ðə stæjənd nɪə ðə sɪŋk]. [hɜː hɛjə ɪz dɜːtɪ ænd
grɪzɪ]. [nɪðə ðə ouldə wumɪn nowə ðə lɪtĮ gɜəl noutɪst ðə nju
kɪtʃɪn kɜːtɪn blouwɪŋ æjəz ðə fɜːst saːn əv ðə raːzɪŋ stɔwəm].

Immigration of various groups of non-English speaking Europeans, especially Swedes, Italians, and Germans, throughout the General American area during the 19th and 20th centuries has added a variety of speech habits and pronunciations in different communities. Other important migrations involved the Mexicans moving to the American Southwest and the Orientals moving to the West Coast. By and large, these groups have become linguistically acculturized, moving away from their native language toward a General American with their own peculiar pronunciations and intonation patterns in the second (Creole) generation, and by the third generation becoming nearly indistinguishable from the General American around them.

For the future, General American pronunciation appears to be the dialect most likely to predominate throughout the United States. It is the largest dialect in both geographic area and in population. In a very mobile society, where people frequently move from one part of the country to another for vocational advancement, the surviving dialect is likely to be that which is most common. Announcers on network TV and radio are mostly speakers of General American, bringing this dialect daily into nearly every Southern and New England Home. Moving pictures, similarly, are largely dominated by General American speech, even though live stage productions are likely to reflect New England or Southern English dialect. Some blending of the three major dialects is likely for the future, with small areas of dialect differences recognized, such as those that follow.

Hawaii

It is not surprising that one finds different sounding speech in the Hawaiian Islands, often called the "melting pot" of the Pacific. Hawaii is thousands of miles from the mainland, it became the 50th state of the Union only comparatively recently in 1959, and it has a history of migrations unlike the rest of the United States. New England missionaries and Yankee sailors in the early 19th century brought English to the native Hawaiians, who spoke a Polynesian dialect. Then came waves of "sugar immigrants" imported to grow cane and pineapple. Between 1875 and 1930, over a quarter-million workers (mostly men) were brought to the Hawaiian Islands, which totaled an area of only 6435 square miles. Each group spoke its own language. They came in successive waves of Chinese, Portuguese, Japanese, Puerto Ricans, Koreans, Spaniards, and the last and largest group, the Philippinoes, who spoke three different languages themselves.

While each group kept its native language at home and in close social affairs, they needed a "business" language for broader communication. Some simple and universal oral language was especially necessary in dealing with the plantation overseers, for buying and selling with other groups, and just in order to be able to talk to their fellow worker who may have been born on a different continent. They adopted and adapted the dialect called "pidgin" English, a name that probably came from a Cantonese pronunciation of the English word "business."

Although the native Hawaiians had their own language, they eagerly learned English in the mission schools. With the flood of immigrants, the common intermarriage of Hawaiians with these groups, and a steady decrease in the number of pure Hawaiians, the original Hawaiian language has had little chance to survive except in place names. Hawaiian has only seven consonants (/h, p, k, w, l, m, n/) and five vowels (/i, ɛ, ɑ, u, o/), remarkably consistent in pronunciation. Intervocalic *w*, as in *Ewa* and *Hawaii*, inconsistently becomes the labio-dental fricative /v/. There are no consonant clusters and no word ends with a consonant. Hawaiian makes frequent use of the glottal stop to separate like vowels as in *Hawaii* [hɑwɑiʔi], *Nuuanu* [nuʔuɑnu], *alii* [aliʔi], and *muumuu* [muʔumuʔu]. To make the strange English words conform to their consonant-vowel sequence, Hawaiians placed a vowel between clustered consonants, and a vowel was added to the end of words. They freely substituted consonants of their own language for English consonants lacking in Hawaiian, so that, for example, the name *Fred* became *Peleke*. The Hawaiians also substituted for consonants of other languages so that the Chinese pidgin word for *food*, "chowchow," became the common Hawaiian word "kaukau."

Pidgin emerged from its early development with plantation terms to its **creole** stage as second generation Islanders learned it as babies. It contained only content words and very few function words, it usually omitted the verb *to be*, and it had little or no inflection—"can do," "bumby" (by and by), "mobetu" (more better), and "savvy" (sabe). At present, citizens of Japanese ancestry and "haoles" (Caucasians) are the largest ethnic groups on the Islands. English is the official language with a mixture of General American and New England pronunciations, but pidgin can still be heard, particularly among non-Caucasian men. Remnants of the immigrants' native languages are still spoken at home and in shops. Original Hawaiian has largely become an artifact in songs and for tourist events.

New York City

This dialect area, which has one of the most concentrated populations on earth, includes the city of New York and its adjoining boroughs, most of Long Island, the eastern portion of New Jersey, the southern end of the Hudson River valley, and southeastern Connecticut. There is almost nothing left from the Dutch heritage of New Amsterdam except here and there an anglicized place name like *Harlem,* where now Puerto Rican Spanish and Black American-English is most likely to be heard. Thousands upon thousands of European immigrants entered the United States through Ellis Island and the Port of New York during the 19th and early 20th centuries. Many stayed in the area from choice because they had relatives or found friends there who spoke their language, or because they either had no money to move away or no desire to move farther into the strange new country. The public schools took responsibility for acculturation of the immigrants, teaching their children the English language as spoken in America. A fine school system and the intense desire of the immigrants to become Americans wrought a linguistic and cultural miracle that, although never since matched, is seldom recognized or appreciated.

The speech of the people of New York City is extremely varied. What is commonly attributed to New York as its dialect is really one among its many dialects that has persisted and has been prominent in drama and public media representations of New York. Here we point out a few prominent characteristics. New York shares the omission of final and preconsonantal *r* with most of the rest of the Atlantic Coast. In some words where /ɔ/ is found in Southern, General American, and New England, a diphthongized [ɔə] is used in New York so that *all* becomes [ɔəl], *law* becomes [lɔə], and *taught* becomes [tɔət] with pronounced lip-rounding. However, the more generally used /ɔ/ or /o/ before /r/ is quite often pronounced /ɑ/ for the following:

forest	[fɑrɪst]
horrid	[hɑrɪd]
orange	[ɑrɪndʒ]

Before the /ŋ/, the usual /ɔ/ also becomes /ɑ/ as in *prong* as [prɑŋ] and *honk* as [hɑŋk]. The *o* before *r* is very rounded as *four* becomes [fɔə] compared with Southern or New England [foə] and General American [for]. But the /ɝ/ of General American is likely to be [ʌr] so that *worry* becomes [wʌrɪ] and *hurry* becomes [hʌrɪ].

A number of sub-standard pronunciations are attributed to the New York dialect in popular media stereotypes. These include unnecessary pronunciation of a [g] in -ng endings so that *singing* becomes [sɪŋgɪŋ] and *Long Island* becomes [lɔŋgaɪlənd]; substitution of a glottal stop for lingua-alveolar or lingua-palatal stops as in [bɑʔl̩] for *bottle* and [trɪʔl̩] for *trickle*, and the substitution of /d/ for /ð/ in *these, those,* and *them*.

New York City is not only a place people like to visit. The "Big Apple" attracts its share of residents from all three of the major dialect areas, adding further variety to the speech one is likely to hear there.

Black American-English

The Black tribes of Africa typically spoke languages different from each other, even though they might have lived in fairly close proximity. Their tribal culture was dominated politically by strong autocratic chiefs, and it featured religious rules and taboos that kept tribes linguistically separated, isolated, and relatively small. Their languages were generally not recorded with formal orthographic systems. When Caucasian and Black slave merchants dipped into this polyglot reservoir during the 18th and early 19th centuries, they assembled on the beaches of West Africa compounds of Black men, women, and older children who spoke a myriad of African languages. Regrouped into masses that were convenient to fill the holds and meet the scheduled orders of "slaver" ships, families and tribes were further separated. Their dispersion continued at the auction blocks of Richmond, Annapolis, Charleston, and other slave trade centers of the American South, as plantation owners bid to buy the strong and healthy worker, regardless of tribe or family relation.

Thus, among the slaves of a plantation there might be no two who spoke the same African language. Restrictions on their travel prohibited meeting other members of their native tribes on neighboring plantations. The overseers spoke to them only in English. Finally, their own names, the last vestiges of their African language, were replaced by their owner with first names from common Anglo-Saxon (Joe, Topsy, Ned), classic Latin (Erasmus, Hannibal, Caesar), King James biblical stories (Amos, Ezekiel, Thomas), and from heroes (George Washington, Martin Luther). Surnames were usually the adopted names of their owners. Under these conditions they turned to the only common language available—English.

Their first new world speech, a kind of English Pidgin, consisted of imitated approximations of the Southern American-English model available to them, and some remnants (tote, voodoo, gumbo) of their mother tongue. Since they were unfamiliar with orthographic systems from their African languages and were not given the opportunity to learn to read and write the new language, they did not have alphabet spelling against which to compare their aural perception of others' speech and their own pronunciation. They taught their children this oral language from the cradle, developing the plantation creole or early native American phase of Black American-English.

In 1880, Joel Chandler Harris published a record of creole, Black American-English dialect in *Uncle Remus: His Songs and His Sayings.* Upon hearing that his work was to be catalogued among humorous publications, he retorted that "-its intention is perfectly serious—to preserve the legends— and to wed them permanently to the quaint dialect." He further noted that the dialect is different "—from the intolerable misrepresentations of the minstrel stage, but it is at least phonetically genuine." By brilliant transliter- ation with our alphabet, he forces his reader to abandon the usual rapid visual scanning, and, at least sub-vocally, delight in speaking the dialect of the uneducated Black slave story teller.

> In dem days, de creeturs kyar'd on marters same as fokes. Dey went inter fahmin', en I speck ef de troof wuz ter come out, dey kep' sto', en had der camp-meetin' times en der bobbycues w'en de wedder wuz 'greeble.

Within this short passage is the characteristic substitution of /d/ for /ð/ (dem, de, dey, der, wedder), the insertion of /r/ (marters, ter, der, inter), substitution of /f/ for /θ/ (troof), omission of unstressed syllables (kyar'd, 'speck, 'greeble), omission of final cluster consonants (kep'), substitution of /w/ for /ʍ/ (w'en), and, of course, omission of /r/ (fahmin', bobbycues, sto').

Creole Black American-English is most accurately viewed as a dialect of Southern American-English, since it developed from that dialect and shares characteristics with it. The English spoken by Blacks in Africa is certainly different from that spoken by Blacks in America. As a dialect for Black Americans today, the early creole has been dissipated first by migrations out of the South to the northern and western United States, and second, by social mobility with adoption of the major regional dialect spoken by other than Black Americans.

Modern Black American-English, sometimes called "Ebonics" or "Merican," is more difficult to define and is usually attributed to low socio- economic status Black persons. Certainly, the speech of Blacks differs greatly depending upon the part of the country in which they live and upon their social status. Many Black people who grew up with Black American-English dialect have adopted one of the major regional dialects but can still speak their earlier dialect. Much that characterizes Black American-English is in vocabulary, syntax, and intonation, but some pronunciations are distinctive. Final and preconsonantal -r is omitted, as in Southern speech, so that *hammer* becomes [hæmə] and *sharp* becomes [ʃaəp] or [ʃɑːp]. Many diphthongs are simplified so that *I* becomes [ɑː], *pie* becomes [paː] or [pɑː], *boy* becomes [bɔː] or [boː] and *time* becomes [tɑːm]. A distinctive feature is the nearly complete substitution of other sounds for the lingua-dental sounds

/θ/ and /ð/. The /θ/ becomes /t/ initially and when following lingua-alveolar /n/, and it becomes /f/ medially and finally as in the following examples:

thumb	[tʌm]	*month*	[mʌnt]
teeth	[tif]	*arithmetic*	[rɪtmətɪk]
bathroom	[bæfrʊm]	*nothing*	[nʌfɪn]

The /ð/ becomes /d/ initially, and becomes /v/ medially and finally, as in these examples:

these	[diz]	*the*	[də]
smooth	[smuv]	*those*	[douz]
feather	[fɛvə]	*bathing*	[beɪvɪn]

Final consonant clusters are simplified by omission of one or more consonants, usually the final one. Note these examples where both members of the cluster are either voiced or voiceless:

locked	[lɑk]	*first*	[fʌs]
wasp	[wɑs]	*hand*	[hæn]
nest	[nɛs]	*rained*	[reɪn]
rubbed	[rʌb]	*messed*	[mɛs]

Final consonants are usually both articulated when one is voiceless and the other is voiced, as in [dʒʌmp] for *jump* and [bɛlt] for *belt*. Final and medial /l/ is often omitted so that *apple* becomes [æpə], *health* becomes [hɛəf], *nails* becomes [neɪəz], and *help* becomes [hɛp]. With omission of medial /l/ and reduction of voiceless consonants in a cluster, *twelfth* becomes [tʌəf].

Omission of the contracted /l/ suggests to the listener a difference in syntax that may originally have been just a matter of pronunciation. When *will* is contracted and the /l/ is omitted, "Tomorrow I'll bring the thing" becomes "Tomorrow I' bring the thing." Similarly, "He'll be here in a few minutes" becomes "He' be here in a few minutes," and "I'll be working tomorrow" becomes "I' be working tomorrow." When language is transmitted to the next generation primarily by speech, these omissions of /l/ may appear to be and then become real syntactical differences. A similar phenomenon occurs with the often omitted *-ed* suffix, so that *named* becomes [neɪm] and *finished* is said as [fɪnɪʃ], suggesting the absence of past tense usage. Omission of contracted *'ve* for *have* and *'s* for *has* also suggests syntactical omissions as in "I' been here for hours," and "He' gone home." A similar phenomenon in General American is responsible for people writing "might of been," derived from "might *have* been" by way of contracted [maɪt əv bɪn] in connected speech.

The use of [ɪn] for the *-ing* suffix is common to many American-English speakers but is almost universal in black American-English as in [sɪŋɪn] for *singing.* Nasalized vowels are sometimes substituted for final nasal consonants as in [mæ̃] for *man,* [rʌ̃] for *run,* and [drʌ̃] for *drum.* This is especially frequent in unstressed positions as in [meəmæ̃] for *mailman.*

DEFECTIVE SPEECH

The foregoing sections describe important ways speech differs as non-standard productions and as dialects. Neither kind of deviation should be considered "defective" or "disordered" speech. Two useful definitions of speech defects are prevalent. Speech defects exist when the speaker wishes to change a non-standard pattern but cannot, and thus some external assistance is needed. Speech is defective also when it poses a significant handicap for the speaker, possibly influencing his social, vocational, or educational potential. The first definition refers to the speaker's own impression of his speech and his difficulty with self-improvement. The second refers to the reaction of his listeners. The speaker might analyze his own speech by comparing it with that of others, but often he is unaware even that his speech is different until he is cued by a negative listener reaction.

The following example illustrates how these definitions of defective speech might be applied. Earlier in this chapter, the difficulty of mastering the /l/ and /r/ sounds was cited. For the young child, non-standard productions of these lingual consonants are considered immature speech patterns and are to be expected. Few children master these sounds before six years of age, and before this, the /w/ substitution is not viewed with concern. If the substitution should persist into adulthood, a number of possible reactions may take place:

1. The speaker realizes, by self-analysis or from listener reaction, that his /l/ or /r/ differs from that of his peers. By careful listening and by trial-and-error attempts at articulation, he may improve his own production to a satisfactory level and have no further problem.
2. Upon realizing his /l/ or /r/ production is different, he may wish to change toward the standard, but his attempts are in vain. He cares about his speech and will need help with his speech defect.
3. Upon realizing his /l/ or /r/ production is different, he may not care to change from what he has always said. He may attempt a change himself but gives up easily with disinterest. Among his peers and in his school, or in his type of vocation, he is not penalized because of his non-standard speech. His speech is intelligible and some listeners may even think it "cute." His speech is non-standard but not defective. It serves him well.
4. Upon realizing his /l/ or /r/ production is different, he may not care to change from what he has always said. He persists in his non-standard patterns. In school classes in which oral recitation is required, his

classmates laugh at him, and later he finds he cannot get the jobs he wants because of the reactions of listeners to his speech. He retreats from communicative situations and works at menial occupations well beneath his intellectual potential. He is severely penalized by his defective speech.

5. He realizes his /l/ or /r/ production is different, but in school, where he is an outstanding athlete, he is popular and his peers take his different speech as a matter of course. He would like to change his speech but is not bothered enough to make a serious effort. In college he cannot make the varsity team, and now his fellow students sometimes laugh at his speech or imitate him. They do not seek him out or look up to him. He knows his speech defect will handicap him and he seeks professional help. Even though there was no change in the degree of difference in his speech, it has shifted from merely non-standard to defective because of the situation and his reaction to it.

In these examples, even though the speech a listener might have heard was the same, whether or not it should be considered "defective" depended upon the situation, upon the reaction of listeners, and upon the speaker's perception of his speech pattern.

Imagine, now, the problem of determining the incidence of speech defects in our population. Before the age of 9 or 10 years, since it is natural for children to be developing their articulation, many differences will be prevalent in their speech patterns, particularly among preschoolers. Then too, some listeners may judge a minor deviation in pronunciation of an adult to be a defect when the speaker does not think of it as such. It is not surprising to find studies of the incidence of speech defects giving widely varied reports. Surveys have ranged from less than 1 percent to over 20 percent of the school age population having defective speech, with summary estimates at about 5 percent. In some studies, children just developing speech have been considered defective, and in others, foreign accents and dialect differences were included in the defective group. Differences in severity, the type of defect, the speaker's reaction to his speech, and the handicap it gives him may make the task of determining incidence of speech defects in general a nearly impossible one. Those who have tried, by and large, have been speech pathologists whose professional field is enhanced by reports of high incidence and who are untrained in surveys.

REVIEW VOCABULARY

American-English—that English spoken within the United States.

Colloquial speech—the common, familiar, and informal speech of cultivated people.

Creole speech—refers to the speech of the first generation of native born speakers descended from immigrants from a foreign language background.

Defective speech—that which poses a handicap for the speaker, or that which the speaker wishes to change but cannot without assistance.

Dialect—the words, language forms, pronunciations, and speech habits peculiar to people of a geographic region who are part of larger group using the same language.

Enunciation—clarity or precision of articulation, sometimes referred to as diction.

Immature speech—those patterns different from the prevalent speech patterns of adults within a dialect group that an individual uses because of lack of experience and/or maturation.

Intelligibility—the quality of being understandable, usually limited to the recognition of speech units rather than comprehension of their meaning.

Metathasis—reversal of consonant order in connected speech.

Non-standard speech—that which is notably or remarkably different and considered poorer than general standards of speech.

Pidgin English—an adaptation of English by foreign speakers, using essential content words for conducting business and essential communication.

Pronunciation—selection among available phonemes in producing a unit of speech.

Shibboleth—a peculiarity of speech distinctive to a particular group; a password or watchword.

Standards of speech—a variety of criteria for general acceptance or approval of speech, either stated or implied, against which an individual's speech pattern is commonly judged.

Vernacular—native common usage learned from childhood by educated persons.

Voice quality—that which distinguishes one person's voice from others. The combination of fundamental frequency plus overtones, but usually includes characteristics of articulation and speech rhythm.

EXERCISES

1. Pronounce each of the listed variations for the following three words. Compare these with your own typical pronunciation and with that indicated in dictionaries.

library	temperature	February
[laɪbrɛrɪ]	[tɛmpɚətjur]	[fɛbruwɛrɪ]
[laɪbrærɪ]	[tɛmpɚətur]	[fɛbjuwɛrɪ]
[laɪbɛrɪ]	[tɛmpɚətʃɚ]	[fɛbəwɛrɪ]
[laɪbɚɛrɪ]	[tɛmpɚtʃɚ]	[fɛbwɛrɪ]
[lɑbrɚɪ]	[tɛmpɪtʃɚ]	[fɛbɚɛrɪ]
	[tɛmpətʃɚ]	[fɛbrɪ]
	[tɪmpɪtʃə]	[fɪbjɪɛrɪ]

2. Ask several friends to say each of the following sentences as they usually would speak it:

   a. "I believe my library book is extensively overdue."
   b. "Today the barometric pressure and temperature are lower than yesterday."
   c. "It begins to get just a little warmer in February and March."

   Transcribe in IPA symbols the key words *library, temperature,* and *February.* Compare to the pronunciations in exercise 1, above. Do not say the sentences to them yourself or tell them the key words. Let them read each sentence silently on a card before saying it from memory.

3. After your speakers have said all three sentences in exercise 2, ask them for the "correct" pronunciation of each of the key words. Transcribe and compare with the transcription of their usual production in connected speech.

4. From the variations in pronunciation described in this chapter, compile a single list of no more than 10 "shibboleth" words that will differentiate speakers from General American, Southern, and New England dialect areas. If possible, test the list on appropriate speakers.

5. Ask several friends or instructors to read and give you "the correct pronunciation" of the following familiar words:

   with ([θ] - [ð])
   herb ([hɝ] - [ɝ])
   often ([ft] - [f])

> data   ([eɪ] - [æ] - [ɑ])
> was   ([ʌ] - [ɑ])

After they have said the words, ask such questions as, "Is it supposed to be [wɪθ] or [wɪð]?" "Is it supposed to be [hɜ˞b] or [ɜ˞b]?" Note in their responses (1) the standards criteria they employ compared with those in this chapter, (2) their level of certainty about the "correct" pronunciation, and (3) any embarrassment or emotional response related to their uncertainty about pronunciation.

6. Ask several friends or instructors to read and "say" each of these probably less familiar words:

> struthious
> lucubration
> omphaloskepsis
> metathasis
> sesquipedalian

Observe the strategies utilized, not only in settling upon the pronunciation but in determining the accent pattern.

SUGGESTED READING

Winitz, Harris: *Articulatory Acquisition and Behavior*. Englewood Cliffs, N.J., Prentice-Hall, Inc., 1969.

A good basic text on speech development of children from a psycholinguistic viewpoint, for the speech pathologist, especially.

Wise, Claude Merton: *Applied Phonetics*. Englewood Cliffs, N.J., Prentice-Hall, Inc., 1957.

Chapters 6, 7, 8, and 9 deal with the speech of General American, Southern American, and Eastern American speech patterns. Chapter 16 on "Mountain Speech" is very well done. The book also describes the speech of several foreign languages.

Carr, Elizabeth B.: *Da Kine Talk: From Pidgin to Standard English in Hawaii*. Honolulu, University Press of Hawaii, 1972.

A scholarly account of the development of neo-Pidgin spoken in Hawaii today, especially its derivation from the various languages that have been spoken in the Islands, and a description of the present variations from island to island.

Dillard, J.L.: *Black English: Its History and Usage in the United States*, New York, Random House, 1972.

This basic treatise on Black American-English traces the roots of the dialect, especially pointing out "Africanisms," related to tribal languages, and the influence of Black American-English on other American-English dialects.

Chapter VIII

SENSORY PRODUCTS OF SPEECH

- **INFORMATION FOR THE AUDITORY SYSTEM**
  - **THE FREQUENCY-INTENSITY SPECTRUM**
  - **DIFFERENCES IN DURATION**
- **INFORMATION FOR THE VISUAL SYSTEM**
- **INFORMATION FOR PROPRIOCEPTION**
- **SPEECH PERCEPTION**
- **REVIEW VOCABULARY**
- **EXERCISES**
- **SUGGESTED READING**

Another important way to describe speech is to consider the results of speaking. The processes of respiration, phonation, resonation, and articulation, described in earlier chapters, result in the production of acoustic energy or sound waves that carry the code of speech to our auditory system. These sounds are the intended and the primary product of speech production. But sounds are not the only result of speaking. A number of other results occur that may be considered by-products, providing secondary level information that is available to our senses. Among these are **visible** lip movements the observer, but not the speaker, has available for the process called "speech reading," the **tactile** [tǽktɪl] impressions of touching and friction available to the speaker during his articulation, and the **kinesthetic** [kɪnɛsθέtɪk] impressions the speaker senses from muscles moving and stretching.

INFORMATION FOR THE AUDITORY SYSTEM

Acoustics [əkústɪks], the branch of physics concerned with the physical properties of sound, collaborates with phonetics to form the specialized field of study called **acoustic phonetics.** Those who pursue acoustic phonetics seek to describe the important acoustic features of speech and how they relate on the one hand to speech production and on the other hand to speech perception. All speech sounds can be described in terms of three acoustic parameters: frequency, intensity, and time. We begin with the parameters of frequency and intensity.

The Frequency-Intensity Spectrum

The process of phonation was described in Chapter II. The rate of opening and closing of the glottis is the fundamental frequency, F_o, of voice. The physical term **frequency** refers to the number of complete cycles of openings-closings, oscillations, or vibrations of any object over a given period. For sound waves, frequency refers to the number of cycles of compression and rarefaction of air molecules that occurs within one second. When the pulses of compression and rarefaction occur periodically, one of a variety of complex tones results. A special case for illustration is the simple back-and-forth motion of a tuning fork. For the resulting simple sound or "pure" tone, the cycles of compression and rarefaction may be represented graphically by a sinusoidal wave, as shown in Figure VIII-1. Frequency is described by the number of cycles per second, written as **Hertz [hɝts]** (for the German physicist, Heinrich R. Hertz, 1857–1894) and abbreviated **Hz.** As frequency increases, the sound is heard as higher in pitch. A sound of 100 Hz, for example, is very low in pitch, whereas a sound of 8000 Hz (8 KiloHertz) is very high in pitch.

Intensity of sound is determined by the amount of compression of air molecules or pressure that occurs for a sound wave, related somewhat to the frequency of the sound but primarily to its **amplitude.** Amplitude refers to the extent of excursion from the center or equilibrium of a vibrating body or for voice, to the extent of openings of the glottis. The greater the amplitude, the greater the intensity of the sound. Intensity, which is related to dynes **[daɪnz]** (unit of pressure) per square centimeter, is described in ratios written as **deciBels [dɛsɪbɛlz]** (for Alexander Graham Bell, 1847–1922) and abbreviated **dB.** As intensity increases, the sound is heard as louder. A sound of 30 dB, for example, is very soft, whereas a sound of 100 dB is very loud.

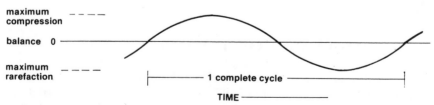

Figure VIII-1.   Sinusoidal wave representing cycles of compression and rarefaction of air molecules.

The wave-like motions of the vocal folds in their gradual opening and closing of the glottis during phonation produce a complex sound consisting not only of the fundamental frequency but also of several **overtones.** These are a succession of higher frequencies or partials of the fundamental frequency. In a periodic sound like voice, the overtones are whole number multiples of the fundamental frequency and are called **harmonics.** The harmonics, whose amplitudes combine to coincide with the amplitude of the fundamental frequency in a given period, will each be less intense or weaker than the fundamental, and each successively higher harmonic will be less intense than the previous one. A description of the acoustic **frequency spectrum** of a complex sound, therefore, requires consideration of the relative intensity or amount of energy at various frequencies.

The complex sound produced by phonation has a frequency spectrum consisting of the fundamental frequency plus harmonics of successively decreasing intensity. The rate of their decrease in intensity is about 12 dB per "octave," or doubling of frequency. Figure VIII–2(a) is a line spectrum representing the various frequencies and their relative intensities that would be produced by a glottal sound source. A sound of this type would be heard by a listener as a buzz with a particular pitch related to the fundamental frequency, having a particular **quality** of sound that is influenced by the intensity relations among the various frequencies represented in the sound.

However, the sound from the glottis is never heard in its original condition because it is immediately influenced by resonation in the vocal tract above it. The process of resonation was briefly described in Chapter II. Imagine the vocal tract in a relaxed condition, with the tongue lying flat and the mouth opened, but the nasal cavity closed off at the velopharyngeal port,

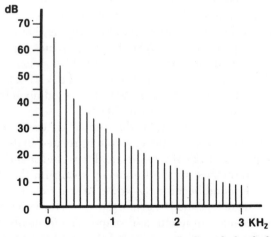

Figure VIII-2. (a)   Frequency-Intensity line spectrum of an idealized glottal sound with a fundamental frequency of 125 Hz (a buzzing sound).

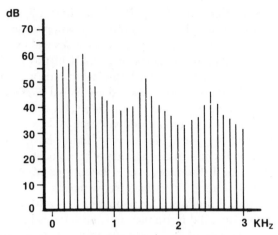

Figure VIII-2. (b) Frequency-Intensity line spectrum resulting from the glottal sound *(a)*, acted upon by an idealized and relaxed vocal tract with a resonant frequency of 500 Hz (an /ə/ sound).

much as the situation would be for the unstressed natural vowel /ə/. In this situation, the oral and pharyngeal cavities would act like a resonating tube open at one end (the mouth) and closed at times at the other (the glottis). Its resonance characteristics would be especially influenced by its length, averaging 17.5 centimeters or about 7 inches for an adult male. Pulses of compressed air can reflect through a tube of that length at a rate of about 500 round-trip reflections or cycles per second, giving the tube a resonant frequency of 500 cycles per second, or 500 Hz. Thus the vocal tract, open as a resonant tube, would tend to reinforce a 500 Hz component more than all others. The new spectrum of frequencies for the resulting sound would show a peak at 500 Hz, sloping off in the higher frequencies, but with a fairly regular pattern of other overtone peaks of energy at about every 1000 Hz above the major resonant peak at 500 Hz. This creates a pattern of peaks followed by valleys at odd multiples (1,3,5,7,9) of the resonant frequency of the tube: 500 Hz, 1500 Hz, 2500 Hz, etc. Figure VIII-2(b) shows a line spectrum of the glottal sound of Figure VIII-2(a) acted upon by an idealized vocal tract with a resonant frequency of 500 Hz.

    This new sound would be quite different from the glottal buzz. The listener would still hear it as having a low pitch, related to its lowest tone or fundamental frequency of 125 Hz, but its quality would sound like the vowel /ə/. The peaks of resonance in the frequency spectrum that form the new quality to make the sound become the vowel /ə/ are called speech **formants** [**formænts**]. They are determined by characteristics of the vocal tract and change as the vocal tract changes in length and shape. The formants are numbered from low to high frequencies and are called the first formant, F_1, the second formant, F_2, the third, F_3, and so on. Remember that the fundamental frequency of a sound is written F_0.

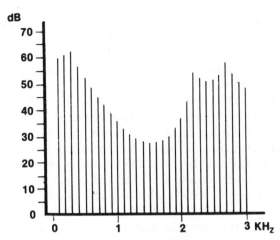

Figure VIII-2. *(c)* Frequency-Intensity line spectrum resulting from the glottal sound *(a)*, acted upon by an idealized vocal tract positioned to produce the vowel /i/.

The frequency locations of the formants, especially F_1 and F_2, are closely influenced by the configuration of the vocal tract. It is these formants that especially contribute to perception of vowels. The factors that contribute most to the position of F_1 and F_2 are (1) length of the vocal tract, (2) location of constriction in the tract, and (3) narrowness of the constriction. The greater the length of the tract from the glottis to the lips, the lower the formant frequencies. Thus, since the average length of the vocal tract in women is about four-fifths as long as that of men, the location of formants would be one-fifth higher than that in men, with the same spacing of odd numbered multiples (1,3,5,7,9) of the resonant frequency of the relaxed vocal tract. And an infant with a vocal tract one-half the length of an adult's would have a resonant frequency of the open tract of twice that of an adult. It is not surprising, then, that lip rounding, which usually includes lip protrusion and therefore lengthening of the tract, tends to lower the frequencies of formants. Thus the vowel /ɔ/ has a lower F_1 and F_2 than /ɑ/ from which it differs primarily in lip rounding.

Although there are not always one-to-one relations between specific configurations of the tract during connected speech and the frequency positions of formants, here are two rough rules-of-thumb for these relations:

1. **F_1 is lowered by increasing constriction in the front half of the tract.**
   Thus the /i/, the highest of the front vowels, has a very low F_1 associated with the narrow space between the front of the tongue and the palate-alveolar ridge (see Chapter IV). Each of the other front vowels, /ɪ/, /ɛ/, and /æ/, has a successively higher F_1 corresponding to less constriction. The /u/ has the narrowest frontal constriction at the lips and thus has a lower F_1 than most other vowels, including those that have lip rounding but a wider opening such as /ʊ/ and /ɔ/.

2. **F_2 is lowered by increasing constriction in the back half of the tract.** Thus the /u/, the highest of the back vowels, has a very low F_2 associated with the narrow space between the back of the tongue and the velum (see Chapter IV). With reduced back constriction, as for back vowels /ʊ/, /o/, /ɔ/, and /ɑ/, the F_2 would tend to rise.

The alterations of the oral cavity to form vowels is reflected in considerable movement of the frequency positions of the first two formants. For example, the /u/, which has constriction in the front by the lips and in the back by the elevated tongue, would have lowered formants, fairly close together. Average F_1 would be about 250 Hz with an F_2 of about 850 Hz for /u/. The /i/, with constriction in the front and no constriction in the back, would have an average F_1 of 250 Hz but an F_2 of over 2000 Hz (often written as 2KHz, for KiloHertz). Figure VIII-2(c) shows a line spectrum for the vowel /i/. Compare this irregular pattern with that of the idealized and relaxed vocal tract of Figure VIII-2(b).

Some average frequency positions of the first two formants of steady state vowels and resonant consonants, produced by a male speaker, are shown in Figure VIII-3. The relation between configurations of the vocal tract and formant positions is apparent, especially for the front vowels /i/, /ɪ/, /ɛ/, and /æ/. Positions of formant bands are well displayed by a filtering device called a "speech spectrograph." Figure VIII-4 shows a resulting spectrogram of /i/, /ɪ/, /ɛ/, and /æ/ in which the formant bands stand out in contrast to the softer background. Time is the horizontal parameter in this figure.

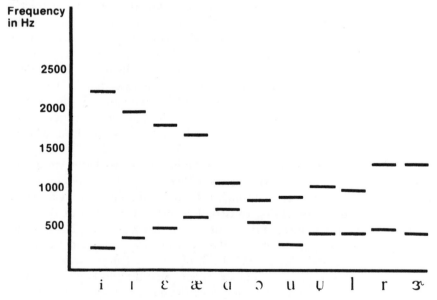

Figure VIII-3. Average frequency positions of the first two formants of steady state vowels and resonant consonants produced by a male speaker.

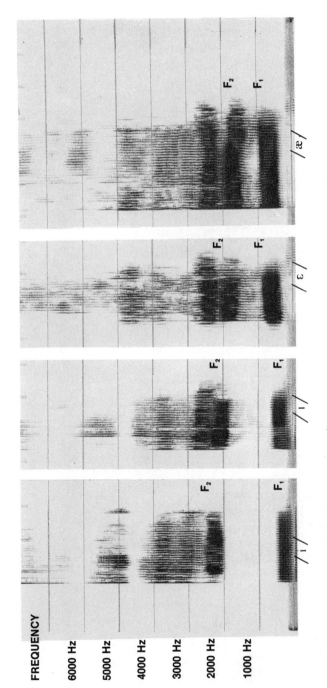

Figure VIII–4. Speech sound spectrograms of isolated vowels /i/, /ɪ/, /ɛ/, and /æ/.

223

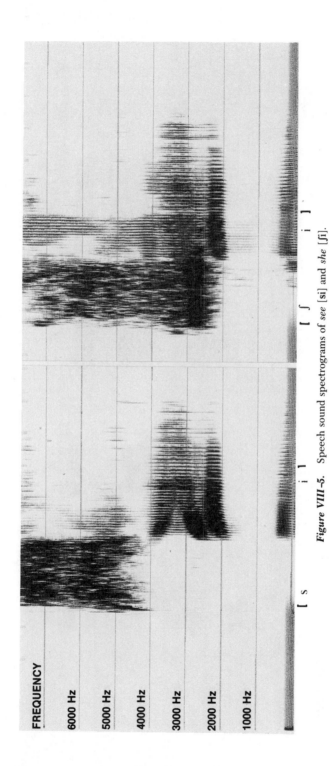

Figure VIII–5. Speech sound spectrograms of *see* [si] and *she* [ʃi].

Fricative consonants appear on spectrograms as areas of sound energy from aperiodic or inharmonic sound production. Notice the difference in Figure VIII–5 of the frequency spread for the /s/ and /ʃ/ sounds. Fricative consonants yield frequency information both from their position on the frequency spectrum and from their spread of sound energy over the spectrum.

Nasal consonants, produced with the velopharyngeal port open, have a complex frequency-intensity spectrum. While the oral cavity is especially resonant for some frequencies, and thus amplifies them, the nasal cavity may be "antiresonant," diminishing those same frequencies, and vice versa. On spectrograms, the nasal consonants show resonant bands or formants, like vowels, but the formant bands are broader in frequency spread and more sound energy exists between the bands than for oral resonant sounds. Since opening of the velopharyngeal port for nasal sounds increases both length and size of the total resonating cavity that may act upon the glottal sound, a large concentration of lower frequency energy is created, usually at 250 to 300 Hz.

In addition to the relative intensity of certain frequency areas for each phoneme, the overall intensity of the sound varies from phoneme to phoneme. When averaged, the phonemes of American-English have a range of intensity of 28 dB, or a power ratio of approximately 1:680 from the weakest /θ/ to the strongest /ɔ/. The vowels are the most powerful and thus the loudest sounds. When stressed (see Chapter VI), vowels may have three to four times as much power as in unstressed syllables. Resonant consonants are next in power, followed by /ʃ/, /tʃ/, and their voiced counterparts. The stops and fricatives follow, with /f/ and /θ/ being the weakest sounds. Of course, the actual intensity of speech sounds, particularly vowels and resonant consonants, would vary from speaker to speaker, as would the range of their intensities. The intensity of voiceless consonants are less influenced by such individual speaker differences.

Just as description of the production of isolated phonemes in Chapters III and IV needed to be modified by the important effects of context and coarticulation described in Chapter V, so too must the static displays of acoustic characteristics of isolated phonemes be considered in the context of the flow of connected speech. Figure VIII–6 is a spectrogram of connected speech produced at a normal rate. Here, formant bands that appeared level in the isolated displays of Figure VIII–4 bend up and down and sometimes do not even attain their target frequency positions. The transitions between phonemes appear as prominently as do the phonemes themselves, and indeed, the transitional characteristics seem to have an important influence on speech perception. The bending of vowel formants, for example, lends an important cue to the place of production of adjoining consonants.

Speech rhythm features are also reflected in the frequency-intensity spectrum over the time period of the connected speech signal. As pointed out in Chapter VI, the physiologic force of production for accent and em-

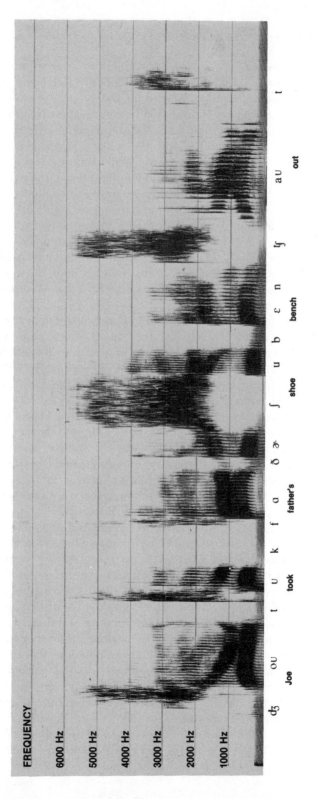

Figure VIII-6. Speech sound spectrogram of connected speech unit, "Joe took father's shoe bench out."

phasis produces perceptible changes in intensity, frequency, and duration of the stressed word or syllable. Intonation consists primarily of variations in fundamental voice frequency over the period of a phrase. Phrasing and rate are related to the parameter of time or duration.

Differences in Duration

Along with the frequency-intensity spectrum, duration appears to be a significant contributor to speech perception. For example, given the same phonetic context, the /i/ is longer than the /ɪ/. This may be a useful difference for perception in words that are similar such as *beet* and *bit*, since the frequency-intensity difference in the two vowels is small. However, the duration of all vowels is systematically influenced by the consonants around them, particularly by the consonants that they precede. A vowel is longer in front of a fricative than in front of a stop consonant, helping the listener to determine the manner of production of that consonant. The duration of a vowel is greater before a voiced consonant than before its voiceless counterpart, so that the greater length of the [i] in *bead* compared to the [i] in *beet* is a cue to perceiving the voiced-voiceless distinction of the final consonant. Because of this influence of phonetic context, the [ɪ] in *bid* may actually be longer than the [i] in *beet*. Stress patterns also influence duration, with the vowel of a stressed syllable typically longer than the same vowel of an unstressed syllable. Of course, individual differences in rate of speaking also determine phoneme duration, especially for vowels and resonant consonants.

Fricative and stop consonants are marked by important durational differences, in addition to their frequency positions and frequency spread, and their intensity characteristics. Stops are shorter than fricatives in overall duration, with affricates falling between the two in length. The voice onset time (VOT) following an aspirated voiceless stop, such as the [pʻ] in [pʻi], is significantly greater than that of a voiced stop [b], as in [bi]. This durational difference is also an important cue to the listener in perceiving the voiced-voiceless distinction of a stop consonant preceding a vowel.

INFORMATION FOR THE VISUAL SYSTEM

In producing the sounds of speech, the jaw, lips, and tongue make movements that are generally visible to an observer. These movements, or articulatory gestures, may provide the observer with important information about the speech sounds produced. The process of using these gestures as a means of speech perception has been called "lipreading." The term "speech-reading," now more common, takes into account the movements of jaw and tongue, buccal tension, upper neck movement, nose movement, and general facial expression, as well as information from the lips.

A listener-observer with normal hearing may occasionally supplement his auditory perception with speechreading in difficult listening situations. In a noisy background, for example, the acoustic distinction between *free* and *three* may be so obscured that only the visual gesture of the lower lip approximating the upper front teeth can assure the listener-observer that the initial consonant was [f] and thus the word must have been *free*. We may also be assisted by speechreading when speech production is unusual. When listening to a person with a speech defect, a foreign speaker, or a young child who is just developing speech, most of us avail ourselves of speechreading to receive visual cues, in addition to the acoustic cues, some of which may be ambiguous. Speechreading is often helpful, also, when spoken language content is difficult to comprehend, as when we hear unfamiliar words in a lecture. The necessity of supplementing auditory speech information with visual information is especially pronounced when we listen to nonsense syllables or to an unfamiliar language for purposes of phonetic transcription.

An observer-listener with a serious hearing impairment may habitually supplement hearing with speechreading in all situations. Or, when hearing loss is even more severe, he may depend upon speechreading as the primary source of speech reception, using hearing as an important supplement. For persons with profound deafness, without recourse to acoustic amplification by hearing aids, articulatory gestures may be the only source of speech information.

It is generally agreed that visible speech gestures carry only a portion of the information necessary for complete and accurate comprehension of the speech message, perhaps less than 50 percent. When only the visible gestures of articulation are perceptible, the remainder of the message may be supplied by (1) contextual information from the subject under discussion, (2) knowledge of linguistic rules so that a recognized word suggests what the word next to it probably was, (3) familiarity with the speaker's typical language style and choice of subject, and (4) a facility for "filling in," utilizing the first three factors, as well as a knowledge of relative frequency of occurrence of words and phrases in spoken language. It is also apparent that, when supplemented with even minimal acoustic speech information, our ability to speechread can improve markedly. Acoustic information that gives cues about manner of production, voicing, and nasality appears to be especially helpful as a supplement to speechreading.

Analogous to the phoneme of auditorally perceived speech is the visual phoneme or **viseme** [vízim]. Visemes are the visible speech positions that form recognizable categories of optical contrast, with variations, like allophonic variations, caused by coarticulation. There is no consensus concerning the number of visemes in English. This fact reflects the greater degree of variability in both producing and perceiving visemes as compared with acoustic phonemes. It is the conventionally accepted acoustic signal, and not the optical signal, that the typical speaker consciously produces. An acceptable acoustic signal for a phoneme may be produced by very different articulatory gestures, as was pointed out in Chapters III and IV. Friction for /ʍ/, for example, can be created by tongue placement without the typical lip rounding. Therefore, we cannot expect as much similarity in how the viseme for /ʍ/ looks from speaker to speaker as in how the acoustic phoneme sounds. One of the marked visual variations among speakers is the nearly immobile upper lip, habitual with some speakers who never really round the lips but may compensate to produce an acceptable acoustic result by changing tongue position. This is an action essentially invisible to the observer.

Ability to perceive speech visually also varies greatly among individuals. Moderately hearing-impaired observers typically read speech better than do those with normal hearing, but there is an immense range of ability among normal-hearing speechreaders. Most people improve in ability to recognize visemes after a short period of training.

Regardless of the habits of the speaker or the ability of the observer, articulatory gestures for all speech sounds are not equally visible. The bilabial /p/, /b/, and /m/, with front articulation and lip closure, are easiest to see. The labio-dental /f/ and /v/ and the vowels with lip rounding are also easily observable. Lingua-alveolar /t/, /d/, /l/, and /n/ are harder to see, and the lingua-velar /k/, /g/, and /ŋ/, made in the back of the mouth, are not visible at all during normal speech production. Among those speech sounds that are visible, however, not all are discriminable. The easily visible /p/, /b/, and /m/, for example, are virtually indistinguishable from each other so that *pie*, *by*, and *my* would look alike. These very similar looking visemes are referred to as being **homophenous** [homáfinəs], and words that are visually indistinguishable are called homophenous words. Acoustically **homophonous** [homáfonəs] words such as *bare-bear*, *write-right*, and *so-sew* were mentioned in Chapter I. Speechreading makes available to the observer information primarily about the place of production of speech sounds. However, the presence or absence of voicing, the use of open nasal resonance, and much about the manner of production is absent from the visual speech signal. Voiced and voiceless cognates, such as /v/ and /f/, and /d/ and /t/ cannot be discriminated. The nasal /m/ also looks exactly like the oral /b/.

A promising approach to research on the parameters of visual information available for speech perception is the description of contrasting features or oppositions. This effort parallels the search for acoustic distinctive features that influence auditory speech perception. Figure VIII–7 shows a model of some visual oppositions at seven levels of increasing subtlety. The levels may correspond to progress in early speechreading development by deaf children, and could be predictive of confusions on visual perception tasks.

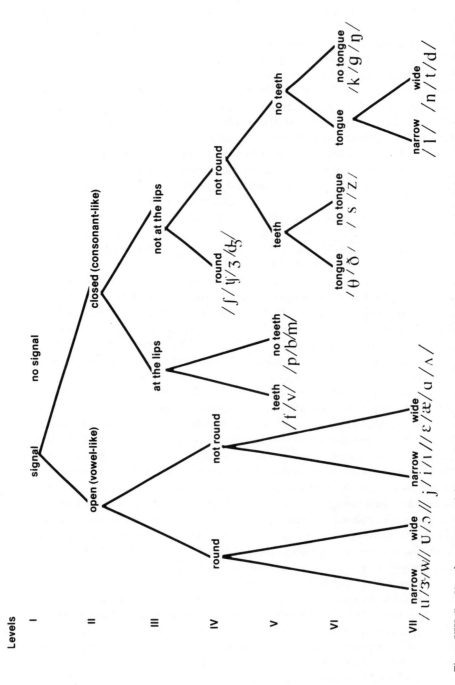

Figure VIII-7. Visual oppositions of the speech signal at seven levels of subtlety (courtesy, Carol DeFilippo, Central Institute for the Deaf).

INFORMATION FOR PROPRIOCEPTION

Speech not only produces acoustic and optical information propagated for perception by other listeners and observers, but it also results in sensory information about speech movements that is fed back only to the speaker. Such information is available for the speaker's internal perception or **proprioception** [próprios*έ*pʃən]. Proprioception for speech serves several important purposes:

1. Proprioception provides instantaneous and continuous feedback about speech movements that helps the speaker **monitor** his speech production. Such monitoring helps him make adjustments in place or manner of production, which result in desirable acoustic output, as he is learning and developing speech. It also helps in correcting occasional speech errors or "slips of the tongue" during rapid connected speech.
2. Proprioception provides sensory information basic to the memory patterns necessary for producing speech. In the absence of hearing for speech, as would occur in a very noisy environment or with temporary hearing loss, we continue to speak by using our memory for how speech feels as it is being produced.
3. Proprioception provides a probable basis for speech perception by the listener or observer. The "motor theory" of speech perception maintains that we perceive speech in the way that we produce it, and that hearing the acoustic events of a unit of speech calls up our proprioceptive memory for how we would produce that same unit.

Proprioception includes two major kinds of sensations, tactile and kinesthetic, which apparently supply complementary information for a unified motor memory pattern.

Tactile speech information comes from touching parts of the speech mechanism; from friction and turbulence as air flows over the surfaces of the tongue, lips and palate; and from vibration associated with voicing called **vibro-tactile** information. A review of speech sound production in Chapters III and IV will reveal that not all phonemes yield equal tactile information. Bilabials /p/, /b/, and /m/ require touching of the tactually sensitive lips, and the lingua-alveolar /t/, /d/, /n/, and /l/ involve touching the alveolar ridge with the sensitive tongue tip. Whereas these sounds provide considerable sensation from touching, the lingua-velar /k/, /g/, and /ŋ/, which involve the less sensitive back of the tongue and the velum, give little information from their touching. Some consonants, such as /s/, /ʃ/, and /r/, do not require touching another part of the speech anatomy and thus provide no tactile feedback to assist in monitoring their appropriate place of production. The same is true of the vowels and of the consonants /w/ and /j/. The fricative consonants, particularly the voiceless fricatives /f/ and /θ/ which require close labio-dental or lingua-dental approximation, provide tactile sensations from the flow of turbulent breath. Less tactile sensation is available from the more open fricatives /h/, /ʍ/, /s/, and /ʃ/. Combined touching and friction occurs in the affricate /ʧ/. The voiced fricates /v/, /ð/, /z/, and /ʒ/ provide less tactile friction sensation than do their voiceless counterparts, but they have vibro-tactile information from voicing. The vowels, which have no touching or friction, possess strong voicing vibration. The strongest vibro-tactile information comes from the nasal resonant consonants /m/, /n/, and /ŋ/.

Kinesthetic speech information comes from the movement of structures and from the stretching of muscles. The kinesthetic sensory receptors lie between muscle cells, in the surface of joints, and in the interior of tendons. They are sensitive to position, movement, and tension. Speech sounds vary in their yield of kinesthetic information as they do of tactile information. Although there is very little stimulus from movements of the velum and pharynx in closing the velopharyngeal port, movement of the lower jaw, the lips, and the tongue provides considerable kinesthetic sensation. The lip rounding /ɔ/, /u/, and /w/; the wide jaw opening /ɑ/ and /æ/ and the diphthongs /ɔɪ/, /ou/, and /aʊ/ offer considerable kinesthetic feedback. If the lips are drawn back for /i/ or if the tongue is retroflexed for /r/, these sounds can yield great kinesthetic sensation. The voiceless stops and affricates, particularly the /p/ and /t/, require pressure for closure, which gives some information. Among the weakest sounds, kinesthetically, are the /ʌ/, which requires no tongue elevation; the /h/, which has no position of its own; and the lingua-velar /g/ and /ŋ/, where little movement is required of either the tongue or velum.

Proprioception for speech usually occurs subconsciously but can be brought to the level of consciousness when needed for analysis of speech production. The fact that tactile and kinesthetic speech feedback information alone is inadequate for monitoring completely normal speech production is borne out by the different sounding speech of profoundly deaf persons deprived of auditory feedback. By the same token, the value of such feedback is demonstrated by those who either lost their hearing or were born with profound deafness and who nevertheless maintain functional use of speech for communication in the absence of auditory feedback. The importance of proprioception for speech is readily apparent for all of us when perception is impaired as with topical dental anesthetic influencing the tongue.

SPEECH PERCEPTION

In the previous chapters, speech has been described as a chain of discrete phonemes linked together by coarticulation. Linguistic theory suggests that speech may be recognized by the human auditory system converting the acoustic code of the 40 or so phonemes that constitute the limited set of American-English phonemes. Allophonic variations of phonemes, despite a multitude of idiosyncratic differences from speaker to speaker, from dialect to dialect, from context to context, and from time to time, are assumed to be sufficiently like each other and distinct enough from allophones of any other phoneme class so that the phoneme intended may be clearly perceived. This view of speech perception suggests an analogy to reading by recognizing each character in a string of alphabet letters forming words and sentences. Recognition of phonemes from within a variable acoustic signal is thought to occur by a process of determining a number of **distinctive features** characteristic of each phoneme. Early studies from confusion matrices of single syllables suggested that the distinctive features of phonemes might be such as (1) whether voicing was present or absent, (2) whether voicing was nasal or oral, (3) whether friction was present, and (4) where the place of articulation occurred. The traditional classification of consonants, as shown in Figure III–1, suggests a rudimentary set of distinctive features. Recognition of /f/ by this approach, for example, would not depend upon the particular acoustic (frequency, intensity, duration) characteristics peculiar to a produced [f] but would be based on determination that the sound (1) was voiceless rather than voiced, (2) was made with friction, and (3) was made at a labio-dental place of articulation. Since no other speech sound has these three characteristics, the phoneme intended must be /f/. A more elaborate theoretical set of distinctive features includes such binary opposites as vocalic-nonvocalic, nasal-oral, tense-lax, compact-diffuse, grave-acute, front-back, interruptive-continuant, and fricative-sonorant.

A number of observations cast doubt on this discrete phoneme code theory of speech perception. First is the extreme acoustic variability among the allophones of a single phoneme when analyzed in connected speech. Figure VIII–6 showed the distortions of vowel formant positions in connected speech context. The acoustic differences between the /t/ and /d/ when produced naturally as in *a liter of wine* and *a leader of men* seem almost to disappear. Many of the assumed distinctive features do not relate directly to acoustic information in the speech signal, the information that must be transmitted to the listener. Another observation is that speech can be followed by listeners at rates as high as 400 words per minute, or about 30 phonemes per second, a rate approaching the known temporal resolving power of the auditory system for non-speech stimuli. At that rate, discrete acoustic events are likely to merge into an indistinguishable buzz. Furthermore, electronic apparatus designed to recognize speech through its phonemes has not been able to succeed beyond recognition of a very few distinct sound patterns in the speech of a very few individuals. When speech-like sounds have been synthesized by electronic equipment, perception appears to be greatly influenced by the transitions between phonemes whether some of the actual phonemes are present or not.

One view of understanding speech to help account for these observations is called the "motor theory" of speech perception. Noting the close linkage between auditory feedback channels and motor control of articulation, this theory suggests that memory for speech is related to memory for how speech is produced. The speech of others is perceived with reference to the listener's knowledge of his own speech mechanism and the motor patterns that we would use to produce the same speech units. The listener, recalling the neuromuscular patterns he would use to produce the unit he hears, associates these patterns with the meaning of the speech units. Tactile and kinesthetic speech feedback is an important part of these motor patterns. It is not necessary that the listener actually move his speech mechanism through the pattern in order to perceive it. However, it is a common observation that when learning a new language or hearing an unfamiliar word, we find ourselves saying the word "under our breath" to get more familiar with it or to help recognize it. The author has observed a number of young deaf children who, having difficulty first learning to lipread, seem to need to say the word to themselves or out loud before they can recognize it. These overt manifestations of motor assistance with auditory perception may be related to the way we perceive rapid connected speech.

This theory of speech perception leaves unanswered what acoustic information must necessarily be transmitted to the listener in order for him to connect the speech unit he hears with his own neuromuscular patterns of speech production. There are clearly a number of questions still to be answered about how we perceive speech. A thorough understanding of descriptive phonetics may be one route to those answers.

REVIEW VOCABULARY

Acoustic phonetics—the field of study concerned with the acoustic features of speech.

Acoustics—the branch of physics concerned with the physical properties of sound.

Amplitude—the extent of excursions of a vibrating body, or extent of openings as in the glottis.

DeciBel, (dB)—a widely used unit for the level or strength of a sound. One-tenth of a Bel, named for Alexander Graham Bell.

Distinctive features—acoustic or visual features characteristic of a phoneme that distinguish it from other phonemes.

Formants—bands of energy in a frequency spectrum associated with vowel perception.

Frequency—the rate of the vibrations of a sound, described in Hertz or the number of cycles per second.

Frequency spectrum—the relative intensity of frequency components of a given sound.

Harmonics—overtones that are whole number multiples of a fundamental frequency.

Hertz, (Hz)—a unit of frequency used for "cycles per second." Named for Heinrich R. Hertz, a German physicist.

Homophenous—optically indistinguishable units of speech, as in *pie, buy,* and *my.*

Homophonous—acoustically indistinguishable units of speech, as in *write, right,* and *rite.*

Intensity—the magnitude of the energy of a sound, described in deciBels.

Kinesthetic—the sense of movement and position available from the stretching of muscles, tension on joints, and moving body parts.

Monitor—to maintain control by making adjustments based on sensory information fed back to the producer during an action.

Overtones—a succession of frequencies higher than the fundamental frequency.

Proprioception—sensory information perceived internally by the producer of an action, as with the tactile and kinesthetic feedback during speech production.

Quality—the intensity relations among the fundamental frequency and overtones of a sound.

Tactile—the sense of touch including that available from touching of parts of the speech mechanism, friction caused by air turbulence, and vibrations as with phonation.

Vibro-tactile—vibration that can be detected by tactile perception, as with the vibration produced by phonation.

Viseme—visible speech positions that form recognizable categories of optical contrast associated with phonemes.

EXERCISES

1. Line up six empty soft drink glass bottles, exactly alike and not touching each other, on a table. Leave the first bottle empty, add one inch of water to the second, two inches to the third, three to the fourth, four to the

fifth, and five inches to the sixth. Tap lightly the neck of each bottle in turn with a metal spoon and note how the pitch of the resulting sound rises as the size of the resonating air cavity decreases.

2. Write at least ten pairs of words that are **homophenous** but not **homophonous.** Example, *bait-made.*

3. By saying each of the following units of speech aloud several times, and by producing each in "slow motion," analyze and describe first the various kinds of **tactile** information, and then the **kinesthetic** information each one yields:

[du]	[sæk]	[lʌntʃ]
[θʌm]	[fju]	[mɑmə]
[sɪŋ]	[æpl̩]	[hɛvən]

4. Analyze the proprioceptive products (both tactile and kinesthetic) of the following sounds, first describing what feedback information is available to the speaker, then placing them in rank order for the strength of overall proprioceptive information they provide.

/t/, /f/, /m/, /ʌ/, /s/, /u/

SUGGESTED READING

Denes, Peter B., and Pinson, Elliot N.: *The Speech Chain: the Physics and Biology of Spoken Language.* Garden City, N.Y., Anchor Press/Doubleday, 1973.

A paperback of the Anchor Science Study Series, written by two speech scientists at the Bell Telephone Laboratories, relates speech production to speech recognition with a simplified presentation of the physics of sound and the acoustic characteristics of speech.

Pickett, James M.: *The Sounds of Speech Communication.* Baltimore, Maryland, University Park Press, 1980.

A technically sound text on acoustic phonetics with some references to speech perception. A well illustrated introduction by a research scientist in acoustic phonetics.

Lehiste, Ilse (editor): *Readings in Acoustic Phonetics.* Cambridge, Mass., The MIT Press, 1967.

This frequently reprinted collection of articles serves as a resource of basic references for a number of original ideas developed by their authors. The single volume includes some of the world's foremost authorities on acoustic phonetics, with articles reprinted from a variety of journals. Some knowledge of acoustics is needed.

Calvert, Donald R., and Silverman, S. Richard: *Speech and Deafness.* Washington, D.C., A.G. Bell Association for the Deaf, 1975.

This text for teachers of hearing-impaired children features a section on the perceptual features of articulation and voice in Chapter I, "Speech and its Production," (pp. 6–39) with tables of ratings for strength of sensory feedback available for consonants and vowels. Chapter IV, "Instructional Analysis of Consonants and Vowels," (pp. 89–146) describes the kinds of tactile and kinesthetic feedback information from each of the American-English speech sounds.

INDEX OF SPEECH SOUNDS (IPA Symbols)

INDEX